Roger Nash Baldwin
and the
American Civil Liberties Union

Roger Nash Baldwin
and the
American Civil Liberties Union

Robert C. Cottrell

COLUMBIA UNIVERSITY PRESS

NEW YORK

Columbia University Press
Publishers Since 1893
New York   Chichester, West Sussex
Copyright © 2000 Robert C. Cottrell

Library of Congress Cataloging-in-Publication Data

Cottrell, Robert C., 1950–
    Roger Nash Baldwin and the American Civil Liberties Union / Robert C. Cottrell.
       p. cm.
    Includes bibliographical references and index.
    ISBN 0-231-11972-0 (cloth : acid-free paper)
       1. Baldwin, Roger Nash, 1884– 2. Civil rights—United States—Biography. 3. American
    Civil Liberties Union—History. 4. Civil rights—United States—History.   I. Title

    JC599.U5 B353 2000
323'.092—dc21
[B]
                                                                    00-043129

⊗

Casebound editions of Columbia University Press books are printed on permanent and
durable acid-free paper.
Printed in the United States of America
c 10 9 8 7 6 5 4 3 2 1

To my mother, Sylvia Light Cottrell

Contents

CONTENTS

Preface

A full-scale biography of Roger Nash Baldwin, founder and longtime director of the American Civil Liberties Union, is clearly overdue. For the first three-quarters of the twentieth century, Baldwin was intimately and uniquely associated with prominent left of center circles in the United States and internationally. Indeed, only his good friends Norman Thomas and A. J. Muste were as inextricably linked to the foremost progressive movements of that era. Consequently, those three men—and especially Baldwin—helped to recast American liberalism and radicalism. However, Baldwin, most determinedly of all, sought to safeguard civil liberties at home and human rights abroad. Baldwin's journey, as he "traveled hopefully," was particularly characterized by his birthing, nurturing, and sustaining of the modern civil liberties movement in this country. Thus, despite lacking legal training himself, Baldwin influenced the course of American jurisprudence and the general political landscape in the United States.

Along the way, however, his passage was marked by compromises, vacillations, and mistakes—both his and the American Left's—including an early and seemingly enduring fascination with Soviet Russia. That resulted in Baldwin's being accused of having a double standard and worse, as did the American Civil Liberties Union's (ACLU's) apparently tepid stance regarding the internment of Japanese Americans during World War II. By that point, Baldwin had largely abandoned the Popular Front approach of the Depression era, when liberals and noncommunist leftists readily joined with their communist brethren in antifascist alliances. Thus by the time the cold war evolved, Baldwin had already adopted an anticommunist stance, but one far removed from the then ascendant red baiters and communist chasers. Increasingly, he devoted his legendary store of energy to the field of international human rights while remaining a mentor for many ACLU members.

The Harvard-educated Baldwin (1884–1981) first acquired national prominence as a social worker in St. Louis, befriended by the likes of Jane Addams and Lillian Wald, during the early twentieth century, the so-called progressive era. With the advent of U.S. involvement in World War I, Baldwin—along with Thomas—began operating under the auspices of the American Union Against Militarism and the National Civil Liberties Bureau, before he landed in a federal penitentiary because he had deliberately violated the Selective Service Act. Influenced by the prewar and bohemian-tinged Lyrical Left—and, no doubt, his philandering father—Baldwin boasted an unconventional marriage and lifestyle. In 1920 he helped establish the ACLU and through that forum proved more instrumental than any other individual in fighting to safeguard the individual freedoms protected by the First and Fourteenth amendments to the U.S. Constitution. In the period just ahead, Baldwin steered the ACLU toward involvement with the Sacco and Vanzetti, Scopes (Monkey Trial), and Scottsboro Boys cases. At the same time he was a leading figure in the American Old Left, which emerged after World War I and proved enormously controversial because of its close identification—organizationally, emotionally, and intellectually—with the Soviet Union.

Severely disillusioned by the 1939 German-Soviet Nonaggression Pact and worried about the ACLU's very viability, Baldwin began withdrawing from the Left, all the while reaffirming the importance of core liberal values, ideas, and practices. Previously an archetypal progressive, unaffiliated radical, and Popular Fronter, he now became a model liberal anticommunist. In 1940 he orchestrated the exclusion of communists like Elizabeth Gurley Flynn from high-level positions inside the ACLU; some saw this as setting the stage for anticommunist machinations by both private agencies and government officials in the period just ahead. By contrast, and charges to the contrary notwithstanding, Baldwin strove to provide legal protection for the Japanese Americans and Japanese nationals who were rounded up starting in 1942, due to the insistence of military officials on the west coast and the acquiescence of the Roosevelt administration. He also courageously defended freedom of speech, of the press, and of assemblage for political pariahs, spanning the ideological spectrum from Trotskyists to anti-Semites and German-American Bundists.

After the war and as a domestic red scare flowered, Baldwin continued to argue that infringing on the rights of any group, no matter how disliked or unlovable, resulted in an abridgment of the rights of all. At the same time he became more concerned about international civil liberties, traveling to Japan, Korea, and Germany at the behest of military commanders like Douglas MacArthur to help devise legal protections for occupied lands.

Retiring as ACLU director in January 1950, Baldwin established an international branch of the organization while working for human rights agencies associated with the United Nations. For the next three decades he continued his involvement with civil liberties and human rights campaigns and supported the antinuclear, civil rights, and peace movements of the period. In 1981 Baldwin, for so long reviled and admired, was awarded the Presidential Medal of Freedom.

Through it all contradictions abounded in this epochal figure in the pantheon of American liberalism, reform, and radicalism. Baldwin maintained friendships with leftists—or those who had departed the train of the revolution—like John Reed, Scott Nearing, Bill Haywood, William Foster, and Max Eastman. At the same time he delighted in his associations with some of America's wealthiest and most powerful families, including the Morgans and the Rockefellers. He perceived the need to create organizations like the National Civil Liberties Bureau (NCLB) and the ACLU to check government encroachments on personal freedoms. At the same time he considered it only fitting that government agencies open their doors to the civil liberties chieftains, all well-heeled sorts like himself. A classical libertarian who regularly corresponded with the anarchist Emma Goldman for three full decades, Baldwin was dictatorial—sometimes brutally so—in the workplace. To the dismay of many friends and colleagues, he respected and frequently admired authority figures such as General MacArthur and FBI Director J. Edgar Hoover. Baldwin's own lifestyle was colorful, to say the least, yet he could be judgmental and dogmatic when examining that of others. A highly visible public figure, he strove to keep his private life—especially his bedroom—closed to public purview. Considered more than frugal by family members and ACLU compatriots, he long commuted between a Greenwich Village townhouse, an estate in the New Jersey countryside, and Martha's Vineyard. His modus operandi in the domestic arena was viewed by some, and only somewhat tongue-in-cheek, as approximating the *Life with Father* childhood in Wellesley, Massachusetts, he mentioned so often.

Despite such inconsistencies, Roger Baldwin deservedly was acclaimed "the patriarch of the American civil liberties movement." That movement, although surprisingly ignored or given short shrift in history textbooks, was a remarkable undertaking, one as important as the momentous civil rights crusade. Significantly, the two movements have worked in tandem to extend individual liberties in this land in a hitherto unprecedented manner. Friends and antagonists alike acknowledged Baldwin's unparalleled role in bringing that about.

Acknowledgments

A legion of archivists, librarians, and clerical workers scattered across the country helped me carry out this project. Staffs at the following institutions (in alphabetical order) were among the most helpful: Columbia University, Dartmouth College, Duke University, the Federal Bureau of Investigation, the Franklin Delano Roosevelt Presidential Library, the Harry S Truman Presidential Library, the Harvard Law Library, Haverford College, the Hoover Institution, the Illinois Historical Society, the Library of Congress, the Lyndon Baines Johnson Presidential Library, the National Archives, the New York Public Library, New York University, the New York State Archives in Albany, Princeton University, Smith College, Southern Illinois University, Swarthmore College, Syracuse University, the University of California at Berkeley, the University of California at Davis, the University of Oregon, the University of Texas, the Washington State Historical Society, the Wisconsin State Historical Society, and Yale University.

At my home institution, California State University, Chico, interlibrary loan officers Jo Ann Bradley and George Thompson were especially helpful and supportive. The archival staff at Princeton's Mudd Memorial Library, which houses both the Roger Baldwin and the ACLU papers, was wonderfully professional and cheerful. Special thanks go to Ben Primer, Nanci A. Young, Monica Ruscil, Paula Jabloner, and Daniel Linke. I am also grateful to Phi Alpha Theta for allowing me to include material from an article of mine that appeared in *The Historian*.

The National Endowment for the Humanities, the American Philosophical Society, and California State University, Chico, provided financial assistance that enabled me to complete this book. At CSUC the Graduate School, the College of Humanities and Fine Arts, and the Department of History offered me necessary financial support from the inception of this project to its near completion. I am particularly appreciative of the support afforded by Jeff Wright, Bob Bakke, and Juri Brilts of the Office of Sponsored Projects and by Don Heinz. And a bit more lucre came my way thanks to my agent, Robbie Hare, and Columbia University Press.

Drafts of this manuscript, in whole or in part, were read by Bob Miller, Dale R. Steiner, Sam Walker, Bill Preston, and Sharon and Steve Gerson, my sister and brother-in-law. Bob and Dale, two of my best buddies, have supported my work from the outset. Sam encouraged me to undertake the project in the first place, while Bill actually pored over what was then an even bigger tome. David Levy and Rob Griswold have long been supportive of my scholarly endeavors. My copy editor, Polly Kummel, labored mightily to refine *Roger Nash Baldwin and the ACLU*, as well as to query me about potentially troublesome matters.

The folk at Columbia University Press, especially editors Ron Harris and Kate Wittenberg, were enormously helpful.

My own family, as always, was incredibly supportive. As she completed her own graduate studies, my wife, Sue, listened patiently to my tales of Roger Baldwin and took on added burdens as I engaged in yet another cross-country trek. Then there were Adrienne, grappling with teenage angst, and Jordan, my precocious third-grader, who never ceases to teach me about certain wonders of life.

Roger Nash Baldwin
and the
American Civil Liberties Union

CHAPTER ONE

Growing Up in Wellesley Hills

Roger Nash Baldwin was born in Wellesley Hills, Massachusetts, on January 21, 1884, into the comfort and affluence of an old-stock New England family. He was the first of seven children of Frank Fenno Baldwin and Lucy Cushing Nash; his family lineage dated to the time of William the Conqueror, and his ancestors arrived in the Americas on "the inescapable *Mayflower.*" More than five centuries before the Pilgrims, "Baldwins of rank" had appeared in England. One Loammi Baldwin was credited with producing the Baldwin apple. Roger's maternal side boasted Chaffees, Cushings, and Nashes—long considered among the most prominent names in Massachusetts society—as well as a Revolutionary War general.[1]

By the antebellum period the Baldwins exuded the kind of social conscience often exhibited by leading families in the American Northeast. Roger Baldwin's paternal grandfather, William Henry Baldwin, was in his early forties when he gave up his successful dry goods business to found the Boston Young Men's Christian Union in 1851. The union offered adult education in addition to recreation and social services. William, attracted to abolitionism, was a kind of Unitarian lay preacher who befriended "non-conformist Brahmins" like Phillips Brooks, the renowned Episcopal minister who would write the words to "O Little Town of Bethlehem," and Thomas Wentworth Higginson, the early abolitionist who would lead the first regiment of black troops in the Civil War. William Baldwin corresponded with Ralph Waldo Emerson, Henry Wadsworth Longfellow, and Oliver Wendell Holmes, and he knew Henry Ward Beecher, who headed the nation's largest Protestant congregation at Brooklyn's Plymouth Church.[2]

When Roger Baldwin was a young child, his paternal grandparents lived at 63 Pinckney Street, where he visited them often. Grandfather Baldwin spoke frequently of the operations of the Young Men's Christian Union, which held Christmas parties for poor children, sent emissaries to their homes, ran an athletic program for young men, and offered library services, among other functions. While walking with his grandfather around the streets of Boston, Roger was impressed with how respectfully members of the organization greeted the elderly gentleman. And he came to consider his grandfather's famous pen pals, especially Brooks and Holmes, as family friends.[3]

Roger also often visited his uncle, William Henry Baldwin Jr., who eventually served as president of the Long Island Railroad. Like his father, William Henry Jr. was something of a reformer and held a seat on the Southern Education Board, which contested the exploitation of minors in the workforce. He became director of the National Child Labor Committee, which brought together northerners and southerners who considered learning the key to racial understanding, and chaired the Committee of Fifteen, which spearheaded a campaign against prostitution in New York City. He also was a trustee of Tuskegee Normal and Industrial Institute. William Henry Jr. would insist to his somewhat disbelieving nephew that only a few individuals worked hard, saved their earnings, and became rich.[4]

William Henry Jr. had married Ruth Standish Bowles, the daughter of newspaper editor Samuel Bowles. She helped found the National Urban League, served as a trustee of Smith College, and joined the Socialist Party. Her acquaintances included social reformers and critics like Lillian Wald, Paul U. Kellogg, and Jacob Riis. She and Roger became particularly close, especially after William Henry Jr. died in 1905.

Roger's father, Frank Fenno Baldwin, was a successful leather merchant who ran several factories. When Roger was a teenager, his father was a partner in the Boston Counter Co. and traveled widely to great shoe centers. Later he served as a vice president of the American Hide Leather Co. and still later became an officer of the New York, New Haven & Hartford Railroad. Frank was considered "a charming and fascinating person, flinging himself into any thing [sic] which claimed his interest or appealed to his sympathies with ardor and abandon—a man, too, of driving force and ardent emotions." He married his neighbor in the affluent Union Park area of Boston, Lucy Cushing Nash, who was "a lovely, quiet, gentlewoman." The daughter of Israel Nash, a successful importer, Lucy was taken with music, order, and thoroughness.[5]

Frank would leave home for his office at seven in the morning and return at five or six. He exuded authority—certain of his relatives called him the Grand Duke. Articulate and possessed of a disciplined mind, Frank was, in Roger's estimation, "very positive, very decisive. He felt in command of things. He was the head of the works." He commanded a good salary, and the servants viewed him as "the Boss," Roger remembered. Frank was generally upbeat but could become angry or irritated, in a manner foreign to his wife. Although he was a devoted father, his children "were a bit fearful of crossing him." Indeed, the family made frequent references to Frank's acting as a semi-tyrannical patriarch, in the fashion of the protagonist of Clarence Day Jr.'s *Life with Father*. Nevertheless, Roger considered him "a very loving father and very companionable." While his father was determined to keep up appearances despite the turmoil in the household, Roger "saw right through him." His father allowed Roger to have everything he wanted and rarely disciplined or reprimanded him. Still, Roger acknowledged, "I think among all of us children there was a little sense of restraint, not through direct action but you didn't contradict or question. Fear is too strong a word. All of us, all six of us, were not fearful, but we wouldn't cross him."[6]

The Baldwin household did not use corporal punishment. Instead, when one of the six surviving children (one died in infancy)—three girls and three boys—became unruly, Lucy would lead that child by the hand to the closet and lock the door. The angry and frightened seven- or eight-year-old Roger "used to kick the door, yell, finally I would give in and say I'll be good. I may have fought with my brothers and/or sisters or disobeyed my mother to have earned that punishment."[7]

Small, slight, and soft-spoken, Lucy Baldwin possessed certain unconventional beliefs, albeit in a "quieter, self-effacing way," in contrast to her husband's more brusque and grandiose manner. She was appreciative of "good music, good solid books—no trash around our house—and good talk about things that mattered," Roger recalled. A friend related that Roger acquired from his mother his love of music and "his orderliness and thoroughness." Equally significant, Lucy seemed to believe in change, which Frank merely accepted. She was something of a supporter of women's suffrage. In contrast, their other children never expressed the same concerns about social issues that Roger did.[8]

For the first seventeen years of his life Roger Baldwin lived in the family home on Maugus Avenue in Wellesley that Lucy had received as a gift from her father. The spacious Victorian was perched high on a hill, surrounded by about fifteen acres of open land, woods, and streams. The house, which a friend called indescribable, underwent many additions as the Baldwin family expanded. Above the house were five acres of pasture, and Frank took to farming as a kind of gentleman's hobby. The estate was home to pigs, sheep, cows, and horses. When Roger was about twelve, his father purchased a four-hundred-acre farm about twenty-five miles outside of Wellesley in Hopkinton. The Baldwins' existence was privileged and sheltered, attended to by a number of servants, including a nurse and a laundress. The maids and cooks were Irish, the gardeners Italian, and the coachman English.[9]

Wellesley was a suburb of Boston, which included the eastern sector of Wellesley Hills, where the Baldwins resided. The suburbs of Wellesley, Brookline, Chestnut Hill, Milton, Needham, Dedham, and Dover were home to proper Bostonians. The townsfolk were generally comfortably middle class, with wealthier individuals serving as community leaders. Both proper and Unitarian, the Baldwins considered their religion superior to others, particularly the Catholicism practiced by those of Irish stock and domestic help. "Class distinctions were remote," Roger later insisted, but they clearly were present in Wellesley and in the circles to which the Baldwins gravitated. They also had an enduring influence on Roger. In the public schools he attended, Roger became acquainted with the children of immigrants. However, such schoolmates were not invited to Baldwin family parties. He was one of "the better people," young Roger understood, whose family did not associate with certain sorts. While in high school, he was attracted to a young Irish Catholic girl, Anastasia Kilmain. One of his parents pointedly insisted, "Now Roger, I wouldn't ask a girl like that to come to the house to your birthday party." Roger never considered questioning the admonition.[10]

Not surprisingly, the lone extant correspondence from Roger Baldwin's adolescence reflects various prejudices, as well as stark class consciousness. He corresponded regularly with Charlotte M. Ryman of Wilkes Barre, Pennsylvania, whom he met in the summer of 1897 at the Hotel Humarock in Sea View Station, Massachusetts. The Baldwins and Rymans were vacationing there, and the trip marked the start of a three-decade friendship with Charlotte Ryman, whose husband owned a coal mine. She had two daughters and became greatly fond of the thirteen-year-old Roger. He returned the affection of the forty-nine-year-old woman he came to call Ma Ryman or Grossmutter; she referred to him as "Ritterino." Ryman became the kind of second mother he often sought out, and he visited her home on several occasions. Her family was well off, "genteel middle-class," and he "fell right into its social circle in Wilkes-Barre," he recalled. There he became enamored of a niece of Ryman's, Marjorie Rose, to whom he later drew even closer. Around 1898 the Rymans invited him along on a trip to Washington, D.C., his first visit to the nation's capital. They also took him to New York City, where they stayed at the Waldorf-Astoria, which became his social center when he visited Manhattan during his college days.[11]

In a letter to Ryman dated April 18, 1898, he referred to the city of Norfolk, which he was visiting with his family, as "the worst and dirtiest" he had seen, "most full of lounging niggers that I ever saw." Departing from an electric car, the fourteen-year-old found himself "accosted by about five niggers," all of whom sought to carry his bag to the boat his family was boarding. Roger informed Charlotte Ryman that he refused their offers, choosing to carry the luggage himself.[12]

In another letter, written on February 11, 1899, he spoke of a masquerade ball held at his school that resulted in "a *corking* time." He wore "a 'killing costume,' which undoubtedly would have shocked the leading angel in Heaven." Sporting a great tan, he attended the ball as "a negro dude, with a face of immense proportions." He was attired in an old stovepipe hat, his father's dress suit, gaiters, a loud necktie, white gloves, and a diamond ring the size of a "chicken's egg."[13] His flippant attitude about racial matters, every bit as much as the language itself, was all too characteristic of many Americans of his era. This was true even of well-educated people, including some of those who were viewed as reformers in their day. It remains startling, nevertheless.

Such transparent biases notwithstanding, his racial attitudes remained malleable, undoubtedly because of an already well-developed sense of noblesse oblige. On April 30 he sent a brief letter to Booker T. Washington—whom he had recently met at his uncle's home in Brooklyn—and enclosed a $20 contribution from the Baldwins to the Tuskegee Institute. This was in keeping with his family's friendship with Washington and its support for various reform efforts. Roger admitted he was "only a school boy" but suggested that made him "feel more for fellow school boys and girls of the South." William Henry Baldwin Jr.'s service as a Tuskeegee trustee also fed Roger's interest, as did Washington's status as arguably the nation's leading black spokesperson.[14]

Shortly afterward Roger again wrote disparagingly to Charlotte Ryman, this time about people he met at the coast. "They aren't the very best," but there was "a little Jewish girl from New York, who is 'perfectly killing.'" Her father was a German Jew, but to Roger she was "only German *percent!*"[15]

In addition to prejudices of various types, his letters to Charlotte Ryman reflect the class consciousness that would always mark his life. He had taken up croquet and golf and planned to write "a grammar of the Golf Language," without synonyms, he told her. He had seen a performance of *Cyrano de Bergerac*, with a lead actor who was "*très excellent*." He was writing in French, he clarified, "not to 'show up'—honestly now—but because English can't express it." He also told Ryman how he and his friend Lawrence Grose had visited Faneuil Hall markets and the docks in Boston, then ventured over to La Touraine for crackers and milk in the coffee room. The hotel was every bit as grand as many in New York City while exuding a comfortable air of homeyness.[16]

Late in the summer of 1899, having tired of playing cards, croquet, or pool, Roger shared intimate thoughts with his friend. He enjoyed lying in the sand, a solitary enterprise that enabled him to "think my little thinks all to myself," he wrote her. He had matured in the past six months. Now, it seemed, he could "see much further into things." In fact, "it seems that I can't think enough." Already highly ambitious, he had long wondered "what good it was to have this life unless one were going to become a President or Prince or other noted 'big.'" Things seemed clearer now, thanks to sermons of the Reverend Edward Everett Hale, the renowned pastor of Roger's maternal grandmother. Still, Roger acknowledged, "I don't want to get 'grown-up' yet." He asked Ryman, "Don't you think it best that I should keep 'kiddish' as long as I can?" He was not, he assured her, aspiring to become "a digni-fied person," and he believed that "the true way to fun is to let oneself go, and be free." Others, including several teenage girls, had tossed out "some unfavorable remarks" regarding his immaturity in "playing with little chil-dren." Roger dismissed such comments as coming from a generally "shallow lot."[17]

Roger now displayed symptoms of depression, to which he was some-times prone—despite a belief held by others and nurtured by him that he was perpetually optimistic. One night he had cried, wondering what "I was ever made for, and how far 'space' went, and such things." In a letter to Ryman in February 1900 he expressed concerns that "I can't keep at any one thing." What this augured, he prophesied, was "certain failure if I keep on." Maybe he should become an editor of a publication engaged in yellow jour-nalism, he mused. But "perhaps I'm too young to judge myself." He acknowl-edged, "My opinions and beliefs are all in a very muddy stage, and I am lost in a depth of uncomfortable 'slum' of confusion." No matter, he was "happy and quite satisfied with school and everything." His parents "have been so good to me in everything I have wanted."[18]

Frank and Lucy Baldwin were not regular churchgoers and gave their eldest to understand that they were "agnostic Unitarians." Nevertheless, the local Unitarian church served as Roger's "social center"; he even taught Sunday school there. Little concerned about questions of immortality, he developed an "unquestioning belief in man, if not God." While still a youngster, he rejected atheism, reasoning that some ethereal force held the universe together. Such a force also suggested the possibility that striving for a common good was a worthwhile endeavor. As a teenager Roger was attracted to the works of Jesus, whom he revered "not as a divine figure but for what he said." Roger participated in the social service efforts of the Unitarian church, including its "Lend-a-Hand Society," founded by Edward Everett Hale. The nonsectarian organization was identified with the mottoes "Look up and not down," "Look forward and not back," "Look out and not in," and "Lend a Hand." Roger helped raise money for the Boston Floating Hospital and joined with other children to collect wildflowers for patients in Boston hospitals. The Floating Hospital gave free medical care to infirm children younger than six, and it did not discriminate on the basis of race or creed, although it refused to treat those with contagious diseases. Roger believed that "lend a hand meant helping people that couldn't help themselves." As he later acknowledged, "I took it all quite seriously." This was not surprising, for "there was always lots of talk in our family about social problems."[19]

Both Frank and Lucy Baldwin were intellectually and artistically curious individuals, and Wellesley residents included several experts in their respective fields. Many were willing to cultivate a young boy's curiosity. He was befriended by Marshall L. Perrin, superintendent of Wellesley public schools, who invited him in for readings in German, which he "dimly understood and hugely enjoyed." Most of his teachers were principled New England puritans, devoted to learning.[20]

Wellesley was only a half-hour train ride from Boston, and Roger frequently went into the city, taking the trip alone from the time he was twelve. Usually, he stopped off at the Young Men's Christian Union, headed by Grandfather Baldwin. There Roger attended Christmas parties orchestrated by his grandfather. On one occasion he accompanied his grandfather to Harvard and met its president, Charles William Eliot, a good friend of the family.[21]

As his brothers recalled, Roger "was one of the most unathletic boys by nature," but he loved the outdoors. At one point he drove off with a horse and carriage, but the animal soon nibbled shrubbery beside the road while its erstwhile driver looked at birds. His interests ranged widely, from the arts to languages.[22]

He was drawn to nature studies because of his father's interest in the outdoors, an interest shared by acquaintances of the Baldwins, including a renowned naturalist who lived in Wellesley, Bradford Torrey, who also was Henry David Thoreau's literary executor. Recognizing that his son thoroughly enjoyed the Hopkinton countryside, Frank Baldwin constructed a shingled cabin, in the pine woods, encircled by a stone wall and with a shingled privy. Throughout high school and afterward Roger and his friends made use of the "camp" during vacations and on weekends. There they rode farm horses over unpaved roads, swam in ponds, and cooked "the most monstrous dishes over the camp stove," Roger recalled. On various occasions his father and Nathaniel P. Kidder, president of the Massachusetts Botanical Society, took Roger along on fishing excursions.[23]

Around the age of twelve or thirteen, he became attracted to the study of birds, following the lead of his friend and classmate Lawrence Grose. The son of a Baptist minister and editor, Lawrence lived next door to Roger. Lawrence, multitalented in the arts and literature, invariably chased after birds with a pair of binoculars in hand. At first Roger was reluctant to join in but "soon caught the infection." This proved to be "a good game, so full of speculation and chance, taking me far afield into places I would never have gone otherwise, and furnishing surprise and adventure, often excitement," he later wrote. Like Lawrence, Roger began tracking his bird studies, which he compared with those of other friends.[24]

Roger avidly read Torrey's weekly column, "Clerk of the Woods," in the *Boston Transcript*. Torrey was a shy bachelor who became a kind of mentor for Roger. The teenager would meet Torrey at his boardinghouse or in the field. Torrey often helped Roger to identify particular birds while telling him about Thoreau. Torrey and another naturalist, a Mr. Purdy, dissuaded Roger from removing bird eggs from nests, which he would gather in a box filled with cotton wool. Purdy exclaimed, "You should know that taking bird eggs from birds' nests is against the law in Massachusetts, and I am not going to identify any unlawful eggs for you."[25]

Botany also appealed to Roger and here again a well-regarded individual, the author Isaac Sprague, along with his wife, helped with identifications.

Roger became knowledgeable about most of the flowering plants in Wellesley. He dabbled in watercolors and took to painting flowers. He also helped
to cultivate a wildflower preserve around the family home.[26]

His other hobbies and interests ranged from sketching to music. His
brother Bob, who was eleven years younger, believed that Roger had innate
music ability and was jealous of Roger's ability to draw. Lawrence played the
guitar and the mandolin; Roger was ten when he began piano lessons, so
mutual musical interests undoubtedly cemented their friendship at this
stage. Roger performed duets with his mother and was drawn to classical
music. During his teen years he frequented the Friday afternoon concerts of
the Boston Symphony and attended the Metropolitan Opera when it performed in the city. He saw such performers as Caruso, and Fritzi Scheff, who
became a star at the Metropolitan Opera, on Broadway, and in silent films.
Roger began playing classical music, eagerly studying and practicing scores
and enjoying Wagner most of all.[27]

He also was thrilled by Revolutionary sites such as Lexington and Concord, visited the historical shrines, and read works that examined colonial
and Revolutionary New England. As he later recalled, "We were proud of the
fact that we were right near where all these things had happened. That
Boston was a part of it. I got that feeling that Bostonians get. That they are
kind of the center of history, the hub of the universe."[28]

Roger also was drawn to the icons of the region, particularly Thoreau—
whose cabin beside Walden Pond he visited—as attractive sorts, "independent, odd, nature-loving." A great uncle who lived in Lexington was prone
to make light of Thoreau, to whom he referred as "that loafer," and to criticize Emerson for having left the ministry. Nevertheless, as Baldwin later
wrote, "the unconventional, the dissenters, the 'different'" appeared to
flourish in the Boston area. And in Boston they were viewed respectfully
and appreciatively. Indeed, the notion prevailed—which Roger subscribed
to—that freethinkers were the "best people." Roger referred to Frank Baldwin, a man of enormous energies and decidedly strong opinions, as
"understanding of heresy." As Roger acknowledged, "In our family it was
hardly respectable not to be a little queer." Consequently, "John Brown . . .
was the family hero, Robert G. Ingersoll the family prophet, and Unitari-
anism the family religion, probably because it was the closest thing to free
thought." Frank admired Ingersoll, the politician and orator known as "the
great agnostic," attended his public addresses, and sifted through his writings.[29]

Consequently, Roger developed an early affinity for the rebel, the heretic, the radical. He later referred to this as "the dualism in my life—conformity and radicalism . . . in the Boston pattern. . . . I consciously identified myself with these people . . . gentlemen radicals, aristocratic radicals" like Thoreau. Inherently contradictory, this pattern characterized Baldwin from his youth onward. It fostered inconsistencies and paradoxes, which often proved more troubling to others than to Baldwin himself.[30]

Roger graduated from the local public high school, finishing third in a class of twenty-five. His education was somewhat in the classical mode, involving the study of Greek, French, geometry, algebra, and American history. Although Greek proved difficult, his French course, as he stated in a letter to his friend Charlotte Ryman, was a particular favorite. An avid reader, he delved into the classics, historical studies, biographies, and the *Boston Transcript* and was quite fond of *Youth's Home Companion*; however, his friend Lawrence was a far more serious student of the classics. In the Grose family library Roger encountered Gibbon, John Fiske's *The Nature of God*, Edward Bellamy's *Looking Backward*, and Ingersoll's lectures. When Roger was fourteen, he attended a lecture by Fiske, the American philosopher who did much to popularize the theory of evolution.[31]

Despite his lack of athleticism, Roger nevertheless was persuaded to try out for the high school football team. During the initial scrimmage he ended up at the bottom of a stack of players. "Please get up," he implored his teammates. "You're hurting me." Several of his good friends were also intellectually inclined lads, drawn to nature, the arts, and music. And he gained an early reputation as something of a social butterfly.[32]

In Wellesley Hills, Roger, Lawrence, and two other boys became close friends who "were able to talk about anything and everything," Lawrence recalled. They were, he said, "kind of renaissance boys reaching out in all directions, art, nature, literature, music." Lawrence's father, the minister, edited a Baptist weekly in Boston and was viewed by his southern brethren as an atheist; the boys saw themselves as pagans. They possessed no conception of God but were concerned about religious and ethical dealings. In the Grose family library they discovered books by Charles Darwin, the British physicist John Tyndall, and Thomas H. Huxley. "I caught on to them," Lawrence recalled. "They were my meat." Influenced by his friend, Roger read Huxley and Darwin and found *The Voyage of the Beetle* to be "quite an exciting book." The Groses were not as well off as Roger's family, but they, like the parents of most of Roger's friends, seemingly attended to their children's every desire. Roger and Lawrence would visit New York City for exhibitions at the Metropolitan Museum of Art, taking the Boston & Albany Railroad. Roger would buy the tickets.[33]

In Lawrence's eyes something was "kind of picturesque about Roger. He was always well-dressed, not dudeish—but his clothes had the quality of old Boston. He was a sort of Prince Charming, his manners always pleasant and affable. He was a great smiler, a smiling prince. He was never grim, the reverse of grim, and he was always very sharp in the sense of being keen. . . . [He] was full of humor and bright wit, a terribly likable person." At the same time Roger walked down the street, Lawrence reflected, "with an air and had an air in everything that he did." Although some friends later referred to Roger as a sissy, Lawrence thought that "he was a good deal of a conqueror of girls—how could he help not being so! He was a kind of personality; he had a way with them." In his brother Bob's estimation Roger "had a streak of femininity in him that came from his relationship to Mother."[34]

Years later Lawrence noted that the Baldwin home life could not have been untroubled. He saw Lucy Baldwin as "refined, a little bit retiring, not a colorful person at all. She didn't seem to me as the kind of woman who would satisfy a vigorous, hearty man like Mr. Baldwin was." Lawrence remembered going with Roger to a farm in Ashland, where Frank Baldwin— who "had a fire in him"—kept a young woman. It is not clear when Roger became aware of his father's philandering, and Lawrence later recalled that Roger seemed little fazed by the events at the farm; however, Lawrence believed "it must have had an influence." Bob noted that their sister, Margaret, who was two years Roger's junior and the oldest girl, also was affected by their father's wanderings, of which she too was aware. "She remained a spinster all her life," Bob said.[35]

Roger and close friends like Lawrence undoubtedly discussed sex a good deal, including masturbation, which was "our own problem. It was considered a terrible thing," Lawrence said. However, nobody considered seducing "nice girls." Apparently, none of the boys at his high school was sexually involved with female classmates, which "would have been quite a scandal." When Roger was twelve or thirteen he began an affair with an Irish maid in his parents' home. "She seduced me," he later asserted. "I knew everything that was to be known, even how to prevent getting her pregnant." This affair continued for two or three years, "right under the noses of my parents," whose bedroom was adjacent to Roger's. The woman eventually returned to Ireland to raise a family. For Roger this relationship involved "no emotion, a purely physical thing. She knew I was ready for business. She had seen me taking a bath and was aware I was prepared for an experience."[36]

Perhaps Roger's sexual precocity was furthered by his father's antics. Unquestionably, the hold that Frank and Lucy had on their son was considerable. His father's liaisons clearly troubled him while providing a model of sexual behavior outside the mainstream. Frank's authoritarianism also notably affected Roger, offering as it did yet another example of adult behavior that he would later duplicate. His parents' class, racial, and ethnic prejudices, no matter how frequently Roger denied their existence, affected him in other ways. Class biases were never far removed from Roger's dealings with various individuals, while the racial and ethnic stereotypes imprinted early in his life proved impossible for him to discard altogether.

At the same time Roger was equally influenced by the liberal atmosphere that permeated the Baldwin household and that of other close relatives, such as his paternal grandfather and Uncle William. He was attracted to the rebel heritage that was held up for public acclaim in Boston and surrounding communities. Likewise, he took to heart the tradition of service and support for reform campaigns, a trait that would become even more evident while he was at Harvard.

CHAPTER TWO

The Inevitable Harvard and Beyond

Roger enrolled at Harvard College in the fall of 1901, a matriculation he regarded as inevitable. As a member of an upper-class, socially prominent family from a Boston suburb, he thrived there. All the while he became aware of the great progressive movement unfolding across the land, thanks in part to the ascendancy to the White House of Theodore Roosevelt, a Harvard alumnus. Progressivism involved the first nationwide effort within the capitalistic framework to address many of the problems resulting from rapid modernization. Progressives believed in their ability to right the wrongs plaguing an urban industrial country and relied on the rationality, scientific knowledge, and professional expertise associated with the modern American university. Cambridge, not surprisingly, was "full of excitement, all of the time," with a host of activities and Roger "curious about it all," he recalled.[1]

Life at Harvard was thoroughly enjoyable, he acknowledged, because it was "dominated by the Boston society in which I grew up, and everything about it seemed so familiar." His fellow undergraduates, Roger later noted, considered him "a young aristocrat, highly connected, clever and musical." Frank Baldwin gave his son, already known for his thrifty ways, $4,000 and paid his tuition. Roger first lived alone in a ground-floor apartment in Weld Hall, located in Harvard Yard. The carpeted apartment contained a small bedroom and a sitting room but no plumbing or heat; it did hold his piano, comfortable armchairs, a desk, study lamp, and bookshelves. In his sophomore year he roomed with his double cousin, Herbert Nash Jr., in Dana Chambers, a private dormitory. Later they moved to one of the so-called Gold Coast buildings, Westmorly Court, on Auburn Street; the Gold Coast

dormitories were constructed around the turn of the century to accommodate well-heeled undergraduates. There another proper Bostonian, Francis
B. Sears Jr., joined them. Westmorly Court, with its large rooms and swimming pool, was considered the premier residence for Harvard students.
Roger usually dined with other bright young men who were fond of music
and the arts.[2]

While at Harvard he had no contact with Lawrence Grose, whose high
marks in Greek had secured his admission. Only two or three other students
from Wellesley Hills attended Harvard, and Roger didn't see them, either.
Lawrence did not find this strange—"He had social connections and I did-
n't." Clearly, Lawrence believed that such considerations resulted in the termination of their friendship. Roger did bring friends home from college, fellows he considered respectable.[3]

He demonstrated his sociability, always attending "the proper parties" for
"the best people" in Boston and Cambridge while he was at Harvard. He was
quite popular, as befitting a "handsome, gay and well-born" lad. Roger was
able to "sing, play the piano, draw and paint in better than mediocre fashion," the *American Mercury* reported. He could also "balance a tea cup gracefully" and "was admired alike by beautiful girls and nice old ladies." He continued to acquire what were later adjudged "the best manners, probably, to
be found anywhere in America; manners so simple and yet so classic as to be
a fine art." Roger attended "swanky dances" at the Somerset Hotel, as did
both Franklin Delano Roosevelt, whom he knew casually, and Franklin's
cousin Eleanor.[4]

As in high school, Roger became involved in a host of activities, joining
the music, natural history, and art clubs and singing with the Freshman Glee
Club. He belonged to the Natural History Society and the Nuttall Ornitho-
logical Club, where he encountered his classmate Harry Greenough. The
Nuttall Club was an exclusive organization that gathered at the Natural History Museum of William Brewster, who was the most esteemed ornithologist
in Massachusetts. Roger considered the Nuttall Club to represent the essence
of "Harvard culture—restrained, sophisticated and so, so genteel." Its members included various distinguished students of birds, as well as relative
novices such as Roger. He tried out for the freshman rowing team but again
found athletics alien.[5]

He was not invited to join the top club, the Porcellian, largely reserved for
a small number of wealthy New Yorkers, or Alpha Delta Phi, to which
Franklin Roosevelt belonged. However, "I made myself well enough known

by my activities and connections to get into larger clubs," Roger later recalled. In his sophomore year he was elected to the Institute of 1770, which had an exclusive clubhouse with an English butler, and dined there for two years. The Institute of 1770 admitted one hundred sophomores each year; Roger's selection, in his estimation, bespoke "a sort of mark of social acceptability." Nevertheless, at one point he participated in a rebellion of sorts, when he backed the successful candidacy of a young man from Kansas—who had not been asked to become part of the top clubs—for class president. Later Roger joined the Memorial Society, the Signet, and Hasty Pudding; Hasty Pudding's membership then included Harry Hopkins.[6]

According to Roger, he had no desire to affiliate with one of the prestigious fraternities, made up of "those concerned about social position." Baldwin later maintained, "I was kind of on the edge of the club system. I wasn't actively opposed to it, but I didn't think it important. I didn't know enough people in the final clubs to want to associate with them. They weren't my natural colleagues." However, such protestations ring hollow. Clearly, Roger, like so many Harvard men, desperately wanted to be included in respectable circles and that required becoming a club man.[7] This also ensured his estrangement from an old friend like Lawrence Grose, who lacked comparable social connections.

His concerns about being accepted were evident when his uncle William Henry Baldwin Jr. delivered a lecture on prostitution to a packed throng at the Harvard Union. Both Roger and his cousin Herbert Nash Jr. sat "bursting with self-importance" and were delighted that prominent students, who had previously ignored them, no longer did so. In 1905 Uncle William died of cancer. During the funeral at Cambridge's Mount Auburn Cemetery, Roger played the organ, concluding the service with "Fair Harvard."[8]

Throughout this period involvement in reform endeavors was hardly controversial at Harvard and indeed was viewed as eminently respectable. Harvard undergraduates—including Franklin Roosevelt—joined the Harvard Service Society, supported union campaigns, championed women's rights, or favored other reform efforts. Roger, influenced by friends at Phillips Brooks House, a Harvard center for religious and public service, volunteered to teach at the Cambridge Social Union on Brattle Street, just next to Harvard Square. The Social Union was led by professors and offered adult education classes for workers. Roger first gave piano lessons and delivered weekly lectures to crowds of 150. The next year Roger—who admittedly "was always organizing things"—was placed in charge of recruiting other students to serve as instructors for the Social Union. He also helped to organize the Harvard Entertainment Troupers, a group of singers and musicians that offered amateur performances in the Boston area for the poor.[9]

His academic performance was merely adequate, not nearly as spectacular as he later remembered it to have been. In fact, of the thirty-seven courses he took, he received mostly gentlemen's C's, pulling down only 5 A's and a dozen B's. The C he got in Music 1, Baldwin reported at the time, "petrified me and has sapped all my ambition for work in music and for a 'cum laude.'" He managed only C's in English too but garnered A's in advanced geology and botany. He studied Greek and Spanish—which, in his estimation, "were of no use"—along with literature, art, music, geology, and history. However, he took no social science courses and only a single political science class.[10]

The Harvard faculty of the early twentieth century comprised, as one former student of that period recalled, an "Olympian roster." Harvard, still expanding under President Eliot, had entered something of a golden age. Roger most revered the kind of "independent and odd characters" he had come to admire back in Wellesley. The philosopher George Santayana had no appeal for him. The philosopher Josiah Royce appeared too remote. Their colleague, Hugo Munsterberg, was "forbidding and Prussian." George Herbert Palmer seemed distant. By contrast, Nathaniel Southgate Shaler was such an attractive instructor that Roger took every one of his geology classes, which somehow fused philosophy, history, social science, and the natural sciences. Charles Townsend Copeland made literature vibrant, and his "tart remarks were common student currency," Baldwin recalled. Barrett Wendell, Roger remembered, stood as "an earthy gentleman whose salacious wit" helped to make English literature bearable. Abbott Lawrence Lowell, who taught government and later became president of Harvard, proved "the most forceful lecturer of them all," Baldwin reflected.[11]

During his last summer as an undergraduate Roger joined an anthropological expedition of fifteen Harvard students led by Professor William C. Farabee to the American Southwest. This was Roger's first trip across the American heartland, and it began with a visit to the St. Louis World's Fair. He was thoroughly impressed with the fair's "architecturally unified and beautiful" grounds, which soon became part of newly established Washington University. The students spent a great portion of the summer traveling through the pueblos and reservations of New Mexico and Arizona. They acquired no college credits in the process, only the adventure of covering six hundred miles on horseback. They traversed the rough desert terrain with a chuck wagon for supplies, aided by a Native American guide and a cowboy cook. Roger pronounced the countryside "magnificent," his compatriots "congenial," and the Indians they encountered "fascinating."[12]

At the conclusion of their anthropological studies of Native Americans, Roger and two or three of his classmates continued on to California, Washington State, Vancouver, and Montreal, which afforded a look at the magnificent Canadian Rockies. They also ventured across the Mexican border, supposedly to witness "a nauseating bull-fight" in Tijuana.[13]

His friends assumed that Roger, pleasure loving and popular as ever, would marry shortly after graduation, obtain a well-paid job, and begin a family. Instead, having completed his bachelor's degree in three years, he began graduate studies, now coupling anthropology and philosophy. In the process he encountered the philosopher Ralph Barton Perry, whose lectures he deemed "abstract and high-minded," different from any he had experienced. As he would at other times, Roger found it difficult to get anything down on paper. The result was a "very pedestrian" master's thesis, which garnered "an undeserved B."[14]

Roger left Harvard in 1905 as still "a not unconventional Boston product." The atmosphere in Cambridge had been "quite conformist," he said, and he felt no pressure to operate outside respectable circles. The progressive currents of the times had honed certain humanitarian instincts from his childhood, and he was considered socially attractive, well versed as he was in the arts and high culture. However, he possessed "no training for any job" and "no practical utility for earning a living."[15]

Following his graduation from Harvard, he returned to his family's home in Wellesley, which was about to be sold. The Baldwins were building a new home in West Newton, which was closer to Boston, where other family members lived. In the meantime it was determined that Lucy Baldwin and the children, along with her widowed sister, Emma, would spend a year in Europe. Frank supposedly was unable to get away for that long but intended to join the family outside Florence for a month or so. As it turned out, Frank and Lucy were separating, perhaps because of his long-standing affair with a widow, Mrs. Clarkson Balch (although it is not clear, she apparently succeeded the woman whom Roger and Lawrence met at the Ashland farm). Frank had bought a cottage for Balch near the Wellesley estate and later settled his lover and her children at the farm in Hopkinton.[16]

Within a week of Roger's commencement, he, his mother, aunt, and siblings sailed for Liverpool on a tour steamer, the S.S. *Bohemia*. Bob later referred to this period as "the year that Roger took us to Europe." Roger was forced to take the lead, Bob said, because "our sweet gentle mother would not have had the remotest idea how to buy so much as a railway ticket." They traveled through Wales, Ireland, and Scotland before heading on to London. From there they proceeded to the Continent and made their way to Florence. Roger left his family at a *pensione* while he searched for a more suitable dwelling. Whether it was planned or a fortuitous coincidence is not clear, but Charlotte Ryman and her family, including her niece Majorie, were staying at a nearby villa. They proposed that Lucy and her clan remain in Florence for the fall season. The Baldwins agreed and rented the Villa i Cedri at Bagnop a Ripoli, once the home of the duke of Connaught, who had been visited there by Queen Victoria. Located up the Arno River from Florence, it offered forty rooms of "medieval elegance," for $100 a month. A superintendent, his wife, two cooks, and five additional servants made the Baldwins' stay quite comfortable. When guests came for dinner, the Baldwin boys donned dinner jackets.[17]

Frank visited at Christmas, and afterward Roger, then almost twenty-two; his sister Ruth, who was about eighteen; and their brother Herb, who was about thirteen, left the family behind in Rome and toured the Mediterranean. The trip, marked by inclement weather and rough seas, took them first to Sicily, where they discovered Greek, Roman, and medieval artifacts. Then they journeyed to Tunis, Crete, and Athens, which Roger, who had long studied Greek and the classics, wanted to see most of all. Led by a guide, they traveled by train and carriage to Corinth, Delphi, Olympia, and Patras.[18]

The Baldwins sailed for New York City on the S.S. *Romanic* on May 18, 1906. On May 31 they arrived in Boston where they were met by Frank, who, as Roger saw it, appeared "nervous, tired and irritable." By now he was having an affair with his niece, the daughter of Lucy's sister, Emma. Lucy, "broken-hearted and bereft" in Roger's eyes, poured out her troubles to her eldest son. At one point Roger went to see his cousin and urged her to break it off. When his father drove up in his carriage, Roger pleaded, "You've got to hold the family together." Lucy and the children went to stay at the Hotel Victoria in Copley Square in Boston, and Roger informed his Aunt Ruth, the widow of Frank's brother William, of what had transpired. Ruth, who was Roger's faithful confidante, phoned her brother-in-law and told him, "Frank, Frank. You can't do this to your family." Frank then informed Roger, "I want you to know, my son, I don't want to hear from my brother's widow. This is to be kept in the family."[19]

Roger bluntly informed his father that his behavior was disgraceful, and he became determined to support his mother, who exuded resignation. As Roger saw it, she "depended on her oldest son to sympathize with her. When she lost her husband's love, it broke her up." All the children, Bob Baldwin later acknowledged, sided with their mother. Roger saw her as both "a devoted wife and a devoted mother to all of us. There never was a day when all of us didn't think that we could depend on our mother. She was loyal and we were loyal."[20]

After more than two decades of marriage, Frank and Lucy Baldwin, in the manner of their class, in 1906, chose to live the next forty years apart and never divorced. Frank lived at the Hopkinton farm until he sold it in 1921 and followed his business interests to Brookline, Cuba, Ecuador, Chicago, and back. He retired in 1930 and spent winters in Geneva and the Balearic Islands off the coast of Spain. Frank frequently visited West Newton for a few days at a time and on holidays and family members' birthdays. Through it all he continued to pay the bills, and Roger never heard discussion of monetary issues. As he put it, "There was enough of it." Lucy lived in West Newton until her daughters Deborah and Ruth married and left home. Later she lived in Cambridge with Margaret; Lucy died in 1943. By that time Frank was residing with Bob or Deborah or stayed in Altadena, California, with his lover, Balch, or with another friend in San Francisco. Roger refused to speak with his father for several years after the separation, even avoiding his presence when Frank came to West Newton. Eventually, Roger heeded his mother's implorings and smoothed over the rupture with his father. They then remained close until Frank's death in 1950. Seldom did anyone refer to the marital separation.[21]

Familial strife unquestionably cemented the next decision Roger made in 1906: to leave Boston for the Midwest. Roger said he sought "to escape Boston," where he invariably was viewed as "my grandfather's grandson, my uncle's nephew, and my father's son." Before he broke with his father, Roger had spoken with the president of Frank's company, who offered him a job in personnel. But Frank urged Roger to talk to Louis D. Brandeis, the attorney for both Frank's company and the Baldwin family. Brandeis, a proponent of sociological jurisprudence and one of the most prominent progressive legal theoreticians, was something of a controversial figure. He evidently examined Roger's Harvard transcripts and, taking his background into account, discussed the possibility of public service. "He showed me that I was already committed in spirit," Roger recalled. Moreover, Brandeis pointed out that Roger could make a "decent living in it." Roger had $2,000 in his savings account—including $500 he had received from his father upon turning twenty-one for not smoking and $250 he had been given for guiding the family through Europe. Furthermore, he "was always canny in a New England sense," he later acknowledged. He had no interest in making money but recognized that he had to get a job. He left his meeting with Brandeis "pretty well sold on a reformer's life." Brandeis had concluded their conversation by taking hold of Roger's shoulders and stating, "Leave Boston. I started my career in Saint Louis and I don't regret it—it's the center of democracy in the United States."[22]

Consequently, Roger paid little heed to anything others might have said to dissuade him. To Roger's surprise, his father strongly supported his decision, as did Uncle George, his father's brother. E. M. Grossman, a lawyer and Harvard alumnus, offered Roger a job in philanthropic work in St. Louis: to both head a settlement house and establish a department of sociology at Washington University. The pay was $1,800 a year, with free lodging at the settlement house included. Grossman offered to pay Roger's way to St. Louis to check out the city and the job offer. Roger was also recruited by Mary Buckley, a professional bookbinder and artist, soon to become another of Roger's surrogate mothers. One of his Harvard professors had recommended Roger to Grossman and Buckley because of his work with the Cambridge Social Union.[23]

Several of Roger's friends also urged him to accept the St. Louis positions. Roger accepted Grossman's offer and traveled to St. Louis, where he visited Washington University and the neighborhood house, Self-Cultural Hall, founded by the St. Louis Ethical Society and situated in a dilapidated part of the city. His hosts obviously wanted to impress him, for Grossman arranged a canoe trip to the Meramec River, which delighted Roger. Roger enthusiastically accepted the twin job offers. He looked forward to teaching at the university level, working at the settlement house, and living in "Ozark country."[24]

Unfortunately, Roger's class work at Harvard had in no way prepared him for his work in St. Louis. Harvard then offered no formal course work in sociology, as the faculty viewed the still new discipline with disdain. Professor Thomas Nixon Carver, a dyed-in-the-wool conservative, was the only instructor who offered anything akin to a course in sociology. Luckily, Carver was teaching that very class in the summer of 1906, before Roger was to leave for St. Louis. The course induced Roger to carry out his "own explorations" of intellectual developments, which resulted in his "quickly becoming a devotee of Herbert Spencer [the English philosopher who was an early advocate of the theory of evolution and a proponent of social Darwinism]. As Roger remembered, Spencer "seemed to have all the answers, big and little, and he had a system."[25]

Roger's Aunt Ruth, who had devoted herself to public causes since her husband's death, was undoubtedly delighted with his decision to become involved in social work. When he visited her in New York City, where she maintained a home, she introduced him to the cream of the social work field. Thus Roger began to establish the kinds of remarkably impressive social, political, and personal connections that his parents had cultivated throughout his adulthood. This was tremendously important to one who remained so heavily influenced by his upper-class Bostonian background. Roger now met Lillian Wald, from the Henry Street Settlement House; Jacob Riis, muckraking author of *How the Other Half Lives*; Owen Lovejoy, of the National Child Labor Committee; and Felix Adler, of the Ethical Culture Society, among others.[26]

If Roger had needed reassurance regarding the merits of a career as a social worker, he received it from "these bright and busy saviors, who struck me as living not only significantly but with unexpected gaiety of spirit and a buoyant optimism." Only Adler lacked such an exuberant nature, yet he too was "impressive . . . high-minded, sensitive, dead-serious." Moreover, Adler had helped to inspire the establishment of Self-Cultural Hall in St. Louis. Buoyed by these already legendary figures in the field of social work, the twenty-two-year-old Roger Baldwin, "full of enthusiasm, ignorance and self-assurance," headed for St. Louis in September 1906. He was to remain there until the winter of 1917.[27]

CHAPTER THREE

The Progressive as Social Worker

Freed from familial restraints and tradition-laden Boston, Baldwin found St. Louis in 1906 to possess a fresh "fluidity, almost a disorderliness." St. Louis was a relatively young city, located near lovely Ozark rivers and hills, although Baldwin later insisted, "It's always been a rather shabby, mediocre town." Nevertheless, it seemed to exude democracy, again in sharp contrast to stratified turn-of-the-century Boston.[1]

During his first year in St. Louis, he lived in Kerry Patch, an Irish-Jewish-Polish district, at 1832 Carr Street, the site of the neighborhood house where he was employed. Its sole occupants were Baldwin and the janitor and his wife. Indeed, throughout his stay in St. Louis Baldwin lived on the east side of town, rather than in the affluent west section where most of his friends resided. According to Baldwin, when news of his apostasy reached Boston, a "washing of hands" occurred in the fashionable Back Bay region. The following year he lived at the home of Mrs. Atlanta Hecker, a teacher and the mother of a Harvard classmate. Her house was packed with boys remanded to her custody by the Juvenile Court. Baldwin then moved to "a really elegant pension" that housed about thirty people, including several other Harvard graduates. Baldwin, in turn, felt welcomed by Mary E. Buckley, the professional bookbinder who had helped to recruit him to St. Louis and who "made her home mine whenever I wished," he remembered.[2]

Baldwin continued to spend weekends in the country; indeed, his interest in the outdoors drew him to both the Linnaean Society and the Audubon Society. He often saw his childless aunt and uncle—his father's youngest brother—who lived in a suburban home in Kirkwood. Or, he showed up at the Meramec Canoe Club in Valley Park to row along the Meramec River. Once he took a canoe trip with Dwight Davis, the tennis star and later secretary of war in the Coolidge administration; Thomas McKittrick, later vice president of Chase Manhattan and president of the Bank of International Settlements; and Robert Minor, a cartoonist for the *St. Louis Post-Dispatch* and a leading figure in the American Communist Party after World War I. In typical fashion Baldwin and his cohorts sunbathed in the nude (years later he received messages from his three companions, asking him to destroy a photograph that had captured them face up). As always, he was refreshed by the woods, waters, and hills—which he considered his natural habitat.[3]

While Baldwin lived in St. Louis, his connections included "all . . . the respectable people," a matter of great significance to him, both personally and professionally. He remained on friendly terms with E. M. Grossman, the Harvard-educated lawyer and counsel for the Board of Education who had induced him to come to the midwestern city in the first place. Another good friend was Luther Ely Smith, one of the community's leading progressive lights.[4]

More a "crowd man," as he put it, than ever, Baldwin maintained an active social life, taking girlfriends to dances, parties, and functions at the University Club. He participated in the Public Question Club, whose young, socially conscious members met twice a month to discuss social issues. He joined the Artists Guild, "a collection of odd and more or less creative personalities" in his estimation. Its fifty or sixty members hosted monthly lunches, and Baldwin recalled that he "liked the informality, the kidding, the wit and good fellowship." He participated in a "super supper club—a gilt-edged, high-brow establishment" whose members dressed the part for monthly dinners. He frequented the St. Louis Club, which hosted society balls. An eligible young bachelor, much in demand, he loved playing the social butterfly. "It was a crowd that I was thrown into by my background; I liked the parties and I liked the people. Their conversation was very pleasant," he told Peggy Lamson years later. "It certainly wasn't consistent with anything I was doing. I mean they weren't people who were interested in civic or social reform— they were rich people who had beautiful homes and gave nice dances and I enjoyed it all very much."[5]

In the process, however, he earned a reputation as a tightwad. He maintained a dinner coat, dress suit, and top hat for proper occasions, a not inexpensive proposition. Yet he refused to accept a regular salary for his services at the settlement house or the university. He believed that the cause of civic reform needed the money more than he did. For him, money "was just never a problem," and he accepted reimbursement only for actual expenses. Consequently, he took to keeping a little black book to record cash expenditures. He also got into the habit of always checking prices, taking subways or, later, buses instead of taxis, reading menus "from the right to the left," shopping in bargain basement stores, traveling second or third class, and avoiding first-class hotels.[6]

He was briefly engaged to Dr. Anna Louise Strong, a beautiful social worker from Seattle. Strong came to St. Louis to set up a major exhibit on child welfare, which Baldwin helped to support financially. The two met and fell in love, Baldwin intrigued by this "powerful dame." However, a cultural divide separated them. She was the daughter of a minister and had been raised in a puritanical home. Consequently, Strong insisted that she was unable to marry Baldwin if he smoked, drank, or played cards. He now smoked a pack of Turkish cigarettes a day, which he failed to inhale, and possessed a batch of pipes for when he "felt like sitting down and reading a book and being calm and philosophical." If cigars were passed out at dinner, he took one. He drank but not to excess, because he was concerned about the possibility of losing control. As Strong saw it, such self-indulgence "was a sin," he said. Baldwin hardly considered abstinence from such vices to entail any great sacrifice. However, his Aunt Belle Baldwin led him to believe that this "was just the beginning of a domination that would destroy me." Informed that he intended to marry Strong, Belle responded sharply, "See that crack in the floor? The line you'll walk if you marry her will be narrower than that." As Baldwin conceded, "I love her but I love my independence more." Strong called off the three-month engagement following his visit to her home, in spite of an emotional outburst by Baldwin. They remained good friends and continued to write and visit one another. She became a writer and a noteworthy supporter of first the Bolshevik and then the Communist Chinese revolution.[7]

Later Baldwin almost became engaged once again, this time to a very different sort of woman. Ann Drew was the petite, black-haired, blue-eyed daughter of a prominent banker and a St. Louis socialite. An item on the society page expressed hope something permanent might be in the offing: "It would be rather a good match in almost every way as Roger and Annie are so well suited in their tastes and ideas, and both are blessed with plenty of this world's good." The article called Baldwin "the nicest and most educated young bachelor in sight and equal to coping with the rather self-centered

Annie." Her large family lived in a great house and employed a butler who always wore a white coat. Ann, "demure and lovely and graceful" in a formal evening gown, would await Baldwin in the drawing room. The object of attention of numerous would-be suitors, she was hardly self-effacing and served as an officer of the Women's Trade Union League and engaged in Catholic public works. Baldwin referred to her as "the real love of my life" and spoke of their "idyllic relationship. No spring was ever so fresh and beautiful as it was when I saw it with her. None has ever been so since." They dated for three or four years and discussed how her Catholicism might preclude them from getting married. She determined that he should sign a pledge that they would be married by a priest in church and raise their children as Catholics. Meanwhile, there existed a rival claimant for her affections, who happened to be Catholic and a strong-willed individual himself. He convinced her to marry him, after a press announcement of the impending wedding was released. Ann was evidently not ready for such a commitment, and Baldwin attempted, unsuccessfully, to undo it.[8]

During the first decade of the twentieth century, progressive reform was in vogue in many communities across the land, and St. Louis was an exemplar of municipal reform. The St. Louis Post-Dispatch set the tone under the tutelage of Joseph Pulitzer (whom Baldwin, after lunching with the publisher, pointedly referred to as a Jew in a letter to his mother). The crusading district attorney, Joseph W. Folk, had just conducted a campaign to rid the city government of corruption; that effort, Baldwin said, had resulted in the conviction of "leading political crooks and grafters." A cleansing atmosphere supportive of reform had followed, involving, in Baldwin's estimation, the better elements in the city.[9]

When Baldwin arrived in town, "full of uplift and self-confidence" and having read Lincoln Steffens's Shame of the Cities, reform efforts and social services were flourishing. Consequently, civic and political leaders welcomed the experimental enterprises in which Baldwin was engaged. Washington University was still in its infancy, and Baldwin's assignment was to initiate a department of sociology there. The university, in Baldwin's view, seemed to lack "the pretensions to superiority" that characterized "the assured Harvard community" and instead exuded "democratic free inquiry." The faculty included the philosopher Arthur O. Lovejoy, the economist Thomas Sewell Adams, and John Livingston Lowes, a professor of English. Among Baldwin's first students were some "live-minded" individuals who became celebrated figures in their own right. They included the novelist Fannie Hurst; the playwright Zoe Atkins; Thomas D. Eliot, later a sociology professor at Northwestern University and afterward an administrator at his alma mater; and Hugh Fullerton, who became involved in juvenile justice in St. Louis.[10]

Using the Socratic method, Baldwin focused on issues ranging from race relations and government activities to crime and poverty. Baldwin's own attitudes on race during this period were not terribly enlightened. In a city still adhering to Jim Crow standards, Baldwin was, nevertheless, controversial. In early 1909 he invited two black school administrators to speak on racial matters at an optional class meeting. Local newspapers headlined the affair WHITE WOMEN STUDENTS FORCED TO HEAR NEGROES and WASHINGTON U. PROFESSOR ADVOCATES MISCEGENATION. Fifty people, instead of the expected fifteen or twenty, showed up. The *St. Louis Star* presented "a much distorted and perverted account of the incident," Baldwin charged in a letter to the editor of the campus newspaper. For his part, Baldwin declared, "whatever criticism turns on the single fact of colored men addressing a group of students who came voluntarily to hear them needs no comment from me." Although Chancellor David F. Houston and Baldwin's students supported him, "unthinking" folk in the area now called him a "nigger lover," he recalled.[11]

Baldwin continued to seek out leading black educators and social workers, who had never been accepted by St. Louis's civic agencies. When he helped to establish the city's first social service conference, blacks were invited. Baldwin was also instrumental in the formation of the first interracial group, the St. Louis Committee for Social Service Among Colored People. Comprised of professionals, the committee sought to remove discriminatory obstacles but professed not to be striving to transform race relations. In St. Louis the committee was the precursor of the National League on Urban Conditions Among Negroes, established in 1910 in New York City; Baldwin's Aunt Ruth played a key role in that organization.[12]

In August 1911 Baldwin asked Chancellor Houston about the advisability of setting up "a special course for colored people" to be run by the School of Social Economy. Such a course, he implied, would avoid the kinds of embarrassing questions likely to arise if "colored people" were allowed in regular classrooms. In January 1913 Baldwin served on the biracial Special Committee on the Housing of Negroes that condemned a Jim Crow ordinance before the St. Louis Municipal Assembly.[13]

During his first two years in St. Louis, Baldwin's work at Washington University and the Ethical Society's Self-Cultural Hall ensured that he was in "the thick of reform" in the city. Within a short while he was instrumental in organizing the Social Service Conference, which brought social workers together from throughout Missouri. He was also a leading figure in setting up the Council of Social Agencies, comprised of representatives from various social welfare organizations. He helped to create a council of neighborhood civic associations and a coordinating body of such agencies. These organizational efforts, combined with the Civic League—established in 1901 to bring about good government—provided a nucleus for urban reform.[14] Baldwin also became a leading member of the Civic League, which he would later head (in 1910).

Now Baldwin was in his element. He was displaying a skill—which he never lost—for establishing and running organizations. Undoubtedly influenced by the authoritarian makeup of his father, Baldwin took control of agendas, strategies, and logistical matters in general. He also clearly thrived on being the boss, just as Frank Baldwin did. At the same time Roger Baldwin's Boston background, with its tradition of support for reform endeavors, proved equally instrumental in steering him in the direction of good government campaigns.

Baldwin's neighborhood work often compelled him to attend the St. Louis Juvenile Court on behalf of boys in the district. His efforts drew the attention of George H. Williams, the young juvenile court judge who sought to improve the treatment of delinquent and neglected children. Williams— later a U.S. senator—offered Baldwin a job in September 1907 as the first chief probation officer for the juvenile court. To Baldwin this "was a job which my interest could not refuse," and it involved overseeing the welfare of about two thousand children, mostly delinquent boys. The board of Self-Cultural Hall agreed to allow Baldwin to take on the new assignment, which paid $2,500 a year and took up more of his time than his university teaching or settlement house work. Baldwin put together a professional staff, carried out probationary reforms, devised new approaches, and "brought together the child caring agencies." The juvenile court in St. Louis was innovative and looked to Judge Ben Lindsey's pioneering efforts in Denver. Baldwin traveled to Colorado to attend Lindsey's court. Seeking other models, he helped to establish in 1908 a loose confederation, the National Probation Officers Association. Formed after the annual conference of social workers, this association—with Baldwin serving as its secretary—included about five hundred probation officers, as well as juvenile court judges Harvey H. Baker of Boston, Julian W. Mack of Chicago, and Edward Waite of Minneapolis.[15]

Unable to rearrange his university schedule to his satisfaction, Baldwin, on March 20, 1909, tendered his resignation, effective that summer, to Houston. Baldwin continued to put together a first-rate probation staff, comprised of ten to fifteen teachers and social workers of various faiths. To ensure professional standards he helped to write Missouri's first set of civil service regulations. To prevent political patronage the regulations required employees of the probation department, including Baldwin and any incumbents, to take a civil service exam.[16]

State legislators, many of whom considered Baldwin too young and inexperienced, passed legislation in 1909 that required probation officers to have attained their twenty-fifth birthday. Baldwin, as it happened, had just turned twenty-five; however, another part of the new law led him to feel compelled to pay a portion of the salary of a young assistant. Fortunately, the juvenile court judges were a politically independent lot and received strong public backing for their operations and financial backing from the government.[17]

Soon St. Louis's juvenile justice system, like Denver's, became something of a model for judges and social workers across the country. The constant influx of interested visitors resulted in changes in the municipal government as well. Judge Willis Brown, visiting from Salt Lake City, startled Baldwin and his colleagues by proposing that the juvenile court be abolished. The court, Brown reasoned, stigmatized the children who entered its chambers. Community welfare agencies could undertake preventative measures to handle wayward children. Like Judge Brown, Baldwin was drawn to the school of thought that held environmental causes responsible for many social ills. Heated debate arose among St. Louis social workers that eventually determined Brown's suggestion had some merit. Subsequently, they refused to heed complaints regarding children that might be dealt with by the public schools. Criminal prosecution was not always necessary, it was argued, as police officers could mediate neighborhood squabbles concerning problem children. Such changes reduced court dockets.[18]

Because of his involvement with juvenile court Baldwin "inadvertently" became legal guardian of two orphan boys of "dubious parentage"—they were the sons of prostitutes—ten-year-old Otto Stolz and twelve-year-old William Oral James. Baldwin had no such intention until the juvenile judge convinced him that no better alternatives existed. "You find a place for them," the judge told him. Otto—called Toto by Baldwin and others who knew him well—had been neglected by his mother and sheltered in the city home. Oral had a foster mother, a reformed prostitute who was ill equipped to care for him. Baldwin took Toto, "a warped little fellow who distrusted everyone until he found I really cared for him," to live with him at Mrs. Hecker's house. Toto warmed up to Baldwin after the two spent a few weekends at a neighborhood house tent camp. Late one evening Baldwin had just completed a swim and returned to the river bank, when he spotted Toto holding a lighted candle for him; this was Toto's first display of friendship. And after they entered their tent, the youngster sat on Baldwin's cot and hugged him. As Baldwin later wrote, "I knew then that he would not leave and that I had to keep him. I told the judge I would do the best I could."[19]

Nevertheless, he maintained a certain reserve or outright coldness when dealing with his young charges; he appeared ambivalent at best regarding the responsibility he had acquired in caring for the two lads. Toto, for instance, always referred to him as Mr. Baldwin, which Baldwin did nothing to discourage. Clearly, then, an emotional distance colored Baldwin's relationship with Toto in particular, as it often did his relationships with male family members.[20]

Baldwin's work at the juvenile court exposed him to diphtheria, German measles, and a host of children's diseases he had managed to avoid in his own sheltered childhood. While in the hospital after contracting diphtheria, he acquired Vincent's angina (a now-obsolete term for ulcerative gingivitis), which produced a boil in his throat that had to be lanced. He communicated with the doctor by writing notes. Baldwin asked, "Am I going to get well?" The doctor replied, "I don't know. Why do you ask?" Baldwin responded, "I have a will that has to be signed." The doctor declared, "You better sign it." Baldwin instructed E. M. Grossman to bring his will and, in the belief that he was going to die, told his doctor, "If I am not going to get well, please let me have morphine." Lucy Baldwin was en route from Boston, and her son told the nurse to say good-bye for him. The morphine, he later stated, "sent me up to heaven." And within a few days he was out riding a horse.[21]

During this period it is clear that Roger Baldwin stood as a progressive who viewed matters from an elitist perspective and believed that American institutions and American society required, at most, fine-tuning. Soon, however, his work with the juvenile court compelled him to analyze the social conditions that had helped to produce neglected and delinquent children like Toto and Oral. He determined that "the basic evil was poverty." Sociology, he believed, offered no answers. Then he attended a public address that profoundly influenced him.[22]

While he was still teaching at Washington University and working at the settlement house, Baldwin first encountered a woman whom he later credited with transforming his intellectual life. Cynthelia Isdrig Knefler, an upper-class woman with a businessman husband and "terribly radical ideas," goaded Baldwin into attending a speech by Emma Goldman, the "Red Queen of Anarchy." Baldwin's initial response had been one of scorn. He would not deign, Baldwin informed Knefler, to go listen to "that crazy woman." She retorted, "You Harvard men think you know everything, but you're really just smug and narrow. You ought to want to hear the other side." Finally, Baldwin agreed. The hall was packed, with workers in abundance. A short homely woman, Goldman impressed Baldwin greatly, demonstrating a selflessness and absolute dedication to "the social problem." To his amazement Goldman spoke passionately and cogently in a way he had never heard before. "Here was a vision of the end of poverty and injustice by free association of those who worked, by the abolition of privilege, and by the organized power of the exploited." Moreover, Goldman was focusing on the same concerns, including poverty and injustice, with which he was wrestling. The effect was electrifying.[23]

Through his radical friend William Marion Reedy, a leading reformer in St. Louis and publisher of the *Mirror*, an internationally acclaimed literary magazine, Baldwin gained an introduction to Goldman. He found her to be "charming, witty, warm, and intellectual in fields unknown to me." Indeed, her vast knowledge of anarchist literature made him feel ignorant.[24]

Baldwin invited compatriots of his—social workers, attorneys, and journalists—to attend lunch with Goldman. "Her wit, charm and modesty" seemed to win them over. Consequently, he arranged for her to lecture on the dramatist Henrik Ibsen before the Women's Wednesday Club and later at one of the better hotels in the city. Baldwin subsequently denied that he had suffered from his sponsorship of Goldman. Rather, "it was regarded as an interesting philosophical excursion natural to a reformer and sociologist— and I saw to it that I had plenty of respectable company." At the same time the probate court judge was less than pleased with Baldwin's apparent sponsorship of the notorious anarchist. Baldwin should either resign as probation officer, he insisted, or toss aside his "scandalous associations." Lacking familial responsibilities, Baldwin declined to do either, refusing "to surrender intellectual freedom for intellectual bondage in the best job on earth." Fortunately, the judge changed his mind.[25]

Initially, Goldman was little impressed with Baldwin. As she recalled in her autobiography, he appeared to be "a very pleasant person, though not very vital." She saw "rather a social lion surrounded by society girls whose interest in the attractive young man was apparently greater than in his uplift work."[26]

In September 1909 Baldwin received a letter from Goldman asking for assistance in renting the Ethical Society's Self-Cultural Hall for another public address; this was the first of hundreds of letters, spanning three full decades, between those disparate souls. The continuation of the settlement house, Baldwin responded, depended on patrons' good graces and public opinion. Furthermore, the board was unlikely to "consent to its use for such subjects as you would desire to speak on, altho [sic] many personally are very much interested." The following year, however, Baldwin did act on her behalf, after being informed that administrators at Washington University had denied her the right to speak on campus.[27]

His association with Emma Goldman induced Baldwin to examine a world of literary and philosophical thought previously foreign to him. He had already begun to look outside the field of social work for answers to the widespread poverty, grave inequalities, and injustices afflicting democratic America. He sought out leading socialists in the community but considered them too enamored "with a scheme of salvation . . . too doctrinaire, too German and too old." When the Socialist Party leader Eugene V. Debs spoke in St. Louis, Baldwin chose not to see him. Baldwin's friends, Frank and Kate O'Hare, who edited the *Rip-Saw*, a national socialist publication, twitted Baldwin about his refusal to do so. He met with militant labor chieftains but viewed them as "too arrogant, too scornful of intellectuals and reformers." The anarchists, with their libertarian emphasis, seemed infinitely more attractive. As he later acknowledged, Baldwin found appealing "their goal of a society with a minimum of compulsion, a maximum of individual freedom and of voluntary association, and the abolition of exploitation and poverty." He viewed their approach as scarcely practical but took satisfaction in having discovered a vision to which he could subscribe. He proceeded to explore "the literature of protest, the utopias, the kind of non-conformist authors not taught at Harvard," like the Russian prince Peter Kropotkin, the foremost theorist of the anarchist movement. Baldwin examined the full panoply of scribes that the anarchists claimed as their own, including Socrates, Jesus, Ibsen, Tolstoy, Emerson, Thoreau, and the German and British libertarians.[28]

As Baldwin later reflected, it was not surprising that a Bostonian "reared in the Concord tradition should take to anarchist ideals." Convinced that anarchism was intellectually respectable, his attraction to Goldman's worldview blossomed. He managed to dismiss acts of violence committed by anarchists as irrelevant; after all, "misguided idealists" of all types acted in desperation. His attraction to the philosophy of anarchism would be extended by his personal relationships with its proponents. Eventually, they ranged from Goldman herself to Harry Kelley, a local businessman, fellow member of the good government Civic League, and "the most unlikely anarchist you could ever find." This gentle and thoughtful soul was well traveled and had met many leading European anarchists, including those who had flocked to Kropotkin during his exile in England. Goldman thought Kelley was hypnotized by Baldwin, who retorted, "He has quite captured me." Kelley, like Goldman, particularly encouraged Baldwin to read Kropotkin. Kelley and Baldwin became part of what was jokingly referred to as "a Crank's Table," comprised of ten or twelve argumentative individuals. Baldwin viewed such men as the most entertaining souls around. "Of course they were all slightly nutty," he said.[29]

The appeal of anarchist tenets and the attraction of noteworthy anarchists notwithstanding, Baldwin remained one of the leading progressives in St. Louis and the Midwest. In the process he initiated another lifelong pattern: involvement with both reformist and radical circles. Reform campaigns during the progressive period were eminently respectable, which was comforting to Baldwin, who was quite concerned about appearances. Now, however, his interest was also piqued by ideas and movements of a more controversial cast. His association with anarchists undoubtedly allowed him to identify with the Boston rebels whose legend loomed so large during his childhood. That tie, along with Baldwin's standing as a well-regarded progressive, enabled him to consider himself at the cutting edge of the reform and radical movements that flourished before World War I.

Throughout his stay in St. Louis, Baldwin demonstrated great interest in the plight of unfortunate children. From 1910 onward he served as president of the State Conference for Social Welfare. At the mayor's behest he joined the Municipal Commission of Children, established by city ordinance in 1911. He was gaining a national reputation from his work with the juvenile court, advocacy of pioneering legislation for children, and association with other social movements. He attended national conferences where he met leading figures in various social welfare enterprises. He was particularly attracted to Denver's Ben Lindsey, whom Baldwin considered a man of courage and a visionary selflessly devoted to children. Lindsey could be "tactless as a crusader," Baldwin recognized, and many saw the judge "as a wild man off the social work reservation." Baldwin, in contrast, looked at the good judge as "the major promoter, certainly the advertising specialist, in the field of juvenile neglect and delinquency." Baldwin believed his own contributions to juvenile justice to be largely technical in nature, as he devised "a thoroughgoing system of supervision and of investigation and report."[30]

From May 19 to 26, 1910, the 37th Annual Session of the National Conference of Charities and Correction met in St. Louis. Undoubtedly to Baldwin's delight, the foremost actors in the field of social work were present, including Jane Addams, who delivered the presidential address, "Charity and Social Justice." Homer Folks spoke about the National Children's Bureau, Louisville attorney Bernard Flexner discussed juvenile justice, Owen R. Lovejoy focused on the national child labor movement, and Paul U. Kellogg examined occupational standards. The session entitled "Statistics" featured talks by Florence Kelley, the well-known social worker who toiled with Jane Addams at Hull House in Chicago; Julia C. Lathrop, a pioneer advocate of child welfare laws and public assistance to the indigent; and Roger N. Baldwin. In his speech, "Statistics Relating to Juvenile Delinquents," Baldwin contended that only children who threatened to become "habitual offenders" or apparently lacked the "capacity for normal moral conduct" should be considered juvenile delinquents.[31]

In 1914 he related his experiences in juvenile justice in *Juvenile Courts and Probation*, a textbook he co-authored with Flexner. The book was derived in part from a series of answers to a lengthy questionnaire that they had sent to top figures in the field of juvenile justice, including Judge Lindsey, Julian W. Mack, and Homer Folks. The questionnaire asked these experts what treatments might prove effective in dealing with perpetrators of false fire alarms, knifings, sex offenses, auto thefts, manslaughter, and murder. Baldwin and Flexner traveled between St. Louis and Louisville as they drafted the manuscript, which came to be recommended by leading authorities on juvenile courts. Juvenile justice, the authors insisted, must be committed to "the training of the child to make him as good a member of society as possible. Every disposition should be based on the idea of what is best for the child's welfare." A determination to mete out punishment, they asserted, should not guide judges in juvenile courts. Probation also had to be handled differently. It must be instituted "to adjust the forces of the community to the child's life." All social agencies had to be employed in an effort "to surround the child with a network of favorable influences which will enable him to maintain normal habits of life."[32]

With Baldwin as a key player, both the city of St. Louis and the state of Missouri stood in the vanguard of reform legislation concerning children. In 1915 the governor set up a statewide commission on children, inspired by Baldwin's work. The commission's charge was to examine legislation affecting child care. Baldwin and his compatriots discovered other allies in Kansas City, particularly attorney Frank P. Walsh, later chairman of Woodrow Wilson's Commission on Industrial Relations.[33]

In 1916 Lucille Milner (then known as Lucille Lowenstein), a young widow recently graduated from the New York School of Philanthropy who had carried out part of her field research on Hester Street, returned to her native St. Louis seeking employment. She received a call from Baldwin, who stated, "We have a tailor-made job for you." Milner went to see Baldwin at his Civic League office, a beehive of activity, with the telephone ringing constantly and staff members popping in, especially Oral James, who was acting as a kind of gofer. To Milner the thirty-two year-old Baldwin was "tall, wiry, handsome and vigorous." Baldwin informed her, "We want you to administer the Children's Code Commission which Governor Gardner has just appointed. It's an interesting and worthwhile job; not an easy one, but that only makes it all the more interesting."[34]

He then stated, "Our laws relating to children are conflicting, some overlap and many are outdated and inadequate." Few people were concerned about child care, while private charities and the state legislature, particularly the upper house dominated by the Pendergast machine, would oppose any reform efforts. Funds were nonexistent, and Milner would be compelled to canvass the state to bring pressure to bear on politicians. "The burden of the task—and it may seem hopeless at times," Baldwin acknowledged, "will be on you as executive secretary. Will you take it?" Milner responded, "When do I start?" Interestingly enough, given his generally parsimonious ways, he insisted that she not operate as a volunteer but rather as a paid professional.[35]

By now Baldwin was a well-respected progressive, who possessed intimate ties to both leading reformers and a growing number of radicals across the land. In fact, because of his activities to a certain extent, St. Louis was considered one of the bastions of early twentieth-century progressivism. St. Louis progressives like Baldwin strove to ameliorate the worst aspects of industrial capitalism while engaging in a wide range of reform activities.

CHAPTER FOUR

The Civic League

In 1910 Baldwin was named secretary of St. Louis's Civic League, a good government organization supported by "all the best people," as he liked to put it; consequently, it was precisely the kind of association that mainstream progressives were comfortable with. To Baldwin's satisfaction the Civic League intended to deal "with the political and civic problems of the whole community." Once again he refused a full salary, despite the tremendous workload involved, because the Civic League was often strapped financially.[1]

In accepting the secretaryship of the Civic League, he had declined other offers, including one tendered by the Association for Improving the Condition of the Poor. The guiding force behind the association was R. Fulton Cutting, who, along with the board, offered Roger a handsome salary, $6,000 a year, and the chance to live in America's most vibrant metropolitan area, New York City. Proclaiming that he did not seek to "improve the poor," Baldwin chose to replace Mayo Fesler—who had moved on to take a similar job in Cleveland—at the Civic League.[2]

As Baldwin's reputation continued to grow, he turned down other job offers that would have enabled him to return east. Indeed, a reform group known as "Boston 1915" initially viewed with appreciation his accomplishments in St. Louis. The reformers involved with "Boston 1915," headed by the muckraker Lincoln Steffens, sought to break the stranglehold of the Democratic political machine. Steffens envisioned a committee, to be led by Edward A. Filene, the department store mogul and philanthropist, that would seek to convince grafters and corrupt politicians of the need for political reform. As Steffens reasoned, such individuals were natural leaders who relished a good fight. "Indeed," Steffens had intimated, "it was the fighting which might convert these bad men to carry on where good men commonly lay down." Baldwin saw himself as "a pretty solid citizen" and was little impressed by the "romantic crusading" of the "Boston 1915" crowd. After he met with the "Boston 1915," its members evidently were not taken with Baldwin, either.[3]

Still more groups sought Baldwin's services. The Northern American Civic League for Immigrants, championed by his aunt Ruth Baldwin, offered him an opportunity to serve as its secretary general. However, a colleague, Homer Folks, the New York state probation commissioner, convinced Baldwin that the league was a private organization that sought to operate as a public agency but lacked sufficient support. Upon the recommendation of Florence Kelley of Hull House, Baldwin also received an offer to become secretary of the Minimum Wage Commission, which was associated with the National Consumers' League, in Washington, D.C. Kelley spoke of Baldwin's accomplishments in St. Louis. She referred to him as "a Harvard graduate and a man of unusual ability and power to conciliate and persuade people of many different kinds and dispositions." Baldwin declined this position too, because he was convinced that the secretaryship of the Civic League afforded even greater opportunities.[4]

Later Baldwin revealed that he never again possessed "such a feeling of certainty and exhilaration, certainty that reform was the answer to social evils than in that period." Still a confirmed progressive, he remained convinced that public ownership of utilities, the graduated income tax, the safeguarding of trade union rights, civil service reform, regulation of child labor, and the institution of the initiative, the referendum, and the recall "would bring a pretty good society."[5]

Joining Baldwin as key members of the Civic League were reform-minded businessmen, lawyers, and social gospel ministers such as John Gundlach, Luther Ely Smith, and Willard Boyd, respectively. The Civic League, formerly dominated by big businessmen, had concentrated on bringing honesty and efficiency to city government, along with public improvements and growth. Its new architects favored "democratizing the city instead of just a city beautiful."[6]

To his delight, Baldwin's colleagues in the campaign to bring about civic reform in St. Louis were prominent individuals, among them some of St. Louis's most distinguished citizens: Charles A. Stix, president of the city's largest department store, Stix, Baer, and Fuller; Mrs. Philip North Moore, president of the General Federation of Women's Clubs; Dr. Percival Chubb, who headed the Ethical Society; and Dwight F. Davis, the donor of the Davis Cup for international tennis competition, the city park commissioner, and later governor-general of the Philippines. Nevertheless, Baldwin relied even more on William Preston Hill, a retired physician who favored the single tax panacea devised by Henry George and was a powerful presence in the city's potent labor movement. Baldwin felt that to bring about reform, he would need support from Hill and his allies, who included the socialists. Hill and J. P. McDonough, a leading labor figure, seemed to accept Baldwin, albeit with some suspicion. Baldwin's more socially respectable supporters viewed Hill and McDonough as cranks.[7]

For the next seven years Baldwin strove to expand the Civic League's emphasis on civic betterment to include "thoroughgoing political reform." Backed by business and professional groups, the Civic League under Baldwin's guidance supported numerous municipal reforms, including "social welfare, slum clearance, clean streets; abolition of nuisances, charter revision and smoke abatement . . . [as well as] cultivating popular forces to assure good government," according to the historian James Neal Primm. In 1912 Baldwin helped to form the Civic Federation, which successfully brought together businessmen, professionals, workers, and religious leaders to support a bond for bridge construction.[8]

Reformers in St. Louis, such as Baldwin and his compatriots with the Civic League and the juvenile court, were part of the progressive movement that had dominated U.S. politics since Teddy Roosevelt's presidency. They sought to reform—not transform altogether—existing political, economic, and social structures, and Baldwin continued to work comfortably within such a framework. The Civic League never boasted a membership greater than three or four thousand, drawn from an urban area of about 750,000 inhabitants. Nevertheless, it riveted public attention on issues big and small, including the inauguration of participatory democratic devices, efforts to curb social ills, and a campaign to rein in "predatory special interests."[9]

Early in his tenure as league secretary, Baldwin joined in a campaign to revise the city charter and to construct a free metropolitan bridge. The revision called for giving voters the initiative, the referendum, and the recall, three of the political devices championed by progressives. Such mechanisms, they believed, could empower the local citizenry. The call for charter revision had begun in 1908 to institutionalize the "business government," with its focus on efficiency, inaugurated by Rolla Wells, Democratic mayor of St. Louis from 1901 to 1909. The revised charter would have strengthened the executive powers of the mayor and resulted in a unicameral legislature. Workers, socialists, Germans, owners of small businesses, and various reformers—all of whom believed big business was supporting charter revision—combined to urge its defeat. The People's League, headed by Dr. Hill, Baldwin's sometime ally, condemned the "Plutocratic-Oligarchic" conspiracy to turn the citizenry of St. Louis into "serfs of the Big Cinch," the dominant West End businessmen and professionals. The voters responded in 1911 by defeating the proposed charter by a nearly 3–1 margin.[10]

Leaders of the Civic League now recognized the need to invoke greater public cooperation. Consequently, Baldwin, along with Charlotte Rumbold, superintendent of the St. Louis Park Department's public playgrounds and recreation; the local progressive leader Luther Ely Smith; and John Gundlach, a real estate agent, helped to celebrate the founding of St. Louis by the Frenchman Pierre Laclède Liguest a century and a half earlier. Backed by the local historical society, the Businessmen's League, labor unions, and nearly one hundred other professional associations, the Civic League sponsored the Pageant and Masque of May 28–June 1, 1914. Baldwin termed the spectacle "the greatest civic drama ever projected in the United States." To his delight, virtually every government agency, ranging from the public schools to municipal administrative branches, joined in. About seventy-five hundred men, women, and children participated, acting on a massive stage set inside a natural amphitheater with a seating capacity of sixty thousand. The purpose of the pageant was to depict the history of St. Louis and "the struggle of civilization the triumph of the city and of democracy," he wrote.[11]

"If we play together, we will work together" was the slogan adopted by the pageant's architects. This was a lesson, Baldwin wrote, that St. Louis needed to learn. The Pageant and Masque, he hoped, would "visualize the city's life, and bring forth into expression all the latent power for a new citizenship." City dwellers of all types, native born and immigrant, black and white, businessmen and laborers, served on pageant committees together. Such "democratic contact in the cause of a celebration of the common civic life," he hoped, would enable a new spirit to arise that would allow St. Louis to accomplish "big things and to do them through her citizenship as a whole." New democratic devices like the initiative and the referendum, if adopted by St. Louis, would mean that the entire community, rather than businessmen only as in days past, would be "the doer of deeds," he wrote.[12]

The city charter was antiquated, Baldwin and other leading members of the new Civic League believed, and had to be revised "to serve the citizens rather than the politicians." This latest effort to gain charter revision was bitterly contested, even within the ranks of the Civic League, despite the celebratory spirit generated by the St. Louis Pageant and Masque. Newspapers in the city, led by the *Post-Dispatch*, favored charter revision. So did civic organizations and political parties but not many politicians or businessmen, who preferred business-as-usual practices. The city council would not set an election for a charter commission, it appeared likely, thanks to pressures from ward politicians. Baldwin solicited the help of John Gundlach, the Republican businessman, political figure, and fellow Civic League officer who lived on St. Louis's prosperous north side. Gundlach, in turn, convinced the chairman of the Republican Party in St. Louis, John Schmoll, to support the proposed election. Schmoll informed Baldwin that "he would line up 'the boys' " on the city council and then proceeded to do so.[13]

The charter drafted by the commission in 1914 possessed, as Baldwin saw it, the types of "popular safeguards we advocated," including the initiative, the referendum, and the recall; civil service regulations; a smaller city council; and municipal ownership of public utilities—all favorites of early twentieth-century progressives. In fact, Baldwin contended that this latest version of the charter was considerably more radical than the one rejected by voters three years earlier. Additionally, this charter was the by-product of open discussions, advice from experts throughout the United States, and suggestions from all classes of citizens, which undercut the opposition of the radicals; again, progressives favored just such an approach. Baldwin believed that the charter commission had earnestly attempted to craft the type of charter that the people of St. Louis desired. But most significant, in Baldwin's estimation, was that the charter was "the first big thing that the progressive forces of the city have achieved in many years." Following the pageant as it did, Baldwin later noted, the charter campaign "was the response of a new spirit in a city which has been divided, torn, hampered and hobbled by suspicion, apathy and conflicting issues." It replicated, Baldwin insisted, "the old story of plunderer and plundered, of special interests versus the public."[14]

Not surprisingly, then, the good government forces now backed this effort, while political bosses and industrial magnates opposed it. Baldwin, in a tactic that was becoming increasingly familiar to him, remained in the background, helping to devise strategy to support revision of the city charter. Mayor Fred Kreismann supported the transformed charter, as did citi-

zens' organizations, the improvement associations, and neighborhood business associations. Baldwin's compatriots purportedly felt "that a professional
reformer [like Baldwin] would be no great asset out front." In 1914 the voters approved the new charter by a scant 2,681 votes. The *St. Louis Post-Dispatch* applauded Baldwin's "single-handed efforts," and Gundlach credited
the pageant, which had cultivated "a sustained public spirit for a more
humane city." Baldwin too claimed that the "great democratic civic pageant
and masque" had turned the tide.[15]

The St. Louis Pageant and Masque and the charter campaign, Baldwin
believed, had revitalized progressive forces in the city. In 1915 voters approved
a bond sale of $2.75 million by a 7–1 margin, marking what Baldwin called
"the last act in St. Louis' greatest municipal drama, the free bridge fight,"
which allowed for its completion. Baldwin considered this a classic fight that
pitted the people against a railroad monopoly; moreover, as he saw it, "the
issue of the 'Big Cinch versus the people' came to the front." In June 1906 voters had approved an $11.2 million bond issue, which included more than $3
million for bridge construction; however, the Businessmen's League had continued to oppose the building of a toll-free bridge. "Scandal, bribery, corruption and intrigue" had resulted from the conflict. The curbing of the power
of the Terminal Railroad Association, a large freight and passenger operation,
Baldwin wrote—using language characteristic of the progressive movement—had proved to be "a tremendous educational force in developing the
power of democracy." It had instilled a progressive spirit and was further
indication that "St. Louis is a city today where 'the people rule,' perhaps not
always wisely or well, but they do really control. Political bossism and public
utilities in politics are doubtless influences all of the past," Baldwin wrote.[16]

However, to Baldwin's dismay, but consistent with the beliefs of a certain
wing of progressivism, once St. Louis voters had the initiative, they began a
drive to mandate segregated housing. Overt racial strife had been little
apparent in St. Louis, perhaps because blacks continued to comprise a mere
6 percent of the population and had generally lived in the central river dis-
tricts and on the outskirts of downtown. Schools, hotels, restaurants, and
barbershops were segregated; libraries, department store elevators, street-
cars, and the theater were not. In 1896 the U.S. Supreme Court's decision in
Plessy v. Ferguson had given a judicial imprimatur to segregation, and the
next fifteen years had proved to be particularly violent in regard to race relations. Following Baltimore's lead, a number of cities in the South and in border states like Missouri enacted residential segregation codes.[17]

In 1911 white neighborhood associations in St. Louis, fearing a shift in residential patterns, formed the United Welfare Association, which had the backing of the powerful Real Estate Exchange. Lacking support in the Municipal Assembly, the association in 1915 sought to use the initiative to produce "an ordinance to prevent ill feeling, conflict and collision between the white and colored races" by mandating "the use of separate blocks for residence," in addition to segregation in churches and dance halls. No individual of any race could reside, one provision held, on a block where three-quarters of the inhabitants were of another race. The election was set for February 29, 1916.[18]

A bitter political contest unfolded, with Baldwin leading the opposition forces. He served as coordinator of the various organizations, including the seven-year-old National Association for the Advancement of Colored People (NAACP), which sought to ensure rejection of the "Baltimore Law." Baldwin joined with Luther Ely Smith, Judge Selden P. Spencer, and other leading community members in drafting a petition that condemned the proposed segregation ordinance. They deemed it "opposed to American traditions and principles, thoroughly undemocratic, and degrading to our city and the people of both races." They proposed the formation of the Citizens' Committee Opposed to the Legal Segregation of Negroes. With election day approaching, however, proponents of the measure played on racial fears, asking, "How can we afford to let the Negro whip the white man in this election?"[19]

To Baldwin's chagrin, St. Louis voters overwhelmingly supported the housing initiative, approving the segregation measure by a nearly 3–1 margin. In a letter to local newspapers Baldwin sought to assure the black citizens of St. Louis that the new city charter still had merit. Terming himself both a charter supporter and a foe of segregation, he pointed out that a comparable ordinance would likely have resulted under the old charter as well. He and other charter supporters, Baldwin acknowledged, had recognized that the initiative could result in the submission of segregation measures. They nevertheless believed that "in the long run the control of legislation by the whole people is best for all of us, white and colored." Under the new charter, he contended, special interests and professional politicians could not control the public agenda as they had previously. "A vote of the people," he insisted, "will come out fairly for the right on almost any other question but one involving race prejudice."[20]

Happily, however, the U.S. Constitution and the court system afforded the individual and the minority protection against tyranny. Acting on behalf of the Civic League, Baldwin helped to bring a test case in federal court, where Judge D. P. Dyer, a veteran of the Union Army, granted a temporary injunction in April 1916. Dyer made the injunction permanent in March 1918, following a U.S. Supreme Court ruling, *Buchanan v. Warley,* which held unconstitutional a similar ordinance approved by voters in Louisville, Kentucky. As matters turned out, the judicial victory did little to stem the tide of private restrictive covenants used to enforce residential segregation.[21]

The segregation initiative transformed Baldwin's "too simple theory of democracy," as the writer Dwight Macdonald termed it. As befitting a good progressive, Baldwin had believed that the people simply required the means to participate more fully in the democratic process. And displaying the elitism that also was characteristic of many progressives, he determined that "the prejudices of the majority" must be checked in some way. The judicial branch, he hoped, could perform such a function.[22]

During his tenure as secretary of the Civic League, Baldwin's interests ranged beyond those of the organization. In 1910, the same year he became a key figure in the Civic League, Baldwin helped to establish the St. Louis City Club. The club was run by Gus Tuckerman, a former Episcopal priest and one of Baldwin's closest friends in St. Louis. The City Club hosted luncheons for about two thousand businessmen and professionals who worked in downtown St. Louis; over lunch they held wide-ranging discussions on important public issues of the day. Theodore Roosevelt, William Howard Taft, and Woodrow Wilson were among the speakers Baldwin helped to bring to St. Louis. More controversial figures spoke too, from the socialist mayor of Milwaukee to a British advocate of women's suffrage, Sylvia Pankhurst.[23]

His City Club functions led to Baldwin's involvement with various speakers whose message was received with trepidation by many. One morning in 1912 he was disturbed to learn that city police had prevented the birth control advocate Margaret Sanger from delivering a talk at a private hall. Because he regarded himself "as a guardian of good government," he felt compelled to act. He contacted Sanger, suggesting that she hold the meeting in front of the hall as a symbol of protest only, and offered to chair the proceeding. A small crowd gathered but was met by a large contingent of the city's finest. Baldwin introduced Sanger, she engaged in her symbolic protest, and "excellent press publicity" followed. This was Baldwin's "first free speech meeting," and he later pronounced it "an exhilarating success as a matter of principle."[24]

When the Wobblies—members of the radical labor organization, the Industrial Workers of the World (IWW)—came to town, ran out of money, and were forced to sleep in public places, Baldwin befriended several of them. The penniless Wobblies headed into restaurants, ran up tabs, and then insisted that the restaurant bill the mayor. They soon were arrested and sent to a workhouse. Baldwin believed the city had to craft a better solution, and he helped to establish St. Louis's first municipal lodging and its first soup kitchen. The IWW men struck him as possessing both vision and courage, along with their "simple working-class resistance to 'capitalism.'" As he had with the anarchists, Baldwin sympathized with the Wobblies' general belief in a free society and anarchosyndicalist ideals. Once again, however, he "yet could see no effective way of practical daily service."[25]

Although he dabbled in controversial causes, Baldwin remained thoroughly respectable throughout his days in St. Louis, as did the progressive movement of which he was a part. "I knew that I was part of a movement of hopeful reform and useful social work," he recalled. "My backing was 'respectable' and assured; the best people and the press were with me. I belonged to the right clubs, and associated with the right people. I was not regarded as a busybody, as I might have been." In fact, a poll taken around 1915 named him "one of the ten most influential citizens of St. Louis," even as he was acquiring "the reputation of being a friend of radicals, if not one myself."[26]

Lucille Milner, whom Baldwin hired about this time for the Children's Code Commission and who worked with him for many years, later referred to him as "an outstanding civic figure" in St. Louis who had all the women sitting "on his doorstep." Indeed, Milner reported, "he was the idol of the women and all the leaders of civic causes idolized him. It was often said that Roger could be a big business man if he wanted to and they were amazed that he would give all this up to go into the public service." For a full decade Baldwin had appeared content to be operating out of St. Louis; he "was absolutely the top man in social welfare" in the state, Milner told Joseph Lash.[27]

Increasingly, however, Baldwin, who was now reading the *Masses*, the radical political and literary journal edited by Max Eastman, and the *New Republic*, felt dissatisfied with his work and the solutions afforded by the early twentieth-century progressive movement. Both social work and the kind of reform efforts possible in St. Louis were becoming less satisfying. His work to date had led to more critical analyses of social ailments. Thus the report issued by the U.S. Industrial Commission in 1915 concerning labor-capital strife, particularly the testimony by the libertarian Theodore Schroeder regarding the right of workers to free speech, resonated with Baldwin. Subsequently, he wrote to his friend Frank P. Walsh, now chairman of the commission, and declared that the report would "do more to educate public opinion to the truth of existing conditions than any other one document in existence." Many wanted to remain oblivious to the real struggle the nation was experiencing, Baldwin feared, yet he questioned whether halfway remedies alone could bridge the chasms of class. A sense of impotence overcame him, Baldwin acknowledged, when he reflected on "the great problem of poverty . . . and the need of tying up fundamental reform." More and more, even progressive reforms appeared to be inadequate.[28]

Baldwin must have felt as if he were living in multiple worlds, one involving social gatherings and parties, another his civic work and various reform efforts, and yet another his growing identification with radical thought and individuals. The latter made him feel inadequate and desirous of doing more to address the fundamental problems of poverty and injustice. At the same time he recognized something he would contend with from this point forth: "the block created by my traditions and temperament to 'unclassing' myself and joining a revolutionary movement aimed at the very evils I most deplored, and my satisfactions in the practical reforms and services of the moment."[29]

With talk of the Great War in Europe all around, reconciling his reformist and radical inclinations proved increasingly difficult. His work for the Civic League no longer seemed as significant as it once had. Social ills appeared to demand new approaches and perspectives.

CHAPTER FIVE

Early Civil Liberties Career

Baldwin's comfortable world was shattered and the progressive movement was transformed as the guns of war grew louder on the European continent. He summarily turned down a request in mid-1916 to join the Citizen's League for America and the Allies, telling the organization, "Let me say that I am not of your persuasion. I do not believe that anything is being served by propaganda in the interests of any one of the belligerents, and I do not see the issue in that light. I believe that Americans can do more now by opposing war as an institution and by building up those constructive agencies of international harmony with which we are already familiar in principle."[1]

In early March 1917 he received a letter from Roy Smith Wallace of the Seybert Foundation, which attempted to care for poor children, in Philadelphia, expressing concern that the antiwar stance of Jane Addams and her friends was leading the administration of Woodrow Wilson to view social workers as "pacifist and queer." This had caused the profession to lose standing with government officials. Would Baldwin, Wallace wanted to know, lead a drive in St. Louis to draft a telegram to the president that recognized not all social workers were "extreme pacifists" or pacifists of any kind? The telegram should acknowledge great respect for such individuals, Wallace suggested. It also must profess "loyal support for such measures, social, industrial and military, as should enable us to meet the obligations, both national and international, and to protects [sic] the rights, of this country."[2]

Baldwin's response was hardly what Wallace had wanted or anticipated. First, Baldwin announced that he "would fall in line with almost anything in the world that you proposed." Then, he stated, "I am thoroughly with Miss

Addams and the pacifists now and all the time. I am unfortunately one of those who take the Sermon on the Mount pretty seriously, which does not square with the current conception of patriotism." Baldwin continued, "I am enough of a democrat to really put the interests of all the people of the world before some of the people. That means the world comes before any country." Consequently, Baldwin asked his friend, who was also well connected, to "excuse me from being patriotic in standing behind the president." However, he noted somewhat haughtily, "No doubt there are plenty of patriots out here in social work and I shall be glad to discover one of them and turn your letter over to him if you like."[3]

The outbreak of World War I, as much as any other development, predis-posed Baldwin, along with Norman Thomas and A. J. Muste, a Dutch Reformed minister who adopted a pacifist stance—both men were soon to become close compatriots of Baldwin's—to a more radical perspective. The mass bloodletting compelled Baldwin to contend with "new and trouble-some issues in my thinking." He sought to examine modern nation-states, the role of capitalistic competition in engendering warfare, and the morality of resorting to war to bring about desired ends. He was for the Allies yet had responded sympathetically to the antiwar preachments of Jean Jaures, the French socialist who had been assassinated in 1914. However, Baldwin was most moved by accounts of British conscientious objectors, whose message he had never heard before. He read stories about the young Englishmen who were relying on Christian and humanitarian tenets in refusing military ser-vice, even if that resulted in their incarceration. Baldwin determined that, if circumstances warranted, he would act as they had. Thus he now considered himself "a convinced pacifist," opposed to all wars and a willing participant in none. As an agnostic, he "had no God to turn to, no sanction other than the 'inner voice.'" He possessed only some vague notion that humanity's interests superseded those of individual countries. He also became more sympathetic to arguments by socialists and anarchists that wars were ruling-class instruments.[4]

In January 1915 Baldwin turned down an offer to serve as secretary of the American Union Against Militarism (AUAM), established by the Henry Street Peace Committee. He questioned how effective the organization would be. Nevertheless, he soon headed the AUAM's small and largely inef-fectual St. Louis branch. The AUAM shared his sentiments regarding "oppo-sition to conscription and the protection of conscience." The committee, which had evolved from the famed settlement house on New York City's

Lower East Side, originally included Jane Addams; Florence Kelley; Paul U. Kellogg, a social worker; Lillian Wald; and John Haynes Holmes, pastor of the Unitarian Church in New York City.[5]

By 1917 a series of occurrences—some fortuitous, others the product of Baldwin's reputation and ambition—enabled him to move on to a larger stage. He had clearly tired of his operations in St. Louis and longed to head back east. He had made his mark as an organization man, able to deal easily with those who supported reform efforts. His own political philosophy was still evolving, an amalgam of progressive ideals and, increasingly, radical ones too. In 1916 Woodrow Wilson had won reelection as both a domestic reformer and peacemaker, yet the drumbeats of war were growing louder.

In February 1917 Baldwin wrote to the AUAM's national office, urging that it hold mass meetings in opposition to U.S. involvement in the war. Baldwin considered American entrance into the war in Europe imminent. Fearing that "civic reform would disappear into background," he resigned from all his posts in St. Louis—Louis Budenz, later an important figure in the American communist movement, replaced him as director of the Civic League—and volunteered his services to the AUAM. In March he received a telegram from the AUAM, asking him to replace the ailing Crystal Eastman Fuller as the organization's secretary. The telegram was signed by such friends as Oswald Garrison Villard, who would become editor of the *Nation* in 1918; L. Hollingsworth Wood, a Quaker lawyer; Amos Pinchot, a progressive reformer who was determined to protect the constitutional rights of pacifists; John Lovejoy Elliot, who spearheaded the Ethical Culture Society; and Owen Lovejoy, of the National Child Labor Committee. Baldwin knew the social workers in the AUAM, like Florence Kelley, Kellogg, and Wald, and he knew Villard through family connections. Influenced by both the war overseas and his determination to leave the Midwest, Baldwin headed for New York, the nation's intellectual center, and the AUAM's headquarters in the Munsey Building on Fifth Avenue. He agreed to become AUAM secretary, with the understanding he would remain just for the duration of the war. Concluding that he should reap no financial gain, he received but $125 a month to cover his expenses. Because he was single, Baldwin believed that he "could afford the luxury of a conscience." Typically, he was pleased that the people affiliated with the AUAM were "so much more prominent nationally than in any other peace organizations." Indeed, these were the kind of people who "had such high standing that they could go right in to see Wilson," which seemed only natural to him.[6]

The New York metropolitan area appeared, in his estimation, "the right place for any pacifist then." Antiwar sentiment abounded and fueled the mayoral campaign of Morris Hillquit, a labor lawyer and top figure in the American Socialist Party. The Irish opposed what they saw as England's war, whereas German Americans were divided in their loyalties. Jews harbored doubts that the United States should become involved. Socialists, along with sympathetic unions, viewed the conflict with disdain. Baldwin, who was hoping to stem war fever, worked on behalf of Hillquit and delivered the only speech for a socialist candidate that he ever made.[7]

In New York City Baldwin initially stayed with his aunt Ruth Baldwin and her friend Elizabeth Walden, both staunch pacifists. The three of them "all lived in a fellowship of heresy to the times, reasonably safe in the cosmopolitanism of the great city, as we would not have been elsewhere." It was "a lively pacifist menage."[8]

The American Union, with its array of pacifists, Quakers, socialists, and liberals, offered another kind of home for Baldwin. In the organization he found "plenty of sympathetic company." His closest pacifist compatriots were Norman Thomas, who was still a Presbyterian clergyman; John Nevin Sayre, the Episcopal minister; Agnes Brown Leach, the well-heeled Quaker reformer; John Lovejoy Elliott; John Haynes Holmes, Wood, Villard, and Addams. Through Sayre, Baldwin became involved with the pacifist Fellowship of Reconciliation and served on its board of directors for many years.[9]

As the United States officially entered the war, the AUAM took on, in Baldwin's words, "a defensive role." It became most concerned about protecting the rights of conscientious objectors and safeguarding the civil liberties of those who opposed Wilson's policies. Above all else it sought "to moderate the war hysteria." Other organizations, such as the Socialist Party, the International Workers of the World (IWW), and the Non-Partisan League, a militant farmers' group, adopted more solidly antiwar positions. Unlike those groups, the American Union was guided "by pacifist and civil libertarian principles," and few of its members "thought in class terms." Baldwin felt sympathetic toward the radical organizations but did not identify with "their class concepts." He appreciated, nevertheless, that they might "restrain the excesses of the war fever."[10]

In the process the modern civil liberties movement was spawned. This was the first sustained effort to safeguard the personal liberties guaranteed under the Bill of Rights against encroachments by federal or state agents. In 1878 the National Defense Association had been founded to counter the Comstock Law, which banned use of the mails to ship materials deemed obscene. A more expansive outlook was afforded by the Free Speech League—established in 1902—that challenged free speech restrictions in general. Such a precedent was significant, but the Free Speech League's legacy remained limited because of hostile court rulings, the organization's identification with both anarchists and sex radicals, who condemned the vestiges of the Victorian era, and the often prickly leadership provided by its iconoclastic administrator, Theodore Schroeder.[11]

Federal officials had earlier targeted anarchist immigrants, the IWW, and foreign nationals who were radicals, efforts that the Free Speech League often gamely but unsuccessfully contested. The U.S. Supreme Court in particular remained enamored of the "bad tendency test," the common law directive that precluded prior restraint of speech but allowed for "the subsequent punishment of such as may be deemed contrary to the public welfare." As David M. Rabban has persuasively reported, a handful of legal scholars began challenging restrictive court rulings, contending that broader protection of First Amendment freedoms would diminish the possibility of social disorder. However, their viewpoints failed to convince many state or federal judges before the United States entered World War I.[12]

A more vibrant civil liberties campaign emerged only after socially respectable AUAM members, under Baldwin's directorship, determined to protect First Amendment freedoms. They believed a crusade was necessary because they were worried about the heavy-handed practices of government and private forces in dealing with a seemingly still vibrant antiwar movement. Clearly, the upper-class and upper-middle-class backgrounds of its leaders proved instrumental in ensuring that the movement was taken seriously, even by those who viewed its emergence with disdain or trepidation. Such figures possessed the ability, at least initially, to acquire access to the highest government circles.

The American Union operated out of its offices in New York City and Washington, D.C., under the guidance of Charles T. Hallinan, a quiet, diligent journalist, and Crystal Eastman Fuller, who eventually recovered sufficiently to shoulder anew certain organizational responsibilities. Baldwin had met her when she was involved in the women's suffrage campaign and viewed her, unlike the self-effacing Hallinan, as a natural leader. She was, in his eyes, "outspoken (often tactless), determined, charming, beautiful, courageous—

the very picture of the intellectual feminist then associated with New York, particularly Greenwich Village." However, neither Hallinan's nor Fuller's style matched his. Hallinan considered Baldwin impulsive and thought that Fuller's approach was obscure. Somehow Baldwin and Fuller avoided open clashes, but their partnership was always uneasy.[13]

During his first year in New York Baldwin's schedule found him spending half the week in Washington. He unfailingly attended the AUAM's Monday lunches in New York at which organizational matters were discussed; while in the capital, he stayed at the Cosmos Club or with friends or relatives. He was delighted that the American Union possessed access to high places. Some of its members were old associates of Secretary of War Newton Baker or President Wilson, and several members of Congress initially sympathized with the group's agenda. Following the U.S. entrance into the war, an AUAM delegation, which included Addams, Wald, and Thomas, went to see Wilson to discuss the status of conscientious objectors. On May 18, 1917, Congress passed the Selective Service Act, which required the registration of all male citizens and males who were "not alien enemies" who intended to become citizens. It applied to men aged twenty to thirty and afforded conscientious objector status to members of religious groups that historically had been opposed to war. AUAM leaders viewed Baldwin, who had just taken over the directorship of the organization, as too young and inexperienced to be invited to attend the meeting, although Thomas was no older.[14]

Their work on the AUAM board marked the beginning of a half-century friendship for Thomas and Baldwin. As the historian Bill Preston later eloquently pointed out, the two men had a good deal in common. Born in 1884 into comfortable homes with distinguished family backgrounds, they had attended Ivy League institutions. Each left his initial profession—social work for Baldwin, the ministry for Thomas—because of the war and heartfelt attraction to pacifist ideals and the antiwar movement. Both were charismatic, energetic figures who drew others to their causes. And, according to Preston, they also had in common "humor, curiosity, and self-confidence."[15]

Baldwin found his work with the American Union riddled with "high tension, perpetual pressure" but exhilarating. After all, as he later put it, "I was doing what my deepest convictions demanded and working with people who shared them." At the same time he required an outlet for his pent-up energy and looked to the countryside outside New York City. He wanted a weekend country place and consulted an assistant at Abercrombie & Fitch, a fellow known for his canoeing expertise. "Try the Hackensack River," the Abercrombie man told Baldwin.

So Baldwin bought a train ticket to North Hackensack and walked up the tracks to the dam in Oradell. He would squat there on water company property for the next four or five years, using the same canoe he had in St. Louis. Roger eventually signed a lease with the water company for his camp in Harrington Park, where the river flowed for a mile or two before it ran into the reservoir. He had grain ground at an old grist mill below the camp. During his first summer there he erected two tents on platforms. In the fall he resorted to a portable one-room structure with a kitchen, a washroom, a fireplace, two porches, and a couple of double-decker bunks.[16]

Early companions at his New Jersey haunt included Oral James, Baldwin's former foster child who was now working in the New York office of an adding machine company, and Tom McKittrick, a Harvard graduate. Another was John Williams, a big outdoorsman Baldwin had met while fishing. Williams would stop at Baldwin's camp, and the two would hike the Catskills or the Ramapos. A girlfriend of Roger's, Vida Milholland, the daughter of a wealthy businessman, also stayed with him on the Hackensack River.[17]

Following Woodrow Wilson's lead, Congress issued a declaration of war on April 2, 1917. Four days later the president, resorting to the 1798 Alien Enemies Act, framed guidelines for restraining enemy aliens. On April 14 Baldwin sent telegrams from the Washington headquarters of the American Union to dignitaries around the country. He solicited signatures to a statement by Jane Addams, among others, requesting that the president render a precise accounting of "his views on free speech, free press and assemblage during the war." This was considered necessary for "these have been grossly violated in many places."[18]

At the end of the month Baldwin telegrammed Addams, with whom he remained in close consultation during this period. He urged her to contact Newton Baker, the secretary of war, regarding the inclusion of provisions for conscientious objectors in the Selective Service Act, which was pending before Congress. As the vote approached, Norman Thomas and Baldwin on May 1 discussed the need to preserve liberty of conscience in wartime America. They reminded the conference committee, then drafting the bill, that while "autocracies may coerce conscience in this vital matter; democracies do so at their peril." They spoke "not from love of cowards or slackers," the

AUAM officers insisted, but rather from a determined belief that the United States not dishonor "her glorious heritage."[19]

After Congress approved the Selective Service Act, Baldwin helped to establish "a bureau for advice and help to conscientious objectors throughout the United States." The bureau's board was led by L. Hollingsworth Wood and included Thomas, representing the Fellowship of Reconciliation; Villard; Elliot; Alice Lewisohn, the champion of New York settlement houses; the socialist and labor organizer Joseph D. Cannon; and Scott Nearing of the People's Council of America for Democracy and Peace, a new radical group that sought to spearhead antiwar opposition. The bureau, like its parent organization earlier, sought but failed to win a liberal provision in the Selective Service Act regarding conscientious objection. During this period an AUAM pamphlet deemed liberty of conscience "essentially an Anglo-American tradition for which our ancestors fought and died, and for which thousands emigrated to America." An AUAM-backed petition signed by Wald, Villard, Holmes, Thomas, and Baldwin, among others, urged young men to "register—and when you register, state your protest against participation in war."[20]

During this period Baldwin and other AUAM officers maintained a steady correspondence with government officials, repeatedly reassuring them of the organization's honorable intentions. In a letter to Assistant Secretary of War Frederick D. Keppel, dated May 18, Baldwin sought information regarding procedures the War Department intended to follow in dealing with conscientious objectors. Baldwin told Keppel that a number of groups opposed registration. By contrast, the AUAM was "strong in advising even those who may seek exemption as conscientious objectors to fully comply with the law."[21]

Baldwin was instrumental in the AUAM's decision to align with Nearing's People's Council, which was demanding a rapid end to the fighting, government that was more representative, and the safeguarding of the civil liberties of critics of the Wilson administration. Founded in late May 1917, the People's Council garnered a good deal of its support from socialists, independent radicals, and labor leaders. Baldwin, ever the organization man, served on its board of directors. He did so in the belief that, unlike the pacifist groups, the People's Council offered "the strongest expression of antiwar forces" and therefore had a slim chance of influencing government policy. Nevertheless, Baldwin was never completely comfortable with the "socialist politicians" associated with the People's Council. Although he and Nearing were close friends, Baldwin was not pleased about Nearing's intransigence regarding overt opposition to the administration's wartime policies. Baldwin continued to feel the greatest kinship with Quakers and other religious pacifists because of their determined resolve and principled commitment, "so free of the qualifying motives of the socialists and other leftists."[22]

Nevertheless, Baldwin's association with the People's Council, like his friendship with Emma Goldman, was a sign that radical ideas were increasingly attractive to him. At the same time he remained very much a member of the well-educated, privileged class of his youth and young adulthood. Moreover, he continued to believe that the better sorts must necessarily be involved in matters of state, whether through government service or organizational efforts designed to pressure public officials for the greater good.

At a special meeting of the AUAM on June 1, 1917, held at Villard's Manhattan office, the organization's leaders tentatively decided to separate the conscientious objectors' information bureau from the AUAM. The AUAM would henceforth provide only goodwill and assistance. Furthermore, the executive committee determined that Roger Baldwin should continue to head the bureau.[23]

Baldwin continued to believe that the AUAM could influence certain government officials, among them Keppel of the War Department. On June 2 he informed Keppel, "We don't want to make a move without consulting you." A note from Baldwin to Secretary of War Baker on June 15 referred to the dilemma of what to do about conscientious objectors. Baldwin told Baker that he had placed the bureau's members "entirely at the service of the War Department in rendering any assistance that you think lies in our power to give."[24] Baldwin's statements were consistent with his progressive background, demonstrating his continued belief in the ability of rational individuals—particularly those with the proper pedigrees—to resolve political disputes and social maladies.

On the morning of June 22 Baldwin and Villard spoke with Baker regarding the treatment of conscientious objectors. The War Department "would follow the letter of the law," Baker affirmed, and anyone who refused to serve would be treated severely and incarcerated. But the secretary disclosed that many could become noncombatants in the manner of Quakers and members of other peace churches. Baker solicited information from Villard and Baldwin regarding the number of those disinclined to serve, hinting that dealing with them vigorously would dissuade others from choosing the same course. As Baldwin recalled, Baker expressed his belief that "any recognition of individual conscience would open the doors too wide to slackers." The meeting ended with Baker expressing "warm appreciation" for the AUAM's offer to help; Baldwin and Villard came away with the impression that Baker would be amenable to cooperation in the future.[25]

That same month Baldwin attended an antiwar session at the National Conference of Social Work in Pittsburgh, Pennsylvania, that he had organized. In contrast to many of their colleagues, leading figures in the social work movement like Jane Addams and Lillian Wald refused to adopt a pro-war stance. Many social workers backed the AUAM's efforts to defend the rights of conscientious objectors but were reluctant to express such convictions openly. Generally, even social workers like Addams, who despised the war and sought to shield dissenting thought, remained silent about the conflagration itself. The Pittsburgh gathering drew a good deal of attention, with police ringing the speakers' platform, supposedly to protect orators like Baldwin, Owen Lovejoy, and Florence Kelley. Soon, opposing the war would become even more controversial.[26]

At a meeting of the AUAM's executive committee on June 4 in New York City, Baldwin revealed that he had spoken with Justice Department officials. Hallinan, who was serving as an AUAM lobbyist in the nation's capital, recounted that federal agents had visited the Washington office. They supposedly had determined that the AUAM was operating "within the law" and subsequently informed Hallinan and Baldwin that the organization's work "would not be interfered with."[27]

Nevertheless, the *Washington Post*, as Hallinan related at the executive committee's next meeting, reported that the AUAM was under government surveillance. Hallinan found this so unlikely that he considered suing the *Post* for libel. (The United Press expressed a willingness to mail a story to its members that would serve as a retraction, if the organization produced one.) As it turned out, the AUAM members were terribly naive.[28]

Equally ominous to the AUAM leadership was the determination of reformers Elizabeth Glendower Evans, Lillian Wald, and Paul Kellogg to resign from the organization. Wald regarded Baldwin and Crystal Eastman Fuller as "activists and radicals." Norman Thomas, Wald declared, "is reasonable and has judgment, but Crystal, Mr. Hallinan and Roger Baldwin much as I like them personally, are more than I can manage single handed." With America now at war, Evans expressed her unwillingness to impede government operations. "Even defense of free speech in opposing the draft," she believed, was "contrary to a sound public policy." The AUAM's support of conscientious objectors, Kellogg reasoned, had diminished its "influence and power in the 'drive for peace.'" The executive committee nevertheless asked Fuller to prepare a response to their disgruntled former colleagues that expressed the AUAM's opposition to military exigencies that threatened basic rights, including freedom of speech.[29]

Congress's approval of the Espionage Act in June compelled the AUAM to charge unequivocally that the law would seriously abrogate constitutional rights. The Espionage Act allowed for prison sentences as long as twenty years and fines as high as $10,000 for individuals convicted of willfully issuing "false statements" intended to interfere with American military operations during wartime, such as through promoting draft resistance or military insubordination. The U.S. Post Office was authorized to ban from the mails materials considered treasonous. The AUAM asserted its intention to stand "for the maintenance in war time of the rights of free press, free speech, peaceable assembly, liberty of conscience, and freedom from unlawful search and seizure." In addition to preserving civil liberties, the organization sought the end of militarism, movement toward international government, and "the ultimate abolition of war."[30]

While such lofty goals increasingly appeared unattainable, given wartime realities, Baldwin and the AUAM believed that the Wilson administration was guided by progressive principles. Baldwin remained convinced that gentlemen in the inner reaches of Washington, D.C., and those outside it, could resolve disputes in an amicable manner that would sustain democratic principles. On June 30 he again wrote to Secretary Baker, urging passage of new legislation to forestall "the brutalities and scandals" resulting from the enforcement of the Selective Service Act by lower-level military officials.[31]

The historian Charles Chatfield has reported that the organization was informed that some conscientious objectors had been subjected to "beatings, bayonets, torture, and unreasonable confinement." In closing, Baldwin declared the services of the AUAM to be "entirely at the disposal of the War Department in doing whatever we can to help solve this difficult problem."[32] Generally, he took great pains to assuage any fears by administration officials regarding the operations of the AUAM and its bureau to safeguard conscientious objectors. He also went out of his way to praise the liberal bent of the president and other top government officials.

On July 1 the AUAM announced the formation of a national Civil Liberties Bureau, to serve as a clearinghouse for information pertaining to conscientious objectors. In a document issued later that month the CLB asserted that its purpose was neither to assist nor encourage individuals to violate the Selective Service Act. Rather, the CLB insisted that "a liberal, statesman-like solution of the problem of liberty of conscience" could be worked out, something Baldwin genuinely believed was possible.[33]

Baldwin became immersed in the CLB's operations, putting in long hours analyzing key issues and casees. The CLB board met weekly and included house counsel Walter Nelles; it eventually was joined by Albert DeSilver, a wealthy New York attorney. Nelles, a Harvard classmate of Baldwin's and a scholarly and judicious sort, left his law firm to help the CLB. DeSilver, an affable man, also resigned from his law firm to concentrate fully on civil liberty concerns. Baldwin, Nelles, and DeSilver comprised a triumvirate of sorts, with the former providing "the techniques of a social case worker, an organizer and a publicity man," as he put it. Commuting between Manhattan and Washington, D.C., Baldwin strove to articulate the CLB's position before the key departments of war and justice, as well as the Post Office. Although he was treated cordially, his efforts generally proved unavailing. Not even the support of Wisconsin Senator Robert LaFollette—who was himself increasingly viewed with distrust because of his antiwar stance—helped. Nevertheless, the CLB director held fast to his optimistic view that people of reason and good faith could work together to mitigate injustices resulting from American participation in the war.[34]

Each Monday, the CLB's Directing Committee—its executive committee—met for lunch at the Civic Club on West 12th Street in Manhattan to discuss civil liberties issues. During the sweltering summer months, the committee sat on backless benches around a bare woden table in the Civic Club's paved backyard. A lone ailanthus tree provided but a modicum of shade. Committee members included the artist Helen Phelps Stokes, Rabbi Judah L. Magnes, Wood, Thomas, Holmes, Sayre, Fuller, Baldwin, and, later that summer, Lucille Milner.[35]

The actions of the CLB proved controversial, both within the ranks of the Wilson administration and inside the AUAM itself. And it did not help that Baldwin was walking a tightrope. He was urging that the CLB do more than simply funnel information to and from conscientious objectors, even as he sought to maintain old school ties with government officials. Despite his denials that he and Crystal Eastman Fuller comprised "a party of opposition

. . . we are not, by habit or temperament, troublemakers," Baldwin favored a more militant posture. His public speeches, Kellogg charged, amounted to a championing of conscientious objection, no mere defense of the rights of the objectors themselves.[36]

Certain government officials, both then and later, viewed many of Baldwin's actions as nothing more than subterfuge. A letter he wrote to the journalist Louis Lochner regarding the People's Council Convention would be viewed as evidence of his less-than-sincere motives:

> Do steer away from making it look like a Socialist enterprise. Too many people have already gotten the idea that it is nine-tenths of a Socialist movement. You can, of course, avoid this by bringing to the front people like Senator Works, Miss Addams, and others, who are known as substantial Democrats. . . . I think it would be an error to get the public thinking that we are launching a political party in Minneapolis. To be sure, we are launching a political movement, but that is quite a different matter from a political point. We want also to look [like] patriots in everything we do. We want to get a good lot of flags, talk a good deal about the Constitution and what our forefathers wanted to make of this country, and to show that we are really the folks that really stand for the spirit of our institutions.[37]

While damning to government officials, Baldwin's suggestions were sensible, even politically astute. Perhaps more than any other figure involved in the early civil liberties campaign, he recognized the importance of public relations. Thus he naturally urged that nonsocialists be prominent at the convention, a reflection of his determination to include forces from throughout the left side of the political spectrum. He wisely called for a highlighting of patriotic ties, something many American radicals foolishly sought to avoid, which enabled antagonists to toss loaded epithets their way.

Through the summer of 1917 the American radical movement remained a potent force that the Wilson administration had to contend with. Thousands attended rallies orchestrated by the People's Council; in the West the IWW carried out potentially crippling strikes; and the Socialist Party's staunchly antiwar pronouncement attracted twelve thousand new members, while the group's candidates for elective office soon reaped the benefits of that stand. Determined to silence opposition to the American war effort, the federal government moved more forcefully to repress the peace movement. To that end it relied on the Espionage Act, deportations, a rounding up of foreign nationals for placement in internment camps, military intelligence for gathering information about dissidents, and army officers to "sternly repress acts committed with seditious intent" and to safeguard public utilities deemed essential to U.S. overseas operations. Also instrumental in attacking radicals were state and local politicians, vigilantes, and the American Protective League, a privately financed group that had close ties to the Justice Department.[38] The league was a volunteer spy organization that gathered information about purported violations of wartime measures.

"A common understanding between the peoples of the earth," not war, Baldwin now believed, would resolve international disputes. In a letter to the *St. Louis Star*, dated August 23, 1917, he noted that leading radical labor organizations sought an end to the fighting. This movement was not simply antiwar, Baldwin insisted. Rather, it was "a great resurgence of democratic power from the bottom," involving "the revolutionary, radical forces" across the globe that demanded "a peace without victory." Such a victory, Baldwin was certain, would not occur with the demise of "Prussianism" "but of autocracy everywhere." And "the new internationalism will be established on a radical democratic basis."[39]

Clearly, Baldwin now increasingly adhered to a radical perspective. He viewed structural change, both domestically and internationally, as necessary for democracy's growth. The kinds of reforms sought by progressives, who included the president and many key administration officials, appeared woefully inadequate.

Remarkably, however, the often politically astute Baldwin failed to appreciate how his pronouncements in the *St. Louis Star* might be received by the federal government. After all, the Wilson administration, to carry out its European crusade and to thwart domestic opposition to its wartime policies, was laying the foundation for the national security state. Perhaps the more conservative elements in the AUAM recognized the danger involved in a public posture of a militant cast, or perhaps they simply viewed such a perspective with dismay.

Nevertheless, in succeeding months the CLB director appeared more determined than ever to maintain a friendly association with well-placed members of Wilson's war cabinet. Baldwin repeatedly reached out to Secretary of War Baker and Assistant Secretary Keppel, both friends of the social workers drawn to the AUAM and the CLB. On September 14 Baldwin wrote to John Henry Wigmore, provost marshal general, the army's chief law enforcement authority. The CLB merely desired "something like a solution on the part of the War Department which would make it unnecessary to raise this issue [the status of conscientious objectors] further during the conduct of the war." Two days later Baldwin proposed a meeting with "representative outsiders" concerned about conscientious objectors. The representative outsiders included Thomas, Wood, Hillquit, and Nearing. Nothing came of Baldwin's suggestion.[40]

A letter from Baldwin to Felix Frankfurter, then judge advocate general for the War Department, expressed hope that it might be possible to "avoid making the conscientious objector a continuing issue during the war." A letter to Woodrow Wilson himself, signed by Baldwin, Thomas, Wood, Pinchot, Elliott, and Holmes, registered "vigorous protest" against the section of the Trading with the Enemy Bill that would have severely curtailed press freedoms and abrogated individual rights. The letter denied that its signatories favored an obstruction of the war effort or actions that would in any way embarrass the government. They simply viewed "freedom of discussion, even of peace and war, [as] absolutely essential to preservation of our democratic liberties." Consequently, they urged a presidential veto.[41]

In the first several months of U.S. involvement in World War I, Baldwin and his closest compatriots had given rise to the modern civil liberties movement, a remarkable accomplishment. Members of the upper class or upper-middle class, they possessed entrée to high government circles. Still something of progressive elitists, they nevertheless acted courageously in challenging government encroachments on personal freedoms that flew in the face of the country's long professed devotion to the Bill of Rights. No individual was more instrumental in shaping the civil liberties movement, or in devising myths surrounding it, than Roger Baldwin. Every bit the upper-class Bostonian, he remained conflicted by his desire to remain in good standing with the Wilson administration and his growing attraction to radical thought and action.

CHAPTER SIX

The National Civil Liberties Bureau

The formal separation of the civil liberties group from its parent institution occurred on October 1, 1917, following a meeting of the AUAM's executive committee. The new organization, initially named the Civil Liberty Defense League, soon became the National Civil Liberties Bureau (NCLB). Its officers deemed free speech no "empty legal right" but rather "the living essence of democracy." Civil liberty would not be guaranteed anywhere, they asserted, until "international agreement and organization . . . make disarmament possible." The bureau, Baldwin believed, was now "a national independent organization . . . free . . . for a larger work than some of our conservative friends in the AUAM committee are willing to stand for."[1]

The bureau's headquarters were located in the same building in Manhattan as the AUAM's but in separate offices. Other organizations, all avowedly antiwar and situated at 70 Fifth Avenue, included the Emergency Peace Federation; the Bureau of Legal First Aid, which largely concerned itself with conscientious objectors in the New York metropolitan area; and, eventually, the People's Council. The NCLB, by contrast, was basically pacifist and professed neutrality regarding the war.[2]

Immersed in the bureau's operations, Baldwin pored over countless cases involving conscientious objectors or violations of civil liberties. The board, chaired by Hollingsworth Wood, met weekly and included John Haynes Holmes, Rabbi Judah L. Magnes, Norman Thomas, John Lovejoy Elliott, and Helen Phelps Stokes.[3]

The bureau selected its cases from those reported by both the mainstream and radical press and from correspondence with individuals whose rights had been abridged in some fashion. The board solicited legal counsel for each case the bureau took to court, publicized the issues at stake, battled with government officials, and, on occasion, helped raise defense funds. Through its bulletins the board diligently acted to keep sympathetic attorneys across the land apprised of key cases, rulings, and regulations. Baldwin continued his visits to the nation's capital to meet with government officials. Soon, however, the bureau's congressional allies were reduced to increasingly ostracized figures like Senator Robert M. La Follette. One day Baldwin went to La Follette's office for help about some matter. The esteemed senator placed his hands on Baldwin's shoulders and exclaimed that "it was hopeless to try for justice, so fanatical had the country and government become." Baldwin managed to take "the hysteria in my stride—often shocked, often indignant" and refused to give way to depression.[4]

On two occasions Baldwin visited the military prison at Fort Leavenworth, where he was received as an honored guest by the commandant, Col. Sedgwick A. Rice. Baldwin was allowed to roam about the camp and to speak freely with both officers and prisoners. He was much taken with Rice. For one who was now a confirmed pacifist, Baldwin was curiously drawn to military figures; perhaps this was attributable, at least to some extent, to his *Life with Father* upbringing. He saw Rice as a thoughtful and progressive military officer who had applied many modern methods to running the prison. Yet even Rice, Baldwin determined, was constrained by regulations issued by the adjutant general. These involved the treatment of prisoners in military camps, including shackling and solitary confinement and a diet of bread and water for extended periods. Baldwin saw these as vestiges of "medieval forms of punishment," although he was unable to convince Rice of this. Nor was he able to make clear to any military official "the new democratic viewpoint in running prisons. The craving for a degree of liberty in prison—for self-expression." Still, Baldwin viewed the commandant as "the chief good point" at the camp.[5]

Ironically, Oral James, one of the two lads Roger had looked after in St. Louis, was a prisoner at Fort Leavenworth, incarcerated because of his conscientious objection to military service in any fashion. While at Fort Leavenworth, James led a strike to protest the treatment accorded resisters. Toto, Roger's other charge, had been drafted and sent to the front lines in France.[6]

In the fall of 1917 several other issues loomed large for the NCLB. The conservationist and Yale professor Gifford Pinchot, now AUAM chairman, informed Baldwin of his decision to resign from the bureau's Directing

Committee. Among those asked to fill the vacancy was Dr. James P. Warbasse, a surgeon who was deeply involved with the Cooperative League of the United States (which later became the Twentieth Century Fund, a research and advocacy agency for socioeconomic reform) and who expressed delight at the decision to split the NCLB off from the AUAM. As he saw it, "The American Union has long since ceased to be against militarism." In a note to John S. Codman, a consulting engineer in Boston, whom Baldwin also invited to join the Directing Committee, he promised that the NCLB had no intention of "backing anti-war or anti-draft propaganda."[7]

The willingness of so many well-regarded individuals to risk their reputations and perhaps considerably more in their quest to protect freedom of expression in wartime is remarkable. There were few precedents of individuals who spoke critically of their own nation's participation in a war, and fewer still of such criticism being received with anything but heavy-handed repression. Nevertheless, during the nineteen months that the United States was a combatant in World War I, a fair number of esteemed attorneys, academicians, businessmen, social workers, and others displayed a hearty determination to ensure the preservation of the Bill of Rights.

Thanks to such support, the efforts of the NCLB to ameliorate the fate of conscientious objectors succeeded to a limited degree. Those who failed to convey opposition to conscription before being drafted were inducted into the U.S. Army. If they defied military authorities, they were placed in military camps and court-martialed. The boards of courts martial handed down brutal decrees, including capital sentences—always commuted—and life imprisonments. The bureau, along with other organizations, eventually convinced Secretary of War Newton Baker that objectors should be given furloughs to engage in civilian service and not subjected to military control. However, the absolutists, who refused any service at all, received no such treatment. Baldwin considered such individuals courageous and appreciated their dissenting, nonconformist opposition to the power of the state.[8]

Baldwin, who still wanted a window into the Wilson administration, must have been displeased to receive a letter from David Lawrence (governor of Pennsylvania, 1959–1963) of the Judge Advocate Department on October 24 indicating that Newton Baker wanted the NCLB members to rein themselves in. Lawrence referred to the secretary's belief that it was "extremely dangerous and inadvisable to have any publicity about the method of the treatment of conscientious objectors." Such publicity could do much harm, Lawrence argued, "to the cause itself." He strongly advised, at Baker's behest, that Baldwin not "write anything yourself." Baldwin referred to Lawrence as "the old back-slider" in regard to the administration's wartime policies and said Lawrence was in such good standing with the Wilson administration "that he is very helpful to us on this particular matter."[9]

Nevertheless, for a good while longer Baldwin reasoned that key members of the War and Justice departments were willing to communicate with bureau representatives. He viewed Baker as "always approachable" and Frederick Keppel, a top aide to Baker, as even more so, perhaps because Keppel and Hollingsworth Wood were friends. U.S. Attorney General Thomas Watt Gregory was markedly unreceptive, but his assistants, John Lord O'Brian and Alfred Bettman, appeared committed to the defense of civil liberties. However, the Post Office, with Albert Sidney Burleson at the helm, was simply "a graveyard," as Baldwin termed it. Baldwin went with Clarence Darrow, the famed iconoclastic attorney, to see Burleson at one point. Darrow, a supporter of the war effort, tried to appeal to Burleson in his typically folksy manner. Burleson proved immune to Darrow's charms, simply dismissed his request, and spun a tale about his native Texas.[10]

In notes to Baker and Keppel, Baldwin delivered the type of veiled threat he used repeatedly during this period: if conscientious objectors in military camps continued to suffer abuses, he would have to publicize the "present injustices." On November 22 Baldwin warned Baker—whom he addressed as "My Dear Mr. Secretary"—what that might mean: should word of "brutalities of such shocking character" get out, "a widespread campaign of opposition to the present arrangements" could result. By late December Baldwin had written to individuals like John Dewey to solicit liberal support for a meeting in New York the following month to "put before the public the case for the maintenance of American liberties during the war."[11]

The New York meeting was held on January 13, and it was packed, but a number of organizations, such as the NAACP, refused to be associated with the bureau. They viewed the NCLB as pacifist despite Baldwin's less than sincere statements to the contrary. Theodore Schroeder; Louis F. Post, an assistant secretary of labor; Charles W. Eliot of Harvard; and Charles A. Beard, the historian who was an influential progressive, were among those who declined to participate. After he was denied the use of Carnegie Hall, Baldwin rented the Liberty Theatre. Speakers included the journalist Lincoln Steffens, the Reverend Harry F. Ward of the Union Theological Seminary, and Norman Thomas. The meeting, Baldwin informed David Starr Jordan, president of Stanford University, was "the beginning of a campaign to secure a Congressional inquiry into the causes of mob violence and violations of constitutional rights, particularly the use of war by commercial interests to crush labor." Despite considerable press coverage, however, this was the lone public meeting the NCLB held during the period of direct U.S. involvement in the war.[12]

By the beginning of 1918, despite Baldwin's efforts to remain in good standing—or what he perceived to be the same—with the Wilson administration, reports that called his operations into question were increasingly being circulated in government circles. The Justice Department's Bureau of Investigation began keeping tabs on the civil liberties organization. A report from the Naval Intelligence staff charged that after an informant had said he was German born, Baldwin had told him, "Well my friend I am fighting for Germany." Supposedly, Baldwin then had declared that he required no financial assistance but could use some "trusted men who would secretly distribute seditious literature in the military camps and naval training stations." Baldwin was a German agent, the informant was convinced, and a friend of such leading radicals as Emma Goldman; Elizabeth Gurley Flynn, then a Wobbly; and Carlo Tresca, the Italian anarchist who had emigrated to the United States in 1904. Only the information about Baldwin's friendships was true. The informant also claimed that Goldman had stated that Baldwin possessed "the best known system of anti-draft organization." But the informant additionally termed him a *Yalie* and alleged that "he must have been in [Pancho] Villa's employ" while in Mexico. Baldwin was, of course, a Harvard man through and through and had been south of the U.S. border only briefly, well before the time of Villa's notoriety.[13]

Word of Baldwin's purported involvement with Villa led to the one instance in which a government agency insisted that he clarify what was in his dossier. The inspector general of the U.S. Army asked Baldwin to come to Washington. He did so, along with John S. Codman, a member of the NCLB's governing body and a pro-Wilson liberal who backed administration policies in Europe. With the dossier in plain view the inspector general asked Baldwin whether he knew Villa. He did not, nor had he ever been in Mexico, Baldwin insisted, curiously forgetting an early excursion into Tijuana in 1905. The report, the inspector general stated, said that Baldwin had helped Villa conduct a raid across the Arizona border. Baldwin replied that he had not visited that state in years. Moreover, he was a pacifist. He told the official he "could not conceivably have had anything to do with a bandit," a statement perfectly in character. The interview terminated with the inspector general looking bewildered.[14]

On December 19, 1917, the acting division intelligence officer for the 34th Division sent a memo entitled "Suspects" to the chief of the Intelligence Section of the War College in Washington, D.C., calling for an investigation of Baldwin's activities. Less than two weeks later Col. R. H. Van Deman, a member of the general staff and chief of the college's Intelligence Section, called that memo to the attention of Maj. Nicholas Biddle, an intelligence officer. Van Deman asked that Biddle deliver the memo of December 19 to intelligence operatives.[15]

The NCLB's board scrupulously sought to avoid encouraging draft resistance in any overt fashion, for that would have violated the Selective Service Act. However, military intelligence operatives in the War Department began insisting that the NCLB had more than crossed the line. In early February Van Deman sent a confidential memo to intelligence officers throughout the U.S. military in which he called the NCLB "a prolific producer of . . . literature and circulars having the obvious intent to disrupt American patriotic sentiment." Van Deman, in turn, received a memo from the office of the chief of staff of the War Department affirming that Justice Department agents were convinced that speeches delivered at AUAM meetings were "near seditious." The activities of AUAM and NCLB members, the report went on to say, "have been pernicious from the beginning; their whole attempt has been to preach down patriotism."[16]

All the while, Baldwin, oblivious to these machinations and to the placement of an informant in his own office, had maintained the NCLB's campaign of correspondence with top government officials, including Col. Edward M. House, the president's personal secretary. In a letter to House dated January 22 Baldwin complained about "the suppression of liberal opinion" by various federal departments. Such action presented "a serious menace to getting liberal and radical thought behind the President's war aims," Baldwin said. On February 8 he expressed concern about the impending trial of leaders of the International Workers of the World in Chicago. The government had indicted 166 Wobbly leaders under both the Selective Service Act and the Espionage Act and charged them with conspiring to induce draft refusal, desertion, and military insubordination. Baldwin was determined to keep track of their fate. One week later he spoke again of the need for a definitive government policy regarding "liberal and radical opinion."[17]

On February 13 he fired off a letter to conscientious objectors engaged in a hunger strike at Camp Upton, New Jersey. He exhorted them to await action by Secretary of War Baker, because much "depends on not making a public issue of it at this time."[18]

Despite such attempts to be conciliatory, however, Baldwin and the NCLB were increasingly viewed in a different light. Government operatives masquerading as conscientious objectors sought him out. By early March officials were telling one another that "this man Baldwin should be checked in some way and . . . his organization should be broken up." Thus the civil liberties movement was in danger of being slain during its infancy; it is quite possible that only Baldwin's impressive social connections, and those of his NCLB colleagues, prevented this from happening. Keppel of the War Department saw fit to inform Baldwin that "an embarrassing situation" was unfolding, for military authorities viewed the NCLB's activities as leading to "a direct conflict with the Government." Keppel warned that he might have to terminate further communication with the NCLB altogether.[19]

Keppel's warning must have been deeply disturbing to Baldwin, for the NCLB's relations with the War Department were most important of all; it undoubtedly was painful to Baldwin personally too. On March 1 Baldwin wrote to Keppel, declaring the NCLB "entirely willing to adjust ourselves in the matter of dealing with the conscientious objectors . . . whatever policy seems wise in your judgment." The civil liberties organization had always apprised the War Department of its operations on behalf of objectors. It had acted, "as we thought, entirely in harmony with the Secretary's general policy," Baldwin told Keppel. Moreover, the NCLB had engaged in no propaganda following congressional approval of the Selective Service Act. It had operated as a clearinghouse, and chiefly a legal clearinghouse, in order that "through one office the matter might be handled with the War Department as an administrative problem, more effectively than it could be handled in dealing with a dozen or more separate agencies," Baldwin wrote. Consequently, the directors of the organization failed to understand how they might have run afoul of federal law or why their relationship with the government should now change. Still, the NCLB could not maintain silence when "brutalities" involving the treatment of war resisters by British military officials—avoided in the United States because of "the Secretary's [Baker's] position"—came to light. In fact, various military officers, Baldwin reported, were "openly hostile" to Secretary of War Baker's supposedly evenhanded treatment of conscientious objectors. Thus they were deeply resentful of an organization like the NCLB, which had maintained "friendly relations with the Department," Baldwin contended.[20]

The NCLB would "continue to serve the cause of liberty of conscience" during wartime, Baldwin exclaimed to Keppel, "unless we are put out of business by the government." It was up to Secretary Baker, the letter continued, to determine "the exact method of that service." At the same time the NCLB remained committed to fulfilling its obligations to the young men who looked to it for assistance. However, in a note to Baker, Baldwin asserted that his agency sought conscientious objector status "only for those men whose conduct was entirely beyond the suspicion of avoiding military service for personal interests or safety." A follow-up letter from Baldwin to Keppel—who meanwhile was seeking guidance from Van Deman on how to respond to Baldwin—suggested that perhaps NCLB representatives needed "to go directly to those who misunderstand our operations and frankly explain."[21]

Once more Baldwin viewed the apparently changed relationship between the NCLB and the government as merely the result of some kind of misunderstanding. Thus he continued to believe that simply getting together with government officials or corresponding with them on a one-to-one basis, in gentlemanly fashion, would overcome any mistaken perceptions. Baldwin failed to appreciate that both he and the NCLB were increasingly viewed as some kind of "other" by top government officials.

At the same time Baldwin now served as secretary of the Liberty Defense Union, which was designed "to organize popular support in behalf of persons prosecuted for the exercise of their constitutional rights of free speech and free press," as Baldwin put it in a March 7 letter to Jane Addams. Other officers included John Haynes Holmes, Helen Phelps Stokes, and the socialist Harry W. Laidler; on its executive committee were Max Eastman, the prominent radical writer and editor; Scott Nearing; and Amos Pinchot. As Baldwin advised Addams, the founders of the Liberty Defense Union appreciated the need for such an emergency organization, which would work closely with groups like the Socialist Party and the NCLB. The Liberty Defense Union intended "to carry the appeal to the whole country" and therefore sought "a national committee of well known liberals and radicals." Baldwin's involvement in such an organization undoubtedly only further antagonized government agents.[22]

Baldwin nevertheless attempted to diminish concerns expressed by certain members of the armed forces that the NCLB encouraged resistance to military authority. He implored Major Biddle to undertake an official inquiry into the NCLB's activities regarding conscientious objectors. However, by this point Biddle had determined that Baldwin's activities were beyond the pale. In contrast, Baker and Keppel considered Baldwin "absolutely sincere" and his concerns about civil liberties "not entirely groundless." Admittedly, they were not as certain about the NCLB. As Biddle had requested, Baldwin sent him all the materials the NCLB had published in regard to conscientious objection. Amazingly enough, Baldwin went still further and included the NCLB's mailing list. Baldwin also offered to deliver to the War Department an accounting of all those with whom the NCLB had privately corresponded.[23] He failed to appreciate that such a proposal, if accepted, could have caused grave difficulties for the organization's supporters.

The NCLB wanted to make clear, Baldwin continued, that it was "acting wholly within the letter of the law and within the spirit of the Secretary's policy." But despite his efforts to convince officials of his agency's good intentions, what Baldwin seemed to fear most of all—loss of access to the inner recesses of the federal government—soon came about. On March 9 Colonel Van Deman sent a memo to Keppel affirming that dealing with the NCLB made for "a decidedly awkward and difficult situation." Van Deman did not seem much concerned about the genuine conscientious objectors but rather those who sought to avoid their military obligations and were encouraged by the very organization Baldwin represented. Moreover, Van Deman pointed out, it was quite likely "that our friend the enemy will use this organization for the promulgation of enemy propaganda." In fact, Van Deman offered, "I am inclined to think that it is now being done."[24]

Van Deman acknowledged "how difficult it is to attempt to suppress the activities of an organization such as the National Civil Liberties Bureau." After all, its aims were "praiseworthy in so far as they not conflict with the interests of our country at war." In addition, Van Deman predicted, "forcible suppression" probably would not work. Such action "on the contrary will be apt to throw them into the martyr class and, therefore, help the German agent in his work." The wisest approach would be to deal with Baldwin directly. Maybe it would be possible to convince him that if he did not confine his activities, and therefore those of the NCLB, along certain lines, they would be treated as unpatriotic pariahs. Clearly, Van Deman recognized Baldwin's sensitivity in that regard. The authorities should use force only as a last resort, Van Deman said.[25]

Keppel sent Baldwin a copy of the Van Deman memo. Amazingly enough, Baldwin had no inkling of what lay in store for his organization. Instead, he suggested that while "a satisfactory understanding" had been worked out between the NCLB and the War Department, "it is evident now that we must make an adjustment with other branches of the service." However, in other correspondence during this same period Baldwin demonstrated an awareness of the potential gravity of a rupture with the government. The dealings between the NCLB and the War Department, he recognized, had reached a critical juncture. Military intelligence already viewed the NCLB with suspicion, although Baldwin incorrectly believed that he had just concluded "a satisfactory conference" with Major Biddle. Still, he understood that his organization was suspected of engaging in propaganda in order to spur conscientious objection. Thus it seemed clear that two different approaches were possible. One demanded a "break with the War Department" and a turn toward the radical press. That would undoubtedly result in an indictment and end with the NCLB's being "put out of business." The second approach—which the NCLB had chosen out of necessity—involved inducing military officials to accept the organization's perspective, even if that required a tempering of its tactics.[26]

On March 16 Grant Squires, a New York City attorney, reported to Major Biddle on a meeting with Baldwin the previous day. Squires said that Baldwin had acknowledged that "in any other country of the world his ideas and his dissemination of them would have long since resulted in him and his associates being promptly made to suffer the death penalty." At the same time, Baldwin contended, "A democracy that interferes with the freest of free speech, is not worthy to survive."[27]

Another report, dated March 18 and filed with Colonel Van Deman, contained Baldwin's supposed admission that the AUAM, the NCLB's parent organization, "had published seditious literature and should not have been allowed to continue." The author of this latest study said he had examined government reports and NCLB documents and concluded,

> I am of the opinion that this organization serves no good purpose and that their activities should be stopped. Baldwin, himself, impressed me, and the others of this office who interviewed him, as being decidedly "hipped" on this subject of conscientious objectors. He is a Socialist and a believer in all sorts of Socialistic agitation and although he, personally, makes a good impression on those with whom he comes in contact, to the general mass of people who do not see him, his organization stands simply for a method by which the

"slacker" as well as the conscientious objector can and does attempt to evade his duty. There seems to me very little difference between their methods of obtaining recruits by the means of pamphlets and other propaganda than in writing direct to men of draft age, and some of their literature is certainly very near the borderline of sedition. Even assuming that Baldwin himself is sincere in his statements and endeavors to see that the conscientious objector is properly placed, the people associated with him, both individuals and organizations, have very unsavory reputations.[28]

In his private correspondence Baldwin confessed to being "thoroughly disgusted" with the "hearty assurances" objectors would be treated fairly that were delivered by government officials like Colonel House and George Creel, the journalist who directed the government's wartime propaganda. However, Baldwin continued to hold out an olive branch to members of the Wilson administration. Writing to Major Biddle yet again, Baldwin plaintively confessed to having searched his agency's documents once more to verify the absence of "the slightest appearance of any intention on our part to encourage resistance to military authority." He abjectly acknowledged that perhaps the NCLB had helped spread propaganda, which was "a wholly unintentional blunder." A British antiwar play that "can be construed as propaganda," he acknowledged, had been slated for distribution by the NCLB. No longer was this true. Obviously attempting yet again to convince Biddle of the organization's good intentions, Baldwin pointed out that he was now personally examining all the materials mailed to potential conscripts. Baldwin closed with the reassuring thought that "we want to be absolutely frank with the Department about all our activities." He had "never had the privilege of meeting Col. Van Deman," Baldwin also pointed out, an encounter that he believed might have prevented misunderstandings or misconceptions.[29]

Despite such obsequious efforts, Baldwin continued to condemn violations of civil liberties that were taking place in army camps or those likely to result from proposed amendments to the Espionage Act. The latter—which came to be known as the Sedition Act—seemed to the NCLB "to threaten the elementary rights of discussion of public policies during the war," or so Baldwin apprised Colonel House.[30] The Sedition Act, passed in May 1918, outlawed the issuance of "false statements" that hindered war bond sales or recruitment or employed "disloyal, profane, scurrilous, or abusive" language in regard to the U.S. government, Constitution, armed forces, the flag, or American military uniforms. Also banned was language designed to engender "contempt, scorn, contumely or disrepute" for those entities.

Not surprisingly, many public officials continued to view Baldwin as dangerous. A naval Intelligence officer based in San Francisco urged that Baldwin "be arrested and all his effects seized." Major Biddle informed his superior in the Office of Military Intelligence of attempts to plant a government operative in a job as a publicity agent in Baldwin's office. Referring directly to Baldwin, Biddle also insisted that "the time has come when his activities should be curbed." Baldwin's attempts to assist conscientious objectors, Biddle cautioned, spawned discontent in military camps. By contrast, the author of another government report, written on April 22, 1918, spoke favorably of the NCLB: "I do not find anything upon which to base any prosecution. The purpose of this Bureau, as set forth in its declaration of purpose, strikes me as not only lawful but a good one." But even this official urged that the NCLB be apprised of the government's ongoing interest in the organization in order to induce it to "carefully avoid any anti-war or obstructive propaganda." A short time later Keppel exclaimed to Colonel Van Deman that Baldwin's "typewriter ought to appeal to the Labor Department for relief."[31]

Also during April the NCLB published a fifty-six-page document entitled *The Truth About the I.W.W.*, which professed to provide a fair statement about the Wobblies "by thoughtful and unprejudiced observers." However, the editor of the little pamphlet, Roger Baldwin, was hardly a disinterested viewer when it came to the Wobblies. In fact, their anarchosyndicalism appealed mightily to Baldwin, who dismissed their charged rhetoric as "almost all talk." Rather, he pointed out, it was the Wobblies themselves who were often physically attacked. Furthermore, self-proclaimed patriots out to destroy the IWW were issuing the charges that the Wobblies intended to obstruct the war effort. The ongoing conspiracy trial of the Wobbly leaders in Chicago, Baldwin believed, involved no overt acts and should be terminated.[32]

To Baldwin and other leading figures in the NCLB, the government had targeted the IWW both because of its antiwar stance and its advocacy of militant unionism. Baldwin well recognized the danger posed by the NCLB's association with the IWW, acknowledging that "we have risked the whole organization on it." However, the NCLB considered a fair trial for the Wobbly leaders "of the greatest public necessity to the industrial future of America." Moreover, the NCLB was "deeply concerned for the whole cause of liberty in America," reasoning that the government could not carve out exceptions, even for the likes of the IWW. The Justice Department denied the

NCLB express mailing privileges for *The Truth About the I.W.W.*, and the Post Office withheld it from the mails.[33]

The trial of the Wobblies, with federal judge Kenesaw Mountain Landis presiding, had begun on April 1 in Chicago. The NCLB provided office space to Lee Chumley, a member of the IWW's General Defense Committee. The committee raised money, selected legal counsel, devised trial strategy, and solicited publicity favorable to the defendants. Attorneys for the NCLB expressed concern that the IWW had called for industrial sabotage, much as the indictment contended. But the NCLB demanded that due process be afforded the defendants and sought nonpartisan support for them. Distinguished liberals—including some prominent backers of the war effort—put themselves on the line by insisting on a fair trial for the Wobblies. During the five months that the trial lingered on, Baldwin went to Chicago at several points, attended court proceedings, and became acquainted with the defendants. These trips reinforced his impressions of the Wobblies from his days in St. Louis. He viewed these men as "a rare lot of upstanding and intelligent workers, determined, courageous, articulate" and was impressed by their "thoroughly American character."[34]

Baldwin drew closest to William D. "Big Bill" Haywood, secretary-treasurer of the IWW; Vincent St.-John; "Red" Doran, also a Wobbly leader; and Wobbly poet Ralph Chaplin, editor of *Solidarity*. Baldwin was aware of Haywood's somewhat notorious reputation, derived in part from his arrest for the assassination of former Idaho governor Frank Steunenberg (Clarence Darrow won Haywood's acquittal). The public image of Haywood as a terrorist was at odds with Baldwin's impression of "this quiet man, who spoke softly but with conviction and determination." He visited Haywood at the offices of the General Defense Committee, which under Haywood's leadership had secured nearly $1 million in contributions. The Post Office had held up one mailing, Haywood informed Baldwin, because of its purported incitement to violence. The front page of its newsletter was dripped in red ink that read "with drops of blood," a reference to attacks on the IWW. "It's getting harder for us to reach our mailing-lists," Haywood told Baldwin. The Post Office had acted because it assumed "we are after somebody's blood," Haywood said. As he explained to Baldwin, the circular did nothing more than tell "the story of the bloody attacks on the IWW, and it's all our blood. Perhaps your outfit can help clear it." Attorneys for the NCLB met with solicitors at the Post Office and got the document released for circulation.[35]

The NCLB established a committee to raise money for the Wobblies' defense; it was chaired by John A. Fitch, an editor of the *Survey*, the leading social work journal. Helping Fitch was John Graham Brooks, the biographer of William Baldwin and a labor relations expert. Brooks set up a lunch date at New York City's Century Club for Baldwin and top government officials, including David F. Houston, the secretary of agriculture and Baldwin's former boss at Washington University; Francis Caffey, New York's district attorney; and an assistant U.S. attorney general. Two contrasting stories, told by Baldwin himself, described the meeting. In one account Houston, who had always been friendly to Baldwin, seemed cold and wholly unmoved by his defense of free speech. The government, it was made clear, would not allow a group like the IWW to sabotage the war effort. However, in another recollection of events Baldwin said that the government had considered "calling off the [IWW] trial because of its effect upon the production of timber in the Northwest." Such litigation, the government feared, would only antagonize IWW supporters. Baldwin left the meeting with an assurance that Houston was prepared to advise that the trial be postponed until the war's end. Consequently, Baldwin was stunned when Brooks later informed him that the government intended to proceed immediately with the case.[36]

On May 13 A. B. Bielaski, chief of the Bureau of Investigation, sent a memorandum about Roger Baldwin to Attorney General Gregory. Bielaski, like other government officials, was obviously impressed by Baldwin's background. Baldwin, Bielaski's report said, was a pacifist, a leading figure in the People's Council, and director of the NCLB. He was "looking after the interests of radicals generally" and was determined that their rights not be abridged without due process of law. "Some of the purposes" of the civil liberties organization, Bielaski acknowledged, were "good in that they tend to act as a check upon excessive zeal of officers of the law in a time when excesses are likely to occur." His memo acclaimed Baldwin as a graduate of Harvard College "and a very intelligent young man of pleasing personality." Nevertheless, Bielaski contended that Baldwin was "headed in the general direction of a penal institution," although he had thus far managed to avoid violating the law. Having spoken and corresponded with Baldwin at length, Bielaski considered him "a pretty decent sort of fellow, but a very much misguided [*sic*] citizen." Still, Baldwin's determination to protect civil liberties, Bielaski wrote, was producing some good.[37]

But increasingly, the perception of Baldwin and the NCLB was that expressed by Colonel Van Deman. On May 15 Van Deman condemned Baldwin altogether. "Baldwin's entire work," Van Deman insisted, "may be summed up in wise—'You supply the man, we'll supply the conscientious objector.'" Consequently, Baldwin was simply "a seditious pacifist" who should be prosecuted under the new Sedition Act.[38]

On May 19 Keppel, an assistant secretary of war, moved to sever altogether ties with the NCLB; Colonel Van Deman was pleased that a changed attitude had taken hold in the War Department, producing "a distinct improvement in this particular matter." In a letter to Baldwin, Keppel declared that "it would not be in the public interest for us to continue to supply information pursuant to your request, or otherwise to cooperate in any way with the NCLB." Keppel also wrote to Hollingsworth Wood, who often took on cases for the NCLB, and pointed out that a special report had proved highly critical of the organization. Therefore, Keppel was forced to "terminate what was developing into an embarrassing situation."[39]

Baldwin reacted as might a wounded suitor, obviously stunned by the rupture between gentlemen and undoubtedly mortified that a top government official considered communication with him, the very embodiment of rectitude, to be embarrassing. This type of misunderstanding simply could not be allowed to continue. Moreover, he undoubtedly feared that such a development might destroy the still budding civil liberties movement.

Consequently, in his letter of May 27 Baldwin sought to speak directly with Keppel, affirming that the NCLB had to maintain certain of its activities but adding that "we would not for a moment undertake anything regarded as questionable by the Department." In a note the following day to Colonel Van Deman, Baldwin promised that the NCLB would refrain from any activities concerning conscientious objectors that might "be open to criticism." Baldwin continued to write to Secretary of War Baker during the early summer months of 1918, praising him for his "unfailing liberal and sympathetic attitude" toward the conscientious objector. Baldwin counseled that the government should treat resisters of a nonsectarian sort with respect.[40]

All the while the government maintained close tabs on Baldwin and the NCLB. One military intelligence document charged that the "real executive meetings" of the NCLB were held during informal luncheons at the Civic Club. "In this way the real activities of the organization are camouflaged, and those attending meetings held for the larger groupes [sic] do not realize the true state of affairs in the organization."[41]

On June 19 a memo from the Office of Naval Intelligence in Washington, D.C., to the Office of Military Intelligence asserted that Baldwin "favors extreme radicalism and violence." He did, after all, subscribe to *Mother Earth*, Emma Goldman's journal. Another intelligence report revealed that R. W. Finch of the Justice Department viewed Baldwin as "one of the most dangerous men in the United States today," who should not be allowed on any military installation. Philip J. Termini, the intelligence officer at Camp Dix in New Jersey, accused Baldwin of telling a soldier that he could avoid combat. Termini considered this "the first positive statement that I have been able to procure which shows an attempt on the part of Baldwin to interfere with the military force, contrary to the Espionage Law."[42]

Through it all Baldwin attempted to maintain correspondence with Keppel, sending him a plaintive note on August 3. It termed the present state of affairs "highly unsatisfactory and frequently embarrassing." Would he not "be good enough to let me have definite word which will settle my difficulties?" Baldwin asked Keppel. Ten days later Keppel responded pointedly: "I can readily see that the situation is an embarrassing one for you." Like Van Deman earlier, Keppel knew the man he was dealing with. Given the nature of the NCLB's operations, Keppel failed to see how the breach could be avoided. By this point Keppel would only ask military intelligence whether the War Department should avoid any dealings with the NCLB.[43]

On August 17 Baldwin wrote directly to Van Deman. Military intelligence officers, Baldwin stated, had "frequently called into question" NCLB activities on behalf of conscientious objectors. This had brought about "an embarrassing and difficult situation, which is likely to throw the whole matter into the field of public controversy." That would result in an unraveling of "much of the quiet and effective work toward a satisfactory solution, which has been made possible by Secretary Baker's liberal ruling" regarding conscientious objectors.[44]

The government had never told NCLB's officers, Baldwin continued, "what activities of ours are considered improper." The organization remained ready "to discontinue efforts which the Secretary of War may not think to be helpful."[45] Even at this late date Baldwin still held out hope for a pipeline to the government, something others were more determined than ever to prevent. This demonstrated a certain naïveté, even foolishness, on Baldwin's part and was another example of his elitism too. He simply refused to accept that government officials refused to deal with him and his colleagues as equals or partners in the campaign to maintain civil liberties.

Thus Baldwin may have welcomed the series of interviews conducted by government agents that began on August 22. They asked his opinion of the Wobblies, inquired about the financing of *The Truth about the I.W.W.*, and sought to learn whether Morris Hillquit of the Socialist Party had been paid for legal services rendered on behalf of the *Masses*. Once again Baldwin proclaimed that "no other Government in the world" would tolerate the kind of criticism emanating from organizations like the NCLB. When queried about men stationed in various army camps but serving "as informants for your Bureau," government documents claim that Baldwin replied, "I have three or four men who are sending the comments of our other men, and shall be glad to give you the names."[46]

In late August the NCLB became the subject of heated discussion in several government agencies, despite Keppel's attempt to deflect some of the most serious criticisms from military intelligence. On August 26 Nicholas Biddle, now a lieutenant colonel, wrote to the chief of the Military Intelligence Branch of the War Department and proclaimed that MIB's New York office was eager to assist the Justice Department's actions "against Baldwin and the Conscientious Objector group."[47]

Two days later a fourteen-page report on Baldwin arrived at the War Department. It quoted a brigadier general, who termed the NCLB "one of the most insidiously active anti-war organizations in existence. It is nearly treasonable, undoubtedly disloyal." It referred to Baldwin's intimate associations with Emma Goldman and her declaration that he possessed "the best system of anti-draft organization known, with its quota of 10,000." A series of government officials, the report claimed, agreed that the NCLB was "carrying on a very insidious and dangerous campaign." This was "all the more harmful because of the subtlety with which it is conducted" and Baldwin's emphatic belief that he was "keeping within the spirit and letter of the law." Affidavits from military officers specified that the NCLB had constantly "worked against the military authorities and that its activities have been to the hindrance of military authorities." The NCLB, the report asserted, sought "to retard the draft by any method that did not constitute an open violation of the law."[48]

The report further claimed that disseminating propaganda in the manner Baldwin did was tantamount to an attack on "every high impulse and altruistic motive animating our President and Cabinet in this epochal cataclysm, and helps to indoctrinate our youth with a spirit of disloyalty and treason that taking root would bankrupt us in faith, hope and patriotism." Further-more, Baldwin had "become associated in the west with some kind of negro movement," although it was unclear what brand of propaganda he was spreading "among the colored people." This supposedly proved that Baldwin "was not tied body and soul to the Conscientious Objector's movement."[49]

On August 31 the solicitor of the Post Office Department also wrote to military intelligence to seek information about the NCLB, Roger Baldwin, Walter Nelles, John Haynes Holmes, John Nevin Sayre, and other key figures in the organization. They were among the individuals who had sued the postmaster in New York City to gain release of materials, including the pam-phlet about the Wobblies, being held in the metropolitan post office. The solicitor saw the NCLB as the American Union's legal wing and believed Baldwin's agency was involved "in many matters which are manifestly inim-ical to the Government in the prosecution of the present war."[50]

That same day Nicholas Biddle of the Office of Military Intelligence con-firmed that the Justice Department "had taken up the case of Roger Baldwin seriously." Biddle believed that Baldwin undoubtedly could be indicted for violating the Espionage Act. Because Justice wanted still more documentary evidence, Biddle decided to send six men from his office to NCLB head-quarters.[51]

Later that same day—as Judge Landis was handing down harsh sentences to the IWW defendants—federal agents, along with members of the Ameri-can Protective League, stormed into the NCLB offices. The federal agents arrived with a search warrant that authorized them to seize any materials believed to encourage obstruction of the war effort. The American Protec-tive League members were led by Archibald Stevenson, an attorney and pro-ponent of the 100 percent Americanism propounded by self-proclaimed patriots. Baldwin temporarily abandoned his usual politesse and excitedly told the government men "that he did not give a damn about anything"—and that they should "go ahead, lock him up, shoot him, hang him, or any-thing else," as the agents' report put it. Once Baldwin calmed down, he allowed the agents to remove the organization's files and "anything . . . required for prosecution." Moreover, a federal agent said that Baldwin told him—no doubt sarcastically—that "plenty of indictments could be secured from the minute book itself." Military Intelligence seemed to agree with such an analysis. The government had copies of correspondence between Baldwin and young men in which he advised them "at what point they could resist service in the Army," a government agent claimed.[52]

At this point the still fledgling civil liberties movement appeared in danger of extinction. That's what government operatives wanted, and they had at their disposal repressive legislation, the backing of the Justice Department, and compliant federal courts. Once again chance and commitment would determine the fate of the leading national organization dedicated to upholding the Bill of Rights.

CHAPTER SEVEN

The United States v. Roger Baldwin

After the raid on NCLB headquarters, Walter Nelles warned those who sat on its executive committee that "all or most" might be indicted. Baldwin called John Haynes Holmes at his summer retreat in Maine and exclaimed, "I think you had better come to town. Come right away." Holmes responded, "Why, what's the matter?" Roger replied, "They raided our offices yesterday. They took away all our . . . books and papers, all our files. They stripped us clean. From other sources, we hear that the Attorney-General is preparing indictments against the officers . . . and that we shall soon be placed under arrest. You'd better come down." Holmes assured Baldwin, "I'll come down tonight. See you in the morning."[1]

Baldwin also sent a wire to Norman Thomas, then in Kansas visiting his mother. The two agreed with L. Hollingsworth Wood's suggestion that the board hire George Gordon Battle, a conservative southerner who worked with Tammany Hall. This was the period, beginning in early September 1918, when a sweeping raid on "slackers"—those viewed as not sufficiently supportive of the war effort—was carried out by the American Protective League in New York City. League members eventually rousted more than twenty thousand young men. The *Nation*, edited by Oswald Garrison Villard, cried, "Civil Liberty Dead."[2]

As matters turned out, another kind of indictment was about to come Baldwin's way. Now thirty-four, he could still face conscription into the U.S. military. In early August 1918 he had submitted his resignation as NCLB director, effective upon the signing of the Selective Service Act at the end of the month. Because of the raid on the NCLB's headquarters, Baldwin temporarily withdrew his resignation until "the critical period was past." Then on September 12 he refused to report for his physical and delivered to his draft board the following statement:

> I am opposed to the use of force to accomplish any end, however good. I am therefore opposed to participation in this or any other war. My opposition is not only to direct military service, but to any service whatsoever designed to help prosecute the war. I am furthermore opposed to the principle of conscription in time of war or peace, for any purpose whatever. I will decline to perform any service under compulsion regardless of its character.[3]

Government harassment may well have compelled Baldwin to adopt such an absolutist stance. Perhaps he saw the gentlemanly world in which he had operated coming apart. Or perhaps his association with rebels, heretics, and political misfits now stirred in him still greater empathy, and he was acting with less of the sense of noblesse oblige to which he had long been prone. In any event Roger Nash Baldwin had come to believe he could no longer simply pull strings from the sidelines while younger men suffered the consequences.

Indeed, Baldwin's identification with the dispossessed, with a kind of American lumpenproletariat, was now clearer than ever. After he left St. Louis to join the American Union, Baldwin maintained ties with old associates in the field of social work. The National Conference of Social Work (NCSW) published two of his editorials calling for greater involvement with radical movements. Baldwin—who served as vice chairman of the NCSW's Division on Industrial and Economic Problems—spoke of a new world aborning in which old institutions would be challenged as never before. At present, he insisted, social workers were merely "caseworkers patching up the evils and the miseries of the industrial system; or propagandists for reform legislation; educators; collectors of facts or figures; or neighborhood and community workers." However, "outside our work, we can join in the radical political movement of socialism; we can get the facts of economic injustice, and talk and write them, helping indict the present economic system."[4]

His more radical stance suggested how far Baldwin had veered from the comfortable progressive camp. Yet he continued to champion incremental reform measures while expressing sympathy with revolutionary movements abroad or calling for the socialization of the U.S. economy. Once more, he stood as if in two camps, but circumstances and his own identification with the dispossessed and wartime resisters were leading to another confrontation with government forces.

On September 16 Baldwin wrote once more to Frederick Keppel at the War Department seeking return of NCLB materials held by the Bureau of Investigation since the August 31 raid. Baldwin expressed hope that no individual would be punished for communicating with the NCLB during the very period it had engaged in "active cooperation with the War Department." At the same time the civil liberties group anticipated that the authors of any documents "expressing disloyal sentiments, a defiant attitude, or participation in propaganda . . . would be held fully responsible for them." Baldwin could not recall having received such materials.[5]

On September 24 the director of military intelligence for the War Department, Brig. Gen. Marlborough Churchill, disclosed that Baldwin was being investigated by the U.S. Post Office, the Department of Justice, and the Military Intelligence office in New York City, which had been keeping tabs on him for some time now. "Some definite action," General Churchill announced, was expected "in the near future."[6]

George Gordon Battle's efforts and his personal ties to leading figures in the Wilson administration probably saved the NCLB from prosecution at this point. John Nevin Sayre, a member of the NCLB executive committee, asked his brother Frank, who happened to be President Wilson's son-in-law, to find out whether Attorney General Thomas W. Gregory would meet with NCLB representatives. What actually transpired at the meeting is unclear, but Gregory, perhaps because of pressure from the president himself, declined to bring charges against the organization. Unquestionably, the distinguished connections of leading NCLB figures like Sayre helped to avert such an occurrence and may have prevented the government from crushing the still new civil liberties movement. One story has it that Norman Thomas was the first to receive word, albeit unofficially, that no prosecution would be forthcoming. Thomas told Assistant Attorney General Alfred Bettman, "I can't see what protection civil liberties will have in America if the Civil Liberties Bureau itself is to be prosecuted." Bettman replied, "It's not my business to discuss that. But, Mr. Thomas, I think you and your colleagues are pretty safe. You can go back and tell your friends that." Bettman acknowledged that the government had lost its prosecutions of the editors of the *Masses* and Scott Nearing. (Postmaster General Albert Burleson had withdrawn the *Masses*' second-class mailing privileges and suppressed the June and August 1917 issues; Nearing had been indicted on a charge of treason.) Bettman then told Thomas, "What we've found out is this: in New York City it's very hard to convict any of you folks who can make a good speech to the jury. And you've got John Haynes Holmes and Roger Baldwin and yourself—there would be too many speeches. We're not taking the chance."[7]

An obviously perplexed Nicholas Biddle, writing to his boss from the Office of Military Intelligence in the heart of New York City, asked why Baldwin and other NCLB leaders had avoided indictment. Frederick Keppel also wanted to be apprised of Roger Baldwin's status. As Keppel divulged in a letter to the Military Intelligence Division, he had suggested that Baldwin "go out of business as an evidence of good faith and sincere desire to carry out the stated purpose of his organization."[8]

On October 7 Baldwin was ordered to take a physical examination at his local draft board two evenings later. He sought out Agent Raymond W. Finch of the Justice Department—the same operative whose reports about Baldwin had been so damning. Finch jokingly promised to arrest Baldwin for violating the Selective Service Act, making it "the greatest little arrest ever pulled in New York," with "half a dozen cow-bells and tin-cans." On October 9 Baldwin informed District Attorney Francis G. Caffey that he was "respectfully" refusing to appear before Local Board 129. Once again he expressed his opposition to conscription of any type or to the use of force even to bring about noble ends. Such beliefs, he bluntly acknowledged, would lead to his incarceration. Nevertheless, "it seemed to me more honest to make my position clear at the start by refusing even to register." All he sought was a speedy trial; he planned to represent himself and plead guilty. In the meantime he would refuse bail, which was not available to the indigent.[9]

A government agent, decked out with Liberty Loan buttons, showed up at the elevator in Baldwin's apartment building on West 83d Street to arrest him for violating the Selective Service Act. They went upstairs, where Baldwin was allowed to make some phone calls and cancel appointments; he managed to convince the agent not to handcuff him. He was taken to the basement of the American Museum of Natural History, where the draft office of Local Board 129 was located. He appeared before Julius Henry Cohen, the chairman of the draft board and a well-known lawyer, and was afforded the opportunity to recant. Baldwin recalled that Cohen strongly urged him "not to be so 'contumacious.'" Cohen exclaimed that the "more obdurate I was, the harder it would be." Baldwin declined the offer and was taken to a police station to think things over. There he was "searched, booked, questioned, and locked up in a cold, hard cell, with nothing in it but a board bench . . . and a toilet." The desk sergeant ordered an officer, "Take everything away from him." Somehow Baldwin, using a newspaper for a pillow, was able to sleep. At one point a guard came by to give him some water and asked, in a thick Irish brogue, "And can ye till me why so mauny intelligent men are conscientious objectors?" Baldwin replied, "Because they're intelligent, I guess." The jailer left without responding. The only other occupants of the cell, deposited there in the early morning, were two loud drunks.[10]

That morning, instead of being returned to the draft board, Baldwin was let out of his cell by "a group of hilarious FBI agents," some of whom he had met during the raid on the NCLB's headquarters. Sent by the district attorney, they appeared, he reported, "delighted to take me in charge." They were led by Agent Finch, who seemingly found "nothing could strike his funny bone more keenly than arresting a fellow who had walked himself right into jail," Baldwin related. A great limousine awaited the distinguished arrestee. "Amid great merriment," Baldwin was taken to "a bang-up breakfast," allowed to shave, and then carted off to the Bureau of Investigation office. As he later recalled, "My sense of humor was not lacking either, and it all struck me as good clean fun." The levity with which Baldwin responded to his situation was somewhat characteristic but bordered on the absurd.[11]

A number of assistant U.S. attorneys interviewed Baldwin, attempting to convince him, as he recalled, that "I would ruin all my future prospects of usefulness by being so cantankerous." Like Baldwin, many of the government lawyers were Ivy League graduates. One assistant U.S. attorney, Leland Duer, had been a Harvard classmate and appeared highly distressed regarding "the reflection on our class," as Baldwin put it. The lawyers' efforts proved unavailing, and Baldwin was indicted that morning, charged with violating the Selective Service Act.[12]

That evening Baldwin was placed in a cell at the Tombs, the old city jail. On the same level were federal prisoners, including draft dodgers, German nationals, an Indian revolutionary sought by the British, the feminist Agnes Smedley, and drug offenders. The dimensions of Baldwin's cell were approximately 8 feet by 6 feet, with an 8-foot ceiling. It contained a pair of iron bunks attached to the wall, a basin, toilet, and wooden stool. It held an electric light, which came on at 5:30 in the morning and was shut off at nine in the evening. The bunk beds had wire springs, two blankets, sheets, a pillow, and bed bugs but no mattress. Prisoners were handed only a spoon to contend with "half sour bread, luke-warm, unsweetened 'coffee,' sodden mush for breakfast at 7,—a steamy stew of meat and vegetables at 11; pale 'tea,' sour bread and tasteless 'stewed' fruit at 4, all served in the cells in tin mugs." After one long day of such fare Baldwin purchased his meals from the prison kitchen.[13]

At 6:15 A.M. the jailer ran his key against the bars to awaken the prisoners. Before breakfast Baldwin swept his cell, made up his bed, and was shaved by the prison barber. After two hours of exercise in the corridors the prisoners returned to their cells. Those who paid for the privilege were allowed to roam the corridors throughout the day.[14]

On the morning of October 11 a deputy U.S. marshal handcuffed Baldwin before marching him down Broadway to the local headquarters of the Bureau of Investigation. Worrying that some acquaintance might recognize him, Baldwin strode ahead of the official, "dragging him along as if he were my prisoner." Upon their arrival at the government office, Agent Finch expressed outrage that Baldwin, "his pet prisoner," was in handcuffs. Finch ordered the deputy never to repeat that mistake. As Baldwin recalled, Finch believed that "I could be trusted to go wherever I was wanted, since I had locked myself up."[15]

Unexpectedly, Finch—who had ensured that Baldwin's trial not take place immediately—asked Baldwin whether he would help the Bureau of Investigation to organize the NCLB files, which were in hopeless disarray. Baldwin readily accepted the proposal in the belief that "orderly files would prove our complete innocence." Thus for the next three weeks Baldwin slept at the Tombs, was picked up in the morning, and was taken over to the Bureau of Investigation's office. Fortunately, the deputy U.S. marshal, a Yale graduate assigned to watch Baldwin, was opposed to the war and conscription. Unwilling to buck the system, he had obtained his present position to avoid military service. But apparently the marshal was unhappy with his decision, for "he atoned a bit by giving me every privilege within his limited power," Baldwin recalled. He was treated as something of a guest and was frequently taken out to dinner and the theater. Baldwin's friends were invited to lunch with him, and on one occasion he was driven over to Norman Thomas's home for a meal. As Baldwin informed his mother, all the government men were "extraordinarily decent to me"; however, such treatment was hardly shared by others imprisoned because of political beliefs or on grounds of conscience. He was also allowed to visit his dying aunt, Sally Briggs, who sought to understand why her nephew was in his present predicament. Finally, she declared, "I do not know whether you are right or not, but I do know you have good blood in you and that will tell."[16]

Holmes, acting on behalf of the NCLB's Directing Committee, congratulated Baldwin for his faithful and zealous service to the organization. The NCLB, Holmes asserted, had contributed in a "not unsubstantial" fashion to defending personal freedom in wartime. "And that it is to you, above all others, that credit for this achievement properly belongs."[17]

Sitting in his cell one morning, Baldwin drafted his speech to the court. On October 30 he was brought into U.S. District Court in Manhattan. Ironically, the presiding judge, Julius Mayer, had served as the first judge of New York City's Children's Court. The courtroom was packed with friends and colleagues of Baldwin's, along with his aunt Ruth Baldwin. Those in attendance included Florence Kelley, Norman Thomas, Crystal Eastman Fuller, Scott Nearing, the socialist Rose Pastor Stokes, and the antiwar proponent Rabbi Judah Magnes. Baldwin's fiancée, the journalist and lawyer Madeleine Doty, was bedridden with a severe cold and could not be present.[18]

In his opening statement the district attorney announced that the case involved a willful violation of the Selective Service Act. Baldwin responded with an eloquent oration similar to the one so recently made by Eugene V. Debs, who had been convicted under the Espionage Act. To Roger, Debs had come to embody "pure socialism; his was a voice of protest and humanity above parties."[19]

Now Baldwin had the opportunity to display his own mettle and place himself firmly on the side of radical, even revolutionary, forces both at home and abroad. He had shown his statement only to Thomas, who had proposed minor editorial alterations. Baldwin acknowledged that he was deliberately violating the Selective Service Act and had informed his draft board that he would not take his physical examination. Having reordered the NCLB files for the Department of Justice, he was now prepared to be sentenced. Baldwin thanked all the officers of the court and the Department of Justice for the exceptional courtesy he had been afforded.[20]

His uncompromising opposition to conscription, Baldwin affirmed, compelled him to violate the Selective Service Act. He regarded conscription as antithetical to all democratic and Christian tenets. Furthermore, "I am opposed to this and all other wars. I do not believe in the use of physical force as a method of achieving any end, however good." His opposition was not merely "to direct military service but to any service whatever designed to help prosecute the war."[21]

Some might deem Baldwin's refusal to register an act of deliberate defiance, as he acknowledged. And he could well have avoided this controversy. "I answer that I am not seeking to evade the draft; that I scorn evasion, compromise and gambling with moral issues." He was unwilling to accept any service, morally objectionable or not, if he was compelled to serve.[22]

Baldwin explained how he had come to adopt such an extreme position. He had grown discouraged with the pace of social work and reform. Challenged by the example of the Wobblies, he considered "getting out altogether, throwing respectability overboard and joining the IWW as a manual worker." He had decided against that course of action.

> But ever since I have felt myself heart and soul with the world-wide radical movements for industrial and political freedom—wherever and however expressed—and more and more impatient with reform. Personally I share the extreme radical philosophy of the future society. I look forward to a social order without any external restraints upon the individual, save through public opinion and the opinion of friends and neighbors. I am not a member of any radical organization, nor do I wear any tag by which my views may be classified. I believe that all parts of the radical movement serve the common end—freedom of the individual from arbitrary external controls.[23]

After the United States entered the war, he strove to safeguard the ideals of liberty that had laid the foundation for radical economic thought: "the radical political view" of the Founders, and religious freedom. Consequently, he joined the American Union's anticonscription campaign and, to protect freedom of speech and of the press in wartime, helped to establish the NCLB. He also was determined to uphold "the Anglo-Saxon tradition of liberty of conscience" by defending conscientious objectors.[24]

With great conviction and considerable drama Baldwin professed, "I seek no martyrdom, no publicity." He asked for a court-martial and incarceration in a military prison. There he might join two to three hundred other objectors. He would "refuse to conform to the rules for military salutes and the like," which would undoubtedly result in solitary confinement and shackles. No matter—he, like other absolutists, Baldwin continued, was "prepared even to die for our faith, just as our brothers in France are dying for theirs. To them we are comrades in spirit—we understand one another's motives, though our methods are wide apart. We both share deeply the common experience of living up to the truth as we see it, whatever the price." He asked for no favors from the court.[25]

Judge Mayer conceded that he had no doubts about the defendant's sincerity. Baldwin seemed to stand apart from others similarly accused. The judge referred to Baldwin's self-respect, clearly articulated principles, and "manly" willingness to face the consequences of his actions. Then Mayer stated that he was ruling simply as a matter of law. The defendant had failed to appreciate something essential and fundamental regarding the maintenance of American freedoms. "A republic," Mayer suggested, "can last only so long as its laws are obeyed." A free government could not continue if any individual, guided by noble or ignoble intentions, could break the law. History might later prove such an individual to have been in the right. However, "with those possible idealistic and academic speculations a court has nothing to do."[26]

Baldwin was quite correct about one thing, the judge continued: "There can be no compromise." An individual who knowingly violated the law must suffer the consequences. In the present case a final determination was an easy matter because of the defendant's intelligence and clear assertion of his position. The war, Mayer emphasized, could not be waged successfully if Baldwin's attitude became widespread. It would lead to disorder and the demise of "a real people's government." Consequently, Mayer said, he had no choice but to levy the full statutory penalty. Allowing Baldwin into the army would be unwise, for he would "become a disturbing element." Having asked for no compromise, he would receive none. Mayer sentenced Baldwin to one year in the penitentiary, with credit for the twenty days he had already served.[27]

The case of *U.S. v. Roger Nash Baldwin* received wide press coverage. A story appeared on the front page of the *New York Post*. "Two strong men looked each other between the eyes, and though one of the men sentenced the other to a term in prison, each of the men found no fault in the other," the paper told its readers. On October 31 the *New York Times* headlined its report on the trial PACIFIST PROFESSOR GETS YEAR IN PRISON. The following day the *Times* included an editorial on Baldwin's case, "He Chose Words in Haste." Baldwin, dubbed "the pacifist martyr" by the *Times*, was quoted as opposing the use of physical force for any purpose. The editorial then cuttingly affirmed,

> It would be unfair, probably, to assume that any man not obviously insane entertained that belief in the literal and strict sense of the words used by Professor BALDWIN. If he did, he would be deprived, among other precious privileges, of that of raising to his lips a glass of what the Prohibitionists are fond of calling "pure, sparkling water," however burning might be his innocent thirst. Physical force must be used, as even every pacifist knows, for the achieving of about all the ends there are.[28]

Copies of Baldwin's speech before the court appeared in the *Nation* and the *Survey*, while a private copy was printed and circulated among his friends. Baldwin, the *Nation*'s editorialist predicted, would likely emerge from imprisonment unscathed. After all, the writer had "never met a more socially-minded, more useful, or more patriotically devoted American." In a note to Doty, Baldwin denied deserving plaudits for simply "standing out for what I believe—when not to stand out would be pain [*sic*]." He had done "the most obvious and natural thing in the world."[29]

Family members, friends, and associates immediately reacted to the verdict and sentence. Baldwin worried about the response of his father, mother, and siblings, having become the first "jailbird in the known heritage" of the Baldwin family. However, he was pleasantly surprised that all said they understood his actions, with even his mother nodding her approval. Only Uncle George Baldwin, a millionaire from operations in the stock market, chastised Baldwin by letter, reading "him out of the family." Roger's brothers, Bob and Herb, both serving in the U.S. Army, later came to see him in jail. His father, although unhappy with his eldest son's activities, proved "tolerant in the tradition of Boston heresy." Frank Baldwin expressed regret that his son had felt compelled to defy the law. Yet Roger Baldwin's statement to the court "was well expressed and showed a finer feeling of spirit than could be expressed from mere man," his father said, adding "I admire your spirit and strength of character in holding to convictions and wholly respect you." Nevertheless, Frank Baldwin informed Roger that he shared Judge Mayer's sentiments that his son's beliefs had "led you to a defiance of the law." Still, Frank reluctantly revealed that he was proud of his son. To his daughter Margaret, Frank insisted that their relatives were "not big enough to comprehend 'the nobility of the boy.'"[30]

Margaret and his aunt Ruth S. Baldwin were virtually overcome by Roger's courtroom performance. Margaret found it difficult to express what she felt "about this wonderful thing you have done and the way in which you have carried yourself all through your hard experience." Ruth Baldwin told Roger, "Never shall I forget that scene in court, nor cease to be grateful that I was there and could see you and listen to your words. I felt it was the most deeply moving experience of my life, and your bearing, simple and noble, your address beautiful, direct and convincing beyond what any words of mine can express."[31]

Crystal Eastman Fuller kept Madeleine Doty posted on the court proceedings: "I am desperately sorry that you missed Roger's wonderful appearance in court this morning. It was a beautiful and moving and at the same time brief and logical statement. Altogether we all felt it was a historic occasion." Jane Addams, although strongly disagreeing with Baldwin's rationale, greatly admired his stance. Norman Thomas wrote to Lucy Baldwin, who by then was living in Cambridge with Margaret, to applaud Roger's "courageous stand." Lucy Baldwin must be quite proud of her son, Thomas offered, and should appreciate that a year in jail was far better than the fate he would have suffered at the hands of military authorities. Thomas closed by declaring that Baldwin's oration in the courtroom had resulted in "one of the rare experiences of a lifetime." Even Mayer wrote to Roger Baldwin, expressing his belief the younger man could "be of very great service."[32]

Members of the Justice Department could not have disagreed more strongly. On November 4 an Associated Press dispatch reported that government operatives considered a number of organizations—all purportedly fostering disloyalty—to be "federated." Officials therefore warned against making contributions to "so-called 'civil liberties,' 'liberty defence,' 'popular council,' 'legal advice,' or anti-war organizations." Such financial assistance could end up in the coffers of other organizations seeking to impede the U.S. war effort. One such agency, these officials reminded the public, had until recently been headed by Roger Baldwin, now imprisoned for violating the Selective Service Act. Wood, the NCLB chairman, believed that the reference to Baldwin was intended as a warning. Wood then announced Baldwin's retirement from the NCLB and stated, "His peculiar loyal and efficient service to the cause of civil liberty and of liberty of conscience" clearly spoke for itself.[33]

It now appeared questionable whether the civil liberties movement could survive into the postwar period. Even Baldwin had once wondered whether the campaign would remain viable when U.S. involvement in the war ended. The man most identified with the movement was presently behind bars. His incarceration, which removed the most spirited leadership of the civil liberties campaign and provided ammunition for its bitterest antagonists, could well have proved fatal to the movement.

CHAPTER EIGHT

Prison Life

Those who thought or hoped that the government or Roger Baldwin himself had closed the chapter on his civil liberties career were, of course, sorely mistaken. Months earlier Baldwin had considered the demand for the NCLB's work so dependent on wartime exigencies that it was difficult to predict whether the organization would remain in operation after hostilities ended. At the time Baldwin believed that the organization's work would undoubtedly "be incorporated into a larger national radical labor movement." Ironically, R. W. Finch, the Justice Department agent, recognized that Baldwin's incarceration was merely "the beginning of an adventurous career which, apparently, he has mapped out for himself."[1]

In the reports he continued to file on Baldwin, Finch referred to the belief held by radical leaders in New York—including Baldwin, Scott Nearing, Socialist Party organizer Kate Richards O'Hare, and John Reed—that revolutionary uprisings were likely to occur worldwide. Those individuals placed great emphasis on what might unfold in England, where the young Labour Party was becoming a formally socialist party and was committed to full employment, a minimum wage, a maximum work week, public ownership of industry, progressive taxation, and expanded social services. U.S. radicals saw the English as establishing precedents that might enhance their efforts in the United States. Finch reported that the goings-on in England could mean that workers would become a more potent political force and bring about land redistribution. Baldwin and the other radical leaders, Finch stated, had "agreed that the Russian situation will not affect the U.S."[2]

In one report Finch wrote that John Nevin Sayre, the brother of President Wilson's son-in-law, "like a great many other well meaning liberals, considers Mr. Baldwin only an idealist." Such a belief, Finch continued, was "a dangerous error. I have always been convinced that Baldwin did not fit into this work as gracefully as some people believe." Finch, like Kate Richards O'Hare, had once thought Baldwin was engaged in intelligence work. But the agent had learned "that Baldwin is out on a great adventure." In the postwar period Baldwin intended to devise "a world-wide organization of the leaders of radical thought," if he could manage to find funding, a government report charged. However, Baldwin had to "win his spurs first and have the usual penitentiary record behind him." Thus Military Intelligence charged that Baldwin sought out manual labor to acquire "a little further reputation among the working classes."[3]

Because Baldwin was "an unusually intelligent man," Finch planned to remain in contact during his incarceration. Moreover, Baldwin seemed to be connected to radical leaders throughout the United States. Most important, the government agent wrote, "I believe that what Baldwin states now is the composite view of the leaders of American radical thought." Given Baldwin's affinity at this stage for staying in touch with figures on the cutting edge of radical movements, Finch's analysis was astute, at least in that regard.[4]

Their relationship was curious and foreshadowed others Baldwin had with certain government figures. He viewed Finch as well intentioned and even respectful. Finch, however, considered Baldwin dangerous and a man to be vigilantly watched by the government. All the while, Finch played to Baldwin's need to be well regarded by the same government officials who had arrested and imprisoned him.

While at the Tombs, Baldwin was hardly treated like other prisoners. At one point Carroll Binder, another Harvard man, came to see him. After Binder departed, Baldwin recalled something else he had wanted to share with his visitor, so he simply ran out of the penitentiary to find his friend, now two blocks away. He then returned to jail, and not a word was said about the incident.[5]

The preferential treatment he received throughout his incarceration troubled him not one bit. Indeed, he took it for granted and would, one suspects, have been distressed had it not been forthcoming. His ready acceptance of such treatment is suggestive of the continuing paradoxes that abounded in him. On the one hand, he had moved to adopt a more radical, absolutist stance concerning government's ability to conscript men into the military. And his general perspective on social and economic affairs was increasingly influenced by revolutionary developments abroad, leading to sympathetic pronouncements concerning workers' control of industry. Yet he had hardly escaped his upper-class background, which afforded a sense that he was still viewing matters as an observer, despite his own imprisonment.

On November 11, 1918, Baldwin was escorted by two federal marshals from the Tombs to the Essex County Jail in Newark. It was Victory Day, ironically enough, and New York City exuded a celebratory atmosphere. The trip to Newark ended with Baldwin's treating the marshal to a drink at the corner saloon. Forewarned about the conditions of the jail slated to serve as his residence for the next nine months, Baldwin was pleasantly surprised to encounter a brick brownstone in an old residential area. The clean prison grounds contained a bricked yard, with chickens below the yard and birds perched in the trees ringing the sidewalks. Baldwin was booked and informed that no written rules existed. He had to relinquish only sharp objects and medicines but was allowed to take clothes, books, and other belongings into his small second-floor cell. That first evening the prisoners celebrated the end of the war, with Baldwin playing the piano and joining the chorus.[6]

Between 8 A.M. and 8 P.M. inmates were allowed to roam the narrow corridor. They spent most daytime hours reading, writing, playing games, walking, and talking with one another. The prison food, brought to the cells, was much better than at the Tombs, and inmates could buy extra portions or special dishes. Baldwin exercised and took a sponge bath before eating breakfast at 7:30, when he received an apple, a large pitcher of milk, two soft-boiled eggs, and four slices of bread and butter for 25 cents. The regular prison breakfast, comprised of excellent bread and coffee, was served at 8:30 A.M. Baldwin elected to eat the standard prison lunch at 2:30, then purchased coffee, a sandwich, and pie for his 8 P.M. supper. He paid one lad 50 cents a week to clean his cell and do his laundry; his ability to afford such assistance apparently caused him no misgivings. He spent the day perched on his stool in the corridor, reading and writing, composing letters and a bit of poetry. He took time out only to exercise in the yard or the corridor, go to the barber, attend religious services on Wednesday and Sunday—for a brief while— or see visitors. The prisoners had unrestricted mail and visitor privileges twice a week for two hours at a time. On becoming a trusty—one of a half-dozen in the prison population of 250—Baldwin's right to see visitors proved virtually unrestricted. The visits were carried out through heavy iron-mesh screens, which Baldwin naturally found embarrassing.[7]

Herb and Bob Baldwin, who served in the U.S. Navy and Army, respectively, during the war, both wrote to their brother in jail. Herb, who frequently disapproved of his older brother, hinted that it was "too bad you had to 'enlist' for so long beyond the duration of the war, but then I am not going to lavish any sympathy or condolences on you for I know you don't want it." After all, Roger had chosen his lot, which was no more difficult than that experienced by many others. Bob revealed that he felt closer to Roger than ever but could not understand "where your bolshevism or red flag policy would ever bring any kind of peace or happiness to the world." Such a radical philosophy, Bob continued, would require "more bloodshed, murder, rape, the world over, and there has been enough of that."[8]

While he was imprisoned, Roger Baldwin also received letters from a young fellow he had first met at an IWW gathering in St. Louis. Harold K. Brown, known to Roger as "Brownie," was an astonishingly precocious young man who read widely to his father, a socialist with limited sight; they covered works ranging from the proceedings of the British House of Commons to the writings of Karl Marx. Brownie cuttingly admonished Baldwin (to whom he referred as "Unk"), "You must not let your 'Red' tendencies carry you away, my dear, remember you're a true pacifist, and can surely have no sympathy with the unpleasant whiskered Bolsheviki, whose way of solving any problem in the way of politics that itself is to more or less indiscriminately turn on the machine-guns."[9]

In his typical fashion Baldwin was pleased to be "saving so much useless expense!" Increasingly, he viewed his year in prison as "but 'taking the veil,' a 'retreat'—or a 'sabbatical year.'" Having directed offices in both St. Louis and New York, which entailed endless committee work, appointments, and travel, he welcomed life as "reduced to simplest terms."[10]

His breezy, almost dismissive, attitude concerning his incarceration begs for an interpretation, albeit one perhaps best left to psychoanalysts. Was it simply a desire on his part to alleviate concerns of friends and family about his well-being? Did it demonstrate the propensity for denial that sometimes afflicted him? Or was it simply an example of the flightiness he was often accused of?

The treatment accorded him by the Irish guards at the Essex County Jail undoubtedly made his stay more comfortable. As Baldwin told his mother, he was determined "to feel useful to the management here. They seem to be a fine set of men—good fellows all—and I look forward to the pleasantest associations"; although he was a federal prisoner, he thought it only natural that he should assist the jail administrators. Again, on the surface this was an example of an astonishing degree of hubris, with Baldwin planning to help administer the very institution that held him prisoner. But it also pointed to his sense of self, his seemingly never-ending belief in his ability to direct matters, and his feeling regarding the appropriateness of doing so. Fortunately for him, the guards were hostile to "England's war" and viewed with favor any opponent of the conflict. Warden McGinnis was himself a staunch Sinn Feiner who had been suspected of running guns to Irish rebels. Most of the guards were Irish; one, having read Baldwin's declaration to the court, came to him to express outrage that he was behind bars. Consequently, the jailers all viewed Baldwin as something of a celebrity and afforded him special privileges. In the evening, when other prisoners were safely in their cells, Baldwin's door was left open so that he could continue reading and writing in the corridor. During the evenings he often joined in discussions in the office with the guards and a few prisoners. Baldwin and McGinnis frequently discussed world events from Ireland to India.[11]

Initially, Baldwin's job was to serve meals purchased by prisoners, as well as meals sent to the infirmary and inmates who had been hospitalized. Along with four or five others, he wielded large pots of stew, vegetables, and meat, ladling out portions. He helped out in the kitchen, where an old drunk named Bridget held forth, frequently bellowing at Baldwin, "God damn it, and haven't I tould ye a dozen times that it's the turnips for the paid dinners and cabbage for the diets?" His class consciousness evident once more, Baldwin found it amusing to be acting as "the cook's servant." Other female kitchen helpers were in jail for shoplifting, prostitution, and various minor offenses and addressed him as "Roger," while he referred to them as "May," "Clarice," and "Stella." Offered the chance to sleep in a dormitory where the kitchen help stayed, Baldwin decided to remain in his jail cell, preferring the privacy and the closeness to the "real prison life" it provided. Within a short while he was also attending to the greenhouse. After watering the plants one evening, he discovered that the entrance into the prison grounds was locked. He found a night bell, rang it, and informed an old guard that he had been locked out. The guard replied, "I don't know you, and I have no orders to let you in. But if you say you belong here, come on in, but don't do it again." The guard also exclaimed, "This ain't no place for a feller like you!"[12]

Throughout his incarceration at the Essex County Jail, Baldwin maintained a steady correspondence with leading figures in the radical camp. In mid-November he felt compelled to explain to Scott Nearing why he had determined not to join the Socialist Party; like the progressive movement—battered following U.S. involvement in the war—it now appeared too tame for him. Unlike the Socialist Party, he no longer believed that "the vote, the State and majority control in political units" would help to liberate humanity. Rather, he had determined that they were "illusory and therefore dangerous." The ideal society, he wrote, would be "wholly free of external, arbitrary controls," other than the associations one willingly opted to join, such as labor unions and voluntary societies. The state, he insisted, was only "a means for enslaving some group or groups for the benefit of others." A more effective approach, he pointed out, was that followed by the Non-Partisan League, backed by European socialists, and shared by the Bolsheviks. All supported the direct takeover of industry by worker, farmer, and cooperative associations and the use of political power to preclude the other side from wielding the power of the state against them.[13]

A number of Baldwin's friends began to agitate for his release from prison by way of a presidential pardon. To his credit Baldwin responded by writing a letter to Albert DeSilver that was intended for broader dissemination. Baldwin declared, "I would refuse to be the beneficiary of any such personal discrimination if it were made." He simply could not allow himself to take advantage of politically well-placed friends, while hundreds remained imprisoned "for precisely the same convictions that brought me here." Like others convicted of violating the draft act, Baldwin was interested only in a general amnesty, "not so much for the sake of our own liberty, as for the country's liberty." He and his fellows, Baldwin argued, were no little band "of protesting cranks." Rather, "we are part of the vanguard in the fight for a new order of society, freed of the compulsion and arbitrary restraints of an all supreme State."[14]

While he was in prison, Baldwin's concern for social issues reached well beyond daily correspondence with other political activists. His own relatively privileged position notwithstanding, he recognized that many prisoners lacked the intellectual or financial resources required to ameliorate their plight. For them jail was "often a place of real torture," involving awful monotony, privation, and diminution of both spirit and body. On December 17, 1918, he had written to John J. Hanley, warden at the Tombs, and offered suggestions for improving the lot of those incarcerated there. Baldwin complained of the lack of ventilation, poor quality of food, unsanitary conditions, and long hours of confinement to cells. At the Essex County Jail, with the warden's approval, he helped to devise a Prisoners' Welfare League, which he called the "Essex County Jail Soviet." Thus even in jail Baldwin remained the classic organizer, trying to better conditions for all concerned and to direct matters as he saw fit. A committee gathered money to hire an attorney, Jim Smith, son of the former head of the state Democratic Party, and asked him to serve any inmate with a good cause. As reform-minded women in the area, particularly the wealthy Caroline Bayard Colgate, became concerned about prisoner rights, the prison committee convinced the public library to send books to the jail and got welfare agencies to help prisoners' indigent families. It also held educational classes and led discussion groups on such issues as public ownership of the railroads and women's suffrage. Thanks to the committee, the prisoners staged musicals, put together a glee club, offered dances, and provided classes in English, mathematics, and foreign languages. To Baldwin the entire prison atmosphere changed, with order and hope making an appearance.[15]

Although they were well intentioned, many of Baldwin's suggestions were unrealistic, more suited to the genteel class of which he was a part or to public organizations like St. Louis's Civic League. His support for them demonstrated that, despite his more radical perspective, he was willing to champion reforms of a less than sweeping nature. His call for prison reforms was in keeping with the very progressivism he had so recently rejected.

Eventually, however, Essex County Sheriff Flavel got wind of what was occurring at his jail and sent for Baldwin. Flavel asked, "What are you doing, spoiling those criminals? I won't stand for it." Baldwin replied, "Half the men had not even been tried in court and were no criminals." "Well," Flavel responded, "if they are not criminals, why are they in jail?" Point-blank, he ordered that the prisoners' group be disbanded, but Baldwin refused. Instead, he leaked the story to the *Newark Daily News* and the lady reformers; the resulting publicity compelled the sheriff to back down temporarily. Also, nearly two hundred prisoners signed a petition asking Flavel to reconsider his decision. He had acted as he had, Flavel charged, "because Professor Baldwin was teaching members of the League socialism." Baldwin responded sharply, denying Flavel's accusations and challenging anyone to cite a single incident in which "I have voiced any views on socialism or any radical subject likely to be objectionable to the authorities." However, the sheriff urged that Baldwin be transferred to another county facility, which Baldwin had been requesting. The transfer order came from the U.S. attorney general without prior notice; Baldwin was the only federal prisoner transferred in such a manner. As the sheriff expected, the prisoners' league did not long survive Baldwin's departure on May 13.[16]

Perched on a high hill and surrounded by gardens, the county prison in Caldwell, New Jersey, appeared to Baldwin "even more home-like than jail." It was a work farm, designed for short-term offenders and a small number of federal prisoners like Baldwin. He was allowed to keep only underwear, socks, shoes, ties, and pajamas and was handed a blue shirt, a dark wool suit, and heavy work shoes. This time he retained all his toiletries, including a razor blade, and his books. His jail cell was approximately 5 by 8 by 9 feet and had been freshly painted white. The cell held a bunk with a straw mattress and pillow, small table, and toilet and basin. After the lights came on at 6 A.M. the prisoners cleaned their cells, made their beds, dressed, and washed up. Breakfast was at seven and included coffee, bread, and a hot cereal. Following breakfast, the inmates returned to their cells until eight, when they were let out for chores. Along with a gang of nine or ten, Baldwin was assigned to work in the fruit and flower gardens, under the watchful eye of a German guard "so radical that when the Spartacus revolt took place [in Berlin in January 1919] he went on a drunk for three days. He and I got on fine after that." Baldwin earned 30 cents a day for his labor, which he deemed an appropriate sum for the quality of his farming. Planting, hoeing, and weeding put Baldwin in better shape than he had been for years. The work continued until lunch and then again until 4:45 P.M. After dinner—generally a meal of vegetables, meat, bread, and coffee—he watered and planted, sometimes until eight or nine o'clock at night. Like other gardeners, he had free run of the farm.[17]

On Saturdays the prisoners at the Caldwell facility mopped the cells, changed sheets and pillow cases, washed their clothes, and showered. Many were given the day off, and they often held ballgames in the afternoon. Sundays were for rest and religious services, and visitors were allowed on weekends. On Sunday evenings the prisoners were allowed to play music, and Baldwin performed on a concert grand piano. Once or twice a week they were permitted various forms of entertainment or lectures.[18]

Rules and discipline were less strict in Caldwell. Once again serving as trusty, Baldwin worked outside from eight in the morning until five in the evening. At first his mail was read and was limited to two letters a week. But after two weeks he was moved to an area reserved for the trusties and accorded greater freedom. No lockup was required, except between the hours of 8:30 P.M. and 6 A.M. No guard was directly in charge, and the prisoners disciplined themselves. They ate their dinners at small tables, which seated eight and were decorated with gay red geraniums. Baldwin again befriended a couple of younger men, who constantly played tricks on him, even sticking a pair of fat toads into his pocket at one point. The three sat together at the dinner table, making up "a talkative, merry little family."[19]

An "easy, genial spirit" prevailed throughout the prison grounds. A type of comradeship seemed to exist between the jailers and the prisoners. The warden was accessible; he handled the men democratically and exuded an air of informality. On May 30 the warden held a track meet, during which Baldwin landed flat on his face after the first twenty yards of a hundred-yard sprint. Prizes were handed out in the evening, following a talk by the warden concerning the relationship between prisoners and jail keepers. The prisoners were allowed their own organization, which amounted to "a self-government and welfare association" in Baldwin's eyes, and they published a monthly paper, the *Spokesman*. At a prison store the inmates purchased tobacco, writing paper, stamps, toilet articles, and newspapers. The prisoners had library privileges and could borrow books on a weekly basis. Other books and periodicals could be shipped in from the outside but were subject to inspection. The warden eventually lifted the restriction on the number of letters Baldwin could receive.[20]

The prisoners had a type of social organization, encouraged by the warden, who was a member of the National Conference of Social Work. In fact, while Baldwin was in Caldwell, the warden attended the national convention of the social work organization, where he voted to reelect his celebrated prisoner to the standing committee for industrial and economic problems. Committee chair Florence Kelley had nominated Baldwin, but George Thorne, a New York social worker, jumped up and demanded that Baldwin's name not be considered. "I make this motion," Thorne cried, "because . . . I do not believe we can be party to an action that makes this conference in the eyes of the public endorse a man now in prison for having violated the laws of the United States in time of war." David I. Kelley, who worked for the New Jersey Department of Institutes and Agencies, seconded Thorne's charges: "We have too much of this sliding back, we have too much of this excusing of persons who stab Americans in the back because of their convictions. I warn you that your entire organization will be cast aside and injured materially if you allow your sympathies and friendships to carry you in voting this matter." Despite support from social workers Florence Kelley, Arthur Dunham, and Edward T. Devine, among others, the vote was 262–216 against Baldwin's election.[21]

During this same period the National Probation Association—which Baldwin had helped to establish—convened in Atlantic City. Once again controversy unfolded with the discovery that Baldwin's name was on the program. Judge Charles W. Hoffman, from the domestic relations court in Cincinnati and the presiding officer of the National Probation Association, was said to be "indignant that a program with Baldwin's name upon it should have been 'put over,' on him by some of Baldwin's personal friends in New York." A meeting of the executive committee was called and Baldwin sharply condemned.[22]

It was not merely Baldwin's newly discovered apostasy that induced leading figures in his former field to attack him so vociferously. His own criticisms of social work no doubt had rankled many who now determined to treat him like a pariah. For his part Baldwin—who seemed desirous of cutting a symbolic umbilical cord with his old compatriots—denounced what he termed "the immorality of social work." While professing to provide service to society in general, he asserted, it sustained "the class interests of private capitalism," working at the behest of "the propertied for the propertyless." As a consequence, radicals in the profession, like those in teaching and the ministry, were either being forced out or—like Baldwin himself—departing "for other fields of service."[23]

Between mid-May and July 19, 1919, Baldwin was housed at the Caldwell facility. However, because of a clerical error and the time off he had earned for good behavior, he was released nearly three months shy of his yearlong sentence. Judge Mayer had allowed Baldwin credit for time served before sentencing, but the commitment papers read ten months and eleven days, instead of eleven months and ten days, as they were supposed to. Baldwin wrote to Mayer to ask that his papers be corrected, but the judge refused. For many jailers and prisoners alike, Baldwin had indeed served as a model prisoner. Brownie had suggested Baldwin behave in such a manner, undoubtedly to ensure both better treatment while in jail and an early release.[24]

Attired in a light gray summer suit and holding several parcels and a satchel, Baldwin left the Caldwell penitentiary at 9 o'clock on the morning of July 19, 1919. Only three people awaited him, including Madeleine Doty and a reporter from the *New York Herald Tribune*. Baldwin characteristically discussed his experience in the most favorable light possible. "It is the most profitable year I have ever spent," he told his companions. "It has given me a view of the whole administration of our law in practice, and it has brought me in contact with a great stream of men going in and out of the penitentiary in a way that no reformer or social worker can possibly obtain." His opinions about conscription had not changed one bit: "I object to conscription by any government. I don't care whose it is. I would rather die than submit to conscription."[25]

In the fall he planned—in his wholly quixotic fashion—to join the Musicians' Union or the IWW's culinary union to learn more about American labor. He intended to become part of "the revolutionary social movement." He bluntly stated: "I am through with social reform as a method, because I think the world has passed it by, just as it has passed so-called political democracy. I am going to do what a so-called intellectual can do in the labor movement and aid in the struggle of the workers to control society in the interests of the masses."[26]

To his friends he declared his intention to remain "as close to the radical labor movement as my training and abilities permit." On the very evening Baldwin was released from prison, Norman Thomas hosted a party for him at the Thomas home on East 17th Street. Among those present were Norman's brother Evan, a conscientious objector just released from Leavenworth Penitentiary; John Haynes Holmes; Oswald Garrison Villard; the Wobbly Lee Chumley; Roger's fellow inmate at the Tombs, Agnes Smedley of the Friends of Freedom for India; Elizabeth Gurley Flynn of the Workers' Defense League; and Herbert Croly of the *New Republic*.[27]

Albert DeSilver proclaimed, "There's not going to be any public stuff tonight. This is just a chance for you to say howdy to Roger upon his return from, shall we say, his vacation? . . . Make a few remarks on the state of the nation, Rog; you can say anything you doggone please from Gesundheit to the Ten Commandments." All devoured the chocolate ice cream and cake Lucille Milner had purchased from a nearby bakery. "I feel like a deb at a coming out party," Baldwin chortled. As the evening concluded, it was clear that those in attendance awaited the guest of honor's return as NCLB director.[28]

Two weeks later Villard informed readers of the *Nation* that "one of the fairest and squarest and best of Americans" had just been released from jail. After nine months of incarceration Baldwin had emerged "as clear-eyed, as fresh, as unbroken in spirit as when he entered." In determining to join up with militants in the labor movement, Baldwin favored peaceful action, "for he is an absolute non-resistant and wholly opposed to force." Hoping "to live down" his Harvard education, Baldwin "has chosen to wander."[29]

Shortly after his release from prison Baldwin spoke with U.S. Attorney General A. Mitchell Palmer about his incarceration. Palmer had informed friends of Baldwin's that he wished to see him; undoubtedly, Baldwin hardly found this surprising. They met in Palmer's office at the Justice Department, and the attorney general acknowledged, "Mr. Baldwin, I want you to understand that I'm not unsympathetic with the position you have taken yourself." Palmer's family members were all Quakers, he said, and he too hated war. The conversation was low key and cordial, just "a conversation between two gentlemen which might take place anywhere," Baldwin later recalled. It was precisely the kind of discussion he had hoped and even expected to have with top government officials during the war, though that seldom happened.[30]

The meeting with Palmer and the decision to join the Wobblies exemplified the dualism still besetting Baldwin. His increasingly radical beliefs and declarations notwithstanding, he readily accepted invitations to deal with public officials, whether behind prison walls or in august government buildings. Simultaneously, he expressed sympathy for and sought to identify with those deemed wholly beyond the pale by the same officials. Whether by design or not, he thus continued the pattern he had adopted in St. Louis and maintained throughout U.S. involvement in the war. What all this portended for both him and the causes with which he was associated remained to be seen.

CHAPTER NINE

An Unconventional Marriage

Upon his release from prison Baldwin had one immediate goal in mind: to marry Madeleine Z. Doty, the thirty-nine-year-old journalist, lawyer, prison reformer, and feminist whose celebrity at this point was every bit as great as his. Doty had returned from Europe, where she spent most of the time Baldwin was incarcerated. They had met in 1913 at the National Conference of Social Work, when he was working for the Civic League in St. Louis and she for the New York City Prison Reform Commission. He had immediately been attracted to her. She appeared to be "the rare type of independent professional women [sic]," with strong opinions of her own and a commitment to social justice. She was a socialist but no revolutionary, had published in national magazines, and was, like Baldwin at the time, "essentially a social reformer." He was also drawn in "by her gaiety and humor, her clear blue eyes, her trim figure and her professional women's [sic] style of dressing." Moreover, "she seemed to know everybody in the New York crowd which dominated the social work fraternity"—which undoubtedly made her even more appealing to Baldwin.[1]

They saw each other only briefly at another conference before his move to New York in early 1917. They met again through her involvement with the Women's Peace Party and her friendship with Crystal Eastman Fuller of the AUAM. They kept running into each other at antiwar gatherings and at social occasions orchestrated by mutual friends. She considered him "gay and handsome. His charm was irresistible." He seemed interested in everything with which she had been involved, no doubt particularly the time she spent in Russia during the Bolshevik Revolution. She was writing about "revolutionary justice" for the *Atlantic Monthly* and planned to complete an article on the Russian soviets for the *New York Tribune*. He invited her to go canoeing at his camp in Oradell, New Jersey, and easily displayed his knowledge of all the birds and flowers in the area. Several subsequent canoeing adventures followed, and Baldwin frequently visited Doty at her studio apartment in New York. Their friendship continued to blossom, and he was introduced to her parents, who lived in Manhattan, and her brothers, Ralph and Douglas; Douglas served as an editor at *Harper's*.[2]

Later Baldwin determined that "Madeleine was almost abnormally devoted to her parents," particularly her father. Nevertheless, her considerable desire for independence and privacy compelled her to live alone. However, whenever Doty became ill, she immediately asked for her father, a soft-spoken and charming elderly man who had made something of a fortune in the insurance trade. The family could afford a trip to Europe virtually every summer, with Madeleine going along, determined to pay her own way. During her most recent visit abroad she "managed to see radicals everywhere, from Bertrand Russell to Trotsky," Baldwin wrote. In New York she lived frugally, seldom eating out or attending the theater. A modern woman, Doty had experienced a number of affairs, as she acknowledged to Baldwin, some with well-known authors, including the muckraker and novelist David Graham Phillips, and one with a member of the Cabot family of Boston.[3]

By the summer of 1918 Baldwin and Doty had fallen in love and planned to wed. However, uncertainty regarding his draft status compelled them to put their plans on hold. On September 26 he wrote a letter to her bemoaning their time apart and likening himself to "a bunch of dynamite—ready to explode." He refused to assign her any part in his battle against the government, reasoning that he was "stronger alone." Nevertheless, Baldwin, clearly relying on an idealized vision of Doty, acknowledged that her absence on the day of his sentencing pained him.[4]

Writing her from the Essex County Jail in early January 1919, Baldwin discussed their marriage plans. He agreed that they should wed in the countryside, serving as their own witnesses. Freddy Farnum, a fellow draft resister and inmate, was to stand as his best man; Baldwin referred to Farnum as a kind of "American Rupert Brooks with a dash of Thoreau in him." Freedom and love, Baldwin wrote, came from within. All efforts to restrict their behavior, he declared, were "only fetters to hold us down. How I rejoice in the prospect of a free marriage. It is a sort of respectable free love!"[5]

During the first several weeks of his imprisonment in New Jersey, Doty went to see Baldwin regularly, even posing as his attorney to obtain unlimited visiting privileges. The warden allowed them to meet in the prison greenhouse. However, their relationship became strained because of the pressures—her telephone was tapped, which meant their private talks were becoming public property. Even Baldwin's seemingly boundless cheerfulness flagged. Eventually, she sailed for Europe to attend the Congress of the Women's International League for Peace and Freedom. Soon he spoke of his desire that they were "more of a mind in cheer, in nonsense, in gaiety—freedom to banter." This was an area, he believed—presciently, as matters turned out—that required "careful attention by us both."[6]

At the end of March Baldwin wrote about a new brood of three young lads he had befriended; during the decade that followed his jail term, he became guardian to another pair of boys and the namesake of numerous others. Playing the older brother to troubled young people, Baldwin acknowledged, was "flattering to one's vanity." He possessed "much of that protégé instinct . . . a form of ego of course, all directed to developing youth." However, "the boys need you—some of them fully as much as me, & more," he proclaimed to Doty. "And you need them, my dear—for the same reason I need them. They are the eternal tests of our own integrity of mind and heart—the youthful examiners of our faith, the guarantors of our eternal childhood. I am young with them. I feed off their inquiring search for purpose and experience of life as if it were my own."[7]

In early April Baldwin wondered how he and Doty, separated by such a great distance, could be "such happy fools." Perhaps it was because "we are destined to make new rules anyway! I still feel the absence of all bonds but common purposes and common love. But they get stronger!!" In July he asserted, "I really quite seriously am falling too deeply in love with you—and you must help me recover. It is disturbing."[8]

Because he had been released from the Caldwell County facility one week after Doty sailed from Liverpool, he was present, along with her parents, when her boat docked. He and Madeleine went to Boston where she was warmly greeted by Lucy and Frank Baldwin and their grown children. On August 8, 1919, Roger and Madeleine, each having paid 50 cents for a marriage license, were wed in a civil ceremony in New York City. They then went to her parents' summer home in Sparta, New Jersey. Madeleine's parents were there, Lucy Baldwin soon arrived, and Freddy Farnum showed up too. The "real wedding," in Madeleine's estimation, took place in Sparta. The simple outdoor ceremony was performed by Norman Thomas, still an ordained minister. The bride wore everyday apparel, no wedding dress or veil, and they did not exchange rings. Madeleine "was a lovely person" and "very high-minded," Roger's brother Bob thought, but he interestingly enough considered this "a marriage of convenience."[9]

To demonstrate their commitment to each other and to the idea of an unconventional marriage, Baldwin and Doty recited their own vows. They were starting, Doty began by declaring, "on a great adventure. We enter into partnership, the great partnership, the union of man and woman. [Love] is a test greater and beyond all law and all clergy." Love required absolute freedom, she exclaimed, the freedom "to love whom you will, to go where you will, to be your own master total and absolute." She wanted her love for Baldwin to be unfettered by possessiveness or jealousy. In truly unconventional fashion she asserted that "one cannot promise to live together as man and woman always." This type of union would plant the seeds "for the new brotherhood for which we strive, when all men shall live together in love and harmony, bound by no laws, subjected to no force—dominated wholly by love."[10]

Baldwin's response was even more striking, declaring that "to us who passionately cherish the vision of a free human society, the present institution of marriage among us is a grim mockery of essential freedom. Here we have the most intimate, most sacred, most creative human relationship shackled in the deadening grip of private property, and essentially holding the woman subservient to the man." But as women achieved their economic and political freedom, the bonds would be broken. As for the two of them, Baldwin intimated that they were agreeing to this contractual bond "only because it seems a matter of too little importance to resist or ignore it." Similarly, they were concerned about family members and friends. Nevertheless, they saw monogamy as "a tyranny of emotional repression," they denied exclusivity and jealousy, and they welcomed other friendships and "many loves." Their marriage, he continued, should further "my primary interest and joy . . . the great revolutionary struggle for human freedom, so intense, so full of promise." To that end they were determined to retain their economic independence and the liberty to chart their own courses of action.[11]

They headed off for the summer home of Caroline Colgate in the Adirondacks. Doty was not pleased to find that Freddy Farnum was tagging along, and she insisted that Roger's friend allow them two weeks of uninterrupted honeymooning. Blessed with fine weather, Roger and Madeleine cooked outdoors, canoed, swam, and climbed mountains. On their return to Manhattan they settled in at her cold-water, third-floor apartment just off Washington Square in Greenwich Village. The apartment was carved out of an old house and contained a comfortable living room with an open coal fire and three bedrooms.[12]

Later Baldwin denied having ever "entered Village life. I see it around me and avoid it." His friend Joseph Freeman acknowledged that "there was nothing bohemian about him." Yet as early as 1912 Baldwin recognized that the Village served as "a magnet for the dissenters and radicals," and he first visited there two years later for a meeting of the Liberal Club. Discussion of socialism, Freud, and women's suffrage filled the air. Indeed, "the talk was so sophisticated and witty that its substance didn't matter," he said. After he moved to New York, Baldwin's office was located on Fifth Avenue in the Village. Many NCLB associates, naturally enough, were identified with "the dissenting left, pacifist and libertarian," he said.[13]

Clearly, Baldwin and Doty were part of "the Greenwich Village Left," or its remnants, at the end of World War I. Moreover, one or both were friends of, among others, Max Eastman, Crystal Eastman Fuller, John Reed, the radical journalist Floyd Dell, Margaret Sanger, and Dorothy Day, then a journalist drawn to socialist and antiwar causes. Any number—like Baldwin, Fuller, and Reed—were graduates of elite institutions. The women tended to be professionals, either social workers or lawyers, whereas Doty, of course, was both. All were attracted to the social and political movements that influenced what the historian John Patrick Diggins terms the Lyrical Left, such as women's emancipation, sexual liberation, and the avant-garde in the arts. They were increasingly disillusioned with the gradualism and reformism associated with the now badly weakened progressive movement. Although chastened by the repression unleashed during the war—which led some to head for other locales, ranging from Paris to Moscow—the Greenwich Village intellectuals were determined to defy conventionality in their personal relationships. Consequently, all condemned Victorian double standards, and many championed birth control, open marriage, and the discarding of rigid gender roles. Some engaged in homosexual or extramarital affairs.[14]

Baldwin had been planning for months to take to the road as an itinerant worker. Doty was not enthralled with the idea, while Scott Nearing had argued that Baldwin, because of his background and temperament, was better suited to the kind of work he had conducted for the NCLB. The labor activist Elizabeth Gurley Flynn, Nearing reported, agreed that Baldwin's joining the IWW would be a mistake. Nearing apologized for lecturing Baldwin but reasoned that he had "a real function in the big mission and I don't want to see you get sidetracked."[15]

Despite Doty's reservations and his friends' concerns, Baldwin began his great adventure. He remembered what Jim Maurer, head of the Pennsylvania local of the American Federation of Labor, had told him: "You will never understand the labor movement until you have worked with other men with your hands and know that's your only support. And if you go hungry, so much the better." Even if he returned to the field of civil liberties, Baldwin reasoned, he needed to understand the plight of workers better, for labor was certain to be "our major client."[16]

Baldwin also felt cheered or goaded by correspondence he had received while in jail from Evan Thomas and Harold Lord Varney of the Metal Machinery Workers Industrial Union, who championed militant unionism. The IWW's philosophy, Evan contended, best matched his own because it preached "self-reliance, true individual responsibility and effort for freedom." Varney wondered whether Baldwin would "choose to still cling to the class where you have been rooted." Some individuals, he suggested, acted in a manner befitting their beliefs, no matter what peril threatened. Others "turn to radicalism in a mood of dalliance. Their natures are dual." Although such people wanted to act, they remained physically detached from the fray. In Varney's estimation these were "our reformists and compromisers."[17]

In mid-September, as Baldwin prepared for his trip, he wrote to the IWW's Bill Haywood, offering his assistance in building up the union's defense fund. Haywood responded immediately, declaring that Baldwin could do nothing better for the IWW than to carry out a fund-raising effort himself and to obtain favorable publicity in the liberal and radical press. Baldwin's time could be more effectively spent, Haywood wrote, than "in rustling a job and bustling around the country in box cars. Excuse me, please, for expressing myself so bluntly, but this is really what I think."[18]

But with the labor movement in ferment throughout the Midwest, Baldwin headed there, determined to provide for himself by dint of hard labor; he carried little cash and no bags. He was thirty-four and in good physical shape after his stint in prison. He went first to Chicago, where he stopped off at IWW headquarters and ran into Haywood, then out on bail during the appeal of the verdict in the mass conspiracy trial. Baldwin admired the Wobblies; he believed that they had "guts, hope, a philosophy." Haywood still did not seem to think much of Baldwin's plan, warning, "Don't try to get a job cooking in any of our camps. Our boys like to eat good." Nevertheless, Haywood agreed to sponsor Baldwin for membership, and he was initiated at a party in the IWW hall. Baldwin was already acquainted with a number of the men and reported that he felt at home.[19]

While in Chicago, Baldwin stayed at Hull House, where he wrote to Doty on October 2, proclaiming himself both "a full fledged I.W.W." and a member of the Waiters' Union. He described his stay in the Windy City as joyous and exulted in hanging out with Emma Goldman, the Wobblies and Bill Haywood, and Jane Addams and other Hull House workers.[20]

Despite Haywood's half-joking warning, Baldwin had thought he might be able to get a job as a cook and applied for membership in the Chicago local of the Cooks and Waiters Union. The union was stationed in a swank clubhouse whose restaurant employed black nonunionized waiters. The initiation was formal, in striking contrast to the Wobblies' fraternity. Now, with two union cards in hand, Baldwin was nearly ready for work. First, he joined the picket lines in south Chicago and Gary, set up to support a great steelworkers' strike. He then hopped a freight train to St. Louis, where he stayed with old friends for a few days and visited Toto. His friends were taken aback by Baldwin's latest endeavor, and a local newspaper informed the police, who then questioned him about bumming rides from the railroad. News got around that the city's former top young reformer had hoboed into town. Military Intelligence got wind of Baldwin's presence in the city too and filed a report entitled "Radicalism in St. Louis." Baldwin supposedly had agreed to avoid speaking at radical gatherings or engaging in direct work for the IWW, because the Secret Service—just one of several agencies that tailed him regularly—had warned him "he would be jugged again."[21]

Traveling incognito, Baldwin ventured from St. Louis to the lead mines in southeastern Missouri, which he described as "the wildest barbarian lands in the West." There he worked the night shift, shoveling lead ore into a smelter. He was subsequently fired from another job, after bricks he tossed from a wheelbarrow bounced off other workers. Back in St. Louis, Baldwin was delighted when, dressed as a worker in faded clothing, he passed an acquaintance at the railroad station and was not detected. Next he spent several days at railroad labor in Youngstown, Ohio. When he landed in Pittsburgh, Baldwin was welcomed by William Z. Foster, who was heading the bloody steel strike there. Foster's strike committee needed a labor spy, and Baldwin was selected.[22]

In Homestead, eight miles east of Pittsburgh, Baldwin was ordered to clean out hot ovens and replace burned-out bricks. In the evenings he recorded the presence of morale problems, inefficient scab labor, and general problems in the production line. After a week on the job Baldwin was fired and told to pick up his pay in the morning. When he returned to his hotel room, he discovered it had been ransacked and his papers and notes pilfered. Fully cognizant of how labor spies were dealt with, Baldwin refused to be cowed into leaving town without his pay. After a sleepless but uneventful night he picked up his pay and returned to Pittsburgh, where Foster enjoyed a good laugh at his expense.[23]

Baldwin appreciated as never before Clarence Darrow's observation that "I'd rather be the friend of the working man than a working man; it's a lot easier." Broke but contented, Baldwin returned to New York City, where he let his union membership lapse.[24]

Lucy Baldwin had written a letter to her new daughter-in-law to express concern about the antics of her "runaway boy, Baldwin. I wish he could come home to his wife and stay put where he belongs! He is allowing you to carry all the burdens of living." The problem was that her son "has reached a too visionary state of mind. He would better come home and be practical for a while."[25]

Back at Doty's apartment in Greenwich Village, he quickly pitched a tent on the roof to shelter "his waifs and strays," including the seemingly ever-present Freddy Farnum. The constant influx of young men was somewhat annoying to Doty, who did not take kindly to having her face powder used and the bathtub left unwashed. Still, as she later acknowledged, "Life was gay. There was never a dull moment." Other guests included such leading figures on the American Left as Freda Kirchwey, an editor with the *Nation*; Upton Sinclair; Bill Haywood; Elizabeth Gurley Flynn; Norman Thomas; and "Mother" Bloor, later an important figure in the American Communist Party. They also regularly saw other old friends of Baldwin's, such as Caroline Colgate.[26]

They had stuck both of their names on the street-level door to their house, which led certain individuals to gawk. For his part Baldwin delighted in referring to "Miss Doty, my wife." Baldwin penned a skit, "Why My Wife Should Not Take My Name," which expressed his opposition to any woman's adopting his surname. After all, "it's all I've got to identify me, and I am not going to give it away to a woman . . . only the Lord knows what she would do with it." Furthermore, he had his "own masculine reputation as a cook to protect."[27]

Although Baldwin was supposedly determined to maintain a working-class lifestyle, he and Doty entertained frequently and for a while employed a maid who cleaned and prepared dinners. As he departed one morning, he left a note for the maid: "Soup No. 5; Entree 18; Meat 7; Dessert 21," all references to entries in a cookbook. He also wrote, "Clean thoroughly and wipe behind all the pictures." When Doty returned home that evening, she discovered that no work had been attended to and found a note that declared, "I see I am not satisfactory, I am leaving."[28]

Once again incongruities abounded even in Baldwin's household. Although he had recently held an IWW card and professed to identify with the working class, he obviously saw nothing ironic in having a maid or in treating her like the servants he had grown up with in Wellesley. Similar difficulties would arise within his marital relationship.

Baldwin and Doty proceeded to divide the domestic chores, as befitting their intention to have a "50–50 Marriage." They each pitched in $60 a month to cover the rent and other expenses. However, the rent alone was $50. A full year into their marriage, a reporter from the *New York Evening Mail* asserted that the home on Waverly Place was "as beautiful as conscientious care can make it." Doty was spending four hours a day away from her writing career to do housework, for which she charged her husband 50 cents an hour. However, because they shared everything equally, she refunded half that amount to him. She considered their arrangement perfectly sensible, for Baldwin had to pay a stenographer to take care of the work in his office. "Every self-supporting wife," Doty asserted, "should be paid for the drudgery she does which breaks into her professional day." As part of their fifty-fifty arrangement, Baldwin attended to the cooking. Together this modern man and woman were striving "to work out a new and wonderful relationship," the *New York Evening Mail* reported.[29]

They generally spent the weekends at Baldwin's camp along the Hackensack River, only thirty minutes from midtown Manhattan. Much to his delight the riverbanks were home to blue heron, woodcock, muskrat, beaver, bass, and deer. He declined to hunt or fish but swam, canoed, watched birds through his field glasses, and instructed local youth in woodcraft. Many daytime parties, with guests ranging from millionaires to communists, were held.[30]

However, Doty's and Baldwin's efforts to devise a new style of marriage soon ran afoul of the best intentions. She wanted her husband at home dur-

ing the evenings, while he continued his seemingly endless round of meetings and other encounters. Most of his friends held little appeal for her, so he
saw them away from their apartment. Compromises proved unavailing, and
she was distressed by his failure to mend his ways. As Baldwin later reflected,
"I was too obstinate to yield my presumed freedom to marriage obligation."
Doty also made decisions on her own; she apparently terminated a preg-
nancy early in their marriage. She increasingly felt frustrated with her own
work, finding it difficult to get published in the manner she once had. Thus
friction continued to build. They loved one another, but the differences
mounted. Although an ardent feminist with supposedly advanced views
regarding sexual freedom, Doty disliked Baldwin's female friends, even
begrudging him the time he spent with Aunt Ruth Baldwin.[31]

Later Baldwin acknowledged, "I wasn't as attentive as I should have been.
I wasn't as thoroughly married as I should have been. I should have made her
Number One and I didn't. It wasn't that there was anyone else who was
Number One. It was just all the things that I was doing that were Number
One and a man should make his wife feel that she is Number One." However,
he also acknowledged with a grin, "I never had occasion to give my wives
cause to charge me with infidelity, but I wasn't always faithful, but they were
incidental affairs." One of the women with whom he maintained "an affectionate relationship" was Dr. Anna Louise Strong, his former fiancée who
had visited him while he was in jail.[32]

Disturbed by her inability to get much writing done, Doty sailed for
France aboard *La Touraine* with her parents in May 1921. Words of appreciation from a New York editorial writer on the ship helped to restore some of
her confidence. In June Baldwin acknowledged that Doty's "insistence on
seclusion and solitude" made sense. He wondered whether sometimes she
actually was even more desperate about their relationship than she appeared
to be. She had put up with a great deal, he acknowledged, as he constantly
interrupted her and was a "thoughtless comrade" in general. But he told her
he had expected her "to get your rights by fighting for them, like all others in
the world—& you've done a noble job & won!" Putting up with him on a
daily basis, he acknowledged, was difficult.[33]

He simply did not choose to live "a la Fanny Hurst." However, he recognized that perhaps she did. "You are the chief sufferer from domestic malad-
justments," he wrote, "& it is you to whom the solitude of a man-free life
would bring peace and calm." As for him, he was "pained most, when I see
you pained." Thus he would prefer that they live apart "rather than continue

that condition indefinitely." Yes, it was true, he was "a bum husband," not like those in the best literature or families, as she desired. "But that's what you dream in a moment of folly!" he exclaimed. He did feel married, "not 'more than I want to,' but just so."[34]

In a letter to Doty that July Baldwin pointed to a disparity between her intellectual beliefs regarding an open marriage and her emotional state. If she had an extramarital affair, he insisted, that "would *never* upset me." He would not hesitate to have one if it would not trouble her. However, until she could bridge the chasm between her ideas and emotions, he was "taking no chances!" Undoubtedly, Baldwin was being disingenuous. The easiest way to overcome her quandary, he believed, was by "developing such an 'outside' relation yourself!" All this—where honest and generous people were concerned—seemed so petty, he continued. However, on just such an issue, he knew, many a relationship had foundered. For now he saw himself in his typically blunt, sometimes callous, manner—"a settled married man. Lord! how I hate the phrase!"[35]

In October 1921 Doty finally returned home and took a job with the Bray Moving Pictures Corp., which produced educational films. Her assignment was to cut and splice pictures together and compose titles. While the weekly paycheck of $75 eased financial concerns, she continued to chafe at her "haphazard existence." Unlike Baldwin, she loathed uncertain dinner hours, having to catch a train to Oradell on the spur of a moment, and missing engagements with each other or friends. The differences in their personalities were becoming starker still. As she remembered it, Baldwin's "ideal of freedom applied to everything. To me freedom was intellectual and spiritual, a daily routine had nothing to do with it." She considered some basic order in one's everyday affairs to be essential. However, her husband had led, as she saw it, "a carefree, irresponsible life for 35 years" and chafed at any restrictions.[36]

Greater and greater strains developed. One apparent source of discontent was her continued dissatisfaction with her own work and Baldwin's growing stature. As a public figure, still larger demands were placed on his time. All the while her views regarding matrimony began to change. She came to appreciate the worth in running a home and creating a nurturing environment. Baldwin likened what they were attempting to do to walking "a tightrope over Niagara." While he remained generally upbeat, he became distressed or concerned "because I don't like to see you *want* so much from Life, knowing that for me anyhow the road to happiness is the way of No-Desire."

In the spring of 1922 Doty again sailed for Europe with her parents and returned in mid-September.[37]

On July 17, 1922, Baldwin informed his old friend Mary Buckley that he was living very comfortably at the Greenwich Village apartment, alongside "occasional other deserted men." His temperament, Baldwin wrote, enabled him to "survive this depression of radical spirits which has submerged most of my friends in the movement. What I am after in the world is too far beyond a communist revolution to worry about accomplishing now. . . . I am a more thorough anarchist the longer I live,—for which I shall be justly hung on the day of the Revolution!"[38]

Because she had experienced the hyperinflation that was wrenching German society and the horrific damage wrought by World War I, Doty's political perspective was changing, whereas Baldwin remained drawn to the Left. By now, as she later acknowledged, "I no longer thought the world was evolving and gradually growing better; that material advancement was improving mankind." She was particularly disturbed by the willingness of some of Baldwin's radical associates "to use any means to get their end." They were exploiting her husband, she thought; he was continually invited to join and frequent one organization after another. In her estimation, "if the object of the organization was worthwhile, he didn't question the personnel." But for her "no object however worthy can be achieved without people of integrity."[39]

One meeting Doty attended proved cathartic for her. She listened as striking workers, in her estimation, appealed only to self-interest. "Socialism and economic change now seemed to me useless if the people who came to the top were as greedy and ruthless as their predecessors." She believed that people, not laws, needed to change, and she was drawn back to religion. Soon she was regularly joining her father for services at First Presbyterian Church, where the liberal Protestant minister Harry Emerson Fosdick was associate pastor; Doty's turn toward religion greatly displeased Baldwin. Doty was also influenced by Malini (Emmeline) Pethick-Lawrence, who was married to Frederick Lawrence, the British politician who, like his wife, was a leader of the British women's suffrage movement. Malini Pethick-Lawrence was attracted to the teachings of Rudolf Steiner, founder of the movement called anthroposophy, and began studying this branch of theosophy. In the winter of 1923 she heard Émile Coué discuss thought control during his visit to the United States.[40]

Lucy Baldwin, undoubtedly reflecting on her own marital state, felt compelled to write to her son regarding his deteriorating marriage. She reported that a recent letter from Madeleine had implied that she "couldn't possibly stand in the way of Baldwin's happiness." Even though it would not be easy to give Baldwin up, for "she loved him and always will," Doty told her mother-in-law that she believed that their circumstances had dramatically changed along with "his emotional being." His mother then wrote, "Baldwin dear—if you are to be a member of a *home*, do you realize you will have to make a great change in your way of living? The *Home* should have some claim on a man's time, after his day's work is done." Baldwin and Doty had grown apart, his mother acknowledged, and had acquired "different interests and ways of thinking." In that sense she was surprised only that they had remained together as long as they had.[41]

In the spring of 1924 Doty attended the convention of the Women's International League for Peace and Freedom (WILPF) in Geneva. One newspaper report characterized her as "probably the most active woman in the whole Convention, the best press representative of any large meeting coming here this season." Shortly after the conference ended, her father, who had been despondent and increasingly drug dependent since his wife's recent death, announced that he was heading to London with a young lover. His daughter felt compelled to go along. Consequently, she resigned from Bray Production Corp. and spent a difficult week with Baldwin at his camp before doing so. Freddy Farnum had just committed suicide. As Doty saw it, Farnum "had not been able to live up to Baldwin's ideals and he had no God to sustain him." Later that year her father left his lady friend behind in Paris and sailed home with Madeleine.[42]

Unfortunately, her father remained a source of great anxiety and required constant attention. Her brother Douglas had gotten a divorce and decamped for Hollywood to write screenplays. The studio apartment at Waverly Place, which Baldwin had maintained—he intended to sublet it until Doty returned—increasingly fell into disrepair. Doty was unable to sleep and feared that she might suffer a breakdown. As Doty later acknowledged, she worried most of all that "my views had changed and were often not in accord with Baldwin's."[43]

She now was secretary of the WILPF's New York chapter, at half the salary Bray Studio had paid her. Soon she offered to give up her position with the WILPF, which had afforded her a limited but steady source of income, so that she might attend to their housekeeping and take care of both Baldwin and her father. Neither man proved amenable to the proposition, however, and Baldwin again suggested that they acquire separate domiciles. That, she knew, would resolve nothing. "It would be one more place to visit. I would wait and wait and Baldwin would not return, and after I left he would come. It was better to make a clean break temporarily," she later wrote. On July 9, 1925, he wrote her a letter in which he declared that their marriage was, in effect, over. He referred to "our present unhappy state," indicating that if they were of like mind, compromise might be possible. Such was not the case, it was clear to him. Only strain and unhappiness beckoned if they attempted to live together. For both their sakes, he was "unwilling to be party any longer to the kind of strain we have both suffered under the last year particularly."[44]

Then he bluntly stated, "You are unhappy with me most of the time, and I am unhappy with your unhappiness." Her state of mind, he recognized, probably resulted from his inability "to meet what you have a right to expect of a husband and a comrade for life." In spite of it all, "there is however no question of my love nor yours. I have tested mine a hundred times. I am tied to you by profounder ties than to any other human being." And still, he acknowledged, they might not be "very profound." It was true that

> next to my freedom in my work you come,—but you come only as the largest single human tie, not as the chief nourishment of my energies. That comes from many sides. I am a crowd man. I need a variety of contacts to keep going in work and friendships. Without them I feel restless and unfulfilled. I know it is a shortcoming that I cannot also concentrate on a great personal love as do many other men who also are equally social. It is a beautiful expression of a fuller life but it is not mine.[45]

Cutting and blunt, Baldwin's acknowledgment offered an astonishingly lucid self-analysis. He was clearly determined to place his career and the social relationships derived from it above even familial ties. His declaration amounted to an admission that, in his closest relationships, he was ready to put his own needs ahead of anyone else's. Yes, he was socially committed, but he remained as determined as ever to carve out the good life for himself. Certain friends and family friends would consider him as egomaniacal as ever.

To Lucille Milner, Doty was simply pathetic: "She was so madly in love with him and he was so cold." Unable to take it any longer, Doty soon chose to return to Geneva. Milner viewed the couple as possessing sharply contrasting personalities, whose differences were mirrored in their physical makeup. She "was a dainty sort of person. I remember her with white hair and blue eyes—a very gentle face while Baldwin was sharp, staccato, forceful."[46]

While Doty was attending a WILPF national board meeting, she discovered that the post of international secretary of the organization was vacant. Her offer to serve in that capacity was immediately accepted. For Doty "it was as though God had offered me a solution. He was again tapping me on the shoulder." Although leaving Baldwin was not easy, neither she nor he thought that the break would be permanent. After some time apart, she hoped, "Baldwin would be willing to give up some personal freedom for the sake of a home." He, on the other hand, hoped that Doty would "learn to take things more easily and not get upset." On October 10, 1925, Doty and her father sailed for Europe.[47]

A little more than a year later Baldwin let the lease lapse on the Greenwich Village apartment. He was bound for Europe to join his wife for a spell. During this period overseas they were together a great deal, skiing, hiking, and visiting friends and colleagues. They spent a week together in Paris before traveling to Geneva, where she lived with her father at the Maison Internationale. In London they stayed at Lincoln's Inn with her friends, Malini and Frederick Pethick-Lawrence; he was now a member of Parliament, having defeated Winston Churchill in the 1923 elections. When Baldwin returned to the United States, this latest separation "almost broke my heart," Doty said. Their time together convinced her that they possessed "something that cannot be taken away." She expressed joy over their last evening together. "I loved lying against you last night like a tired overwrought child," she wrote. "It was good to surrender to you and feel your strength."[48]

However, their relationship, as friends recognized and they themselves soon realized, had changed little. Writing to Baldwin from London, Malini Pethick-Lawrence spoke of Doty's growth and "her great richness." Given the changes her friend was experiencing, Pethick-Lawrence considered it advisable for the separation to continue. What Doty required was "certainty & peace in her emotional life—*even if* it be the peace *& certainty of the desert*." The adjustments Baldwin sought were simply too demanding. Doty should not be compelled, Pethick-Lawrence continued, to submerge "her emotional self to your vision, or to your intelligence." When her emotions were more under control, a reconciliation would be possible. The break had to come from Baldwin, Pethick-Lawrence insisted: "Tell her plainly that you want your freedom."[49]

That is precisely what Baldwin desired and insisted on. In many ways he was duplicating the pattern established by his father, who had considered his personal needs over those of his wife and six children. Baldwin had "children" of his own—albeit of the adopted and often temporary nature—who had to contend with the sometimes flighty or tempestuous quality of his temperament. To an even greater degree so did his wife, whose attraction seemed to dim as she aged and her luster dulled, even as his star rose. Names and recognition meant a great deal to him, as they had since his earliest days growing up just outside Boston.

Another formative influence established during his youth involved his fascination with rebels of various types. His self-image demanded distinctiveness, which to some extent explains the allure of both the Wobblies and anarchists. His adoption of their programs, even if short-lived, promised to set him apart from other well-intentioned Brahmins, who accepted reformist and progressive programs. Yet his dealings with prison officials, guards, and workers, and with laborers and servants, demonstrated a class-conscious haughtiness hardly in keeping with revolutionary pronouncements.

CHAPTER TEN

The American Civil Liberties Union

While Baldwin was imprisoned, the plight of political dissidents and the American Left in general worsened. A proliferation of walkouts on the labor front, a series of terrorist bombings, and the emergence of not one but two American communist parties sustained the antiradical hysteria that had evolved during the period of direct U.S. involvement in World War I. By 1919 the steel and coal industries were saddled with major strikes, policemen had abandoned their posts in Boston, and a general strike had unfolded in Seattle. The still-feared IWW loomed large in the labor unrest on the west coast. A substantial minority broke away from the Socialist Party to form the Communist Party of America, which was dominated by foreign federations, and the U.S.-based Communist Labor Party, the adherents of which were certain that a Bolshevik America lay just ahead. Thirty-four bombs were uncovered in the post office in New York City; they were addressed to John D. Rockefeller, J. Pierpont Morgan, Supreme Court Justice Oliver Wendell Holmes Jr., and cabinet officials A. Mitchell Palmer and Albert Burleson.

On January 25, 1919, both the *New York Tribune* and the *New York Times* cited an ongoing investigation by Military Intelligence of "a 'Who's Who' of . . . pacifist and radical intellectuals." The investigation was headed by Baldwin's old nemesis, Archibald E. Stevenson, now chief of the propaganda division of Military Intelligence. Its findings were reported by the Senate's Overman Committee, which was examining German propaganda. The newspaper articles quoted from an exchange between Stevenson and Senator William Henry King, the Utah Democrat who asked, "Can there be any question but what the activities of these organizations contributed to the cause of Germany and were harmful to the United States and the morale of the American people?" Stevenson answered his own question by offering a list of sixty-two names, including Norman Thomas, John Haynes Holmes, Eugene V. Debs, Oswald Garrison Villard, Scott Nearing, and Roger Baldwin.[1]

On June 6, 1919, a report filed by the New York bureau of the *St. Louis Post-Dispatch* discussed the "Who's Who in Leadership of Organized Bolshevik Movement in the U.S." The story referred to the NCLB as "one of the most active propaganda bureaus in the entire country today," owing to the influential nature of its members. While the newspaper account acknowledged that the NCLB had not officially championed bolshevism, it deemed the NCLB forces "extremely active in defending every anti-military and Radical advocate" who ran afoul of the law. It called Baldwin "a brilliant Radical" who had been jailed for "evading the conscription act."[2]

During this same period Military Intelligence continued to view Baldwin with suspicion. A report issued in September 1919 noted his attendance at a gathering of the pacifist Fellowship of Reconciliation in Highland, New York, purportedly held to concoct plans "to cooperate with the ultra radicals of this country." Among those who appeared at the conference were Elizabeth Gurley Flynn; James Weldon Johnson, the great black writer and artist; and Jane Addams. Most participants at the Highland meeting, the report said, were individuals of some financial means who provided funds "to assist in furthering the movement for a revolution in America, and at the same time [were] buying themselves protection should the revolution materialize."[3]

With tensions already high from the summer's race riots, especially in Chicago and Omaha, Congress authorized the funding of antiradical investigations, which Attorney General Palmer encouraged through the operations of William J. Flynn, head of the Bureau of Investigation. Flynn ordered a young government attorney, J. Edgar Hoover, to establish the bureau's General Intelligence Division. Within a short while Hoover had index cards on 200,000 individuals. In November the Bureau of Investigation kicked off the so-called Palmer Raids, which initially focused on the Union of Russian Workers, comprised of immigrant radicals. The New York Senate's Lusk Committee, relying heavily on papers taken from the NCLB, carried out raids of its own. In late December the Justice Department booted 249 aliens, including anarchist leaders Emma Goldman and Alexander Berkman, out of the United States. More systematic raids began on the evening of January 2, 1920, resulting in massive violations of civil liberties. On January 7 the New

York Legislature voted to deny five Socialist state assemblymen the right to hold office, thereby duplicating a congressional move to prevent Socialist Victor Berger of Milwaukee from serving as a member of the House of Representatives.[4]

The NCLB's executive committee awaited the return of Baldwin, who believed that "the world of slow reform as the answer was pretty well shattered by World War I and the Russian Revolution." Hundreds of individuals, including many conscientious objectors, remained behind bars. However, Baldwin was concerned that his own prison record and extolling of pacifism might be used against the organization. Thus, while he engaged in his labor pursuits, NCLB leaders polled the membership regarding the advisability of Baldwin's return as director. According to Baldwin, no one voted against him.[5]

Determined to have a greater effect and undoubtedly influenced by the postwar Red Scare that arose on the heels of the bombings, Baldwin hesitated to accept the position until members agreed that the organization would both assist war protesters and serve "the cause of freedom of expression in the industrial struggle." He insisted that he would spend only half his time on the operations of the civil liberties organization; he wanted to devote time to other enterprises. Baldwin foresaw that the NCLB would greatly expand the scope of its operations by sending organizers and speakers into the sharpest industrial conflicts. Civil rights, he insisted, would be secured "by exercising them."[6]

Baldwin also determined that the organization should be renamed the American Civil Liberties Union, which came into existence on January 20, 1920. Its office, along with those of the *Liberator*, edited by Max Eastman, and the *Dial*, where the writers Van Wyck Brooks, Kenneth Burke, and Lewis Mumford worked, was located in an old three-story red-brick house on West 13th Street. The ACLU occupied the ground floor. Its "Statement of Purpose" proclaimed that "all thought on matters of public concern should be freely expressed, without interference. Orderly social progress is promoted by unrestricted freedom of opinion." To support First Amendment rights, the ACLU dedicated itself to "an aggressive policy of insistence."[7]

Unquestionably, Baldwin sought to determine the program of the civil liberties group. During his prison stay he had been highly critical of Albert DeSilver's leadership of the NCLB and believed that his major accomplishment had been cosponsorship of an Anglo-American civil liberties conference. In fact, DeSilver had striven diligently to gain repeal of the Espionage

Act and to obtain amnesty for those imprisoned because of opposition to the war or conscription.[8]

As Baldwin saw it, the ACLU's evolution from the NCLB provided the first means to highlight the full range of issues involving civil liberties in the United States; indeed, no other organization had done so on a national basis. Ad hoc groups had existed earlier, with the abolitionists, women's suffrage campaign, and the labor movement at various points championing freedom of speech and of the press. But until now only Theodore H. Schroeder's Free Speech League, formed in 1902, had been specifically set up to defend freedom of expression. Because he viewed Schroeder as something of an egocentric and a crank, and perhaps a competitor as well, Baldwin never considered asking him to join in the ACLU's fight to defend civil liberties. He was unable to associate with the Free Speech League, Baldwin later said, due to Schroeder's eccentricities and prejudices.[9]

Baldwin's attitudes concerning DeSilver's temporary directorship of the NCLB and Schroeder's earlier civil liberties involvement were of a piece. For one thing, he never trusted anyone else's leadership of the civil liberties movement. For another, he was unwilling to bring into the movement anyone who might vie with him for control. Clearly, Baldwin possessed a dogged determination to spearhead the organizations and movement he, more than any single individual, had established and strove to nurture.

Nevertheless, the original national committee of the ACLU was hardly lacking other strong-willed individuals. It was noticeably less drawn from pacifist ranks than the NCLB had been because Baldwin had deliberately sought out labor leaders and pro-war liberals, in addition to those who had been associated with the earlier group. The ACLU leaders were overwhelmingly members of the American upper crust or, at the very least, the good middle class. The ACLU's national committee included Jane Addams; Charles F. Amidon and George W. Anderson, both of whom had resigned from the federal bench; Felix Frankfurter of the Harvard Law School; and William Z. Foster from the American Federation of Labor (AFL). Among the other board members were Scott Nearing, Norman Thomas, Crystal Eastman Fuller, Oswald Garrison Villard, Robert Morss Lovett of the University of Chicago, and Elizabeth Gurley Flynn. New to the organization was its chairman, Dr. Harry F. Ward of the Union Theological Seminary in New York, who had backed the war effort but supported the rights of labor and the maintenance of civil liberties. Imbued with Marxist sentiments, Ward viewed the Soviet Union favorably as a workers' state. Director Baldwin also served as vice chairman of the board, while other national vice chairmen included U.S. Representative Jeannette Rankin, the Montanan who had opposed U.S. participation in World War I; Dr. Frank Graham, president of the University of North Carolina; Duncan McDonald of the Illinois Mine Workers; Mary Wooley, president emeritus of Mt. Holyoke College and a respectable conservative Republican; Bishop Edward L. Parsons, a socialist assailed as the "red bishop"; and Fremont Older, a staunch liberal from San Francisco.[10]

Key to the organization were its secretary, treasurer, and counsel. Lucille B. Milner, Baldwin's friend and sometime lover from his St. Louis days, efficiently performed her duties as secretary. Helen Phelps Stokes served as the ACLU's first treasurer, signing checks and maintaining an account of expenditures and contributions. Expenses often hardly amounted to much, thanks to Baldwin's legendary economical ways. As a good New Englander, he was reputed to be more than thrifty. At the very least, the organization suffered no deficits.[11]

Baldwin cooperated most closely with ACLU attorneys Albert DeSilver and Walter Nelles, who had worked with the NCLB. Operating out of the home office, their dealings with Baldwin remained intimate. The three men, Milner later related, "loved each other. They were very close friends." But, most important, as Baldwin later reported, "We made a team which was never after equaled in the Civil Liberties Union. DeSilver contributed the quick unerring judgment, with a gay and easy approach to tough problems; Nelles, the reflective opinions of a studious lawyer sometimes aroused by hot indignations; and I, the techniques of a social case worker, an organizer and a publicity man for such limited publicity as was open to us."

Baldwin initially relied on the counsel of DeSilver and Nelles; in late 1924 DeSilver suffered a fatal fall from a railroad car. Another key ACLU figure was Baldwin's old friend Wolcott H. Pitkin, who had served as attorney general of Puerto Rico and as an adviser to the government of Siam. Pitkin resigned from the organization in 1925, his place as general counsel filled by board member Arthur Garfield Hays, who was noted for his defense of the underdog.[12]

Hays was a civil libertarian in the classic sense and remained with the ACLU until his death in 1954. Baldwin deferred to his judgment, except where compromise was needed. Hays was generally unwilling to compromise, whereas Baldwin considered it essential except when core principles were involved. Soon after his appointment as general counsel, Hays suggested that Morris Ernst, who had done considerable work for the ACLU on censorship, be hired as joint counsel. Ernst came to handle cases involving censorship, legislation, and government policy. Hays and Ernst coexisted somewhat uneasily, but each offered something the board occasionally required: "Hays was ever the wise counselor Ernst the smart 'fixer,'" Milner said.[13]

Like its predecessor, the ACLU relied on well-known lawyers nationwide to volunteer their services in cases that grabbed their attention. The selection of attorneys, considered an operational matter, was largely made by Baldwin. He would ask, "Who is the best lawyer? Who would be most persuasive?" Among the lawyers he turned to were Albert Bettman of Cincinnati, a former assistant U.S. attorney general; Frank P. Walsh, the one-time colleague of Baldwin's in St. Louis; Felix Frankfurter; Grenville Clark of New York, a partner of Elihu Root's; and Clarence Darrow of Chicago, probably the most celebrated and controversial litigator of his generation.[14]

Baldwin—who was initially paid $2,400 a year—directed the ACLU's national office from its inception. He continued to do so for the next three decades, with only a two-year hiatus along the way. The work was taxing but exhilarating; Baldwin loaded his briefcase with documents to which he would attend in the evenings and on weekends. He was constantly on the phone—both at the office and in his apartment—planning out-of-town trips, meetings, and conferences. As an administrator his skills were at best mixed, perhaps because he viewed himself in a different light: "I thought in terms of a crusade for civil liberties, and of myself as the responsible guardian of it." Baldwin continually denied that the office was "a one man affair," although he admitted to directing and supervising its operations, maintaining calendars, devising a tickler system to attend to all important matters and writing twenty to fifty letters daily, the kind of correspondence "as deserved the attention of the 'boss.'" Because he disliked many of the everyday chores he was supposed to undertake, he left them for others to handle, like righthand man DeSilver, until his death.[15]

Baldwin's running of the national office proved a mixed blessing for the organization. His own puritanical attitude toward money initially resulted in a refusal to arrange to accept a $100,000 bequest that he thought posed the "real threat of riches." He deliberately sought to restrict the ACLU's membership and the number of affiliates, reasoning that "a small cadre of true believers" would best serve the cause of civil liberties. The ACLU had one thousand members in the first year of its existence, a mere twenty-five hundred at the end of the 1920s.[16]

The executive committee's meetings opened with Baldwin's delivering the "Report on the Civil Liberty Situation for the Week." Spirited debate generally followed, and certain members looked back on the sessions "as the most exciting part of their lives," according to the ACLU historian Sam Walker. Invariably, Baldwin controlled the agenda, declining to bring up an issue if he thought his point of view would not prevail. Committee members, many of whom had been drawn to the ACLU by Baldwin, often deferred to him. As Ben Huebsch, James Joyce's U.S. publisher, acknowledged, "I'm in the civil liberties union for a reason that has made some thousands of people become members, because of Roger Baldwin."[17]

Baldwin considered the members of the board—who also generally joined at his request—a remarkable lot who shared his abiding commitment to civil liberties. He viewed his staff in the same light and sought to recruit individuals who possessed the same passion for the First Amendment and were as financially secure as he. DeSilver actually gave money of his own to the ACLU, whereas Nelles received expenses only. Baldwin's secretary, Lucille Milner, worked without salary for the first several years, until her personal circumstances changed. Other associates in the early years included Louis F. Budenz, who had replaced Baldwin as secretary of the Civic League in St. Louis. Unable to support a family on his meager ACLU salary, Budenz became the editor of *Labor Age* before moving into the leadership ranks of the Communist Party.[18]

The halftime position of public relations man, which required Baldwin's close supervision, continually experienced turnover. Joseph Freeman served in that slot in the early twenties and again later, displaying "a rare integrity" that endeared him to Baldwin. Freeman, who also joined the Communist Party, refused to allow his political beliefs to intrude in his office work. Eugene Lyons, another key figure in the American Old Left, joined the ACLU staff after serving in the labor defense organization headed by Elizabeth Gurley Flynn. In his antiradical tract, *The Red Decade*, Lyons later claimed that a few of "Stalin's henchmen" had sat on the ACLU board along with "a bevy of active fellow-travelers." On the other hand, Lyons declared that Baldwin was "not easily classified."[19]

After Freeman worked in the national office, he portrayed Baldwin as "a thin, sharp-eyed New England puritan of extraordinary energy and efficiency . . . a demon for work." To Freeman, Baldwin was most interested "in political power, rather than in the arts, in nature or in abstract social justice." Freeman viewed Baldwin as possessing "a *'faustian'* nature wearing a *'magian'* mask, a John Adams who imagined himself a Prince Kropotkin." Freeman believed that Baldwin "fancied himself an anarchist of the philosophic kind, devoted to the ideal man in the ideal society, contemptuous of practical politics; a libertarian above the battle, impartially appealing to labor, capital and the government to exercise justice and forbearance toward each other." With that vision in mind, Baldwin used his tireless energy to participate in scores of committees and organizations, toiling from morning into the evening, "playing the very politics he despised, from which he always longed to escape and to which he always returned."[20] Baldwin's involvement with so many organizations led to his being called "the pope of the liberals."

Early during his ACLU directorship, Baldwin acquired a reputation as a keen, driven, stingy, and often ill-tempered employer. He paid staff members meager salaries and continued to treat them oppressively. On one celebrated occasion the ACLU staff almost walked off en masse when Baldwin refused to allow them to take Columbus Day off. Fearing public repercussions, he relented.[21]

An outsider like Phil Taft, then a Wobbly, later referred to Baldwin as "an autocratic man. He would never say to anybody just 'come in.' He'd have them sitting outside his office for a while." Baldwin, Taft asserted, was a tyrant. He was "an executive type," as well as "a shrewd Yankee, a good horse trader." Taft also saw Baldwin running "the ACLU on the basis that reasonable men can come to some kind of agreement." Thus Baldwin would even go to lunch with his old antagonist, Archibald Stevenson, "to get him to do or not to do things—and would talk to him as one member of the club to another." Once again, given the temper of the times, Taft acknowledged, such an approach might have been necessary. It was also in keeping with Baldwin's aristocratic makeup and his "always [being] conscious of his social position."[22]

Anna Friedkin was a friend who worked for Baldwin for a couple of years at the League for Mutual Aid, another agency he headed. (Her husband, Mike, was one of the Wobblies indicted in Chicago.) Friedkin appreciated Baldwin's willingness to fire a fellow employee she despised. "As an administrator," Friedkin remembered, "he was quick and short." And yet she found Baldwin "very warm and easy to work with."[23]

Morris Ernst, referring to Baldwin's directorship, termed him "the dictator" but said that "without him there would not have been an ACLU." Moreover, "he ran it so well that no one minded. He kept it under his thumb so that we have no problems of groups running off the reservation." Although Ernst could not recall Baldwin's ever pounding on the table at a board of directors' meeting, "he ran that organization with an iron hand." Baldwin was "very interested in power," Ernst told Joseph Lash. "He got his pleasure out of the use of power to the point where he didn't need mass applause like J. L. Lewis," the labor leader. Baldwin's name, Ernst noted, never came to overshadow the organization he founded. Happily too, "he was catholic in his tastes, ready to conciliate and compromise, sane." Fortunately, Baldwin had a flair for publicity and found a sympathetic audience in the *New York Herald Tribune*, which proved more favorably disposed to civil liberties issues than the *New York Times*.[24]

Baldwin's modus operandi with the ACLU was considerably different than for its predecessor. Instead of working behind the scenes, corresponding and meeting with government officials to arrive at some kind of compromise, Baldwin was now more involved in publicizing the activities of the new organization and in bringing civil liberties issues to the forefront of public discussion. The possibility of doing so had served as a type of veiled threat when he had communicated with Justice and War department officials during the period of the NCLB's existence. Taking to the hustings, Baldwin now delivered public addresses dealing with civil liberties and traveled widely to observe conditions across the country. His first extended trip, stretching from the east coast to Washington state and California, took place in May and June 1920. It began with a series of speaking engagements by Baldwin and Elizabeth Gurley Flynn; he lectured on "Civil Liberty and Industrial Conflict," while she discussed "Amnesty for the I.W.W." Baldwin was a good friend of both Flynn and her lover, Carlo Tresca, and occasionally shared spaghetti and salad at their Staten Island beach cottage. Baldwin and Flynn began the tour in Rochester and Buffalo on May 13, then went to Ohio, Michigan, Illinois, and Wisconsin, before stopping off in St. Louis, Indianapolis, Cincinnati, and Pittsburgh.[25]

In the August 1920 issue of the *Socialist Review*, published by England's Labour Party, Baldwin discussed his trip and said that freedom of speech and the press appeared to be sorely lacking in the United States. Abridgment of fundamental freedoms, in his estimation, was part of the campaign to cripple organized labor. As he put it, "The lid is on. There is no doubt about that. Everywhere in the United States the hysterical anti-red drive has clamped the lid on free speech and free assemblage. In substance it is an attack on the right of labor to organize, strike, and picket. Organized business is engaged in a colossal anti-labor campaign." Such a campaign was waged through injunctions, statutes that made syndicalism and sedition crimes, and the abuse of the police power.[26]

Freedom of the press and freedom of assemblage, Baldwin argued, prevailed only where workers or farmers were potent enough to safeguard those rights. Significantly, "the fiction that constitutional American rights can be maintained through law has been pretty well exploded. Everywhere the realization is growing that legal rights are hollow shams without the political and economic power to enforce them. The road to industrial freedom is the way to all freedom."[27]

On its face, such a declaration by the director of the ACLU was astonishing. Fundamental American freedoms, he was asserting, could not be upheld in a court of law or a legislative assembly by invoking the Bill of Rights alone. However, when one considers the unwillingness of federal tribunals, including the U.S. Supreme Court, to safeguard the First Amendment, Baldwin's analysis was more clear-sighted. Yet this type of pronouncement was, at the very least, politically unwise.

In the preface to the ACLU's first annual report, issued in September 1921, Baldwin and Albert DeSilver noted that the organization was being criticized from all sides. "The disheartened liberal" urged that the struggle for free speech be postponed until "the reaction" (repression) had passed. The ACLU leaders noted that the revolutionary would insist that the fight for "industrial and political control" of the means of production was paramount. The reactionary would claim that the "so-called free speech fight is just a camouflage to put over the radical movement." Then Baldwin and DeSilver fed notions of the organization's radical bent. Backing repressive moves, they declared, were

> the property interests of the country, so completely in control of our political life as to establish what is in effect a class government,—a government by and for business. Political democracy as conceived by many of America's greatest leaders, does not exist, except in a few communities. This condition is not yet understood by the public at large. They are drugged by propaganda and blinded by a press necessarily subservient to property interests. Dazed by the

kaleidoscopic changes of the last few years, the rank and file citizens accept the dictatorship of property in the name of patriotism.[28]

Only radicals, the most militant workers and farmers, and a small number of liberals, the ACLU report suggested, were "conscious of this condition and capable of outspoken resistance to it." Untrammeled freedom of opinion helped to bring about "orderly progress." Should class warfare mount, that crusade "must have the effect of softening the conflict, both by making easier the way for the new forces and by creating a general distrust of the shams of our political system." Regardless of such possibilities, Baldwin and DeSilver argued, the ACLU provided succor to those "who are prosecuted, or mobbed, or whose rights are restricted inside and outside the law." In the process "the friends of progress to a new social order make common cause." Along the way the ACLU "makes no distinction as to whose liberties it defends; it puts no limit on the principle of free speech." At the same time its national committee, comprised of well-known persons, recognized that civil liberty could not be obtained "as abstract principles or as constitutional guarantees. Economic or political power is necessary to assert and maintain all 'rights.'" Moreover, the freedom of workers to strike without having to face federal troops, protection against unreasonable searches and seizures, the right to a fair trial, academic freedom, immigration policies that did not target radicals, and racial equality were essential too.[29]

Such pronouncements would pique the ire of those who already viewed the ACLU skeptically. The declaration that democracy was virtually nonexistent in the United States was certain to antagonize those ill disposed toward the civil liberties organization. So too would analyses Baldwin drew in the April 1922 issue of the *World Tomorrow*. There he asserted, "Yet we admit that no ideal of social and intellectual freedom can be real for any great number, until we are rid of this competitive struggle for property. We readily accept in theory the ethics of a communist society, 'to each according to his need, from each according to his ability.'" At the same time, he wrote, "It is a long, long road from where we are to that goal."[30]

Baldwin's professed belief—however theoretical—in the communist vision was sure to antagonize further certain government and corporate powers. Thus Baldwin, once again, had perhaps spoken too freely, which could result in the civil liberties movement's being tagged with an unwelcome label. Often politically facile, Baldwin was at other points candid to the point of being foolish.

As Baldwin's own political perspective continued to undergo changes during the ACLU's formative period, the organization—to his infinite credit—adopted an expansive view of civil liberties. It championed the rights of communists, socialists, anarchists, Wobblies, and even "the unspeakable Ku Klux Klan." Baldwin had insisted on such an approach, a move that was both politically astute and morally courageous but engendered disagreement among the ACLU's natural allies.[31]

During the early twenties the bulk of Baldwin's attention was now focused on the ACLU, which served as an organizational touchstone for the badly splintered American Left. At the same time he was engaged in other endeavors that involved him in the affairs of a host of different radical and reform groups. One such enterprise, the American Fund for Public Service, was incorporated on July 5, 1921, by the *New York World*'s Lewis Gannett, the University of Chicago's Robert Morss Lovett, and Baldwin. The fund was made possible by the generosity of Charles Garland, a native of Boston, son of a railroad baron, and an opponent of capitalism who sought to rid himself of a million-dollar inheritance. Hearing of the young man's plight, Baldwin met with Garland at his mother's small farm in North Carver, Massachusetts. Baldwin proposed the establishment of a private foundation to support the kind of "new social order" Garland favored. Baldwin called for the fund to provide seed money for left-wing and pioneering efforts—"nonpartisan and unconventional"—in a way no other foundation would. Attorneys in New York drew up the proper papers, which took effect when Garland reached the age of maturity. "We were taking no chances on time to change his mind," Baldwin recalled. Garland's trustee handed over the gilt-edged securities housed at the First National Bank of New York to a group of individuals involved in various quests to transform the existing social and economic order. In typical fashion Baldwin reached out to the Rockefeller, Russell Sage, and Carnegie foundations to ascertain how they handled grant requests.[32]

The fund's board members spanned the full range of the left side of the American political spectrum. They included Harry F. Ward; Norman Thomas; Scott Nearing; William Z. Foster; Sidney Hillman, a leading labor attorney and top figure in the Socialist Party; Freda Kirchwey, an editor with the *Nation*; Ben Gitlow, a founder of American communism; James Weldon Johnson of the NAACP; Lovett; Gannett; and Flynn. Garland allowed the trustees free rein to spend the money as they saw fit, asking only that it be doled out without strings attached and spent for the "benefit of mankind."

While foremost ACLU figures like Ward, Thomas, Ernst, and Walter Nelles, were prominently positioned on the board, Baldwin strove mightily to avoid any direct conflicts of interest. The Garland Fund did, nevertheless, award grants to legal defense committees and put up bail money in cases in which the ACLU was involved.[33]

As the initial executive secretary of the trust and the man who had urged its establishment, Baldwin felt great responsibility in allocating what he termed "Garland's Million." Fortunately, a spirit of cooperation prevailed during the first years of the fund's existence. Eventually, however, the board was riddled by sectarian differences, its members becoming increasingly partisan in determining how the fund—which doubled at one point—should be spent. This turn of events paralleled the increasingly fratricidal developments afflicting U.S. radical and labor camps during the 1920s. The board appeared to divide into a left wing and a right wing, with a small number of centrists tipping the scales. Another source of contention involved the parsimonious manner with which some, including the fund's secretary, believed that it should be allocated. The pool of money, others feared, provided the board members with considerable leverage over left-wing movements that attracted them, with Baldwin acknowledging, "We could make or break a project."[34]

Both Baldwin and his good friend Norman Thomas believed that "things were stirring; things were changing and going our way." They admired the activism of communists, regardless of their dictatorial makeup, reasoning that "they were active in the right direction" and that "their program despite the dictatorship was aimed at ultimate democracy," Baldwin said. Nevertheless, in a note to Emma Goldman in September 1922, he acknowledged that American comrades made the civil liberties fight difficult. "It is pretty grim business, too, to be fight-now [sic] and then for the rights of free speech for radicals who have swallowed the worst of the evils of the present State, and who would save the workers by substituting their dictatorship for capital's." Even the Wobblies, Baldwin acknowledged the following February, "have become dogmatists, sectarians, heresy-hunters." By November Baldwin was saying, "All the rebels have gone almost flat in their public expression. The communists alone, with their dreams of power, have any enthusiasm." For his part, Baldwin declared, "I plug away for a voice for the rebels, whoever and wherever they are. It is all I can see to do effectively."[35]

On June 22, 1925, Baldwin posed the kind of question he would later revisit: "Whether we want to elect anyone to the Board who is not free to make up his or her own mind independent of outside direction. Workers Party members are presumably subject to Party control even as members of our Board—and we have frankly recognized that in allowing a Party official to sit with us as Foster's proxy." He then expressed concerns regarding Scott Nearing's proposal that two additional party members be added to the board.[36]

Many observers would later contend that Baldwin first became troubled during World War II about communist machinations involving groups with which he was associated. The 1940 ouster of Elizabeth Gurley Flynn, a Communist Party member, from the ACLU's board of directors springs to mind. As evidenced by his involvement with the Garland Fund and other affairs, Baldwin long viewed communist antics with concern.

The Garland Fund's board had early determined not to give money directly to political parties, religious groups, or sectarian forces. Rather, grants were handed out to movements engaged in pioneering efforts on behalf of workers and minorities. Decision making was guided by a basic opposition to capitalism, like Charles Garland's, and a belief that workers could craft "a new political and economic power to replace capitalism," as Baldwin put it. It provided money for labor publications, the radical press, research and investigative work, strike relief, legal assistance, and workers' education. Its board hoped that the Garland Fund, in sustaining movements of a national scope rather than local efforts, would bolster both experimental and more established radical endeavors.[37]

However, the general economic prosperity of the times, the legacy of the Red Scare, and internecine struggles involving the Russian Revolution made the 1920s a less fruitful period for the American Left than it had envisioned. Consequently, the board of the Garland Fund was continually implored to deliver a financial lifejacket to one radical enterprise after another. These included the socialist Rand School, the labor school Commonwealth College, and Brookwood Labor College, founded by A. J. Muste and whose guest lecturers included Reinhold Niebuhr, Norman Thomas, Bill Haywood, William Z. Foster, and Roger Baldwin. The fund gave considerable sums to the Furriers Joint Board and the International Ladies' Garment Workers' Union. It also awarded grants to the Federated Press—the left-wing press syndicate established in 1919—the NAACP, the League for Industrial Democracy, and the American Birth Control League. It assisted a wide range of communist-dominated enterprises, such as the International Labor Defense, the *Daily Worker*, the *New Masses*, and the Russian reconstruction farms in the Caucasus.[38]

Eventually, however, a sense of futility set in, resulting in a decision to accept only applications personally sponsored by a board member. While that ensured greater scrutiny of proposals, it also converted board members into advocates and heightened political partisanship. Indeed, the board itself soon delivered proposals and tendered funds that had not even been requested. It allocated its largest appropriation, $250,000, to workers' education but generally to little avail because of sectarianism. Another $150,000 went to establish the Vanguard Press, which published radical works in inexpensive editions and produced a number of books on the Soviet Union. Unfortunately, the press lost a great amount of money before being sold. The Garland Fund also published a number of works on American imperialism, edited by a committee of scholars headed by the historian Harry Elmer Barnes, a critic of U.S. entrance into World War I. These works were handed out free of charge to public and university libraries.[39]

Many quarters, including the increasingly conservative American Federation of Labor, viewed the Garland Fund with disdain and believed its board was comprised of "disreputable reds." Charges that the trust was subversive flowed from AF of L headquarters after the fund dismissed as too conservative a 1923 request by an AF of L affiliate, the Workers Education Bureau. Of little help was Baldwin's explanation for the board's decision. The fund would "favor those organizations and institutions which instilled into the workers the knowledge and the qualities which will fit them for carrying on the struggle for the emancipation of their class in every sphere." Thus it would support only "those definitely committed to a radical program," Baldwin said.[40]

Like the AF of L, self-proclaimed professional patriots "always tied us to the Bolshevik kite, regarding the Fund as no better than outright Moscow gold," Baldwin later recalled. Even the composition of the board, derived from all quadrants of the American Left, was considered "proof of an interlocking directorate of all the radical agencies united on overthrowing the government," he said. One projected vehicle for an alliance of left-of-center forces was the New Masses, a journal that received backing from the Garland Fund, thanks in no small part to Scott Nearing and Baldwin.[41]

Baldwin nevertheless believed that the fund was administered in a manner above reproach. He questioned whether board members should "become officially involved with enterprises substantially aided by the Fund" and whether they should remain on the board if that occurred. No board members received a stipend of any kind, as he had insisted; a public stenographer carried out necessary clerical work; and an accounting firm kept the books. Legal counsel was usually donated. Thus in the nineteen years of its operation overhead amounted to a mere $50,000, 2.5 percent of all moneys involved.[42]

Both Baldwin and Nearing, Ernst later recalled, were "hairshirt people— a little ashamed of money—they never gave anyone enough to do a job." Rather, "they starved them," including Muste's Brookwood College and the Vanguard Press. Baldwin seemed to believe that "money was corruption," Ernst said.[43]

Charles Garland had another trust, the Personal Service Fund, that produced about $10,000 annually, which he turned over to Baldwin and a group of trustees to hand out to individuals engaged in "creative social work" for progressive causes. For a time Anna Davis, a wealthy Quaker from Brookline, Massachusetts, managed the fund, along with Muste, Nearing, and Baldwin.[44]

Baldwin's directorship of both the ACLU and the Garland Fund established a pattern that would soon become familiar. He was now heading the latest version of the civil liberties organization first established during the war and one that proved much longer lasting than its predecessors. His stewardship of the ACLU was sometimes rocky, due to missteps undertaken or misstatements delivered along the way, often by Baldwin himself. Yet it was steadfast and exemplified his determined belief that the civil liberties movement was of paramount importance. It was also characterized, and thankfully so, by the fervent support of the expansive reading of the First Amendment to which Baldwin subscribed.

His association with the Garland Fund, and the resulting necessity to deal with groups all along the left side of the political spectrum, was one of his first efforts at presenting the Left as a united front. From this point on, Baldwin, as much as any other figure on the American Left, became involved with a series of such campaigns, which sought to join reformers and radicals of disparate sorts. Yet even at this stage such alliances, as Baldwin well recognized, were often tenuous affairs, particularly because of communist forces that often behaved less like brethren than as diehard opponents of his "no enemies on the left" approach.

CHAPTER ELEVEN

The ACLU Under Suspicion

The ACLU's parentage and Roger Baldwin's directorship ensured that controversy would soon envelop the organization. Military Intelligence referred to Baldwin as a member of the League for the Amnesty of Political Prisoners, which it termed "a revolutionary, radical organization"; a report from an intelligence officer called him a Wobbly and a dangerous individual. In 1920, its first year of existence, the Lusk Committee of the New York Senate published *Revolutionary Radicalism*, a four-volume report that lumped together liberals, pacifists, and civil libertarians as pathfinders for the international communist movement. Volume 1 pointed to Baldwin's efforts during World War I on behalf of the American Union Against Militarism, where "the old German-Socialist-Internationalist pacifism" was supposedly converted to "international revolutionary Socialism." Baldwin's subsequent heading of the Civil Liberties Bureau, the Lusk Committee argued, resulted in "entirely new machinery for hampering the military strength of the country, during the war and afterward."[1]

A lengthy section in the Lusk Committee report contained other cutting analyses of Baldwin. It included a reference to the letter he had written to Louis Lochner urging the People's Council Convention to rely on patriotic symbols and themes. The committee charged, "The advice to have plenty of flags and to seem patriotic in everything was particularly characteristic of Baldwin, to the naked eye a charming, well-bred liberal, of good American stock and traditions, in reality a radical to the very bone, with a strong leaning toward the I.W.W." Now Baldwin's new organization, the ACLU, was termed "as active as ever working up sympathy for revolutionaries, influencing public opinion, and generally spreading subversive propaganda."[2]

Volume 2 of the Lusk report referred to Baldwin's testimony before the committee that "the advocacy of murder, unaccompanied by any act, is within the legitimate scope of free speech." ACLU national committee members opposed the doctrine of constructive intent; they believed in the right of individuals to advocate the overthrow of the government by force and violence. Such a position, the Lusk report alleged, did not involve protected political rights but rather "license" that went beyond the Constitution. The ACLU operations, the report continued, served "to create in the minds of the ill-informed people the impression that it is un-American to interfere with the activities of those who seek to destroy American institutions." The ACLU, the Lusk report concluded, "is a supporter of all subversive movements and its propaganda is detrimental to the interests of the state. It attempts not only to protect crime but to encourage attacks upon our institutions in every form."[3]

J. Edgar Hoover, as head of the Department of Justice's General Intelligence Division of the Bureau of Investigation, produced a series of publications that dismissed civil libertarians and liberals as pro-Bolshevik sympathizers, perhaps even communists. He termed them "parlor pinks," while his *General Intelligence Bulletin* blasted "leading radicals," including the likes of Morris Hillquit of the Socialist Party and the liberal cleric John A. Ryan, along with the ACLU's John Haynes Holmes and Roger Baldwin.[4]

The initial Bureau of Investigation report on the ACLU, dated March 1, 1920, was specifically prepared for Hoover. The memorandum was drafted by George F. Ruch, a close friend of Hoover's who offered background information for the latter's attacks on communism. Ruch's paper—a condensation of a lengthier one by secret agent 836—argued that the new organization was launching a nationwide campaign to condemn the Palmer Raids and champion freedom of speech and of the press. For Ruch the phrase "free speech" was used to enable "anyone, no matter whether anarchists, IWWs, Communists, or whatever else . . . to speak and write all they wished against this government or any other government!" Ruch exhorted Hoover to order agent 836 to watch "nothing else."[5]

Within a short while Hoover's agents had amassed an extensive file on the ACLU. They gathered information about board and executive committee meetings, as well as the organization's financial state. One agent was assigned the task of attending all of Roger Baldwin's public addresses, which he duly recorded. As the Hoover biographer Curt Gentry notes, because the minutes of ACLU meetings were not published, Hoover's men could have obtained such information only from a bugging device, a well-placed informer, or by burglarizing the national office. Burglary was how the government acquired the ACLU's mailing list; someone mailed copies to local Bureau of Investigation offices, which considered them reliable lists of American radicals.[6]

A message was transmitted to Hoover on June 2, 1921, that purported to relay the contents of an address by Baldwin; the sender urged that "a very prompt decision" be made regarding the ACLU. Such a decision was forthcoming. Attorney General Harry M. Daugherty determined that the organization had, to date, carried out "no act which could be construed as being in violation of any federal statutes now in existence and for that reason action by the government is precluded at the present time." Nevertheless, the investigation of the ACLU—which one agent referred to as a collection of "Pinks and Reds" and "all the tints between"—continued. The ACLU was now proclaimed "big brother to them all, from the bomb-throwing Anarchist to the wrist slapping pacifist, and the preferred occupation, slacker," according to the historian Theodore Draper.[7]

Federal officials could hardly have been pleased by Baldwin's role, during the fall of 1922, in the formation of the Labor Defense Council. The LDC was designed to "unite all radical, liberal and conservative organizations . . . to raise bail money, to hold defense meetings and to carry on agitation" on behalf of members of the Workers Party of America (Communist) rousted by federal officials in Bridgman, Michigan, on August 22. Baldwin was a member of the LDC's "provisional National Committee," along with Eugene Debs; Elizabeth Gurley Flynn; Dennis M. Blatt of the Proletarian Party; Robert M. Buck, editor of the *New Majority*; William Z. Foster, now of the Trade Union Educational League; and William F. Dunne, Charles E. Ruthenberg, and Moritz J. Loeb of the Workers Party of America.[8]

On November 21, 1922, Hoover asked Ruch for a memorandum on "the antecedents of Roger Baldwin." The report said that Baldwin was directly descended from Miles Standish, mistakenly declared that he had graduated from the Harvard Law School, and stated that he had "specialized in defending radicals." Because of his education and professional experience, the memo continued, Baldwin would "approach his work in an entirely different manner than the average red worker."[9]

In September Daugherty had received a letter from an officer of the International Reform Bureau, yet another right-wing organization, urging close scrutiny of the Garland Fund because of the prominent roles played on its board of directors by Baldwin and William Z. Foster. "It would be a national misfortune," the author asserted, if the fund "should be used for a radical propaganda."[10]

In 1923 the Bureau of Investigation expressed alarm that Baldwin was to give a speech on radio station WJZ in New York City. The anarchist Carlo Tresca, a report revealed, had urged Baldwin to respond to charges by William J. Burns, director of the Bureau of Investigation, that Baldwin was a "paid agent" of the Communist Third International and Moscow; Burns, who had founded the detective agency that bore his name, similarly viewed the ACLU as a danger to national security. Burns was a "son of a bitch," Baldwin had retorted. It did not bother him to be called an anarchist, "but to be confused with that Moscow crowd was too much." Thus he planned to deliver a radio talk to counter Burns's accusation "the way he deserved."[11]

Burns asked Lawrence Richay of the U.S. Department of Commerce to investigate the proposed radio transmission by Baldwin, to whom Burns referred as "a notorious radical and agitator." Burns expressed concern that Baldwin would attack government agents who were curbing "the activities of ultra-radicals." Burns then ordered one of his G-men to inform the head of the Radio Corporation of America of Baldwin's activities and those of the ACLU. The agent was to urge "as strongly as possible" that Baldwin "or any of the radicals" not be permitted to air "their rotten propaganda." A member of the RCA board of directors had told the Bureau of Investigation, a follow-up report said, that no individual "with extreme radical tendencies" would deliver a speech on its airwaves. The RCA director also promised to let the Bureau of Investigation know whether the ACLU corresponded with his company.[12]

In February 1924 Burns received a letter requesting all derogatory information about Baldwin and the ACLU. The correspondent, whose identity was blacked out by the FBI after the ACLU demanded its FBI files in the 1970s, expressed his belief that Baldwin was "an arch-slacker." Burns suggested that an examination by the New York Joint Legislative Committee on seditious activities might be in order. The writer also expressed a readiness to discuss Baldwin and the ACLU in person.[13]

On the morning of March 28 Baldwin was apprised of materials that the ACLU had collected on Burns, as well as purportedly illegal operations by the Department of Justice, private detective agencies, and so-called patriotic groups. An ACLU contact, to Baldwin's delight, expressed a determination to get "Burns' scalp" and publicize the activities in question. Baldwin frequently corresponded with W. Jett Lauck about the Bureau of Investigation, declaring that the continued existence of the William J. Burns Detective Agency suggested graft on the part of its namesake. In the same vein Baldwin recognized that Burns had received generous funding from Congress to battle the "red menace" but had produced meager results. Only a small number of political cases involving the exercise of free speech by radicals had resulted but no capture of bomb-throwers, Baldwin told Lauck. The development of an elaborate spy system within the Bureau of Investigation helped to produce massive industrial espionage. This "un-American institution," Baldwin insisted, had been forced on this nation because no one had challenged its "wholesale illegal activities." The Bureau of Investigation had repeatedly delivered information to patriotic organizations that cast radicals and labor unions in an unfavorable light while denying others access to its files. Additionally, secret lists of purported radicals were handed over to the patriotic groups to use as they saw fit.[14]

Throughout the year Baldwin led the ACLU in calling into question the practices of the Bureau of Investigation. The government agency resorted to "lawless propaganda," the ACLU charged, to lambaste labor and radical organizations. Deeply troubled about the machinations of the Bureau of Investigation and other violations of civil liberties, Baldwin applauded Montana senator Burton Wheeler's resolution condemning industrial espionage. Baldwin argued that the proposed measure was designed to call attention to "reactionary" groups that had fostered red scares, attacks on labor unions, and legal action to curb free speech. The Bureau of Investigation, Baldwin charged, encouraged such practices and, indeed, the entire "spy system" that American industry had concocted. Both William J. Burns's agency and private detective forces had to be prevented from drafting "secret lists of persons 'suspect,'" or such lists needed to be made public.[15]

Having received no sympathetic hearing from the Harding administration, Baldwin was delighted that access to high government officials was once again open to him, now that Calvin Coolidge was president. The departments of Labor and the Post Office were somewhat receptive, but the greatest change occurred at the Department of Justice. During the spring of 1924 Coolidge appointed Harlan F. Stone, dean of the Columbia University Law School, as the new U.S. Attorney General, replacing Harry M. Daugherty who had resigned because of the Teapot Dome scandal. Baldwin sent

Stone, whom he had met during the war, a congratulatory note declaring that all Americans concerned about civil liberties were delighted by his appointment. The ACLU's relationship with the attorney general's office, Baldwin remarked, heretofore had been distressing. All too often "propaganda, not law, has dictated its activities in relation to civil liberties." But now hope abounded for a return of the department "to its old and honorable tradition."[16]

The ACLU attempted to urge the U.S. Senate Committee on Appropriations to reduce funding for the Bureau of Investigation. Baldwin told the committee that the bureau had won large budgetary increases from Congress by hunting down pacifists during the war and radicals ever since. The Department of Justice had played the Red Menace theme and demanded passage of a peacetime sedition law to criminalize expressions by radicals. Many of the Bureau of Investigation's activities lacked statutory authority, including the dissemination of propaganda to patriotic groups and the tendering of evidence for prosecutions involving state crimes of syndicalism or sedition. The bureau had also provided assistance to private detective agencies involved in industrial espionage and had carried out illegal searches and seizures. Such practices, Baldwin insisted, were uncalled for, unsound, and in violation of civil liberties.[17]

ACLU members, he argued somewhat disingenuously, were "concerned solely with the issue of civil rights." They possessed "no radical program to promote or defend" but recognized that the Bureau of Investigation often considered efforts to maintain civil liberties part of "the radical program." Such a notion was absurd, as those who supported free speech championed it for all, regardless of political viewpoint.[18]

Although Baldwin, to his credit, had promoted such a civil liberties perspective, the statement that his colleagues had no other agenda was simply untrue. From the outset Baldwin had acknowledged that the ACLU would stand beside organized labor as industrial conflict continued. Unquestionably, Baldwin and many ACLU leaders viewed the civil liberties movement as intimately tied to the broader effort to usher in radical change in the United States. In that regard the lens through which the Bureau of Investigation viewed the early ACLU was strongly tinted but not entirely blind.

Attorney General Stone's decision to reorganize the Bureau of Investigation and to terminate "its political and propaganda activities" delighted Baldwin and other ACLU board members. Following Stone's selection of J. Edgar Hoover on May 10 to replace William J. Burns as director of the Bureau of

Investigation, Baldwin sought to inform the labor and radical presses of changes the federal agency had undergone at the instigation of the new attorney general. As Baldwin acknowledged, however, in a letter to Stone in June 1924, he believed that bitter experience made it difficult for many to view "the secret service agency" favorably. Baldwin, for his part, had no intention of affording the Justice Department "any general absolution." Despite his appreciation for Stone's good intentions, Baldwin remained skeptical of how faithfully other Justice Department officials—particularly those, like Hoover, who had worked for Burns—would adhere to the new policies.[19]

Baldwin mailed a copy of the ACLU's pamphlet, *The Nation-Wide Spy System Centering in the Department of Justice*, to Stone, who sought a response from Hoover. In a seven-page letter the new Bureau of Investigation director defended his actions, attempted to blame Burns and Flynn for various abuses, and referred to Baldwin as a former convict. Stone asked the two men to meet for a frank discussion. Baldwin called on Hoover, with the attorney general present. On encountering Hoover, Baldwin was pleased to find him "polite, and very lawyerlike." Hoover insisted he had performed an "unwilling part" in assisting A. Mitchell Palmer, Harry Daugherty, and William J. Burns. Hoover discussed the new guidelines articulated by Stone and explained how he had attempted to adhere to them. Saying precisely what Baldwin wanted to hear, Hoover stated that the Bureau of Investigation was initiating a new chapter and would scrupulously observe the rights of American citizens; this proved to be a patently false assertion. The General Intelligence or Anti-Radical Division of the Bureau of Investigation, Hoover reported, was being closed. Infiltration of labor unions or political organizations would end, and his agency would no longer rely on private detective agencies. Hoover urged Baldwin to contact him if further allegations of wrongdoing involving the Bureau of Investigation surfaced. Not surprisingly, Baldwin was more than a little impressed and considerably mollified. His demands, he reasoned, had largely been met. Baldwin left the meeting, Hoover told Stone, "in a particularly friendly state of mind." However, Hoover retained control of the master index and personal files compiled by the Bureau of Investigation. Only Congress, not Attorney General Stone, could do anything about those.[20] Since its inception in 1908 the Bureau of Investigation had, after all, compiled such documents under its vague but seemingly ever-elastic mandate from Congress.

After his initial meeting with Hoover, Baldwin told Stone, "I think I owe it to him and to you to say that I think we were wrong in our estimate of his attitude." Stone's termination of political surveillance appeared to satisfy all ACLU complaints, as Baldwin acknowledged to the press. In mid-October he again met with Hoover and was informed that the Bureau of Investigation would become more centralized, rely on the civil service, and gradually release its antiradical detectives. Hoover told Baldwin that he was seeking information about operations by federal agents pertaining to radicals. Military Intelligence could not obtain access to the Bureau of Investigation's confidential files without his personal approval, the director promised. The War and Navy departments, Hoover insisted, were not entitled to any information about radical and pacifist activities.[21]

Once more Baldwin was impressed with the Bureau of Investigation chief. Hoover's administrative acumen was clearly apparent, as was his "amazingly retentive memory," much like Baldwin's own. Hoover reiterated his determination that the Bureau of Investigation start afresh and his intention to investigate only alleged violations of federal law, not personal opinions or beliefs. But best of all, Hoover assured Baldwin that the ACLU had never been investigated by his agency—a blatant falsehood. Such assurances were worth little, but Baldwin seemingly heard what he wanted to hear when communicating with Hoover. The ACLU, like its predecessor, had indeed been watched by government operatives. Furthermore, the surveillance would continue throughout the 1920s and beyond, despite Hoover's assertions to the contrary.[22]

By the beginning of 1925 Baldwin had come to believe that Hoover could trusted. Stone, about to take on his new role as an associate justice of the U.S. Supreme Court, wrote to Baldwin about Hoover. Stone referred to the propensity of radical newspapers to vilify Hoover "as a product of the Burns School of Detective Agency." In fact, Stone asserted, it was Assistant Attorney General John Lord O'Brian—with whom Baldwin had dealt during the war—who had ushered Hoover into the Bureau of Investigation. In Stone's eyes Hoover was loyal and efficient and deserved to be supported, not condemned, "at least until there is some ground for attack." Following the attorney general's lead, Baldwin believed that the ACLU should contact Hoover to find out whether certain individuals worked for the Department of Justice.[23]

Repeating a pattern established during the war, Baldwin was elated whenever he believed that he had a pipeline to the inner circles of government, with top officials treating him respectfully. Falling back on the elitism natural to him as an upper-class Bostonian, he continued to assume that this was only proper, despite his wartime record and subsequent notoriety as an

American heretic. This resulted in Baldwin's being something of an easy mark for an operator like J. Edgar Hoover, who led him to believe that their interests were not in conflict. Over the course of several decades the two men developed a strange relationship; Baldwin always insisted that Hoover was friendly or at least not inimical to the ACLU.

While Hoover, his agents, and other government operatives viewed the ACLU as an appropriate target for investigation, labor leaders like the American Federation of Labor's Samuel Gompers and the United Mine Workers' John L. Lewis, along with right-wing critics, also viewed the civil liberties organization with disdain. A librarian in the War Department drew up a "spider-web chart" that sought to demonstrate how a Wobbly-Communist-pacifist-ACLU plot had been conceived to harm the United States. Baldwin, for his part, continued to back radical labor forces and edited a book entitled *The Professional Patriots*, which sought to expose the activities of their antagonists. He carried out his own examination of "the professional patriots racket." Baldwin believed that no one fighting for civil liberties or other progressive causes should underestimate such groups, which included the revitalized Ku Klux Klan, the American Legion, the Daughters of the American Revolution, and the Civic Federation. In his estimation these forces were characterized by "stand-patism; fear; lawlessness; violence of the law; *their* law!; militarism; anti-labor." They were class conscious, and the worst comprised "the lunatic fringe of reaction." At the same time many so-called patriotic groups clearly were engaged in money-making rackets. For others property was "their god."[24]

Baldwin's clear identification with left-wing movements led some to view him as part of "a red web" designed to subvert the U.S. political system. In 1924 Richard Whitney, who headed the American Defense Society, a super-patriot group, wrote *Reds in America*, relying on documents seized by the Bureau of Investigation at the national convention of the Workers Party; J. Edgar Hoover himself gave Whitney the materials. Whitney termed Baldwin a "draft dodger" and "slacker" during World War I and "an intimate friend of the most radical of Communists." The ACLU, the author insisted,

is definitely linked with Communists through the system of interlocking directorates, so successfully used by the Communist party of America in penetrating into every possible organization with a view to getting control so that when the time comes for the great general strike which, they believe and hope, will lead to the overthrow of the United States government by violence, they will already have these bodies definitely aligned with them.[25]

The ACLU, Whitney argued, was spawned by "the notorious pacifist organizations of wartime fame, which were presumably financed by German agents in this country working desperately, and for a time successfully, to keep the United States from entering the war." The ACLU, he charged, was derived from a host of groups formed during the war whose members "were pacifists, defeatists, German agents, radicals of many hues, Communists, I.W.W., and Socialists." The ACLU afforded a haven for radicals of all types. From the very outset all radicals had relied on the ACLU "to fight the existing government of the United States." Whitney insisted that to leaders of the civil liberties movement, freedom "means the license of treason and sedition." Not surprisingly, "the Union creates in the minds of Communists, anarchists, and all classes of radicals the idea that it is improper for anyone to interfere with their activities aimed at the destruction of American institutions."[26]

Whitney singled out Baldwin for attack, accusing him of cynically urging other ACLU members "to look like patriots in everything we do." The ACLU itself, Whitney wrote, was "closely identified with groups in practically every city in the country known as 'parlor Bolsheviki,'" comprised of "dilettante radicals."[27]

In his 1925 book, *The Red Web*, Blair Coan, formerly a member of Harry Daugherty's Justice Department, pointed to ACLU national committee members Elizabeth Gurley Flynn, William Z. Foster, Helen Keller, Scott Nearing, Seymour Stedman, Norman Thomas, and Baldwin as "well known communists, socialists and reds." Baldwin—referred to as "an ex-convict . . . convicted and imprisoned for draft-dodging during the war"—and his colleagues were characterized by Coan as "birds of a feather." Many leading ACLU figures, Coan charged, were also involved with the communist-led Labor Defense Council.[28]

Ironically, given how government agents and those phobic about radicals viewed Baldwin, he spent a great deal of his time during this period attempting to convince the communist Workers Party of America to adopt a more tolerant attitude toward civil liberties. Throughout 1925, for instance, he felt compelled to warn party officials that disruption of public addresses and a cavalier attitude toward the Bill of Rights would prove disastrous for the

Workers Party and the American Left as a whole. After an incident in New York City that resulted in the termination of a speech by Dr. Rafael Abramovich—a socialist critic of communist Russia—Baldwin on January 31 wrote to his old friend William Z. Foster, now the party's chairman, to condemn the actions of "over-zealous party members." Such actions placed the ACLU in a difficult position, for it defended the communists' rights to freedom of speech and assemblage. "We don't object to heckling or to demonstrations from the audience," Baldwin wrote. "But there is a line beyond which they can't go without raising an issue we'll have to act upon."[29]

Ten days later Baldwin fired off a letter to the editor of the *Daily Worker* regarding the publication's declaration that free speech could be denied to capitalists as it was denied to workers by them. He asked whether the *Daily Worker* held contradictory views regarding free speech: that it should be afforded communists but denied in the United States or anywhere else to Russian radicals who opposed the Soviet government. Common sense called for the American comrades to take a different approach. In closing, Baldwin declared, "None of us who are outside that family now relish this spectacle. You don't encourage the support of people who believe in free speech by denying to others the rights which you demand for yourselves."[30]

Earl Browder wrote back on February 17, declaring that the Workers Party's approval of heckling and demonstrating matched the ACLU's position. Baldwin denied that any similarity existed between the ACLU stance and the disruption of public gatherings. Communists seemed determined "to fight out a Russian issue on American soil," without considering the repercussions. On March 7 William F. Dunne, coeditor of the *Daily Worker*, asserted that the ACLU's attitude concerning the purported disruption of public talks was outrageous. Workers Party members and their compatriots, not Abramovich and his ilk, were being beaten and arrested across the land. Dunne's statement that the ACLU's position was outrageous, Baldwin retorted, "is ridiculous in face of the facts." Clearly, communists had sought to prevent Abramovich from speaking. Furthermore, Baldwin had attended a Town Hall Club meeting in New York City on March 9 on the issue of political prisoners around the globe, including those held in Russia. The scheduled topic of discussion led an official delegation of the Workers Party, comprised of Ludwig Lore, an independent communist journalist, and Juliet Paynts, a party member, to visit Baldwin, who was to serve as temporary chairman of the meeting. One scheduled speaker considered unfriendly to the communists would not be allowed to deliver his speech, the committee informed Baldwin, and made good on that promise. Intriguingly, Baldwin urged Dunne to recall Lenin's admonition that communists accept support from the "petty bourgeois" in "preparing the way for the dictatorship."[31]

In responding to correspondence from Baldwin regarding the Abramovich and Town Hall meetings, Browder spoke for the Workers Party's Central Executive Committee. The demand that free speech be afforded Dr. Abramovich, the "enemy of the workers' government of Russia," Browder wrote on March 12, had been converted "into a fight, not for free speech, but to slander and discredit Soviet Russia—to assist the capitalist governments of the world to intimidate the workers and prepare for new warfare against the stronghold of the world's workers." This was the only conclusion the Workers Party could draw in watching the *New York Times* merrily standing side by side "with the friends of 'free speech.'" It was not surprising, Browder submitted, that capitalist publications were suddenly welcoming letters and even editorials by Baldwin, for he was "rendering their owners a great service. You are being placed in the position of sponsoring the lies which they have been unable to make the workers of America believe."[32]

Soon more troubled than ever, Baldwin wrote to Robert Morss Lovett, an ACLU board member who was well regarded on the Left, asking him to convince members of the Workers Party to stop disrupting political gatherings. Because William Z. Foster, Charles E. Ruthenberg, and James P. Cannon—the last two were founders of the American communist movement—were overseas, Baldwin reasoned, the party was dominated by underlings "who apparently are incapable of statesmanship." On March 14 Baldwin replied to Browder, saying that the ACLU supported the right of Catholics to criticize birth control and Margaret Sanger's right to advocate it; the right of the Ku Klux Klan to hold meetings unmolested and the right of the Knights of Columbus to condemn that terrorist organization; and the right of both socialists and communists to hold rallies damning one another. The bottom line was that the ACLU and the Workers Party of America viewed free speech differently. "You regard it as a means to an end. We regard it as an end in itself," he told Browder.[33]

On March 19 Baldwin received a letter from Morris Ernst that damned "the High-Priest of the Communist Party [Browder] and their order takers." Ernst advised, "Real human beings should not take their words as 'gold,' nor relate to them anything of any importance. For tomorrow or whenever it may be, the spirit of the Communist International may call on them to sell their father and mother or the very best that is in a human being for 'tactics,'

Strategy 'United Front' or for other outstanding words that's on the line of every Red Army soldier in Russia."[34]

In early April 1925 Browder, the Workers Party's acting secretary, fired off a note to the ACLU in response to a letter of inquiry from its executive committee. The party, Browder reminded, was "not yet the ruling party in the United States" but rather was the wing of the U.S. labor movement "most outrageously persecuted and oppressed." Thus to demand that it either respect or acknowledge the civil rights of its foes was ridiculous. The only civil rights issue of concern to the party involved its determination that the American working class not be "intimidated by the capitalist dictatorship." Capitalists and supporters of capitalism, the Workers Party held, were "the only real enemy" of civil rights for the working class. Thus the Workers Party wanted to find out whether the ACLU supported or opposed "the new concentration of capitalist reaction thruout [sic] the world against Soviet Russia? Is your committee with or against Abramovich in his open call to overthrow and destroy the first republic of workers and peasants?"[35]

Writing to "Dear Earl," Baldwin proclaimed that the ACLU "has no official interest" in the battle between the working class and capitalists.

> We take no position on any struggle whatever, except to see that the participants all get a chance to be heard openly, freely and fairly. Theoretically, we are just as much concerned about civil rights for capitalists as we are for workers . . . for the worst reactionary as for the extremist radical. Practically of course, the nature of the struggle about us and the personnel of the organization brings to us chiefly working-class cases.[36]

His misgivings about the communist stance regarding civil liberties notwithstanding, Baldwin continued to serve on the national committee of the Labor Defense Council. The LDC had been established to defend Workers Party representatives prosecuted because of their opinions or beliefs. Other officers or national committee members included Eugene V. Debs, who was the vice chairman; the Reverend John A. Ryan; Foster, George Maurer, and John Haynes Holmes. In late May, Maurer, who was secretary of the LDC, issued a call for the organization to sponsor a national conference to discuss foreign affairs and domestic developments. Baldwin and the ACLU leadership declared their opposition to such a conclave, because they were concerned that communists intended to dominate the LDC. On June 12, after an exchange of letters, Maurer wrote again to Baldwin to express the hope that he would continue working with the LDC and not against its interests. However, it was obvious to Baldwin that the Wobblies, socialists, and anarchists would not support the LDC's call for a united front; rather, it would attract only Workers Party members, sympathizers, and liberals "who don't understand radical politics." Finally, on June 12 Baldwin warned Edward C. Wentworth, the LDC chairman, that he would withdraw from the national committee if Maurer—whom he viewed as lacking the requisite tact and skill to deal with disparate groups—was making decisions without consultation. Baldwin also wanted to know whether the party cadre was plotting the LDC's strategy, had proposed the conference, and was instructing Maurer how to operate.[37]

After Wentworth said that he viewed the LDC "as an adjunct of the Workers Party under Party control," Baldwin tendered his resignation. He had joined the national committee in the belief that the organization was "an independent non-partisan agency" established to defend the civil rights of Workers Party members. Now, however, it was clear that the LDC was independent no longer but rather "subject to the orders of that Party's officials." Consequently, "it is not honest to stand before the public as an independent non-partisan agency, and I am unwilling to be party to any such pretense," Baldwin wrote. He expressed his belief that "the sooner the Labor Defense Council becomes frankly and openly an arm of the WP, the better for all concerned." Despite his actions, he remained determined to defend the civil liberties of party members. The ACLU, for its part, was unwilling to participate in any conference focusing on foreign affairs.[38]

The formation of the International Labor Defense, which provided legal defense for communists, in the summer of 1925 pleased Baldwin little better. As he told Debs, "The plain fact remains that it is an organ of the Workers' Party pretending to be independent and non-partisan." Baldwin was not opposed to the communists heading a defense organization for all parties. He appreciated "their energy and ability." But the sham of independence riled him, and he thought that "the public responsibility for the work ought to be where the control is." He also doubted whether "a united non-partisan defense organization" would be viable. He expressed some of the same concerns to Maurer, although Baldwin acknowledged that the new defense group had "a mighty good program."[39]

His dismay over the Workers Party's attitude toward civil liberties in no way lessened Baldwin's belief that U.S. capitalism needed to be transformed, nor did it diminish his identification with the Left. Rather, he contended that the party's sectarianism and its dismissive attitude regarding the personal liberties of opponents would only play into the hands of reactionaries. In early 1926 Baldwin bluntly declared that "the only power that works is class power." "Political liberalism," he insisted, "is dead." Present-day radicals, Baldwin insisted, had to identify with organized workers and farmers, not "a phantom public." Among those radicals were individuals—like himself— who in times past would have joined political crusades or engaged in social work. Driving the new radicals was "the same fine faith and love of their fellow man" that guided those earlier efforts. Thus "radicalism does not die; its forms change."[40]

Baldwin's identification with both the civil liberties campaign and the American Left made him a feared figure in certain circles but a revered one in others. In August 1925 the *American Mercury* ran a lengthy article entitled "The Legend of Roger Baldwin." Baldwin, this "last American who believed in free speech," the author offered, must be some ethereal being. Baldwin's opinions were said to be thoughtfully considered. "He is no half-baked follower of Rousseau. He does not believe in natural rights, and when he invokes the Constitution and the Declaration of Independence it is because they are weapons conveniently left available by a dominating class."[41]

But the *American Mercury* piece did not simply paint Baldwin as a one-dimensional figure. After all, Baldwin maintained "contact with the world of wealth and conservatism into which he was born," despite favoring "the plainest sort of living." He was "a perfect woodsman and a rare naturalist" who could easily walk all day long with a heavy pack on his back, paddle a canoe, and swim expertly. Those who spent time with Baldwin in the country were kept on the go and amazed by his stamina and energy. His indoor accomplishments were also said to be considerable and included decent watercolor sketches, near-professional piano playing, and cooking "like an angel." This was a man, the *American Mercury* confirmed, who "is never dull, and never, so far as anyone can tell, depressed. He is in deadly earnest about many things; yet he has humor and irony, and there dances in his eyes, which remind one of Bertrand Russell's, at times a half-mocking Ariel."[42]

Such kudos notwithstanding, Baldwin's explicit identification with the American Left continued to make him a suspect figure in the eyes of government agents. While the Bureau of Investigation had supposedly terminated its surveillance, Military Intelligence still tailed him. A report was mailed to the War Department in April 1926 regarding an ACLU meeting that Baldwin had attended at the City Club in Chicago. Deemed a "disloyalist," Baldwin was said to be heading for the west coast to agitate against a California law that criminalized syndicalism and to support the imprisoned Charlotte Anita Whitney. Whitney, a California patrician, was convicted under a 1919 state measure that criminalized the advocacy of force and violence to transform the industrial or political system. Baldwin allegedly sought to "stir up strife through the spurious plea of freedom of speech." The report likened him to "other radicals and Communists" such as Baldwin's former fiancée, Anna Louise Strong, a radical journalist; Paul Blanshard, a former Congregational minister who became a trade union activist; and Kate Richards O'Hare. Another report, labeled "Extra Special," also termed Baldwin a disloyalist.[43]

Early that summer the office of the corps area commander at the Presidio in San Francisco sent yet another report on Baldwin to Washington. The occasion was a dinner at the Palace Hotel in Baldwin's honor. The guest speaker was said to possess "great personality" but to be "a very ordinary looking man, cheaply and sloppily dressed." Early in his speech, Baldwin confirmed he was no communist, but the government agent charged that "he showed decided communistic tendencies in all he said later" and had acknowledged he was a close friend of William Z. Foster's. The ACLU appeared to be at a standstill—it had a few thousand members but lacked recent converts. Displaying the elitism so characteristic of him, Baldwin stated that the American people in general were "simply members of an unthinking herd, and they must be awakened by constant talk and printed propaganda, persistent and unceasing," the commander reported. The ACLU was to "play the part of a fly or mosquito, buzzing and stinging repeatedly until it makes itself felt." According to the commander's report, Baldwin called himself a pacifist but "an extremely militant" one who would fight for any cause but his country.[44]

Thus both Baldwin's ready association with the radical movement and his directorship of the ACLU made him a target of certain government agencies, including the Bureau of Investigation and Military Intelligence. As during the war and its immediate aftermath, top officials viewed him as suspect, even seditious, and were determined to keep a close eye on his operations. Had even higher officials followed their lead, the ACLU and Baldwin, the nation's top civil libertarian, would have been put out of business. What remains striking is how frequently various statements or actions by Baldwin put his beloved organization and movement at risk.

CHAPTER TWELVE

Turning to the Courts

The ACLU's executive committee, guided by Baldwin, carefully selected the court cases in which the organization would become involved. At times Baldwin acted on his own, seeking board approval only after the fact. The committee usually declined to take on cases it perceived as hopeless or those lacking a clear issue. However, on occasion the ACLU did willing battle against considerable odds to publicize an important issue. To influence judges, the ACLU played the public relations game, firing off press releases to newspapers, writing editorials, reaching out to the liberal editors, and sending letters that appeared in "voices of the people" columns. Once an issue grabbed the attention of Baldwin or the executive committee, the ACLU mailed a wire or letter, offered the organization's services, protested to officials, and sought publicity.[1]

A favorite tactic, particularly during the organization's first years, involved directly contesting actions by local officials that the ACLU viewed as repressive. It sent teams to the sites of industrial strife to challenge restrictions on free speech and assemblage. ACLU activists often were arrested and unceremoniously ushered out of town. Arthur Garfield Hays was celebrated for heading to the Pennsylvania and Kentucky coal country to contest restrictions on civil liberties. And on various occasions Roger Baldwin followed suit. One such affair involved the walkout in the fall of 1924 by eight thousand laborers in Paterson, New Jersey, orchestrated by the Associated Silk Workers. An injunction banned picketing and meetings by the strikers. The union asked for the ACLU's help in reopening a private hall where its members had congregated. The ACLU planned to hold a meeting in the forbidden hall, but the chief of police surrounded the building with his men and declared that no such gathering would take place.[2]

Unable to find anyone willing to go immediately to Paterson to forge strategy, Baldwin went and met with the strike committee. Only a public protest would suffice, it seemed clear, as public halls were unavailable and the injunction remained in place. The previous week he had attended a packed meeting disrupted by the police as a strike leader spoke. Consequently, Baldwin—recalling his first free speech fight on behalf of Margaret Sanger—now urged a march to city hall, where the strikers could carry out a public protest. Carrying American flags and a copy of the U.S. Constitution, thirty or forty workers and Baldwin headed for the town plaza and met up with hundreds of strikers along the way. Heeding Baldwin's suggestion, John C. Buttersworth of the Associated Silk Workers Union started to read from the Bill of Rights. Such a move, Baldwin had reasoned, would preclude the bringing of charges involving seditious statements or incitement to violence.[3]

After Buttersworth had spoken but a few words, however, a squadron of more than fifty police officers appeared and terminated the protest. While the police captain later reported that the police chief had "read [the protesters] the riot act"—literally an eighteenth-century statute—none of the demonstrators heard him do so, although one account has Baldwin calling out, "I protest!" Police clubs fell swiftly on the heads of workers, bloodying two. The crowd, attempting to escape from the police, dispersed; only the handful of flag bearers and speakers remained. Nine individuals were arrested but not Baldwin, who had orchestrated the protest. He had never witnessed "so flagrant an exhibition of unprovoked and unnecessary police lawlessness."[4]

Bewildered by the turn of events, Baldwin went down to police headquarters to seek a meeting with Chief John M. Tracey to find out what charges were being brought. Denied entrance, Baldwin asked that his card be delivered to Tracey, but it was handed back, along with a message that the chief refused to see him. Baldwin then phoned Tracey and exclaimed, "If anyone should be arrested, it should be I." He drafted a press release for the local paper that discussed the incident at city hall and the role he had played. The night editor urged that Baldwin also be arrested; Baldwin readily agreed.

The following morning Baldwin learned that Chief Tracey was looking for him, so he went to police headquarters, according to court testimony and a memo Baldwin wrote at the time. When they met, Tracey placed his hand on Baldwin's shoulder "in a fatherly sort of way" and blurted out, "Boy, you are in wrong." Baldwin replied, "Chief, I am not in near as wrong as your men are with me for that disgraceful spectacle on the steps last night. It was an outrage." Tracey retorted that he would not allow "any communist" to speak in the manner one worker had: "We can't have that kind of thing in this town." When Baldwin asked what the worker had said, Tracey charged that the man had vilified President Coolidge. Baldwin remarked, "Why John W. Davis is doing that. Abusing the President isn't a crime." Tracey told Baldwin that he would not allow such speech at strike gatherings. Baldwin in turn accused the police chief of seeking to determine who could say what in Paterson. Tracey agreed and blurted out, "I am the law." The conversation concluded with the police chief warning that he would make Baldwin "kiss the Constitution and the flag" in front of city hall during his next visit to Paterson. "Why, you couldn't make me kiss my own mother, if I didn't want to," Baldwin chortled. "I wouldn't do anything for a police officer just because he told me to."[5]

A warrant for his arrest was then issued on a charge of violating the 1796 antiriot statute, and bail was arranged by the strike committee; front-page headlines reporting the news rang out across the country. The publicity had the desired effect. Paterson immediately rescinded its ban on public gatherings, and Baldwin attended a crowded strike meeting the next evening at the same hall whose doors had been closed to the union. With Baldwin pulling the strings, the silk workers decided that Buttersworth should march down the center aisle toward the platform, where he would once again read from the Constitution. A welter of applause greeted both Buttersworth and Baldwin. The strikers were revitalized, and within two weeks management had met the union's demands.[6]

However, the Passaic County grand jury brought indictments against ten individuals, including Baldwin and Buttersworth. They were charged under the 1796 law, which had never been used before; the indictment charged that the defendants, along with "other evil-disposed persons . . . unlawfully, routously, riotously and tumultuously" breached the public peace, causing "great terror and disturbance." The ACLU put up the $3,000 bail for Baldwin and took care of $50 bail bonds for the other defendants. Baldwin had been delighted with the union's success and his part in it. A friend of his remarked, "I see Baldwin's stock is going up; he's been arrested again." Once he read the indictment, John Haynes Holmes wondered whether Baldwin was "really yourself or the mighty Behemoth of Holy Scripture." The charges, Holmes declared, sounded as though Baldwin were "some prehistoric monster who had gone on a rampage." While this seemed like a joke, Holmes remembered Elizabeth Gurley Flynn's warning that an arrest in Paterson was not to be treated lightly (Flynn was recalling earlier antilabor antics in Paterson). The ACLU would, of course, attend to Baldwin's legal costs, Holmes promised in a letter, for "what you did was on our behalf and as our agent. Furthermore, the issue involved belongs not to you personally but to the cause that we are fighting. While this sort of thing is possible our Union certainly has a mission."[7]

The facts were not in dispute, and the only legal issue to be determined was whether a reasonable person would have been "put in fear" by the public protest. The case was argued in Judge Joseph A. Delaney's Court of Common Pleas. Baldwin had hoped to deliver a moving oration celebrating freedom of assembly and petition, but he became "unusually tongue-tied" in the presence of an impassive judge and "the polite remoteness" of his own lawyer, Addison F. Rosenkrans, a local practitioner. Baldwin did acknowledge that he had triggered the incident at city hall.[8]

At the trial's conclusion Delaney pointedly stated, "At the outset, Baldwin, you were primarily at fault. You felt that a test case should be made. The court feels that it should deal with you more severely than with the others." He levied $50 fines against all defendants except for Baldwin, whom he ordered to serve six months in the county jail.[9]

The noted New York attorney Samuel Untermyer offered to take the case on appeal, and Baldwin accepted for himself alone, while the other defendants retained local counsel. The first appellate review sustained the convictions. While Baldwin appeared little worried about what might lie ahead, the ACLU attorneys were concerned because of his wartime conviction. They believed that Untermyer, a wealthy Jewish corporate lawyer, had not been well received in New Jersey. So they turned to Arthur T. Vanderbilt, the best-known attorney in Newark, a former president of the American Bar Association, and later a law school dean and chief justice of the New Jersey Court of Errors and Appeals, the state's highest tribunal. Members of the Garland Fund's board battled with Baldwin, who attempted to dissuade them from allocating any money for his appeal. Arguing that such assistance would not violate the board's "policy of supporting causes to the exclusion of persons," Walter Nelles insisted, "the case is an appropriate 'cause.' . . . Roger is himself a cause. And if he's one that warms the heart as well as the mind, so much the better." Eventually, Baldwin's lead attorney, paid a grand total of $150 for his fee and expenses, persuaded the New Jersey Court of Errors and Appeals; in 1928 it voted unanimously to overturn the conviction, while highlighting the need for freedom of assembly to prevail.[10]

In a sharply worded opinion, Justice Samuel Kalisch expressed doubt that the gathering before the Paterson City Hall could have made a reasonable individual fearful of a threatened breach of the peace: "We find an utter absence of any such proof." Sam Walker has proclaimed the ruling—which the *New York Times* applauded—as "the most sweeping First Amendment victory of the entire decade."[11]

While the free speech fight in Paterson resulted in an important legal victory, another case, where questions of law were not ultimately determined, engendered far greater publicity for the ACLU. The Scopes, or Monkey, Trial—so named by H. L. Mencken—involved the Butler Act, a Tennessee law prohibiting the teaching of evolution in public classrooms, and was a cause célèbre of American liberals and intellectuals during the 1920s. The ACLU became intimately involved with this case when Lucille Milner, scouring through newspapers, spotted a news report that Governor Austin Peay of Tennessee had signed the Butler bill into law. Somewhat excitedly, Milner showed the item to Baldwin, declaring, "Here's something that ought to have our attention," while her boss reportedly "saw its import in a flash." He ordered her to bring the Tennessee law to the board's attention when it met the following Monday. At that meeting board members immediately agreed that this was a case of great significance, one that might end up before the U.S. Supreme Court. The board fired off a press announcement that the ACLU stood ready to support any teacher in the state who challenged the act's constitutionality. The ACLU's determination to get involved at the trial level, hardly an everyday occurrence, demonstrated how board members viewed the case. Within a few days the ACLU received a telegram reporting that a high school science teacher, John Thomas Scopes, would be arrested for having violated the Butler Act.[12]

To the ACLU's dismay William Jennings Bryan, three-time Democratic Party presidential nominee, religious fundamentalist, and secretary of state under Woodrow Wilson, tendered his services as legal counsel, to serve on behalf of the Tennessee attorney general. As Baldwin recognized, the case would represent "the Good Book against Darwin, bigotry against science, or, as popularly put, God against the monkeys." Bryan's entry also all but ensured that his chief antagonist would be Clarence Darrow, the great court-room litigator and agnostic, who had volunteered to defend Scopes.[13]

Certain board members, particularly Arthur Garfield Hays, strongly urged that Darrow be allowed to represent Scopes. However, those who thought the case should be fought strictly on constitutional grounds initially dangled the name of Bainbridge Colby, another former secretary of state, before Scopes. Nelles and Baldwin, already troubled by the circus-like atmosphere that had developed, opposed Darrow's appointment. Nelles had envisioned an examination of whether the Tennessee law abridged the establishment clause, whereas Baldwin wanted to emphasize the issue of academic freedom. They sought to have Darrow removed as counsel and even attempted to find out whether a more "respectable" figure could replace him. Those considered included John W. Davis, the 1924 Democratic Party presidential nominee, and Charles Evans Hughes, the former associate justice of the U.S. Supreme Court who had resigned his seat to run against Woodrow Wilson in 1916. In contrast, Arthur Garfield Hays defended the selection of Darrow, declaring, "I never yet have found any conservative lawyer who, at the beginning, wants to undertake a case which *might* reflect discredit upon him." Spirited discussion followed, with the decision made, "but just barely," to select Darrow and Hays as cocounsel.[14]

In the steamy courtroom in Dayton, Tennessee, histrionics flourished, with Bryan attempting to defend the sanctity of fundamentalist tenets as revealed in the Book of Genesis and Darrow striving to ridicule his opponent as a bigoted, unenlightened buffoon wielding a paper sword against the forces of modernity. Refusing to admit testimony regarding science and religion from the ACLU's expert witnesses, the judge determined that the issue in question involved the authority of the state legislature to develop the public school curriculum. This effectively undercut the ACLU's case. Consequently, Darrow concocted a plan to trap the prosecution's star attorney into declaring his fundamentalist religious beliefs on the stand. Although Bryan was made to appear the fool, Scopes was convicted and fined $100. The ACLU readied a federal appellate brief, and certain board members again sought to remove Darrow from the case. However, the Tennessee Supreme Court reversed the lower court's ruling, stating that the fine should have been levied by a jury, not the sitting judge.[15]

Perhaps surprisingly, perhaps not, the ACLU director never saw fit to travel to Dayton to witness the courtroom theatrics. "I didn't want to go because I was in New York raising money and paying bills," Baldwin later recalled. He continued, "I never had the habit of attending trials. They're a waste of time, most of them. And besides I was managing things from New York." Baldwin had decided not to attend the proceedings because he recognized that the lawyers, not he, would be making the tactical decisions in the case. The ACLU's strategy in Dayton largely was decided on the spot, in the courthouse, or from a rented house referred to as the Mansion, which sheltered counsel and expert witnesses alike.[16]

Therefore, even had Baldwin gone down to Tennessee, he would not have been able to orchestrate events in his usual manner. That was not something Baldwin would easily or lightly have accepted. Nor would he have welcomed being perceived as a minor actor in a drama pitting Darrow against Bryan or evolutionary theory against the biblical version of creation.

During this period the ACLU was only peripherally associated with three other celebrated cases—Sacco and Vanzetti, Mooney-Billings, and the Scottsboro Boys; however, Baldwin became personally involved with each. Nicola Sacco and Bartolomeo Vanzetti, both anarchist immigrants, were accused of committing felony murder in April 1920 during the robbery of a paymaster and his guard in South Braintree, Massachusetts. They were convicted the following July, despite the controversial strategy used on their behalf by Fred H. Moore, the celebrated socialist attorney who had regularly defended the IWW. Moore had sought to show that the defendants' political views were on trial and orchestrated a public campaign to support their cause. For the next six years he appealed their convictions and sought to win a new trial.

In the case involving Sacco and Vanzetti, unlike the fight in Paterson, the role of the ACLU's national office included little more than a listing on the letterhead of the defense committee and help to raise funds. However, almost from the case's inception Baldwin became intimately involved, communicating with the defense committee, the defendants, and their attorneys. The trial was held in Boston and attracted many of his acquaintances. He came to view Sacco and Vanzetti as personal friends, whom he "admired and loved." Their political perspective seemingly dovetailed with his "own anarchist past connections and sympathies." He treasured the time he spent with Vanzetti as "one of the most inspiring experiences of my life."[17]

Like many others, Baldwin remained unsure about their culpability, although at one point he specifically declared that they had not committed murder. He was certain that the prosecution never met the standard of guilt required by American criminal jurisprudence—beyond a reasonable doubt. Moore, whose behavior Baldwin considered irresponsible, informed him, while the convictions were under appeal, that Sacco's alibi witnesses appeared to be unreliable. That was particularly troublesome, for Sacco's defense depended heavily on those witnesses. Others involved in the defense, including Baldwin, were less disturbed by inconsistencies in how people would testify. They recognized that anarchist groups might well have carried out the heist and the murders or that the defendants might know who had done so. In fact, Baldwin helped defeat a proposal before the Garland Fund trustees to investigate whether anarchist groups were directly involved; he feared that the study might compromise Sacco and Vanzetti. He was content for the campaign to highlight that the prosecution of the defendants centered around their ideas and nationality. Baldwin recognized that "language confusion," caused in part because the prosecution was carried out in English and the defense in Italian, hardly helped matters. But most important in his estimation was the sheer improbability that two such idealistic defendants—one, Sacco, a family man—had carried out such a criminal act in midafternoon. He particularly saw Vanzetti—to whom he gave Italian poetry—as a "poetic man" who "could never have murdered anybody."[18]

The defense effort for Sacco and Vanzetti garnered support from liberals and radicals of all stripes. Individuals like Gardner Jackson, a wealthy newspaperman, devoted great amounts of time and energy to devising strategy and public relations for the defense. In Baldwin's estimation Jackson and Elizabeth Glendower Evans, a social activist, did more than anyone else to keep the case in the limelight.[19]

At one point Sacco asked Baldwin to speak with the state prison commissioner about transferring him to the state penitentiary. Should that prove impossible, Baldwin hoped that "some creative job" outside Sacco's cell might be possible; romantically and unrealistically, Baldwin appeared to compare the plight of Sacco and Vanzetti behind bars with his own wartime incarceration. In a note to U.S. Prison Commissioner Sanford Bates, an old acquaintance, Baldwin referred to Sacco's agitated nervous condition and the "serious mental collapse" he had recently suffered.[20]

On October 17, 1920, Baldwin received a disturbing letter from Fred Moore. The attorney asked whether Baldwin would accept anything less than a complete legal defense if he were innocent but facing the electric chair. The defendants, Moore pointed out, favored "an effective international agitation." "You will note that I have put in the words *if you were innocent*. This is the test." Moore recognized that an individual who had committed a crime in order to challenge the existing social order might be contemptuous of a legal defense. However, he found it inconceivable that a man would allow himself to be "railroaded to the electric chair or to a penitentiary for a crime of which he is not guilty." He also urged caution in dealing with the defendants, who opposed all judicial institutions and who "look upon the State as their natural enemy." Consequently, Moore admonished Baldwin not "to throw the weight of your own personality into the scales."[21]

Upton Sinclair was troubled enough by Moore's doubts that he visited Baldwin to discuss the matter. Baldwin informed the distinguished novelist that others involved with the case, such as Glendower Evans, a close friend of Louis and Alice Goldmark Brandeis, considered the attorney's concerns overwrought. Nevertheless, Gardner Jackson worried that Baldwin "was passing by word of mouth doubts about Nick" Sacco.[22]

In October 1924, after Moore's motions for a new trial were denied and he was subjected to sharp judicial criticism, the attorney resigned from the case. Baldwin helped to retain William G. Thompson, a well-regarded Boston lawyer with respectable credentials, to carry out the appeal. The Garland Fund delivered a $20,000 interest-free loan to the defense committee, with $2,500 eventually canceled outright. The only security, as Baldwin acknowledged, was "the good faith of the Committee and the ability of friends of the defense to meet its cost."[23]

During his years in prison Vanzetti corresponded with Baldwin, but Baldwin, who normally kept all such materials, inexplicably failed to do so. He did retain one of the last letters he received from Vanzetti, dated June 25, 1927, which contained the following closing: "With a strong and most cordial shake hands, alway [sic] your friend BARTOLO."[24]

The case ended with the electrocutions of Sacco and Vanzetti on August 23, 1927, which stunned Baldwin, who was abroad at the time but had continued to hope for a last-minute reprieve. After he returned to the United States, he became one of three trustees who watched over about $15,000 that French supporters had collected to ensure an education for Sacco's son and daughter.[25]

The Mooney-Billings case began in 1916 after a bomb exploded in the midst of a Preparedness Day Parade in San Francisco, killing ten. Tom Mooney was the head of the radical wing of the California Federation of Labor and Warren Knox Billings a close associate. Renowned as a fiery orator and writer,

Mooney, like Billings, appeared friendly to anarchists and supportive of the doctrine of "propaganda of the deed," which was associated with anarchists and terrorism. Mooney had already been charged with blowing up property held by the Pacific Gas and Electric Co. in San Francisco, whereas Billings had been convicted of bringing dynamite aboard a passenger train. By 1916 Mooney strongly opposed U.S. entrance into World War I and backed a drive—as did Billings—to organize workers of the United Railroads of San Francisco.

The deadly bomb exploded on July 22. Mooney and his wife, Rena, were some distance away, but they, along with Billings, Israel Weinberg, and Edward D. Noland, were charged with the crime. Mooney was convicted of first-degree murder and Billings of a second-degree capital offense; initially, Mooney was sentenced to hang and Billings to life in prison. Within a year evidence emerged that perjured testimony had been used against the defendants. The federal Wickersham Commission, made up largely of respectable conservative figures, determined that the prosecution had been out to get the accused. The trial judge and jurors acknowledged that their handling of the case had been in error; this later led Baldwin to proclaim the case "one of the outstanding judicial scandals in this country." A firestorm of protest occurred, and the death sentence meted out to Mooney was commuted, but he and Billings remained locked up.[26]

The ACLU established a national Mooney-Billings committee, which received the defendants' blessing. Because Billings allowed Mooney to determine their mutual defense and because Billings was incarcerated at Folsom Prison, Baldwin failed to meet him until after his release. But Baldwin visited Mooney at San Quentin on a number of occasions and considered him "a jolly, breezy, vigorous man" determined to win his freedom and clear his name. At the same time it was clear that Mooney was strong willed, even "a prima donna by temperament," not a man inclined to allow others to devise legal strategy for him and his codefendant.[27]

In early 1929 Baldwin became still more involved with the Mooney-Billings case. In characteristic fashion he urged the formation of a committee in California, comprised of "the most respectable liberals possible." Such a group, he believed, should contact the governor, deliver public speeches, compose articles for the popular press, and support sympathetic resolutions in various organizations. In short, they should afford "responsible backing" to the petition seeking pardons for Mooney and Billings. Should "enough prominent people" become involved in such a campaign, he reasoned, the governor would have to listen. So too, Baldwin hoped, would Tom Mooney, whose own committee, in trying to orchestrate the defense, had antagonized Warren Billings.[28]

In August 1929 Baldwin termed the Mooney-Billings case "the most scandalous of any frame-up of labor leaders in our history." To him it was even more egregious than the Sacco and Vanzetti case, because there, at least, no parties involved with the prosecution had confirmed the defendants' innocence. The judge who presided over the trial of Mooney and Billings called it "one of the dirtiest jobs ever put over, and I resent the fact that my court was used for such a contemptible piece of work." Moreover, "subsequent revelations damned every witness who testified before me against them as perjurious or mistaken." Nevertheless, top legal and political circles opposed a pardon. Those who condemned "this frame-up," Baldwin argued, should "never rest till these men step out of prison, vindicated and free."[29]

That day did not arrive for another ten years. Baldwin, along with Robert Morss Lovett, A. J. Muste, James Cannon, a founder of the American communist movement, and J. B. Matthews, a leading fellow traveler, joined the National Free Mooney Council in 1933. However, the so-called New York crowd, comprised of Baldwin and the attorneys—including Arthur Garfield Hays—who appealed on every ground they could think of, remained the strongest supporters of pardons. Lawyers in California were less inclined to become involved, fearing the case's association with industrial unrest and the need for the state's highest tribunal to acknowledge legal errors. Despite the implorings, Mooney and Billings remained in jail until Governor Culbert Olsen had them released in 1939. Pardons were issued to Mooney and Billings in 1939 and 1941, respectively.[30]

The Scottsboro case involved nine young black men aged thirteen to twenty-one who were arrested on March 25, 1931, and accused of raping two white women, Victoria Price and Ruby Bates, on a freight train close to the small town of Paint Rock, Alabama. The accused, lacking adequate defense counsel, were convicted three weeks later on the basis of meager evidence; eight received death sentences. The NAACP, which was headed by Roger's old friend, the staunchly anticommunist Walter White, proved unable to afford consistent support for the "Scottsboro Boys." For one thing, the Communist Party, through the International Labor Defense, had acted quickly to provide counsel for the defendants. At first reluctant to place the NAACP at the service of nine young men accused of a heinous crime in the heart of Old Dixie,

White also was little disposed to work alongside the communists. Then, in hiring Arthur Garfield Hays and Clarence Darrow to serve as NAACP defense counsel, White blundered badly. When they found the Scottsboro Boys were represented by communist attorneys sent by the ILD, Hays and Darrow withdrew in disgust. As both the ACLU director and a friend of White and the two attorneys, Baldwin found himself "caught in the middle of it." He believed that the ACLU had to defend all parties whose civil liberties had been abridged, even as he expressed concern that Communist Party members were attempting to use the defendants' plight to political advantage. He blamed the NAACP for acting carelessly and in bad faith, because the organization had failed to obtain consent of the minors' parents to hire the attorneys. Baldwin sent a series of heated missives to White.[31]

Baldwin spoke at mass meetings held on behalf of the defendants. He considered the Scottsboro Boys "just a bunch of unlettered Negroes," victimized by the unwritten code in the South that made it all but impossible to free blacks accused of raping white women. He went to see the defendants in jail, and later met with them following their release, but developed no lasting impressions "of character or personality." He recognized that they had been "idealized as symbols of race prejudice."[32]

The Scottsboro Boys were clearly not the kinds of defendants Baldwin could identify with in any manner. They were, as he put it, unlettered and not just lacking formal education. They possessed no political philosophy that interested him or to which he subscribed.

The communists controlled the Scottsboro Defense Committee, but Baldwin served on it, reasoning that the defendants had accepted the communists' support, albeit under extenuating circumstances. The Scottsboro Boys and their families considered the communists—an apparently increasingly influential political force—"the only active white folks" to express a belief in racial equality. Baldwin was little troubled by whatever ulterior motives were guiding the communists, rationalizing that he often dealt with individuals and groups "whose motives could not be regarded as so pure as to be confined to principles alone."[33]

As the controversy between the NAACP and the ILD continued, Hays and Darrow issued accounts backing the civil rights group. The blame for the clash, Hays held, should reside with the ILD, not the NAACP, as Baldwin had charged. Darrow fired off a letter to White, declaring absurd the notion that he and Hays had been misled by the NAACP. However, neither Hays nor Darrow insisted on remaining as the attorneys of record. Both had offered to work with ILD counsel and operate independently of any organization, in order to defend the Scottsboro Boys. This offer had been refused by the ILD, and Darrow and Hays in turn were given the choice of accepting that organization's lead or withdrawing from the case. "Of course we refused," Darrow said.[34]

In mid-May Martha Gruening, who had been a member of the executive committee of the New York Bureau of Legal First Aid, examined Baldwin's file on the Scottsboro case. As she informed him, she found little to substantiate his charges that the NAACP had acted both carelessly and in bad faith in hiring Darrow and Hays. Absent any additional information, the NAACP, she believed, was "entitled to the benefit of any doubt." Gruening viewed such treatment as "wholly unjustified." Furthermore, Baldwin's accusations should never have been made "except with the fullest publicity." Such a statement by the ACLU director was "extremely damaging to the NAACP," which had not been fully apprised of the accusation or afforded an opportunity to respond. "The whole procedure seems to me terribly inconsistent with the principles for which the American Civil Liberties Union stands," Gruening said.[35]

Curiously, Baldwin seemed far more inclined to accept the Communist Party's participation in the Scottsboro case than the NAACP's, as well as the Communist Party's version of events. Although he was close to NAACP leaders like Walter White, Baldwin perhaps retained a certain distrust of the organization, which dated to his days in St. Louis when followers of W. E. B. DuBois had clashed with those of Booker T. Washington. In a letter dated August 12 Baldwin acknowledged that many were displeased with the communists' bent for propaganda. Nevertheless, he declared, "Personally I don't think it has done any harm and has indeed dramatized all over the world the kind of justice Negroes get in southern courts."[36]

During this same period Walter White attempted to heal the rift with Baldwin, acknowledging what he considered their mutual disdain for Communist Party antics. On August 17 Baldwin, in a note to White that he declared "Not for publication," expressed displeasure with Earl Browder's accusation that the ACLU had urged a cessation of contributions to the Scottsboro fund. Both the ACLU and the NAACP, White reminded Baldwin, had been forced to contend with "tactics of duplicity, treachery, dishonesty and untruth" emanating from the Communist Party of the United States.[37]

On November 7, 1932, the U.S. Supreme Court, in the case of *Powell v. Alabama,* overturned the convictions of the Scottsboro defendants. Justice

George Sutherland determined that the indigent defendants were entitled, under the Fourteenth Amendment's due process clause, to a fair trial, which includes the right to counsel. A second Scottsboro trial in March 1933 resulted in another guilty verdict, which ensured that the case remained a cause of great concern for the American Left. The Communist Party established the National Scottsboro Action Committee, whose members included J. B. Matthews, Adam Clayton Powell, Heywood Hale Broun, A. J. Muste, and Baldwin.[38]

At that point, the ACLU had attempted, in its own words, to "help give these boys the best possible break at this second trial." The organization had tried to ensure that the defendants had expert counsel. A month later, on April 13, 1933, the *Chicago Daily Tribune* condemned the ACLU's role in the case; this followed an Alabama circuit judge's ruling that ordered yet another trial. The *Tribune* termed the ACLU "a fraud. Its managers have no regard for civil liberties except when they can be pleaded for the protection of radical mischief makers and criminals. They are communists and sympathizers with bolshevism, which has destroyed civil liberties wherever it has gained power."[39]

The *Tribune* then pointed to a recent speech by Baldwin, in which he had termed political democracy flaccid and called for a united front of communists and liberals to battle fascism. The paper denounced the very idea of such an alliance.

> A union of communists and genuine liberals would be a union of the snake and the bird. The Civil Liberties union is such a union. Liberals who support it are either gullibles or they are not liberals. There are no civil liberties remaining except where political democracy exists, and so long as the Civil Liberties union is run as it has been and is, by enemies of democracy, its title is a flagrant hypocrisy which can no longer deceive any but liberal sentimentalists befogged by mere phrases. Even these ought to be shocked at its methods in the Scottsboro affair.[40]

Baldwin immediately fired off a letter to the editor of the *Tribune* and called into question every charge made by the paper concerning the ACLU's role in the Scottsboro case. The appeals were genuine, he responded, seeking to afford the defendants their full constitutional right to a fair trial. The architects of the ACLU—who numbered men of the cloth, socialists, and liberals—did more than assist "radical mischief makers and criminals." They also dealt with many issues unrelated to the political Left, including censorship, academic freedom, civil rights, and labor rights. Yes, political democracy was being discarded for dictatorship, Baldwin declared, but that hardly made ACLU members "enemies of democracy."[41]

Baldwin's response to the *Tribune*'s accusations was necessary and pointed. His need to counter the newspaper's accusations, however, again demonstrated a surprising propensity to issue sweeping, charged statements that could prove damaging to the ACLU. For such a politically discerning individual—indeed, one often accused of being calculating—the continued exposition of such rhetoric remains largely inexplicable. At the same time it was in keeping with the temper of the times, and Baldwin's intimate involvement with the American Left.

The ultimate resolution of the Scottsboro case proved unsatisfactory, notwithstanding the continued involvement of ACLU leaders, including Baldwin and ACLU attorneys Osmond K. Fraenkel and Walter Pollak. In 1937, following an attempt to bribe one of the witnesses and then another trial, a curious plea bargain led to the release of four defendants and lengthy prison sentences for the others. The final defendant remained imprisoned until 1950.[42]

The ACLU board under Baldwin's direction singled out particular cases believed to involve important constitutional issues or key members of the organization's perceived constituency. Focusing on First Amendment freedoms, the ACLU initially displayed little interest in adopting the expansive perspective of old libertarian radicals like Theodore Schroeder and the members of the Free Speech League. Thus the organization proved little desirous of staking out a position on Prohibition. Rather, the board of directors, Baldwin recalled, was concerned about "violations of citizens' rights in . . . enforcement" of the Eighteenth Amendment, which took effect on January 29, 1920. Illegal searches and raids, entrapment, and the use of *agents provocateurs* all occurred, but the ACLU nevertheless challenged few of the government's actions. Regarding the ACLU's disinclination to contest Prohibition, Baldwin later said, "I think we were wrong in ignoring the issues." Although John Haynes Holmes was one of the few on the board who supported Prohibition, "We were all of like view that it was not our business," Baldwin said. With the advantage of hindsight, Baldwin suggested that the ACLU should have helped to combat official lawlessness by joining in protests of the government's illegal methods, both in court and through discussions with law enforcement representatives. Limited financial resources and personnel, Baldwin argued, also would likely have made any overt ACLU opposition to Prohibition negligible at best. However, such constraints did not preclude the organization from taking on other campaigns in which the odds appeared equally long.[43]

In the early years of its existence the ACLU did wrestle with the issue of censorship of controversial writings, especially those deemed indecent or obscene by authorities. In 1926 Arthur Garfield Hays defended H. L. Mencken and his *American Mercury* from an attempted ban by the Boston Watch and Ward Society. The society first sought to prevent distribution of an article in Mencken's journal that made light of fundamentalists, then broadened its attack to include sixty-five books in all. The expression "Banned in Boston" became commonplace. The ACLU board was split over whether to become involved in such matters. Baldwin, Norman Thomas, and John Haynes Holmes adopted a cautious approach, the by-product of both a puritanical bent and their belief that First Amendment protection of political speech remained of paramount importance. Given Baldwin's somewhat unconventional lifestyle, his own attitude toward racy literature was paradoxical, at the very least, and arguably hypocritical. Holmes, for his part, believed that local communities could restrict supposedly indecent books such as *Lady Chatterley's Lover*. Thomas supported the ban on the film *Birth of a Nation*, because he feared it would stir racial tumult.[44]

Hays and Morris Ernst, both "secularized Jews," as Sam Walker described them, saw censorship differently. They argued that the Constitution protects private consensual sexual activities. Baldwin was sometimes shocked by Ernst's use of expletives. As Baldwin acknowledged, "He was the first I ever heard use the word 'fuck' at a meeting with ladies present." Ernst—who also served as counsel for Planned Parenthood—considered Holmes and Baldwin old-fashioned because of their belief that certain words, like *damn*, should not be completely spelled out in books. Decades later, Baldwin reported, "I still am shocked by these words in print." So-called blasphemous words or expressions, such as the use of *Jesus Christ* in an exclamation, Baldwin also reasoned, "should remain in the realm of privacy." Similarly, he contended, "Private sexual life should be private, not in public places. You don't have public fornication or public homosexuality. Some things you don't do in public view. The Puritan ethic had something to be said for it." And while he did not favor limiting expression involving public issues, "on private matters, a certain sense of propriety and decency has to be observed." Furthermore, "the right of freedom of expression runs up versus the sensitivities of people."[45]

In early 1929 censorship in Boston nevertheless compelled the ACLU and Baldwin to act. The mayor had permitted a lecture that attacked birth control but had prevented Margaret Sanger from speaking. As he had two decades earlier, Baldwin came to his friend's rescue, declaring that "a square issue of discrimination" had been raised. The ACLU produced a pamphlet, *Censorship in Boston*, signed by Zechariah Chafee, a Harvard law school professor, but drafted by Baldwin. It condemned any kind of prior restraint, although it said that "subsequent criminal proceedings against indecent books and plays" did not violate the Constitution. This was a lesser standard, of course, than the clear and present danger test the ACLU supported when political speech was in question.[46]

Later that year Baldwin, his own prudishness notwithstanding, successfully proposed that the ACLU board support judicial interpretation regarding the shipping of controversial literature into the United States. That would take the determination of indecency out of the hands of customs officials. Then Baldwin and the ACLU went further and called for shifting to the prosecution the burden of proving indecency.[47]

In early 1931 Baldwin helped to organize the Committee Against Stage Censorship. Members included Ernst, Mencken, Harry Elmer Barnes, Walter Lippmann, Eugene O'Neill, Lewis Mumford, and Elmer Rice. They sought to lead a national campaign to prevent censorship in the "literary arts, the press, motion and talking pictures, the radio, and the scientific discussion of sex." The ACLU began to challenge censorship in all its guises through its National Committee on Freedom from Censorship. In 1933 Ernst obtained a federal court ruling in *United States v. One Book Entitled "Ulysses"* that James Joyce's epic work was not obscene. A book must be examined "in its entirety," the opinion held, to determine its effect on "a person with average sex instincts."[48]

Baldwin and the ACLU's reliance on the courts was striking, given his increased identification with the Left and supposed disdain for reform palliatives. It was, at the same time, in keeping with his elitist nature and his long-standing willingness to rely on the judicial branch to overcome perceived injustices meted out by private citizens or state agents alike. The turn to the courts was hardly avoidable, of course, because of the ACLU's very reason for existence: sustaining the Bill of Rights.

This tactical decision ultimately proved remarkably fruitful, as ACLU attorneys—often spurred on by Baldwin—helped to rewrite constitutional law. That process began with the *Gitlow* decision in 1925, with U.S. Supreme

Court Justice Edward T. Sanford proclaiming that "we may and do assume that freedom of speech and of the press—which are protected by the First Amendment from abridgment by Congress—are among the fundamental personal rights and 'liberties' protected by the due process clause of the 14th Amendment from impairment by the states." While the Court upheld the conviction of Benjamin Gitlow, one of American communism's early leaders, subsequent rulings, sometimes featuring ACLU representation, proved still more expansive. In 1931 Chief Justice Charles Evans Hughes issued the majority opinion in *Stromberg v. California*, which declared that the Fourteenth Amendment protects symbolic speech from state encroachments. That same year, in the case of *Near v. Minnesota*, Hughes asserted that freedom of the press could not be abridged through prior restraint.

In *Palko v. Connecticut* (1937) Justice Benjamin Cardozo stated that freedom of speech, freedom of the press, freedom of religion, the right to assemble, and the criminal defendant's right to counsel are guaranteed by the Fourteenth Amendment's due process clause against state infringements. These rights, Cardozo insisted, "represented the very essence of a scheme of ordered liberty . . . principles of justice so rooted in the traditions and conscience of our people as to be ranked fundamental." In *Hague v. Congress of Industrial Organizations* (1939) Justice Owen J. Roberts, with Cardozo among those concurring, proclaimed streets and parks public forums shielded by the First Amendment. This decision particularly delighted Baldwin, who had been involved in something of a running battle with Jersey City mayor Frank Hague. While Baldwin had damned "the tyranny and corruption of the Hague machine," the mayor had called Baldwin, Arthur Garfield Hays, Morris L. Ernst, and fellow ACLU member Abraham J. Isserman "the leading Communists in this country."[49] Over the next several decades, with the ACLU often providing counsel or amicus briefs, more and more sections of the Bill of Rights came to be considered "fundamental" by the Supreme Court.

CHAPTER THIRTEEN

International Human Rights

Although he virtually dominated the early ACLU, Baldwin initially was unable to convince board members to become involved in international affairs. Consequently, in 1920—the year the ACLU was founded—he began to branch out, helping to establish the International Committee for Political Prisoners and the American League for India's Freedom; the following year, he became involved in the planning of the Kuzbas Autonomous Industrial Colony in the Ural Mountains. The war had both energized and radicalized Baldwin, as it did many others. It helped to crystallize, albeit only to a certain degree, his previously ill-defined political perceptions and to transform him into one of the leading figures on the American Left. It led him to discard more completely the progressivism of his social work days in favor of anarchist and syndicalist tenets, yet his ideological grounding remained flexible and nondogmatic.

Some saw this as characteristic of Baldwin's readiness to move from one ideological position to another or, even more coldly, as demonstrating a kind of political flightiness on his part. Nevertheless, throughout this period he remained committed to certain principles: a firm belief in American civil liberties and support for workers' movements around the globe.

Shortly after his release from jail in mid-1919, he became involved with the American League for India's Freedom. In the midst of the war his old friend Mary Buckley had introduced him to Dhan Gopal Mukerji, a student, writer, and Indian patriot who conveyed a sense of his nation's misery and subjugation. Then while jailed at the Tombs, Baldwin had met an Indian nationalist sought by the British, and Agnes Smedley, an American feminist and lifelong anticolonialist; both were inmates. Baldwin had first followed the Indian anti-imperialist campaign through Lala Lajpat Rai's articles in the *New Republic*. In the belief that India's sheer size made it the "most vital country" under the imperial yoke, Baldwin was drawn to the league, along with other members of "the pacifist-socialist-middle-class left" like John Haynes Holmes. Should India achieve independence, they reasoned, colonial rule would collapse. Working with the Indian League in England, Baldwin and his colleagues met such leaders as Villabai Patel, Shaukat Ali, Mrs. Sarojini Naidu, and Rabindaranath Tagore. Tales of Mahatma Gandhi were spun by Baldwin's friend Richard Gregg, a graduate of Harvard College and Harvard Law School, who became an ardent proponent of nonviolent resistance.[1]

Although Baldwin was a firm supporter of Indian nationalism, the bulk of his legendary energy now concentrated on the civil liberties organization he had helped found and on the new workers' state in Russia. It was increasingly clear that he viewed international affairs through a different prism than he did events in the United States. Violations of civil liberties in his own country, particularly those involving pacifists, labor activists, or political radicals, he believed, perverted the Bill of Rights and Anglo-American jurisprudence. Throughout this period he stood as an absolutist when individual rights were abridged in the United States. When he discussed British imperial policies in India or the treatment of the Irish, he was indignant. When he analyzed feudal dictatorships in Eastern Europe, his anger was equally aroused. When he watched Mussolini's fascists terrorize their opponents, he denounced such practices as barbaric. But when he focused on events in communist Russia, Baldwin's political sympathies overshadowed his concerns regarding authoritarian practices.

In one sense he readily acknowledged this bias. He repeatedly denied standing as any kind of apologist for the Soviet state, but this was at least somewhat disingenuous. As for so many progressives of this generation and the one to follow, communist Russia occupied a unique place in his heart and mind. He had been delighted by the February 1917 takeover by Alexander Kerensky, which had resulted in the deposing of the czar. Baldwin had been still more elated by the Bolsheviks' triumph in October of that year and their call for "All power to the Soviets." Baldwin eagerly awaited all accounts of the revolution and had no sympathy for the old Russian nobility.[2]

At first, the American Left, which ranged from militant socialists to anarchists, seemed united in its support of the Bolshevik Revolution. "I had no doubt that this was the beginning of a world shaking change which no country could escape," Baldwin later wrote. "I saw in it the hopes of freedom for the masses, a new spirit of liberty, an end to tyranny and exploitation, and so a fresh new power for good in the world." Others initially shared the Left's enthusiasm for developments in Russia. A friend from Baldwin's St. Louis days, Charles Nagel—who had served as secretary of commerce and of labor under President William Howard Taft—informed Baldwin that "Lenin was the only real statesman to have come out of the war, and Russia the only country to have won anything from it." Baldwin tried to follow the civil war between the White Russians and the Bolsheviks that developed in the wake of the revolution. He was appalled by the intervention of Allied forces, including American soldiers, and rejoiced when the Red Russians prevailed.[3]

The appearance of the Soviet state had caused a splintering of left-of-center ranks in the United States and elsewhere. The U.S. Socialist Party fragmented; its more militant elements veered off to form first one, then a second, communist organization. Baldwin's sympathies lay with the militants, but as a member of no political party he remained out of the sectarian fray, or at least the direct line of fire. The crushing of the anarchist sailors' revolt in Kronstadt in March 1921 appalled and shocked him and lessened his opinion of Lenin and Trotsky. So did word of the Bolsheviks' repression of other left-wing opponents.[4]

Nevertheless, Baldwin agreed to serve on a committee formed to examine charges publicized by the social democratic *Jewish Daily Forward* in July and August 1922 that the Friends of Soviet Russia had mishandled relief funds. Established in 1921, the Friends of Soviet Russia sought to mitigate the devastating effects of a famine resulting from drought and an economic blockade. The group collected relief money, sent tractors to Russia, and built homes to house children. The *Forward*, edited by the stridently anticommunist Abraham Cahan, complained that relief moneys had been diverted for propaganda purposes. In August Baldwin, Robert Morss Lovett, Norman Thomas, Walter Nelles, and Timothy Healy of the Stationary Firemen's Union, gathered to examine the charges. In mid-October committee members issued a report fully exonerating the Friends of Soviet Russia, declaring that it had carried its work out with dedicated commitment to famine relief. Nelles declined to sign the report because he had a potential conflict of interest involving the appointment of his law partner as counsel for the Friends of Soviet Russia. The rest of Baldwin's committee, led by its chair, noted that "practically all" of its members opposed the ways of the Soviet government and "most of the Communist tactics" in the United States. They professed to have approached their task without prejudice, determined only to obtain the truth. The committee suggested that Friends of Soviet Russia bar its representatives from participating in political activities while serving with the organization. The charges brought against the Friends, Baldwin's committee concluded, resulted from divisions within the radical working-class movement.[5]

Cahan immediately attacked the committee's report, denouncing it as a whitewash and its members as suspect because they had been selected by the very organization they purported to investigate. Baldwin issued a statement saying it would be inappropriate to respond to Cahan. On behalf of the committee, however, he asserted that Cahan's broadside was determined "more by partisan feeling and political considerations than an interest in famine relief."[6]

Baldwin also readily responded to a request by some Wobbly friends and engineers that he join the board of the Kuzbas Autonomous Industrial Colony; the Kuzbas experiment was spearheaded by Americans who sought to demonstrate what a worker-led colony could achieve. The Kuzbas colony was to operate in the Urals under contractual agreement with the Russian government. It was to be free of government control, and the Soviet regime appeared ready to assist in any way the colony desired. Americans planned to send technical assistance in the form of labor and equipment, which eventually was to include a giant steel mill. Hundreds of Americans, enraptured by the promise of the new workers' paradise, prepared to depart for Russia. They raised $500,000 and shipped machinery and equipment across the Atlantic.[7]

Baldwin, like other sponsors, viewed the Kuzbas colony as a means to build socialism. Or, as he put it, to help construct "the promised land." In April 1923 he agreed to serve on an advisory committee created to support the Kuzbas colony. However, he also clearly expressed his unhappiness with the move toward greater Communist Party dominance that had occurred in regard to Kuzbas. Still, he believed it but temporary and expected the original autonomy to be reestablished. Kuzbas would help to make Russia productive, Baldwin hoped, but once that was accomplished, he wanted "to see democratic management and free contract replace State control."[8]

He was troubled by reports that about fifty Kuzbas colonists—each of whom had paid $300 for transportation, food, and tools—had returned to the United States embittered by their experiences. Many found the primitive standard of living troubling, as was the mismanagement seemingly characteristic of the colonial venture. Some said they had been so misled by the prospectus that they had expected considerably different conditions. Some former colonists made formal complaints to the New York City district attorney's office, and a New York County grand jury on April 17 handed up an indictment of the American fund-raisers, including Baldwin, for grand larceny that cited the misrepresentations in the prospectus. The indictment did not accuse the defendants of personally profiting from these misrepresentations. All those indicted had served on the American Organization Committee, which had attempted to locate workers, engineers, and equipment for the Kuzbas colony.[9]

The ACLU's executive committee dismissed Baldwin's indictment as preposterous and politically motivated. Involved with the prosecution from the outset were John Haas, a Justice Department official concerned about radicalism in the United States, and two detectives from the New York City Bomb Squad. The purpose of the charges, the ACLU executive committee asserted, was to discredit the Kuzbas colony and the ACLU. Already, the National Civic Federation, a progressive-era reform organization created to conduct a study of social and industrial problems, had applauded the indictment. The ACLU executive committee expressed complete faith in its director and unanimously declined to accept his offer to take a leave of absence until the case was resolved. John H. Gundlach, Baldwin's old friend from the Midwest, expressed complete confidence in him. There was "no man in the World I would rather trust," Gundlach exclaimed. No matter what Baldwin's political foes said about him, Gundlach continued, "there is one man in St. Louis that will never lose faith in your honesty."[10]

Responding to the charges, Baldwin characterized them "as ridiculous as they are extraordinary." Expecting to be completely vindicated, he insisted that his involvement with the Kuzbas committee amounted to only "a very trifling piece of public service." Somewhat disingenuously, he claimed that he served on the committee as any individual concerned about public service sat on a board of directors. In reality, of course, Baldwin had been placed on the committee because of his public notoriety and his well-known sympathies for the Soviet "experiment." Again, in less than believable fashion he proclaimed this service to involve "an entirely non-political work." He proceeded to deny that he was a communist or even a communist sympathizer: "I am opposed to the political practices and principles of the Soviet government."[11]

In a sworn deposition, filed in the Court of General Sessions in New York County, Baldwin refuted the charges of first- and second-degree larceny. But in a rather astonishing section of testimony Baldwin professed that he had agreed to serve on the committee "purely from a sociological point of view" and because he hoped the project would help the Russian people. While the latter was certainly true, the notion he was acting from a kind of academic vantage point defies credulity, to say the least.[12]

Arthur Garfield Hays received a $5,000 fee to defend Baldwin and the other nine members of the American Organization Committee board who had been indicted. Hays urged the court to compare the grand jury minutes and the testimony of returned Kuzbas colonists. On September 24 the judge ruled that he had found no deceit, only bad luck and poor management, and dismissed all but two charges; the latter related to two technical issues involving the American Organization Committee's treasurer. The Kuzbas colony continued, with many Americans remaining part of the enterprise. However, the Soviet government proceeded to take over operations, expropriating the investments from abroad.[13]

On December 26, 1923, Thomas Reese, the American representative on the Kuzbas's managing board, told Baldwin that the American Organization Committee had been disbanded. Baldwin responded by saying he thought that power in Kuzbas should be in the hands of one administrator. The colony had suffered from too many squabbles and too little planning. Baldwin, for his part, was characteristically leery of doling out responsibilities. "The most workable administrative systems the world over," he declared as if speaking about the ACLU, involved "one-man direction, checked by a committee, group or superior." Almost immediately thereafter, in a note to an American stationed in Siberia, he expressed concerns that political considerations had resulted in the government's takeover of the colony. This troubled Baldwin, who claimed he had "no political connections in the radical movement itself," for the autonomous nature of the colony had been most attractive of all. Nevertheless, he offered to assist the Kuzbas colony should the need arise and expressed the "warmest regards to you who are doing such devoted work for the reconstruction of Russian industry."[14]

Despite the disappointment and embarrassment caused by his involvement with the Kuzbas colony, Baldwin almost immediately joined the board of another project related to the communist experiment, the Russian Reconstruction Farms. This involved a fertile agricultural expanse in southern Russia, where workers were to apply American mechanical means instead of old peasant practices. Once again U.S. supporters raised a considerable sum of money to purchase the machinery by buying bonds guaranteed by the Soviet government. As it turned out, the Soviets ignored the guarantee, but the farms prospered. That they did, Baldwin believed, was due to the leadership of an American agronomist, Harold Ware, the son of Mother Ella Reeve Bloor, a leading communist in the United States. When Baldwin visited the farms in 1927, he likened the region to Kansas, with its multitude of wheat and machines.[15]

In an oral history he later completed for Columbia University, Baldwin acknowledged he had handled various sums of money, so-called Moscow gold, on behalf of the Kuzbas colony and the Russian Reconstruction Farms. One check, for $1 million, was drawn on a bank in Manhattan by the Soviet government, in consideration of the good public relations the colony and farms engendered. It was passed on to Baldwin and two other trustees of a fund established to purchase equipment. Had word of such a transaction gotten out, Baldwin acknowledged, it might have come back to haunt him.[16]

It also could have proved crippling, at the very least, to the still burgeoning civil liberties movement. Had it come to light, Baldwin would have had to resign from the ACLU and such a revelation might have set back the modern civil liberties movement for a long time. It also would have removed from the movement the man who most helped to spawn and sustain it.

Although ever hopeful that the Soviets were giving birth to a new social order, Baldwin continued to be disturbed by accounts of political repression. The wielding of a red fist against the Russian aristocracy failed to faze him. However, he was taken aback by the imprisonment and forced exile of revolutionaries. He was troubled by the reaction of his friends Emma Goldman and Alexander Berkman, both of whom had been deported to Russia in December 1919 during the postwar Red Scare. After the Kronstadt uprising was crushed, they had left Russia in late 1921, initially to live in Berlin. There Goldman was completing *My Disillusionment in Russia*, an embittered critique of the repression meted out by the Bolsheviks. Like Baldwin, Goldman remained a celebrant of the revolution, but she was enraged by the communist oppression and statism enveloping Russia.[17]

On February 12, 1923, Baldwin acknowledged in a letter to Goldman that he was feeling "less militant than I wish," for he was engaged in "such a respectable business!" Nevertheless, his work on behalf of the ACLU did appear "for the time important, though it is aside from the main current."

Revolution seemed even less likely in the United States than it had a decade earlier, because "Russia has so disillusioned hopes." That November Baldwin announced that he was appreciative of Bertrand Russell's critical book on Russia "and all that it stands for in human conflict." He expressed the need "to get away from American conditions" to appreciate the small role "for any of us to play." In the United States "we are so elementary, fighting on such stodgy lines, the heavy old fight for a hearing—and with no response to any revolutionary fire there may yet be burning in us."[18]

In March 1924 Goldman, writing to Baldwin, condemned "the lying face of Bolshevism" and denounced Lenin as "the modern inquisitor." She asked whether Baldwin agreed that "the silence of the American liberals in the face of such horror [is] the most damnable thing." She found inexplicable those individuals who demanded amnesty for political prisoners but remained mute when " 'their own pet government' is guilty of such heinous crimes." Any publicity Baldwin could generate regarding "the unfortunate victims of Leninism," she said, would be welcomed by whose who were concerned about liberty.[19]

In response Baldwin revealed that he and others were working to bring the issue of Russian political prisoners before the Soviet regime. The Americans were determined to address the matter directly with the government. Wielding the tactic for which Baldwin had long been known, they hoped "to use the threat of publicity as a means to getting action," he said. This reflected an amazingly unsophisticated reading of communist Russia, particularly for one as worldly as Baldwin. But at this point he, like many other Western intellectuals, seemed to view the Soviet leaders as superprogressives of a sort.[20]

Shortly thereafter Baldwin affirmed more clearly his disagreement and that of others with Goldman's reading of Soviet Russia. He told her he had spoken with a number of individuals who also condemned "the Bolshevik dictatorship" but who believed another indictment of the government to be unwarranted. Then, he clearly stated, "I would not be interested in it myself. I am through with indicting evil in the world merely for the sake of satisfying myself that I have spoken out."[21]

In typical fashion Goldman, who considered Baldwin's approach very naive, responded by both criticizing and flattering him. In a June 3 letter she insisted that "so many lives could have been saved, so many truly worth while [sic] people rescued from despair and suicide if most of the radicals had not been so completely under the hypnotic influence of Moscow." Goldman deemed that influence, to which she herself had once fallen prey, to be unavoidable. However, she decried as a religiously spun myth the notion "that Bolshevism, Leninism and the Russian Revolution are identical." As for Baldwin, she knew that he "would take up the cause of the persecuted, and prosecuted politicals of Russia. . . . In fact I know no one else among the radicals of A. [America] in whom I have so much faith as I do in you." Still she wondered "how long it will take you to realize the whole enormity of the crimes against the spirit of man going on in Russia." Leninist terrors, which involved inquisitional torture of noncommunist radicals as well as "continued murder" of nonpolitical figures, surpassed those of the czar, Goldman insisted.[22]

In a November 6 letter Goldman condemned "the myth foisted upon the world by Moscow." She then dismissed Baldwin's claim that no evidentiary material existed to condemn the Soviets. "You are putting yourself in the position of the average Catholic, to whom no amount of data and historic facts as regards the crimes committed by the Catholic Church will be convincing." She continued, "Now, listen, dear boy: We sent you a list of a thousand names of Soviet victims in prisons, concentration camps and exile. This list is only a very small part of the many thousands who have been incarcerated, starved, tortured, or even shot."[23]

Neither Tolstoy's nor Kropotkin's veracity had been questioned when they challenged czarist practices, she aptly noted. Yet the czar, unlike the Bolsheviks, had allowed political prisoners to receive correspondence and visitors. Now, however, the ACLU viewed with suspicion materials regarding repression in Soviet Russia sent by lifelong revolutionaries. She then declared that Baldwin would have to free himself from believing that communist Russia was "a workers' experiment." She concluded by insisting that the Soviet government had "a most deteriorating and disintegrating effect both on revolutionary thinking and organization. In fact, it has poisoned the whole Social and revolutionary movement."[24]

While "not by nature timid," Baldwin subsequently reflected, "I am cautious when it comes to making statements of fact which I cannot back up." Furthermore, he considered events in the Soviet Union far more complex and important "from a revolutionary standpoint than you." When a national economy was reconstructed, vast practical difficulties resulted that revolutionary ideas alone could not resolve.[25]

Two points were clear to him. Persecuting foes of the communist regime was unnecessary and injurious to "revolutionary progress." Repression victimized the very people such a society needed and foisted "the temper of tyranny on the ruling class." Centralizing power prevented "spontaneous experimental growths toward communal production and distribution" that could produce the economic stability essential for personal freedoms.[26]

Baldwin's reading of conditions in Russia was shaped by his determination not "to feed the reactionaries with material" while presenting incontestable facts before the government. The Soviet regime, he continued to believe, was "a dictatorship in the interests of workers and the peasants." Goldman viewed Baldwin's analysis as wrongheaded. "You well know," she asserted, "that you and others of the same persuasion would be the first to swing, or rather, to be shot, since that is their favourite method of punishment. I assure you that people have been shot in Russia for much less than you have said." The terror was "inherent in the Dictatorship," while Soviet supporters must subscribe to the "Divine Right of the Bolsheviki," she said. The Soviet dictatorship was like any other, serving "a privileged class which happens in Russia to be the Communists and others who are working for the Communist Party."[27]

Increasingly, Baldwin was devoting time and energy to the International Committee for Political Prisoners (ICPP), which had emerged as a response, however belated, to the deportation of radicals spurred by the Palmer Raids of 1919 and 1920. He had formed the committee in New York, relying on "a little group of friends and colleagues." The U.S. government had shipped many anarchists, communists, and Wobblies to Bolshevik Russia, others to Scandinavia or France, even if that entailed the separation of spouses. Because of his involvement with the NCLB earlier and the ACLU at present, Baldwin was seen as someone who might be able to help. After all, the ACLU had attempted to assist many of these individuals before they had been exiled. Baldwin then had joined a number of ACLU backers to create the ICPP in early 1920. Among those who participated in this new campaign were Jane Addams, Clarence Darrow, Eugene V. Debs, Felix Frankfurter, and Norman Thomas. Acting as chairman, Baldwin poured a great amount of energy into his latest crusade, which involved writing letters to government officials and publishing a news bulletin and reports.[28]

Speaking before the Foreign Policy Association on January 17, 1925, Baldwin delivered an address on political prisoners in Russia. Drawing on personal experience, Baldwin said at the outset that his subject was "the hottest political potato in the world." One was either denounced as a Bolshevik or a counterrevolutionary. The communists adopted the latter tack, believing that "either you are 100% with them or 100% against them." Those who championed free expression were considered courageously naive or altogether hostile to the Soviet state. Terming himself in sympathy with Russia's economic reconstruction, Baldwin insisted that political prosecutions worked against that nation's best interests. Such repression prevented necessary criticisms of bureaucratic centralization and calls for greater power by workers and peasants. Unfortunately, officials had stifled or quashed the spontaneous appearance of trade unions. This made no sense to Baldwin, who viewed the Soviet government as Europe's strongest. Thus political persecution appeared "so unnecessary and so vindictive," however "natural enough," given the Soviet government's behavior. But more had been expected "from a working-class government."[29]

Reports regarding political repression in Russia, Baldwin told the Foreign Policy Association, were shrouded in partisan analyses. Nevertheless, he acknowledged that those concerned about the issue had failed to heed warnings made by "our socialist and anarchist friends" regarding the plight of their comrades. They had refused to come to their assistance until presented with incontrovertible facts. That had occurred after a visit to Russia the previous summer by ACLU chairman Harry F. Ward. Ward's account, which relied on official government records and reports of imprisoned radicals, supposedly had been verified by other observers. Indeed, the Russian government itself had acknowledged that it held about fifteen hundred political prisoners. That number would be greatly magnified if one counted the thousands exiled for political offenses. It remained difficult to verify how many individuals had been imprisoned in the Soviet Union for what Americans would regard as political offenses. But the creation of an atmosphere in which "freedom of opinion is impossible" was most significant. There existed in Russia, all parties agreed, "no political freedom as we understand it here," Baldwin said. The only freedom to be found was within the ranks of the ruling party, but even there, he acknowledged, dissenting views were suppressed once a decision had been made. Trotsky's writings were off-limits, no opposition press existed, and no opposition party was allowed. Furthermore, censors dissected every written document before publication.[30]

He was uncertain, Baldwin acknowledged, whether Russian prisoners in general suffered a fate worse than that experienced by others elsewhere. A fair test, in Harry Ward's estimation, would be to compare the treatment of political prisoners in Russia and communist prisoners of capitalist states.

Political control was more fully advanced in Russia, Baldwin acknowledged, than in any other dictatorship. Because that control was so absolute, the need for force and prosecution appeared to be less than in Hungary, Italy, or Spain. He incorrectly believed that stabilizing the Russian economy and lessening the threats from outside would bring about a relaxation of "the severity of the control" in Russia.[31]

Now Baldwin determined to write an introduction for a volume entitled *Letters from Russian Prisons*, edited by Alexander Berkman and published by Albert and Charles Boni, magazine and book publishers, in 1925. As its lengthy subtitle indicated, included in this book were "reprints of documents by political prisoners in Soviet prisons, prison camps and exile, and reprints of affidavits concerning political persecution in Soviet Russia." Isaac Don Levine, a journalist for the Hearst newspaper chain, had gathered the Russian material. The volume also contained letters from a series of "celebrated intellectuals" from Europe and the United States, including Albert Einstein, the Norwegian novelist Knut Hamsun, Sinclair Lewis, Thomas Mann, Romain Rolland, and Bertrand Russell, all present or future Nobel Prize winners.[32]

"Russia presents the unique spectacle of a revolutionary government based on working-class and peasant power imprisoning and exiling its political opponents in other revolutionary parties," read the first sentence of Baldwin's introductory essay. Former comrades, once exiled and imprisoned side by side, now were bitterly divided. The ruling Bolsheviks were meting out the same fate to those who had also suffered the wrath of czarist officials before the revolution. *Liberty Under the Soviets*, Baldwin explained, sought to depict the treatment of revolutionary political prisoners—including socialists, social democrats, syndicalists, anarchists, and Tolstoyan pacifists—in the workers' state. It did not explore what happened to those who had engaged in violence against the state, including "counter-revolutionary military" action. Against such forces, Baldwin asserted, the Soviet state "naturally proceeded," as did any government encountering attempts to overthrow it. Although the ICPP professed to stand for freedom of opinion for all groups, *Liberty Under the Soviets* also excluded from discussion nonradicals who had been incarcerated or banished from their homeland.[33]

Thus Baldwin's work contained a highly selective interpretation of political repression, with some cases clearly viewed less favorably than others. Baldwin's approach in this instance—and in many others regarding the Soviet Union, for two full decades, in fact—was at odds with his expansive view of civil liberties on the home front. For his own nation he insisted on the need for political liberties to be afforded all, including the despised and the weak. For communist Russia he was far more willing to accept infringements on the rights of those condemned as foes of the revolutionary state.

The Bolsheviks argued that the treatment of political opponents was a small matter, considering the tremendous problems confronting the Soviet nation. They also contended they were still in a transitional period, when hostile forces naturally were treated harshly. Furthermore, they considered the treatment accorded political antagonists a good deal less severe than in reactionary Italy, Spain, Poland, Hungary, Germany—under both socialist and nonsocialist governments—and in California, which also saw antiradical and anti-union activities. However, Baldwin insisted that a higher standard was demanded "of a new State devoted to the revolutionary conceptions of 'the cooperative commonwealth,' producers' control and the abolition of classes." Those who saw themselves as friends of the Soviet state considered a retention of czarist practices unnecessary. Additionally, changes in Russia could continue for a half-century and might be relied on to justify political tyranny—although "the Soviet Government appears to be the most secure one in Europe," Baldwin wrote.[34]

Baldwin and other ICPP members sought to avoid the animus coloring other accounts of political repression in Russia. The committee approached the subject in a nonpartisan manner, Baldwin claimed, but believed that the presence of political prisoners impeded progress by quashing "ideas and forces necessary to growth." At the same time he acknowledged that many committee members considered the Russian Revolution "the greatest and most daring experiment yet undertaken to recreate society in the interests of the producers and in terms of human values, however faulty its course may have been and however discouraging its many compromises. Many of them look upon Russia today as a great laboratory of social experiment of incalculable value to the development of the world." Thus they were concerned that the first workers' state not replicate the ways of reactionary regimes. Partisan communists, the committee recognized, undoubtedly would dismiss this collection as "a counter-revolutionary attack." Others would turn to it to vilify the Soviet state. Yet even sympathy for the revolutionary endeavor could not overcome the need to condemn the repression experienced by political prisoners, or at least certain ones.[35]

Baldwin soon wrote a letter to the editor of the *New Leader*, a social democratic publication, reiterating his belief, and that of many ICPP members, that the Russian Revolution was "the most significant event of this generation." He further proclaimed "the Soviet experiment [as] . . . the heart of the struggle toward a world run by the producers." Baldwin then exclaimed,

> I prefer its dictatorship with all its suppression, to any capitalist dictatorship. On all its advancing fronts it is to be commended and supported. Only in its retention of the evil practices of Tsardom is it to be criticized, not only in the interest of the radical minorities persecuted for opinions but also for the working out of an experiment depending for its very success on constant criticism and change.[36]

His attempts to reconcile support for the Soviet experiment with his belief in political liberty proved difficult for Baldwin, as they did for so many other American liberals and radicals. Indeed, this remained a dilemma for more than twenty years after the Russian Revolution. In many ways the attitudes concerning the Soviet state displayed by those on the left side of the political spectrum helped to shape American liberalism and radicalism for the better part of the twentieth century. Like many others, Baldwin was drawn to the "cause" of Soviet Russia, believing that a workers' state was aborning. He saw the possibility that greater economic equity would unfold there, which he considered necessary for a better world to emerge. Ever the upper-class Bostonian, he had nevertheless come to identify with the masses, albeit at a distance and generally from the perspective of his comfortable existence in Greenwich Village or ACLU headquarters in Manhattan. Thus he considered a number of Wobbly leaders friends, retained acquaintanceships with those high up in the Workers Party, and viewed the communist nation as a model of a kind, albeit for another land. All the while he stood as the foremost civil libertarian in the United States and now was attempting to champion human rights in the international arena as well. At the same time he drew distinctions between developments in communist Russia and those taking place in countries where conservative or right-wing forces held the upper hand. A stark kind of double standard emerged, in which his evaluation of machinations in various countries was guided, to a considerable degree, by political sympathies or hostilities. This led others to damn Baldwin and those of like mind as hypocrites or something worse altogether.

CHAPTER FOURTEEN

A European Sabbatical

During the mid-twenties Baldwin experienced a series of personal crises, similar to one that had befallen him a few years earlier. He determined to camp out in the summer of 1926 in a tent by the shore of the Hackensack River and attempt to write. However, as he later acknowledged, "I never was a writer." The location of his camp was now along the upper Hackensack, the water company having run him off. Madeleine Doty was one of those who came to visit him at his "portable camp." Baldwin believed that he was experiencing a "period of renunciation. You renounce the world, the flesh and the devil. I wanted to renounce city life, making money. I was in a Tolstoyan mood."[1]

At Doty's urging, Baldwin—who recognized he was undergoing "a time of confusion in my values"—agreed to see a psychiatrist in Manhattan. The physician had treated the daughter of a good friend, and Baldwin knew him on a first-name basis. The psychiatrist asked Baldwin to record his dreams on a note pad kept close to his bed. After reading through about fifteen pads' worth of dreams, the psychiatrist suggested that Baldwin was trying to placate his father or other authority figures of a paternal sort. Baldwin should "leave his wife and go into a new line of work," the doctor concluded.[2]

Baldwin's angst resulted in his temporary departure from the ACLU and heightened involvement with the ICPP in 1926. The fatal drug overdose the previous year of his friend Freddy Farnum must have been deeply disturbing. Baldwin and Doty attended the funeral services for the tormented man they considered almost as a family member. Freddy was a restless, adventurous sort who nevertheless had been a devoted and cheerful friend. Meanwhile, Baldwin and Doty's marriage, long a tenuous affair, became more troubled still. The marriage was over, he now informed her, but neither acted to finalize matters. Instead, they remained intimate in their on-again, off-again manner, continuing to be involved with each other's lives as they lived a continent apart or were together during his trips abroad.[3]

With Doty in Geneva working as secretary of the Women's International League for Peace and Freedom, Baldwin felt adrift, perhaps for the first time during his adulthood. Writing to her in November 1925, he blurted out, "You are all over the place, and I'm glad that you are." He then brought up a matter that had evidently caused hurt feelings in the past. He wanted her to agree to let lapse his $10,000 life insurance policy, which was costing about 10 percent of his salary. He intended to take the amount due on the policy and invest it. That would raise his total assets to about $11,500. In closing he revealed that he had experienced "a few depressions, rather unusual for me, in which life really didn't seem worth living." He attributed this to living alone, to attempting to devise "a new life of effort," and perhaps to his love for her.[4]

As he confirmed in his note to Doty, he was even dissatisfied with his work at the ACLU, around which his life had largely revolved for the past several years. Lucille Milner found him "so tired out" and said years later that he was troubled by a heart condition at this time. Uncertain whether he wanted to remain in an administrative position, he briefly considered returning to teaching or working for the labor movement. In late 1926 he decided to take a leave of absence from the ACLU and was replaced by Forrest Bailey as interim director. All the while Baldwin attempted to remain apprised of ACLU operations, and he came to view the actions of his replacement and other colleagues with a jaundiced eye. Bailey, he soon informed Harry Ward, was becoming more knowledgeable about the issues the ACLU grappled with. However, "he lacks that capacity for indignation which puts drive into the work." Morris Ernst might help Bailey out. But Ernst, Baldwin argued, "finds his [Bailey's] mind too slow and his sensitiveness an obstacle to plain speaking." Ward might wish to keep Ernst "in line" to smooth over Ernst's relationship with the new director. Then Baldwin said that Milner, his longtime secretary, was upset by Bailey's "lack of drive." This feeling on her part, Baldwin noted, was "largely temperamental . . . and she often errs on the side of being too impetuous." Talking to Milner on occasion about her work, Baldwin advised Ward, would mollify her.[5]

He acknowledged he was extremely critical of any work that "I don't boss myself." He was disturbed by what he perceived to be laxity in Bailey's directorship. Moreover, if matters failed to improve, Baldwin warned Ward, he would find it difficult to return as ACLU director. All this troubled him so greatly that he was finding it difficult to concentrate on "the special task I have set myself to." Consequently, if conditions in the national office worsened, another replacement might be in order. Baldwin urged Ward to call on Norman Thomas to help "size up the larger outlines of the job."[6]

Throughout 1926 this normally driven soul continued to founder. For a period Baldwin stayed at the country residence of Morris Ernst before traveling to Carmel, California, to spend three months with Mary Buckley, his elderly good friend from St. Louis. In midsummer 1926 after some time in San Francisco, he undertook an excursion through the Montana woods and mountains. Baldwin also expressed a readiness to visit Brownie, to whom he had remained close over the last several years. "I'd go most anywhere to see Brownie when he's in distress of soul, as he seems to be."[7]

On Christmas Eve 1926 Baldwin sailed for Europe with a series of projects in mind. His work on behalf of the Indian League had resulted in his being named to the American delegation to the inaugural World Congress Against Imperialism in Brussels. He had been handed a press card from the Federated Press, the left-wing labor news service. He held another card from the Quakers, similarly intended to provide Baldwin with entrée to political prisoners on the Continent. He had also contracted with Vanguard Press to produce a monograph for its Russian series; he would examine liberty inside the Soviet state.[8]

Immediately after he arrived in Paris Baldwin went to the ICPP office at 11 Rue Scribe, which served as his headquarters during 1927. He spent a week with Doty in both Paris and the French countryside. He then stayed for a while in Geneva, as Doty had found comfortable quarters for him at the Maison Internationale, where she and her father lived.[9]

Baldwin left for Brussels on February 10; he intended to write an article about the conference for the *Nation*. He was inspired by the sight of black, brown, and yellow people linking up with European workers in an anti-imperialist movement. This was "the greatest collection of subversives ever to get together," he later asserted. Baldwin conversed with the Oxford-educated Nehru; Georg Ledebour of the German Socialist Party; the German communist Willi Münzenberg, a member of the Third International Executive Committee; the French author Henri Barbusse; the Hungarian communist Louis Gibarti; and Edo Fimmen, Dutch secretary of the International Seamen's Union. Present too was Luis Muñoz Marín, then a socialist and advocate of independence for Puerto Rico, whom Baldwin had met on committees condemning the U.S. occupation of Haiti and Nicaragua. The three American representatives included two communists and Baldwin.[10]

After the conference Baldwin returned to Paris and awaited the return of Doty from Geneva; she and her father were to accompany him to England. There they planned to stay with her friends Malini and Frederick Pethick-Lawrence. Frederick Pethick-Lawrence, a member of Parliament, pressured the Home Office, which finally agreed to issue a conditional visa that would enable Baldwin to visit England for two weeks; the difficulty in obtaining the visa stemmed from his left-wing political activism. Baldwin was to "play the game," his friends informed him; the Home Office had made Frederick Pethick-Lawrence personally liable for Baldwin's behavior.[11]

London appeared "smoky, dirty, slow, with the atmosphere of a big village, smug, reserved," Baldwin wrote his mother. Other than a group of young left-wingers, those involved in the radical and labor movements seemed "equally stodgy and uninspired." Ellen Wilkinson, a member of Parliament, hosted a lively party on his arrival. Guests included George Lansbury, who often was referred to as "Britain's No. 1 pacifist"; James Maxton of the Independent Labour Party; and a couple of dozen "assorted agitators."[12]

Having adhered to his pledge to refrain from involvement in controversial matters, Baldwin reported, "The Empire still stands." The Home Office refused to extend his stay and denied him permission to travel on to Ireland. "It is all very silly," Baldwin noted, "but they are scared to death of reds, and I am down as a dangerous agent of revolution." So he was off to Amsterdam with his brother Herb after a send-off by Doty, Malini Pethick-Lawrence, and Norman Ewer of the *Daily Herald*. Doty returned to Switzerland.[13]

In Amsterdam the police tailed Baldwin and his antimilitarist compatriots. At the end of March he and Herb went to Cologne to meet Craney Gratz, who had come over from Paris to pick them up. Gratz was the son of a wealthy ACLU supporter who placed an automobile at Baldwin's disposal. Roger and Herb stayed at a hotel for only $1.50 a day, but Baldwin decided to move in with a family of communists.[14]

The trio then drove through small towns and the German countryside to get to Czechoslovakia. Czechoslovakia did not impress Baldwin, despite what he termed "its republican pretenses." He became enamored with Austria, which struck him "as the freest country in Europe—perhaps excepting Scandinavia." The socialist movement, dominant in Vienna, was "aggressive and constructive" and considerably more militant "than the so-called Socialist movements" across much of the Continent.[15]

The atmosphere in Hungary reminded him of the United States during the war, albeit without the hysteria. He saw no evidence of political repression because the entire nation "has been subdued." Here, where communism had once briefly reigned, the ideology had been thoroughly obliterated. Similarly, socialism was cautious, whereas peasant organizations were illegal.[16]

In late May Baldwin and his fellow travelers traveled third class by train to Italy. His stay in Italy convinced him that Mussolini had been unable to remake the country. The dictator was "a lot of bluff and policemen," Baldwin claimed, and possessed little popular support. Mussolini hardly lacked for soldiers and Blackshirts, "who swarm everywhere." Discontent appeared rampant, but the people seemed more "fearful of being heard" than in any other dictatorship he had yet encountered. Surprisingly enough, Baldwin could speak with anyone he chose to—and did, from the minister of justice to communists—without apparent interference or surveillance.[17]

In Bulgaria he saw both the prime minister and imprisoned communists. "It's a tough place for radicals," he reported, "most of them have been murdered." In Romania Baldwin, Gratz, and Herb were guests of the American ambassador, and a young aristocrat stationed in the foreign press office showed them the sights. Here too they saw the prime minister and the head of the all-powerful secret service, as well as persecuted Jews and communists.[18]

In June Baldwin and Craney Gratz passed into Constantinople, where Fritz Schubert, a young Austrian Quaker, attorney, and libertarian, joined them. Baldwin believed that Turkey was yet "another one-man dictatorship" engaged in "such commendable ends as modernizing the country and destroying the political power of the church." The three men eventually reached Tiflis, in the Georgian Republic of the Union of Soviet Socialist Republics. There Baldwin was shepherded around by Ivan J. Kulik, an editor of the Communist daily, while Gratz and Schubert played the part of tourists. The guide took Baldwin to a local Soviet then in session, where the elegant well-fed individuals dressed in silk shirts impressed him. These were "big shots—revolutionary big shots," and Baldwin's guide warned that questions about political prisoners would get them nowhere. But in the middle of their last dinner in Tiflis, the guide, Baldwin reported, "told me that I would not be told the truth by any official, nor would I read the truth anywhere. He said nothing I had seen really mattered because the real control was the OGPU," the Soviet intelligence agency. The warnings appeared to have no effect on Baldwin, who viewed developments in communist Russia through rose-colored lenses.[19]

In mid-July the three friends reached Moscow. Initially, Baldwin stayed at the Hotel Metropole and acted as a tourist himself. Gratz and Schubert left for Leningrad en route to Berlin. The widow of the sainted anarchocommunist prince Peter Kropotkin had left for her dacha and turned over her apartment at the Kropotkin Museum for Baldwin's stay in Moscow. It featured a large comfortable room with a kitchen, dressing area, and toilet. Baldwin cooked his meals, cleaned up, and went to the local market. He spent his days hosting visitors, setting up appointments, writing, or deciphering documents with the assistance of a translator. The pace of life in Moscow seemed "hard and slow" because of the summer season and heavy-handed bureaucracy. Baldwin likened the Bolsheviks to "high-brow social engineers, with the outlook and technique of social workers, plus a revolutionary base in the dominance of the working class."[20]

The atmosphere at the time, Baldwin later insisted, was freer in Soviet Russia than it would become. In Georgia pictures of both Trotsky and Lenin appeared everywhere. Anarchists seemed to be viewed as harmless. American visitors were abundant and shared Baldwin's general impressions regarding an absence of overt terror. A U.S. labor delegation, led by a socialist, Jim Maurer of the American Federation of Labor, saw signs of "progress and hope." The technocratic intellectual Stuart Chase dismissed talk of repression as "incidental to the vast achievements." Journalist friends—considered by Baldwin as "most helpful and intelligent and fair"—like the *New York Times*'s Walter Duranty and the United Press's Victor Knauth, seemed little troubled by evidence of repression. The *Nation*'s Louis Fischer stridently defended "the great experiment," refusing to tolerate any criticism of the Soviet state. Such reporters would be perceived by others as no better than apologists for communist tyranny.[21]

More remarkably, while he was in Moscow Baldwin met several American critics of communist Russia. These included academicians like Bruce Hopper and Geroid Robinson, later of Harvard and Columbia, respectively. Less reserved in his judgments was the independent radical V. F. Calverton, editor of his own publication, the *Modern Quarterly*. Calverton had come over to the new promised land with high hopes but appeared to be despondent and disgusted by what he encountered. Calverton poignantly asked Baldwin, "Is it for this we had so much faith?" Surprisingly, perhaps, a less critical figure also in the Soviet Union during this same period was Abraham Cahan of the *Jewish Daily Forward*. It seemed astonishing that Cahan had even been granted a visa, given his outspoken condemnation of dictatorships.[22]

Clearly, Baldwin was impressed by what he had seen so far. "I marvel at their optimism and fighting qualities in the face of such obstacles as they have to face." Moreover, the Bolsheviks were few in number and obviously entirely of like mind themselves. Still, everything in this new communist state appeared "orderly; far too orderly, for it is completely controlled. There is fear and repression outside the city working class, which is really free, in the saddle bossing the whole show, but with rather canny understanding of how far they can go," Baldwin wrote to his mother that July.[23]

Madame Katherine Pechkova, former wife of the great Russian writer Maxim Gorky, now headed Russian Red Cross relief for political prisoners. She enabled Baldwin to travel to sites where political prisoners were held. The notorious Lubianka Prison, which held those deemed the greatest offenders against the communist regime, was off-limits. So was the Soviet political police force.[24]

Preparing to leave Moscow in mid-August, Baldwin told his mother,

> I am not a bit sorry to leave Russia. It is an irritating place for one who does not know the language, and it is irritating per se. . . . I admire the heroism of the Communists in tackling such a job, but not being of them, I don't get the sense of enthusiasm that marks my Communist friends from abroad here. Yet I am relieved not to see a privileged class around, and I rejoice in what the revolution did to destroy such terrible inequities. Everybody is poor together. There is much discontent, much regulation of life, but not much terrorism or repression except of the old upper classes. They live in fear, of losing jobs, of exile, some even of death. But they are few among the workers and peasants.[25]

Baldwin's easy dismissal of the plight of the former aristocracy was cavalier at best. It also portended the kind of theoretical slippery slope that papered over or even justified repression meted out to a succession of so-called enemies of the communist government. Coming from the ACLU founder, who continually relied on his prominence as a member of the American upper crust, such a statement was troubling, revealing, and blatantly hypocritical.

Back in Paris in late September, Baldwin reported on his Soviet excursions for the International Committee for Political Prisoners. "There is certainly more liberty of essential sorts for more of the Russian people to-day [sic] than ever before in their history," Baldwin exclaimed, "and more of some sorts than elsewhere in the world." He was pleased at the supposed existence of cultural liberties for racial and national minorities, trade union freedoms, and the immeasurably greater liberties apparently afforded religious worshipers, women, and the peasants.[26]

However, the secret police, with a force of 150,000, conducted a rigid surveillance of all those who opposed the government. "It is the agent of terrorism," Baldwin declared, as it operated in cities, alongside railroads, and at the border. It was impossible to ascertain how many individuals it had detained or forced out of their homeland. Only the OGPU knew and its agents refused to say. This produced an atmosphere of fear and enveloped the activities of the secret police with a sense of mystery. Public trials were carried out for propaganda purposes only. Seeming paranoia regarding "counter-revolutionary plots," Baldwin wrote, "rests on about the same basis as fear of Bolshevik plots abroad." Several thousand individuals had been sent to six special colonies run by the secret police or to isolated villages in Siberia or Turkestan, or had been prohibited from living in six of the Soviet Union's largest cities.[27]

All in all, Baldwin was convinced, exiles and political prisoners were treated somewhat better by the Bolsheviks than under czarist rule. Admittedly, "the system is almost the same." The major difference involved the absence of forced labor and the shorter periods of exile. Also, the treatment of socialists and anarchists was not as severe as that afforded the old bourgeoisie. Non-Soviet revolutionaries were held in separate locations and acknowledged to be political prisoners, whereas the Soviets characterized the bourgeoisie as counterrevolutionaries, a far more damning label.[28]

Baldwin closed his report by asking his fellow committee members to keep things in perspective. "This is the darkest side of the Soviet regime," he wrote. "It is the result of a frankly class dictatorship beset by enormous difficulties, and born of a tradition of government that even a revolution cannot easily change."[29]

Once again Baldwin appeared more than willing to give the Soviet government the benefit of the doubt. That led him to misread the nature of Stalinism and to underestimate greatly the horrors it wreaked. Although it can be argued that the worst Stalinist terrors lay ahead, earlier practices of the communist state provided little ground for optimism. Nevertheless, such a hopeful, even utopian reading of the possibilities suggested by the Soviet experiment led Baldwin, like other Western leftists, to resort to double standards or outright apologies concerning the repression that characterized Stalinism. In Baldwin's case this arguably proved more disturbing still because of his identification with the American civil liberties movement and international human rights.

Baldwin continued to declare, "I regard the soviet experiment as the most significant and hopeful force in the world today." Yet demonstrating the ideological inconsistency to which he was so often inclined, he professed continued admiration for Kropotkin's anarchocommunism and remained good friends with Emma Goldman. While Baldwin was still in Paris working on his book, Vanguard Press published Kropotkin's *Revolutionary Pamphlets*, for which Baldwin had served as editor, written an introduction and biographical sketch, and compiled a bibliography and a collection of notes. In the introduction he demonstrated his appreciation for Kropotkin's "no-government system of socialism." The dictatorial control held by the Soviet Communist Party, Baldwin wrote, was the embodiment of all the Russian prince had so valiantly fought against.[30]

Plugging away at his manuscript for *Liberty Under the Soviets*, Baldwin found the task more daunting than he had anticipated. Thus he was delighted with the assistance provided by two Americans who were in Europe before attending college in Denmark; he also worked with Alexander Berkman—Emma Goldman's companion—who had been forced out of the United States, along with Baldwin's old friend and other immigrant radicals, during the Palmer Raids. Berkman—who "was gentleman enough to hide his view of me as naive," Baldwin said—translated documents Baldwin had compiled during his stay in the Soviet Union. The American students were Brownie, whom Baldwin had known since the young man's childhood in St. Louis, and a school friend of his. Fortunately, both were fine stenographers. They worked with Baldwin in a homey three-bedroom apartment in a working-class district close to Paris's southern gate.[31]

On October 18 Baldwin wrote to Doty and acknowledged that his book "will be more Bolshevik than my previous utterances, not because I was wrong before, but because the perspective is a bit different when you see the other sides of the conflicting life that is Russia today." He had reread *Letters from Russian Prisons* and viewed it as "only one side of the truth, and only one aspect of oppression in a regime marked by many developing liberties."[32]

In early December, as Baldwin prepared to leave for the States, he received a brief note from an R. Abramowitsch, a scholarly critic of Soviet policies, in Berlin. "You appear to hold the view," Abramowitsch wrote, "that in general the condition of political prisoners and exiles has improved. That is an error. The contrary is true." The regime had waged "systematic and ruthless" persecution of socialists.[33]

Abramowitsch's reading of Baldwin was insightful. Since the October Revolution Baldwin had viewed communist rule sympathetically. Although troubled by the most egregious examples of political repression he had witnessed or heard talk of, particularly those involving the Georgian Republic, Baldwin managed to convince himself that the "socialist experiment" was most important of all. In this manner his responses to events in Soviet Russia duplicated those of many other political activists in the West, including a sizable number of his countrymen, who looked on developments in the communist state with hopeful, even millennial, expectations.

In mid-December Baldwin reached New York, planning to divide his time equally between the ACLU and his international work and writing. He was determined to avoid getting ensnared in office work once again, so that he might concentrate on policy making and strategy. Just a short time before, he had declared, "I am through with the nerve wearing drive of a desk from 9 to 6."[34]

Soon after his return to the States Baldwin delivered a speech in Manhattan in which he announced he had ventured to communist Russia "as a libertarian looking for liberty." Admittedly, he had found neither political freedoms nor civil liberties. However, they never had existed in Russia, Baldwin declared. Then, in an astonishing statement for the leading American civil libertarian, he asserted, "People don't miss much what they haven't lost." The Russian people had gained economic liberty, and the workers were "top dog in Russia."[35]

Baldwin posed the obvious question: how could he, a champion of freedom of speech in his own country, view the Soviet Union so sympathetically? His mode of operations in the United States, he realized, would undoubtedly result in exile in Russia. No matter,

I regard the economic experiment of such fundamental importance, I regard economic liberty as basic to all others—that I have faith in the working out of the experiment to a condition of unrestricted liberty. That cannot exist in the midst of class conflicts. Class conflicts still exist in Russia and between Russia and the world. So long as that danger remains, repression will mark the Soviet regime.[36]

This was the kind of analysis on which many Western observers would rely during the first two decades of the communist regime's existence. It served as an apology for Soviet violations of human rights, which had briefly waned but were soon to intensify once again. While adversaries of the Soviet state certainly lurked without and within, Stalin and his henchmen used the presence of enemies, which was often greatly exaggerated, to tighten their stranglehold on Russian life.

On returning to the United States Baldwin wrote a lengthy account of his "sabbatical year of study among the down-trodden and uplifters of Europe." He affirmed his identification "with the struggle of the producers in which civil liberty is a weapon of conflict." He continued, "I do not believe in civil liberty as an abstract principle. I believe in it as I believe in non-violence as the best weapon in the struggle to create a world of freedom. But I am primarily for the growth of power of the exploited classes on whom the hope of any real democracy rests, and I am with that struggle even when the weapons they use are not what seem to me the best."[37]

Clearly, he had no problem with relying on different criteria—what others plainly saw as a double standard—to view different states. Some found it difficult to understand why he did not examine all dictatorial regimes in the same light. But for Baldwin and his compatriots, who held such high hopes for the communist state, analyzing dictatorships through ideologically tinted prisms proved all too easy.

This was perhaps most striking in Baldwin's case, for he was the ACLU founder and the man who, more than any other, spawned the modern civil liberties movement. To acknowledge that he did not believe in civil liberties as "an abstract principle," and to proclaim his allegiance to the class struggle, was both startling and politically foolish, to say the least. It is surprising that such pronouncements did not do more damage to the cause with which he was so identified. They were nevertheless in keeping with the propensity of many libertarian members of the American Left to demonstrate a less than complete commitment to democracy and to human rights.

Emma Goldman suggested to Baldwin that "dear old [Theodore] Dreiser had a much more penetrating eye than you and many others—he at least saw some evils—you saw nothing." Admitting that he did not condemn the evils in Russia in the same manner as comparable ills elsewhere, Baldwin argued, "Such protests might be used by the common enemies of us all—the capitalist and imperialist press." Baldwin then asserted, "I prefer a working-class dictatorship to a capitalist dictatorship, and in this practical world you come pretty near having to choose."[38]

Throughout this period Baldwin continued to defend the Soviet state while turning a jaundiced eye on communist machinations in organizations he helped direct. An entire state, he seemed to believe, could be reorganized through communist directives and at the behest of communist agents, despite the brutal repression to which they were prone. But the groups and associations he was part of, Baldwin repeatedly argued, should avoid being dominated by those who professed to subscribe to the same tenets as the Russian comrades. Here again he was open to charges of hypocrisy.

In May 1928 Baldwin received a lengthy letter from Willi Münzenberg, a fellow member of the executive committee of the International League Against Imperialism, regarding Baldwin's rumored fear that Communist Party members were attempting to take over the organization. The Paris Secretariat, Münzenberg reminded, had been left wholly in the hands of Baldwin and his friends. He repeatedly sought "to push us out of all participation in the movement," Münzenberg charged, by attempting to remove all communists from the league's executive committee.[39]

In reply Baldwin—soon to refer to himself as "notoriously pro-Soviet"—declared his comrade's impressions to be mistaken. For years, Baldwin recalled, he had worked in United Front groups alongside communists. These included Red Aid, or the International Workers' Relief, which was intended to counter Herbert Hoover's Relief Administration for postwar Europe; committees attacking imperialism; and "nonpolitical" organizations that supported Soviet Russia. At present he was a member of the executive committee of the All-America Anti-Imperialist League, whose secretary was a communist. "You will see from all this that I have no political prejudices. I am solely concerned with getting results," he wrote Münzenberg.[40]

Baldwin affirmed, "I know that the Communist movement is the most determined and effective support which the movements for colonial independence have, and I know that support rests ultimately on the solid basis of the organized workers and peasants, not upon bourgeois nationalism." Consequently, he backed the communists' anti-imperialism program, "the only one worth supporting." Nevertheless, nonpartisan, anti-imperialist organizations needed to avoid sectarian hatreds within their ranks. Thus he believed that Münzenberg should resign as league secretary.[41]

In the fall Vanguard Press released *Liberty Under the Soviets*. As Peter Filene has suggested, American liberals accorded the communist state "firm but qualified support" during the 1920s. As Baldwin acknowledged at the outset of *Liberty Under the Soviets*, its title displayed his prejudices. Although the book focused on dictatorial controls the Soviet regime had in place, its author perceived "as far more significant the basic economic freedom of workers and peasants and the abolition of privileged classes based on wealth."[42]

His new book, Baldwin again recognized, would undoubtedly result in criticisms that he subscribed to double standards regarding repression in Soviet Russia and that in capitalist lands. "It is true that I feel differently about them," Baldwin said, "because I regard them as unlike." Repression in democratic countries violated supposed constitutional guarantees, whereas repression in the new communist state involved "weapons of struggle in a transition period to socialism." Most important in Baldwin's estimation was that the communists envisioned a society removed from class struggle and, consequently, repression. He recognized the dangers inherent "in the extreme measures of control" now prevailing. "I deplore them for their unnecessary cruelties," particularly as they threatened the emergence of the popular forces that the communists were said to favor. In fact, much greater liberty could be allowed without endangering the regime. "As for the future, no society seems to me permanently tolerable without unrestricted civil liberty as the means toward its continuing growth," he wrote. In his estimation the Soviet Communist Party appeared "far too alive, too dynamic, too youthful, not to break" the bonds of political repression. In a telling statement Baldwin asserted that the truest gauge of the Soviet model involved progress toward the regime's avowed determination to mold "a free and classless society." Already, its "amazingly devoted if somewhat fanatical little minority" of party members had initiated "the most heroic piece of social reorganization in history"—and in a backward land at that.[43]

In other revealing analyses Baldwin affirmed that Soviet censorship was "more complete and more thorough than has been achieved under any other dictatorship." The censorship extended to journalism, literature, scientific writings, the theater, cinema, and radio. The secret police, the OGPU, were authorized to arrest, exile, and imprison individuals without trial after an administrative inquiry. Dragnet arrests during tense periods heightened the sense of terror experienced by those singled out. The secret police could also condemn to death individuals who had been rounded up and were allowed to carry out such sentences without trial. Nevertheless, Baldwin was convinced that "the G.P.U. keeps pretty well within the bounds of law," and "does not get out of hand," unlike secret police forces elsewhere, such as the Bureau of Investigation in the United States. This was an astonishing statement and again suggested either incredible insensitivity or gullibility on Baldwin's part; at the same time it was in keeping with his reading of certain American intelligence operatives (although curiously enough, evidently not J. Edgar Hoover). To opponents of the Bolshevik government, he acknowledged, the OGPU was "the Red Terror, supreme, lawless, all-powerful, ruthless, shooting at will on suspicion." But Baldwin insisted that to any rational student of Soviet Russia, the OGPU stood as "an exceedingly well-organized and efficient military police, with the function of combating all opposition, but working within definite bounds under the central political authority."[44]

Written shortly after Stalin ascended to power, *Liberty Under the Soviets*, along with John Dewey's *Impressions of Soviet Russia*, helped to shape the attitudes of American liberals toward the communist state. Both works painted the picture of a progressive Russia engaged in a great social and economic experiment, where cooperation rather than selfish individualism was prevailing, in contrast to the United States of the 1920s. Dewey was critical of the repression afflicting the Soviet Union but contended, like Baldwin, that the general populace appeared little affected. Baldwin's major "contribution" to intellectual debate was his separation of political and economic liberties, along with his argument that one could occur without the other. Again, that enabled some to accuse him of hypocrisy and a less-than-wholehearted belief in democracy.[45]

In late 1928 a series of reviews—many laudatory—of *Liberty Under the Soviets* began to appear. The social democratic Milwaukee *Leader* termed Baldwin's work "a most excellent guide through the dark and light places of sovietism" that underscored the need for democracy ultimately to prevail within the communist state. But B. Charney Vladeck, in *Bookman*, accused Baldwin of lapsing into apologies concerning the dictatorship of the proletariat. *Liberty Under the Soviets*, a review in the *Missourian* declared, was "radical, readable, informative, and worth two hours of your time. Not more than two hours." A write-up in the *New York World* termed Baldwin's study unbiased. The *Boston Transcript* called *Liberty Under the Soviets* an important book, although "inevitably biased." Nevertheless, the *(Boston) Transcript* revealed that he was inclined more "to the paradise view than the hell-interpretation of the Russian experiment." The *New York Herald Tribune* disagreed, adjudging *Liberty Under the Soviets* "the fairest statement" yet produced on the subject.[46]

As their correspondence reflects, Emma Goldman hardly agreed. Baldwin's attitude concerning Russia, she stated, exemplified the "indefiniteness" that was "very much characteristic in you." He found her statement understandable but amusing too, considering "all the kicks I get about being too definite, too dogmatic, too absolute." He then wrote,

> What you really object to is that I don't line up with an exclusive black and white, for and against position in the revolutionary movement. I am engaged in the job of helping defend the rights of all revolutionists (and any others attacked by police and courts) and I am for all revolutionary effort, regardless of philosophy. As to Russia, I was too definitely pro-Soviet to suit you not long ago, and I am too definitely against Soviet tyranny to suit the Communists. So, in favor of the economic program of Russia and against its cruel and unnecessary repression, I get damned by both sides, thank you.[47]

Working through the ICPP, Baldwin continued to agitate on behalf of those imprisoned for political reasons in the Soviet Union. In the spring of 1928 he helped to orchestrate a campaign to free Left Social Revolutionist and Maximalist political prisoners in Russia.[48]

Goldman was undoubtedly displeased by Baldwin's continued involvement with the International League Against Imperialism, the first of the great united fronts of the era. Other executive committee members included Münzenberg; Nehru; James Maxton, the left-wing English socialist; Georg Ledebour, the German socialist; Haya de la Torre from Peru; Ellen Wilkinson, the British member of Parliament; Edo Fimmen, the Dutch labor leader; and the Frenchwoman Gabrielle Duchene of the Women's International League for Peace and Freedom.[49]

By the spring of 1931, however, the communists were seeking full control of the International League Against Imperialism and orchestrated Baldwin's dismissal as chairman of the American section. A meeting was held in Manhattan, with Baldwin presiding. The room was packed, however, with party members. They supported a lengthy indictment accusing him of such "deviations" as being a friend of Gandhi, who allegedly was compromising with the British. They also accused Baldwin of not being genuinely committed to the Indian independence struggle. Was he, they asked, "not an accomplice of bourgeois elements and a victim of bourgeois illusions?" They voted to oust Baldwin both as chairman and from the league itself. Baldwin refused to defend himself, and the entire proceeding lasted less than fifteen minutes. Seemingly unoffended, he then bought coffee for the committee members downstairs.[50]

That fall, Baldwin insisted to Goldman,

> I am a rebel, a revolutionist, a heretic at heart, but my associations and background have given me a technique of life that only partly discloses it. I am always therefore between the respectables and the outcasts, damned by sections of both. And I am further so pragmatically minded that I can accept—with reluctance and doubt—the Soviet system because it works toward a far better goal than capitalism, while maintaining the principles of anarchist-communism as the only desirable solution of the world's struggle for liberation.[51]

Not surprisingly, Baldwin's ability to hold onto obviously contradictory beliefs appalled and sometimes infuriated Goldman. Through this period, at least, he seemed able to maintain his absolutist belief in civil liberties for the United States, his desire for economic democracy to take hold in the West, and his support for "the communist experiment." He was hardly alone in this regard, as many Western intellectuals similarly professed support for human rights, democracy, and the Soviet Union. Others found the inconsistencies disturbing, wondering how champions of First Amendment freedoms could defend a regime that was ever more repressive.

CHAPTER FIFTEEN

Free Speech and the Class Struggle

As the 1930s began, the American economy continued the slide first brought to public attention with the previous fall's stock market plunge. Over the course of the next three years, economic indexes grew increasingly grim, with unemployment figures reaching the 25 percent mark or higher, as thirteen to fifteen million workers lost their jobs. About 100,000 businesses went belly up, as did five thousand banks, taking with them nine million savings accounts. The banks foreclosed on countless farms and homes, millions simply milled about, and untold numbers were reduced to scavenging in garbage bins for morsels of food. Personal depression and anxiety took hold at the outset, but anger began to brew as well. Soon talk of the need for action—and radical or even revolutionary action at that—could be heard on various sides along the political spectrum. Some envisioned an American version of the iron heel wielded by Italy's Benito Mussolini or called for by a mustachioed former corporal in the German army who headed a right-wing political party attracting more and more adherents. Others supported a workers' party and foresaw a Soviet America to overcome the lassitude and immorality of an economic system that had resulted in large-scale waste, exploitation, and distress.

By the early thirties, the American Left was experiencing something of a rebirth. Later termed the Old Left, this batch of American radicals was considerably different from the Lyrical Left of the pre–World War I period, which included the Socialist Party, the Wobblies, and cultural radicals of the Greenwich Village sort. The earlier Left was in certain ways more innocent in that time before submarine assaults, poison gas, and trench warfare transformed European society and much of the rest of the world, including the

United States. After the United States entered World War I, the Left of Eugene V. Debs, Big Bill Haywood, and Randolph Bourne, the brilliant essayist who so scathingly attacked American involvement in World War I, began to pass into memory. Officially sanctioned attacks on both the Socialist Party and the IWW, along with private vigilante action, badly crippled those leading institutional forces of the early twentieth-century American Left. After word of the Russian Revolution spread, sectarian divisions also helped to diminish Debs's once-promising political organization. Shortly thereafter, communist political parties appeared in the United States, before the Comintern demanded that American comrades form one workers' party alone. In the meantime the wartime and postwar Red Scares had further weakened the American Left as a whole, resulting in lean times throughout the 1920s.

However, the contradictions that Marx and Lenin had insisted necessarily abounded in the capitalist system had fostered the economic collapse sweeping across the United States and much of the globe during the first part of 1930s. The American Left was reborn, and the Socialist Party under Norman Thomas—the former Presbyterian minister and a close friend of Roger Baldwin's—experienced a minor revitalization. The greatest beneficiary of the depressed economic conditions proved to be the Communist Party of the United States, which was identified with the lone socialist experiment. Furthermore, its call for structural transformations appeared far removed from the impotence of the socialists, so clearly evidenced in central Europe and in the United States, despite Thomas's noble efforts. By 1932 leading American intellectuals—including John Dos Passos, Sidney Hook, Matthew Josephson, Edmund Wilson, Malcolm Cowley, Sherwood Anderson, Theodore Dreiser, Lincoln Steffens, and Langston Hughes—were supporting "the frankly revolutionary Communist Party" and its presidential candidate, William Z. Foster. Although Thomas received four times as many votes as Foster, it seemed both fashionable and intellectually respectable to favor the communist program, as did an increasing number of Left-inclined Americans. Thanks to its obvious ties to the Soviet Union in particular, which then was experiencing a supposedly successful Five-Year Plan, many on the Left viewed the Communist Party of the United States as the wave of the future, whereas they considered the Socialist Party to be long past its prime. After all, the Communist Party of the United States, like the Soviet Union, was identified with economic liberties, which many, in a time of financial crisis, considered most essential of all.

Baldwin kept abreast of international developments, particularly those relating to political prisoners or the status of Soviet Russia. In 1929 he again spent considerable time in Europe, including five days in fascist Italy; he also helped create an international civil liberties bureau in Paris. That same year he reimmersed himself in ACLU operations while maintaining that a larger civil liberties movement had to be considered by ACLU activists. Writing to board members on February 7, he noted that the ACLU had largely focused on the First Amendment freedoms of speech, press, and assemblage. "Incidentally," he noted, the organization also had championed the individual's right, as articulated in the Fourth Amendment, to be shielded from unreasonable searches and seizures. Constitutional rights, Baldwin now asserted, "cover a wider field which we have not touched." Consequently, the executive committee was calling for a broadening of ACLU operations to create "a far larger and more effective constituency." This required greater decentralization, which in turn demanded strong chapters around the country. "It is time," Baldwin continued, "for a union of all forces on the practical issues of struggle against repression, intolerance and race and religious discrimination in all its forms."[1]

To that end the ACLU leadership favored a greatly expanded agenda, parts of which the organization had addressed on an irregular basis. The executive committee urged support for blacks and Native Americans in their civil rights campaigns, foreign nationals facing naturalization and deportation battles, and individuals targeted because of race or religion. It condemned third-degree police practices besetting criminal defendants, unlawful searches and seizures in Prohibition cases, and censorship of literature, radio, and cinema. And it denounced compulsory military training, the sending of U.S. military forces against weaker states, and repression in other lands where American interests were represented.[2]

In a lengthy report penned shortly after his year in Europe, Baldwin presciently predicted a series of constitutional issues that would come before the U.S. Supreme Court. These included state laws prohibiting the wielding of the red flag, a Minnesota statute allowing a lone judge to prevent publication of newspapers deemed defamatory or scurrilous, and measures that targeted supposed sedition and syndicalism. Other questionable government practices ranged from compulsory Bible-reading provisions in public schools to the power of the U.S. Post Office to refuse to ship materials considered obscene, seditious, or defamatory, or that contained birth-control information. Remaining in effect too were discriminatory laws against blacks that attempted to keep them tied to employers, prohibited intermarriage, and mandated segregation of schools and other public facilities.[3]

Baldwin acknowledged that "mere expression" alone was no longer punished. "One may utter the most revolutionary thoughts" to an attentive college audience, if allowed on campus, without suffering legal consequences, he admitted. However, incarceration was likely if someone delivered the same speech to workers in coalfields or steel towns, or if one advocated social equality of the races in the American South, birth control in Catholic and puritanical Boston, "or evolution or atheism in the Bible belt." Because only communists strove to bring such issues to the fore in their quest to organize workers, they stood as "the chief victims of attack," as Baldwin put it. Still, even they generally were not facing the lengthy prison sentences suffered earlier by the Wobblies, Baldwin admitted. The worst treatment occurred in central California's Imperial Valley, where strike activities similar to those of the IWW had been employed.[4]

As Baldwin saw it, the drama being played out in the United States was the same as anywhere else. "The ruling economic class" dominated government agencies and relied on "force, money, power, patriotism, the law, the courts, the press, the church, the colleges." Opposing it were militant unionists, radical political parties, libertarian members of the middle class, the liberal press, and a small number of "intransigent professors and preachers." Resistance proved difficult because the United States had, at the time, only one effective political party, and half the voters failed to cast ballots, "a tribute to their intelligence, for they know it is no use," Baldwin wrote. Only "a tiny minority" stirred things up, suffered the brunt of repercussions for confronting the powers that were, and invoked its right to agitate. In Baldwin's estimation "ceaseless and unremitting struggle wins them" something of a right to speak out, "at terrific cost in defense and propaganda." These agitators underscored "the bankruptcy of our pretenses to equal rights before the law, the myth of law and order."[5]

In the period ahead, Baldwin predicted, as class divisions deepened and capitalism weakened, opposition from below would increase. While class conflict continued, law and government would "serve the masters of property." Only at the end of that struggle might "a world [of] . . . equality before the law" come about. Before that occurred, he suggested, progress would be achieved with less violence, if greater freedom were afforded to expound revolutionary tenets. Civil libertarians had to strive "to keep the powers of government off the backs of a rising class."[6]

Unlike so many others of his class, Baldwin welcomed "the spirit of revolt" evidenced by the Russian Revolution, India's independence struggle, and the ferment in China. That spirit, he believed, had "achieved everything in history" or was the "basis for it anyhow." The ultimate goal of that revolt, he argued, should be greater individual freedom. Repression, such as that identified with fascists abroad and the Ku Klux Klan at home, he was certain, only bred revolution. The immediate losers in this clash included liberalism, democracy, and parliamentary government.[7]

Baldwin insisted to Earl Browder of the Communist Party of the United States in January 1930 that incidents like the disruptions of public addresses by Victor Chernov, a Russian social revolutionist, were counterproductive. After an unhappy response from Browder, Baldwin retorted, "This is the first time that the [Communist] Party has assumed responsibility for breaking up meetings of persons to whom they are politically opposed." Consequently, he wondered "how the Party can claim support of its demand for freedom of assemblage, when it so denies it to others." At the very least such actions would diminish the support the ACLU's friends afforded the Communist Party of the United States "in its struggle for the right to conduct its propaganda without interference." ACLU leaders drafted one statement that warned some ACLU members were arguing against defending communists should the party approve of such disruptions.[8]

In one exchange Browder declined Harry F. Ward and Baldwin's offer of joint support in condemning "police lawlessness" in confrontations with communist demonstrators at New York's city hall "There are, to our knowledge, certain persons connected with your organization who make use of formal protests against the police attacks as a cover for actual solidarity with the police," Browder wrote. The ACLU was comprised, Baldwin responded, "of very diverse elements whose only agreement is on a common struggle for civil liberty, regardless of their political philosophies." In fact, Baldwin acknowledged, "Communist Party members are on our National Committee and in our membership." By year's end, however, William Z. Foster, a Communist Party leader and longtime ACLU member, had resigned from the board in protest. Foster claimed that the ACLU directors had betrayed workers by following the lead of socialist members in refusing a request to help imprisoned communists post bail.[9]

The Special Committee to Investigate Communist Activities in the United States, headed by Hamilton Fish Jr., a Republican congressman from New York, hurled sweeping charges against the ACLU, the Communist Party, and radical labor leaders. Voluntarily appearing before the committee on December 5, 1930, Baldwin acknowledged that the ACLU upheld the right of either a U.S. citizen or a foreign national to advocate the use of force and violence to bring about the government's overthrow. Supreme Court justices Oliver Wendell Holmes Jr. and Louis D. Brandeis held this position. On the other hand, Baldwin noted, the ACLU drew "the line at either the overt act, or attempted act." The theory behind such a distinction was that if individuals were allowed to speak their minds, they would not act on their revolutionary principles. When one congressman stated, "That is pretty good theory," Baldwin responded, "It is the Hyde Park theory, the old familiar theory."[10]

Baldwin may well have thought he was appearing before the House committee in the same social context he had used to deal or attempted to deal with high government officials: as one gentleman speaking to others. If so, his expectations in this instance were sorely wrongheaded, just as they had been in his dealings with the Department of War and Military Intelligence during World War I and J. Edgar Hoover of the Bureau of Investigation in the midtwenties. Although Baldwin had undoubtedly hoped or even expected to refute the committee's charges, his testimony only added fuel to Fish's accusations. The Fish Committee subsequently recommended legislation to outlaw the Communist Party because of its alleged direct advocacy of the violent overthrow of the federal government.[11]

The Fish Committee report, issued in January 1931, blasted the ACLU and Baldwin personally:

> The A.C.L.U. is closely affiliated with the communist movement in the United States, and fully 90% of its efforts are on behalf of communists who have come into conflict with the law. It claims to stand for free speech, free press, and free assembly; but it is quite apparent that the main function of the A.C.L.U. is to attempt to protect the communists in their advocacy of force and violence to overthrow the government, replacing the American flag by a red flag and erecting a Soviet Government in place of the republican form of government guaranteed to each State by the Federal Constitution.
>
> Roger N. Baldwin, its guiding spirit, makes no attempt to hide his friendship for the communists and their principles.

The Fish Committee's direct attack on the ACLU resulted in a series of editorial commentaries. The organization, the congressional committee had charged, was "a supporter of all subversive movements. . . . It attempts not only to protect crime, but to encourage attacks upon our institutions in every form." Such a statement, one editorialist claimed, called into question the report's veracity. In that author's estimation, the charges hurled at the ACLU could hardly have been more wrongheaded. The ACLU, the writer argued, "is a supporter of the almost-forgotten principles of Jeffersonian democracy in their purest form." An editorial in *Law and Labor*, however, challenged the ACLU's argument that the Founders had fought for unlimited free speech. The editorial, in a telling analysis, professed rather, "There is no respectable opinion that any government should take a revolution lying down."[12]

Such criticisms notwithstanding, the ACLU, with Baldwin taking the lead, condemned the Fish Committee's proposal to outlaw the Communist Party of the United States. Such a move, he said, would prove to the communists "that the only way they can bring about their program is by revolution," the same revolution the House committee was trying to stave off. "Any intelligent person will agree," Baldwin wrote in a note to ACLU affiliates, "that this is a childish way of combating Communism." Unfortunately, however, many appeared to lose perspective whenever radicalism was involved.[13]

While the Fish Committee Inquiry was underway, Baldwin wrote an article that appeared in a collection of essays entitled *Behold America!* that might have caused both him and the ACLU embarrassment had it been more widely read. In that article he referred to "the myth of law and order" and "the illusion of democracy." Parliaments, democracy, and civil liberties, he insisted, went "hand in hand. Always they have served the interests of the ruling propertied class in control of the political machinery; and always they have fed the illusion of the people that individual initiative could advance any man, however humble, into the seats of financial and political power." With the emergence of the working class, the unfolding of the Russian Revolution, and the weakening of world capitalism, "the old institutions of democracy are going."[14]

Baldwin said that the international program of the Soviet Communist Party—particularly the threat it posed to property worldwide—"made it at once the central issue of struggle in every industrial country." Concerns about its contagious effect had resulted in legislation throughout the United States. Thus in the United States, as elsewhere, Baldwin argued, "the drama goes on . . . with the ruling economic class controlling the agencies of government in the interest of order!" Liberty was won by those who fought for it and by "disinterested citizens" who empathized with the underdog. "On the one side of the struggle, force, money, power, patriotism, the law, the courts, the press, the church, the colleges; on the other, the more militant sections of labor, the radical parties, the libertarian wing of the middle-class, the liberal press, and a few intransigent professors and preachers." The United States, the world's richest and most powerful land, "tolerates no opposition. Its economic liberties are confined to the right to get rich. Its political liberties are confined to voting for one capitalist party or the other." Baldwin saw "the bankruptcy of our pretenses to equal rights before the law—the myth of law and order."[15]

As class tensions intensified and capitalism faltered, Baldwin predicted, "an opposition will grow from below based on the workers and the farmers." That movement was already stirring in the United States, just as it had emerged in other lands. Only when this struggle was concluded, he said, "may we venture to visualize a world in which equality before the law may become a reality." But in the meantime the greater the freedom to expound even revolutionary tenets, "the less violent will be the process of advance." Thus both those who cherished "old notions of civil liberty" and those who for selfish or altruistic reasons sought "to keep the powers of government off the backs of a rising class" would attempt to stave off "the wreckage of violent struggle." In the United States "no greater challenge could confront us."[16]

Now Baldwin reversed himself, arguing that 1930, like the period just after the war, had been a sorry year for civil liberties. Once again economic crisis had translated into attacks on constitutionally protected rights such as freedom of speech, of the press, and of assemblage. "Depression always means repression," Baldwin asserted in an interview with the *New York World*. However, in the ACLU's annual report, published in June 1931, Baldwin acknowledged that the U.S. Supreme Court was displaying "a new and liberal outlook" regarding the First Amendment.[17]

In the springtime of 1932 Baldwin delivered an address at Mount Holyoke College entitled "Civil Liberties." "I don't want to see the coming class struggle in America fought out in bloodshed as it was in Russia," Baldwin exclaimed, "but violent suppression always leads to violent upheaval." Forcing the communist movement underground, he warned, would "reap a harvest of revolution."[18]

Despite such rhetoric—or perhaps owing to it—the ACLU and its leaders continued to be vilified in the press, legislative assemblies, and Congress. In May the *Chicago Tribune* charged several times that the organization was "identified with radical and communistic activities" and referred to Arthur Garfield Hays and Dudley Field Malone, a top divorce lawyer who had served as Woodrow Wilson's undersecretary of state, as "lawyers with radical backgrounds." Nothing about the ACLU was more radical, Baldwin insisted, than its championing of freedom of speech and assemblage for all groups, regardless of political orientation.[19]

The attacks continued unabated through the end of 1930. In a speech she was scheduled to deliver before the Daughters of the American Revolution and the American Legion in Evanston, Illinois, Elizabeth Dilling, a right-wing polemicist, planned to indict the ACLU as "unqualifiedly connected with communistic activities in the United States." She intended to rely on the investigative work of John A. Kappelman, chairman of the legion's Americanization committee, which had the ACLU and the League for Industrial Democracy (LID) joined in "a national plan to propagandize the United States along Communistic lines." (Originally called the Intercollegiate Socialist Society, the LID was founded in 1905 with the express purpose of "educating Americans about the need to extend democracy to every aspect of our society.") Dilling—soon to produce one of the most notorious anti-radical tracts, The Red Network—informed a local newspaper:

> One need not go to Russia, nor to the slums, to find Communism. . . . The aid given by "intellectual" sympathizers is more powerful than that of many times the number of "gutter" adherents. . . . Its friends usually pose as "neutrals," "liberals," "lovers of mental freedom," seldom as plain Communists. The bitter joke is that these sympathizers are of that very "capitalistic enemy class" which Communism rages to destroy.[20]

The criticisms hurled at Baldwin emanated from the Left as well. James Cannon, a founder of the American communist movement and a Trotskyist by this point, objected to Baldwin's departure from an antiwar gathering held in August 1932 at New York City's Labor Temple. Baldwin left after delivering his speech as the representative of the American Committee for the World Congress Against War. Two resolutions were subsequently offered, the pacifist position presented by Baldwin's committee and a Leninist stance provided by the Communist Left Opposition of "Bolshevik-Leninists." Pacifists, left-wing socialists, and "Official Communists," among others, assailed the Leninist program. Cannon believed that "a pre-arranged plan" called for Baldwin to leave, thus lending "tacit support to the steam-rolling of the Bolshevik-Leninists." Such indirect backing of the effort to quash the Left

Opposition, Cannon asserted, made sense from a political vantage point. "You, and the tendency you represent—pacifism—were indubitably the victors at the conference." A United Front that found both Stalinists and pacifists in the antiwar camp had led to the Stalinists yielding "principle (sic) positions all along the line, from Paris to New York." But while the program, propaganda, and leadership of the movement were pacifist, Stalinists had been allowed to control it organizationally and to silence the Left Opposition they feared most of all. "That is what your united front looks like to us," Cannon wrote to Baldwin.[21]

Still, Cannon wanted Baldwin to clarify his position. Until now, he wrote, Baldwin had defended freedom of speech for everyone, even Russian Mensheviks and American Klansmen. If Baldwin had now changed course and opted "to sacrifice the principle of free speech," he should frankly and publicly acknowledge as much and provide a rationale for this shift in perspective. In the antiwar movement, Cannon argued, nothing was "more dangerous and disarming than ambiguity and deception." At the same time Cannon, who strove to avoid personal attacks, did not doubt Baldwin's sincerity. "It is your program that we oppose," he insisted, along with the lack of clarity regarding the Left Opposition's right to participate in the antiwar fight.[22]

The organizers of the antiwar convention had assured him, Baldwin stated, that all forces opposed to war, no matter their politics, would be included. Because of his experiences in the International League Against Imperialism, he had specifically asked about the communist opposition and had been promised that no discrimination would result. He had not served as chairman at the meeting in question, did have another function to attend, and had reached no understanding with the Stalinists. Later he had sought to learn what had transpired. He received word that members of the communist opposition were seated if they arrived before the police closed the doors. Max Shactman, a leading Trotskyist, delivered a lengthy oration in favor of the resolution Baldwin sponsored. If any group were denied the right to speak freely, Baldwin wanted "to know it in specific terms." He continued to favor such an open-ended approach for the United Front. In fact, his adherence to that policy had resulted in his own expulsion from the League Against Imperialism. "I shall always stick to it regardless of whose interests are at stake," he assured Cannon.[23]

In other correspondence, however, Baldwin revealed that he had received word the communists "so thoroughly controlled" the meeting as to make it unrepresentative. He bluntly stated, "I always fear that in any enterprise in which the Communists participate. They are as intolerant as their enemies." However, he pointed out that the conference was not pacifist but rather anti-war, entailing "opposition to nationalist, imperialist war, which is the only kind we have today." Baldwin then spoke of the defense of communist Russia by arms, declaring that even the great French novelist and pacifist Romain Rolland had acknowledged that, if he were younger, he would so act. Although Baldwin did not agree with Rolland's comment, he understood why communists and their supporters viewed an attack by imperialist states on the Soviet Union as amounting to civil war: "It would be a class war—a workers' state vs. capitalist states."[24]

For his part Baldwin had supported the congress in the belief that war could be staved off only through organized working-class efforts. He considered the congress, no matter how partisan, the only means for mobilizing the forces backed by left-wing intellectuals. Thus individuals like George Bernard Shaw and Albert Einstein were willing to climb on board, despite "any scruples they may have about armed class war or armed defense of the Soviet Union." The greatest danger, in Baldwin's eyes, lay in "nationalist-imperialist wars" like that unfolding in Manchuria. Great war machines were devised for just such conflagrations, and opposition to them required "more than the feeble middle-class pacifists." The fueling of antiwar sentiment without the workers' ability to prevent munitions from being shipped abroad, and to strike against war-related industries, meant little, he said.[25]

Like many on the Left who remained enamored of Soviet communism, Baldwin viewed the Communist Party of the United States critically. The party hierarchy, both domestic and external, reigned in dictatorial fashion. Consequently, the party's appeal was limited, even in the midst of a wrenching economic depression. At the same time Baldwin appreciated the dogged determination of party activists to reach out to the dispossessed, and he remained willing to work with communists in a series of United Front groups.

One year later, in late September 1933, Baldwin was again ensnared in internecine battles on the Left, where communist forces acted provocatively. The First United States Congress Against War convened in New York City on September 29, with more than twenty-six hundred delegates in attendance. As Henri Barbusse, a member of the French Communist Party, entered the convention hall, an orchestra struck up "The Internationale," and hundreds greeted the noted author with a red salute. Subsequently, an attempt to place Jay Lovestone, a leading dissident communist, on the presiding committee was turned aside. As the *Daily Worker* boasted, the nomination of Lovestone—whose leadership of the American Communist Party had been terminated by Stalin himself following a heated confrontation in Moscow—was "drowned out in a thunderous roar of disapproval." Baldwin attempted to reintroduce the issue of Lovestone's nomination, urging that the gathering demonstrate genuine antifascist unity. Once again a disturbance took place, and Earl Browder had to act to restore order. Baldwin's motion was easily defeated. He and other nonparty members of the presiding committee were displeased at the turn of events and threatened to walk out unless some kind of compromise was forthcoming. Subsequently, Charles Zimmerman, a Lovestone ally associated with the International Ladies' Garment Workers' Union, was placed on the committee. But when he spoke, boos and hisses rang out, compelling Browder to intervene once again.[26]

Thus Baldwin was caught up in the whirlwind of events that enabled the American Left to experience something of a resurgence while providing the seeds for its demise. Civil liberties continued to be his foremost concern, but increasingly other issues threatened to loom equally large. Consequently, he was drawn into some of the internecine battles afflicting the Old Left, particularly as he was still enamored of the socialist "experiment" in Soviet Russia. He remained willing to deal with all forces on the Left, which angered some and infuriated others, leading to the contradictory accusations that he was sympathetic to the Stalinists or played into the hands of anticommunists. All the while his championing of freedom of speech, of the press, and of assemblage for all individuals, regardless of political persuasion, equally enraged many on all sides of the ideological landscape. Right-wingers immediately harped on his readiness, and that of the ACLU, to defend the rights of ostracized forces, especially communists. They viewed such a position as truly insidious, dismissing the expansive civil libertarian perspective as resulting in the defense of the rights of those not worthy of having such rights defended. Left-wing sectarians, in turn, adopted the same approach, favoring restrictions on the political freedoms of their foes, whether native fascists or rivals on the "progressive" side of the political spectrum.

Nevertheless, the legend of Roger Baldwin continued to spread. The *World Tomorrow*, a pacifist publication, had recently termed him a "Galahad of Freedom" who moved "easily through the two contrasting lives of our capitalist system, and has devoted friends in both camps." The *North American Review*, in its November 1932 issue, referred to "a sort of mythology" about

Baldwin that had developed. It mentioned the camp he had built back in 1924 along the Hackensack River—a bare half-hour from mid-Manhattan—where wild animals lived. No hunter or angler, Baldwin swam, cooked, watched birds, and taught woodcraft to young people in the area. In New York City he lived in an old flat on West 12th Street, where he served as household manager for his fellow residents: a philosophy professor, a writer, and a civic worker. His cooking was likened to cordon bleu, and he was said to favor sweet wine. He continued to play the piano expertly, painted when the urge arose, and wrote prolifically.[27]

The thin, taut Baldwin was constantly in motion. Contemplation and meditation were foreign to him, the *North American Review* perceptively contended, for he always acted "as part of a programme." Of late, it seemed "a touch of grimness . . . or bitterness" had taken hold of Baldwin. The article speculated that "internal conflicts wear him. He has lived, perhaps, too much with and for too many people, and from a Puritan sense of duty; in his heart he walks with Thoreau at Walden Pond. He is evangelist by birth and pagan by conviction, and there can be little peace for him. He has accomplished incalculable things for incalculable numbers, and he takes joy only in the fight."[28]

On January 17, 1933, Baldwin demonstrated as much, informing a correspondent that the ACLU favored the safeguarding of the right of native fascists to speak freely. The ACLU's position, he wrote, was that "the best way to beat the Nazi propaganda is in the open where you can get at it, not by driving it into obscure channels." He had absolutely no fear that Nazis would amass support in the United States and was determined not to turn them into martyrs.[29]

Two weeks later Baldwin received a letter from a Presbyterian minister in Columbus, Ohio, regarding allegations made by Don R. Falkenberg, secretary of the patriotic Ohio Pocket Testament League, who had deemed the ACLU communistic and bent on stoking a violent overthrow of the government. Falkenberg had particularly emphasized his belief that the ACLU was determined to defend the rights of all notorious criminals in order to get in their good graces; when the revolution came, he contended, all prisoners would be released and then would naturally "line up with the cause." Baldwin denied any communist affiliations on the ACLU's part and affirmed that it championed the rights of communists and all others. Falkenberg's inferences were completely false, Baldwin continued, and if he persisted, the ACLU would be compelled to take legal action. While state and congressional committees accused the ACLU of providing succor to communists, the communists in turn condemned the organization for defending " 'justice in capitalist courts,' the 'illusion of democracy,' and a bourgeoisie liberalism which does not recognize class interests," Baldwin told Falkenberg.[30]

The controversies continued to swirl about the ACLU; those failed to inhibit Baldwin from speaking in the very fashion that engendered such controversies. In March 1933 he, along with Norman Thomas, Malcolm Cowley, and Scott Nearing, among others, responded to an inquiry from the *Student Outlook*, a progressive publication associated with the LID, regarding the notion of class struggle. Baldwin explained that the class struggle was "the most obvious of conflicts." In his estimation progress had always resulted from the demands by "oppressed economic classes" for greater political and economic power. At present the class struggle was fertile. Individuals thought "in terms of their groups and class interests." When a crisis arose, they battled for their interests. A classless social order would emerge when the interests of the community as a whole became paramount. "To that goal we shall doubtless advance, first by state capitalism (as today in Fascist lands then state socialism as in the Soviet Union) and ultimately communism without a state based on violence." By this point Baldwin agreed with Marxist analyses of class struggle and "the goal of a classless society through revolutionary conflict." Like Marxists, he reasoned that the workers comprised the only group that could transform society. As for himself, Baldwin professed, "My only affiliation is with the struggle of those forces advancing toward a classless society with minimum violence."[31]

On the evening of April 5, at a rally orchestrated by the Communist Party of the United States, Baldwin spoke at Madison Square Garden before fifteen thousand onlookers—many party members—and condemned Adolf Hitler's rise to power in Germany. While communist orators predicted that "Sovietism" would supplant Nazism in Europe, Baldwin "ridiculed the value of political democracy, which he pronounced moribund," the *New York Times* reported. He urged formation of a united front of left-of-center forces to battle fascism. A *New York Times* editorial on April 7 bitingly asked "why anybody who thinks democracy moribund should continue to be interested in civil liberties."[32]

Then on April 21 in a letter to the editor of the *Christian Science Monitor* Baldwin referred to a recent editorial that had repeated his statement, "Political democracy is moribund." The editorial expressed wonderment that such an individual could be a defender of civil liberties. Baldwin responded, declaring that "civil liberties, like democracy, are useful only as tools for social change. Political democracy as such a tool is obviously bankrupt throughout the world. Dictatorship in one form or another is rapidly replacing it." Civil liberties too, Baldwin worried, "have gone out of fashion." He for one was determined to support "freedom of agitation," not principally as a political concern but rather as a way to mitigate economic conflict and to do so with the least amount of violence possible.[33]

At the very least, for the ACLU director to make such a statement was unwise. At worst, it opened him up to charges of callous, guileless, or duplicitous behavior. It is both surprising and fortunate that Baldwin's declaration did not prove more damaging to him and the civil liberties movement. After all, his assertion that civil liberties and democracy were "useful only as tools for social change" could easily have resulted in a plummeting of support. Perhaps it was fortunate that the civil liberties movement, at this stage, still relied on small circles of friends, many close to Baldwin himself. Had the civil liberties campaign involved a mass movement during this era, Baldwin's more radical and sometimes thoughtless pronouncements might have proved fatal.

On November 28, 1933, Baldwin wrote to Maury Maverick, then serving as county tax collector in San Antonio, regarding a speech the Texan was to deliver on the American Legion and the ACLU. The legion had supported the Fish Committee, while the latter championed free speech for all political groups. The argument that the ACLU favored First Amendment protections only for communists could be offset, Baldwin noted, by discussing "our recent championship of free speech for Nazis." As he had in his recently published essay in the World Tomorrow, Baldwin argued that the ACLU was compelled to champion the rights of all, unless it became "a class organization." Additionally, experience had demonstrated that propaganda of the Ku Klux Klan or American Nazis was "far better combated in the open than under suppression." Converting such right-wing fanatics into martyrs only served their interests. By contrast, allowing them to propound their foolish doctrines would result in public condemnation. "Nazis can't live long in the open in America." Civil libertarians, Baldwin insisted, were compelled to support freedom of speech for all. In January 1934 Baldwin responded to a pair of letters criticizing the ACLU's decision to adopt such a stance. To one of the correspondents he argued that suppressing Nazi propaganda would merely "breed the very acts of violence which you fear." Allowing Nazis to operate openly, the ACLU reasoned, made better sense. There the hatred they spewed could best be contested.[34]

His expansive reading of civil liberties was arguably Baldwin's greatest contribution to American thought and practice. It helped to redefine American liberalism and democracy and was propounded in the very period when others subscribed to a much narrower interpretation of First Amendment rights. While many on the Left championed the safeguarding of freedom of speech, of the press, and of assemblage for themselves or their favorite groups, they were equally determined to prevent those rights from being afforded to those with whom they disagreed. Not so Baldwin, who insisted, as he had since the ACLU's inception, on full protections for those on both the far Right and the far Left.

Baldwin's consistent civil libertarian stance was all the more remarkable given his greater and greater identification with the radical Left. He saw intensified class struggle looming, not an altogether happy likelihood in his estimation. Yet he believed that a new, more egalitarian day would result, and he hoped it would unfold in as peaceful a manner as possible.

CHAPTER SIXTEEN

From the United Front to the Popular Front

Throughout most of Franklin Delano Roosevelt's first two presidential terms, the American Left continued its resurgence, then suffered a series of blows from which it never fully recovered. The economic collapse had enabled the Left to garner the kind of support it had been unable to muster since the World War I era. When Roosevelt took office in March 1933, the U.S. economy had sunk to the lowest point of the Great Depression. FDR's New Deal programs helped to revitalize the nation as a whole and provided a paradoxical environment in which the Left could operate. The liberal direction of the administration in Washington, D.C.—which was duplicated in a number of statehouses—created a nurturing environment that enabled progressive, even radical, ideas to acquire an aura of respectability. Certain holders of such beliefs and theories obtained a foothold in government circles. At the same time, it was clear, as it had been during the heyday of the Lyrical Left and would be again during the ascendancy of the New Left, that American radicalism was enormously dependent on the goodwill and well-being of the very liberalism it so often appeared to disparage. Throughout the course of the twentieth century, American radicals fared best when liberals held power. When liberals were voted out of office, and particularly when liberalism itself was viewed with disfavor by much of the establishment and the general public, those same radicals and the radicalism they espoused won little attention. The attention they did get usually was not welcome— they were pilloried, denigrated, or reduced to impotent martyrdom.

But access to officeholders also held perils for the American Left, which has tended to thrive to a considerable extent on its outsider status. The Left has required an identification with the masses of working people, not those who shape and make policy. Too close an association with the inner reaches of government, even if more perceived than real, tempers or even mutes the critical perspectives on which the Left thrives. However, at various points during the 1930s forces on the Left seemed to comprise a wing, no matter how tenuous or fragile, of the New Deal administration and various state governments.

The second great American Left of the twentieth century, the Old Left of the 1930s, peaked and plummeted as the fortunes of the New Deal administration ebbed and flowed. In addition, of course, the influence of events worldwide proved of great significance, particularly those pertaining to fascist aggression and developments in the Soviet Union. Significant portions of the American Left had long been attracted to antiwar, even pacifist, sentiments. However, the rise of right-wing aggressor states in the Far East and Europe caused many to support collective security as the only means to stave off another world war. Many did so as well in defense of the great socialist experiment still being played out in communist Russia. Developments in that land likewise affected the staying power of the Old Left, particularly because so many of its adherents remained fixated on occurrences in the Soviet Union. The continued importance of the Soviet Union was strikingly evidenced by the position it held in the hearts and minds of all on the Left, Sovietphiles and anticommunists alike.

Throughout the midthirties most American leftists still viewed the Soviet Union favorably. Its Five-Year Plans were seemingly producing economic miracles, socialism was supposedly being ushered in, and communist Russia appeared steadfast as the leading antifascist state. Its defense of the Spanish Republic in the face of withdrawal, resignation, or cowardice by the leading Western nations, including the United States, England, and France, seemed significant, even noble. Some, of course, had long been disabused of the notion that a new order, or at least a true workers' state, was being shaped in Soviet Russia. Anarchists like Emma Goldman and Alexander Berkman had early been appalled by the heavy-handed practices of Lenin and Trotsky, and social democrats like Bertrand Russell had never viewed the developments in Russia with anything other than dismay and alarm. Trotskyists too were infuriated by the Stalinist terrors evident in the collectivization campaign and in the purges that intensified after the murder in late 1934 of Sergei Kirov, Leningrad's Communist Party leader.

But many on the American Left retained their allegiance, albeit from afar, to the Soviet Union because of its antifascist colors and communist experiment. Equally important in that regard was the seemingly greater flexibility the Soviet Union and Communist parties displayed once they adopted the Popular Front approach in the mid-1930s. The Popular Front called for all forces on the left side of the political spectrum to align in order to stave off fascism, sustain democracy, and defend the socialist state. This suggested that liberals, socialists, communists, and anarchists could join together in antifascist alliances. The Popular Front also was intended to ensure that the Soviet Union and the leading Western democracies stood as one to ward off the threat from militarist Japan, fascist Italy, and Nazi Germany. For the Politburo and the Comintern, of course, this explained the policy shift away from damning socialists as social fascists, breaking up meetings held by other radical groups, and viewing the democracies as weak-kneed sisters no more worthy of respect than that granted by Adolf Hitler. Furthermore, the shift was never as complete as noncommunist leftists had announced or hoped for, with bitter invectives still hurled at Trotskyists, communist machinations directed at the small party of Marxist revolutionaries and at anarchists during the Spanish Civil War, and the Moscow purge trials unfolding.

Few Americans were more prominent in United Front and Popular Front organizations than Roger Baldwin. He continued to believe that alliances of all forces on the Left, even those guided by communists, needed the support of liberals and radicals across the board. To his credit he remained determined that Lovestonites, as well as doctrinaire communists—socialists and anarchists alike—and, of course, liberals of various stripes, be welcomed in antifascist confederations. His own approach, for better or worse, truly appeared to be "no enemies to the Left" or left of center. That led others then and later to term him "the archetype fellow traveler," to whom J. B. Matthews referred, along with himself, as one of the "united front twins." During the 1930s, individuals like Reinhold Niebuhr, Harry F. Ward, Robert Morss Lovett, Matthews, and Baldwin—none of whom was affiliated with the Communist Party of the United States but whose names regularly appeared on organizations' letterheads—provided "a kind of imprimatur for the board of a radical organization, the rally of protest, the appeal for justice, the petition for redress of grievances," as Matthews put it.[1]

Now Baldwin, still a major player in left-of-center circles, delivered the most radical statements he had yet made. He adopted a more explicitly class-conscious position, but then so did many others. Most noteworthy was that the foremost civil libertarian in the United States asserted at one point that economic liberties prevailed over all others; he also championed the working class's right to maintain power by any means once it was acquired. Yet it was precisely during this same period that Baldwin again sought and considered himself to have attained access to top government officials. As was the case throughout the World War I era, he considered this only right, owing to his background and cultured breeding, and something that individuals of goodwill should naturally respect. All the while government agencies, most notably the newly renamed Federal Bureau of Investigation, continued to investigate Baldwin's activities and those of the ACLU. Thus inconsistencies and contradictions involving Baldwin remained plentiful.

During Herbert Hoover's administration Baldwin had sought to influence public policy more directly than at any point since the war. In 1929 Hoover established the Wickersham Commission to conduct the first national examination of the criminal justice system. Through Baldwin's efforts Walter Pollak, a top attorney for the ACLU; Zechariah Chafee, a Harvard law professor; and Carl Stern were authorized by the commission to draft the report on police practices, *Lawlessness in Law Enforcement*. That study condemned third-degree tactics, while an ensuing and widely adopted ACLU model statute insisted on criminal due process. In 1930 Baldwin formed the National Committee on Labor Injunctions, and ACLU members Felix Frankfurter and Nathan Greene wrote a groundbreaking work, *The Labor Injunction*.

In 1932 Congress passed the Norris–La Guardia Act, which proclaimed that workers had a right to "full freedom of association, self-organization . . . [and] to be free from the interference, restraint, or coercion of employers." Before issuing injunctions, judges were required to uncover evidence of violence or substantial harm suffered by employers as a result of the job action. Baldwin also initiated the ACLU Committee on Indian Civil Rights, which sought the restoration of tribal autonomy and control over Native Americans' land. ACLU lobbying efforts provided a spur for the drafting of the 1934 Indian Reorganization Act.[2]

In the final months of Hoover's presidency Baldwin corresponded with such cabinet officials as William N. Doak, the secretary of labor, and Henry L. Stimson, the secretary of state, in an effort to determine whether those agencies were targeting individuals for discriminatory treatment because of their political views. In April Baldwin attempted to find out why the Immigration Bureau, which sought to deport communists and anarchists, had investigated thirty members of Local 28 of the Sheet Metal Workers International Association. The individuals, Doak replied, had been questioned solely to determine whether any were illegally residing in the United States. In December Baldwin wrote to ask Stimson why American consuls had been told to deny Albert Einstein entrance into the United States because of allegations that he was a member of "several Communist organizations under Moscow management." Such charges—bandied about by the Woman's Patriotic Corporation on National Defense, a staunchly anticommunist organization—were unfounded, Baldwin wrote, for Einstein was a well-known pacifist and socialist. The accusations made by the Woman's Patriotic Corporation, Stimson revealed, had been passed on to the U.S. consul general in Berlin to enable Einstein, were he to apply for a visa, the opportunity to answer such allegations. The ACLU would not question the State Department's right or duty, Baldwin replied, to provide U.S. officials stationed abroad with pertinent information about potential visitors to the United States. It did "question the common lack of sense" in forwarding such prejudiced material involving an internationally acclaimed figure. A good number of Americans, Baldwin suspected, would be interested in learning whether the treatment afforded Einstein was common State Department practice.[3]

Yet even at the beginning of Herbert Hoover's last full year in office, Baldwin had reported to the ACLU board that the atmosphere in Washington appeared "more favorable for liberal legislation than it has been for years." And with the arrival of the Roosevelt administration Baldwin's communication with government officials became the warmest since the early days of U.S. involvement in World War I. Like his progressive compatriots at that time, a number of Baldwin's friends and those of other leading ACLU figures had obtained top government positions. Once again Baldwin contacted federal officials when he went to the nation's capital. Eventually, he sensed that the entire atmosphere in Washington had been transformed. To his delight he readily gained access to the Oval Office. Important New Dealers, such as Secretary of the Interior Harold Ickes, Secretary of Labor Frances Perkins, Commissioner of Immigration Daniel W. MacCormack, Commissioner of Indian Affairs John Collier, and Ernest Gruening, a presidential adviser on Latin American affairs, proved sympathetic to the ACLU position on any number of issues. Fewer friends could be found in the House of Representatives, although a small number of representatives, like Maury Maverick of Texas, were staunch civil liberties advocates. In the Senate individuals like Robert La Follette Jr., George Norris of Nebraska, Herbert Lehman of New

York, Bronson Cutting of New Mexico, Edward Costigan of Colorado, and a number of others, proved receptive to many of the ACLU's arguments. New Deal agencies contained numerous sympathetic figures, such as Rexford G. Tugwell at the Agriculture Department.[4]

However, Baldwin's dealings with top officials were not always so productive. In August he deflected warnings by an old acquaintance from Boston regarding J. Edgar Hoover, just chosen to head all Justice Department investigations. Baldwin reported that he had always found Hoover "responsive to every suggestion that we have made." Moreover, Hoover was a consummate bureaucrat who followed orders handed down by his bosses. Thus Hoover had been equally willing to accept Harlan Stone's edict to end political investigations of radicals and Harry Daugherty's diametrically opposite policy. Baldwin also reasoned that Hoover was not apt "to break loose" unless ordered to by "higher-ups." Furthermore, Baldwin continued, "The 'red' business is pretty nearly exhausted."[5]

Nevertheless, he sent an ACLU representative to the FBI after the *New Republic* charged that Hoover had sent sixty investigators into the Pennsylvania coalfields to check on the activities of "reds." A top assistant denied the report, repeating earlier assurances delivered by the director to Baldwin that his agency considered political investigations outside its purview. On August 29, 1933, Baldwin told Bruce Bliven of the *New Republic* that the Justice Department had unequivocally denied having sent G-men to the Pennsylvania coal country. Consequently, Baldwin hoped the journal would avoid "any unjustified comments" involving such accusations.[6]

But Baldwin received word about the start of another Justice Department "red hunt," and on October 2 he asked Hoover to issue an official denial regarding such operations in the coal district. Ten days later Hoover replied, declaring that the Bureau of Investigation of the U.S. Department of Justice was engaged in no red hunt and was not involved in Pennsylvania coal mine operations. The very next day Baldwin declared himself obliged to Hoover for "setting at rest the rumors" the ACLU had been receiving. Hoover's denial, Baldwin hoped, would "set at rest such unfounded statements." Clearly but mistakenly, the ACLU director continued to view Hoover as well intentioned.[7]

By contrast the ACLU's annual report for 1933 showed that Baldwin, fearing the emergence of an Italian-style corporate state, was concerned about the federal government's greatly augmented power under the New Deal. He recognized that Roosevelt's policies had strong support from the American middle class and from many workers and farmers. Yet the administration, he assumed, was "frankly an ally of business." This was troubling because labor-capital relations appeared to be sharper and more contentious as the New Deal sought "to bring order out of industrial conflict." The treatment of minorities, including Native Americans, foreign nationals, and blacks, had improved, Baldwin acknowledged. However, the New Deal had proved "timid or ineffective" in matters affecting "the ruling economic class." Thus, despite its expanded powers, "effective control over the exercise of civil liberties in the United States rests where it always has been,—with the masters of property," the annual report declared.[8]

As Baldwin sought to influence government policy, he remained a major figure on the American Left. On Friday, February 16, 1934, a mass demonstration in Madison Square Garden condemned the attack on social democratic Viennese workers by the right-wing Austrian government. Norman Thomas's Socialist Party and a group of labor unions had called for the meeting and asked workers to participate in a general strike that afternoon before joining the rally at the Garden. Communist-dominated unions backed the strike and party members went to the protest gathering. Attending were about eighteen thousand workers, including one to two thousand from left-wing unions antagonistic to both the AFL and socialist-dominated unions. The latter group—which contained a large number of communists or communist sympathizers—disrupted the proceedings, with tactics that ranged from brickbats to fistfights.[9]

A commission of inquiry assembled by the ACLU—comprised of Professor Henry Pratt Fairchild of Columbia University; Corliss Lamont, a left-wing activist; Alfred Bingham, editor of *Common Sense*; William B. Spofford from the Episcopal Church League for Industrial Democracy, which supported industrial reform, and Baldwin—found that the disturbance was hardly unusual. The commission reported that the disturbance resulted from recurrent hostilities between socialists and communists. It also was the by-product of the communists' deliberate attempt to prevent Matthew Woll, an AFL national officer and ardent anticommunist, and New York City mayor Fiorello La Guardia from speaking; Woll and La Guardia never appeared at the rally.[10]

In a telegram to the Reverend J. B. Matthews, dated February 20, Baldwin said the incident at Madison Square Garden "has destroyed for present possibility of extending united front against war in labor movement." The communists' tactics made cooperation with them ineffective. "We non-communists," Baldwin contended, should pursue another approach.[11]

Baldwin's anger was short-lived, however, for he remained comfortably within the fold of the United Front. Since his release from prison he had participated in a series of such alliances, including the International Committee for Political Prisoners, the Kuzbas Autonomous Industrial Colony in the Urals, and the International League Against Imperialism. Even his ouster from the League Against Imperialism and his involvement in the controversy surrounding the Scottsboro Boys' legal team failed to dissuade him from joining with any forces on the left—including communists—willing to participate in campaigns on behalf of the dispossessed or in opposition to war, imperialism, and fascism. Many in the liberal circles Baldwin frequented also participated in communist-dominated fronts, which included well-regarded noncommunists on their governing committees. Perhaps this was a result of their perception that the Russian communists were on the side of the angels, unlike the fascists in central and eastern Europe.

The International League Against Imperialism had passed from the scene back in 1931, undoubtedly the victim of the same kind of communist-driven sectarianism that had resulted in Baldwin's eviction. The league was replaced by the World League Against War and Fascism, which was established at another conference in Brussels in the same year and promoted by Willi Münzenberg, formerly a communist representative in the German Reichstag. Baldwin had been asked to serve on the board of the American branch, led by J. B. Matthews, until he resigned after the Madison Square Garden incident. Earl Browder, secretary of the Communist Party, and Clarence Hathaway, editor of the *Daily Worker*, went to Baldwin and apologized for the events at the Garden. Browder invited Baldwin to visit him at party headquarters. Acknowledging the league's loss of liberal members, Browder said Baldwin was "the only one who could persuade them to stay." Baldwin agreed to make such an attempt and spoke with ACLU chair Harry F. Ward about replacing Matthews as head of the league. To his surprise, Ward, a staunch friend of the Soviet Union, accepted the proposal.[12]

On March 7 Baldwin delivered an address at Madison Square Garden, "The Case of Civilization Against Hitlerism." Speaking as a strong supporter of the United Front, Baldwin discussed developments in Germany. Hitler was brutally suppressing "all the forces of dissent," from liberals to communists. While such groups previously had been unable to come together, "they are tragically united now—in concentration camps, exile, prison, silence and death." Thus Hitler had devised a united front for them. Such an alliance was needed to contend with "a wholesale terrorism unmatched by any dictatorship," Baldwin said. That terror was wielded by "a handful of adventurers," supported by giant industrialists and landholders. The result had been the quashing of the greatest socialist and communist parties. The Nazi dictatorship, Baldwin insisted, was different from the Soviet version, because the Germans provided "no economic freedom for the masses, no abolition of exploiting classes; no freedom for racial minorities; no larger education for youth; no progress to greater liberties." Mercifully, however, fascism was "the last possible stage of reaction, the last stronghold under the State of the privileged." To quash "this new tyranny of reaction," Baldwin cried, individuals with disparate political viewpoints had to unite.[13]

Fascism could arise "in any western country," he warned, "if socialism does not triumph first." "The tragic lessons of Germany and Austria," he insisted, had to be taken to heart in the United States. Unfortunately, however, the Left remained divided in practice, with noncommunists distrustful of their sectarian brethren. "Can the Communists be trusted in a united front to play the game fair?" Baldwin asked. Was a United Front possible so long as the communists subscribed to the doctrine of social fascism that all bourgeois and democratic parties were fascist at their core? Or was such an alliance workable while the communists carried out a policy of "united front from below," which involved raiding the rank-and-file of other parties? On the other hand, could a United Front be put together without the communists?[14]

For his part Baldwin possessed more than ten years' experience in united fronts, both at home and abroad, devised by communists. "I agreed with the specific objects," he wrote, "and found no other agency ready to tackle them with vigor." Thus he had worked with the International League Against Imperialism, the Friends of the Soviet Union, the Workers International Relief, labor defense committees, anti-Nazi groups, and presently the World League Against War and Fascism. Now, Baldwin believed, the communists had learned hard lessons. They appeared willing to allow others to take a hand in running front groups. They also seemed ready to stop attempting to mechanically dominate meetings. Admittedly, the communists were less apt to discard their beliefs in social fascism and the united front from below. But more important, they apparently were determined to work with leaders of other groups and had promised not to attack them inside the United Front.[15]

In the United States the American League Against War and Fascism, Baldwin claimed, could best serve the interests of the United Front. On July

14 Baldwin—who had recently asked once more to be replaced temporarily as ACLU director—wrote to Browder to suggest how to expand representation in the league. "We ought to have, we all will agree," he acknowledged, "far less Communist Party representation in proportion to the whole than at the first." The league should send out speakers like Philip La Follette of Wisconsin, his brother Robert Jr., and Governor Floyd Olson of Minnesota to spread its antiwar message. Other well-known middle-class figures who would be sympathetic to the calls against war and fascism included Jane Addams, the economist Paul H. Douglas, and the writer Zona Gale. Baldwin suggested that John Bosch of the Holiday Association, a farmers' organization, might canvass farmers, while A. Philip Randolph of the Brotherhood of Sleeping Car Porters might serve as a link to both labor and blacks. Norman Thomas, Baldwin maintained, should be invited to participate.[16]

Writing to Thomas on July 22, 1934, Baldwin spoke of his decision to remain in the American League Against War and Fascism, despite the unhappiness felt by many regarding communist tactics. "I do so because I see no other agency for the job that demands doing," he explained, "and because I find the Communists in the League entirely receptive to any and all proposals to enlist other forces, to minimize their part, proportionately, and to adopt methods which do not smack of Party tactics." Baldwin then referred to the Second Congress Against War and Fascism, scheduled for the end of September in Chicago. The communist influence would be too potent, he feared, unless those who were neither communists nor party sympathizers showed up. The committee orchestrating the convention especially hoped—but to no avail—that Thomas would deliver a talk at one of the major sessions, either as an individual or as a Socialist Party representative.[17]

It was hardly surprising that Baldwin now produced his most radical critique of socioeconomic conditions to date. Civil libertarians, he acknowledged in the September 1934 issue of *Soviet Russia Today*, a procommunist publication, adopted a class position, consciously or not, in the manner of everyone else. The more conservative among them believed that property interests were better protected by allowing opponents to blow off steam. Capitalism could be reformed, the liberals reasoned, and a new social order peacefully established. The pacifists were so enamored of nonviolence that they accepted "the colossal violence of the existing system," rather than "upset it by overt violence by the working class." None of those groups sought to overturn the capitalist system.[18]

Baldwin's own stance was both similar to and different from that of his colleagues:

> I, too, take a class position. It is anti-capitalist and pro-revolutionary. I believe in non-violent methods of struggle as most effective in the long run for building up successful working class power. Where they cannot be followed or where they are not even permitted by the ruling class, obviously only violent tactics remain. I champion civil liberty as the best of the non-violent means of building the power on which workers' rule must be based. If I aid the reactionaries to get free speech now and then, if I go outside the class struggle to fight against censorship, it is only because those liberties help to create a more hospitable atmosphere for working class liberties. The class struggle is the central conflict of the world; all others are incidental. When that power of the working class is once achieved, as it has been only in the Soviet Union, I am for maintaining it by any means whatever.

Such dictatorial control, Baldwin submitted, was only natural in a hostile world, where enemies, domestic and foreign, lurked all about. However, Soviet Russia had "already created liberties far greater than exist elsewhere in the world." While he was concerned about certain Communist Party practices that precluded democratic developments and resulted in unwarranted persecution, Baldwin insisted, "The fundamentals of liberty are firmly fixed in the USSR." Most significantly, they were "fixed on the only ground on which liberty really matters—economic." Thus no class existed to exploit the masses, the running of economic organizations was in the hands of workers, and any wealth created was considered common property.[19]

Political opponents encountered "rigid suppression," Baldwin acknowledged, as the road to socialism continued. This was symptomatic of the difficulties and insecurities resulting from the carving out of socialism in a world dominated by capitalists. Referring to his own trip to the Soviet Union, Baldwin said that he had heard many tales of communist brutality. Then he revealingly acknowledged,

> While I sympathized with personal distress I just could not bring myself to get excited over the suppression of opposition when I stacked it up against what I saw of fresh, vigorous expressions of free living by workers and peasants all over the land. And further, no champion of a socialist society could fail to see that some suppression was necessary to achieve it. It could not all be done by persuasion. Doubtless there has been at times far more coercion than was necessary. The Party has itself repeatedly said so. But "workers democracy" in

action is no product of coercion. It is genuine, and it the nearest approach to freedom that the workers have ever achieved.[20]

Next Baldwin analyzed how long the proletarian dictatorship would remain in existence. International circumstances and internal developments would answer that question. The concentration of power at the apex of the Soviet government would surely dissipate. The state and the power of police agencies would gradually disappear. Civil liberties would once again be safeguarded, this time by the socialist society. However, no one would oppose such a social order, "for who will want to?" Baldwin asked, demonstrating his continued belief in utopian possibilities. The expansion of educational opportunities and the emergence of a new generation of Soviet citizens would diminish autocracy at the top.[21]

Should American laborers—possessing no genuine liberties other than the right "to change masters" or, on occasion, the ability to rise through the ranks—grasp their class interests, Baldwin continued, the "Soviet 'workers' democracy'" would be their goal." And should American civil libertarians view economic freedom as the ultimate goal, they too would consider "workers' democracy" to be "far superior to what the capitalist world offers to any but a small minority. Yes, and they would accept—regretfully, of course—the necessity of dictatorship while the job of reorganizing society on a socialist basis is being done."[22]

From a pragmatic viewpoint Baldwin's statement was clearly wrongheaded. For the ACLU director to be declaring, in effect, that the defense of civil liberties was intended to serve the interests of workers alone was politically misguided. Affirming that the defense of right-wingers was designed for the same purpose could only call into question the sincerity of his belief in an expansive interpretation of First Amendment freedoms. Similarly, Baldwin's acknowledgment that he considered political repression necessary in Soviet Russia would certainly result in a firestorm of criticism. So would his declaration that the class struggle was most significant.

From another and still more troubling perspective Baldwin's analysis could lead to doubts regarding the campaign he had long waged on behalf of civil liberties. If civil liberties served as a kind of club to be drawn against propertied interests, what place did civil liberties really have in the American pantheon Baldwin and the ACLU sought to create? Why would anyone other than committed revolutionaries drawn from the ranks of the American working class insist on protecting civil liberties? Although the article in

Soviet Russia Today might have enabled Baldwin to show, even flaunt, his radical colors in the period when the Old Left was becoming more prominent, it seemed to fly in the face of the crusade he had waged for nearly two decades now. It also was hardly conducive to fostering the kind of government access he sought.

Corresponding in January 1935 with Joseph Wood Krutch of the *Nation*, Baldwin agreed that the ability to criticize was essential to any government system. Such a right existed—admittedly in a very limited way—inside the Soviet Communist Party and among peasants and workers who had been encouraged to register complaints. At present, Baldwin argued, "a political opposition would strike at the very frame-work of a Socialist state." Like Krutch, Baldwin deplored the terrorism and the authoritarianism of Soviet Russia. "I can tolerate it only as preferable to far less hopeful concentrations of power in capitalist countries."[23]

The correspondence with Krutch was intriguing because another round of purges was unfolding in the Soviet Union. Just a month earlier Sergei Kirov, the Leningrad Communist Party chief, had been assassinated. One hundred and eighteen Soviet citizens were rounded up, denounced as White Guardists by Joseph Stalin, and then executed after show trials like those in Nazi Germany. On January 18 Baldwin, John Dewey, Arthur Garfield Hays, Sinclair Lewis, and John Haynes Holmes, among others, sent a letter to Alexander A. Troyanovsky, the Soviet ambassador to the United States, to express their concerns about developments in his land. Acting on behalf of the International Committee for the Defense of Political Prisoners, they proclaimed themselves representative of no particular political philosophy. They had stood up for antifascists, anti-imperialists, labor unions, and revolutionary parties, communist ones chief among them. At times they had condemned political persecution in Soviet Russia. Frequently, however, they had refused to do so, declining to give comfort to "reactionary opponents" of the communist state. Nevertheless, they opposed the penalties being meted out to individuals for mere expressions of opinion or nonviolent activities. Where such penalties were legally authorized, they urged that defendants be afforded full legal rights and not summarily tried or made to suffer excessive punishment.[24]

The spate of arrests and executions following the murder of Kirov compelled members of the international committee to speak out. The Soviet government had acted, it seemed clear from official accounts, with "shocking severity . . . unwarranted by any facts yet disclosed." Even the normal, largely summary methods of dealing with political cases had been discarded in the latest incidents. Scores of individuals had been shot—some mere hours following their arrest—without any trial but after a special secret tribunal had been convened. The committee "would not for a moment make representations on behalf of assassins or their accomplices, nor terrorists or conspirators engaged in carrying out or plotting overt acts against the Soviet state," the committee wrote. (These, of course, were the kinds of justifications made by the communist regime for conducting the purges.) However, it continued, "the terroristic methods themselves necessarily shock and dismay even those friendly to the Soviet Union." Similar practices had occurred during previous crises. Their use at present, when the Soviet Union was so much stronger both at home and abroad, signified "insecurity, fear or tyrannical and vengeful habits of rule," the committee said.[25]

Committee members implored the Soviet ambassador to inform his government about their protest, which they had withheld until now because they had expected some reasonable explanation might be forthcoming. Now they were confronted with "the ruthless suppression of opponents or critics guilty of no overt acts." The committee stated in closing that it was sending the letter "in a friendly spirit," despite charges of partisanship that might arise.[26]

On February 15 Baldwin wrote to the editor of the *Daily Worker* and declared that the International Committee for the Defense of Political Prisoners had drafted the January statement to condemn actions by the Soviet regime that "played into the hands of reactionaries." Baldwin took exception to a recent editorial in the *Daily Worker* that had lumped committee members with White Guardists out to destroy the Soviet Union: "Certainly no test of friendliness to the Soviet regime can be gauged by uncritical acceptance of its every act."[27]

In June Baldwin sent a brief note to be included in the thirtieth reunion classbook of the Harvard class of 1905. Perhaps deliberately provocative, the statement proved to be one of the most controversial he ever made:

> My "chief aversion" is the system of greed, private profit, privilege, and violence which makes up the control of the world today, and which has brought it the tragic crisis of unprecedented hunger and unemployment. I am opposed to the new deal [sic] because it strives to strengthen and prolong production for private profit. At bottom I am for conserving the full powers of every person on earth by expanding them to their individual limits. Therefore, I am for socialism, disarmament, and ultimately for abolishing the State itself as an

instrument of property, the abolition of the propertied class and sole control by those who produce wealth. Communism is the goal. It sums up into one single purpose—the abolition of the system of dog-eat-dog under which we live, and the substitution by the most effective non-violence possible of a system of cooperative ownership and use of all wealth.[28]

Again, the impolitic nature of the statement is striking. One reason for its delivery was, of course, Baldwin's leftward shift during the midthirties. In typical fashion he might have been thumbing his nose at his own kind, former Harvard classmates, most of whom would naturally be appalled by his pronouncements. Such a possibility would undoubtedly have amused him. However, he again failed to consider how this response could prove costly to both the ACLU and the civil liberties movement.

His hardened class analysis, coupled with a lingering distrust of government action, led Baldwin, along with the ACLU board, to oppose passage of the Wagner Act, which established the National Labor Relations Board and safeguarded the right of workers to organize. Baldwin's perception was in keeping with a recent conference, "Civil Liberties Under the New Deal," sponsored by the ACLU, along with other liberal and radical organizations. In his minutes of the gathering, held at Howard University Law School in Washington, D.C., in December 1934, Baldwin claimed that the New Dealers had not lived up to their promises to support the right of workers to bargain collectively. Indeed, he wrote, "the New Deal's labor policy is obviously confused, vacillating and timid."[29]

Now, on April 1, 1935, in a letter to the bill's sponsor, Senator Robert Wagner, the New York Democrat, Baldwin insisted "that no such federal agency intervening in the conflicts between employers and employees can be expected to fairly determine the issues of labor's rights." Instead, only strong militant unions had managed "to achieve anything like an unrestricted exercise of their rights." However, an opposite determination by labor leaders and ACLU attorneys, including Morris Ernst and Arthur Garfield Hays, compelled the board to poll national committee members and affiliates, who overwhelmingly supported the measure. In early July 1935 organized labor's "Magna Carta" was signed into law. ACLU leaders, including Baldwin, soon recognized that the NLRB was a spur to union organizing.[30]

That same month Fred Beal—a former member of the Communist Party who had headed the 1929 strike in Gastonia, North Carolina, before fleeing to the Soviet Union to escape charges of murdering the Gastonia police chief—penned an open letter to a series of American "liberals" in hopes of inducing them to condemn the Stalinist dictatorship, just as they had fascist ones. The "liberals" were Harry F. Ward, John Dewey, Norman Thomas, Mary van Kleeck (a social activist and dedicated director of the Russell Sage Foundation's Department of Industrial Studies), and Baldwin. Baldwin fired off a note to the *Daily Worker* that called Beal "a weak and vacillating man" who had written a series of devastating critiques about the Soviet Union. Baldwin accused Beal of selling out to the staunchly anticommunist Hearst press, resulting in the vilification of "the first great attempt in the world's history to liberate the masses from their exploiters." For Baldwin—who was again using double standards—to ask pro-Russian Americans to castigate the Soviet and fascist dictatorships equally "is to put a dishonest question. Everyone with a grain of political sense knows that it is not forms of government but the purposes of government which constitute the only sound basis for judgment. Fascism crystallizes the slavery of the existing economic system; the Soviet Union is abolishing it." Beal thus stood as "a weak tool of reaction."[31]

In a somewhat more temperate letter Ward, Kleeck, and Baldwin wrote to the Hearst Newspapers and declared Beal's challenge "naive and insincere." Criticism, no matter how well intentioned, they believed, was invariably used by those who had no concerns about Soviet workers. The "crocodile tears" of those criticizing the USSR served to conceal the readiness to break "the world's first experiment in building socialism" and to bring about a return to capitalist exploitation and czarist despotism. At this stage Baldwin refused, as he had at other points, to provide the Soviet Union's critics with ammunition, regardless of what that entailed.[32]

Later that year the Hearst Newspapers initiated a campaign to expose the purported communism of the ACLU and Roger Baldwin. In an editorial ominously entitled "Unmasked," the chain reported that the ACLU was defending the rights of communists, and it deemed the ACLU director no authentic champion of free speech but a communist. In a letter to the *San Francisco Daily News*, dated October 21, 1935, Baldwin held that American traditions required protection of the right of all political groups to speak freely, regardless of their composition, provided no acts of violence resulted. Concerning the charges hurled at him personally, Baldwin declared unequivocally,

> I am not and never have been a member of the Communist Party. My goal and method, political and economic, is based wholly on reducing and ultimately

abolishing all violence in human relations. I am sympathetic with the economic system being worked out in Soviet Russia. I believe in the economic
goal of communism—namely, sharing in common the world's wealth. To my
mind there is no higher ethical principle than that which marks the ethics, not
of political Communism as it is understood today, but of Communism in its
early Christian sense—"From each according to his ability; to each according
to his needs."

Baldwin referred to the Hearst papers' efforts to portray him as "a political
Communist." Those publications were relying heavily on the statement he
had delivered for his Harvard classbook, but that note, he pointed out, was
clearly intended to refer to economic communism. However, to expect others to draw such a distinction was wholly unrealistic.[33]

By 1936 Baldwin's political perspective had changed little. He continued to
express his preference for "any form of a cooperative society to capitalism."
Thus he remained supportive of the Soviet Union's economic policy,
although not of "its dictatorship or atrocities," which he had often condemned. He favored "any venture in collectivism on the road to what I
believe will ultimately be a society in which individuals can be socially
free." By contrast, the New Deal remained, in his estimation, "a mild collection of reforms." For Baldwin the adoption by communists the previous
summer of "a people's anti-Fascist front," and the realities of fascist aggression, required "that all forward-looking forces make common cause against
reaction."[34]

Baldwin's perspective on international events compelled him to adopt a
different stance than he had a generation earlier. Increasingly, in the face of
right-wing aggression abroad his acceptance of a pacifist perspective began
to change—although he still referred to himself as "an extremist . . . in pacifism." In early December 1936 he said that the pacifist principle was inherently correct, should be supported vigorously, and would eventually win out.
At the same time he viewed it as "wholly impractical in the present day
world." At present, he maintained, the pacifist was required to choose
"between absolute non-violence and violence." Already, pacifists were well
aware of where they stood on the great issues of the day: the Japanese
encroachment against China, the Italian invasion of Ethiopia, and the
Falangists' attempt to overturn the legally constituted government of Republican Spain. Baldwin believed that pacifists needed to recognize the economic origins of war, support the working class and its representatives

against reactionary forces, and envision "the building of a Socialist state as the means to eliminate war."[35]

On December 11, in a letter to Maj. Gen. Smedly D. Butler, one of the most popular speakers on the American League Against War and Fascism's lecture circuit, Baldwin expressed concerns regarding critical comments about the organization's support for the Spanish government. The league did not want to infringe on Butler's right to speak, Baldwin wrote, and respected his belief that the United States should remain on the sidelines. The league felt otherwise, Baldwin reminded the good general, because it believed that it had to stand beside the Spanish regime in confronting "Fascist revolt."[36]

As fascist aggression mounted, Baldwin argued that the most important question facing the world now was whether a democratic nation like the United States could experience economic change peacefully. Or, must submission to dictatorship and the possibility of international and civil war take place? Developments in the Soviet Union, he reasoned, provided clues to these fundamental queries. On December 13, in an address entitled "Liberty in the U.S.A. and the U.S.S.R." at Boston's Community Church, Baldwin discussed what he perceived to be hopeful developments involving the Soviet Union. The country, he explained, was carving out alliances with democratic nations, its new constitution held great promise, and it welcomed communist support for the Popular Front.[37]

The notion that the Soviet Union was being democratized, Baldwin reasoned, was certain to engender distrust. Then Baldwin—speaking as the Moscow show trials were taking place—acknowledged that he, like others who still viewed events in the USSR hopefully, believed that great accomplishments were being made. The Soviet proclamation of the importance of civil rights, he argued, was "a great gain." He was pleased as well that the communist dictatorship remained "committed to an ultimate democracy" and the architect of economic liberties. And he found it fortunate that the German "catastrophe" had convinced the Soviets of the need to discard "the struggle for world revolution" in the fight to defend democracy against fascism.[38]

The United States possessed "political democracy limited by industrial autocracy," Baldwin concluded, whereas the Soviet Union experienced "a political autocracy limited by industrial democracy." However, for the average individual, Baldwin proclaimed, again in improvident fashion, economic liberty superseded political liberty, thus establishing the Soviet Union as a guiding force. Recognition of this fact led individuals like him to defend the

Soviet Union, despite its dictatorial makeup. This was only natural, Baldwin asserted, for as the capitalist economic system changed, democracy would eventually be carried over into the industrial realm. Political democracy alone, Baldwin intemperately insisted, "is useful only as a tool of peaceful change. The substance of change is the control of the whole business of production by the community itself. The vision of the socialized democratic state today stands even clearer than ever as a promise of mankind's ultimate liberty."[39]

For Baldwin the Russian Revolution still held "immense significance." As he saw it, the obliteration of economic privileges was "in itself a vast step to a freedom the world has never before known." The quest to replace such economic privileges with a great cooperative effort was "a contribution recognized even by Russia's enemies," who attempted five-year plans of their own. Despite the Soviet dictatorship, the revolution continued to provide the only proven means of abolishing the class conflicts that afflicted all societies and forestalled movement toward democratic liberties.[40]

Now Baldwin had determined there were but three vehicles for bringing about the redistribution of property and two had major shortcomings. The general strike appeared impractical and unlikely ever to occur. At present armed insurrection seemed too risky and even the communists had abandoned it after the Comintern was convened in 1935.[41]

That left democratic action to usher in radical change. Apparently discredited by the Great Depression—which had resulted in a surge of support for both fascism and communism—democracy had, for a time, increasingly fallen out of favor with many on the Left. Capitalists had proven prone to abandon democracy when they thought their property interests were in danger. "Our embryo Fascism" could be witnessed in "their strong-arm men, their spies, their strike-breakers, their subservient police and sheriffs, their complacent government," Baldwin said. Simultaneously, however, workers, farmers, and socialist movements praised democracy. Since the Nazis had cemented their hold on Germany, the communists too had come to view democracy in a different light. Now they had joined with socialists and middle-class reformers in supporting "people's fronts." In both France and Spain the result had been the "greatest contemporary laboratories of social change," which offered the means to bring about revolutionary transformation in a different manner. Armed resistance might well result, but peaceful and legal change would continue unless civil war broke out. Thus for Baldwin there existed the contrasting models provided by France and Spain to usher in socialism and thereby produce the "industrial democracy which is the heart of the democratic ideal," and the Soviet Union, whose economic liberties made it "the most democratic country in the world."[42]

Once more Baldwin's faith in the ongoing developments in the Soviet Union appears astonishing, particularly as the Moscow show trials were underway. His declaration that the USSR, with its "economic liberties," was the world's "most democratic" nation, demonstrated astonishing naïvêté or crass cynicism. Given Baldwin's sometimes marked inability or unwillingness to analyze events in the communist state, the former was more likely the case. For some, however, who well appreciated his calculating, manipulative qualities, his reading of the USSR was more deliberate, even devious. In this regard, of course, Baldwin's continued identification with the Soviet Union was hardly unique, nor was his readiness to dismiss or paper over stories of certain horrors increasingly characteristic of Stalinism. What is most curious, ironic, or hypocritical about Baldwin's perspective is that it was delivered by the very man who personified the civil liberties movement in the United States and had argued, quite convincingly, that protection of fundamental freedoms was essential for American democracy. Unquestionably, Baldwin, at a bare minimum, remained capable of requiring different standards from different governments, depending on their ideological makeup.

Throughout 1937 Baldwin continued to serve as a leading figure in the ranks of the American League Against War and Fascism. In late August, however, he objected to a draft statement that explored the international situation. His major objection involved a sentence that indicated democracy had been obliterated in Italy and Germany. It had also been crushed, Baldwin asserted—to his credit—in Russia, Austria, and significant parts of Latin America.[43]

During this same period Baldwin proposed to Harry F. Ward that the antifascist organization change its name to the American League for Peace and Democracy. This was to underscore its determination to "protect and extend democratic rights for all sections of the American people." The league was especially intended to protect labor unions from mounting attacks by corporations and government officials and to help usher in legislation outlawing lynching. The name change also allowed the league to skirt the issue of whether it was opposed to war, fascism, and communism, a question that could hardly be answered adequately, given the sectarian nature of many of its members.[44]

Spain, and France for a brief period, stood as embodiments of the Popular Front. Both countries, as Baldwin acknowledged, "continue to grip me as the battle-front of the forces of progress." He remained "almost prayerful" regarding the Loyalists' success in battle. This was "a fine emotion for an anarchist and pacifist!" he acknowledged. "Such is the fate of ideals!" In a letter to Madeleine Doty, Baldwin said, "No, sir, my pacifism goes completely under when it comes to defense of democracy against Fascism. What way out have you other than arms? How would you resist the Fascists? If you don't, you just invite an endless tyranny."[45]

Ensnared in the struggle to support the Spanish Republic, Baldwin backed a number of Popular Front efforts to champion the Loyalist cause. He joined with V. F. Calverton, Sidney Hook, A. Philip Randolph, Upton Sinclair, and Carlo Tresca, among others, in the Friends of the Debs Column, designed to raise money and obtain volunteers to fight in Spain. In early 1937 Baldwin served as chairman of the executive committee of the North American Committee to Aid Spanish Democracy. Apparently, he was the one individual that groups with highly divergent ideas would accept in such a role. That organization soon merged with the Medical Bureau to Aid Spanish Democracy to found the Spanish Refugee Relief Campaign, for which Baldwin was also an officer. Due to the fierce allegiance to the Republic by socialists and anarchists, sectarian divisions were all but inevitable. The board contained Quakers too, as well as august names, including those of Ernest Hemingway, Louis Brandeis, Malcolm Cowley of the *New Republic*, the actress Helen Hayes, the playwright Lillian Hellman, the poet Edna St. Vincent Millay, and the artist Rockwell Kent. Noncommunists were determined that communists not dominate this latest Popular Front manifestation. Fortunately, Herman Reissig, a Protestant minister, acted as the organization's executive secretary. Great rallies were held across the United States, with war documentaries depicting atrocities. While this committee refrained from actively soliciting volunteers to join the good fight, Baldwin delivered a speech applauding those individuals who engaged General Francisco Franco's Falangists. Although still a self-professed pacifist, Baldwin justified such involvement as sustaining a police action undertaken by a legally constituted government.[46]

Through the early months of 1938 he continued to hope that a confederation of antifascist forces might prevent another world war. He refused to view collective security and isolation as mutually exclusive. Thus he was "in favor of withholding our economic reserves from aggressor nations and making them available to their victims." He also called for the removal of U.S. troops from foreign service, a refusal to use the military to safeguard American financial interests or citizens in other lands, and the nationalization of the arms industry. Similarly, he urged the paring down of the U.S. military "to the proved needs of national defense of our shores" and the approval of the Ludlow Amendment, proposed by Rep. Louis Ludlow, D-Ind., to require, except in cases of invasion, that "the authority of Congress to declare war shall not become effective until confirmed by a majority of all votes cast in a national referendum." [47]

On July 12, in a letter to Leonard Bright of Keep America Out of War, Baldwin expressed general satisfaction with the National Anti-War Congress. At the same time he was displeased with the committee's refusal to address the question of the embargo on Spain. Such an approach, he affirmed, was "the keystone of any realistic foreign policy in dealing with the struggle for democracy throughout the world." He would support a worldwide cessation of arms shipments by the United States. Barring that, he argued that the United States should withhold munitions from countries at war with a democratic state, as in Republican Spain. [48]

Thus by 1938 Baldwin, while still proclaiming himself a pacifist, had come to support action against the right-wing aggressor states. That might entail restriction of trade, an arms embargo, or even fighting by soldiers—Spaniards and international volunteers alike—who defended the Spanish Republic. Above all else Baldwin readily backed the Popular Front and the call for an antifascist alliance, which continued to be identified with communist support and the Soviet Union.

At the same time he appeared more troubled than ever by events involving the supposed communist experiment. The Moscow trials reinforced his earlier misgivings regarding Stalinist practices. Indeed, Baldwin had come to couple Soviet and Nazi repression in a manner he previously had refused to do. Yet at this point, he, like so many American leftists, still viewed the Soviet Union as prominently involved in the antifascist fight.

The six Baldwin children, ca. 1898, in Wellesley Hills: Roger,
14; Margaret, 12; Ruth, 10; Deborah, 8; Herbert, 5; Robert, 3.
A seventh child, Frank F. Jr., died when he was a year old.

Roger Baldwin at Washington University in
St. Louis, 1906

Roger Baldwin in St. Louis, ca. 1911
PRINCETON UNIVERSITY LIBRARY

Roger Baldwin rowing, ca. 1915 PRINCETON UNIVERSITY LIBRARY

Madeleine Zabriskie Doty,
ca. 1917 PRINCETON
UNIVERSITY LIBRARY

Roger Baldwin with group at brook in Sparta, N.J., 1919 SMITH COLLEGE LIBRARY

Freddy Farnum, 1919

Reunion at Caldwell Penitentiary: from left, Freddy Farnum, Roger Baldwin, Alexander McCabe, Warden Hosp, Caroline Colgate, Milton Bauman, 1923

Roger Baldwin and Madeleine Doty, Geneva, 1927; the two youngsters are not identified.
SMITH COLLEGE LIBRARY

Roger Baldwin, 1934 PRINCETON UNIVERSITY LIBRARY

Roger Baldwin, Columbia University antiwar rally, April 12, 1935
PRINCETON UNIVERSITY LIBRARY

Roger and Evelyn Baldwin, ca. 1940
PRINCETON UNIVERSITY LIBRARY

Roger Baldwin with students at Tokyo Imperial University, 1947

Roger Baldwin at meeting of the judicial council and guests, Berchtesgaden, Bavaria,
October 28, 1950

Norman Thomas and
Roger Baldwin, ca. 1960
PRINCETON UNIVERSITY LIBRARY

Roger Baldwin at Leonard Bernstein's apartment, 1964
PRINCETON UNIVERSITY LIBRARY

Roger Baldwin on the *David Frost Show* talking about the ACLU's fiftieth anniversary, January 31, 1970 PRINCETON UNIVERSITY LIBRARY

Roger Baldwin (second from right) at thirtieth anniversary celebration of the United Nations, 1975 PRINCETON UNIVERSITY LIBRARY

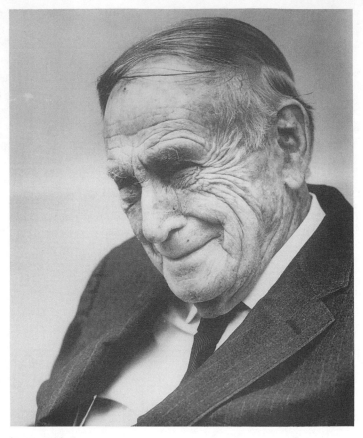

Roger Baldwin, ca. 1975 PRINCETON UNIVERSITY LIBRARY

CHAPTER SEVENTEEN

The Home Front

While Baldwin's involvement with organizations ranging from the ACLU to the American League for Peace and Democracy remained both enormously controversial and a constant source of excitement and satisfaction, his personal life continued to be riddled with uncertainty. For more than a full decade after he and Madeleine Doty first separated, their unconventional marriage was still unbroken, sustained by the fierce bonds that bound them and by an unwillingness to change a situation affording each some measure of security. In 1929 and 1931 Baldwin again visited Doty in Geneva, where she remained stationed with the Women's International League for Peace and Freedom.[1]

The first trip resulted in Baldwin's confinement to a French sanitarium for ten days, one leg afflicted with both phlebitis and a skin infection. He had been attending morning meetings of the World League Against Imperialism and visiting old friends, when he awakened one day with a fever, chills, and a swollen and painful leg. Initially, he attributed his physical ailments to his "shock at meeting my wife." A communist member of the Reichstag—perhaps Willi Münzenberg—referred Baldwin to a homeopathic physician. Baldwin asked what his chances were and the doctor replied, "It can go to your head or your heart." Baldwin wrote a farewell note to his family, placed it next to the bed, and fell asleep. Eventually, chamomile tea dressings were applied to Baldwin's leg, and he was given an herbal remedy. Still more exotic measures followed. At the sanitarium he was given hay tea, and a bitter potion helped him pass gallstones.[2]

Shortly after his return to the United States, Baldwin had to share with Doty the tragic news of the twin suicides of two of his "boys," Toto Stolz and

Brownie Brown. These latest tragedies followed Freddy Farnum's apparent suicide a half-dozen years earlier.[3]

During the summer of 1929 Baldwin had spent some time with Toto in England and France. After Toto returned home, he quit his job in St. Louis and headed for the warmer climate of Los Angeles. Dissatisfied, he found a better-paying job in a Santa Fe oil camp. But he was still unhappy and moved back to Los Angeles without a job. Unwilling to return to his hometown of St. Louis, thirty-three-year-old Toto drove his Ford roadster to a public park on the evening of February 5, 1930, and shot himself. Baldwin's Aunt Belle, one of Toto's few friends in Los Angeles, where she too now lived, delivered the following message: "He came to my house every five days and always started talking about you, for time and again he said he could not understand your line of thought. He would have liked to live nearer you, but after his visit last summer he said 'that was all over.'" Toto left no note explaining his suicide.[4]

Baldwin asked for no displays of sympathy and asserted in a note to friends, "I am satisfied to have done my best in raising him to what was for over 15 years a pretty contented and successful life of his own, and to have had the fun and friendship that went with fathering a growing youngster." Baldwin planned to set up a trust fund to benefit needy children with the approximately $10,000 estate left him by Toto.[5]

Baldwin declined to attend Toto's funeral and left the arrangements up to a public administrator. He asserted that Toto "could not have been more companionable; he was the closest of anyone to me for a decade, but it was not the closeness of love." Frances Bowen, Brownie's sister, told Baldwin on February 17, "Toto was the most tremendously lonely person I know." Thanks to Baldwin, Toto "had learned to find distasteful a vapid glamour of tinsel and roadhouse parties"; having done so, however, Toto had nothing to turn to. On February 20 Baldwin received a letter from Oral James offering condolences—"My heart goes out to you, Baldwin, you know that without my saying it on paper"—yet it contained a cutting edge as well. First James exclaimed, "What an original way to go OUT!" Then he termed Baldwin's note to his friends a "unique document . . . . Sounds like a WHITE HOUSE memo."[6]

About six weeks after Toto died, Brownie too committed suicide. Two years earlier Brownie had unsuccessfully worked for the ACLU as a publicity man. At one point in 1928 Baldwin had fired off a sharp letter to Brownie regarding his resentment of wages and working conditions for staffers. "Your attitude makes it hard for me to deal with you," Baldwin wrote, "because you insist on regarding me as an employer from whom you must wrest whatever favorable treatment you get." Forrest Bailey, Lucille Milner, and Baldwin considered Brownie the source of "constant friction and misunderstanding." They determined to let him go, the first employee fired because of "a temperamental disability to adjust to the organization," Baldwin informed Brownie.[7]

On March 25, 1930, troubled by the collapse of a love affair, Brownie shot himself through the heart. Baldwin acknowledged to Mary Buckley that he too had experienced "a good deal of pressure and strain." Now "added to the shock of Toto's death comes a fresh tragedy." Baldwin did "not yet know the inside reason" for Brownie's action, "but he was full of conflict over life." Sadly, Baldwin wrote, "I just can't tell you what this suicide on top of Toto's has done to me."[8]

As his Wobbly friends Anna Friedkin and Phil Taft later reported, Baldwin now had an affair with Friedkin's friend Peggy Tucker. Tucker, a native of England, and her late husband had been associated with the ACLU's San Francisco branch. In 1924 she traveled to the east coast as a representative of the Committee of 48, a group tied to the Farmer-Labor Party, and backed the presidential bid of Sen. Robert M. La Follette of Wisconsin. According to Taft, Tucker had lived with the Wobbly poet-singer Ralph Chaplin for a spell. Friedkin believed that Baldwin was not sincere about his relationship with Tucker, but Lucille Milner thought "they were madly in love." If Doty would only divorce Baldwin, Tucker said, they could be together, something Friedkin thought that he never seriously considered. Tucker, who was quite feminine, possessed "the nerve of a brass monkey," Friedkin declared. The radical artist Art Young thought well of her. Although older than Friedkin and some others in their circle, she was "so vivacious you didn't think of that," Young said. She had been married twice and had four children.[9]

On one occasion Baldwin and Tucker and her young son Allen showed up unannounced at the Friedkin home in Brooklyn. They exclaimed, "Oh, Ann, Allen is going to spend the night with you." Off Baldwin and Tucker went, infuriating Friedkin. She contacted Tucker and asked, "How can you put that boy out of your house just because Roger was coming to spend the night with you?" That episode, Friedkin contended, was all too characteristic of Baldwin and Tucker's relationship; he had no respect for Tucker, Friedkin believed. Most tragic of all, however, that "most gorgeous child" later went to a farm and hanged himself.[10]

Throughout this period Baldwin maintained a camp in the New Jersey countryside, which served as a sanctuary for him and various friends. In 1930, after the water company threatened to evict Baldwin from his latest site on the upper Hackensack, he purchased two acres beside the river at Old Tappan and relocated his camp there. Although he planned to make that site the permanent location for his camp, he gradually became involved with Dell Brook, a ninety-five-acre tract in Oakland with a nineteenth-century farmhouse, a frame barn, and three other outbuildings. By 1932 two groups of friends, including James Reid of Harcourt Brace; Dorothy Kenyon, a lawyer who worked with the ACLU; and Bob Gessner, were helping Baldwin to rent Dell Brook for $1,000 a year. Baldwin sold the Old Tappan property in 1940.[11]

Dell Brook, about eight miles northwest of Paterson, had been a self-sufficient farm, with good river-bottom land that flooded at times and a brook that was never dry. The brook served as a pond for swimming and boating during the summer and as a skating rink in the winter. Throughout the year Baldwin and his friends played tennis, canoed, and hiked the mountain trails. When Baldwin and his friends took over Dell Brook, the land was largely open pasture, much of it covered with brush. Eventually, Baldwin and his friends bought other land beside the river as well as another plot nearby. The going price was only $100 an acre. Baldwin, who joined the board of directors of the National Audubon Society in 1934, delighted in the time he spent in the New Jersey countryside.[12]

In 1934 Doty, who had resigned as secretary of the Women's International League for Peace and Freedom, returned home from Geneva to obtain an apartment next to Baldwin's on West 12th Street in Manhattan. Baldwin shared his apartment with Eduard Lindeman and Travis Hoke, both friends from his St. Louis days, and for a brief while with Bob Gessner. Baldwin and Doty tried a reconciliation but to no avail. He was now involved with a younger woman, Evelyn Preston. In the twenties Baldwin had first heard of a wealthy, well-educated young woman who had joined the labor movement after graduating from Barnard College, receiving her master's degree at the University of Wisconsin, and doing postgraduate studies at the Brookings Institution. Her father, Ralph Preston, who had died in 1917, was a man of impeccable taste who, rather than ply his trade as an attorney, had lived off money he had inherited from his wife, Elizabeth Thompson, who had died when Evie was only two.

Evie Preston was raised mostly by her aunt, Geraldine Thompson, a powerful figure in the Republican Party. Staid and proper, Thompson, who was married to the son of the Standard Oil Co.'s treasurer, was involved in reform efforts, including campaigns to improve prison conditions, hospitals, child welfare, and the treatment of the mentally ill. The Thompsons were neighbors of the Roosevelt family in Hyde Park, and Geraldine Thompson was a good friend of Eleanor Roosevelt's. Evie, influenced by the reformist bent of her aunts, Geraldine Thompson and Ruth Morgan, worked in England for a while as secretary to Ellen Wilkinson, a Labor Party member of Parliament. On returning to the United States in 1927, Evie Preston became involved with Brookwood Labor College, which the Garland Fund helped to sustain, and the League for Industrial Democracy. A millionaire at least a couple of times over, she caused a furor in her family when she donated money to Brookwood.[13]

In 1927 Baldwin attended an ACLU luncheon at the Civic Club at 12th Street and Fifth Avenue. A number of young people, including Evie Preston, came over to speak with committee members. To Baldwin she was "a breezy, queenly sort of girl with a hearty laugh and a ready smile." Afterward he was informed of her work at Brookwood Labor College. In the summer of 1928 they met once more, when both were guests at Barn House on Martha's Vineyard; she had been invited by the ACLU lawyer Dorothy Kenyon. Barn House was "a cooperative, intellectual venture," founded after the war by a group of left-leaning attorneys, artists, businessmen, academics, and reformers. One member of the group was the artist Boardman Robinson, who had contributed to the foremost radical publications of the Lyrical Left, the *Masses* and the *Liberator*, both edited by Max Eastman. The participants sought something of "a communal utopia" to serve as a seaside summer retreat; at the same time Barn House members were all well-off and could easily return to more comfortable surroundings. After a day at the beach they would gather in the afternoons for conversation and entertainment. After dinner all washed and dried the dishes, then headed off to read in the spartan cabins, or "coops," spread out over Barn House's forty acres. For many years the coops lacked running water or indoor plumbing. Baldwin had visited Barn House once before, shortly after its founding in 1919.[14]

For some time Martha's Vineyard residents viewed Barn House with distrust. The secretiveness enveloping Barn House provoked all sorts of questions. Who were those individuals living communally in such crude circumstances? One theory had it that "they must be Communists . . . living promiscuously, holding wild beach parties," as one local writer put it years later. Stories abounded of nude bathing along the private beach.[15]

Preston and Baldwin proved inseparable, discovering that they shared the same interests and a good number of friends—including Alex Meiklejohn, the renowned professor of philosophy at the University of Wisconsin and an ACLU compatriot, and his wife, Helen, who were also at the Vineyard that summer. Baldwin was delighted with Preston's interest in the outdoors, including birds and wildflowers. And they were both part of the New York Left. But Baldwin was still mired in his unconventional marriage to Doty, while Preston was engaged to Steve Rauschenbusch, who was on the staff of Pennsylvania governor Amos Pinchot. Rauschenbusch's family lineage was every bit as distinguished as Baldwin's, for he was the son of the great social gospel minister Walter Rauschenbusch. Baldwin was acquainted with both Steve Rauschenbusch and his family. He knew Steve's mother, who lived in Rochester; his sister, who briefly worked as the ACLU publicity director; and his brother, Paul, son-in-law of Supreme Court Justice Louis Brandeis. Evie Preston's background was still more privileged, of course. Helen Meiklejohn informed Baldwin that Preston lived in "the swank . . . big house, servants, racing stables and endless acres." Preston invited Baldwin to spend a weekend at her family's estate at Red Bank, New Jersey. There he met Geraldine Thompson, and the three had a grand time, conversing, riding through the countryside, and sauntering along the woods behind the grand house.[16]

Evie Preston married Rauschenbusch in 1928. With Dorothy Kenyon, Steve and Evie wrote a brief arguing that prices would drop if New York City took over the Con Ed electrical plants. Mayor James J. Walker became "rather rattled and nervous" by the report, but his successor, Fiorello La Guardia, later purchased a few plants. At first Evie maintained her New York City apartment on Washington Square; after the birth in 1929 of her first child, whom she named Roger, she bought another apartment at 1 Fifth Avenue. Eventually, she and the baby moved to Harrisburg to join Steve, and she mostly lost touch with Roger Baldwin. But soon after the birth of another son, Carl, in 1931, she decided to leave Rauschenbusch. "She found her marriage dull, Harrisburg impossible and New York the only place to raise her children," Carl said years later.[17]

She then bought a cooperative on 11th Street, along with friends who had established Bleecker Gardens, but did not move in until 1933. Eventually, she owned the townhouses at 282, 284, and 286 West 11th Street; Baldwin, along with several roommates, leased the house next to hers. Because she wanted a weekend retreat near the city, she had recently paid $50,000 for Windy Gates—280 acres of land in Chilmark on Martha's Vineyard. She invited Baldwin to visit and joined his group at Dell Brook in 1933. The following year, when a pending sale threatened an eviction from Dell Brook, she bought the property for $25,000 and paid $250 more for all the furniture in the buildings. Baldwin later tacked on another twenty acres.[18]

On July 6, 1934, Baldwin informed Mary Buckley that if Doty divorced him, "I suppose Evelyn and I will marry." He told his old friend, "We have a perfect relationship in every department, tested over a considerable period." The Rauschenbusch boys, he wrote, "are gems." Happily too, "she is economically independent, and I would be taking on no family burdens which my income could hardly swing." He continued, "It is the right kind of life for those who can afford it and who find stimulus and content in it. I have never been so completely at peace and so happy in a love relation."[19]

Lucy Baldwin learned of her son's plans from Doty, and she was not pleased with the turn of events. On November 2 she thanked Doty for "thinking only of Roger's happiness," apparently a reference to an earlier note from Doty that had confirmed for Lucy what "had been merely a hazy suspicion." The woman, Lucy wrote from sad personal experience, always appeared to end up "deserted and lonely." She was "distressed at the thought of the break" although somewhat steeled for it by the lengthy separations and recognition that Doty and her son were "growing farther and farther apart." His mother retained "grave doubts about Roger's future being a happy one." She questioned whether her son would find "as generous and patient" a partner as Doty, one who would grant "him his freedom to go and come as he pleased. It has been his habit and life for many years to be 'out about' amongst people. He loves a crowd!!!" His mother also wondered whether he could provide the kind of time and attention a family required. Then she dramatically declared, "The 'lady' will make trouble if he doesn't." Although Doty would always be welcome at the Baldwin home, Lucy neither expected nor welcomed the prospect of meeting "the lady."[20]

In the summer of 1935 Baldwin spent a considerable amount of time with his father in Geneva at a lakeside villa as he planned for a friendly divorce from Doty. In September he signed a legal document, in which he agreed to pay Doty $50 a month while his ACLU salary remained $2,400 a year and a similar proportion if it were reduced (before the depression required the

ACLU to cut costs, his annual salary had risen to $4,000). He also agreed to bequeath to her one-half the value of his assets on his death. Baldwin and Doty intended to create a $5,000 fund to which she could turn in emergencies, but they never did so. When they entered a Swiss court together, the clerk asked in French if they had tried to get along. They responded, "Only for ten years." The divorce was granted.[21]

Preston and Baldwin decided to wait "a respectable time" before supposedly getting married. Then on Sunday morning, March 6, 1936, without any fuss or public announcement, they participated in a simple, Quaker-like ceremony on the lawn at Dell Brook. Dorothy Kenyon, who was now a judge, was among the guests who gave their blessings to Baldwin, who was fifty-two, and Preston, who was about fourteen years his junior. Their union, Baldwin later acknowledged, occurred "quite informally under the New Jersey common law marriage law"; in fact, New Jersey did not recognize common law marriages. His personal attorney acknowledged that Baldwin and Preston never were officially wed; an FBI report filed several years later noted that agents could find no reference to such a marriage in the clerk's office at the Oakland (New Jersey) Marriage Bureau. The couple maintained something of a subterfuge, never acknowledging that they were not married.[22]

Baldwin came to view Evie somewhat differently than he had when they first met. He saw her as possessing "at heart a retiring personality." Her shyness seemed to derive from her height—she was taller than six feet—and her lack of physical beauty. At the same time she was strong willed and "knew exactly what she expected of life and what she rejected. She could turn her face on a person she found dull or unresponsive and forget his or her existence. She just refused to be around people who bored her or to make efforts to be nice when she didn't feel it." With others, however, she displayed "a wonderful hearty sense of humor" and a "deep rollicking laugh."[23]

Some close friends, such as Osmond Fraenkel, a top ACLU litigator, "never could understand that marriage." Preston, Fraenkel acknowledged, "always struck me as an unfeminine type of woman." Lucille Milner considered them a strange combination. As she put it, "He was always interested in attractive women and I never thought Evie attractive."[24]

For the next twenty-seven years, until her death in 1963, Doty continued to communicate with Baldwin, often seeking some kind of financial assistance. She remained a remarkable figure in her own right, serving as director of the Smith College junior year abroad program in Geneva for a time and as director of a tour of American students from a series of universities, orchestrated by the University of Delaware. When she was sixty-five, she became the oldest person to obtain a doctoral degree from the University of Geneva.[25]

Preston and Baldwin were determined to establish a family of their own, but she suffered a pair of devastating miscarriages. Then in 1937 she became pregnant once again. To avoid another miscarriage she took to bed for six months. In a letter to Mary Buckley dated January 7, 1938, Baldwin expressed hope for "a girl off-spring, too, not only to balance the family, but to vary my record. The propriety of my adopting girls might be questioned, but there can't be any about producing one." As Baldwin reported, he was "improving on the usual pattern of spending the last part of my life as most men spend the early,—raising a bunch of kids in domestic routine. But I love it all despite the assumptions of my friends that I am not adapted to domestic living. I just needed the right girl." On May 4 Helen Baldwin—named after Helen Meiklejohn—was born, a joyous occasion all around. Roger Baldwin came to Preston at Harkness Pavilion; pale and semiconscious, she muttered, "Go and see, Bunkle, if her ears are flat. I could not stand a baby with sticking-out ears." The newborn, Baldwin informed Doty, "looks terrible, but no parts are missing and they tell me it will improve. It can't do anything else."[26]

Evie's boys, Carl and Roger, along with the children's nurse, lived on West 11th Street, until Helen was about three. At that point the live-in nurse departed, making room for middle-aged Roger Baldwin. For more than twenty years that residence remained the Preston-Baldwin home. A feminist, Preston was reluctant to relinquish her surname, doing so only after the birth of her daughter and without any announcement to that effect.[27]

No disagreements about money ever arose. Baldwin agreed to pay "each month only what I would have paid if I had been living alone." He avoided learning about her income or finances. They filed a joint income tax return, but he always covered the figures when signing his name, "so I wouldn't know how much she had." She was a millionaire but adopted a "kind of modest and spartan" lifestyle, to a certain extent. In keeping with Baldwin's New England sense of thrift, "she never wanted to put on the dog. Simple living was her taste—with comforts," he said. She had few clothes, and many of those were rustic. Evie Baldwin owned one hat, which she kept for a very long while. At the same time she contributed generously to public causes and those in need. But it is clear that her considerable wealth enabled them to afford to do whatever they chose to, throughout the Great Depression and beyond. Her financial standing allowed Baldwin to maintain his low salary with the ACLU—in the manner of his friend Norman Thomas of the Socialist Party—which led him to expect others to as well.[28]

Thanks to her money, Baldwin could partake of the physical comforts that so delighted him. Indeed, now both Dell Brook and her beachfront property on Martha's Vineyard provided getaways from the pressures of the ACLU national office and the seemingly interminable battles afflicting American liberals and radicals. At the same time, because she owned these estates, Baldwin could retain his feeling of purity about not being immersed in mundane financial matters.

Evie Baldwin's interests included the theater, which she could never get enough of, but not opera, despite Roger's implorings. She read often and widely and enjoyed having him read Shakespeare to her. She treasured her solitude, savoring her books, dogs, music, and art. When they were first together, she played the piano, sometimes performing duets with Roger. But she recognized her lack of skill and chose to give up the piano, preferring to listen to Roger instead; perhaps a type of competition with her husband—or his critical nature—led her to do so. With the passage of time she also gave up bridge, tennis, and golf, although she once had been proficient at all. Social life was even less stimulating. "Even with her few close women friends, a little was enough," Roger Baldwin once revealed. However, Evie Baldwin's behavior suggests that she may have suffered from depression.[29]

Undoubtedly, his explosive temperament and critical nature helped matters little. At times she pointedly told him, "Roger, you need a two-week vacation." Her good friends were sometimes outraged by his treatment of her.[30] Roger's temper and criticisms of Evie, along with his egocentric ways, disturbed them.

Like her husband, Evie Baldwin came "most fully alive" in the countryside. Both reveled in nature in all its guises. The weather and the constellations meant even more to her than they did to Baldwin. She shared his particular interests, including birds, flowers, and trees. At various times they engaged in nude bathing at Windy Gates, an innovation of the Barn House crowd. Baldwin said his wife "was less conventional than I was." And they hoped the children would avoid "a false sense of prudery about the body." On one occasion a female visitor gawked as Baldwin prepared to go swimming. At some point, however, the Baldwins determined that nude swimming was "rather pretentious and self-conscious."[31]

Despite Roger Baldwin's repeated attempts to paint an idyllic picture of family existence, all was not entirely rosy. Roger Jr., as he was known, and Carl concocted a "hostile nickname" for their mother's lover: Bunkle. Disturbed that Baldwin was "coming from out of nowhere"—one minute he wasn't there, then the next he was a part of the family—the boys began referring to him as "Uncle Bunkle Baldwin," Carl said. As Carl later reflected, "So there was just more than a little bit of hostility there. Maybe we were trying to say, 'He's the bunk.'" Eventually, the name stuck but with the passage of time, "the acerbic element was lost and it became a nickname that a lot of people used and that he seemed to like and that was fondly in use in the family," Carl remembered. The children came to think, "Well, what's Bunkle going to do?" or "Well, what's Bunkle think of this?"[32]

The children's referring to Baldwin as "Bunkle" was in keeping with the practices of certain well-educated folk of the time, who considered it retrograde to have parents called "Mom" or "Dad." Thus Roger Jr. and Carl could refer to the new man in their mother's life as "Bunkle" or "Roger," while she was "Evie."[33]

The relationship between Baldwin and the two boys proved troubled from the outset, at least from their perspective. As Carl recalled, this "was a complicated family situation." After all, the boys already had "a perfectly fine father," who had been displaced. Not surprisingly, "I couldn't really relate to the guy [Roger]," Carl reflected. "I think I regarded him as sort of an intruder. I mean, where was this perfectly good father of mine who was given the gate?" Looking back, he acknowledged that this had perhaps been his mother's decision, not Baldwin's. Carl believed their thinking was, "'Oh, it's going to be too confusing to the boys. They'll have two fathers. Come on, let's try to help them get used to the Baldwin father. Let's sort of discourage the Rauschenbusch father.'" Consequently, Carl stated, "I think my brother and I grew up not quite knowing whether either one of these fathers would figure prominently in our lives." Their mother explicitly told Steve Rauschenbusch "to stay clear," and he acceded to her demands. "A long period of being a little bit in limbo" resulted, with the boys "not knowing who this Rauschenbusch guy was," Carl remembered. They received Christmas cards and sometimes presents from their father but for years saw him infrequently at most. Whenever Rauschenbusch's name came up, Baldwin resorted to being "a put-down artist," according to Carl. He "could be quite ungenerous," Carl recalled, and would dismissively contend, "He's not interesting," or, "That would never have worked out."[34]

This proved deeply disturbing to the two boys. An emotional wall was erected that prevented them from getting close to Baldwin. They were not made part of the world of social engagement so appealing to both Baldwin and their mother. It was as though they were being told, "Don't get too close to Roger Baldwin and all this important stuff. Go your own way; you'll be happier that way." As Carl remembered, "I never felt that I was sort of tossed into this exciting maelstrom of activity and politics." Nor was Baldwin's namesake, who naturally assumed that he was Roger's son.[35]

Psychosomatic ailments, especially asthma, afflicted Helen and Carl, who fifty years later pinpointed two telling events. Troubled by asthma as a four-year-old—a condition perhaps brought on or exacerbated by his mother's growing attachment to Baldwin—Carl was sent to Arizona, where a nanny cared for him for a time. Acknowledging that this perhaps "was the sort of thing that was done at the time," Carl nevertheless deemed the decision "a little odd-ball or off-base." Then, when he was twelve or thirteen, he attended the progressive Putney Work Camp in Vermont. Among the speakers at the camp was Baldwin's old friend Scott Nearing, who delivered a rousing talk condemning American capitalism. Afflicted with a host of psychosomatic ailments, including asthma, the frail and feeble Carl was confined a good deal while at camp. There a slightly older and politically savvy boy exclaimed, "Tell me about Roger Baldwin, this father of yours." All Carl could think to say was, "Well, I think he was a conscientious objector in World War I" and "He's working on civil liberties and all."[36]

The encounter demonstrated to Carl how little he knew about Baldwin. At the same time he still felt somewhat estranged and had no intention of trying to find out more when he returned home. He hardly anticipated that would be welcomed. Particular topics were not forbidden, but it was made clear to the younger boy, at least, that "these powerful parents didn't like too many questions about themselves." As Carl said, "I think I just got this kind of feeling, and therefore I rarely asked. I had a very passive role: 'You tell me what you want to tell me.'" Baldwin would typically state, "Carl, you're practicing the flute, you're painting, according to what your mother says. Good, that's fine, you just keep doing that." Never did Carl feel privy to the issues Baldwin was involved in, such as the ACLU's reaction to the internment camps holding Japanese Americans and Japanese nationals. "I never got that kind of invitation to sort of march along on the campaign trail," Carl said. Later he became quite resentful about that. As Carl put it, "I guess my irritation is just that I wasn't given an invitation to follow in his footsteps, and I had to kind of flounder around, trying to find out who was I and did I fit in."[37]

Adolescence proved equally difficult for the younger Roger Baldwin. He seemed less articulate than other members of the family but became a star athlete, in contrast to his namesake, who invariably had displayed a lack of prowess on the playing field. However, neither the elder Roger Baldwin nor the boy's mother deigned to attend his high school basketball games, nor would they visit him later when he was stationed at Fort Dix.[38]

Still, the children were clearly influenced by the socially conscious bent of both Roger and Evie Baldwin. Encouraged by their mother in particular, they all attended City and Country School, then located on West 12th Street. Thus they began a pattern of attending private schools, apparently in contradiction to their parents' belief in "what was good for the people," as Carl put it. However, as Carl later said, "We were full of inconsistencies. We never were really part of the people in, let's say, a public school. This is very elitist stuff." At City and Country they were exposed to "all the good progressive political ideas and ideals" and sang songs like "We Are the Peatbog Soldiers, Meadowlands," and a host of pro-labor tunes. The director of music, Margaret Bradford Ponar, favored homages to Irish immigrant workers and Negro spirituals. Carl was enamored of the school and its emphasis on both art and shop. "We all learned to do things with our hands."[39]

The boys were four and five when they entered City and Country. Students were placed in classes according to their age and referred to as "the fours, the fives, the sixes, the sevens." The school avoided traditional approaches to education, which presented certain difficulties when they reached high school; City and Country graduates were unfamiliar with the greater number of courses required. As their graduation from City and Country neared, Roger Jr. and Carl both decided to change their last name to Baldwin. Thus "by the time we hit high school we were Baldwins or we certainly tried to be Baldwins," Carl said.[40]

On graduating from City and Country, the boys were sent to separate high schools. Roger Jr. attended Fieldston, the tony Riverdale prep school. Helen, still beset by asthma, went to a boarding school in Woodstock, Vermont. However, Carl, who had wanted to follow in his brother's footsteps, studied at Birch Wasson in midtown Manhattan. He was troubled by a recurrence of asthma and sinus problems, and his parents believed that a subway ride to Sixty-Eighth Street would somehow be less taxing than the ride all the way to Fieldston in the upper Bronx.[41]

Soon Carl was sent off to Colorado Springs to attend a good prep school, Fountain Valley School. This proved "to be kind of a miserable experience," which he likened to *Lord of the Flies*. Carl later wondered whether his physical difficulties best explained why he had been sent to Colorado. Was the real problem his relationship with his mother and Baldwin, "these two very dominant figures in my life?" Carl remembered "sort of walking on eggs at West Eleventh Street." Nevertheless, he returned to New York for his junior and senior years at the Millbrook School in Dutchess County, an institution William F. Buckley Jr. and his brother James also attended.[42]

After he graduated from Fieldston, Roger Jr. considered attending Harvard but decided against it at the last minute. Reasoning that "this was getting too close for comfort," he opted for Cornell University. Cornell boasted a socially progressive program, Telluride, whose admittees were expected to become community leaders following their graduation. Helen, whose relationship with Baldwin was considerably different from that of her brothers, attended Radcliffe College. But Carl never thought about going to Baldwin's alma mater. "I guess I must have felt that I don't want to be treading too close to these footsteps," Carl reflected. "I mean, I'm likely to somehow or other get crushed by the weight of the tradition, the weight of the example. To be associated with this man, to be considered a son of Roger Baldwin, would be too crushing an expectation." Instead, Carl first went to Oberlin College, then to Pomona College in Claremont, California, before ending up at the University of Arizona in Tucson. Carl hoped that the desert climate would alleviate his asthma but later came to believe "that was all just balderdash, you know. If I'd got my head screwed on right, I wouldn't have. . . ."[43]

The distance between Baldwin and the boys resulted, at least in part, because of the role he adopted: companion to the children. So, as Carl readily acknowledged, Baldwin "made every effort to do a lot of fun things with the boys, and he did that." Every Friday afternoon—except during the summertime—Roger Baldwin left his office at the ACLU and walked home to the Preston-Baldwin brownstone on West 11th Street. Roger, Evie, and Helen got in the family car—invariably a large, comfortable vehicle—and around 4:30 picked the boys up at City and Country School. Their mother was behind the wheel, because Baldwin could barely handle an automobile. The family then undertook the hour-long drive to Oakland, New Jersey, crossing the George Washington Bridge and traveling north on Route 17, before heading west on Route 202 toward Norwalk for the weekend. The Preston farm was actually located in Norwalk Township, just south of Sutter, New York, and north of Bergen County, New Jersey.[44]

The Oakland farm was perched on several acres of beautiful, rugged, rocky terrain. The house was wired for electricity by 1936, and oil heat replaced the coal furnace a dozen years later. Other buildings also underwent alterations. A fire burned down the garage. The icehouse at the base of the pine woods was pulled apart for lumber to help repair the large chicken house below the barn, which was converted into a residence. Another structure replaced a burned-out log cabin that was perched on the hill. A grain house for chickens was remade into a cabin for a tenant. The family tore down a rickety shed and a grain crib behind the barn. Another chicken house was moved into the woods, between the big house and a cottage on the property, to provide a studio for other tenants. Some animals were kept there at various points, including ducks, pigeons, chickens, and rabbits. Family dogs ranged from a mongrel called Jack and the farm dog named Penny to Scottish terriers and Evie Baldwin's Welsh terriers, Buffie and Surprise. No wild animals were tolerated—Roger Baldwin and the other residents trapped and drowned skunks, woodchucks, raccoons, possum, squirrels, mink, fox, wood rats, deer, and snakes.[45]

The two-story house, built early in the nineteenth century, boasted white shingles, columns, and a covered porch. As Carl Baldwin remembered, "It kind of meandered along the terrain." The house contained a somewhat elevated music room, a living room–dining room area, a medium-sized kitchen, two downstairs bedrooms, and three more bedrooms upstairs. From the porch, one could see the rolling Ramapo River. The farm "was just a very cozy, kind of a friendly place, really a delightful place to be," Carl Baldwin recalled. Along with Windy Gates, the other estate Evie Baldwin owned on Martha's Vineyard—nearly three hundred acres' worth—the Oakland farm was the kind of retreat only the very wealthy could afford. That hardly troubled the Baldwin-Preston clan; in Carl's words it "was just sort of like something we accepted—this is our lot. In a way it kind of [made] us a little different from other people, but maybe that [was] all to the good." It clearly demonstrated that there was "a bit of snobbism in our family."[46]

The estates in Oakland and Martha's Vineyard "were kind of beautiful, kind of wild places, though nicely trimmed . . . kept up," Carl recalled. His mother made certain that the old houses on the properties were well attended to, which took a good deal of time and cost a considerable amount of money. At the same time, as Carl pointed out, "If you were to walk into any of these places, they would have struck you as being almost spartan, almost like a Shaker house. Very tastefully done, rather tasteful and spartan."[47]

At the Oakland farm outdoor activities abounded. Baldwin taught the boys how to canoe and paddle, working the stern and taking the boat through the rapids, but Roger Jr. and Carl handled duties in the bow. Invariably, the Baldwins and their guests went bird watching and hiking or trespassed on other people's property in the wintertime to ski; during other seasons they trespassed to swim in various lakes. Baldwin himself "was a terrible skier, he had no form as a skier," according to Carl. But more important, whatever the activity was, it "was just part of this tramping out there, of going down, just tramp up this hill and go down—everything was by dint of sheer physical energy." For young boys all this was great fun.[48]

Baldwin also delighted the boys with his storytelling, which "was just part of his being. He put that to wonderful advantage," Carl recalled. He and his brother shared a room at the Oakland farm, where Baldwin often read stories to them. Br'er Rabbit was a particular favorite, introduced by Baldwin's affected "pseudo-Southern accent or . . . pseudo-country accent." So too were fairy tales, which piqued Carl's imagination. Thus Baldwin the storyteller "was a great guy to have in the house," Carl said.[49]

Life at the New Jersey farm or the estate in Martha's Vineyard "was very easy," he said. Evie Baldwin and the children headed to the Vineyard when school let out in early June, and Baldwin would join them sometime in August. At Oakland a local couple, the Beamers, tended to the property when the Baldwins were away; Zed Beamer served as caretaker and plumber, and Ona Beamer cooked pies, pumpkins, or other culinary delights. Meals were enjoyable, with all pitching in to clean up afterward, as the boys and their mother washed dishes, while Baldwin, relying on Brillo and sheer muscle, tackled the pots and pans. He frequently baked cakes, cookies, or bread and put up preserves, applesauce, and jellies. Conversation flowed easily during the weekends, as the elder Baldwins spent Friday and Saturday evenings reading publications like the *Nation* and the *New Republic*. Whenever the need arose, Roger Baldwin attended to ACLU business as well. But the atmosphere remained relaxed in the large living room, where the children read or played cards, checkers, or chess.[50]

On Saturdays Baldwin generally had some strenuous physical activity or project planned. For him, escaping to the country was a religious undertaking. There he participated "in all the juvenile sports in a rough wilderness retreat," Carl recalled. On the pond, frozen rock solid during the winter months, the boys played ice hockey, sometimes with school friends who had been invited to the farm. After breakfast on Sunday the family would return to New York City. Back at West 11th Street in the Village, the children completed their homework, while Baldwin prepared for some upcoming meeting.[51]

Every August Baldwin boarded a train from Manhattan to Falmouth, then took the ferry to Martha's Vineyard, where the family picked him up at Vineyard Station. The Windy Gates estate was located on the southwestern corner of the island, at Chilmark, and contained the most beautiful beach on the island. The estate was referred to "as the Baldwin place," and the waterfront as "the Baldwin beach." Neighbors eventually included "good, liberal, well known people" like Trude and Joe Lash, later the Roosevelts' biographer, and Eddie Greenbaum of the law firm Greenbaum, Wolfe, and Ernst. Guests included Rita and Thomas Hart Benton, the great social-realist artist; David Lilienthal, formerly head of the Tennessee Valley Authority; and Helen and Alexander Meiklejohn. "All the right kind of progressive people were there," Carl recalled, and his mother and Baldwin were in their element.[52]

Baldwin became somewhat infamous on Martha's Vineyard because of his attempts to navigate a Jeepster along backcountry roads. His driving was "extremely perilous," as an easily distracted Baldwin crept along, frequently with a canoe poking out of the back of the vehicle. Although the Vineyard lacked rivers, it had ponds, and Baldwin invariably "would insist on befriending somebody who had property on a pond and getting this canoe onto the pond." In contrast to their stepfather, the boys became adept in the water, sailing an eighteen-footer and a fifteen-footer. One summer the boys, whom their stepfather had taught to sail, won a silver cup in a race; the trophy was lost when Evie Baldwin left the family car outside the townhouse on West 11th Street one night—it was normally parked in a garage in the Village—and thieves rifled through it.[53]

Distance continued to mark Baldwin's relationship with the boys. He seldom took them to visit his relatives in Boston, and they had little involvement with their Preston relatives. Thus, as Carl later reflected, "We were surrounded with beautiful things, with nature, great books, good ideas, art and music, but still there was a feeling of not knowing exactly who we were in terms of actual people." Young Roger Baldwin too felt a type of "depersonalization" in the family's makeup. In his estimation his stepfather was not a "back porcher" but rather "a raconteur" who logically analyzed what he was discussing. Both Evie and Roger Baldwin were more inclined to focus on issues than individuals.[54]

Roger Baldwin's relationship with Evie, his assuming responsibility for a household of children, and the satisfaction of settling into her comfortable existence affected him professionally as well as personally. Unquestionably, Baldwin was drawn to the affluent lifestyle Evie Baldwin's wealth allowed for. He also enjoyed moving in the well-heeled circles to which she was inclined. Indeed, Helen later referred to his "fondness for the best people" and pleasure in acquiring friendships with the "topnotch rich of the country," including the Rockefellers.[55]

This was the same period when Baldwin's dealings with top government officials were friendlier than ever. The ACLU insiders comprised a kind of Left-liberal wing just outside FDR's New Deal administration, which similarly favored a more expansive interpretation of First Amendment freedoms. Yet inconsistencies continued to mark Baldwin, who had so recently expounded his most radical analyses of capitalism and communism.

CHAPTER EIGHTEEN

Controversies on the Path
from Fellow Traveling to Anticommunism

In the mid-1930s Elizabeth Dilling produced two books, *The Red Network* and *The Roosevelt Red Record and Its Background,* that purported to reveal a vast web of subversive forces both within and outside government circles. Each work contained lengthy sections on the activities of the ACLU and Roger Baldwin, said to be furthering the interests of "the Red Movement." The ACLU, Dilling wrote, was "directed by Communist and Socialist revolutionary leaders and their sympathizers." The freedom of speech propounded by the civil liberties organization, Dilling insisted, served as a cover for the advocacy and commission of "sedition, violence and murder." The ACLU itself, the author proclaimed, was at "the very forefront of the Red revolutionary movement, the defender of atheism, obscenity and Communist revolution."[1]

Although many viewed Dilling's studies as the rantings of a fanatic, another attack on the ACLU and Baldwin was not so readily dismissed. In December 1936 ex-Wobbly Harold Lord Varney, Baldwin's former friend and political ally, produced a scathing critique for the *American Mercury.* The ACLU, Varney charged, was "doing the most fruitful work to advance the so-called Class War in America." Thus the genius of the director and "his militant coterie" shielded their revolutionary designs "under the deceptive insignia of liberty." The reality was "the recurrent Leftist purpose which animates virtually all Mr. Baldwin's furious crusades for civil liberties." His occasional forays to the contrary, Varney wrote, were "little more than window-dressing." The ACLU provided "a vast insurance system for revolutionists" [in other words, a shield for leftists], as it all but paralleled the ever-changing line of the Communist Party of the United States. As for Baldwin, Varney asserted, he had been mired for "ten years in the Comintern strait-jacket." All the while Baldwin had "stage-managed himself in masterly fashion as a courageous David challenged the Goliath of intolerance."[2]

In a letter to Ben Huebsch, founder and publisher of Viking Press and ACLU treasurer, Baldwin called for only a curt response to Varney. It should also, Baldwin insisted, be "particularly direct in exposing Mr. Varney's openly Fascist connections, his acting as a paid agent of the Italian Government, his decoration by Mussolini and his editor ship [sic] of 'The Awakener,' a fascist sheet, using that word." Additionally, Huebsch would need to underscore the ACLU's composition as a united front. Baldwin continued by noting that the letter also should emphasize his "plain denial that I have been or am a Communist in any political sense. I happen to believe that the economics of socialism or communism, call it what you like, are vastly superior to the economics of predatory capitalism. That's as far as my 'communism' goes."[3]

Under Baldwin's direction the ACLU opted for a multipronged approach to ward off the kinds of criticisms it received from Varney and others. In March 1937 the board adopted "A Restatement of the Principles and Attitude of the American Civil Liberties Union." The organization, the manifesto said, sought only "the maintenance of democratic rights." The ACLU was a united front whose members only agreed to defend civil liberties. Possessing "no political or economic direction whatever," the ACLU desired simply "to protect orderly and peaceful progress through the exercise of traditional American civil rights."[4]

The ACLU also initiated legal action, charging Varney and the *American Mercury* with libel. H. L. Mencken, the publication's founder, who had relinquished control in early 1934, proposed a meeting of the concerned parties; he would act as something of a mediator. The encounter resolved little, but Mencken determined to give his own account of both Varney's analysis of the ACLU and the organization itself. Arthur Garfield Hays agreed to withdraw the suit, provided a letter from the ACLU board were included in the same issue that Mencken's article appeared.

In October 1938 the journal reported Mencken's findings. After dismissing Varney's accusation that the ACLU was advancing the cause of class warfare in the United States, Mencken accused certain of the most influential ACLU leaders of being sympathetic to the Left. Baldwin, Mencken wrote, was "a man of great energy, notable courage, strong convictions, and engaging personality." Although no communist, the ACLU chief justified the different ways civil liberties were handled in his own country and Soviet Russia. In the process, Mencken wrote, Baldwin expounded a standard communist argument that was contrary to the ACLU's founding principles. As for Mencken, he could not "imagine any thorough-going friend of civil liberties" acting in such a manner. At the same time he recognized that Baldwin had at various points criticized the communist approach to civil liberties. Baldwin's career in the United States showed that he "is in favor of civil liberties in themselves, as essential to the primary dignities of man." However, he needed to "say so in a clarion voice, with no ifs or buts in favor of the Hagues of Russia." In their written response members of the ACLU board of directors pointed out that a good deal of their work did not concern the Left at all. The board also denied that Baldwin's personal beliefs involving matters outside the purview of the ACLU influenced the organization.[5]

The ACLU letter noted that the organization worked side by side with Catholics and communists to defend the Bill of Rights. It acknowledged that both Catholics and one Communist Party member—an obvious reference to Elizabeth Gurley Flynn—served on the ACLU board. The ACLU, board members insisted, "should be judged not by the personal views or associations of its officers but by its record." But two passages in the letter later were repudiated by the actions of the ACLU itself. One section contested the "amazing position that defenders of civil liberties cannot cooperate or consort with those who do not accept 100 per cent defense of civil rights for all." The other even more freely asserted: "We make no political, religious, or racial distinctions in our membership or in our boards. Any other position would violate the tolerance for which we stand and limit the forces available for defense of civil rights."[6]

Despite the *American Mercury* controversy, by 1938 the ACLU appeared to be in good health. It boasted about six thousand members scattered throughout the United States. Leading the ACLU was a national committee of eighty individuals and a smaller executive board in Manhattan. Thirty-one states had local civil liberties groups affiliated with the ACLU, and attorneys and representatives worked on behalf of the organization in every major urban center. Special national committees had sprung up to attend to issues of particular interest to ACLU members. These included the National Committee on Labor Injunctions, the National Council for Freedom from Censorship, the Committee on Academic Freedom, and the Committee on Religious Liberties, in addition to committees pertaining to the rights of foreign nationals and Native Americans and a Committee on Fair Play to Puerto Rico. As it had since its founding, the ACLU joined in test cases involving alleged violations of constitutional rights, in attempts to prevent the restriction of civil liberties, and in campaigns to pressure elected officials to champion the Bill of Rights. Significant too was the "freer exercise of civil liberties" that the ACLU had noted in its annual reports since the beginning of Franklin Roosevelt's presidential term.[7]

In the spring of 1938 Baldwin delivered a pair of lectures at Harvard University in which he proclaimed that the civil liberties campaign was "the history of political democracy." The American experience, he stated, involved "an expanding public democracy enlisting larger sections of the people and wider functions of control." The overwhelming triumph by New Deal liberals and President Roosevelt in the 1936 campaigns had convinced Baldwin that so-called economic royalists had lost public support.[8]

A far sharper conflict, he argued, was unfolding worldwide, supposedly requiring unreasoning choices "between equally unacceptable dictatorial alternatives. . . . No supporter of the democratic principles can tolerate either." To avoid "the unwelcome choice between Fascism and Communism," political democracies had to undertake significant economic changes to overcome the worldwide economic crisis. Fortunately, there had emerged "the most significant popular force in politics over the last fifty years": movements of workers and farmers. This hopeful development could be seen in socialist or labor governments in New Zealand and Australia, in England's Labour Party, the French and Spanish Popular Fronts, and Scandinavia's socialist, cooperative, and labor governments, he told the Harvard audience.[9]

Clearly, Baldwin's political and ideological perspective was in flux. No longer did he view New Deal–style reforms, to whatever extent, as mere palliatives incapable of ushering in the broader changes democratic societies demanded. Now Baldwin was coupling fascism and communism as authoritarian revolutionary solutions to be avoided. The appearance and extension of welfare states in the United States, Europe, and elsewhere made communist solutions less attractive, whereas fascist states always had been wholly repugnant to him.

Nonetheless, U.S. Rep. Martin Dies of Texas delivered a radio broadcast on August 29, 1938, in which he alleged that the ACLU was communist controlled and "carrying on the work of the Communist Party under [the] guise of democracy." Speaking from the House floor, Dies termed the ACLU "an instrument of communism" and referred to Baldwin's statement in the 1935

Harvard classbook: "Communism is the goal." ACLU counsel Arthur Garfield Hays challenged the chairman of the newly formed House Committee to Investigate Un-American Activities to produce evidence to substantiate such allegations. "Such irresponsible statements," Hays contended, had resulted in the Dies Committee's suffering ridicule.[10]

As a matter of principle, the ACLU did not oppose congressional investigative committees. It had consistently applauded the La Follette Civil Liberties Committee in the U.S. Senate, which examined violations of First Amendment rights involving "the right of labor to organize and bargain collectively." The ACLU had also supported the La Follette Committee's investigation into right-wing activities.[11]

Now, however, Baldwin and other ACLU leaders, through sworn depositions delivered on December 31, 1938, attempted to stave off damage to the organization. Baldwin's own willingness to speak his mind, and the increasingly radical perspective that he had adopted during the first half of the decade, now threatened to haunt both him and the cause to which he had devoted a good portion of his life. As always, particularly controversial were Baldwin's testimony before the Fish Committee back in 1930 and the statement he had delivered for the Harvard classbook of 1935.[12]

In his deposition Baldwin referred to his response to the Harvard questionnaire that "communism is the goal." It was clear from such a declaration, Baldwin insisted—drawing a distinction few others would—that he was using "communism . . . in its ordinary dictionary sense to designate the common ownership of property, not the political movement of Communism." He stated for the official record, "I am not, nor have I ever been, a member of the Communist Party."[13]

His own reading of economic and political affairs, like that of all ACLU members, Baldwin insisted, was purely personal and had no bearing on the organization's projects. Given the weight he had carried with the leadership of the ACLU since its inception, such an analysis was hard to take seriously. Baldwin also stated that the ACLU "has no economic or political program" and that its members possessed widely divergent views.[14]

In another deposition Baldwin joined with ACLU vice chairman John Haynes Holmes and treasurer Huebsch in refuting charges made by people who had testified before the Dies Committee. The ACLU, the three insisted, "has never been a front or part of a united front for the Communist Party," nor was it either directly or indirectly involved with any political movement. It sought to champion the civil liberties of all individuals and thus had defended alike communists, Nazis, Silver Shirts (American anti-Semites), Ku Klux Klansmen, Jehovah's Witnesses, Catholics, Jews, antifascists, blacks, Quakers, the Congress of Industrial Organizations, and Henry Ford.[15]

On January 3, 1939, the ACLU board decided to consider pushing for a joint congressional resolution that would maintain the operations of the La Follette Committee on civil liberties as well as the Dies Committee's "legitimate portions," which included the exploration of "anti-democratic movements." Thus the ACLU leaders, in a blatantly political move, affirmed that the Dies Committee was not wholly illegitimate. Similarly, on January 23, the board of directors voted 8 to 4 to send the following resolution to the full board: "The American Civil Liberties Union is opposed to all totalitarian governments,—Fascist, Nazi or Communist,—as the antithesis of civil liberties but will support and defend the right of persons to express or advocate peacefully these economic and political theories."[16]

On the evening of January 24 Baldwin delivered a speech, "Should the Dies Committee Die?" over the National Broadcasting Co. network from station WEAF in New York City. He was speaking, Baldwin opened by insisting, "for no interest save that of American democratic liberties." Like all American patriots, he welcomed the genuine exposure of elements antagonistic to democracy. And like other U.S. citizens troubled by fascist aggression worldwide, he believed that the U.S. government should strive to protect "our own institutions from that infection, whether from abroad or from within." Such a menace had led to the creation of the Dies Committee. However, Chairman Dies and his committee had devoted little attention to examining the activities of fascist groups in the United States such as the Silver Shirts, the Black Legion, or the Ku Klux Klan. Rather, Dies and his committee had concentrated disproportionately on allegations involving American communists.[17]

For his part Baldwin asserted that he "held no brief whatever for the Communist party." Like other members of the ACLU and all patriotic Americans, he was "wholly opposed to any form of dictatorship which would undermine our liberties and our democracy." But it was clear to him that the communist movement was "far less a menace to the democracy of the world than the Nazi and the Fascist regimes." Unfortunately, communism was being used as a bogeyman by the Dies Committee to attack progressive and liberal movements.[18]

At the ACLU board's meeting on January 30, Baldwin declared, "All efforts to sidetrack the Dies investigation have apparently failed." The organization's Washington advisers considered the proposal for a joint congressional resolution to be impractical, and the ACLU was making new attempts to ensure the Senate's examination of civil liberties issues would continue. Two weeks later the ACLU's national committee members and its standing committees again urged support for the La Follette subcommittee in the Senate while denouncing Dies's inquiry as "so unfair."[19]

In early March Baldwin—still striving to influence government officials—wrote to Martin Dies and expressed an interest in getting together; Baldwin had some suggestions for the "thorough exposure of forces hostile to our democracy." On Friday, March 31, in Room 3026 at the Hotel New Yorker in Manhattan, Baldwin testified before Rhea Whitley, counsel to the Dies Committee, and J. B. Matthews, its research director, who once had served on the ACLU board. The ACLU had not concerned itself, Baldwin asserted, "with any issue outside of the United States" and had never dealt with any movement or agency; in reality, of course, the ACLU had in its infancy been tied to the American labor movement.[20]

Baldwin's former compatriot, Matthews, stated for the record that he was convinced of one thing: "Your own connections with all of the United Fronts that I knew anything about were wholly devoid of any *ultimate* political purpose." Moreover, as Baldwin had long held, Matthews added, "Your sole interest has been in the immediate objective."[21]

Attorney Whitley asked Baldwin to respond to allegations regarding active communist involvement in the ACLU. The organization, Baldwin pointed out, made "no distinction based upon the political views of those who seek to join it. We accept anybody who applies, and who pays their dues. We have people on the lists of every political persuasion and from every economic class." He believed that there were probably fewer than fifty communists among the ACLU's six thousand members. There were more communist sympathizers but probably only two to three hundred. No staff member, with the lone exception of Joseph Freeman, who had served as publicity director about ten years earlier, was or had been a Communist Party member. No party member, Baldwin mistakenly reported, had been elected to the ACLU's national committee or board of directors; William Foster and Elizabeth Gurley Flynn became communists some time after joining the ACLU. By contrast, socialists like Norman Thomas and Helen Phelps Stokes did serve on the board. Although the ACLU had never taken formal action to prevent the election of communists to its board, Baldwin noted that "communists have never been known to be whole-hearted supporters of civil liberty for their opponents."[22]

As for himself, Baldwin affirmed, "I have never belonged to any political party. The reason I have not belonged to any political party is that I don't happen to be politically minded." True, Baldwin had never lined up with an established party and had always refused to support Norman Thomas's seemingly perennial bids for the presidency. However, insisting that he was not "politically minded" involved dissembling at the very least; indeed, it could be argued that such a statement was absurd on its face.[23]

Baldwin sharply declared, "I am not, of course, a member of the Communist Party." Rather, he believed in "the economics of an ultimate communism, that is, the common ownership of property of the ethical principle formulated as 'from each according to his ability; to each according to his need' seems to me the only possible basis for reconciling economics with social ethics." Given the criticisms coming his way, this certainly was a courageous, albeit impolitic, admission on his part.[24]

In the summer of 1939 Congress approved a relief appropriation bill that precluded awarding funds to "any person who advocates, or who is a member of an organization that advocates the overthrow of the government of the United States through force or violence." Roosevelt also signed into law the Hatch Act, which denied federal employment to anyone belonging to "any political party or organization which advocated the overthrow of our constitutional form of government in the United States."[25]

The Moscow show trials, Baldwin said in a letter of May 9, tragically revealed "how dangerous is dictatorship to the progress even of a workers' state." Yet he continued to believe that the interests of Soviet foreign policy and the American League for Peace and Democracy were not divergent. Then the signing of the German-Soviet Nonaggression Pact was announced in late August. It was "like a bombshell" to Baldwin and many others on the American Left. He had been walking along the beach in Chilmark, he later recalled, when someone informed him about the agreement. "I think it was the biggest shock of my life. I never was so shaken up by anything as I was by that pact—by the fact that those two powers had got together at the expense of the democracies." To the delight of his old friend Emma Goldman, he no longer believed that communists could be trusted. "The Nazi-Soviet pact made you feel that suddenly the Communists were different people," he recalled. "They had abandoned us and got into bed with Hitler. It changed everything, of course." He soon resigned from the American League for Peace and Democracy.[26]

Popular Front groupings disintegrated, sometimes torn apart by those who, like Baldwin, had so willingly supported such alignments or by party members now enraged by the changed Soviet line. Genuine distrust and anger certainly played a part in such determinations. So too, increasingly, did politics, pure and simple, including the desire to distance oneself or one's organization from those who were increasingly viewed as beyond the political pale. This process hardly proved smooth or consistent, as evidenced by the ACLU's tortured stance regarding its previous readiness to have board members with wholly antagonistic political perspectives. On October 9 Baldwin, responding to a charge that the participants at the National Conference on Civil Liberties included communist fronts, dismissed such a concern. No such gathering, he asserted, "could fairly exclude anybody from its deliberations who is interested in discussing the issues." Consequently, "we invited all those organizations engaged actively in the defense of civil liberties on one front or another, wholly without regard to whatever political connections they might have." Insisting that the ACLU "takes no part in politics," Baldwin stated that it "will cooperate with any organization, whatever its character, which aids in any way the defense of civil rights. We do not demand of such organizations an agreement with our own platform." He then concluded, "I think on reflection you will agree that no conference on civil liberties in the present emergency could fairly exclude anybody from its deliberations who is interested in discussing the issues."[27]

Two days later the *New York Times* applauded Baldwin's "sound position." Its editorial, which read as if it were written by a Baldwin accolyte, proclaimed: "But civil liberties mean nothing if they merely guard the rights of those in whose arguments we can see some merit. Civil liberties take on meaning and become precious to us as a people only when they protect, to the point where public safety is actually endangered, free speech and action of persons whose views we may vehemently detest. A conference on civil liberties that itself withheld such liberties would be comic indeed."[28]

Baldwin's declarations and the *Times*'s editorial notwithstanding, however, many on the ACLU board determined that the organization's position was potentially precarious. They reasoned that the ACLU's acceptance of Communist Party members had led to the greater number of invectives hurled its way. Consequently, Arthur Garfield Hays and Morris Ernst soon went to see Martin Dies in Washington, D.C., where they struck an accord of sorts, or so both Lucille Milner and Corliss Lamont, a left-wing activist, later charged. They said that Dies had agreed his investigative committee would no longer attack the ACLU, provided its top leaders promised to remove communists from the board of directors. Baldwin repeatedly denied that Hays and Ernst had approved any such arrangement, and Hays opposed attempts to exclude communists from the ACLU board. Moreover, during this same period Elizabeth Gurley Flynn—now a Communist Party member—expressed concerns to Baldwin that she might be squeezed out of the ACLU board. Flynn feared that other board members might resort to a technicality—she had missed too many meetings during her recent trip undertaken to speak to miners, for example. According to Helen Camp, Flynn's biographer, Baldwin laughed and advised, "The Board needs people who get around the country in the struggles of the workers."[29]

In a November 22 letter to Mary McLeod Bethune, president of Bethune-Cookman College, Baldwin declared, "I think the position of each of us depends on how we feel on cooperation with Communists on international affairs. I have come to the end of my rope on that since the Soviet Government has followed so questionable a course. It is plain now that Communists will always follow the Soviet Union whatever it does, and I don't care to be committed to working with people of that state of mind."[30]

Few could have predicted the result of Baldwin's changed perception of American comrades. Nor could they have readily seen how that altered stance could provide a blueprint for the kind of red scare he had so consistently opposed. The postwar red scare would dramatically influence the course of American political life while producing a wholesale violation of the civil liberties of particular groups and individuals. All this was terribly ironic, because the man who did more than other figure to safeguard First Amendment freedoms would be blamed for devising a model to restrict those same liberties. Yet perhaps this series of events was inevitable, given Baldwin's greater determination to curry favor with government officials. After all, he believed that there presently existed "a better understanding" between ACLU members and the administration than had existed for two full decades.[31]

It soon became clear that the ACLU could hardly remain immune to the political earthquake caused by the German-Soviet Nonaggression Pact, which had shaken the American Left and interred the Popular Front. At this time two longtime allies stood on opposite sides of a political fault line. One was the ACLU's national chairman, Harry F. Ward, whom many viewed as a Soviet sympathizer or even an apologist. The other, Roger Baldwin, who until now had been one of the strongest of the United Fronters, had determined that communists, like the Soviet Union, could not be trusted. In late November at the Town Hall Club in midtown Manhattan, the ACLU's executive board gathered amid newspaper reports of a move to force Ward's resignation because of his involvement with "Communist-inspired organizations" such as the American League Against War and Fascism; such involvement, it was feared, would compromise the ACLU. Those refusing comment about the charges until the meeting was over included Baldwin, Norman Thomas, and Ernst. After the meeting Baldwin strongly denied anyone had made a move to oust Ward.[32]

The calls for Ward's removal, however, refused to abate. Lillian Symes, writing in the *Call*, a socialist periodical, confirmed that a revolt was brewing inside the ACLU's national board concerning Ward's chairmanship. There existed "a notorious contradiction," Symes wrote, in having the ACLU chaired by a man who "has demonstrated his complete contempt for civil liberties." For the past half dozen years at least, Ward "has functioned as the number one clerical stooge and trigger-man of the Communist party," Symes charged. "Dr. Ward not only travels in the same train as the C.P., he sleeps in the same berth." But "genuine innocents, fellow-travelers, party members and Roger Baldwin" had allowed Ward to remain as ACLU chair, to the dismay of many members, including Symes herself.[33]

The announcement of the Nazi-Soviet pact in the summer of 1939 had triggered a controversy among the American intelligentsia that brought matters to a head. The Committee for Cultural Freedom, a new organization led by John Dewey, had delivered a manifesto condemning totalitarianism in all its guises. Another manifesto, drawn up by The Committee of 400 and spearheaded by Corliss Lamont, condemned the Dewey-led group for putting forth "the fantastic falsehood that the U.S.S.R. and the totalitarian states are basically alike." The Soviet Union, where the Moscow show trials were still underway, was nevertheless said to be undergoing "steadily expanding democracy in every sphere," Symes charged. Those who argued to the contrary were proclaimed "fascist sympathizers," she said. As matters turned out, several national board members of the ACLU had joined with the Dewey group, while Ward was on The Committee of 400.[34]

Symes deemed this "a nice kettle of fish, a situation which seems to have stumped even Roger Baldwin's well-known talents for fence walking." While Baldwin had resigned from the American League for Peace and Democracy, Ward "stuck by the league and by the pact, just as he had stuck by every twist and turn the C.P. has taken since 1932," Symes charged. ACLU member Sidney Hook, who was among the first U.S. scholars to analyze Marxism and was a steadfast opponent of all forms of totalitarianism, proceeded to pose "some embarrassing questions," Symes reported, while "the genuine liberals" on the ACLU board hoped for Ward's resignation. It was even bandied about—although Symes gave little credence to this notion—that Baldwin had backed such a proposal. "After all, it is rather embarrassing to have a fellow-traveler of the Moscow-Berlin axis leading the struggle for free speech, free press and free assemblage in the U.S.A.," she wrote.[35]

The ACLU's cauldron was bubbling. Meeting in Arthur Garfield Hays's Manhattan home on December 4, the board declared that "members of the Union differ sharply in their economic and political views, and all are free to express them without involving the Union." Baldwin felt compelled to defend himself and the national office against charges hurled at a recent board meeting; John Haynes Holmes came to his friend's rescue. "Shocked and grieved" that Baldwin had responded in such a manner, Holmes insisted, "There has never been the slightest suspicion in anybody's mind that you were under any Communist influence or were being used for any other purpose other than that of the most rigorous services of the principles of civil liberties in this republic."[36]

That same month Baldwin wrote to John Dos Passos, who had resigned from the ACLU: "I don't believe that however any of us feel about Communists, we can afford to take the position of excluding anybody from the Union because of political views, or to remove from our Board anybody whose views of international affairs differ from the majority. Once we begin drawing such a line, there is no end to it." At this point Baldwin continued to believe that he could finesse the increasingly great differences dividing board members. While a sizable minority on the board had acted, in Baldwin's estimation, as "partisans of the defense of Communist rights and of the Party line on rights," he had managed to prevent the board's consideration of "touchy issues" unless he was certain "that a majority would be present of disinterested members." As he acknowledged, "I controlled the agenda, since the board passed on such matters as the office put before it, rarely from other sources."[37]

However, on January 3, 1940, John Haynes Holmes wrote to Baldwin expressing dismay over the schism that had developed regarding the issuance of an ACLU committee report on the Dies Committee. By placing on the ACLU committee a series of strong anticommunists, including Morris Ernst and ACLU moderate Roger Riis, Baldwin had ensured what its report would say. The first draft attacked the Dies Committee's methods but concluded that "The Dies Committee has performed a useful service" in unveiling communist propaganda. In response to demands by Osmond K. Fraenkel, Gardner Jackson, and others, the final report deleted much of the favorable language toward the Dies Committee but accepted the legitimacy of congressional inquiries involving political beliefs and associations. Referring to the previous day's meeting of the national board, Holmes insisted that "the opposition" engaged in "its familiar work of 'boring from within.' They gnawed here and gnawed there; they nibbled away this paragraph, and then bit away that. Always they acted in full accord, until at last there was little left that meant anything at all." By contrast, "we liberals did what we usually do—instead of fighting for what we believed in, we sought to make concessions and compromises, adaptations and adjustments, revisions and corrections, thus playing right into the hands of the opposition."[38]

If not for his enduring affection for Baldwin and other board members, along with his lifelong belief in the civil liberties crusade, Holmes disclosed, he would have resigned the day before. At one point the board was wholly concerned about civil liberties and fought for them "no matter whom we hit or hurt." Now "we seem to be under the strange control of a minority," led by Harry Ward, that was not concerned with civil liberties but rather "the interests of a radical minority group which follows the party line as laid down by Moscow." That group would abandon civil liberties, Holmes charged, whenever they conflicted with its own interests.[39]

As his radio address from New York's Town Hall Club on January 4 shows, Baldwin was in no way willing to give the Dies Committee the benefit of the doubt, as John Haynes Holmes evidently did. Baldwin asked, "Should the Dies Committee be continued?" Even though Martin Dies had acknowledged that the ACLU was not a communist organization, Baldwin continued to view the committee as an agency of "intolerance and repression." It made no sense, Baldwin argued, for the Dies Committee to single out only communists for exposure. After all, "Stalin has done a vastly better job than Dies in reducing to impotence the appeal of Communism to any element in American life." The Dies Committee should be taken to task, Baldwin contended, for failing to examine those "closely allied in spirit if not in fact with Nazi propaganda," including Father Charles Coughlin and his Christian Front, the Ku Klux Klan, the Black Legion, and other groups engendering "racial, religious and class strife." Such "home-grown propaganda by the enemies of democracy in our midst" imperiled the American people, Baldwin said.[40]

Nevertheless, it was soon evident that Baldwin's position had dramatically shifted from the previous fall when he had claimed that ostracizing communists amounted to hysteria. Still angered by the course of events in Europe and worried about the very fate of the organization he had so long nurtured, Baldwin, ever the pragmatist, devised a new strategy. As he later acknowledged, he had determined "that the board could not continue to function unless policy was made definite on the character of our directing personnel." On January 18 the ACLU board held a special meeting to vote on the following resolution, which Baldwin had drafted:

> The National Committee of the American Civil Liberties Union regards it as inappropriate for any person to serve on the governing committees of the Union, of its affiliated bodies, or on its staff, who is a member of any organization which supports totalitarian dictatorship in any country, or who by his public declarations and connections indicates his support of such a principle. Within this category we include organizations in the United States supporting the totalitarian governments of the Soviet Union and of the Fascist and Nazi countries, such as the Communist Party, the German-American Bund and others; and native organizations with obvious anti-democratic objectives or practices, such as the Ku Klux Klan, the Silver Shirts, Christian Front and others.
>
> While the American Civil Liberties Union does not make any test of opinion on political or economic questions a condition of membership, and makes no distinction in defending the right to hold and utter any opinions, the personnel of its governing committees and staff is properly subject to the test of consistency in the defense of civil liberties in all aspects and all places.[41]

By a single vote the board defeated the resolution and opted for one that read: "It is the sense of the Board that there is no occasion to adopt a resolution setting up standards of qualifications for membership on the National Committee or Board of Directors, and the National Committee should be so notified." Relying on ACLU by-laws that allowed for any five national committee members to appeal board decisions, John Nevin Sayre, John S. Codman, Sherwood Eddy, Agnes Brown Leach, A. J. Muste, William Pickens, Amos Pinchot, Oswald Garrison Villard, and L. Hollingsworth Wood called for a reconsideration of the initial resolution.[42]

On January 20 another leading ACLU figure, Roger Riis, leveled a series of accusations against the organization's leadership. The board, he charged, no

CONTROVERSIES ON THE PATH

longer stood for civil liberties. It was too greatly influenced by a cadre of individuals who owed allegiance "to the Communist idea." That group had effectively brought the board's work to a standstill. In contrast to this pro-communist contingent, Riis asserted his determination to back the right of Earl Browder and Henry Ford to express themselves. However, Riis noted, "so do not our left wing members." The basic division within the ACLU ranks, he stated, involved contrasting views of civil liberties. While one group considered civil liberties "a universal truth," the other perceived them as "an instrument in the so-called 'class war.' "[43]

For twenty years numerous statements by Baldwin fit into the second category. On various occasions he had explicitly termed civil liberties an instrument in the class struggle. He had also deemed economic liberty paramount to all freedoms. Now he was placing civil liberties above the political fray while enmeshing the ACLU more fully in the new sectarian wars that were splintering the left side of the ideological spectrum.

Three days later Villard too spoke of his dissatisfaction with the board's actions. "We of course should set up standards of membership," he wrote. "I do not think any one affiliated with the Communists or the Nazis should have any place on our board. They are *ipso facto* unfitted to be with any organization demanding civil liberties." Should the board's action stand, Villard warned Baldwin, he would be forced to withdraw from the national advisory committee.[44]

Seeking to resolve the quandary, Baldwin and Ward proposed that the full executive board resign, to be replaced by the national committee. The suggestion, however, got nowhere. Additionally, they unsuccessfully argued that the embittered opponents on the board depart from it. Instead, on February 5 the executive board and the national committee passed a resolution precluding anyone who supported totalitarianism from holding a position of leadership in the ACLU. The 1940 Resolution, as it came to be known, adopted the language of the board's nominating committee by affirming that both those serving on governing committees and staff members were "properly subject to the test of consistency in the defense of civil liberties in all aspects and all places." The civil liberties campaign, it was asserted, "is inevitably compromised by persons who champion civil liberties in the United States and yet who justify or tolerate the denial of civil liberties by dictatorships abroad."[45]

In a letter to the board of directors on February 19, Baldwin stated, "I wholly support it, though regretting greatly the situation which brought it about."

Various statements and writings of his from the past, he now acknowledged, might cause "some question as to my own consistency." Quotations could be made to look as though he had favored economic ends over civil liberties; certainly that was true regarding the Soviet Union, before the pact. Now, he stated unequivocally, "I repudiate the implication of any such position in the light of events in the world which have more convincingly than ever affirmed my devotion to civil liberty and the democratic process above any end."[46]

The national committee's latest decision led to Harry Ward's resignation as ACLU chairman. He was replaced by the staunchly anticommunist John Haynes Holmes. What followed was the celebrated "trial" of longtime board member Elizabeth Gurley Flynn, an old-time Wobbly and current Communist Party member, viewed even by those on the opposite side of the ideological spectrum as "engagingly honest."

As early as mid-1938 Baldwin had expressed concerns about the propensity of board members like Mary Van Kleeck who sought "to inject their political or economic beliefs into the defense of civil liberties." That had led to "almost unprecedented dissension," Baldwin reported, "and an atmosphere of wrangling which will alienate some of our friends." He also contended that the appointment of "some strong conservatives," should ideology not color their civil libertarian stance, would help "our standing before the country." While Flynn's official tie to the Communist Party was acknowledged, other board members—Abraham Isserman, a left-wing lawyer; Robert Dunn, a labor radical; and Van Kleeck—were similarly affiliated, a fact evidently not known to all their ACLU compatriots. Less than three months before the Flynn episode, Baldwin, in responding to a demand that communists be removed from "responsible positions in the Union," had questioned "how we could adopt any such policy without doing violence to our fundamental principles."[47]

Nevertheless, Baldwin had earlier urged the adoption of such a litmus test, again under circumstances that he believed could imperil the ACLU. At a board meeting in March 1933 he had introduced the possibility of "dropping from membership persons on our lists proved to be agents or informers for patriotic societies." The proposal had not been adopted, although the board agreed to keep track of such individuals "so that no special information may be given them."[48]

Writing to Holmes on February 21, 1940, Arthur Garfield Hays discussed the call for Flynn's removal from the ACLU board, which Baldwin favored.

Hays expressed no desire to speak with Flynn about the matter. She clearly appreciated how board members felt about her continued presence on it. In Hays's view, "We have no right to expel her from the Board of Directors," and it would be a mistake to attempt to do so. Nor did he believe that ACLU by-laws should possess "definite qualifications. If they did, we might on occasion find ourselves on a witch hunt," should individuals fail to acknowledge openly, in contrast to Flynn, Communist Party membership.[49]

Attempting to smooth matters over, Baldwin addressed a letter "to our friends." In it he sought to refute the notion that the just-passed resolution augured a change in ACLU policy, although it certainly did. Insisting that it portended no substantial alteration, he declared that the ACLU, in its twenty years of existence, had "never elected nor appointed anybody who supported the principles of civil liberties in the United States and denied them elsewhere or who belonged to organizations which qualified the principle or practice of civil liberty." Thus no Communist Party member had ever been elected or appointed "to any responsible position in the Union"; this was a declaration soon contested by at least one former board member. The 1940 Resolution, Baldwin proclaimed, applied to both top committees and staff members.[50]

The reason for this action, he divulged, related to "the entirely new direction of the Communist movement since the Nazi-Soviet pact." This had resulted in sharp divisions on the ACLU board and produced a host of resignations. A once-dormant issue now "became one demanding action if the Union was to hold together." The national committee's present position, he alleged, augured no rightward swing or a lessening of the determination to safeguard the rights of communists or workers. Terming this a "slight extension of our traditional policy"—although it was considerably more than that—Baldwin wrote that the ACLU was simply reaffirming "that *an organization devoted to civil liberties* should be directed only by consistent supporters of civil liberty." With close allies like John Haynes Holmes, Baldwin acknowledged that it might be difficult to "ever explain an act of expulsion."[51]

On March 18 seventeen "prominent liberals" affixed their signatures to an open letter to the ACLU. Among the signatories were Robert Morss Lovett, governor general of the Virgin Islands; former U.S. Rep. John T. Bernard of Minnesota; professors Franz Boas and Robert S. Lynd of Columbia University; author Theodore Dreiser; and Carey McWilliams and I. F. Stone of the *Nation*. The 1940 Resolution, they prophetically warned, "encourages the very tendencies it was intended to fight. It sets an example less liberal organizations will not be slow to imitate. It places the prestige of our foremost defender of civil liberties behind the idea that Communists or Communist sympathizers or that infinitely extensible category of 'fellow-travelers' are properly to be barred from certain types of offices and treated as less than first-class citizens." Furthermore, the inconsistency of the ACLU's position was clearly apparent, for what did the resolution suggest about "those faithful Catholics who, following the policy laid down by their Church, approve the Fascist regimes in Spain and Italy?" The language of the resolution was "so wide as to make the Union seem a fellow-traveller of the Dies Committee," they declared.[52]

Two days later a sharp attack on Baldwin's position appeared in the *Daily Worker*. Written by Flynn, it asserted, "Mr. Baldwin's 'unwritten policy' is just so much sand thrown in the eyes of the public. Not so long ago this breezy fellow-traveler boasted genially of the broadmindedness of the Union. 'We even have Communists on our board.' All is changed now. . . . Mr. Baldwin says, 'Communists have no moral integrity.' Well, I'll stake mine and any party member's against his any time." Holmes responded by asking for Flynn's resignation from the board.[53] She refused.

Anna Rochester, a radical historian and economist, informed the *New York Times*, "When I was elected to the Board about eleven years go, the fact that I was a Communist was known to Roger Baldwin, Norman Thomas, and other members of the Board. In fact, I was given to understand that one reason they wanted me on the Board was that I would represent the Communist viewpoint. I resigned of my own free will, long before they turned into a red-baiting organization."[54]

Dorothy Dunbar Bromley, who wrote a column that ran in the women's pages of the Scripps-Howard newspaper chain, had urged Flynn's removal from the board because of her Communist Party membership. However, Lucille Milner later insisted that Baldwin had induced Bromley to take such a stand, reasoning that it would look better if a woman delivered the charge. "It's a tough job," Baldwin wrote to Bromley, "but you are the person to do it with firmness and delicacy." The influence Baldwin possessed over Bromley and others regarding the Flynn affair decided matters, Corliss Lamont reported. "Had he chosen to uphold without compromise the basic principles of the Civil Liberties Union, the Flynn trial would never have taken place. His responsibility for this unhappy event was greater than that of anyone else."[55]

At the City Club on April 8 Roger Riis presented an amended charge that Flynn's accusations in the *Daily Worker* disqualified her from continuing as a board member. Ironically enough, during that same meeting the board authorized release of a statement challenging the Dies Committee's "demands for membership lists of organizations under investigation"; the board also confirmed the ACLU's readiness to aid the International Workers Order, a left-wing working-class fraternal organization, to regain materials removed from its headquarters by Philadelphia police officers and Dies Committee agents. One week later the board condemned a measure proposed by Rep. Jerry Voorhis of California that would compel the registration of organizations associated with foreign governments.[56]

What is referred to as "the Trial of Elizabeth Gurley Flynn"—who was brought to the meeting by Baldwin—began at the City Club of New York at 8 P.M. on May 7. The main charge was that Communist Party membership disqualified her from serving on the ACLU board. Flynn deemed this violative of basic principles long championed by ACLU members. She asked why Baldwin should not be expelled as well because of his self-professed anarchist beliefs. After a lengthy and embittered debate that lasted six hours, the board voted—but deadlocked 9–9. Among those favoring the expulsion were Ernst, Huebsch, and Riis. Those voting against it included Fraenkel, Hays, Lamont, William B. Spofford, an Episcopal priest and editor, and Dorothy Kenyon. Baldwin, Milner, and Flynn did not vote (Milner was not eligible to vote, and Flynn was not permitted to do so); Baldwin reportedly refused to utter a word throughout the lengthy proceeding. Officially, Baldwin was not entitled to vote, for he was not a board member. However, he was viewed by many as the individual who had orchestrated the entire affair. Chairman John Haynes Holmes broke the tie, thereby forcing Flynn's departure.[57]

The action has remained one of the most controversial in the annals of the ACLU. Shortly after the board's determination Harry Dana wrote to Baldwin and said that the Civil Liberties Committee of Massachusetts also had voted and had reached the opposite decision by a large margin. Dana, who had been fired from his teaching position at Columbia University for criticizing U.S. policy during World War I, delivered a blistering charge: "The removal of Communists from positions to which they have been elected is a traditional method with which Fascism has begun, in Italy, in Germany, and elsewhere. I hate to see you fighting Fascism by yielding to Fascist methods." Despite Baldwin's condemnation of all totalitarianism, it was clear that "you are yielding to what I call 'Totalitarianism of the Center,'" Dana said, adding that Baldwin had "equivocated long enough."[58]

The Flynn affair, "from start to finish," the writer Geoffrey Perrett contends, "was the kind of hearing that the ACLU had denounced elsewhere." Even the Dies Committee had not acted in such a manner, Perrett argues, but the techniques used by the ACLU "would appear again, in a more public forum, almost exactly a decade later, presided over by a Senator from Wisconsin." The ACLU action, the author Leo P. Ribuffo also reasons, "affected subsequent treatment of the far left and far right."[59]

Corliss Lamont, who later produced a book on the Flynn affair, considered "that whole rigmarole a great blot on Roger's name." The purge of communists from the ACLU leadership, Lamont thought, "not only busted [the] organization wide open" but provided a model for a host of anticommunist resolutions subsequently adopted by labor unions and other groups. The personal relationship between Baldwin and Lamont became quite strained, as the latter believed that Baldwin "was betraying the principle of civil liberties." In his book Lamont also argues that the ACLU action guided its policies for the next two decades. It led to his estrangement from Baldwin, with Baldwin and Evie becoming "a little mean." The Lamonts were denied use of the tennis court and beach at Windy Gates. "We were no longer persona grata."[60]

From Baldwin's perspective Flynn's ouster was necessary to ensure the ACLU's continued existence. Or that is how he rationalized his changed perspective. The Nazi-Soviet pact obviously enraged Baldwin and compelled him to view both the Soviet Union and the Communist Party in a different light. It led to his departure from the front ranks of the Popular Front. However, the timing of the Flynn affair—occurring as threats of resignation by long-time ACLU supporters, even leaders, loomed large—suggests that Baldwin was operating once again in a calculating manner to keep the ACLU viable. His actions and those of Flynn's accusers did establish a clear precedent followed by many other organizations during the cold war. This was highly ironic because of the ACLU's history and Baldwin's own United Front record, as well as his hitherto inclusive approach regarding organizational membership and leadership.

Baldwin had cast his lot with the anticommunists, who gained steam after the announcement of the Nazi-Soviet pact and would become still more potent in the postwar period. His days as a Popular Fronter were over. Not even the wartime alliance of the United States and the Soviet Union caused him to view communists with anything other than distrust. Unlike other former Old Leftists, Baldwin's anticommunism—to his credit—did not lead him to call for the suspension of the civil liberties or political rights of American comrades. Still, his perception of communists as outside the pale was not far removed from the strident anticommunism that led many to support a new kind of double standard. Among those who had left the train of the revolution altogether, a good number proved as willing to go after communists as American Stalinists had attacked others during their short-lived heyday. However, Baldwin remained reluctant to link up with those who assailed the communists and treated them as pariahs.

Ironically, just as Baldwin was refusing to collaborate with communists any longer, government agencies, particularly the FBI, were again viewing him with suspicion. During the midthirties Roosevelt had directed FBI director J. Edgar Hoover to investigate fascist, Nazi, and, eventually, communist groups. In late June 1940—shortly after the Elizabeth Gurley Flynn affair—the FBI prepared a new report on Baldwin that labeled him a communist. This was evidently triggered by two developments: an ACLU press release critical of the FBI's treatment of refugees from Franco's Spain, and a recent letter by Baldwin to the attorney general that condemned the FBI's investigation of individuals allegedly involved in subversive activities or in movements deemed threatening to national security. (During that very period the ACLU board voted to reprint copies of an article written by FBI director J. Edgar Hoover, "Outlaw the Vigilante!")[61]

On April 3, 1941, Hoover recommended that Baldwin "be considered for custodial detention in the event of a national emergency." On October 21 Hoover issued a report on Baldwin that adjudged him an internal security threat. It confirmed that "the Special Defense Unit had placed Baldwin in Group A, comprised of those 'individuals believed to be the most dangerous and who in all probability should be interned in event of War.'"[62]

In typical fashion none of this precluded Hoover from engaging in seemingly cordial correspondence with Baldwin, who was again seeking a link to top government officials so he could influence policy making. According to Florence Isbell, a one-time secretary who became a leader of the ACLU, the exchanges between the two men led some at the time and others later to charge Baldwin with "informing the FBI about ACLU activities and ACLU people." At the very least, Isbell continued, he was said to be "in touch with people at the FBI when it suited him to be." On October 20 Baldwin filed a memo regarding his recent visit with the FBI director. The two spent "a most pleasant hour," during which Hoover "professed his liberalism and devotion to civil rights." The FBI, Baldwin concluded, had a difficult but important task that should not be handled by anyone else. Nevertheless, it might be possible, he suggested, to get the Civil Service Commission to agree to hold hearings and follow procedure when seeking to dismiss those accused of subversive activities. Curiously enough, Hoover felt compelled to express his strong aversion "to any National police idea."[63]

On October 24, 1941, an FBI agent reported to Hoover that Baldwin, in a conversation in the Denver field office of the FBI, had asked whether there was any major communist enterprise in the area. Informed that one agent was unaware of such activity, Baldwin disclosed that he had posed the same question to his colleagues in Colorado. One name had been put forth, which Baldwin now relayed to the Denver FBI office, the agent said. However, the report acknowledged that Baldwin had "apparently intended to infer that . . . [the person he named] probably was a reputable citizen."[64]

Baldwin wrote to Hoover on October 28 urging that local FBI offices not turn over reports of subversive activities to local police departments. Police detectives, Baldwin complained, were ill trained for that kind of work. He then continued, appealing to Hoover's ego: "May I suggest that, in this field at least, instructions be given that such investigations be made only by your own agents who alone are qualified in such tasks?" In a single-spaced, four-page letter dated November 1, Hoover proclaimed himself "particularly gratified" that the FBI's basic investigative policies had received Baldwin's approval.[65]

In early 1942 Baldwin agreed to withdraw an article he had been commissioned to write for the New Republic, "Civil Rights and the F.B.I." In that unpublished manuscript he contended that wartime powers granted to the FBI had heightened "the widespread uneasiness" long felt by liberals and unionists concerning its "relation to civil liberties." Experience taught that democracy and a thought-police did not mix. However, it was clear that since the fall of 1939 the FBI, through congressional and executive edicts, had moved well beyond its usual purview, crime investigation, to examine political opinions and trade union operations. The ill-defined area of subversive activities was as expansive as the FBI determined it to be. Thus J. Edgar Hoover's social and political perspective appeared highly significant. His views approximated those "of the average professional patriot, modified in recent years by professions of liberalism," Baldwin wrote. However, Hoover's analysis of subversion seemed to begin and end with communist association.[66]

In Baldwin's estimation, the FBI would "earn its laurels in war-time only to the degree to which it discharges the grave responsibilities of protecting the country against espionage and sabotage. It has a vastly more serious job to do than heresy-hunting on the Left." Still, Baldwin considered it "inconceivable that it will again sink to the low level which marked its operations during and after World War I, for the whole policy of the government is against it." Furthermore, the FBI was "a vastly improved service, and Mr. Hoover, then a youthful assistant, is a considerably changed man."[67]

Nevertheless, certain FBI operations, Baldwin warned, were "dangerous to our democracy." He wrote, "No bureau of the government charged by law or executive order with wholesale examination of subversive political opinions can escape certain of the damaging implications which go with the words 'Gestapo' and 'O.G.P.U.,'—words which it is gratifying to say are detested by Mr. Hoover and his associates." At the same time Baldwin reasoned that it would require "great restraint" on the attorney general's part to prevent vitally essential FBI functions "from being compromised by its forced excursions into political opinion."[68]

"Civil Rights and the F.B.I.," with its many prescient warnings, never was published, because Hoover convinced Baldwin that the FBI director had "largely changed his views on the dangers from labor and the left." Now Hoover had become "violently anti-Dies and all the witch-hunting for reds," according to Baldwin.[69]

No matter, as late as June 1945 Hoover refused to remove Baldwin's name from the Security Index. Even at that relatively late date he referred to Baldwin's supposed advocacy of the violent overthrow of the U.S. government. Baldwin, he also predicted, could still "exercise considerable influence which would be of material benefit to the Communists or any similar radical group."[70]

Thus the curious relationship of the ACLU director and the FBI chieftain continued. Baldwin, more than ever, seemingly desired influence with top government officials, something Hoover, the ultimate insider, readily possessed. Once again Baldwin appeared to accept Hoover's word as gospel, even as the top G-man connived to place Baldwin on the latest version of the infamous black list first devised during the Palmer Raids. Most ironically, Baldwin seemed willing to have the FBI operate as a type of national police force, which Hoover, concerned about maintaining control of his empire, professed to oppose.

CHAPTER NINETEEN

Civil Liberties During World War II

By the end of the 1930s Baldwin feared that if the international situation worsened or the United States entered World War II, civil liberties would become more precarious. Consequently, in October 1939 he helped orchestrate a campaign to remind the American people of the restrictions placed on political freedoms during World War I. The Conference on Civil Liberties in the National Emergency, convened by Baldwin, heard the featured speaker, U.S. Attorney General Frank Murphy, affirm that the U.S. Constitution and Bill of Rights must not be abridged. The Nazi blitzkrieg in Western Europe, Baldwin warned in early June 1940, had led to "an almost unprecedented strain on peace-time democracy in the United States." The hysteria evident in Congress, he charged in a speech delivered at the University of Chicago Law School, appeared even graver now than a generation earlier. Pending legislation called for denying government jobs to members of the Communist Party of the United States or to German-American Bundists, precluded them from obtaining employment in interstate industry, and refused them federal Civil Service appointments because of their political affiliations. Even more ominous was the portrayal of foreign nationals as "enemies of our democracy operating in the guise of Trojan Horses," as Baldwin put it.[1]

On September 16, 1940, President Roosevelt signed into law the Selective Service Act, which cited "religious training and belief" as the means to determine conscientious objector status and provided for alternative service. Baldwin called a meeting of the foremost pacifist groups in the country, which led to the formation of the National Committee on Conscientious

Objectors, which operated as an ACLU adjunct. At a gathering of the new organization on September 26, he began by declaring that the ACLU had no intention of challenging the draft's constitutionality. This infuriated John Haynes Holmes, who threatened to resign his chairmanship of the new organization. Baldwin continued to meet with Justice Department officials, urging unsuccessfully that political beliefs could establish conscientious objection and thereby keep absolutists out of prisons.[2]

Later both Baldwin and the ACLU were roundly criticized for not having done enough to protest some of the greatest abuses during the war, especially those involving conscientious objectors and individuals of Japanese ancestry. The stance on conscientious objectors by both Baldwin and the ACLU was particularly curious, given his own position during World War I, the decision to found the National Civil Liberties Bureau to provide protections for war resisters, and his continued professed belief in pacifism. While the ACLU had recently opposed peacetime conscription, it declined to protest as Congress moved in the summer of 1940 to establish the Selective Service. Baldwin and the ACLU determined instead to seek more liberal provisions for objectors.[3]

That fall Baldwin claimed that the recently passed Military Service Act treated objectors more equitably; objectors were henceforth to be handled by civilian agencies. Initially, he viewed positively the treatment accorded objectors, stating that they were receiving "surprisingly sympathetic treatment." Later he argued that the law would probably accommodate nonreligious objectors who stressed an "ethical concept equivalent to religion" and applied it universally to wars and armed violence.[4]

He also expressed greater concern about wartime restrictions on civil liberties. In a speech entitled "Liberty in the Shadow of War" he asserted that no reasonable individual approved of the severe restrictions imposed on Americans during World War I. Unfortunately, however, he feared that past and present lessons had made too little impression. Paradoxically, although the United States was involved in a worldwide battle against international fascism, fascism's sharpest antagonists, labor and the Left, remained most controversial and subject to the largest curtailments of their rights to organize or speak out. Even the Roosevelt administration, despite what Baldwin termed its "clearly democratic purposes," discriminated against refugees who had communist or Popular Front connections.[5]

The official entrance of the United States into World War II, following the attack on Pearl Harbor, resulted in a shift in Baldwin's stance on civil liberties. On December 12, 1941, he joined in a discussion, "Propaganda and Censorship in Wartime," on *America's Town Meeting of the Air*, on the NBC radio network. The other participants were Eugene Lyons, author of *The Red Decade*; Morris Ernst; and Reagan McCrary of the *New York Daily Mirror*. All members of this roundtable agreed, Baldwin said, that "our political democracy and the liberties essential to it should be maintained in war as in peace." They also assumed that the government could properly control access to military information. Similarly, they did not disagree that "enemy aliens are subject to reasonable restraints." The government had the responsibility, they acknowledged, to deal quickly and firmly with any acts carried out against it or the public peace. At the same time Baldwin believed that voluntary restraints were much preferable to legal constraints. And he would curb no propaganda except that involving "a direct incitement to some act, committed or attempted, against the Government or against the public peace."[6]

As he had during World War I, Baldwin believed that his reputation well served the cause of civil liberties in dealing with government officials. At the meeting of the ACLU board the day after the Pearl Harbor attack, he reported on a series of conferences held in the nation's capital. Top War Department officials had spoken with him about a rumor that the ACLU was supporting a ban on soldiers attending religious services. Selective Service representatives shared with him information about appeals by conscientious objectors. The Justice Department noted that the case of Harry Bridges, the Australian-born president of the International Longshoremen, held the greatest priority among the more than four hundred cases of deportations involving communists. The attorney general's office also stated that the appeal process involving Minneapolis labor unionists who were members of the Socialist Workers Party would be expedited, with the defendants to be released on bail and facing only minimal sentences. A special board, the Justice Department's Special Defense unit related, would probably handle the question of what foreign propaganda would be banned.[7]

One month later Baldwin more fully discussed the Department of Justice's prosecution of members of the Trotskyist Socialist Workers Party, diehard antagonists of the Communist Party of the United States, under the 1940 Smith Act. That measure made it illegal to "advocate, abet, advise, or teach the duty, necessity, desirability, or propriety of overthrowing or destroying any government in the United States by force or violence." The Smith Act also outlawed membership in organizations that supported the overthrow of the government or published or distributed documents calling for such an overthrow. The trial of the Minneapolis Trotskyists became, in Baldwin's words, "a heresy trial." Guilty verdicts, based on simple utterances and publications, were obtained against eighteen defendants. The 2d U.S. Circuit Court of Appeals sustained the convictions, which the U.S. Supreme Court declined to review.[8]

Thus, unlike numerous radicals and liberals, Baldwin strongly opposed the prosecution of the frequently reviled Trotskyists. He correctly pointed out that words and writings alone, not illegal acts, had resulted in their prosecution. The case was applauded by communists, who lacked the foresight to appreciate that similar moves could and soon would be undertaken against them.

Also, in contrast to many others in leftist and liberal circles, including some ACLU colleagues, Baldwin consistently defended the rights of native fascists and anti-Semites to express themselves in print or at the podium. Early in 1942 he expressed concern that the *New Republic* had basically urged the prosecution of those considered guilty of "treasonable utterances." In a private note to editor Bruce Bliven, Baldwin stated, "I thought the New Republic was way beyond asking for prosecutions for expressions of opinion, whatever their character. There are plenty of people who would testify to the 'treasonable utterances' of the New Republic itself in times past. I hope you will mend your ways."[9]

On April 4 Baldwin and other top ACLU officials wrote to the new attorney general, Francis Biddle, criticizing the Justice Department's decision to undertake the first prosecutions involving opinion since the United States had entered the war. The prosecutions—one involving George W. Christians of Chattanooga, head of the anti-Semitic Crusader White Shirts—seemed to violate the spirit of the very principle Biddle had articulated in December: "The Department has concluded that free speech as such ought not to be restricted by punishment unless it clearly appears that such speech would cause direct and dangerous interference with the conduct of the war." Such an analysis, adopted by the ACLU, was in accord with Supreme Court decisions concerning the pronouncement of the "'clear and present danger' of substantive evils to justify any prosecution for speech or publication."[10]

One week later Baldwin wrote a letter to the *Nation* criticizing editor Freda Kirchwey's call to suppress the fascist press. To his credit Baldwin termed such a proposal "as impracticable and dangerous as it is fantastic coming from" that journal. Only "united democratic forces," he insisted, could defeat American far rightists. "Counter-propaganda is our best weapon," he wrote. The *Nation*'s editors responded by asking, "How can our old friend Roger Baldwin talk such nonsense? Doesn't he really know an out-and-out fascist paper when he sees one?" They then pointed to publications by anti-Semitic "native fascists" that must be silenced—such as those by William Pelley, leader of the Silver Shirts; George E. Deatherage, head of the Knights of the White Camellia; and Father Coughlin—and asked whether the ACLU planned to oppose such action. If so, the *Nation* would be quite displeased, the editors stated, to learn "that Mr. Baldwin and his associates knew so little about the realities of political warfare."[11]

Baldwin and the ACLU were repeatedly criticized for Elizabeth Gurley Flynn's expulsion from the national board because of her Communist Party membership, an action that arguably provided a model for other organizations during the cold war. However, it should also be noted that the demands by the *Nation*'s editorial staff for muzzling right-wingers were a far more egregious example of the kind of ideological baiting increasingly heard after the war ended. The *Nation*, after all, was demanding that the fascist press be censored.

When Morris Ernst urged ACLU support for public disclosure of operations of political organizations and movements, such as the right-wing Christian Front, Baldwin expressed grave doubts that such a move would even prevent "war-time prosecutions for utterances or the censorship of publications." The activities and financial operations of the Christian Front and American fascists like Pelley had long been disclosed. The same was true during World War I, Baldwin reminded John Haynes Holmes, "though the shoe then was on the other foot most of the time. Everybody knew all there was to know about the Socialists and IWW's." Nevertheless, prosecutions were carried out.[12]

In a radio address, "Our Wartime Rights and Liberties," Baldwin discerningly warned about seemingly reasonable calls for suppression of particular publications or individuals. "The danger is that, beginning with a Pelley, a Coughlin and a few other fanatics of long standing, it will spread to any of those charged with creating disunity, racial or class hatreds, and thus tend to silence all criticism."[13]

Once more Baldwin—to his delight—had entrée to the inner reaches of government and was conversing with the likes of Attorney General Biddle and

Ed Ennis, head of the Justice Department's Enemy Alien Control Unit. Ernest Angell, who chaired the ACLU's National Committee on Conscientious Objectors, was welcomed into the Oval Office itself. Top ACLU figures also met with FBI director Hoover, Assistant Secretary of War John J. McCloy, and Paul V. McNutt, chairman of the War Manpower Commission.[14]

Baldwin, Arthur Garfield Hays, and Alexander Meiklejohn spoke with several top officials regarding issues of concern to the ACLU. Justice Department officials reported that they were receiving few complaints concerning seditious conversation and publications. They planned no prosecutions of that sort unless greater pressure arose. No action against Charles Coughlin was likely, as he effectively had been muzzled by the Catholic Church.[15]

Throughout the first several months of 1942 the ACLU board of directors remained divided over how to respond to the government prosecution of American fascists. Christians, the head of the Crusader White Shirts, had been charged with mailing antiwar materials to soldiers stationed at Fort Oglethorpe, Georgia. Also indicted were Robert Noble and Ellis O. Jones of the Friends of Progress in Los Angeles, for antiwar speeches and criticisms of military officials. In July twenty-eight right-wingers—including Elizabeth Dilling, author of *The Red Network*; Silver Shirts leader Pelley; and Lawrence Dennis, the most prominent fascist in the United States—were accused of conspiring to produce insubordination in the armed forces.[16]

As Sam Walker has recorded, "the same conservative-liberal-left coalition" that prevented a more stalwart ACLU stance regarding the internment of Japanese Americans kept the ACLU from defending the American fascists. Whitney North Seymour, a leading New York lawyer, urged that the Justice Department suppress speech that exhibited dangerous propensities. Morris Ernst and the playwright Elmer Rice considered American democracy imperiled and thus favored the prosecutions. The sociologist David Riesman championed "administrative control of propaganda." Wartime exigencies, Corliss Lamont insisted, superseded unfettered freedom of speech. By contrast, Arthur Garfield Hays, like Baldwin, urged the ACLU to affirm its belief that speech be restricted only in cases of direct incitement to violence.[17]

The clash produced a heated meeting of the board, which gathered on October 12 at Walter Frank's apartment in Greenwich Village. Osmond Fraenkel proposed that the ACLU defend any individual except when "utterances interfered with the war effort." To his amazement no one seconded his motion. Rice exclaimed that "he was for America and against anyone who opposed the American way," Walker writes. Criticisms of the war effort, Ernst warned, were causing the ACLU to lose influence within the Roosevelt administration. The discussion stunned Baldwin, Hays, and Holmes. Hays was taken aback by the anti–civil liberties rhetoric, while Baldwin all but said he would resign. The majority, Holmes charged, was motivated by less than classic civil libertarian concerns.[18]

At its October 19 meeting the ACLU board voted unanimously to adopt the following resolution, proposed by Whitney North Seymour:

> Recognizing that our military enemies are now using techniques of propaganda which may involve an attempt to pervert the Bill of Rights to serve the enemy rather than the people of the United States, the American Civil Liberties Union will not participate,—except where the fundamentals of due process are denied,—in cases where, after investigation, there are grounds for a belief that the defendant is cooperating with or acting on behalf of the enemy, even though the particular charge against the defendant might otherwise be appropriate for intervention by the Union.[19]

Despite the apparent agreement on the board, its ardent civil libertarians—Baldwin, Hays, Holmes, and Norman Thomas—were distressed that the Seymour resolution passed. Fraenkel acknowledged, "The all-out for the war group is getting out of hand, it seems to me." Baldwin regretfully acknowledged that "the caution of our majority of the Board pretty accurately reflects our membership." Ernst fired back at Holmes, "You, and Roger, and Art . . . don't represent the Board any more." Once more Thomas threatened to resign but was dissuaded from doing so by Baldwin and Holmes, his colleagues of the past quarter-century.[20]

As his correspondence with Holmes in the fall of 1942 shows, Baldwin disagreed with the ACLU's unwillingness to challenge the government decision to place Japanese Americans and Japanese nationals in internment camps, the use of sedition laws to prosecute American fascists, and administration support for compulsory civilian service, to be determined by the government. Nevertheless, he did "not feel that our job has been compromised nor the cause betrayed. The issues are not so clear as to be beyond debate." Furthermore, he was convinced that the vast majority of ACLU members was in full agreement with the board. He was disturbed about the urging of caution that seemingly emanated from other than civil libertarian concerns. "It is a state of mind in our Board which would rather not act, contrary to my own inclination always to act in cases of doubt," Baldwin told Holmes. Baldwin considered himself free to continue speaking out on civil liberties issues in any manner he chose, no matter the position adopted by the ACLU. This would be done, he trusted, "with sufficient discrimination as not to cause confusion or involve the Union." Thus "the time has not yet come when I am unable to work in the Union within the policies laid down."[21]

As Baldwin reflected on January 30, 1943, the ACLU remained the only national organization that sought—theoretically, at least—to champion the rights of all individuals and groups "without distinction." At the same time the ACLU recognized that certain restrictions were necessary, including the registration of foreign agents, the identification of their propaganda, and the censorship of communications by private citizens with other countries. The organization remained opposed to abridgments of freedom of speech that did not meet the clear and present danger test, any curbs on public discussion, censorship of mail and the press, and racial discrimination of any sort.[22]

In March 1943 the ACLU published an abstract of a speech Baldwin delivered, entitled "War and the Bill of Rights," which displayed something less than an absolutist civil libertarian perspective. Baldwin conceded the necessity of "controls of military information at home and abroad, of enemy aliens, of activities presenting a clear obstruction of the war, and of industrial conflict. We do not accept controls of opinion nor of non-military news, nor of debate and dissent on the critical issues."[23]

The ACLU found it remarkable, Baldwin reported, that in contrast to the World War I era, the United States was now "almost as free of repression as in time of peace." "Great democratic progress" had been made since the last world war. Supreme Court rulings had placed the Bill of Rights on firmer ground than ever, while the Roosevelt administration was generally "opposed to illiberal measures." More than one thousand individuals had been incarcerated or indicted because of spoken or written words at the end of the first year of U.S. involvement in World War I. This time around, fewer than one hundred such actions had been initiated.[24]

Prosecutions under the Espionage Act had resulted in sedition charges, and postal authorities had removed from the U.S. mail publications they considered "to cause disaffection in the armed forces." The government censored communications with people overseas, resulting in the withholding of information from the general public on such topics as discriminatory treatment of blacks at home and anticolonial agitation abroad. More than one thousand conscientious objectors—half were Jehovah's Witnesses—were in federal penitentiaries, while six thousand others toiled in camps modeled after the Civilian Conservation Corps, not the productive farm work to which the conscientious objectors of World War I had been assigned. Still more damaging to democracy's cause, Baldwin reasoned, was the discrimination suffered by blacks, workers, Japanese Americans, and foreign nationals. Additionally, Baldwin reported, "We have refused to lift the enemy alien restrictions from the 200,000 refugees from Hitler who are living in our midst, presumably for fear of being regarded as pro-Semitic, since most of them are Jews."[25]

Baldwin's own recounting of violations of personal freedoms hardly reflected a remarkable absence of wartime repression. He condemned those abridgments, sometimes adopting an unpopular stance in the process. Such blemishes notwithstanding, that wartime record involving the First Amendment and minority rights, he repeatedly argued, was noteworthy. In an earlier time he hardly would have reached such a conclusion. More and more, however, Baldwin appeared to be criticizing government policies as an insider might. To his credit his heightened connections with government officials failed to dissuade him from contesting certain administration decisions. But even then he sometimes made declarations of a rather astonishing cast, given his standing as America's foremost civil libertarian.

On April 27 Baldwin wrote to John Rogge of the Department of Justice regarding the trial in *United States v. McWilliams* of the thirty "native fascists" prosecuted under the Espionage and Smith acts. Baldwin had earlier opposed their indictment on conspiracy charges, arguing that they were "competitors in their respective rackets." Eventually, the defendants were accused of conspiring with the German government to damage the morale of the U.S. military. In a note to Max Lerner, Baldwin referred to "that fool sedition trial." He offered a series of suggestions to Rogge that prosecutors not mention the issues of freedom of speech and of the press during the trial. Accepting the clear and present danger test, the ACLU was not adverse to its being "reasonably applied" to the Espionage Act. That would involve acts committed after the United States had entered the war. Regarding those previously carried out, the ACLU hoped that the government could rely on measures other than the Smith Act.[26]

Then Baldwin, in a rather startling move, suggested other statutes to which the government might turn to prosecute the American fascists. These included the Foreign Registration Act, amended the previous April, that might pertain to individuals "who knowingly worked for or in association with persons representing a foreign country and who even as sub-agents were required to register," Baldwin said. He also cited Title 18, Section 5, of the *United States Code Annotated*, which provided criminal penalties for intercourse conducted "with agents of foreign governments for the purpose of 'defeating the measures of the government of the United States.'" Title 19, Section 98, of the annotated code criminalized "the possession of property or papers in aid of a foreign government designed to violate the penal statutes of the United States," Baldwin noted. An ACLU attorney had also broached the possibility of bringing mail fraud charges against some of the defendants.[27]

Throughout the war Baldwin continued to defend the rights of American fascists, including Gerald L. K. Smith, the right-wing minister and spellbinding orator. The ACLU, with Baldwin playing a key role, helped Smith speak in public halls in Minneapolis, Milwaukee, Cleveland, and other locations. The rabid anti-Semite insisted on dealing directly with Baldwin. On one occasion Smith phoned Baldwin at Windy Gates and was told to go to the New York office. Smith replied, "Oh I can't trust that office; you've got Jews in it." Baldwin—who viewed Smith as "our pet reactionary"—offered advice, recommended attorneys, and encouraged affiliates to safeguard his right to speak.[28]

The *McWilliams* case ended unhappily for the federal government. A mistrial was declared after the presiding judge died. The defendants were reindicted, but an appeals court threw the case out in November 1946, asserting that the defendants had been denied their right to a speedy trial.

Increasingly, Baldwin's attention riveted on the greatest wartime infringements of American civil liberties. In late January 1942 he received word of intensified pressure by the U.S. military to carry out a mass evacuation of Japanese Americans and Japanese nationals. While he was in Washington, he was informed by James Rowe of the Justice Department that Lt. Gen. John L. DeWitt, commander of the Western Defense Command, had "recommended moving the whole Japanese population eastward from the seacoast area." On January 20 Baldwin, "rather fearful that some move may be made, if the emergency should appear great," passed this information on to Ernest Besig, the young director of the San Francisco ACLU. The internment of Japanese Americans, Baldwin now warned, "would virtually suspend civil rights" along the west coast.[29]

On February 19 Roosevelt acceded to military requests to set up military zones along the west coast, where Japanese nationals and Americans of Japanese ancestry would be confined. Two days later Baldwin sent a telegram to the northern California office, arguing that the presidential order necessitated "very careful scrutiny of its administration to prevent injustice." He suggested that Besig and the southern California chapter meet with Assistant Attorney General Thomas Clark and General DeWitt. If they proved unresponsive, Besig and his colleagues should resort to filing writs of habeas corpus. Baldwin also proposed that they contact Japanese-American organizations "to insure full report of deserving cases." Similarly, he considered it "desirable to stimulate public meetings and protests" by religious and civic organizations "to offset hysteria."[30]

Besig sought clarification of the national office's policy regarding the presidential order. Baldwin again wired Besig, asserting, "Executive order concerning military control of prescribed defense areas is undoubtedly legal in principle but may readily result in illegal action." Consequently, the ACLU should strive "to prevent injustices both to aliens and citizens against whom reasonable grounds for removal are not established." The ACLU board affirmed that a "system should provide for hearings in individual cases as with enemy aliens now detained."[31]

The ACLU's concern and Baldwin's own, that procedural guidelines be provided for detainees, was admirable. However, his declaration that the presidential action could withstand a legal challenge bespoke the mind-set of many ACLU leaders: a readiness to accede to general government policy, an acceptance of the constitutionality of the internments, and a determination to oppose only specific excesses or abuses. As matters turned out, the nation's leading civil liberties organization proved unwilling to contest the decision to place 120,000 individuals in detention camps. At its March 2 gathering the ACLU board did authorize the establishment of national and California committees to seek modification of the internment order. The board called for citizens to be afforded hearings, unless "military defense" was essential; in that case the board urged that the government declare martial law. The ACLU leaders also envisioned a court case to test "the legality of the order."[32]

The national board still had to decide what, if any, response it would make to Executive Order 9066. The more conservative members, headed by Whitney North Seymour—whom Baldwin had brought into the organization "as part of the move toward respectability"—believed that the president had full authority during wartime to act as he had. Many liberals, including Morris

Ernst, Roger Riis, Freda Kirchwey, and Alexander Meiklejohn, considered the successful waging of the war most important of all. Meiklejohn contended, "For us to say that they are taking away civil rights, would have as much sense as protesting because a 'measles' group is isolated. The Japanese citizens, as a group, are dangerous both to themselves and to their fellow-citizens. And, that being true, discriminatory action is justified." Corliss Lamont viewed the ACLU's stance as obstructionist and bound to give aid and comfort to foes of the United States.[33]

Most disturbed by Executive Order 9066 were the old-line pacifists, Norman Thomas, John Haynes Holmes, Arthur Garfield Hays, and Baldwin. As Fraenkel recollected, Baldwin "wanted to make a much stronger stand than many members of the Board did." But on more than one occasion, the board members "stood on their hind legs" when Baldwin tried to steer ACLU policy in a different direction. And exactly what position the dissenters wanted to take remains unclear.[34]

On March 20 Edward Alsworth Ross, the ACLU's national chairman; vice chairman Edward L. Parsons; board chairman John Haynes Holmes; general counsel Arthur Garfield Hays; and director Roger N. Baldwin drafted a letter to President Roosevelt. They expressed grave concerns about the recently issued executive order, noting that it was unprecedented, highly questionable on constitutional grounds, and could lead to the deprivation of the rights of U.S. citizens without due process of law. Additionally, the order appeared ripe for significant administrative abuses, affording military officials unchecked power to relocate large numbers of people in defense zones. Consequently, the ACLU asked Roosevelt to allow U.S. citizens to be removed from such areas only after individual examinations to ascertain loyalty, and for nationals of enemy countries to be removed only after examinations similar to those already used by the Department of Justice.[35]

Throughout the spring and into the summer of 1942 Baldwin and the ACLU continued to struggle with the question of how to respond to the internments. At a series of meetings the ACLU board sought to refine its position on the treatment of Japanese Americans. The board planned to write to President Roosevelt and Secretary of War Henry Stimson to highlight the increased vigilantism and civil liberties infringements that were accompanying internment. The board applauded Colorado's governor Ralph L. Carr for offering to accept internees in his state. In April the board also adopted a resolution declaring that the internment order "involves no question of civil liberties," although abuses could result from its vague wording. The board subsequently adopted a resolution affirming that "the government *in our judgment* has the *constitutional* right in the present war to establish military zones and to remove persons, either citizens or aliens, from such zones when their presence may endanger national security, even in the absence of a declaration of martial law." At the same meeting the board voted to oppose a Senate bill that enabled the secretary of war to place Japanese Americans in internment camps.[36]

The ACLU, particularly its west coast affiliates, continued to pursue legal remedies. However, in mid-April the U.S. District Court in Seattle summarily dismissed a habeas corpus challenge to the evacuation orders. Baldwin and Besig maintained their search for an appropriate test case, with Baldwin championing the case of Gordon Hirabayashi, a conscientious objector. On May 18 the ACLU national board accepted Baldwin's recommendation to support the case, which involved the defendant's refusal to accede to the evacuation order. By June Besig of the San Francisco ACLU had obtained approval from the committee to provide counsel for Fred Toyosaburo Korematsu, who had been "arrested for remaining illegally within a Military Zone." However, the national board, Besig came to believe, offered Korematsu only weak support.[37]

A deeply divided ACLU national board backed the government's right during wartime to create military zones where individuals could be placed if their presence was said to "endanger national security." Following the national board's lead, Baldwin wrote to Besig, Mary Farquharson of Seattle's ACLU chapter, and A. L. Wirin, who headed the ACLU in Los Angeles, urging them to remain on the cases as private counsel in order to raise additional constitutional issues.[38]

Speaking for the national office, acting ACLU chairman Walter Frank, counsel Osmond K. Fraenkel, and Baldwin agreed with Wirin's decision not to contest Executive Order 9066. "It seems to us quite unnecessary to do so, and would undoubtedly lead to misinterpretations of the Union's position," they wrote him. While challenging congressional action regarding more discriminatory treatment would not prove fruitful, they had no intention of opposing the Los Angeles chapter's determination to do so. The ACLU officials then urged the following approach:

> We think you should concentrate the attack entirely on the order of General DeWitt. For we think we must concede that Congress has a right to punish criminally the violation of a *proper* military order and that the President has

the right to grant a considerable measure of discretion to those in charge of operations.

Our position must come down to this: that the actual evacuation order is arbitrary (1) because the machinery is set up for excepting from the order those against whom there are no grounds of complaint, and (2) because the order covers so wide an area, and (3) because it bases evacuation solely on national origin. We consider the lack of provisions for hearings within a reasonable time arbitrary. The other items involve questions of degree. In this case, all items taken together show arbitrariness. Under certain exceptional circumstances we might consider classification based on national origin reasonable, provided proper safeguards. . . .[39]

Thus the ACLU's leaders, including its longtime executive director, were acknowledging that Congress and the president possessed ample authority to carry out the internment order. They chose to attack only its arbitrary nature and the basing of the evacuation on national origin. Yet they even conceded that such a determination was proper, if various procedural guidelines were laid out.

Stalwart board member Norman Thomas, not impressed with such reasoning, expressed his concerns about the national office's decisions. He had supported the original determination "to test legally the whole business," including military edicts, the resulting evacuation, federal legislation criminalizing civilians' disobedience of military orders, and Executive Order 9066. Thomas found it incomprehensible "to say that you can properly present the whole issue if you accept the legitimacy of the Presidential order." A large number of ACLU members, he suspected, "will be vastly surprised at the legal scholasticism" that guided the organization in determining policy regarding the internments.[40]

In articles he wrote that were published in August and September Baldwin condemned the unprecedented resort to "administrative exile." What this amounted to, he charged, was the setting up of "concentration camps for citizens." This provided "shameful evidence of our hysterical war-time intolerance, based on race alone."[41]

Nevertheless, on October 8 he joined with Holmes and Hays to send a congratulatory note to Dillon Myer, director of the War Relocation Authority. They considered Myer's decision to place internees at sites throughout the United States as "far preferable to their segregation in virtual ghettoes on the Pacific Coast, and will go a long way toward the process of Americanization. We congratulate the War Relocation Authority on its far-sighted statesmanship in making provisions conforming to a sound national policy."[42]

The note to Myer, which painted his agency's actions in such a rosy manner, was astonishing. However, it was in keeping with Baldwin's desire to maintain access to top officials. Now that he had such access, he was obviously determined not to relinquish it; his growing loss of control over the very organization he had founded might also explain his determination to strengthen his Washington ties. Unfortunately, that led to a relationship with certain government agencies, including Myer's War Relocation Authority, which at best was unseemly for the nation's leading civil liberties organization. Still more disturbing was the readiness of Baldwin and his closest ACLU compatriots to laud the very man, Director Myer, whom he had early determined to oppose.

On November 3, 1942, Baldwin, Holmes, and Hays mailed something more than a conciliatory letter to Lt. Gen. John L. DeWitt of the Western Defense Command. Although they expressed opposition to "wholesale evaluations," the correspondents praised DeWitt's handling of the internments. "We cannot refrain from expressing to you our congratulations on so difficult a job accomplished with a minimum of hardship, considering its unprecedented character."[43]

An enraged Norman Thomas sarcastically told Baldwin on November 7, "Since the ACLU is going in for congratulating the army on being humane, may I inquire whether you have yet practiced on a letter to Colonel Lanser who . . . is an officer of the German Army of occupation in Norway. He also tried to be humane."[44]

One week later Thomas wrote to Holmes and warned that other organizations, such as the National Council of Jewish Women, were referring to the ACLU's position to justify their own support for the evacuation order. Thus the civil liberties group again provided an illiberal model for others, in the manner of the Elizabeth Gurley Flynn affair. As Thomas saw it, the ACLU's "legal stand, such as it is, is due to the Northern California Branch and Roger's skillful manipulation."[45]

Holmes, by contrast, was hardly displeased by the ACLU's wartime relationship with the Roosevelt administration, as he said in a letter to Baldwin on December 14, 1942. He expressed full support for Baldwin's

policy of action in relation to the government. . . . I see perfectly the danger which Norman has in mind, but you are just as conscious of this danger as he is, and there is no possibility of the Board going astray or forfeiting its appointed functions under your direction. I favor working with the government to the accomplishments of our end and aims to the farthest extent possible, and thank God that we have a government with which we can thus work.

In the case of the A.C.L.U. exactly as in the case of the conscientious objectors, there seem to be people unhappy and frightened because we've got some friends in high places. I take this to mean in both cases that we've accomplished something in the last quarter of a century. We have educated a whole generation of people, and this is now reflected in the attitude of government. What we find in Washington is to a great extent our own work, and why should we throw it away? Why not make maximum use of it? That you are doing, and I wholeheartedly approve.[46]

Holmes's analysis was astute, capturing as it did Baldwin's twenty-five-year quest to become a player, to be received as something of an equal in the highest rungs of the federal government. While the civil liberties movement had begun as something of a renegade organization, Baldwin had never been entirely comfortable with that role, seeking at the very outset to deal with top military men, cabinet officials, and even the president himself.[47] Now, as Holmes noted, that access had been attained, to his and Baldwin's obvious delight. They believed that they could use such connections to bolster their cause, but the civil liberties campaign still perhaps required something of an outsider spirit. Lacking that, it would hardly possess the ability or verve required to contest government policies that diminished civil liberties.

The ACLU's annual report, published in June 1943, said as much. Reviewing the events of 1942, Baldwin wrote:

> The striking contrast between the state of civil liberty in the first eighteen months of World War II and in World War I offers strong evidence to support the thesis that our democracy can fight even the greatest of all wars and still maintain the essentials of liberty. The country in World War II is almost wholly free of those pressures which in the first World War resulted in mob violence against dissenters, hundreds of prosecutions for utterances; in the creation of a universal volunteer vigilante system, officially recognized, to report dissent to the F.B.I.; in hysterical hatred of everything German; in savage sentences for private expressions of criticism; and in suppression of public debate of the issues of the war and the peace.

Contradicting his own analysis, Baldwin pointed to "the worst single invasion of citizens' liberties under war pressures": the internment of more than seventy thousand Japanese Americans.[48]

In November 1943 Baldwin continued to demonstrate how seductive and dangerous the ACLU's increasingly close relationship with officialdom could prove. "Our tactics will largely depend upon his [McCloy's] judgment and that of Myer as to the time and place of a suit [regarding the camps], if brought at all," Baldwin wrote. He believed that the War Department was close to rescinding the evacuation order, and he was more determined than ever to adopt a conciliatory stance. At the same time he considered it essential to proceed "with as many suits as we can get" against the internment. On June 2, 1944, he informed A. L. Wirin, who headed the ACLU's Los Angeles branch, of "an understanding with Dillon Myer in Washington that we would not send any persons of Japanese ancestry back into the military zone . . . until we had cleared with him." As Baldwin now saw matters, "defiance of military authorities might do more harm than good."[49]

Meanwhile, abuses abounded at Tule Lake, California, where hundreds of internees had been placed in a stockade and detained for lengthy periods, although no charges had been brought against them. On June 6 Besig wired both Baldwin and Myer to seek verification of a statement by an official of the War Relocation Authority (WRA) that the two men had agreed to prevent Besig from visiting Tule Lake. Informed that the New York office had so concurred, Besig angrily wrote back to Baldwin: "It seems to us as though you have more or less joined forces with the War Relocation Authority, the defendants in the suits which we propose to file."[50]

Besig's analysis, Baldwin shot back, was "based upon a complete misapprehension." Until the ACLU sought injunctions to stop the internments, he agreed with Myer that there was no point in presenting legal issues concerning disloyalty cases. Tule Lake involved national issues, as already determined by the New York office. In a follow-up note Baldwin stated, "It would be quite impracticable for any national organization to allow local affiliates or branches to take positions in conflict with the national body on matters of national policy."[51] Baldwin thus appeared to be supporting the WRA position regarding the northern California chapter. This astonished and angered Besig.

The national office, Baldwin informed Myer on June 23, would select cases to pursue. It anticipated initiating legal action to challenge existing standards for determining disloyalty, after it had sought injunctions to stop the internments. At the same time the national office promised to "clear with you as to the particular plaintiffs." That would preclude having "any cases mooted and . . . [would allow the ACLU to] see that the selection of cases raises precisely the legal points at issue." Baldwin did expect Besig, as the ACLU representative, to receive permission to enter the facilities at Tule Lake.[52]

At this stage some would charge that Baldwin and the ACLU were acting as agents of the federal government. This was quite a turn of events from earlier days when both generally were distrusted and outsiders—which some, like FBI director Hoover, thought they should remain—and it hardly served the cause of civil liberties.

The national office remained troubled by its relationship with its northern California chapter. On November 1, 1944, Baldwin asked Besig to reconsider filing a separate brief in the *Ex Parte* Endo case, with which the ACLU national office had had little involvement. The national board, Baldwin wrote, did "not see how any branch could properly raise the question of filing a brief in the Supreme Court of the United States in a national case without consulting with national office." He asked, "Would you suggest that we approach the Supreme Court from four or five different angles? The proposition appears ridiculous on its face."[53]

The Supreme Court ruled on both *Endo* and *Korematsu* in December 1944. In *Endo* the Court found that the WRA could not "detain" loyal American citizens but explicitly declined to rule on constitutional grounds. On December 18 Justice Hugo Black, writing for the 6–3 majority, handed down the ruling in *Korematsu*. As in the *Hirabayashi* case, the majority fully accepted the military's contention that Japanese Americans endangered military security along the west coast. Black acceded to the military's argument that it could not "bring about an immediate segregation of the disloyal from the loyal." Thus the "temporary exclusion of the entire group" was predicated on a strategic rationale. Black vehemently denied that racism had led to the treatment accorded Korematsu and that the relocation centers were actually concentration camps. Justice Frank Murphy—one of three dissenters (the other two were Robert Jackson and Stanley Roberts)—insisted that the internment was rooted in "the misinformation, half-truths and insinuations that for years have been directed against Japanese Americans by people with racial and economic prejudices—the same people who have been among the foremost advocates of the evacuation." Japanese Americans, he wrote, should have been examined "on an individual basis" through "investigations and hearings to separate the loyal from the disloyal, as was done in the case of persons of German and Italian ancestry." Murphy refused to give his legal stamp of approval to "this legalization of racism." The dissent could have been penned, at various points, by an ACLU attorney or Baldwin himself.[54]

The December 1944 issue of the *American Mercury* contained an article by Baldwin on the internment of Japanese Americans and Japanese nationals. The internees had been "driven from their homes, deprived of their livelihood, kicked about as casually as if they were stray mongrels," Baldwin reported. In the process they became "the victims of the most sweeping and deliberate violation of constitutional rights in our history." Their treatment, Baldwin asserted, "stands as the blackest blot on our civil liberties record in this war—a record, incidentally, that has been, in most other instances, remarkably fine."[55]

Alexander Meiklejohn informed Besig on September 14, 1945, of a meeting that he, Baldwin, and Assistant Attorney General Herb Wechsler had participated in regarding renunciation of citizenship. Signed into law by Roosevelt on July 1, 1944, Public Law 405—also known as the "denaturalization bill"—allowed U.S. citizens to renounce their citizenship. Some claimed this legislation was designed to obtain renunciations from Japanese Americans. In Meiklejohn's eyes the meeting resulted in "good hard plain talking, and the difficulties of the situation seemed to get cleared." Baldwin had performed admirably, Meiklejohn insisted. "With Roger's attitude through all this I think you would have agreed. He fought at every point and to the end, kept pressing the point that wherever we could find a legal issue we would fight it."[56]

Meiklejohn then referred to the very strained relations between the San Francisco chapter and the national office. "The vital question," Meiklejohn reasoned, was whether New York should " 'confer' with the officials in Washington, as Roger has been doing." If the national office possessed such authority to determine policy, the northern California chapter could not maintain its independence regarding the renunciation cases. Meiklejohn then offered,

> It's possible, of course, to reject the whole procedure of conference and to make it our business as an organization to fight the government, to defend civil liberties *against the government*.
>
> That's pretty much your attitude and I reminded Roger that it used to be his. But both theoretically and practically, it seems to me wrong. The officials . . . are quite as zealous in the defense of civil liberties as we are. That's their plain duty—and they live up to it. And, that being the case, "confer-

ence" backed by conflict seems infinitely more sensible than conflict *without* conference.[57]

In a September 17 letter to Besig, Baldwin denied that the national office's disinclination to pursue the Tule Lake disciplinary cases "was due to deference to the W.R.A." The cases involved internees who demanded protection of their constitutional rights and who were accused of participating in disturbances, including both demonstrations and strikes, to make their point. The War Relocation Authority, Baldwin said, wanted to downplay the Tule Lake affair. If the "strongly pro-Japanese elements" at Tule Lake managed to get publicity, the effort to relocate evacuees along the west coast would be damaged. Responding four days later, Besig argued, "It is our job to defend the civil liberties of all without distinction. It isn't our job to sacrifice an unpopular minority for a more popular group." He pointedly asserted, "I hold that you have always been extremely reluctant to differ with your friends in the WRA."[58]

A few years later Dillon S. Myer sent a congratulatory note to Baldwin for "the really magnificent service that you have rendered and the high idealism that you have displayed." Particularly noteworthy from Myer's perspective were "the trying days during my administration of the War Relocation Authority when you and I were battling, along with a lot of other people of good will, to restore the rights and privileges of the Japanese Americans who were evacuated from the West Coast."[59]

Many years later Baldwin acknowledged, "We had compromised on some issues where we should have been more clean-cut—notably the Japanese evacuation." He attributed this, at least in part, to the division of the ACLU board of directors, its attorneys, and the Los Angeles and San Francisco chapters "on the question of security." He also believed that the ACLU had failed to defend as forcefully as it might have people who were accused of collaborating with the enemy. At the same time he attempted to explain the rationale behind his willingness, and that of the ACLU, sometimes to accept half a loaf:

> At times the spirit of compromise so dominated a divided board that Arthur Garfield Hays once said to me in disgust that he'd handle a case of civil liberties himself rather than take it to "that damn board." I sympathized, though I supported compromise to hold the organization together as the lesser evil. I have long had the failing, if it is that, of accepting the philosophy of the lesser evil up to the point of a clear collision with principles I couldn't surrender.

No other philosophy seemed to me consistent with the job of an executive obligated to hold his shifting majority and minority together.[60]

Ernest Besig probably would have agreed with Baldwin's later admission to an interviewer about his failure to challenge the national board's actions regarding the test cases: "I'm ashamed of it now." As Besig saw matters, "There were many friends of Roger's who were part of the administration under the Roosevelt regime. Roger used to go the rounds in Washington and meet with all these guys, and he was more of a government representative than he was an ACLU representative for a while."[61]

Perhaps that explains to some degree Baldwin's curious blindness regarding certain civil liberties violations during World War II. In the ACLU's annual report delivered in July 1945, he praised "the almost complete absence of repression arising from the war." In the same document he contradicted himself again, terming the evacuation of Japanese Americans and Japanese nationals "the most complete and tragic exhibition of race prejudice against a single minority in American history."[62]

The stance of the ACLU and Baldwin's own dealings with government officials regarding the internments hardly amounted to the organization's or his finest hour. Both proved willing to accept the word of officials almost at face value, an increasingly unfortunate propensity of Baldwin and other top ACLU officials. His initial response to the evacuation of Japanese Americans was courageous and more timely than many critics charged. He also stood in the ACLU's progressive camp, which sought to challenge the evacuation orders. However, his desire to ingratiate himself and the ACLU with the wartime administration resulted in a readiness to mute criticisms, both his own and those of others.

CHAPTER TWENTY

"Quite a Dysfunctional Family"

Baldwin sought out platforms apart from the high-stakes, pressure-packed operations at ACLU national headquarters. In the spring of 1931 he had helped put together "a free-wheeling discussion group" called the Dissenters. Beginning in April approximately thirty men gathered at the Marlton Hotel off Washington Square. The depression was on everyone's mind, and they felt a need to meet on a monthly basis and speak freely about public issues. Participants in the first few years of the Dissenters' existence included Adolph A. Berle Jr., later assistant secretary of state; his brother Rudolph, a Wall Street attorney; William Nicholas, subsequently the guiding force behind *This Week*; Robert Bendiner, an editor with the *Nation*; Liston Oak, a member of the Communist Party of the United States; Corliss Lamont; Morris Ernst; and Arthur Garfield Hays.[1]

A kind of executive committee helped to devise programs, select meeting places for the group, and invite guest speakers. Writer and editor James M. Reid referred to it as "a thinly disguised dictatorship of Roger Baldwin's," but ACLU staffer Clifton Read thought that Baldwin was "wonderful presiding over the Dissenters." He worked to bring people out, affording all who attended an opportunity to speak. The executive committee ensured that only individuals able to add something to the discussions could participate. Thus, as committee member Reid acknowledged, "We were pretty ruthless in discarding the inarticulate members, those chaps who came and just sat, making no contribution to the discussion." The committee also favored the presentation of contrasting points of view. There was little difficulty finding willing participants from the American Left or the political center, "but it was always a struggle to find and hold onto conservatives," Reid remembered. "A reactionary was more prized than fine gold!"[2]

One of the liveliest early gatherings pitted Adolph A. Berle Jr. against American fascist Lawrence Dennis and Bill Browder—brother of the American Communist Party leader and a top figure himself in the New York branch—in an examination of "How to Come out of a Depression." Other notable speakers included Norman Thomas; A. J. Muste; Jay Lovestone, who had been excommunicated by the Communist Party; Jan Valtin, author of *Out of the Night,* a tale of the German underground; and Jose Calderon, a Spanish Loyalist. Baldwin regularly served as chairman, occasionally replaced by Harry Craven, another founder of the Dissenters, or Reid.[3]

During the late thirties Baldwin also began serving as a member of the Visiting Committee of the Board of Overseers of Harvard's Department of Economics. He had met Harvard's president, James Conant, through a friend, William I. Nichols, an assistant dean who set up a meeting; Baldwin and Conant spent an entire afternoon discussing economics and the law. Conant, a professor of chemistry by trade, had been an ACLU member. In mid-1937 Conant and Walter Lippmann, the distinguished columnist for the *New York Herald Tribune,* asked Baldwin to join the Harvard committee, along with Alvin S. Johnson of the New School for Social Research, Joseph P. Kennedy Sr., and John G. Winant, the former three-term governor of New Hampshire who headed the Social Security board. Lippmann, who chaired the committee, which acted as an illustrious overseer, suggested that Baldwin's appointment would ensure "a vigilant check" should a threat to academic freedom arise.[4]

Baldwin immediately accepted and soon was embroiled in a controversy surrounding the recent dismissal of J. Raymond Walsh and Paul Sweezy, two radical economics instructors. Later Baldwin recalled that while he had initially been sympathetic to the faculty members, he soon determined that the pair had been more concerned about "their extracurricular radical activities than in academic pursuits."[5]

His work on Harvard's committee continued for more than a decade and was highlighted by his urging that John Kenneth Galbraith be reappointed to the Economics Department. Colleagues included Paul Herzog from the National Labor Relations Board, the banker David Rockefeller, and George Rubles, a Washington attorney and La Follette progressive.[6]

Baldwin's association with Alvin Johnson may have led to Baldwin's short-lived involvement at the New School for Social Research, from the winter of 1938 to December 1941. Baldwin had earlier considered teaching at the New School, and Johnson had told him the previous summer that the institution wanted him to organize a course on civil liberties. At the New School Baldwin discussed theories of social progress and the problems of democracy, bringing in guest speakers like Lawrence Dennis and Earl Browder. Also appearing were Adolph A. Berle Jr., Thomas, and Stephen S. Wise, the Zionist rabbi and social reformer who headed the World Jewish Congress. Baldwin was seeking to use his classroom to train "a selected group of students for professional activities in the field of social action."[7]

All the while the vast majority of Baldwin's seemingly indefatigable energy revolved around the ACLU board, where he "dominated some very bright people," ex-staffer Clifton Read recalled. Many served on the board only briefly, then withdrew altogether because of Baldwin's high-handed ways. Some believed that Baldwin and the ACLU failed to make a careful examination of issues because he was, as Read indicated, "too action oriented." Others sometimes were put off by Baldwin's bluntness or coldness. At one point, Read recalled, Al Wirin came to the east coast from California and showed Baldwin a legal brief. He sat down and "tore it to pieces," Read said. Wirin departed virtually in tears, exclaiming, "And I'm a lawyer!" Worse yet, Baldwin's criticisms made sense to Wirin.[8]

Read, who handled the ACLU's public relations during the midthirties, maintained a diary that tracked developments in the national office. Another staff member referred to Baldwin as "a bastard to work for, [saying,] 'He's very virile, you know.'" Another staffer termed him a "prejudiced, hard man for whom to work." Read himself spoke of writing "bad stories," because Baldwin insisted on heavily editing his work. "The Baldwin locomotive works gets under way on a great number of things but seldom seems to follow up or through. Information to one like myself coming in without wide labor background is scarce and hard to dig out." But most significant, Read noted, was that the office was "in terror of his majesty and rightly, his mind clicks along neatly, smoothly, with power if not entire accuracy." Baldwin demonstrated "little feeling for the individual. His warmth while real has a very narcissistic quality beneath it, sense of how well I do this, how well I make the impression of personally registering on what is going on around me. Distrait [sic], bored, rude while eating." Later Read remembered Baldwin as "a very difficult man, demanding, driving, sometimes destructive, yet we all loved him. He would involve you, hook you in somehow."[9]

Baldwin had a particular gift, Read recalled, "for attaching to himself upper class young men with problems about society and about themselves. He was delightful to them, and there was much hanging on his words, but he could withdraw rather precipitously, too."[10]

Although Baldwin was hardly Read's "beau ideal as boss," he appreciated that Baldwin worked hard and taught him a good deal. Furthermore, after Read demonstrated aptitude for the job, he was allowed to do his own work. Unfortunately, Baldwin continued to insist on editing all the ACLU memos himself, "which gave our publications a choppy, impersonal, humorless, hard-hitting style that he favored." Charley Clift, an ACLU member, once told Read that Baldwin "was the best three sentence letter writer in America, but when he tried to do any more the writing fell down." Lucille Milner, who considered Baldwin "a magnificent public speaker," also believed that he couldn't write. As she put it, "I never understood why the things he said on the platform he could not put down on paper."[11]

Baldwin's well-known penchant for thriftiness affected Read, as it did so many other staffers. Osmond Fraenkel remembered Baldwin as "a penny pincher. He starved staff." First hired as a part-timer at $25 a week, Read began working fulltime for $28 a week and later received a raise to $35. At one point, when Baldwin was away on a trip, the ACLU finance committee—which included Quincy Howe, an editor, author, and radio commentator, and Ben Huebsch—sought to increase Read's weekly salary to $50. He warned them not to, declaring that Baldwin would not allow it. They assured Read that they would take care of his boss. But when Baldwin returned, he was furious. Much influenced by the Wisconsin sociologist Edwin Albion Ross, who argued that "cause people should work for other than wages," Baldwin reduced Read's salary by $10. Baldwin informed Read that he himself made less than $50 a week. While true, Read was also aware that Baldwin was living with Evie Preston.[12]

One night Read was working late at the New York office when he heard Baldwin dictating letters and memos to his secretary, Ida Epstein. On other occasions he had seen Baldwin become so agitated that his face whitened as he stood over Epstein talking "as if he were beating her." Now Read heard "such hostility in that voice," he later recollected, "it made my blood run cold." According to Milner, Epstein was "a devotee" of Baldwin's who adored him.[13]

Not surprisingly, then, Baldwin's departure for a trip resulted in great rejoicing in the home office. He would rush out, typically absorbed in what he was doing, tossing out "uneasy goodbys [*sic*]," Read recalled. Once Baldwin was gone, "there was complete relaxation." According to Read, the general sense was that " 'he left us a lot of work but he's gone at last.' " Nevertheless, Read enjoyed serving at the ACLU office under Baldwin's direction. "He was a stimulating man to know and work with, but not an easy boss. What a mixture of charm and aggression."[14]

Despite the issues the ACLU was tackling, its operations during World War II remained circumscribed. The temper of the times seemingly demanded such an approach, but so did the ACLU's executive director. Baldwin's appearance was increasingly disheveled, with his thinning hair combed across his scalp and his rumpled suits exuding a "clean but careless" image. He appeared constantly on the go, still "full of fervor and violent integrity, emotional, ethical, tirelessly seeking the Grail. A genuine article," or so *Current Biography* had recently described him.[15]

Still the dominant figure in the organization, he remained convinced that only a select few should be involved in the civil liberties crusade. Around 1943 a new recruit to the movement appeared, largely by happenstance. Florence Isbell had viewed herself variously as a communist, a socialist, a Trotskyist, a Shactmanite, and a Lovestonite while in high school and at New York University in Greenwich Village. She never attended her NYU classes and, as she put it, "majored in mimeographing and leaflet giving-out." Thrown out of the Young Communists League, Isbell became a kind of "anti-Communist liberal radical."[16]

She wanted to obtain a secretarial position, and an employment agency got her an interview with a theatrical agent. Heading out of the subway at 23d Street, she walked until she came to an old building boasting a gold-plated plaque that read "American Civil Liberties Union." She went inside to "an incredibly decrepit, dirty office." She asked to see the office manager and was introduced to Lucille Milner. After a brief conversation—during which Isbell lied that she had been to secretarial school—Milner asked, "When can you start?" Isbell responded, "Well, today is Friday. How about Monday?" Milner countered, "How about now?"[17]

She was taken into a common room where two other young women were working as secretaries for Baldwin. She was introduced to Baldwin, who made no greeting or small talk. The women informed her that he had gotten a new secretary at nine o'clock that very morning. He had said not a word to the woman and had dictated continuously until just before noon. Finally, he said, "That will be all." His new secretary said, "I'm going out to lunch" and never returned. Thus the job was vacant when Isbell arrived in the early afternoon. He immediately began dictating, but her shorthand skills left something to be desired. He did not speak that rapidly, but his speech was comprised of "all polished sentences; there were no 'er's' or 'but's,'" she recalled. Nevertheless, Isbell believed that she understood what he was talking about, wrote down what she could, and paraphrased the rest. At six o'clock she took the batch of papers—supposedly transcribed—to him. He came back out and said, "This is wonderful! This is wonderful! This isn't what I said but it'll do."[18]

Consequently, Isbell became Baldwin's secretary. The first year on the job she "was paralyzed with fear." She was only nineteen, and he was approaching sixty. At the same time, Isbell later recalled, "I was crazy about him. I had a terrible crush on him," but no social exchange was allowed and she called him "Mister Baldwin." Displaying his usual coldness, he seemed to have no interest in her life.[19]

Baldwin's relationship with Milner, Isbell reported, was more troubled. "She and Roger were always at loggerheads. He kept her on the edge of her seat all the time. She didn't know what she was doing. It was making her crazy." In Isbell's estimation Milner simply lacked "the strength of character or the intellectual gifts or the personality to stand up against Roger." Furthermore, like others on the staff, "she was very much in love with him and he treated her as though she was the scutter maid." It hardly helped that Milner appeared to be, as Isbell saw her, "stunningly incompetent." Baldwin constantly disagreed with the way she phrased something. He would deal with Milner impersonally, but "she acted like a wounded, rejected lover," evidently for good reason.[20]

The ACLU office in general, Isbell recalled, was filled with "nutty, eccentric people," starting with Baldwin himself. "It was quite a dysfunctional family." The legal director, Clifford Forster, "was living in the fifteenth century." Milner seemed to be "having a nervous breakdown." Dan Eastman, the son of Max Eastman, one of the founders of the legendary magazine, the *Masses*, served for a time as publicity director but had a host of problems, as evidenced by alcoholism and lengthy bouts of psychoanalysis. Then there was Baldwin the great civil libertarian "and yet a totally authoritarian person," Isbell noted. Both Baldwin and his friend Norman Thomas "were very, very much the same, sort of stern New England figures. They were used to having people do exactly what they said and they would become very frustrated," she recalled. In discussing politics, Baldwin was quite respectful of another's perspective. However, "if you were working for him and he wanted you to do something, he would go bananas if you didn't do it exactly the way he wanted you to do it. Everybody in the office who worked for him was terrified of him for that reason," she said.[21]

A series of publicity directors, including Eastman, came and went. Baldwin possessed a notion of publicity, "which was like something out of the 1860s," as Isbell put it. Rather than talk directly to the press, Baldwin produced press releases on the staff mimeograph machine and relied on an antiquated mailing list. Consequently, Eastman frequently wrote out a statement and handed it to Baldwin, who invariably edited it heavily, typically scribbling in the margins. Eastman made the necessary changes and gave it back three days later, declaring, "I've rewritten this," while failing to add that the changes were his boss's. Baldwin then insisted on reediting it once again.[22]

Staff members had to contend with Baldwin's insistence that "things be done in exactly the way he wanted." Eastman's replacement, a capable young woman, quit just as Baldwin was heading off for a two-month trip. Before leaving, Isbell said, he had informed the assistant director, "I have given her a list of instructions and corrections of her work, and I think you'll find that she is now on the right track." However, the new publicity director announced to the assistant director, "Well, I'm quitting." He responded, "Oh, my god! Roger just told me that he had bucked you up sufficiently so that now you are on the right track." She countered, "Well, he didn't quite do that. He bucked me up sufficiently to give me the courage to tell that son of a bitch to go fuck himself!" Then she walked out the door, leaving behind an actual list of things Baldwin believed "that she hadn't done quite right."[23]

In many regards, Isbell pointed out, Baldwin

> was a rotten employer. He was highly critical. He had the idea that people should be busy all the time. He really didn't know, at least as far as other people were concerned, the difference between productive work and activity. . . . He very rarely praised people. He didn't yell, he didn't yell at people who were junior to him, but he could be very icy and very unpleasant when he wanted to be. With people who worked for him but were sort of executives, like Lucille, yes, he yelled at her and he was scornful of her, sarcastic.[24]

At the same time, Isbell acknowledged, Baldwin came to respect her, perhaps because she was highly combative. If he said something unpleasant to her, she responded in kind. Because he liked her—and he had run through

twenty-three secretaries in the six months before she arrived on the job—
"he was willing to put up with a lot of crap." And within a year he had happily promoted Isbell to publicity director. All the while he gave her assign-
ments and said, "Now, the reason I'm doing this is this." Isbell followed his
reasoning—which she viewed as "sometimes convoluted"—uncritically.
While he was difficult to work with, she was his pet, "and most of the time,
he was wonderful to me."[25]

Baldwin was inflexible partly because he continued to believe, as he had
from the outset, "that the ACLU was only for brilliant people." Thus its
membership should remain limited, and all involved "should be a leader of
some kind." Furthermore, such individuals should be willing, as he was, to
work for the ACLU for next to nothing. Thus as late as 1943 the ACLU offered
no retirement or insurance coverage for its employees and low salaries,
which in Isbell's case amounted to $35 a week. At one point she went to Bald-
win and demanded a raise. He asked, "Why do you want a raise?" She
responded, "Because nobody can live on thirty-five dollars a week! Prices are
going up. Do you know what the price of meat is?" He answered with a question of his own, "You eat meat? I eat rice."[26]

To Isbell—although she recognized that Baldwin was very austere and
never thought about money in any way—this was all "a terrific charade." She
was living with her parents, while he was living with a woman "who was
loaded." He continued to cover his expenses, while Evie took care of the
Greenwich Village townhouse, the New Jersey farm, the estate on Martha's
Vineyard, the family car, insurance, and servants. He, on the other hand,
"would pay for the new suit, and his lunch, which consisted of Saltines and
a glass of milk every day. And that was it," Isbell said. Thus he and Isbell were
engaged in something of a sham. He explained, "Well, I can't give you a
raise," and she answered, "Well, I love this job but I'll have to quit." He then
agreed to a $2.50 raise, and they both walked about feeling triumphant.[27]

As Isbell saw it, he "was a control freak. Everything had to go through
him," particularly finances. He divided ACLU income into two groups, "regular" and "special" funds, following "some esoteric formula" she never quite
understood. He presented a budget to the board, which argued with him
"over every comma" on doctrinal issues but had no concern for how the
organization ran. However, as Isbell recognized, "what made the organization run, of course, determined its policy." And he wielded the special
fund—begun with a large gift from Florina Lasker, a wealthy supporter and
board member of the ACLU—to influence the organization's direction. If

someone wanted to do something to which Baldwin was opposed, he would answer, "Well, we have no money in the budget." On the other hand, if Baldwin wanted to get involved in a project and others replied, "There's no money in the budget for this," he would respond, "Well, that is a perfect project for special funds." No one "was willing to take Roger on" concerning financial operations.[28]

In keeping with his parsimonious ways, Baldwin obtained all the volunteer assistance he could to attend to the ACLU's run-of-the-mill tasks. Thus he wrote to any number of psychiatrists, asking if they had any patients "who would benefit [from] doing work in a challenging intellectual atmosphere?" Subsequently, wealthy bored women in their forties would show up at the ACLU's headquarters to be assigned to menial tasks. One woman complained, "If he didn't treat me so miserably, I'd leave the ACLU fifty thousand dollars," Isbell recalled. However, Baldwin continued to deal with the woman as he had previously; he never recalled her name and was invariably critical of whatever she had to say. Isbell once exclaimed to him, "You know, she's got a lot of money. She could leave us money!" He replied, "She's a very underbred person."[29]

Bright young men also were drawn to the national office's inner sanctum. Joe Freeman had worked there in the 1920s before becoming a major figure in the Communist Party of the United States. Howard Fast, later a leading novelist; Ben Bradlee, subsequently editor of the *Washington Post*; and Mike Straight, soon to become publisher of the *New Republic*, also served under Baldwin. So did Bill Butler, a young lawyer who handled Baldwin's personal legal matters.[30]

Baldwin or someone like Isbell, who would follow his lead, generally kept records of board meetings. As he informed her when she was about to attend a meeting, "Somebody else can take the notes. You write the minutes. You're writing history. You write it your way." He often told her, "It's very important to spell this out exactly, so that nobody forgets it." Then he explained matters, and she thought to herself, "Gee, I don't remember it quite that way!" Nevertheless, she acted as he ordered.[31]

Both in the office and away from it Baldwin continued to be involved with other women. Isbell recalled:

> I think, as far as women were concerned, he was a man who liked women, who liked to be with women. If you thought you measured up to his intellectual

standards, he opened himself up to you intellectually. . . . While he was courtly and he liked women's company, and he liked the whole idea of femininity and womanhood, he was not in any way a man who went chasing women because of their physical attributes. But I think he had intimate relationships with a lot of women. I don't mean that he was wildly promiscuous, like a Hollywood star, but just my intuition tells me that he was available. He had an awful lot of women calling him up, and the calls always came to me. He would get women writing to him too.

Dan Eastman often spoke to Isbell about Baldwin, frequently mentioning, "There were a lot of women."[32]

Particularly distressed by the ACLU's determination to stand up for far rightists, Lucille Milner, who later wrote that she "admired him and deferred to his judgment in everything," resigned in 1945 as Baldwin's top secretary. She could not think of any board members who criticized him: "They adored him." But she had been upset by Baldwin's role in Elizabeth Gurley Flynn's expulsion and by the gag order placed on her, presumably by Baldwin, at board meetings. "I felt outraged that on the Civil Liberties Board if you believed in communism you had no right to sit on the Board," Milner told Joseph Lash. No one had suffered for the civil liberties movement in the manner of Flynn, who believed, as Milner did, "that the final solution for this awful world might be some form of communism." Milner viewed civil liberties not as an end in themselves but as "a means to an end. What I was interested in was to abolish poverty, not the right to say that poverty is horrible." Milner, in Baldwin's estimation, was "so immersed in winning the war that she'd pass up all civil liberties for the duration, or at least all of them that matter,—such as the Japanese-American issue . . . and the freedom of opponents of the war to carry on their propaganda."[33]

In the midforties Milner also was troubled because Baldwin seemed to be "reverting to his early life, softening up." Yes, he was as frugal as ever, maintaining a little notebook in which he recorded purchases of postage stamps or the cost of carfare. Nevertheless, Milner too knew that Baldwin "lived exceedingly well." As she viewed matters, "That was the incongruity of it." She had the sense "that Roger—the civil libertarian and radical—was not the real Roger—that he was forcing himself to do these things—that his real loves were comfort and elegance." He clearly reveled in his work: "He loved the glory of the job and the fuss that was made over him." He also "enjoyed power and adulation—not power for power's sake but the praise and honor that went along with power." Still, she sensed that "the real Roger could have been very happy in a conventional kind of career."[34]

Perhaps the long emotional pounding she had received finally proved too much. Milner considered Baldwin a taskmaster, although she claimed to be one too: "I was as big a fool as he in these matters." Still, the constant fighting and ridicule must have worn heavily on Milner, who for so long had carried a torch for her boss. Informed that Milner was resigning, board member Norman Cousins had asked Baldwin what to do. Baldwin acknowledged that it was "very sad for me. I've been associated with Mrs. Milner for twenty-five years, but if she feels like this, there's nothing to do but accept her resignation."[35]

In a note to Mary Buckley, Baldwin reacted far more harshly to Milner's decision. "She quit in a huff," after being informed that "a youngster might soon come in to be her superior," Baldwin reported. Since "she had fallen off badly the last few years anyhow, largely because of home troubles . . . her going is no great loss. . . . But I was distressed to have it come that way. She would not consider any readjustment."[36]

The sometimes helter-skelter nature of operations at ACLU national headquarters was attributable to its executive director, who looked with disdain on many administrative duties. Baldwin was best at getting bright, concerned people at all levels to become involved with the civil liberties organization. He pushed and goaded sympathetic parties and piqued consciences as much as any figure associated with leading twentieth-century American reform organizations. Yet the day-to-day running of the New York office—including personnel relations—was something he often handled carelessly and sometimes thoughtlessly. He was best at promoting the civil liberties movement, through speeches, writings, and behind-the-scenes maneuvers. The slipshod manner in which national headquarters muddled along perhaps enabled Baldwin to continue to feel a kinship with rebellious sorts whose very existence was far removed from much of the work in which the ACLU was engaged. Then again, perhaps it is best explained by his propensity to overwhelm those who worked for him, until they voluntarily departed from the organization altogether or were eased out, to be replaced by others, who were, at least temporarily, more pliable.

CHAPTER TWENTY-ONE

The Cold War, the Shogun, and International Civil Liberties

As World War II neared an end, Baldwin was thinking about an issue that soon would overshadow all others on the home front. Over radio station WJZ at New York's Town Hall on Thursday evening, January 11, 1945, he asked, "Is communism a threat to the American way of life?" Only the united fronts that communists led had acquired many backers; consequently, Baldwin argued, "They are therefore no menace through numbers or influence." Nor were they likely to act outside the law, never having done so. During the war the American comrades stood as a group "of super-patriots" and champions of free enterprise, dissipating "whatever sect appeal they ever had," Baldwin claimed.[1]

Nevertheless, as he saw it, "the fearful" considered the communists "in their sheep's clothing" more dangerous than ever. Conservatives argued, he noted, that communists had penetrated labor unions, political organizations, and political parties, guided by a "program and policies dictated from outside in Russia's interests." In reality, Baldwin insisted, communists controlled few organizations and even then had to accede to the wishes of the far greater number of noncommunist members.[2]

The communists, Baldwin acknowledged, were a nuisance, often a serious one: "They mislead unsuspicious liberals into their political traps. They pervert democratic procedures in many associations to achieve control by a minority. They are adept at concealing their identities; they hide behind false fronts. They have an irresistable [sic] itch for power." They championed civil liberties but only for their brethren. Furthermore, by melding communism and democracy in the eyes of many, they allowed reactionaries to condemn as communist any movement the comrades backed. Consequently, the real menace emanated from anticommunist defenders of the status quo, who held aloft "the red bogey to discredit democratic progress."[3]

As Baldwin feared, the United States was about to undergo a political shift to the right. This occurred as tensions heated up between the former partners in the Grand Alliance: the Soviet Union, Great Britain, and the United States. In January 1946 Joseph Stalin insisted that communist and noncommunist states could not coexist. Two months later Winston Churchill spoke in Fulton, Missouri, and bemoaned the Iron Curtain that was now dividing the European continent; President Harry Truman was there and appeared to agree with the eloquent oration. As the Red Army remained in place throughout much of Eastern Europe, pro-Stalinist communists came to power, often crushing in the process their former partners from the Resistance, who generally were noncommunist radicals. Independence movements gathered steam as nationalism swept across much of the colonial world, headed by leaders as disparate as Gandhi and Nehru in India and Ho Chi Minh in Vietnam.

To Baldwin this made perfect sense: "We have pledged self-government, and the colonies are beginning to take us at our word. The cause of the darker peoples advances in India, Indo-China and Indonesia." Unfortunately, however, "our treatment of racial minorities denies our moral claim to democratic leadership in the world," Baldwin said. Mahatma Gandhi, Baldwin reasoned, served as "the supreme apostle of freedom in a far greater frame than nationalism." India's quest was "the touch-stone to the future of most of the human race."[4]

A changed and less hopeful political atmosphere was soon apparent in the United States, as pent-up energies resulted in labor strife and an antiunion backlash, severe inflation, and a Republican triumph in the 1946 congressional races. Among those winning office were Joseph McCarthy, elected to the Senate from Wisconsin, and Richard M. Nixon, chosen to represent Orange County, California, in the House of Representatives. Nixon was one of the first political figures who wielded the weapon of red baiting and was soon followed by a host of other politicians from both major political parties.

Events abroad and at home provided impetus for a strong anticommunist push by the likes of the U.S. Chamber of Commerce, the Republican Party's right wing, the FBI, and the former Dies Committee, now revitalized in the transformed postwar political atmosphere and referred to as the House Committee on Un-American Activities, or HUAC. Its chairman, Mississippi

Democrat John Rankin, and the committee members, Baldwin warned, seemed eager to attack Communists, liberals, and the Congress of Industrial Organizations alike. Meanwhile, the country was witnessing lynchings, Klan activity, and sporadic terrorism against Japanese Americans who were returning to California. Although often bitterly critical of such actions, many liberals soon began distancing themselves from leftists, who increasingly were viewed as pariahs. The heyday of loyalty oaths, investigative committees, and blacklists was beginning.[5]

As the cold war unfolded, the ACLU's adoption of its anticommunist resolution in 1940 and Baldwin's decision to work closely with government officials regarding the internment camps ensured that both he and his good friend Norman Thomas were treated by the establishment with a greater measure of respect. Nor did Baldwin's association with Evie Preston Baldwin hurt, for she was a woman of independent means and impressive social connections, as was Violet Stewart Thomas. Now both men, former social workers and the heads, respectively, of the ACLU and the American Socialist Party, were about to embark on new careers involving international affairs. In the process they were increasingly viewed, in the words of Evie Baldwin's nephew, the historian Bill Preston, "as the respected elder statesmen of dissent in America."[6]

Baldwin and Thomas, Preston insightfully suggests, were soon to "'pass' and achieve a credit rating next to none with the nation's elite." This historian argues that their "background, education, and personality" counted for "a good deal." Baldwin and Thomas came from comfortable Anglo-Saxon stock, had been educated at Ivy League universities, and possessed amiable, if at times irascible, personalities of a charismatic sort. As Preston put it, "They both knew the lesson of bourgeois interaction and influence, namely that propriety, reasonableness, and moderation (and a dark suit) are the protective coloration of successful subversion."[7]

The changed status of Baldwin and Thomas did not occur without a price. Simply put, their altered perspectives provided cover for the anticommunist drives that would soon characterize U.S. domestic and foreign policy. Along with A. J. Muste, Baldwin and Thomas had long crafted a critical but often well-regarded viewpoint, goading other members of the American upper class and upper middle class to support reform, sometimes radical in scope. Muste, in his role as the nation's leading pacifist, continued to offer an alternative way of examining U.S. policies. Baldwin, increasingly less influential in the ranks of a more conservative ACLU, and Thomas, whose staunchly anticommunist Socialist Party was essentially moribund, now failed to act as trenchant government critics as they had for so long. While Baldwin continued to be referred to as the nation's leading civil libertarian and Thomas as perhaps the one recognizable socialist, their radical fervor had clearly abated. That was unfortunate, for the United States was facing troubled times, when civil liberties were often attacked and calls for economic democracy were seldom heard. In contrast to Muste, who was not identified with any particular group, Baldwin and Thomas, like their organizations, were clearly showing their age—and not just chronologically.

Unfortunately, the ACLU also was showing its age in the very period when First Amendment freedoms were most sorely tested. As the postwar Red Scare evolved, the nation's leading civil liberties organization often failed to challenge fully those determined to narrow political boundaries. Sam Walker contends that Baldwin deserves much of the blame, for he offered increasingly tepid leadership while displaying his own ambivalence regarding the treatment of communists. Key ACLU figures remained divided, as they had been at least since the Flynn affair. Norman Thomas and Morris Ernst hewed to a fervently anticommunist line, whereas Arthur Hays, Osmond Fraenkel, and Walter Gellhorn, a Columbia University law professor, were First Amendment absolutists. Baldwin now was associated with a centrist group that was less stridently ideological but refused to condemn altogether the federal government's quest to ferret out communists in its midst.[8]

In early January 1947, Baldwin was astonished to receive a letter from the War Department's Special Staff indicating that Gen. Douglas MacArthur's headquarters in Japan wanted Baldwin to serve as a civil liberties consultant in Japan and Korea. Baldwin had long urged, generally to little avail, that the ACLU extend its operations overseas. Baldwin—his FBI Security Index card (assigned to those the FBI considered internal security threats) had just been canceled—worried about opposition to his appointment from HUAC members; those congressmen saw anyone who defended the rights of communists as communist sympathizers. "I am and have always been anti-Communist of course, as a supporter of political democracy," Baldwin stated in a blatantly false fashion, "but that does not disturb these gentlemen." He had no desire, Baldwin continued, to embarrass either the ACLU or the War Department, which "must have access to *Who's Who*, which tells my essential story."[9]

On February 7, in a confidential memo to ACLU board officers, Baldwin said that a consultant to the War Department would be compelled "to hold his tongue in dealing with the native peoples." Thus, since the start of his discussions with the War Department, Baldwin had believed he could best operate independently.[10]

On February 27 Baldwin—still concerned that conservatives would strongly oppose his appointment because of his past associations—met with J. Parnell Thomas, HUAC's new chairman and the New Jersey Republican whose district included Dell Brook, to discuss whether the ACLU leader should go to the Far East. Undoubtedly, the Oakland estate, Evie Baldwin's social standing, and the ACLU's changed image opened Thomas's doors to his increasingly respectable constituent. Thomas strongly advised Baldwin not to undertake the venture as a paid employee of the U.S. government. He would not object to Baldwin's going as a private citizen, Thomas said, but he suspected that others would.[11]

The meeting with Parnell Thomas resulted from Baldwin's characteristic determination to deal with government figures on a one-to-one basis. It also was in keeping with his more amicable dealings with public officials since the early thirties. Those relationships once again threatened to terminate altogether the ACLU's outsider status and even its critical reading of untoward government policies. That was significant, given the wholesale violation of civil liberties that numerous Americans suffered early in the cold war.

At about this point, President Harry Truman reacted to the debacle suffered by the Democrats in the recent congressional elections and the continued Stalinization of Eastern Europe. On March 11 his secretary of labor, Lewis Schwellenbach, called for outlawing the Communist Party of the United States. The next day Truman enunciated the Truman Doctrine, which declared that the United States would "support free peoples who are resisting attempted subjugation by armed minorities or by outside pressures." On March 21 Truman initiated a major government loyalty program designed to ferret out "subversives."[12]

The ACLU and its executive director appeared increasingly contented with their greater respectability, standing more and more like rebels of bygone days, now largely defanged and harmless. This little troubled the ACLU's chairman, John Haynes Holmes, who applauded Baldwin's mission, deeming it "a kind of crown of recognition and reward for his many years of self-forgetting service of a basic interest of democracy and peace." Within two weeks Baldwin learned that MacArthur had accepted the ACLU director on his own terms. Baldwin was delighted, reasoning that no one could attack him now, for he was simply "a private citizen going at General MacArthur's personal invitation at his own expense." Arrangements were made, the required military approval obtained, and Baldwin prepared a press release announcing his mission. He also acquired letters of support and commendations from a host of different organizations. Baldwin already was a consultant to the United Nations on civil rights for the International League for the Rights of Man. Henri Laugier, assistant UN secretary general and the honorary president of the International League for the Rights of Man, handed Baldwin "a too flattering" note of introduction. Baldwin's UN ties provided him with credentials as a representative of the World Federation of the United Nations Association charged with helping to establish a Japanese affiliate of the federation. Robert Eichelberger, commander of the 8th Army in Japan, received from his cousin a personal letter praising Baldwin. And Baldwin held an ACLU credential, thanks to a memo he had drafted himself.[13]

Conservative publications, such as the *New York Daily News* and the *Washington Times-Herald,* applauded the announcement of Baldwin's impending visit. MacArthur was adjudged astute for having invited a leading liberal to occupied Japan. As Baldwin recalled, one headline read "Smart Cookie, MacArthur." Friends of Baldwin who worked in the White House, including presidential secretary David Niles and Assistant Secretary of State John Hilldring, who had been skeptical that Baldwin would be appointed, were delighted.[14]

By contrast, a scathing article in the procommunist *New Masses* by Virginia Gardner (later a biographer of Louise Bryant) discussed Baldwin's meeting with J. Parnell Thomas. Clearly, no goodwill remained between the Communist Party and its one-time ally. Gardner supposedly had learned of the encounter when Thomas showed her Baldwin's signature in the guest book in his office and softly declared, "I've been pretty close to Roger Baldwin. He's a constituent of mine." Thomas then stated, "There is between us a strong meeting of the minds. We see pretty much eye to eye. He is quite anti-Communist." Gardner, who had interviewed ACLU board members to find out what they knew, told her readers that Baldwin had failed to apprise the organization of his meeting with Thomas. "Roger Baldwin: What are you hiding?" she asked.[15]

The *New Leader,* a social democratic publication, defended Baldwin, declaring the meeting to have been public and charging that Baldwin and the

ACLU had "become the target of Stalinist vilification." The *New Leader* insisted that Baldwin, unlike the communists, had nothing to hide. Eventually, Baldwin fired back at the *New Masses*, condemning its "scurrilous article," which implied that "improper collusion" with the HUAC chairman had taken place.[16]

On April 12 Baldwin arrived in Tokyo and discovered a private limousine awaiting him. He was taken to the Imperial, the top hotel in the city, where he encountered a large room complete with mosaic bath and meals offered in an impressive dining room for a mere 25 cents, served by attractive Japanese women in long purple kimonos. At his disposal for the duration of his stay was the vehicle used to pick him up, along with its military chauffeur. The windshield prominently displayed the letters VIP. Eventually, he was taken over to U.S. Army headquarters, introduced to all parties concerned, and provided with an office, secretary, and interpreter. Baldwin was also offered a military aide, which he declined.[17]

The following day Baldwin was invited to lunch at the American embassy with Douglas and Jean MacArthur. MacArthur greeted him by exclaiming, "Mr. Baldwin, we have been waiting for you for a long time. I am delighted you have come at last." As they entered the dining room, MacArthur draped his arm around Baldwin's shoulder and conveyed his need for help in the civil liberties arena. The general urged Baldwin to report to him directly if cooperation from his staff proved unsatisfactory. He also told Baldwin, "I want you to see everybody, go everywhere; every door is open to you. I want you to tell me what you think is wrong about the Occupation policies in regard to the democratic purposes that we're trying to instill in the Japanese people." MacArthur's desire to promote civil liberties, Baldwin immediately concluded, was sincere.[18]

In a letter dated May 1 and addressed to "Friends" back in the States, Baldwin termed the general "a charming, wise, witty, most unmilitary man with a strong sense of mission, a genuine democrat who sees his role in large historic outlines and with great confidence in the Japanese."[19] Once again and more graphically than ever, Baldwin demonstrated his propensity to be overwhelmed by an authority figure, particularly one who wielded a good deal of power. Over the years America's most celebrated champion of civil liberties had repeatedly been taken in by FBI boss J. Edgar Hoover. Now Douglas MacArthur simply bowled over a man who had long been one of the nation's leading antimilitarists.

In the days ahead Baldwin was busy from morning until late in the evening, conducting interviews and participating in meetings with Americans and Japanese, top military officials and communists, common citizens and royalty. The purpose of all this, from Baldwin's perspective, was to discover the effectiveness of "this amazing experiment in transplanting democracy." He quickly established three associations that would deal with civil rights, the United Nations, and Japanese Americans, respectively. He spoke before the Tokyo Rotary Club, the Japan America Society, and the Harvard Club of Tokyo. He attended the war crimes trials, the Allied Council, election meetings in rural and urban areas, and a cherry blossom garden party thrown by the emperor. Baldwin spent a weekend at a Japanese villa, dined with other Americans in fine requisitioned Japanese homes, and with Japanese in their own domiciles, and conversed with every interested general. He was invited by Gen. John R. Hodge to visit Korea, and planned to "favor him for a couple of weeks."[20]

In a May 6 letter to MacArthur, Baldwin expressed appreciation for the joint effort undertaken by Americans and the Japanese. The Japanese people appeared readily able to grasp the essence of democratic institutions, he reported. The American military possessed the capacity to undertake such a difficult task. Baldwin indicated to the general, "You have an amazingly effective staff imbued with your own ideals and practical statesmanship." Baldwin then made a number of suggestions to further the cause of civil liberties in occupied Japan. The censorship now faced by the mass media would obviously be ended at some point. International mail service should be resumed to encourage "democratic contacts." To allow Japanese groups to associate with UN organizations, provisions for affiliation should be established. "Suitable Japanese representatives" needed to be able to attend international conferences. American financial support to Japanese educational institutions should be resumed.[21]

Four days later Baldwin sent a confidential letter to the ACLU executive board and national committee. Once more he sang the praises of his host. "His observations on civil liberties and democracy," Baldwin waxed eloquent, "rank with the best I ever heard from any civilian—and they were incredible from a general." Yet despite the best intentions, "a terrific job" remained to be done. The U.S. military had to turn responsibility for government affairs over to the Japanese. As for the timing of such a transfer, Baldwin believed that "General MacArthur's judgment on that is obviously to be trusted."[22]

After a brief trip to South Korea, where Baldwin encountered President Syngman Rhee—to whom he referred as "an agent of reaction," yet "such a charming old gentleman, so kindly and urbane"—Baldwin met with Emperor Hirohito. Baldwin arrived laden with gifts for the royal children—boxes of candy, pencils, and some pens—handed his pass to the palace sentries, and reached an unimposing office building in the Imperial Park. He was greeted by two chamberlains attired in morning coats who left him in an upstairs waiting room and took the presents. At the appointed hour of ten, a chamberlain—who was to serve as interpreter—escorted Baldwin into the administration building's grand reception room. Three men dressed in identical cutaways appeared; the smiling emperor was the middle member of the trio. Hirohito came over, shook hands, and declared, "Mister Baldwin."[23]

For about forty minutes the two men sat on gold and scarlet chairs and discussed the treatment of Japanese citizens in the United States and the relationship between Japanese organizations and UN agencies. As Baldwin moved to take his leave, the emperor grasped his hands and thanked him for the gifts.[24]

In a press release Baldwin insisted that the emperor had appeared very responsive to both liberal and democratic ideas. Concerned about reaction to his comments, Baldwin was relieved to receive a phone call from the Japanese Foreign Office the next day. Could Baldwin have tea that afternoon with the emperor's younger brother, Prince Takamatsu?, he was asked. Japanese newspapers played up the gift of candies to the emperor and his children, and Baldwin's picture appeared alongside those of the thirteen-year-old crown prince, Akihito, and his younger brother. For several years the Baldwins and the royal family exchanged Christmas presents.[25]

All in all, Baldwin considered this, he later reflected, to "have been the two most stirring months of my life in years." He most regretted that he had been unable to capture fully the magnitude of what was taking place in Japan, "one of the great dramas of history." In a farewell note to MacArthur, dated June 8, 1947, Baldwin expressed profound appreciation for the opportunities afforded him and for the cooperation from military headquarters. Baldwin wrote, "I leave with the consciousness of the amazing experiment in democracy here made possible and so promising chiefly by your spirit and vision. No possible criticism of detail can detract from what is a great historical achievement already assured."[26]

In a lengthy report to the ACLU Baldwin called the three months he had recently spent abroad "the most useful period of time I have ever spent toward the Union's objectives." A few weeks after his return from the Far East, Baldwin drafted a document entitled "Shogun and Emperor." He had been astonished by the skepticism that had greeted his enthusiastic evaluation of General MacArthur. Baldwin likened the U.S. military commander to the shoguns of centuries past. MacArthur's power to bring about the American program "of disarming, demilitarizing, and democratizing Japan," although officially subject to alterations by Washington or other Allied powers, was virtually unlimited. Fortunately, General MacArthur seemed "engaged in a crusade . . . a crusade for democracy." The general was an exceptional public figure, in Baldwin's estimation, "with an almost missionary spirit of promoting it."[27]

Later Baldwin's opinion of occupation policies in Japan changed considerably, at least for a time. In a letter of May 15, 1952, to Dick Deverall, who was also involved with the postwar campaign to reconstruct Japan, Baldwin wrote, "Things slipped pretty badly as you know, after you and I quit and the General shifted his policies out of fear of the Communists."[28]

In the summer of 1948 the ACLU received an official letter from the U.S. Department of War inviting the organization, at its own expense, to send three individuals to tour the American-occupied zone of Germany and undertake "an unofficial investigation of civil liberties." As matters turned out, board members Arthur Garfield Hays and Norman Cousins were already heading for Europe, so Baldwin was selected as the third representative.[29]

In late September Baldwin headed for Germany on behalf of both the ACLU and the International League for the Rights of Man. After traveling to Bonn, he reported, "The shadow of the Soviets and of Berlin is of course over everything." Along with the occupation controls, this resulted in German paralysis. Refugees continued to pour in to Bonn from the Russian zone, while "nobody is going east. The nearer you get to the Russians the plainer it is that the Communist cure is worse than the capitalist diseases." Still, things were improving in Germany, "and prospects are brighter in the west, despite the darkness in the east." Baldwin now intended to move on to occupied and supposedly liberated Austria. As he reported, "I hear that the Russians control their zone by kidnapping and losing anybody they don't like; and I also hear that the only Vienna air-port [sic] for Americans is in the Russian zone. And I am flying."[30]

Although he had not believed that his Austrian visit would result in any kind of report, he was wrong. He regarded Vienna as similar to Berlin: "a four-power oasis surrounded by a Soviet desert." The Soviets and the Western powers were sharing control, apparently peacefully, with the democracies sacrificing their ideals—political liberties and civil rights—to maintain the peace. Movement within Vienna was easy, but foreigners needed permits to enter the Soviet zone outside the city. Many Austrians had disappeared; thus traveling in the Russian zone was dangerous, particularly for socialists. The Soviets justified all these machinations on security grounds but held no open court proceedings, as the Western forces did in their zones. Instead, the Soviets arrested individuals, who were never seen again. Baldwin charged that a still more egregious example of the West's acquiescing "to Soviet police state methods" involved censorship of the mails, telephones, and telegrams. Austrian radio was fully under occupation control and subjected to the most severe censorship of communications outside the Soviet sphere.[31]

All in all, Baldwin concluded, "Every day we stay is a shameful compromise with our principles. I am pulling out after four days. I have seen enough of what cooperation with the Russians can do to democratic principles. Maybe I should have known it." At the same time Baldwin contended that Washington policymakers needed to recognize that "only alliance with progressive forces, not the reactionaries, is the way to beat Communism and establish genuine democracy."[32]

By 1948 a domestic cold war had enveloped the American landscape. The Republican Party had taken control of Congress after the 1946 congressional elections, sporting the club of anticommunism to elect figures like Joseph McCarthy and Richard Nixon to the U.S. Senate and the House of Representatives, respectively. Truman responded to the political setback his party had suffered by creating a Temporary Commission on Employee Loyalty. In March 1947 he established the Federal Employer Loyalty Program, while later in the year Attorney General Tom Clark drew up a list of supposedly subversive organizations. The House Committee on Un-American Activities began grilling leftists based in Hollywood and elsewhere, demanding that they "name names" of individuals with whom they had associated in political organizations, meetings, or rallies. As matters turned out, HUAC and comparable committees at the state level usually already possessed that information, often culled from FBI files or presented by government informers. Increasingly, many leftists were viewed as suspect, with some denounced as outright traitors who were supposedly abetting the Soviet Union's determined bid to spread communism's tentacles worldwide.

Throughout 1948 Baldwin continued to argue that civil liberties, despite the "unprecedented tensions," had "not yet suffered serious setbacks in law or practice." Instead, "measurable advances are to be noted in both." Nevertheless, the outbreak of the cold war had established an atmosphere hardly conducive to maintaining civil liberties. HUAC remained the center of the "salvationist drive" that had resulted in "inquisitions, purges and witchhunting," the ACLU board said. At the March 15, 1948, meeting of the ACLU board—which was increasingly divided about how to respond to the Red Scare—Baldwin convinced members "to expose the [un-American Activities] Committee's unfairness." They agreed with his proposals to pressure Congress to curb investigative committees and for the ACLU to document HUAC's history. Similarly, Baldwin's colleagues promised to support other organizations that were condemning HUAC.[33]

Baldwin was concerned enough about the temper of the times to write an article, "Red and Rights," for the June issue of the *Progressive*. He warned that liberals were becoming ensnared in the anticommunist mania. Referring to the loyalty oath now required of federal employees, the HUAC hearings involving Hollywood folk, and the Taft-Hartley Act, Baldwin acknowledged, "The sound old doctrine that no penalties should be imposed on mere belief or association is being subjected to unprecedented strains these hectic days." He claimed that the proposed Mundt-Nixon bill—which sought to compel the Communist Party of the United States and communist fronts to register with the government and to hand over membership lists and financial records—would produce unprecedented results. "It would for the first time in our history pretty effectively outlaw a whole political movement and its sympathizers solely for beliefs and associations in the absence of any unlawful acts whatever," he wrote. Such an approach, Baldwin insisted, would imperil the liberties of all progressives and deliver a victory to the Kremlin, for Americans would be admitting "that democracy cannot work and that liberty is a sham."[34]

In August Baldwin acknowledged in the ACLU's annual report that American liberties remained uncertain. He condemned the federal loyalty oath program as potentially unjust, futile, and unfair. He also denounced HUAC's investigation of supposed communist influence in Hollywood as "a veritable Roman circus." While contending that HUAC had failed to demonstrate the relevance of its questions, the ACLU acknowledged "that they might have been proper had the committee first established Communist influence in the production of films." However, when witnesses received contempt citations because they had refused to name others involved in communist organizations, the ACLU contested HUAC's authority "to investigate in the field of opinion at all."[35]

Harry Truman's defeat of Thomas Dewey in the 1948 presidential race led Baldwin to proclaim that American civil liberties were in less danger. Nevertheless, it appeared likely that the future would bring both the repression of communists and the promotion of civil rights. On March 1, 1949, Baldwin joined in an ABC Radio broadcast discussion entitled "Should Communists Be Allowed to Teach in Our Colleges?" The other participants included Raymond B. Allen, president of the University of Washington, which had just undertaken an investigation of faculty members accused of belonging to the Communist Party; T. V. Smith, professor of philosophy at Syracuse University; and Harold Taylor, president of Sarah Lawrence College. In contrast to Allen and Smith, Baldwin argued, "No lawful political beliefs or associations—Communist or other—should in themselves bar anyone from teaching." Furthermore, he asked why communists alone were being singled out, for there were many others "whose associations are either alien to American democracy or whose intellectual freedom is limited by political or religious dogma." Why should a similar standard not be applied to members of the KKK, anti-Semites, white supremacists, fascist sympathizers, or Jehovah's Witnesses?[36]

Allen and Smith, Baldwin noted, reasoned that only communists were "controlled by a blind party discipline which unfits them as teachers devoted to intellectual freedom." Such a test made sense, Baldwin acknowledged, when applied to economics or political science instructors. Similarly, involvement in the Klan might preclude an individual from teaching ethics or anthropology. However, he opposed "the hard-and-fast general ban" that the other panelists approved of. "I would bar only individual teachers for unfitness to teach their subjects, and I would take into account their associations only as they affect their teaching." Concluding his initial remarks, Baldwin affirmed that he would not consider democracy so weak, American students "so supine," or the faculty so inept that they had to be inoculated against "the dread infection."[37]

Baldwin's declaration that a political litmus test could be applied to instructors in various disciplines was not terribly different from that demanded by red baiters. Considering his earlier support for radical educational experiments and his own involvement with the New School, this declaration illustrated how much his beliefs had changed in regard to the appropriateness of excluding from the mainstream individuals with particular political beliefs. Thus the Elizabeth Gurley Flynn episode had indeed put him on something of a slippery slope during an ideologically charged period.

In contrast to the liberal era that many—including Baldwin—had prophesied was about to return, 1949 ushered in a heightening of the cold war both at home and abroad. The civil rights legislation Baldwin had favored did not become the law of the land, whereas the Taft-Hartley Act, restricting union organizing, remained on the books. HUAC continued to hold investigative hearings; calls for outlawing the Communist Party of the United States mounted. Mob violence erupted in places like Peekskill, New York, to ensure that a supposed Soviet apologist like the actor Paul Robeson could not perform. The trial of Communist Party leaders on charges of violating the Smith Act, which made it a crime to advocate the violent overthrow of the government or to belong to any group that did—a prosecution Baldwin strongly opposed—occurred in the spring in a federal courthouse in New York City. The Soviets' acquisition of the atomic bomb initiated the nuclear arms race, and China fell to Mao Zedong's communist forces.[38]

As the cold war lengthened, Baldwin continued to argue that "civil rights are indivisible" and that "only in a free market can peaceful change be assured." Yet the ACLU itself adhered to its 1940 anticommunist stance, which it had recently extended to new affiliates. Many wondered why it was necessary, Baldwin admitted, to defend "the rights of those who reject the principle, as the Communists do for their opponents." Also difficult to explain was the ACLU's concern for the "public rights" of communists, when the organization excluded them from its leadership.[39]

In November 1949 Baldwin discussed the attacks on communists, saying that the ACLU alone had defended their rights, while acknowledging that public employment in "so-called sensitive positions" could be denied "where their divided loyalties might endanger national loyalty." Any other stance, Baldwin claimed, would drive the communists underground and establish procedures that might readily be used against others. Baldwin charged that the communists' propaganda was doing little to help their case, for they championed only the rights of party members and their allies. Additionally, they were guilty of having "deceived a lot of well-meaning people, including still some well-known liberals who should have learned by now that any Communist participation is prima facie evidence of lack of good faith."[40]

At the same time Baldwin argued that the civil liberties of communists had "not suffered much" over the years. They had been denied government employment, communists who were foreign nationals had been deported, a few criminal cases had been prosecuted—resulting in the recent conviction of eleven party leaders under the Smith Act—and communist aliens had been precluded from entering the United States. Still, "the record shows a very extensive damage to our American concept and practice of civil liberties in the measures taken to combat Communist infiltration, from loyalty oaths to black-lists, legislative inquisitions and an unwarranted hysteria against everything to which the Communist label can be even remotely attached. Experience should enforce the lesson that civil liberties are indivisible: if any are destroyed, all are endangered."[41]

By the close of the decade, as the cold war intensified, Baldwin's reading of the transformed political atmosphere was both characteristically pointed and strangely muted. Unlike many cold war liberals, he clearly recognized the danger to civil liberties posed by witch hunts, investigative hearings, loyalty purges, and repressive legislation. He continued to argue for protections of First Amendment rights for all Americans. Yet his analyses were often less sharply drawn and far less biting than in earlier times. More important, he now began to make exceptions in his expansive reading of civil liberties, which could allow for infringements of those same First Amendment freedoms.

It was equally clear that Baldwin's interest in the campaign to safeguard domestic civil liberties had flagged after three strenuous decades of continuous involvement. Still, he seemed determined to carry that crusade into another arena.

CHAPTER TWENTY-TWO

A Very Public Retirement in the Age of Anticommunism

By the late forties Baldwin's interest in orchestrating the day-to-day operations of the ACLU had slackened more than ever. Always an ambivalent administrator at best, he had been troubled by divisions—largely centered around the communist issue, in various ways—that had afflicted the ACLU since the late thirties. Baldwin was also more determined to become involved in international affairs, as he had long urged his colleagues; he had been delighted by the Declaration of Human Rights, proclaimed in Paris in 1948, which was said to provide the framework for an international bill of rights.[1] His experiences in Japan, Korea, and central Europe had whetted his appetite for additional overseas endeavors.

All the while a revolt was brewing within the ranks of the organization—which now boasted nine thousand members—that he had founded. Now board members determined to take the reins of power from Baldwin, while placating, to some extent at least, the man most fully identified with the ACLU. He was relieved of executive responsibilities and given the title of ACLU national chairman, which he held until 1955 as he strove to bring civil liberties to the world stage.[2]

The decision to depose Baldwin, by according him "ambassadorial status," had been considered at a board meeting held at Walter Frank's Manhattan apartment. A special Committee on Public Planning, commissioned in late 1948 and chaired by Walter Gellhorn, urged a broader campaign of public education, predicted difficulty in acquiring a mass membership but foresaw a larger organization, and recommended that "Roger Baldwin . . . be entirely relieved from . . . executive responsibilities."[3]

Afterward, both Baldwin and the ACLU leadership would attempt to maintain the impression that the relinquishment of power was a mutually agreeable determination. In reality Baldwin was ousted, no matter the new titles accorded him or press releases heralding a bright new day for all parties concerned. He was a still remarkably vigorous man—albeit one in his early sixties—whose health and energy level surpassed that of many far younger compatriots. In that sense the decision was clearly unfortunate, necessarily diminishing the influence within the ACLU of the nation's leading First Amendment champion. That development was even more unhappy, for the United States was about to enter a more virulent phase of the postwar Red Scare. The ACLU soon adopted stances that were frequently less than fully civil libertarian, which might have been avoided had Baldwin remained a more dominant figure. On the other hand, Baldwin had himself equivocated on civil liberties issues at various points and would again in the future.

The internal dynamics behind the decision to remove Baldwin obviously were not conveyed to the general public. On October 27, 1949, the ACLU issued a news release announcing his retirement, effective January 1, 1950. Baldwin, the announcement said, would continue working for the ACLU, focusing on "international standards of civil liberties." He also was going to represent the UN-affiliated International League for the Rights of Man, which he chaired. And he would continue to serve as trustee of the Robert Marshall Civil Liberties Trust, as co-chairman of the Coordinating Committee of U.S. Agencies for Human Rights, on the national committees of the U.S. Ratification of the Genocide Convention and the International Rescue and Relief Committee, and, for a brief spell, on the Overseers Committee for Harvard University's Economics Department. In addition, through Frances Grant, president of the Pan American Women's Association, he joined the western hemispheric board of the International American Association for Democracy and Freedom.[4]

Although Baldwin was out as ACLU director, its long-standing orientation as a largely Waspish organization did not change. Baldwin's successor, Patrick Murphy Malin, who taught economics at Swarthmore College, was a member of the eastern elite, and had attended an Ivy League university, worked in the field of international human rights, believed in pacifism, and was independently wealthy, thanks to his in-laws, the Biddles of Philadelphia. The similarity to Baldwin was no coincidence; Gellhorn's search committee had urged, "Other things being equal . . . the ACLU director should not be one whose interest in civil liberties might be mistakenly ascribed to his being a member of an oppressed minority group." As the ACLU's 1953 Annual Report reflected, Malin's relationship with the FBI appeared to be even warmer than Baldwin's. "A heartening expression of principle," Malin suggested, in discussing an article by J. Edgar Hoover entitled "Civil Liberties and Law Enforcement: The Role of the FBI." Along the same lines Ernest Angell, an American Legionnaire and chairman of a regional Federal Loyalty Board, was named ACLU chairman. Although Malin was said to lack Baldwin's vision and charisma, he oversaw the dramatic expansion of ACLU membership, to about sixty thousand during his first ten years, which made the organization a truly national enterprise. Baldwin, undoubtedly troubled by the organization's changed direction, criticized Malin as being disinclined to act without prior approval from the board. Yet it was Malin, not the board, who recognized the possibility of transforming the ACLU into a mass organization. Baldwin was taken aback too by the $13,500 salary Malin received. At the same time Baldwin "was very careful not to step on the toes of his successor," Alan Reitman of the ACLU's national office recalled.[5]

Following the announcement of Baldwin's retirement, commendations poured forth. Baldwin's ACLU service, Arthur Schlesinger Jr. stated, "marked an epoch of education for the American people in the principles of civil freedom." A. J. Muste called Baldwin's resignation "a national event," and "a great thing . . . especially in the period through which we have lived and are still living, that your name should have become identical with civil liberties in the United States and indeed beyond its borders." Norman Thomas stated, "No man in America has more completely stood before the American public as symbol and spokesman for a great cause than you for civil liberties."[6]

For his part Baldwin undoubtedly most enjoyed the handwritten note he received from the General Headquarters of the Supreme Commander for the Allied Powers in Tokyo. General MacArthur asserted, "Baldwin's crusade for civil liberties has had a profound and beneficial influence upon the course of American progress." Memorable too was the cartoon sketch by Bill Mauldin, complete with a handwritten inscription, "To Roger with admiration." A dog was lying wide-eyed and somewhat fearfully beneath a house. An arrow pointing to the dog read, "The Under Dog," and the animal was exclaiming, "That BALDWIN IS THE ONLY PAL I'VE GOT."[7]

One prominent figure who refused to send a congratulatory note was J. Edgar Hoover, who had been asked by ACLU chairman John Haynes Holmes to reflect on any personal experiences the two men had shared. That Holmes sought such a remembrance suggested a good deal about the perception of

Baldwin's relationship with the FBI director. The ACLU was preparing a handsome volume containing greetings and tributes from Baldwin's friends, and Holmes wrote to Hoover to say, "We know you will want to be included in this company." A top FBI assistant teasingly queried Hoover—who had recently received a letter from "An American" denouncing Baldwin as a communist—"Would director like to give a testimonial for his *Friend*?" After sketching a sharp note, Hoover added, "This is a form letter. Disregard it."[8]

On the evening of February 22, 1950, Baldwin was the guest of honor at the ACLU's thirtieth anniversary gathering, held at the Waldorf-Astoria Hotel. Speaking before the gathered throng, he declared, "It should be accepted as axiomatic that communism can be defeated only by a democracy so strong in satisfying the demands of progress that communism will be deprived of its appeal." But he also predicted that "a revolutionary transition" was ushering in "political world unity, an ordered world economy and internal democracy. . . . This transition toward democracy lies through overcoming first our greatest national failure—inequality in law and opportunity based on race and national origin." Until that occurred, the country's "moral authority in international councils will remain, as it is today, questionable."[9]

In an editorial that ran in that day's *New York Times*, the nation's most celebrated newspaper praised the organization that Baldwin, more than any other individual, was most identified with. Terming the ACLU "fundamentalist," the *Times* asked, "What is fundamental to the American system if it is not freedom of thought, of speech, of worship, of publication? What is more fundamental to the political system of the Western World than the preservation and implementation of those freedoms?" Such tenets, the editorial continued, were rooted in "the most fundamental concept of all, the belief in the nobility and worth of the individual man, the conviction that the purpose of the state is to protect the individual, and not vice versa." The ACLU had been involved "in the thick of the battle to uphold the individual right to these fundamental freedoms." The civil liberties organization, the *Times* asserted, "has been a valiant defender of some American fundamentals at the ground level, where it counts."[10]

Typically enough, Baldwin sent a memo to the ACLU staff regarding various "arrangements" when his resignation took effect; he was obviously determined to maintain as much control as possible while avoiding indignities to his sensibilities. His handling of the ACLU's international work, he said, would require trips to the capital and Lake Success (then the Long Island headquarters of the United Nations), as well as attendance at conferences at home and abroad. Naturally enough, some correspondence, dictation, and press releases would be necessary. In his new capacity he planned to visit the New York office only once a week for four hours at a time, when he would be available for consultations regarding any issues. He planned to show up at board meetings only when asked to do so. His mail was to be sent to his home but only that correspondence dealing with his "new responsibilities"; similarly, he intended to write or speak for the ACLU on international matters alone. His days would be divided—he would spend mornings on office work and afternoons would be taken up by outside appointments. He would visit Washington approximately once a month for a week at a time. He stood ready to carry out special jobs that the ACLU determined could best be performed by him. He also intended to complete a history of the ACLU in booklet form, as well as the thirty-year summary for the organization's annual meeting. His incidental expenses, which he believed would amount to no more than $500 a year, should be covered by the ACLU and would include his visits to Washington, his membership in the Cosmos Club—"virtually my office in Washington," he noted—and phone bills. Additionally, about $300 should be set aside for an entertainment fund to cover his out-of-town lectures. One concession he made was to resign from the Century Club in New York City, where he had been a member since 1927 and which he continued to frequent as a guest of others.[11]

His salary, to be paid out of the "Baldwin Salary Account," had been fixed at $3,600 a year by the ACLU board back in May 1948. Baldwin would receive such compensation, it was determined, so long as he continued to render services to the organization.[12]

In his first full year as the ACLU's international mentor, Baldwin seemed more drawn than ever to liberal anticommunism. After North Korean forces crossed the 38th parallel, he supported President Truman's decision to send American troops under UN auspices. He joined the newly founded American Committee for Cultural Freedom (ACCF), a professedly anticommunist organization headed by Sidney Hook. Its vice chairmen included Reinhold Niebuhr, Arthur Schlesinger Jr., the sociologist Daniel Bell, former radical James Burnham, and Baldwin. Soon Baldwin's good friend Norman Thomas became yet another vice chairman. Later Baldwin warned about the ACCF's propagandistic nature, declaring, "Anti-Communism in itself is an inadequate and negative policy, which only partially contributes to cultural freedom."[13]

In a brief note to Alexander Meiklejohn, Baldwin argued that witnesses before congressional investigative committees should answer questions about their political affiliations. Would it be a violation of the Fifth Amendment to compel a witness to acknowledge his ties to the KKK or the Communist Party, he asked, if those organizations had undertaken illegal activities? In an essay on John Haynes Holmes, Baldwin acknowledged that his steadfast compatriot, "like most of us," had considered the communists "genuine allies" in the antifascist fight and the Soviet Union positioned "in the camp of the democracies." However, the Nazi-Soviet pact had "completely smashed what turned out to be that illusion of Communist good faith, revealing them as thick and thin Russian agents."[14]

In the late summer of 1950, as part of a projected six-month worldwide tour, Baldwin traveled to Germany as consultant for the U.S. State Department. Reporting on October 2 from the U.S. Land Observer's Office in Düsseldorf, Germany, Baldwin noted, "Only the most bigoted communist does not know that conditions are infinitely superior in the West. Food, wages, working conditions, personal liberties, everything (with the possible exception of housing) is better here." Once again Baldwin was clearly pleased by the cordial treatment he received from military authorities. After two months he proclaimed that the German people did not care for the occupation but "endure it for fear of worse—the Russians." Still, Germany appeared calmer, he offered, than the United States did from a distance. "They have lived too long too close to the Russians to be disturbed."[15]

On January 20, 1951, Baldwin linked up with 144 other prominent Americans—including Lewis Mumford, Reinhold Niebuhr, Eleanor Roosevelt, Arthur Schlesinger Jr., and Norman Thomas—in declaring that communism now presented a greater threat to free people than Nazism had in 1939. Thus the Committee on National Affairs, operating out of New York City, argued that the "big lie must be countered by the truth." However, the committee warned against easily tossing about charges of "communistic" and "subversive" activity. "The free world," Baldwin declared, would suffer if it used "star-chamber tactics, or encourages espionage by emotionally disturbed individuals, or otherwise degrades the cause of truth and honesty. In combating the 'big lie,' half-truths and prejudices play into the hands of the enemy."[16]

The declaration that communism was more perilous than Nazism was astonishing on its face. It was even more remarkable that Baldwin would affix his signature to such a document, and it demonstrated how far he had traveled to land in the liberal anticommunist camp. That very statement would have been considered ludicrous by Baldwin just a short time before. Now he and other leading American liberals, no matter how inadvertently, were evaluating fascism of the most notorious variety as less threatening to the democracies than the red tide.

On February 13 Baldwin, along with Christopher Emmet of Common Cause and the writer Dwight Macdonald, issued a petition in support of the "Fighting Group Against Inhumanity" that was battling "the oppressive Communist dictatorship in Eastern Germany." Housed in Berlin and with hundreds of underground volunteers in the Soviet bloc, the organization aided refugees and was engaged in nonviolent resistance "to the terroristic regime" in eastern Germany. The petition discussed the "Offenders Against Peace Law," which allowed for capital sentences to be handed out to political opponents. "As Americans," the letter writers affirmed, "we believe with Thomas Jefferson that the tree of liberty is watered with the blood of martyrs."[17]

The September 1951 issue of *Harper's* contained a glowing tribute by Oliver Jensen, "The Persuasive Roger Baldwin." As H. L. Mencken had suggested a quarter-century before, it appeared at times as if there were only one authentic champion of American civil liberties, Jensen wrote. Baldwin had backed the free speech rights of the foolish, the eccentric, and the despised, including nudists, polygamists, atheists, Jehovah's Witnesses, fascists, and communists. Frequently, Baldwin had little liked those he was defending; moreover, he recognized that given the opportunity, they would readily "destroy his own."[18]

As for Baldwin himself, Jensen reported, he at times became cynical but never gave way to pessimism. And "since he belongs to that wiry, hardy, New England variety of mankind which seems to harden in the middle fifties and never alter thereafter, he is not going into retirement." Thus he was engaged in his new crusade: to take civil liberties on to the international stage, "a wider phase of the old battle." Moreover, given Baldwin's belief that all matters involving personal liberty were "world-wide and indivisible," such a quest was the most fundamental. This was hardly new ground for Baldwin, "a sophisticated and widely traveled man," who had agitated under the auspices of numerous groups, including the International League for the Rights of Man. Now most of those Baldwin encountered outside the Soviet sphere tended to agree with him or believed that he was sincere. In earlier times

Baldwin and his hearty band of cohorts had stood apart, facing threats of imprisonment or worse.[19]

Despite his constancy in supporting freedom of speech, the press, and assemblage for all, paradoxes abounded in Baldwin's life. Raised a Boston aristocrat, he seemed to have suffered few of the pangs of guilt other aristocrats-turned-radicals did. Because of the world's imperfections, Baldwin acknowledged, only a man of "respectable native stock"—like its architect—could have guided the civil liberties movement. During his ACLU tenure he had dealt with all kinds of radicals but also sat next to wealthy conservative individuals on the board of directors of the Audubon Society and as a member of the Visiting Committee of the Board of Overseers of Harvard's Department of Economics. He continued to express belief in a philosophy of freedom that could be likened to classical anarchism, yet he had administered the Garland Fund and the ACLU.[20]

While many reformers were stuffy pious sorts, Baldwin was "affable and witty, adept at bird-watching, sketching, and playing Chopin, and not given to proselytizing for the ideas he believes in so fervently," Jensen wrote. Baldwin reveled in the outdoors, where he canoed, skied, and hiked. Jensen referred to the private camp Baldwin had held along the Hackensack River, where his "adopted" boys frequently joined him. Those young men referred to Baldwin as "a tireless athlete, a good camp cook, and a man who carried a belief in non-violence to the point of not trapping the camp's rats and mice." He also seemed "a man of notable humility who keeps a careful notebook, which he types out every night, systematically recording the events and quotations of his day—a habit which makes him hard to misquote, or to defeat in argument."[21]

The ACLU, with which Baldwin was so identified, was experiencing a growth spurt that had seen its membership double within the past couple of years. Malin was engaged in an active bid to expand it still further and had hired more staff to attend to pamphlet writing, public relations, and battling public officials. Despite criticisms that continued to come its way, the ACLU appeared to have acquired unanticipated respectability, as Baldwin had stated on his retirement.[22]

On May 12, 1952, Baldwin—no longer viewed as procommunist by the State Department—delivered the Annual Felix Adler Lecture for the New York Society for Ethical Culture. Political liberties in the noncommunist world, he pointed out, were imperiled by "the arms race, war tensions and Communist aggression." The determination to arm noncommunist forces clashed with the revolutionary desires of those who sought to abolish poverty, illiteracy, and both foreign and domestic tyrannies. Indeed, "a revolution in our spirit of 1776 marks the whole non-white Asiatic and African world," he said. He viewed this as a hopeful sign, for it "made possible a world democracy." To view national independence movements as simply communist inspired, he presciently warned, "would defeat our democratic goals." More was demanded than support for the status quo, embracing "any anti-Communist as an ally," the maintenance "of white men's empire," the resort to arms, and slow-paced reform that stifled hope. A vibrant American democracy was required to provide "encouragement to leadership for rights and liberties."[23]

But dangers lurked. Basic American precepts demanded that no distinction be drawn "between the rights of good patriots and bad Communists," Baldwin told the society. However, recently, calls to outlaw the Communist Party had been heard, while the ongoing witch-hunt was resulting in unsurpassed hysteria. Guilt by association befell those associated with any of some 150 groups the U.S. attorney general presumptively had adjudged disloyal. Loyal citizens were fired from jobs and faced public scorn, although they had quit Popular Front organizations many years before. This was more striking too because of the minuscule size of the Communist Party and its sympathizers. The assumption prevailed that each communist was an agent of the Soviet Union and thus "a potential spy or saboteur." That served to justify "thought-control measures" and resulted in a departure "from the American tradition of the privacy of political beliefs. We have undertaken a vast dragnet inquisition." Baldwin told the society he had never witnessed such an intolerant political atmosphere.[24]

The likes of senators Pat McCarran, the Nevada Democrat, and Joe McCarthy, Baldwin warned, exuded an anticommunism more threatening to American freedoms than communism. He insisted, "We cannot destroy the rights of Communists without endangering our own." At the same time he believed it fitting that communists be denied "the right to public employment in sensitive positions where their dual loyalties conflict with their obligations."[25]

His attack on McCarthy may have led to Baldwin's condemnation by the senator on the Senate floor. On May 26 McCarthy submitted for inclusion in the *Congressional Record* a report on Baldwin that termed him "a draft evader" and discussed his involvement in United Front and Popular Front organizations. McCarthy noted that the California Legislature's Un-American Activities Committee had referred to the ACLU "as a Communist front or 'transmission belt' organization."[26]

In January 1953 Baldwin delivered a series of radio addresses on the case of Julius and Ethel Rosenberg, sentenced to death by a federal court for passing information on nuclear weapons to the Russians. On January 9 the defendants, still professing their innocence, sought clemency from outgoing President Truman. Baldwin insisted that the case involved no question of civil liberties, which was why the ACLU had not entered the fray. Instead, attorneys for the ACLU had determined that the organization should not contest the death sentences. For his part Baldwin expressed his opposition to capital punishment "on both humanitarian and political grounds." It particularly should be avoided in this case, he argued, lest the communist propaganda machine turn the Rosenbergs into martyrs, said to have been victimized by "barbaric American justice." His analysis of the Rosenberg case was broadcast in France over Voice of America—he had accepted the State Department's request that his talk be carried there. However, he later was stunned to discover that the VOA had excised his opposition to the death penalty.[27]

In a February 2 letter to President Dwight Eisenhower, Baldwin asked for a commutation of the sentences. He expressed no disagreement with the trial verdict: "I believe them guilty. Their trial was fair, their offence among the gravest." Executing the Rosenbergs, he again warned, "would play into the hands of Communist propaganda all over the world." That summer the U.S. Supreme Court lifted the stay of execution delivered by Justice William O. Douglas.[28]

After yet another trip to Western Europe that spring, Baldwin reported that he could directly describe how the congressional inquisition was damaging U.S. prestige. European journalists everywhere termed them witch-hunts, as Baldwin had. McCarthy and McCarran stood for "American denials of the democracy we profess." Europeans viewed the senators simply as fascists. Germans repeatedly asked Baldwin, "You Americans reproached us Germans for not stopping Hitler. Why, may we ask, don't you stop McCarthy?" They wondered about the lessons Americans were supposedly attempting to teach regarding democracy and civil liberties.[29]

Despite such deep-seated concerns about the domestic cold war, Baldwin arguably contributed to it in his own right, which marked quite a turn of events for the ACLU founder. A New York publisher asked him to edit a book on forced labor in the Soviet Union, and the U.S. State Department had promised to purchase a considerable number of copies. Baldwin had been recommended to the publisher by Adolph A. Berle Jr., who had been a member of FDR's Brain Trust. Berle reasoned that a book edited by someone who was not considered "a professional anti-Communist," but rather a leading civil libertarian, would have more influence in the countries where the book was largely to be distributed. Baldwin directed the collection of information and wrote an introduction. In late June 1953 Oceana Publications published *A New Slavery*, derived from materials obtained by the United Nations and the anticommunist National Committee for a Free Europe. In a lengthy foreword Baldwin laid out his personal perspective of "the new slavery." Baldwin acknowledged that he had been one of the skeptics who had discounted talk a generation earlier "of a huge system of forced labor for political dissenters." Although, like many other liberals, he was disillusioned by evidence that had dampened "earlier high hopes for greater human freedoms under a professedly socialist state," he had been reluctant to give credence to such reports. Doing so would also have required a recognition that communism's appeal both in Russia and elsewhere was less than he had imagined.[30]

He had long been cognizant "of the evils of the Soviet police state," having published two books back in the 1920s that documented, to some extent at least, repression inside the Soviet Union. However, those works, particularly *Liberty Under the Soviets*, also exuded an unwarranted optimism that, despite the one-party dictatorship, greater human freedoms awaited. Now the Soviet police state, and, consequently, "its servants, the communist parties," had been unmasked "as politically and morally no different from the fascist states, and through the deception of lofty claims to salvation, even more dangerous to human freedom," Baldwin wrote.[31]

He recounted in the book his own reactions to the Soviet Union and the world communist movement, which appeared to reflect those of many of his colleagues. Such admissions were also meant to suggest that hard facts, rather than political biases, eventually led Baldwin's colleagues to damn one of the gravest developments "of the inhuman communist police state tyranny—forced labor." Such a condition was not limited to the Soviet Union alone, Baldwin charged in *A New Slavery*, but rather was characteristic of all communist states, even renegade Yugoslavia. Moreover, the communists' use of slave labor appeared to be a unique "means of political tyranny," which not even right-wing or military dictatorships like those in Spain and Latin America systematically relied on to retain power.[32]

Once again Baldwin was contending that communism was a greater evil than right-wing despotism. His anger about communist practices was understandable, as was his continued distrust of manipulative undemocratic practices engaged in by members of the Communist Party of the United States. Yet a suspicion remains that Baldwin's conversion was not simply the result of disdain for the antics of comrades at home or abroad. Rather, it suggests his determination to match his political analyses with those adopted by leading liberals and moderates, both inside and outside government circles.

In July 1953 *The New Yorker* published a two-part series by Dwight Macdonald that contested the aura of respectability now surrounding Baldwin. The two men had engaged in something of a verbal and literary wrestling match since 1950. Two summers earlier Baldwin had complained to Harold Ross, *The New Yorker*'s famed editor, that Macdonald's profile of him was "so full of factual error and unsupported conclusions" and contained "such fantastic inventions or perversions of fact" as to be libelous. Morris Ernst, representing Baldwin, insisted that the articles be edited. Baldwin went to see Macdonald on Cape Cod at Wellfleet, Massachusetts, and the two, following a pair of lengthy sessions, supposedly said farewell on the friendliest terms. Or so Macdonald informed William Shawn, his editor at *The New Yorker*, while acknowledging that the departure was "at least as friendly as one can be with an SOB like Baldwin." Both Cliff Forster of the ACLU and Norman Thomas—who had served as one of Macdonald's sources for the articles—read over the work and attempted to dissuade Baldwin from bringing legal action, arguing that it would hurt the ACLU and Baldwin more than anything in the articles. Just before the essays appeared in print, Alan Reitman, now the ACLU's assistant director, warned Baldwin that attempting to review the remaining galleys would suggest censorship.[33]

Macdonald's study, entitled "The Defense of Everybody," was a largely critical piece that nevertheless frequently cast Baldwin in a positive light. His story, Macdonald believed, had its "dark shades, but would not be without its highlights," nor was it lacking a "chiaroscurolike" effect. The piece astutely began by explaining Baldwin's personality as "contradictory—a mixture of idealism and cynicism, of enthusiasm and calculation, of the moral crusader and the smart operator." A similar dichotomy permeated Macdonald's biographical sketch. Most disturbingly, Macdonald saw Baldwin as a representative model of the leftist liberals who "went Stalinoid in the thirties."[34]

In analyses intended to be critical, even cutting, Macdonald referred to Baldwin as "the high-pressure salesman, ingratiating and persuasive; the easy, humorous after-dinner speaker, the confident expert, threading his way among technicalities with brisk mastery; the quick, incisive debater; the crusader in a noble cause, bold and impassioned. He is, in a word, articulate." To Macdonald, Baldwin operated best in committee work and was "an expert chairman," who exuded a deceptively open manner, all the while pulling strings. Baldwin had personally selected the early ACLU board and had dominated its meetings. Working with other "notoriously articulate" individuals, Baldwin had often prevailed through "the force of his personality and also . . . his persistence in bringing up his pet projects, no matter how many times they were turned down."[35]

At the same time Baldwin's career, Macdonald acknowledged, virtually duplicated the history of civil liberties since World War I. Baldwin, Macdonald declared, was committed to the belief that civil liberties were applicable to all and had ensured that the ACLU adopted this stance, regardless of whose ideological ox was gored. "This was a more unusual position than it may sound," Macdonald wrote. Furthermore, the policy of defending everybody assured that somebody would be offended. Thus liberals had been upset by the ACLU's defense of American fascists, blacks by the protection of the rights of the Ku Klux Klan, and Jews by the championing of the rights of anti-Semites.[36]

Macdonald also reported that Baldwin's friends frequently were in a quandary regarding what social philosophy guided him. "They have sensed in him a personal commitment less complete than he said, or thought, it was." Baldwin's perspective, Macdonald argued, was "pragmatic—not so much 'Is it right?' as 'Will it work?'" One unsympathetic sort—perhaps Thomas—complained to Macdonald that Baldwin "has spent his life avoiding final commitments on anything."[37]

Evie Baldwin responded to the articles by breaking down in tears. "How can a man do a thing like that?" she asked. Baldwin became so angered by his dealings with Macdonald that he refused to speak to him afterward. Still, he acknowledged that the author excised "some of the dirty stuff, the insinuations. He wouldn't say it right out." Part of the story Macdonald had told—that involving basic civil liberties—"was very good," Baldwin believed. However, "he told half truths as if they were the whole truth." Consequently, Baldwin claimed he had refused to read the finished product.[38]

Baldwin's reputation clearly survived the Macdonald profile, which contained insightful analyses and some glib generalizations as well. As for Baldwin himself, he continued doing precisely what Macdonald had said he did. "I've had to compromise a lot," Baldwin told Macdonald, "but I've always insisted that civil liberty is indivisible and that unless we defend the S.O.B.'s rights, we'll lose our own." As Macdonald had concluded, "He has indeed insisted."[39]

Macdonald correctly portrayed Baldwin as riddled by contradictions, combining principle and cunning. Baldwin was indeed the brilliant committee man, whose determination often won the day, despite early opposition or disinterest. At the same time he was the individual most responsible for insisting on an expansive reading of civil liberties, for both friends and antagonists. Again Macdonald accurately noted that Baldwin appeared to lack the kind of philosophical grounding that guided friends such as Norman Thomas or A. J. Muste. That led some to accuse Baldwin of lacking principles and of easily shifting from one political perspective to another. Macdonald charged that had resulted in Baldwin's going "Stalinoid" during the 1930s, but such an accusation rang hollow. In reality Baldwin veered left from the early teens onward, making sharp moves in that direction during both the period of U.S. involvement in World War I and the first half of the thirties. He could be accused of having stood as an apologist for the Soviet Union at different points, but he never followed the party line regarding the United States and often expressed concerns about developments in the communist land. At the same time he had hardly stood as the consistent anticommunist he now portrayed himself as having long been.

Although Macdonald had condemned Baldwin's Popular Front associations, others encouraged him to participate in a campaign to resuscitate the American Left. When his old friend A. J. Muste had urged in mid-1956 that the pacifist Fellowship of Reconciliation sponsor a meeting on "America's Road to Democracy and World Peace" at Carnegie Hall, he had turned to Baldwin to moderate the gathering. Sharing the platform were Norman Thomas, the American Communist Party's Eugene Dennis, and W. E. B. DuBois. About two thousand people attended, apparently hoping to discover some means to revitalize the American Left, which had fallen on hard times during the late forties and early fifties. The recent acknowledgment of Stalinist horrors by the new Soviet premier Nikita Khrushchev had caused even resolute communist stalwarts to seek reform within the party or to leave its ranks altogether. With Stalinism more discredited than ever, Muste hoped, some kind of new Left might emerge. But the meeting at Carnegie Hall was too early for that and involved too many individuals scarred by the sectarian wars of the Old Left and the domestic cold war.[40]

In 1957 a number of veterans of the Old Left's internecine clashes, along with many liberals, founded SANE, the Committee for a Sane Nuclear Policy. Among the earliest members were Eleanor Roosevelt, the theologian Paul Tillich, Norman Cousins, and Baldwin. In early October Muste acknowledged Baldwin's reluctance to join the National Committee of the American Forum for Socialist Education, which sought to devise a new alliance of noncommunist leftists and their sectarian brothers. Still, Muste was pleased that Baldwin considered the American Forum's "Statement of Purpose" "a sound basis for socialists of whatever brand to explore their approaches to action." Muste was also delighted that Baldwin was willing to participate in a conference held by the American Forum. Baldwin was asked to say a few words at a reception to honor the efforts of Muste, the nation's foremost pacifist, to support free expression.[41]

Although Muste had told Baldwin he would welcome his participation, Baldwin declined the invitation to speak at the gathering, which Muste had hoped would "promote understanding among the contending schools of salvation on the left." Baldwin—referring to himself as "a mere liberal bystander"—expressed appreciation for Muste's efforts: "I applaud your faith in freedom of speech as a solvent of misunderstanding." However, he wondered what would result from such a gathering. Still, Muste deserved high marks for a campaign Baldwin viewed as quixotic at best: to bring about "peace and harmony among the salvationists of the left."[42]

Baldwin appeared no happier regarding the activities of the Americans for Democratic Action (ADA), the liberal anticommunist organization formed back in January 1947 to serve as a counterweight to the more leftist Progressive Citizens of America. Arthur M. Schlesinger Jr. later referred to Baldwin as "a fellow-traveler of the ADA," who occasionally attended national conventions and was great friends with the likes of ADA leaders Joe Rauh, also a civil rights lawyer, and Jim Loeb. However, in a letter to Robert R. Nathan, dated February 18, 1958, Baldwin expressed reservations about the ADA, declaring that recent analyses of world affairs appeared no different from those made by the Democratic Party's "wholly inept leadership." The ADA's southern ties precluded it from boldly addressing racial issues. Its connection to the policies of Dean Acheson and Harry Truman led to an insistence on what Baldwin termed the bankrupt policy involving containment and a heightened arms race. And while the ADA had once spoken of the need for a war on poverty, it no longer did.[43]

As the 1950s ended, Baldwin appeared little cognizant of the bare beginnings of the youth-based movement that C. Wright Mills referred to as the New Left. Unlike a small number of his fellow veterans of the Old Left, Baldwin would have difficulty empathizing with student activists. The emergence of the New Left was now possible, thanks to the civil liberties campaign. However, the leading light of civil liberties now often seemed more comfortable with various dignitaries, ranging from Nehru to Puerto Rico's governor Luis Muñoz Marín to Ngo Dinh Diem, than with those determined to take to the streets to agitate and protest injustice both at home and abroad.

In mid-1959 Baldwin, now seventy-five, met with such international leaders during a whirlwind three-month tour that took him through twenty-one countries, starting with England and concluding in Japan. Ostensibly, the occasion was in honor of the graduation of his daughter, Helen, from Radcliffe. As a graduation present Evie Baldwin financed the trip for Helen, a college classmate of hers, and Roger, who carried out a mission for the International League for the Rights of Man and UN nongovernmental affiliates.[44]

Baldwin's report on developments in South Vietnam, where the government confronted insurgent forces, revealed his liberal anticommunist perspective. President Ngo Dinh Diem, he insisted, was personally incorruptible, but corruption surrounded him. The police were ever present, although little repression was in evidence. In Saigon Baldwin spoke with top officials, including President Diem, along with Michigan State's Wesley Fischel, who had long been involved with America's nation-building endeavor in Vietnam. In typical fashion—but in a wholly unrealistic manner—Baldwin sought to get Diem "to commit himself as to the direction of democracy." However, Diem was merely vague, asserting only "the need for moral and spiritual unity." Diem discussed South Vietnam's reeducation camp for communists and their sympathizers, insisting that the South Vietnamese were striving for reform. Diem—whom Baldwin termed "a charming idealist but tough on dissenters"—clearly had no conception of the "rights of man." Without comment Baldwin referred to Fischel's report that the camps enabled individuals to learn trades, obtain "unwashed brains," and then return home.[45]

Diem's opponents told Baldwin that communism should be contested by democracy, not by aping communist repression. The Diem regime dealt with

Vietnamese citizens only through the police and the placement of government agents in the villages. Courts were weak and unable to afford any protections, lawyers "too few and too timid." The impotent trade unions had already been dissolved, and elections were but a shield for a police state. Nepotism riddled the government, while both the military and police were used largely to quell "internal unrest or subversion." The people were unhappy but lacked the means to vent their displeasure, fearful of being denounced as communists. Baldwin met with a pair of government critics, both doctors and "good liberals with courage," in his estimation. However, he "thought them somewhat unrealistic about the conditions the government faces."[46]

At the conclusion of his tour Baldwin delivered a report for the ACLU that related his findings. The cold war, he acknowledged, had bolstered authoritarian government in various lands. Fear of communism had inhibited the growth of progressive movements championing human rights. In government circles there existed a phenomenon seemingly attractive to the U.S. government—the crafting of "a facade of democracy" to paper over the brutal suppression of communism. Unfortunately, this had resulted in the suppression of a great deal more than communism. At the same time the nations in the hands of the military or experiencing states of siege, Baldwin argued, did not exude repression. He found no sense of fear in Greece, Syria, Iran, Pakistan, Burma, Thailand, or Vietnam. Still, he was troubled by the resort to preventive detention in use in such countries, with Thailand and Vietnam singled out as the worst offenders.[47]

Baldwin's perception of developments in Vietnam, characteristic of his evaluations from his trip, was both astute and markedly lacking in insight. He recognized the omnipresent nature of Diem's intolerant police forces, the nepotism that abounded, the people's dissatisfaction, and the timidity of the nonrevolutionary opposition. However, for Baldwin to seek to convince Diem of the need to adopt democratic practices was ludicrous, although arguably no more so than the efforts of U.S. officials to do the same. After all, Diem was little more than a neo-Confucian dictator, determined to create a family fiefdom and relying on a thin base of support largely comprised of Catholic refugees from North Vietnam.

The lessons imparted to Baldwin by Diem's political opponents also seemed to produce mixed results at best. Baldwin heard talk that an infusion of democracy was required to best communism, as he had long believed. Yet he considered the regime's antagonists unrealistic about the obstacles it confronted. And, strikingly, he appeared all but oblivious to both the mounting guerrilla insurgency and the pervasive fear that enabled old Vietminh cadres to obtain new recruits.

Baldwin's evaluation of U.S. foreign policy demonstrated both the strengths and inadequacies of the liberal anticommunism to which he now sub-scribed. He refused to view communist-guided forces as necessarily more humane than the right-wing elements they sought to depose. At the same time he, unlike many liberals, recognized that U.S. identification with those same reactionary forces would not win hearts and minds in the Third World. However, Baldwin, in the manner of numerous liberals and consistent with his long habit, albeit from a different ideological perspective, examined developments in other lands through selective prisms. Thus governments that opened their doors to him generally received sympathetic evaluations, as did leaders—including some repressive ones—who possessed a certain style that Baldwin somehow identified with.

CHAPTER TWENTY-THREE

A Man of Contradictions

During the period of his public retirement Baldwin's typical day demonstrated his still-legendary energy. When he was in Manhattan, he read newspapers and his voluminous mail and then planned his day by phone. When the UN General Assembly was in session, he arrived at his office, located in the secretariat building, shortly after 10 A.M. He usually lunched in the delegates' lounge, all the while carrying on conversations involving international civil liberties. In the afternoons he frequently went to the office of the International League for the Rights of Man for consultations. In the evenings social life often took precedence, with ambassadors, high government officials, and students from across the globe visiting his home in Greenwich Village, where he continued to reside with Evie Baldwin. On other occasions he attended to his bird paintings or played classical music on the piano.[1]

At the beginning of the 1960s he continued to spend weekends at the country home along the Ramapo River outside Oakland, New Jersey; he and Evie invariably spent a month at their exclusive summer estate in Chilmark on Martha's Vineyard. Nature hikes, skiing, skating, mountain climbing, or canoeing were typical venues for entertainment. Nevertheless, he inevitably pounded away at his trusty typewriter for several hours daily.[2]

Baldwin remained controversial in certain circles. Mississippi senator James Eastland, in an effort to smear Freedom Riders in his state, referred to the support they received from the likes of Baldwin and Lillian Smith, author of the classic *Killers of the Dream* (1949). Eastland displayed a lengthy compilation of Baldwin's involvement with various committees and organizations in an obvious effort to besmirch civil rights activists.[3]

By contrast, the *Milwaukee Journal* in September 1961 underscored Baldwin's involvement with human rights, pacifism, and the United Nations. "The Underdog's Best Friend," a profile of Baldwin written by Marjorie M. Bitker, a family friend, captured him in his element at Chilmark:

> One of the unique summer sights on Martha's Vineyard island, Massachusetts, has been a gentleman of mature years at the helm of a correspondingly mature jeepster. Under his battered tan cap he wears an expression of dedicated concentration, well suited to his New England puritan features. Atop the vehicle is lashed an inverted canoe of massive proportions, jutting out like a giant beak over the head of the driver who, undaunted, careens lickety split down the road.
>
> This phenomenon is as much a part of the local scene to the Islanders as sea gulls or sand dunes. The doughty skipper of the jeep, they take pride in explaining to curious strangers, is none other than Roger Baldwin, founder and long the moving spirit of the American Civil Liberties Union, en route to one of his nature expeditions around island ponds.[4]

Bitker highlighted Baldwin's interest in physical activities of all kinds, nature study, gardening, and cooking. Afternoons often found him, with field glasses dangling from his neck, engaged in excursions with naturalists young and old. He was considered a tireless gardener, whose green thumb ensured that family and friends remained well stocked with vegetables. He was also an expert cook, who could readily concoct "fast gourmet items" from packaged mixes and canned goods. A believer in "the dishpan as an instrument of family togetherness," Baldwin had only recently consented to allow the installation of an automatic dishwasher at the Martha's Vineyard estate.[5]

The write-up in the *Milwaukee Journal* also discussed how readily Baldwin acted as "a lively, imaginative companion, full of jokes, lore and stories on their level" for children. They referred to him, in the manner of those close to him, as "Bunkle." Invariably young people came to him for advice or simply to say hello.[6]

Roger's seemingly idyllic existence was transformed by Evie Baldwin's death, at the age of sixty-four, on June 11, 1962. Baldwin, apparently unaware of how sick she was, had remained in Puerto Rico to teach a course on civil rights he now offered annually at the island's leading university. Finally, he was called to the Harkness Pavilion at Columbia-Presbyterian Medical Center, where

Carl and Roger Jr. were waiting for him. The boys had determined, Carl reported, to "shield Roger from this terrible news. He was oblivious because we were keeping him oblivious." Now Baldwin realized that "something was terribly wrong." Evie had terminal lymph cancer, the physician informed him. Helen returned from Rome, where she had been studying art since completing her undergraduate studies at Radcliffe. Apparently, her mother was never informed about her disease, despite the radium treatment she was receiving. On the morning she died, she told Baldwin, "Oh Bunkle, I'm feeling so low." Seeking to cheer her up—while engaging in characteristic denial—he responded, "Sweetheart, the doctors say you have to be low before the turn comes. First you sink to a low with this radium therapy and then you turn and you begin to get better."[7]

Her death proved devastating to her family. As Carl later reflected, "That was a very calamitous event in our lives because Mother had been such a powerful presence." Roger Jr. appeared quite shaken, "collapsing in tears" at one point, his brother said. By contrast, Baldwin, who "took great pride in being extremely stoic and not showing feelings . . . just sort of took it on the chin and kept on going," Carl said. Instead, Baldwin immediately began planning memorial services for New York, New Jersey, and Martha's Vineyard.[8]

The New York memorial service, presided over by Norman Thomas, was held on June 19 at the Community Church on East 35th Street. Evie's close friend, Dorothy Kenyon, and Bill vanden Heuvel, a young attorney dedicated to public service whom Baldwin had mentored, delivered eloquent orations. As she had requested, Evie Baldwin's ashes were placed in Dell Brook's forest soil, in the Ramapo Mountains.[9]

Baldwin also received a note from Madeleine Doty expressing condolences and saying that Evie was "far more suitable as a wife" than she had been. Doty, who had moved into a resort hotel in the Berkshires, died the following year. Since their divorce in the midthirties, Baldwin had frequently provided financial assistance to her.[10]

With Bill Butler serving as executor, Evie Baldwin's estate was settled. She left Roger Baldwin the Oakland farm, which stood as "his bailiwick." She gave the home and land at Chilmark to Roger Jr., Carl, and Helen as tenants in common. The Greenwich Village townhouse, where the Baldwins had lived and raised the children, was placed in the care of Butler, who proposed that Helen purchase it for a reasonable price. Roger Baldwin went to live with

Carl and his wife, Mary Ellen, for about a year. He also spent a good deal of time in Rome with Helen, who was involved with Piero Mannoni, a teacher in the school where she was studying art restoration. Baldwin went on to Geneva, Germany, Paris, and London before returning home, and Helen and Mannoni returned to the United States, as she felt compelled to attend to her father. She undoubtedly believed that "this might have been like a five or seven year project. Or one or two," given Baldwin's age.[11]

As Baldwin discovered, Mannoni was already married, and his wife refused his request for a divorce. So Baldwin went to Butler, his friend and personal attorney, and said, "Hey, we've got a big problem on our hands. Helen wants to marry this guy. She thinks she wants to marry him. Well, what do I do?" Butler responded, "The best I can do is I'll send Piero down and get him a Mexican divorce. And when he comes back, we'll get Helen and Piero married in Connecticut." As Butler later recalled, "It was an ex-parte divorce. And I don't think it was worth the paper it was written on." But Helen was eight months pregnant, so Baldwin and Butler drove the young couple to Connecticut to witness their union by a justice of the peace. Still, like her own parents, "Helen never got legally married," Butler said.[12]

Helen, Piero, and their baby, Francesca, moved into the brownstone on West 11th Street along with Baldwin. Another daughter, Alessandra, was born two years later. For the first few years Mannoni still spent a good deal of time in Italy, and Baldwin had some of his "adoptive kids" board with them for a while. The longtime Baldwin-Preston residence in Bleecker Gardens, cluttered but expansive, continued to exude shabby gentility. Roger Baldwin's own routine seemingly changed little, with weeks spent at Dell Brook and summers at Windy Gates with Helen's family. Peggy Lamson, in her book on Baldwin, discussed the manner in which Baldwin and his daughter dealt with one another: "Helen is at once brisk, forbearing, irritated and affectionate toward her father. Roger is very much himself—cheerful, demanding, opinionated and tolerant. The rapport between them is evident. . . . Helen treats him like a parent who is sometimes bothersome but never like an *old* parent who is tedious." Baldwin saw his daughter as "the most critical member of the family" and the one who knew him best.[13]

Evie Baldwin's nephew, Bill Preston, viewed the dynamics at the Greenwich Village townhouse in a far different light. He believed that Baldwin now required Helen to become "in a sense, the daughter who becomes the wife." Baldwin—who enjoyed being attended to—was alone, as he had not been for years. Helen was attached to Piero, which "was a shock to Roger," who asked himself, however subconsciously, "I've got to share this woman, with an Italian?" Moreover, Baldwin wanted Helen to serve as his "Girl Friday," to "run the house, accompany him on trips, take notes, and so forth." Coupled with the never-ending tension between the most important men in her life, all of this proved enormously stressful for Helen.[14]

Beneath the surface things were considerably less than rosy on West 11th Street. The Mannonis occupied two floors, while Baldwin lived on the bottom one, where he slept, had a cluttered office, and continuously conducted business on the telephone. From time to time Helen Mannoni served as hostess for her father's parties. This placed tremendous pressure on her, and on Piero Mannoni as well, as he was unhappy at Baldwin's "very visible and audible presence." When asked what Mannoni did, Baldwin was heard to blurt out quite scornfully, "Well, I think he was trained as a—I don't know what—but he's never had a real job." Little helping matters was Baldwin's belief that Mannoni did not treat Helen well. Later, when Baldwin's health began to deteriorate somewhat, things became more difficult still.[15]

Piero Mannoni, in the midst of his ongoing battles with Baldwin, resorted to sarcastic remarks under his breath. Francesca recalled that her grandfather "did things that he knew on some level . . . would irritate my dad." Piero Mannoni, a superb cook, would spend eight hours preparing some dish. Invariably, Baldwin would loudly exclaim, "Oh, Piero, what's this concoction?" which always perturbed Helen's mate.[16]

Language difficulties, real or exaggerated, made things worse. When Mannoni first came to the United States, he knew only minimal English. At dinner he and Helen spoke in Italian until Baldwin—who had once possessed a facility for the language—complained that he was unable to follow the conversation. Also, because Baldwin was hard of hearing, "he screamed a lot," Francesca said. He spoke in such a manner to Mannoni, who responded with his very thick accent in a quieter voice, all but inaudible. Clearly, they annoyed one another.[17]

The relationship between Roger Baldwin and Piero Mannoni never smoothed out, with the older man viewing the handsome young Italian as an interloper. At one point Bill Butler asked Baldwin what he thought of Mannoni. Baldwin blurted out, "What do you think of a guy that doesn't wear a watch?" Helen, who controlled family finances, loved both her husband and her father. Completely tied to her roots, she was enamored of the Greenwich Village townhouse, Dell Brook, and Windy Gates. She loved City and Country School, which she had attended and her children would as well.[18]

To Francesca Mannoni there existed "an emotional triangulation" between her parents and grandfather on West 11th Street. Baldwin, she came to believe, "wanted to be taken care of. And he missed Evie and there were certain things that he wanted to have in his life, and he wanted them from his daughter." Her father and grandfather vied for Helen's attention, which made for "an impossible situation." Baldwin appeared oblivious to the emotional turmoil his presence engendered. As Francesca recalled, "I . . . never felt like my grandfather sort of stepped back or gave them more space. I don't feel like he was sensitive to what their own needs may have been. He just sort of continued to be himself."[19]

Baldwin's presence ensured that the household functioned at a feverish pitch. As Francesca reported, noise was abundant, with the phone constantly ringing, Baldwin's typewriter clattering, and guests coming over. Exacerbating the pandemonium was Baldwin's "incredibly loud voice," as he and Helen conversed about current events or politics. When Baldwin was away, a type of calmness took hold and the noise level abated. Francesca Mannoni declared, "It seemed like my parents were just taking a deep breath. It certainly felt like that."[20]

The weekend trips to Dell Brook continued. There Baldwin took walks with his granddaughters, canoed, and bird watched. Once a year or so he undertook some extended walk through the estate to visit Evie Baldwin's burial site at the front of a waterfall, next to two pine trees that had split from a favored tree. Baldwin would boisterously relate how he and Evie had discovered the spot and talk about the kind of woman she was.[21]

The atmosphere at Dell Brook tended to be more relaxed than back at the Greenwich Village townhouse; this provided a needed respite for the family. Other family members, including Carl Baldwin and Bill Preston, frequently showed up. So did a host of close friends, such as Bill and Jamie Butler, Ed McCamis, Harrison Starr, and Michael Straight, former editor of the *New Republic*. Thanksgivings and New Year's eves, Francesca Mannoni recalled, were particularly festive occasions, with "lots of games, lots of people, lots of food, lots of conversation. And just lots of fun." Invariably, her grandfather "was the center of attention. He liked being the center of attention." His low, loud voice possessed "a certain flavor," as "he always gave . . . almost a kind of theatrical dynamic to anything he was talking about, in terms of tone."[22]

The Chilmark property, like the Greenwich Village townhouse, had been deeded to the children. Although her brothers used Windy Gates only infrequently, Helen Mannoni returned to Martha's Vineyard repeatedly. The estate "meant more to her," Carl said. As he recalled, "I think she, in a way, felt she was sort of stepping into her mother's shoes and I think that was something important to her." Thus Helen had, in effect, come to control two of her mother's three properties, all of which her father still relied on.[23]

Even more than at Dell Brook, the time spent at Martha's Vineyard often proved harmonious. While Bill Preston, Joe and Trude Lash, Rita and Thomas Hart Benton, Max Eastman, or an occasional visitor like Danny Kaye might be on hand, not all family members were present. Nor was there "that sort of intent to create a happening every day," Francesca Mannoni recalled. Baldwin happily played an upright piano daily, while wearing, as he did at Dell Brook, his country outfit: "sort of khakis and . . . a green outdoor shirt, and his little bird binoculars and a baseball cap and hiking boots." On occasion he could be seen in swimming trunks. As his granddaughter put it, Baldwin "had uniforms for his locations."[24]

Unlike other family members, Baldwin appeared to be "sort of in the same state all the time. He never seemed to more or less relax. He seemed more or less busy," Francesca Mannoni said. Still, "he seemed sort of equally comfortable, sort of in an equal state wherever he was." Yet "he made it a point that he was spending time in the country," she said.[25]

Despite the more relaxed circumstances, putting up with Baldwin for extended periods proved difficult. On one occasion during the midseventies, Helen Mannoni and her father "came to blows," in a sense, Francesca recalled. Shortly after Evie had purchased the Chilmark estate back in the 1930s, rose hips were planted that sprouted all around the house. Unfortunately, their roots began to affect its foundation. Helen and Piero Mannoni desperately sought to maintain the house and the cement walkway, which was cracking. She determined that the bushes had to go. Without informing her brothers or father—whose bedroom was near the bushes—she had removed truckload after truckload of the rose bushes. Shocked by what had transpired, Baldwin and Helen argued about her decision. "How could you have done this?" he asked and then warned, "I'll never come back here again." As matters turned out, Baldwin never stayed at the main house again. He continued coming to Chilmark but took up residence, along with aging Harvard professors, among others, at Barn House, where he had first spent time with Evie Preston.[26]

His daughter viewed Baldwin as "something of a dissembler," who was "quite concerned about appearances." As Helen Mannoni told Joseph Lash, "They are paramount in his life too." Baldwin's personal attorney, Bill Butler, also believed that Baldwin had "carefully cultivated an image of himself and never let his guard down." Her mother, Helen contended, had been considerably more radical and less worried about how she came across to others. Helen too saw her father's behavior as contradictory. He acted "very executive" at the Greenwich Village townhouse, attempting to organize everyone as "junior Roger Baldwins." She found this understandable, for he "has been an executive all his life and has been the boss all his life." At the same time, when her father remembered that he was not supposed to believe in bossing people around, he made a conscious effort to stop doing so. Nevertheless, his daughter considered him "extremely authoritarian" in the workplace, and elsewhere as well: "He treats us all like his lackeys." Typically, Baldwin was concerned that Helen sublet Dell Brook to the right sort of people, worrying that they not drink heavily and would love nature. Helen responded that those who imbibed freely might enjoy nature in their own fashion, but Baldwin remained close-minded about that.[27]

She viewed her father as very manipulative and as constantly seeking praise. "He thinks he's good," Helen Mannoni said, "but he doesn't dare say so. So it's almost pathetic the way he fishes for compliments." Once he asked her, "Do you have any friends whose fathers ever did the great things I did?" He seemed to miss Evie's telling him, "Bunkle, you're wonderful."[28]

He became "very bristly" regarding any criticisms. He often admonished Helen, "Don't talk to your father like that." And he was "very defensive about his record at the ACLU," she recalled. When Corliss Lamont's book, *The Trial of Elizabeth Gurley Flynn*, was published, Baldwin's old friend gave him an inscribed copy that read, "You're a great man but you're not always right and you weren't right in this case." Under the inscription Baldwin wrote, "Yes, I was."[29]

Helen Mannoni, like Bill Butler and so many others, was well aware of her father's parsimonious ways. Butler once said that if he ever billed him, "Roger would fall over in a faint." While her mother had been "penny wise, pound foolish, Daddy does it to excess," Helen said. She recalled Carl's taking their father to Brooks Brothers, but when Roger expressed shock at the prices, they ended up at Harry Rothman's. Baldwin believed in "making do" but became agitated when the tailor stated that vests were not in fashion. Baldwin favored vests, although his suits had spots on them. He complained to Helen about the floor at the house in Dell Brook, which was covered by what she termed a revolting old rug. When she mentioned its disrepair, he refused to admit the house needed a new rug. He was long known for doling out 10-cent tips to cabbies, no matter the fare. When a cabby complained, he fired back, "Well, if you don't like it, give it back to me. I can use it—probably better than you." He was adverse to giving tips altogether, reasoning that they were immoral. Employers, he believed, should pay living wages.[30]

Once, on returning from Martha's Vineyard, Baldwin needed a hat, having lost his—which had cost $7—in Stockholm. He went to purchase another but returned home, complaining he couldn't find one. When Helen Mannoni turned on the television, a commercial blared out that hats were on sale for $15. Baldwin responded, "That's the trouble." On another occasion he informed Evie Baldwin that he would buy a winter coat for Helen. But Evie bought a coat at Bonwit's for $180 and Baldwin never let her forget it. At the same time he gave generously to organizations he supported, believing that tithing to such groups was in order.[31]

He insisted that certain standards of etiquette be maintained. When Helen brought a plate of rice to a weekend meal at Dell Brook, he complained, "That's a kitchen spoon in the rice. You have perfectly good silver." Helen replied that she did not care what kind of spoon it was. "Your mother would be shocked," he continued, "to see a kitchen spoon in the dining room." Once he purchased a small silver creamer and sugar bowl and told Helen, "For your lazy susan." However, she never took her coffee in the dining room: "It was for his lazy susan." And for one who had such refined table manners, Baldwin's habit of spitting out food was disconcerting.[32]

Certain women, Helen believed, helped to "keep him alive." Baldwin had been enamored of his friend Margo Newton on Martha's Vineyard and still "just shines in her presence," Helen once revealed. He exclaimed at times, "I've got to find someone to go out with to the theater." Reflecting about one friend, he remarked, "Yes, yes. She pays her way. Trouble with women is that you've got to pick them up, pay for them and then take them home. Men are much less trouble."[33]

The contradictions that abounded in Baldwin did not go unnoticed by others or by him. In a conversation with Joseph Lash in San Juan, Puerto Rico, Baldwin admitted that he was a man of such contrasts. He preferred to live in a small room close to the University of Puerto Rico rather than at one of the fancy hotels along the coast. "I suppose there's something in me all my life—an irrational desire not to take advantage of what I could take advantage of—a compromise renunciation, people would say." Still, Baldwin acknowledged that others would reason, "You talk like that but you live rich. You live off the inherited benefits you and your children get from your wife. You haven't given up anything."[34]

Baldwin, the self-professed anarchist and believer in capitalism's inherent immorality, "really did enjoy hanging out with the rich. Yeah, the really rich," Bill Preston recalled. At the same time Baldwin was upset by the move of ACLU headquarters to a more fashionable site in midtown, away from its "ratty quarters, and shoddy atmosphere," which its founder preferred.[35]

It was her mother, Helen Mannoni reasoned, who had "really kept up with the times." She read a great deal, including works on Sigmund Freud. At the same time, this bright, well-educated woman would admit that she found it difficult to challenge Roger on certain matters. Evie would say, "I couldn't say that to Bunkle. He is just a man of action. Things are black and white—no nuances. He gets enraged if you qualify your analysis of someone." He also became discomfited, reddening easily, when someone told an off-color joke in his presence. Helen viewed her father as a traditionalist who wanted things to "go on the way they have." Given his more old-fashioned bent, he was characteristically ambivalent about women's rights and regarding their duties and responsibilities. Helen overheard a telephone conversation in which her father asked a woman what kind of operation she had just had. Informed it was a hysterectomy, Baldwin stated, "That's a major operation. That's what makes a woman." Helen became enraged.[36]

Even Francesca was troubled by Freudian-like slips that her grandfather made on occasion. Baldwin had no sympathy for the counterculture and she recalled his complaining, "Helen, did you see that young man? Did you see his hair?" Such statements, Francesca contended, were "never consistent, though. I think that is how he got away with it." Still, she "began to realize that everything wasn't as smooth as it was laid out to be." Francesca also became aware that her grandfather "would say the things that people wanted to hear. . . . He had chameleon-like abilities."[37]

Helen, Roger Jr., and Carl all recognized what a paradox their father was. They appreciated "the difference between what he pays lip service to and what he really feels," as Helen put it. She wondered whether he was aware of the contradiction. She recalled his tale about reading Clarence Day's *Life with Father* to his own father, who clapped his knees and said, "Just like your grandfather." Helen thought, "And just like Roger."[38]

What Baldwin seemed to fear most of all was following in his father's footsteps. For a time Frank had moved in with his daughter Deborah in Hingham, Massachusetts. However, "he became unbearable," Helen declared. "She couldn't take him." Consequently, he had lived in a rooming house close by, while continuing to take his meals at Deborah's. "Daddy is in terror of the same thing," Helen Mannoni asserted. Bill Butler also believed that Baldwin was quite afraid of spending time alone in the house at Dell Brook.[39]

The contradictions that abounded in Baldwin's public life also invaded his private realm. He was thrifty to the point of being cheap but lived the life of the upper crust, hobnobbing with the very rich, living in a Greenwich Village townhouse, holding an estate in the New Jersey countryside, and taking advantage of another family home on Martha's Vineyard. He extolled democracy in the political and economic spheres but was authoritarian in both the workplace and his own family relationships. He demanded his own private space, refusing to allow friends and colleagues alike—let alone would-be biographers—to get too close. Yet through his ever-constant presence he denied his own daughter and her family that same privacy.

CHAPTER TWENTY-FOUR

Matters of Principle

As Baldwin turned eighty, he became the subject of a thoughtful and largely flattering profile by Willie Morris that appeared in the January 25, 1964, issue of the *New Republic*. Visiting Baldwin one evening at his Greenwich Village home, Morris discovered that his subject had just spent the day working at the ACLU's national headquarters, the UN, and the office of the International League for the Rights of Man. Baldwin, Morris reported, "has aged like an old waterfall." He was "a highly likable man, lean and a little rumpled, with quick humor and rapid speech" who appeared "much nearer 60 than 80."[1]

Baldwin alone had been continuously involved in the campaign to strengthen civil liberties, the journalist offered. Now Baldwin had become "a monument and an eminence" as he had witnessed the civil liberties movement "change from a cause for radicals and wealthy eccentrics to one which the most respectable Eastern lawyer might embrace with equanimity and without embarrassing either his social standing or the moderate wing of the Grand Old Party."[2]

As others had commented, Morris asserted that Baldwin, in contrast to most of his peers, had led "an intensely public existence, with few traces of introspection, self-pity, or intellectual anguish." Thus he had experienced no difficulty in simultaneously belonging to the Visiting Committee of the Board of Overseers of Harvard's Department of Economics, the League Against Imperialism, the Audubon Society, or the International Committee for Political Prisoners.[3]

On May 15, 1964, Leonard Bernstein threw an eightieth birthday celebration for Baldwin. President Lyndon B. Johnson's congratulatory note saluted

Baldwin's "long career, your unremitting fight against injustice and intolerance." Former Supreme Court justice Felix Frankfurter, an old ally from the
early ACLU days, expressed deep regret at his inability to attend the gathering.
The ailing Frankfurter applauded Baldwin as one of his few friends "who gave
his life to ameliorating the condition of man without having a grain of self-
righteousness about you." In response, Baldwin recalled a remark of Holmes's:
"A man is not old until he is proud of it. I am not—not yet anyhow."[4]

Long after he had retired as ACLU chief, Baldwin still sought to influence its
direction. He befriended young men, sometimes urging their placement on
the national board or in other positions of leadership, always sounding them
out regarding their views on the topics of greatest concern to him. At the
beginning of the 1960s, for instance, he sought to mentor Norman Dorsen, a
Harvard Law School graduate who had served as an aide to Joseph Welch
during the Army-McCarthy hearings and who had clerked for Supreme
Court Justice John Marshall Harlan. The thirty-year-old Dorsen had just
been hired as director of the Arthur Garfield Hays Civil Liberties Program at
the New York University School of Law. Barely six weeks into the job Dorsen
received a phone call that began, "This is Roger Baldwin." When Dorsen
replied, "Well! Mister Baldwin," the voice on the other end responded,
"Everyone calls me Roger." After asking Dorsen about his work, Baldwin
blurted out, "Do you want to get together?" Dorsen replied, "It would be an
honor," and Baldwin exclaimed, "Great! I'll be over in half an hour." Dorsen
countered, "What do you mean? I'll come to where you are." Baldwin
retorted, "Don't be silly. You're a busy man" and hung up. The two men went
to lunch at the Grand Cuccinno Restaurant, which, Baldwin informed
Dorsen, had been a speakeasy during the Great Depression.[5]

A short while later Baldwin hosted a dinner to introduce Dorsen to the
civil liberties community in New York. One of Baldwin's old buddies, who
had been drinking, chortled at one point, "Roger, this is the third time we've
had one of these dinners and nothing ever happens!" But Baldwin responded
enthusiastically, "It all depends on the man. We've got the right man."[6]

At various points Dorsen would not talk or meet with Baldwin for some
time; instead, Baldwin would write Dorsen regarding ACLU operations that
troubled the former director. Then Baldwin began urging that Dorsen be put
on the board of directors, which irritated some members who must have
feared Baldwin was "coming in over the top," as Dorsen put it. No matter: by
early 1965 Dorsen was sitting on the board.[7]

During that same period Dorsen became involved with what proved to be the landmark case of *In re* Gault, decided in May 1967 by the U.S. Supreme Court, which afforded juveniles facing deprivation of liberty many rights granted to adult criminal defendants. Undoubtedly reflecting on his experiences as probationary officer of the St. Louis juvenile court, Baldwin suggested, "The idea of courts getting involved in this was exactly the wrong thing to do." As Dorsen saw it, "New civil liberties developments left him not altogether in synch." Yet Baldwin expressed his concerns in a very gentle manner, never offending Dorsen, who had argued the case before the U.S. Supreme Court. Dorsen's own responses to Baldwin's criticisms were mixed. "I looked at him as probably somebody over the hill or past it," but "I respected him and we were friends. I sort of welcomed his comments." Dorsen kept telling himself, "Here's somebody who really cares. He's an old man and yet he cares."[8]

In the 1960s the ACLU began to broaden its perspective, adopting a more expansive view of civil liberties; the organization began arguing that the equal protection provisions of the Fourteenth Amendment were just as important as the core First Amendment issues. That troubled Baldwin and other old-timers, who had generally raised the banner aloft for freedom of speech, of the press, and of assemblage. As Sheldon Ackley—who served on the national board from 1967 to 1975—recalled, Baldwin appeared quite disturbed by the ACLU's increased focus on economic issues. To Baldwin the key concerns for the ACLU remained the "First Amendment, due process, and equal treatment." Baldwin was not terribly pleased about the gay rights movement and was ambivalent about the women's struggle. Such issues were hotly contested within the ACLU itself, particularly when younger members, serving as new affiliate representatives on the national board, clashed with old-time civil libertarians. The ACLU, Baldwin remained convinced, should not "stray too far from the middle-class." According to Bill Butler, Baldwin believed that once that occurred, "it's the beginning of the end for the ACLU."[9]

Throughout this period Baldwin was operating behind the scenes in his continued attempts to influence ACLU affairs. At times he attended board meetings; on other occasions he did not. However, three weeks or a month before scheduled meetings Baldwin sought to see those individuals he believed would be most influential. As Ira Glasser, director of the ACLU's New York chapter, viewed matters, this was how Baldwin strove to get his agenda across.[10]

At the same time Jack Pemberton—who had replaced Patrick Malin as ACLU executive director in 1962—seldom sensed that Baldwin "was looking over my shoulder." Generally, Pemberton received no phone calls or memos from Baldwin, who would simply stop by his office and ask a question about some organizational matter. However, at one point Pemberton, seeking to follow the lead of the NAACP's Legal Defense Fund, sought to get the ACLU more involved in litigation through the Roger Baldwin Foundation, which had been established to honor the ACLU founder. Now Baldwin demanded to know why the ACLU was initiating certain suits. "This is being brought in my name," he exclaimed, while making clear that the legal action was in no way honoring him. Consequently, the foundation's name was changed.[11]

On another occasion Baldwin criticized Pemberton's staff appointments—such as the promotion of Mel Wulf to legal director—arguing that too many Jews now occupied high-level positions. Baldwin was deeply concerned about "the perceived Jewishness of the ACLU" and the reputation of the organization. As Pemberton remembered, "Roger felt a great deal of the old white man's burden." He believed "advocacy of those who were denied rights should be brought by those who were not denied rights." All this "partially reflected his patrician attitude," Pemberton said.[12]

He also sensed that Baldwin was displeased with the ACLU's tremendous growth. Baldwin continued to believe that only his social peers should be involved with the organization and that a small membership "could remain pure in face of various kinds of political pressures."[13]

One issue discussed in ACLU circles particularly disturbed Baldwin, perhaps because it could affect how history would view him. Various affiliates sought to overturn the 1940 Resolution, which precluded people from holding staff or leadership positions in the ACLU who also were members of political organizations that supported totalitarianism. Baldwin, who remained "basically an elitist," in the estimation of Alan Reitman and many others, wanted policy to trickle down from the top and had long opposed the building of strong affiliate organizations. Moreover, "It was quite clear that he felt very sensitive to being attacked," Reitman said, adding that Baldwin possessed "a massive ego," like any major leader, and "liked being loved."[14]

Starting in 1964, ACLU members in the Iowa, Massachusetts, southern California, and northern California affiliates began to seek support for a revision of the 1940 Resolution. In April 1965 George Slaff, head of the southern California chapter, informed the national board that his branch desired such a policy change. Slaff's affiliate favored adoption of the following criteria: "Support of civil liberties as guaranteed in the Constitution of the United States and particularly in the Bill of Rights is the one and fundamental qualification for membership or office in the American Civil Liberties Union." The southern California ACLU suggested that the 1940 Resolution fostered guilt by association and an examination of the beliefs and opinions of members. The chapter claimed that the resolution could exclude from the ACLU leadership and staff people who were employees of southern states, for example.[15]

As might have been expected, Baldwin strongly opposed the proposed change in a June 1965 memorandum. The ACLU, he maintained, had always kept individuals out of leadership positions if they held ideas or associations at odds with the organization's fundamental purposes. However, this was clearly not the case, for Elizabeth Gurley Flynn and William Foster were among the Communist Party members who had served on the ACLU board. A private organization, Baldwin nevertheless explained, could certainly decide to exclude those with contrary viewpoints. While some argued that the test for exclusion should involve acts alone, Baldwin stated, "Any test we use to square with our principles must be based on beliefs." Furthermore, "the concept of 'guilt by association,' sometimes abused in the administration of law, is valid when applied to qualifications for a private organization, where associations count like views."[16]

Baldwin's old friend and unwavering ACLU colleague Norman Thomas agreed with him. "We believe in civil liberties," Thomas wrote in a memorandum dated October 14, 1965, "because of our deep conviction of their necessity for the highest human dignity and any true democracy." The 1940 Resolution only indicated that those who championed Chinese or Soviet despotism, Thomas declared, "do not belong on our governing boards."[17]

As of early 1966 ACLU affiliates remained sharply divided about whether to alter the 1940 Resolution. On January 30 the board accepted a revised proposal by the Michigan branch to establish a committee, comprised of the affiliates, the national board, and the national committee, to examine the 1940 Resolution. In March 1967 the board adopted these criteria: "The ACLU's leadership and staff should be comprised of those—and only those—whose devotion to civil liberties is not qualified by advocacy of those communist, fascist, racist or other doctrines which reject the concept of democratic government and of civil liberties for all people in the United States and its possessions." At the same time the board deleted from the organization's application form for membership the sentence that read, "The

ACLU needs and welcomes the support of all those—and only those—whose devotion to civil liberties is not qualified by adherence to Communist, Fascist, KKK, or other totalitarian doctrine."[18]

The necessary two-thirds approval of an amendment to the ACLU constitution, however, was not forthcoming, but another move developed to discard the 1940 Resolution. In December 1967 the board adopted a compromise proposal—which Baldwin helped to draft—declaring that ACLU leaders and staff members had to be devoted to democracy and civil liberties for all. This provision was overwhelmingly accepted by ACLU members.[19]

In a note to Ernest Besig, Corliss Lamont expressed his belief that Baldwin was content with the outcome. At a cocktail party Lamont mentioned to Baldwin that the ACLU had accepted his compromise, which superseded the 1940 Resolution. Baldwin responded, "It was no compromise. It's the same thing, but better expressed." Acknowledging that he had yet to read the text, Lamont lamented, "This seems to me conclusive testimony from the horse's mouth as to the meaning of the new resolution."[20]

By early 1968, in the seventh year of Jack Pemberton's directorship, Baldwin began to express more concerns about ACLU operations. On February 6 he discussed the case of the Boston Five—famed pediatrician Benjamin Spock, Yale chaplain William Sloane Coffin, Institute of Policy Studies cofounder Marcus Raskin, and two others—who had been arrested and charged with conspiring to encourage draft resistance. Baldwin denied that the ACLU had ever defended nonregistrants; it had not done so in World War II nor had its predecessor, the National Civil Liberties Bureau, during World War I. However, he acknowledged, "In doubtful cases I would always take a chance in favor of aid." Although he did not believe that "the ACLU is losing its grip on principle," Baldwin did "see caution in excess in some matters where we should be as bold as we are in draft card burning defense."[21]

Bitterly divided, the ACLU's board of directors initially declined to represent the defendants, arguing that these cases would raise questions regarding the Vietnam War's legality, which hardly involved civil liberties. However, a subsequent vote allowed the Massachusetts branch to provide counsel for Michael Ferber, a graduate student at Harvard, and the poet and novelist Mitchell Goodman, the other two members of the Boston Five. Four of the defendants were found guilty, but an appeals court threw out two of the convictions, ordering retrials for Coffin and Goodman. The Justice Department opted not to reprosecute.[22]

By 1969 Baldwin's misgivings about ACLU developments, including concerns about its repeated financial crises, were greater still. In June he sent a memo to colleagues, arguing that decision making should rest with the professional staff, not the affiliates; after all, this was the way the ACLU had been run during his directorship. Because the executive committee was not likely to meet as frequently, now that Baldwin was less involved, he proposed that a small administrative committee, comprised of no more than five members, should attend to "all office, affiliate and similar relations." The biennial session of the executive committee, he reasoned, should not possess sole authority to determine ACLU policy. Rather, it should serve as a "forum for discussion and recommendation," with the national board holding ultimate authority. Indeed, Baldwin shared his belief that the national board should keep close tabs on the affiliates and could act whenever a branch contested national policy.[23]

In this memo Baldwin also focused on what he termed "matters of principle." He referred to suggestions

> that there is something more to civil liberties than the Bill of Rights and the equality amendments to the constitution or the natural rights principles from which they derive. We could of course embrace the right to eat, or the right to work or the right to a warless world and so take on the cause of world peace and all the phases of the welfare state with its economic and social rights. I sense a certain uneasiness about our commitment as if we were behind the times and a bit old-fashioned.

Having concerns about the ills of American society was certainly understandable, Baldwin continued. However, "democracy in its wide political sense is our business—the processes of change not the substance of it." Should the ACLU depart from such a notion, where would it stop? "We become social reformers." This was a curious concern for one who had long placed the ACLU at the forefront of hotly contested social and political issues, albeit behind a civil libertarian shield. At present, he remarked, "I think we sometimes stretch it pretty far." He failed to understand why the ACLU should defend the right to use marijuana, "unless we would defend all privacy, including the use of heroin." In a note he wrote that fall to Jack Pemberton, Baldwin cautioned, "Passing judgment on what is or is not dangerous is not our business."[24]

On September 29, 1969, Baldwin joined with other members of the national committee, including the historians Henry Steele Commager and

Arthur Schlesinger Jr., to send a memorandum to the board of directors, "In Support of Maintaining Integrity of Purpose." They expressed misgivings regarding the recent call from the biennial session of the national board for the ACLU to "support proposals to deal *substantively* with the problems of poverty and welfare, including educational and medical care." For these distinguished national committee members, the memorandum indicated, the proponents of such proposals "appear to have added a new right 'of every citizen to live' as a concept of civil liberties." Baldwin and his colleagues opposed extending the ACLU's basic principles "to open the doors wide to dealing with war, which is opposed to the 'right to live,' with poverty, with public health, and with the human environment in general." In fact, some affiliates had already joined in environmental suits involving clean air and water. The memorandum was designed to remind other ACLU members that the organization's strength "has always been its strictly limited and defined area, embodied in the Bill of Rights and the ACLU Constitution as well." The ACLU's greatest distinction was its belief that democracy's "basic guarantees" should be afforded "to all equally without partisanship." Such distinction would be cast aside if the ACLU became concerned about the worth of specific causes involving civil liberties: "It would lead the Union to pass on the merits of particular wars, or strikes, or movements, even of governmental taxation as fair or unfair to the poor, and so on to an indefinite limit."[25]

By the midsixties Baldwin, like other thoughtful Americans, had become more concerned about events in Vietnam. In late December 1964 he informed Norman Thomas that the most effective peace advocates were senators like J. William Fulbright, Wayne Morse, Frank Church, George McGovern, and Ernest Gruening. On June 3, 1965, Baldwin received a thank-you note from Morse, the Oregon Democrat who was one of two members of Congress to vote against the previous year's Gulf of Tonkin Resolution that President Johnson viewed as handing him a blank check to wage the war in Vietnam. In August 1965 Baldwin applauded his old friend Norman Thomas's opposition to U.S. intervention in both Southeast Asia and the Dominican Republic. "You labor in this field; I do not," Baldwin wrote. Still, he was troubled by a foreign policy that violated international obligations and seemingly represented the belief that the defeat of communism, but not a new world order, was attainable.[26]

Baldwin's idea of antiwar opposition remained rooted in his own experiences several decades earlier. He envisioned opposition that emanated from elite forces or already well-established and respectable organizations, such as Congress, churches, labor unions, and women's groups. He was not one to readily march in parades and demonstrations, as he acknowledged in a later tribute to Thomas, who did take to the streets to protest the war. Baldwin contended, "I am not of that temperament." Similarly, this one-time violator of the World War I–era Selective Service Act did not believe that burning one's draft card was an effective means of protest. Such actions, he informed a young man in late 1965, "arouse either resentment, misunderstanding or dismissals of protesters as unbalanced." If part of a mass effort, they might result in a conspiracy charge. Baldwin urged his correspondent to "write open letters to the papers . . . join anti-draft or anti-war organizations and participate in their public activities . . . tell your draft board and public officials what stand you take." Terming himself a conscientious objector, Baldwin declared that U.S. intervention in both Vietnam and the Dominican Republic violated existing treaties and "should have been handled only by international agencies."[27]

In late February 1966 Baldwin again corresponded with Thomas about U.S. involvement in Vietnam. He urged that the Vietcong be treated "as a negotiating party" to bring about a cease-fire and establish an interim government until elections could be held. He also called for adherence to the 1954 Geneva Accords, which divided Vietnam at the 17th parallel. Threats of aggression, he believed, should be handled by collective action undertaken by the UN. In reply Thomas said that supporters of the pledge wanted to see the removal of U.S. military forces from Vietnam as soon as a peace agreement was signed. To Thomas, "The great thing is to make some use of political action in 1966." On April 24, 1966, in the Student Center at the University of Puerto Rico, where he offered his seminar on civil rights, Baldwin discussed "Youth and the War." The era of empires and colonialism, he asserted, was at an end. World war amounted to world suicide, while the United Nations sought to usher in international law. However, "the old order of each for himself hangs on, resisting. Our historic task is to dare achieve an order of each for all."[28]

The tumult of the 1960s was disconcerting to Baldwin because it challenged his sense of propriety. In September 1966 he opted to resign from the advisory committee of the Congress for Racial Equality, because of its recent emphasis on racial separateness, the right to self-defense, and black power. The CORE he had supported stood for nonviolence, equality, and integration. CORE chairman Floyd B. McKissick quickly responded, disturbed that

Baldwin was removing his name from the advisory board, which included James Baldwin, Martin Luther King Jr., A. J. Muste, A. Philip Randolph, and Walter P. Reuther. McKissick said he would be happy to speak directly with Baldwin about issues troubling him. CORE demonstrations would remain nonviolent, he promised, but its participants would not relinquish "the right of self-defense . . . a constitutional right." CORE, McKissick insisted, "still *is* for equality and integration" but believed that such goals had to be attained through blacks acquiring power.[29]

In closing, McKissick expressed great concern "that a man of your intellect has been persuaded by obvious untruths which have been directed against us." Why would he take the time to write, McKissick asked, "if I did not sincerely feel that you were needed?" He could not prevent other groups from espousing certain beliefs or the press from lumping CORE with those organizations. However, McKissick reminded Baldwin, "Some years ago, you too were caught in a similar position."[30]

In a subsequent note to James Farmer, CORE's national director, Baldwin reported that he had tendered his resignation because of "the inconsistency of my position in supporting the NAACP, Urban League and CORE when policies differ now so radically." His commitment to the two former organizations—involving "equality, integration and non-violence"—was a long one. However, now CORE, like the Student Nonviolent Coordinating Committee, appeared to have headed in a different direction. He regretted having to take this step, as well as "the unhappy developments that prompted it."[31]

In July 1967 Baldwin revisited Geneva, attending the third biennial UN-sponsored Conference for World Peace Through Law. No theme was more recurrent than the need for a respect for human rights to lay the foundation for peace and law. Absent political freedom, economic justice, and rule by law, Baldwin asserted, "World peace is an illusion." He proceeded on to the Soviet Union, returning to Moscow for the first time in four decades. Now he acted more as a critical observer than the sympathizer who had undertaken the odyssey so many leftists had, if only symbolically, four decades earlier. In Baldwin's estimation the problems afflicting the Soviet Union were not attributable to communism but rather "to Russianism." The Soviet regime, in contrast to other communist ones, was "puritanical, moral, rigid." The people, he suspected, did not feel oppressed and were undoubtedly patriotic and proud of the accomplishments wrought by the Soviet state. They were "defensive, resenting the slightest suggestion of criticism."[32]

Baldwin viewed with dismay the determination to create a new man in the communist state—one that was wholly moral, responsible, devoted to family and country:

I just don't think it can be done or should be if it could. A world of such perfect men and women would be an intolerable nightmare of virtue. It couldn't work; to have virtue anyway you have to have sin, or you wouldn't know which was which. To the Russians I suppose sin is Western and virtue Russian. I doubt if any other communist regime makes so central this concept, none except Mao, whom the Russians reject, tho he is preaching this kind of nonsense.[33]

This time Baldwin was not conducting any investigation regarding the communist state. Instead, he was undergoing "a sentimental journey to a land of such significance to our times, and one in which I could not under present conditions ever feel at home. Not just that it is a dictatorship, but that it is messianic, organizing the hive. I just could never be a good bee." For Baldwin the trip's highlight was revisiting Kropotkin's home, where he had lived for a month during the twenties, and discovering that the great anarchist was the most revered of the pre-1917 revolutionaries. Baldwin was delighted that the house had not been converted into a museum—although the front of the house bore a plaque honoring Kropotkin—but now served as "a school for English-speaking children under the auspices of the American Embassy."[34]

Baldwin continued to believe in the ideals with which Kropotkin was identified: "individual and social freedoms from all sorts of arbitrary power." Kropotkin himself had been unable to chart such a course, and, as Baldwin said, "I am certain nobody can." Thus he often favored reaching goals through "contradictory means and associations." Only such experimentation, Baldwin recognized, "fits a spirit of action like mine." Moreover, "it is not shameful to be wrong; it is shameful not to try."[35]

Increasingly, Baldwin's ruminations on contemporary affairs could be heard in Puerto Rico, where he served as an unpaid visiting professor at the commonwealth's public and most prestigious law school. During visits to Puerto Rico, where he now spent winter months, he conversed regularly with individuals as disparate as Governor Luis Muñoz Marín, the cellist Pablo Casals, and independence leader Pedro Albizu Campos. Baldwin viewed Campos as "a great patriot . . . selfless, a mystic believer who made his wishes into facts, a gentle personality without hate, but one to whom violence, murder, if necessary, revolution certainly were the necessary if deplorable means to the lofty goal of human freedom and justice." For nearly two decades Baldwin would visit Casals in his home in Old San Juan, where they discussed such matters as Franco's continued reign in Spain and the plight of the Spanish refugee committee that the great musician headed.[36]

In March 1968, speaking under the auspices of the Puerto Rican wing of the pacifist Fellowship of Reconciliation, Baldwin bemoaned the failure of the United States to appreciate that the unrest in Vietnam amounted to civil war. Yes, "the North helps the rebels," he admitted, but "we run the war for the government." Baldwin favored an unconditional halt to bombing runs and a willingness to meet with Vietcong guerrillas. Unlike many other American liberals, Baldwin recognized that "the war is in the South, not North, and the North's agreement alone will not bring the end." The antiwar opposition on American college campuses, Baldwin reported, was sharper than ever. The ACLU had elected to stand side by side with objectors of a nontraditional sort, along with Puerto Ricans who refused on constitutional grounds to serve in the U.S. armed forces. The dissidence, Baldwin warned, would continue. The war itself, he hoped, as did many others, would "be the last of the cold war armed confrontations, and the last great power intervention in a civil war."[37]

Back on the mainland some months later the eighty-four-year-old Baldwin wrote, "In extreme cases it is obvious that police intervention may be the only means to restore order." The same students drawn to Students for a Democratic Society, he reminded his audience at the St. Louis Ethical Society, had campaigned for senators Eugene McCarthy and Robert F. Kennedy and headed into the American South to champion voter registration. The failures of top university administrators to respond adequately to student grievances, he charged, had led protesters to resort to sit-ins, strikes, and mass demonstrations. Such tactics "are to be deplored," as were riots, and sometimes resulted in a violation of the law. The ACLU, Baldwin noted, supported a student bill of rights rooted in freedom and democracy in order to avoid disaster.[38]

On December 6 Baldwin was awarded the First Annual Human Rights Award of the International League for the Rights of Man, which he had chaired for twenty years and now served as honorary president. Sponsors of the tribute included his old friend Josephine Baker; England's Philip Noel-Baker, the 1959 winner of the Nobel Peace Prize; and Jose Figueres, who later became president of Costa Rica. A greeting arrived from Supreme Court Justice William O. Douglas, who applauded Baldwin's Jeffersonian defense of minority rights, calm and reasoned pleadings for justice, and support for procedural due process. "Though many of the causes you espoused may seem to have been lost, your advocacy has helped keep alive the conscience of America," Douglas wrote. Baldwin's dear but ailing friend Norman Thomas, who was unable to attend the function, called him "a great and good man" who "will live in history. The United States owes him a great debt." Thomas also affirmed, "I owe him a debt for simply being my friend, Roger Baldwin."[39]

Thomas died on December 19, shortly after Baldwin had delivered a tribute to him in the *New Republic*. Thomas, Baldwin wrote, was ever the public man, prone to debate issues of grave import. Baldwin repeated the frequently told tale of trimming apple trees with Thomas in the New Jersey countryside. Even then Thomas engaged in a monologue about politics, and Baldwin determined not to invite him for another sojourn at his Oakland farm. Toward the end of his life Thomas had been afflicted with painful arthritis, which compelled Baldwin to proclaim that he would not punish himself in such a manner to deliver one speech after another. Thomas had replied, "I know you wouldn't, but you aren't an evangelist!"[40]

Thomas's death shortly followed that of A. J. Muste, the other member of the trio born within a year of one another who had made such a mark in the annals of American liberalism and radicalism. Thomas, like Muste a former minister who never wholly discarded his crusading ways and acted as the conscience of his nation, had revitalized the Socialist Party of America, making it more attractive for middle-class individuals and intellectuals. Muste had stood as the nation's foremost peacemaker, helping to set the stage for a rebirth of the American Left through the emergence of a New Left. Baldwin had helped create and then long nurtured the modern civil liberties movement, which sought to safeguard the First Amendment freedoms of even the most despised of all Americans. The three had often joined together in various crusades to oppose war and exploitation, usher in a more egalitarian and internationalist order, and champion freedom of speech, of the press, and of assemblage. In the waning years of their lives, they had joined together once more to oppose U.S. involvement in Indochina. Then, as so often had been the case, they sometimes argued about tactics or policies, but their goals were invariably the same. Now only Baldwin was left, along with a few other veterans of the scarred, even haunted, Old Left who remained politically engaged.

Like Thomas and Muste, Baldwin continued at times to be disturbed by various antics of the New Left. In the spring of 1970 he delivered a report on behalf of the Civil Rights Commission of Puerto Rico regarding the ROTC program at the University of Puerto Rico campus. The previous fall the ROTC building there had been partially burned. The rights of all, the commission contended, should be upheld on university grounds. Whether to continue the ROTC program at UPR should be decided by the university "without political interference." When acts of violence occurred, the preferable solution was to obtain an injunction to restore order. However, when necessary, the report proposed, authorities should rely on both university rules and criminal sanctions.[41]

Later that year, during an interview at his Greenwich Village townhouse, Baldwin stated, "Democracy works. I have hope, but not optimism. But if you want to put a label on me, I'm an 'unhappy optimist!'" Americans experienced cycles in which reform proceeded ahead and then halted. As for those, such as the Black Panthers and the Weathermen, who desired to bring the war home and radically transform the American system, Baldwin thought that their programs made little sense. Furthermore, "There is no real revolutionary group in the United States because our social welfare state has improved things so we don't have revolutionary urges on the part of the poorer peoples. Democracy works and we don't need revolutionary councils."[42]

His ambivalent attitude toward the movements of the 1960s again demonstrated Baldwin's greater attachment to liberal, rather than radical, solutions. On occasion his rhetoric remained as charged as it had been a generation and a half earlier, when he questioned the inherent worth of the capitalist system. Now an American icon, Baldwin viewed the turbulent events of the 1960s, at least those that did not directly affect the ACLU, in a largely objective fashion. Like any number of other Old Leftists, he watched the antics of the New Left with detachment and, at times, dismay. While he appreciated the anger and frustration that drove it, Baldwin was hardly disposed to the kind of analyses he had once drawn. Nor did he suggest the need to bring all forces on the Left into some kind of united or popular front.

CHAPTER TWENTY-FIVE

The Public Image

In the winter of his life Baldwin continued to be troubled by developments involving both the ACLU and his image. As early as 1949 the publishing house W. W. Norton had expressed interest in Baldwin's story, only to be informed that he was committed to Houghton Mifflin, should he ever write an autobiography. Joseph P. Lash had come closest to producing a study of Baldwin. For more than a year, beginning in the fall of 1971, Lash worked with the editor Gilbert A. Harrison and Baldwin before deciding that the venture was doomed because of Baldwin's lack of cooperation. Lash determined that Baldwin was not likely to "be fully reconciled to a biography that deals with the private as well as public man." In a note to Harrison, Baldwin professed that he had "no private life . . . of any interest to anyone." Baldwin, Lash informed his editor on October 16, 1972, was "very concerned about his private image. He's not going to allow a book to be written that will deviate from his image of himself." Promising to return a $40,000 advance, Lash proclaimed that he did not "want to cause him [Baldwin] pain in the sunset years of his life." Baldwin expressed regrets to Lash but again stated that he would be embarrassed to have the intimacies of his private life "exposed to public view." Lash declared that he had felt it necessary to examine Baldwin's relationships with women, including his two "marriages," which he termed "highly unorthodox in form and as such expressive of your personality and outlook." To Lash, Baldwin's "unconventional style of life has much to say to a younger generation."[1]

As Baldwin admitted, he was particularly worried that Lash "wanted to include my love and sex life," which he considered "irrelevant to what most people would want to know about my life." He and Lash "disagreed about 'going into bed-rooms,'" and the abandonment of the project was a painful experience for Baldwin. "I had not suspected," he later wrote, that Lash intended to unveil "private 'indiscretions.'"[2]

The indiscretions to which he referred undoubtedly included affairs outside of his relationship with Evie Preston and perhaps homosexual ones too. Baldwin had always been known as something of a lady's man. As Bill Preston put it, "He loved women. He loved elegant, attractive women," such as Bill's mother and sisters. "I also thought that was a way that he enjoyed life." Bill vanden Heuvel, a friend for more than three decades, also believed that Baldwin "liked the warm company of women." In his later years Baldwin delighted in the company of lovely young women. He told vanden Heuvel that "he'd had a lot of enjoyable sexual relationships with women," including a number who were married.[3]

However, in the midst of his research into Baldwin's life and times, Lash came across information suggesting that Baldwin's sexual life had been varied. Baldwin's sexual preferences are evidenced most clearly in two sets of Lash's interviews: those with Herbert and Bob Baldwin and with Philip Taft. Bob commented that Roger "had a streak of femininity in him" but more strikingly termed the relationship with Doty "a marriage of convenience." Taft, the labor historian and one-time ACLU staffer, told Lash that Baldwin had repeatedly invited him to visit the New Jersey camp. Although reluctant to go, Taft had finally agreed to do so. When Taft got into bed that night, Baldwin came to him and asked, "Can I get into bed with you?" Taft declined the invitation; Baldwin did not pursue the matter and went to sleep by himself.[4]

Fifteen years after Baldwin's death, several individuals discussed with me the issue of Baldwin's sexuality, generally broaching the matter themselves. Alan Reitman, William Butler, Arthur Schlesinger Jr., vanden Heuvel, and Preston all attested to hearing rumors regarding Baldwin's private life and homosexual activity. Reitman recalled that he "did hear something about bisexuality but never in connection with particular individuals." Preston, who had decided against writing his own biography of Baldwin because of family concerns, knew that before Evie's death, Baldwin had been attracted to other women. But Preston also recalled that Baldwin "always had a young man around." Consequently, Preston said, "I speculated whether he had a bisexual side." Vanden Heuvel said that Baldwin had never spoken of any homosexual encounters and added, "I never saw any aspect of it. And I spent as much time with him. With Roger, I never saw any of it." Still, vanden Heuvel recognized that the rift with Lash had developed over precisely this issue.[5]

Butler pointed out that Lash's exploration of the life and times of Roger Baldwin "was getting pretty intimate, getting to discover some things about Roger that nobody had ever heard about." Baldwin, for his part, was upset. He had a daughter and two grandchildren and "didn't want anything derogatory to be published about him." Butler, who believed that Baldwin was strictly heterosexual, was aware of "a lot of rumors that floated around." The rumors were "that Roger had relations with either men or women that he preferred not to discuss, not to have discussed in a public book. When he [Lash] got to that question, Roger said, 'Forget about it,'" and the project was terminated. Given the atmosphere of the times, Schlesinger suggested, Lash was unable to figure out a means to finesse the issue of Baldwin's rumored bisexuality.[6]

While striving to ensure that biographers viewed him in a favorable light, Baldwin continued to wrestle with changes affecting the organization to which he had devoted the better part of his life. On February 25, 1972, in a note to former U.S. attorney general Ramsey Clark, he expressed reservations about another change being proposed inside the ACLU. Increasingly, moves were afoot that would result in the organization's adopting a political stance on various issues, thus discarding the aura of objectivity Baldwin had long sought. True, early on he had attempted to place the ACLU at the service of the struggling American labor movement. However, with the passage of time it had become clear to him that it was politically wiser for the organization to be identified with as much objectivity as possible. Thus he was greatly displeased with proposals for the ACLU to appraise nominees to the Supreme Court. But to Baldwin this did not simply involve a policy question. Rather, objectivity was mandated by the ACLU's constitution, which required "our non-political and nonpartisan character."[7]

The unfolding of the Watergate scandal in 1973 piqued controversy within the ACLU over what stance, if any, the organization should take. Two years earlier the southern California chapter had urged Richard Nixon's impeachment because of his handling of the Vietnam War. Now a growing number of affiliates followed suit, with Ira Glasser, the New York ACLU's executive director, contending that Nixon had "systematically sought to erode those limitations upon presidential power which define our rights." On September

29 the national board voted 51 to 5 to support impeachment proceedings. Executive Director Aryeh Neier and Glasser drafted a full-page ad, costing $12,500, which ran in the *New York Times* on October 14, 1973. Thus the ACLU became the first national organization to urge the president's removal from office.[8]

On November 5 Baldwin wrote to board chairman Ed Ennis expressing concerns about the ACLU action. He would not contest the right to back Nixon's impeachment "on grounds of his wholesale violations of civil liberties." Nor would he have opposed the ACLU's support, relying on evidence of particular concern to the organization, for an inquiry into whether grounds for impeachment existed. However, the ACLU had not demanded an inquiry but rather the ouster of a sitting president. Baldwin appreciated emotional reactions to "such shocking betrayals of trust by a president without principles or moral convictions." Still, he wondered whether that demanded "so emotional a crusade as we have conducted. It isn't like our style; it looks a bit hysterical." Clearly, this was hardly Baldwin's style. True, it had resulted in increases in membership and contributions. However, such an outpouring of support, he reasoned, would not have occurred but for Nixon's defiance of court orders.[9]

In a newspaper interview in March 1974 Baldwin discussed the ACLU decision to call for Nixon's impeachment without revealing any of the internal disputes or anguish that decision had provoked. He referred to presidential abuse of power in relying on "the CIA, the FBI, the Internal Revenue Service, and espionage, burglary, and other criminal acts in order to spy on people or to deny them of their rights." Baldwin deemed the employment of government power to defeat political opponents disreputable. Even he had not appreciated "the web of corruption of civil liberties in the U.S. government."[10]

This was all the more unfortunate, because federal and state governments had adopted many functions of the civil liberties organization. The U.S. Department of Justice contained a Civil Rights Division, a federal Civil Rights Commission existed, and its state counterparts abounded, all seeking to preclude discrimination on the basis of race, religion, and gender. This demonstrated the existence of "a greater awareness of rights than there used to be and more government action to protect them," Baldwin maintained. At the same time, he continued to believe, "The courts are our ultimate protection."[11]

The next year witnessed the publication of a volume of essays commissioned by the ACLU to honor its first half-century. Entitled *The Pulse of Freedom:*

American Liberties, 1920–1970s and edited by Alan Reitman, the ACLU's associate director, the book contained an essay on the 1930s by Jerold S. Auerbach, a professor of history at Brandeis University who had written the well-regarded *Labor and Liberty: The La Follette Committee and the New Deal.* Auerbach referred to the statement made by Baldwin in 1938 that the struggles for civil rights for blacks, religious liberties, academic freedom, and freedom from censorship were "on the whole trifling in national effect compared with the fight for the right of labor to organize." But Baldwin was most troubled by Auerbach's recounting of the 1940 decision to expel Elizabeth Gurley Flynn from the ACLU's national board and his analysis of that action. Consequently, in a virtually unprecedented move Baldwin demanded the right to frame a rejoinder to the Auerbach essay. A revised edition of *The Pulse of Freedom* contained Baldwin's effort to set the historical record straight.[12]

In Baldwin's estimation Auerbach afforded disproportionate attention to "this single internal dispute." This reflected Auerbach's belief, Baldwin reasoned, that the ACLU had discarded its principles in adopting the 1940 Resolution and refusing leadership roles to those who championed "dictatorships and anti-democratic movements." As he had nearly four decades earlier, Baldwin attempted to refute the charge. "No principles were changed," he proclaimed, while denying that the resolution was hatched by certain board members, including him. Rather, "it was the result of a situation long debated." Once more he acknowledged having written the controversial document; however, Baldwin insisted that he had done so "at the request of some Board members."[13]

Consequently, "the author's account is incorrect, biased and misleading," Baldwin charged. Moreover, he pointed out, the resolution had been in effect since its passage. Auerbach was also incorrect, Baldwin stated, in arguing that a deal had been cut with Martin Dies for the ACLU to discard "Communist influences" if the congressman stopped attacking the organization. In fact, Baldwin wrote, Arthur Garfield Hays and Morris Ernst had sought the meeting with Dies to ensure the House committee would abide by "a simple civil liberties requirement of fair hearing." Dies's subsequent decision to exonerate the organization, Baldwin wrote, was not the by-product of any deal; it resulted from Baldwin's session with committee investigators.[14]

The 1940 Resolution had been drafted shortly after the announcement of the Nazi-Soviet pact, Baldwin reminded readers, which produced a "strong feeling of betrayal of democratic principles by the Communists." Then, in biting and somewhat illogical fashion Baldwin charged, "The author thinks that they [communists] still should have been welcome allies in civil liberties. To have been anti-Communist then, he concluded, was to be anti-civil liberties. He does not say the same for being anti-Nazi."[15]

In Bill Preston's estimation Baldwin "had his story down." Thus he was determined to insert "a counter-argument into the historical page." While this seemed pretty astonishing to an historian like Preston, he also recognized that "if you look at a guy who's willing to be defamed and attacked, you've got to have an ego structure that's . . . big." Baldwin certainly had a sizable ego, Preston acknowledged. Otherwise, "he couldn't have done that much."[16]

With an ever-watchful eye on posterity's evaluation of his life story, Baldwin in 1975 produced a five-page note stating why the last twenty-five years had been "the most significant . . . most satisfying and exhilarating." He referred to his continued involvement with the ACLU, particularly in the field of international affairs. He discussed his support for an international bill of rights and his "enthusiasm for world order." Those were based, he declared, on "the two moral principles that had dominated my whole public outlook, freedom and equality." He reasoned that "if the greatest revolution in human affairs, the abolition of war, could be possible . . . then the second greatest, the end of subjection by one people over another was at hand." The cold war struggles had thwarted the effort to turn UN ideals into reality, as had the revolt against colonialism and the arms race, yet he remained as optimistic as when he had begun his second career a quarter-century earlier.[17]

In the spring of 1976 Baldwin was deeply distressed by a decision made by the ACLU board. The issue that had been bandied about for a full decade now came to a head: rescision of Elizabeth Gurley Flynn's expulsion. To Baldwin, the issue involved "the propriety, indeed morality, of Communist Party members in our leadership." But as Frank Haiman, a member of the national board and president of the Illinois board, later reflected, it was clear that "Roger's personal sensitivities were wrapped up in the situation."[18]

On February 1, 1974, seventeen members of the ACLU National Advisory Council sent a letter to the national board declaring that "no useful reason appears for reopening at this late date" the decision to expel Flynn. The signatories to the letter—who included U.S. Rep. Robert F. Drinan of Massachusetts, who was also a Catholic priest; the actor Melvyn Douglas; the columnist and university professor Max Lerner; Arthur Schlesinger Jr.; and

Baldwin—had gotten word that George Slaff of the southern California chapter again sought to defang the 1940 Resolution. At its April meeting the national board readily accepted Slaff's proposal, which stated, "No member of any political party or any other association in the United States is ineligible for membership on the Board of Directors of the Union or of any affiliate or on the staffs thereof merely by reason of being a member of such party or association."[19]

In November 1975 Slaff again sought a rescision of the 1940 Resolution. Baldwin tried to mobilize support in opposition to the proposal, warning Edward Ennis on February 23, 1976, that Flynn's reinstatement would be viewed as a reversal of long-standing ACLU policy and, consequently, would have disastrous repercussions. Writing to Norman Dorsen four days later, Baldwin revealed that he favored extending the exclusionary policy to prevent Klansmen, anti-Semites, and communists from joining the ACLU.[20]

Flynn's reinstatement, Frank Haiman contended, would amount to "a symbolic act of self-flagellation for which I see no rhyme or reason." The ACLU board in early April voted 32–18 to accept the motion reinstating Flynn. Aryeh Neier, the ACLU director, acknowledged that Baldwin must be aggrieved "to see your prodigal child behaving in this way." Alan F. Westin lamented, "What was done on Elizabeth Gurley Flynn seemed to me right out of the history rectification program of George Orwell's *1984*." The action, Westin declared, "strikes me as a total confusion of constitutional and organizational principles."[21]

That same year Peggy Lamson's book, *Roger Baldwin: Founder of the American Civil Liberties Union*, was published, complete with glowing blurbs from Arthur Schlesinger Jr.; Drinan; and Alan Reitman, ACLU associate director. Frequently illuminating, Lamson's work was largely a series of annotated interviews, with a running exchange between the author and her subject. Lamson's completion of the project followed numerous other attempts to capture Baldwin's life and times, all terminated largely because of his unwillingness to divulge personal information.[22]

But Lamson's book pleased Baldwin little better than one by Joe Lash might have. She appeared, he complained, to "regard me as an odd species to be analyzed with the condescion [*sic*] of superior good sense. Peggy professed to love me but she managed to convey the impression of a character I told her I would not like if he were somebody else!"[23]

Revelations of ACLU contacts with the FBI, made public in the fall of 1977, also disturbed Baldwin. That relationship could be traced in the nearly forty-two thousand pages of documents just released to the ACLU under the Freedom of Information Act. The massive FBI file demonstrated the extent of the agency's probe of the ACLU and its predecessor, the National Civil Liberties Bureau, over six decades. The FBI had "infiltrated, burglarized, and wiretapped" the ACLU since its founding in 1920. As Rob Warden and Bob Tamarkin, reporters for the *Chicago Daily News*, wrote, "FBI 'confidential operatives' infiltrated the organization at every level, providing detailed reports on closed meetings, membership lists, financial contributions and—in some cases—copies of private correspondence between ACLU officials and other private citizens."[24]

With his eye on history once more, Baldwin joined with Alan Westin to present a critique of ACLU-FBI relations. In an article that appeared in the November–December 1977 issue of the *Civil Liberties Review*, the two men, in conversational fashion, concentrated on the early years of the ACLU's existence. The ACLU had no idea, Baldwin concluded, that such extensive surveillance was taking place. Characteristically, he remarked, "If we had known, we would have gone directly to higher authority to stop it." But he also expressed belief that before World War II, the ACLU appeared to have little reason to complain about FBI operations. Moreover, Baldwin noted, Hoover opposed the internment of Japanese Americans and Japanese nationals during the war. By contrast, during the early postwar period Hoover was fixated on the red peril, which had led to ACLU protests of the FBI director's actions.[25]

Even at this point Baldwin viewed the ACLU-FBI relationship in a favorable light. He still believed that his own association with Hoover, and that of other ACLU leaders, had possessed the kind of leavening influence on top government officials he long sought to wield.

When asked what the files collected during his tenure as ACLU director suggested, Baldwin replied, "The FBI should not be concerned at all with the political opinions and activities of citizens." The "improper political surveillance" the ACLU had early condemned had been curbed for some time but then returned in full force "during the Cold War hysteria of the 1950s," and again in the 1960s when the civil rights, antiwar, and student protest movements were targeted. The recent Watergate scandals demanded recognition "that a democracy and a political police cannot live comfortably together."[26]

Grabbing the public's attention, however, were clear reports of ongoing exchanges between five ACLU leaders and the FBI during the 1940s and 1950s. Irving Ferman, who headed the Washington office of the ACLU from

1952 to 1959, was said to have regularly delivered information about ACLU members to the FBI. In a letter to Reitman, Baldwin wondered why such a big deal was being made "of our FBI relations." In his estimation "they add up over the years to so slight a part of our activities that this treatment distorts their importance." And as Aryeh Neier had reported to the press, ACLU members had scarcely reacted to the revelations. Baldwin deemed the "wholly personal conduct" to be "so exceptional" in the ACLU's long history and so lacking in effect on its campaign for civil liberties "that it should be discounted as personal aberrations."[27]

Nevertheless, the ACLU established a special commission headed by Shepard Lee to examine the relationship between the ACLU and the FBI. On May 5, 1978, Baldwin sent a memorandum to the committee, asserting, "The great error that tainted the ACLU record was to seek or give information to a police agency about the ACLU's internal affairs." Admittedly, "several ACLU officers crossed the line of propriety in dealing with the FBI secretly about Communist infiltration, and compounded the grave error by not reporting it to the elected officers or board." Still, Baldwin reasoned that no guidelines were required to prevent a recurrence of such errors. Rather, common sense should dictate a different course of behavior.[28]

The ACLU, he argued, should be willing to provide the FBI and other law enforcement agencies with "information within our field when asked, but not to express opinions about persons or movements." As for past dealings, Baldwin believed that the ACLU should not seek additional information, particularly involving regional offices. After all, FBI documents were highly suspect, "and we risk damage to persons who may be unfairly named." He considered the cooperation that had occurred between the ACLU and the FBI short-lived and confined to the Washington office.[29]

As the ACLU special commission moved to wrap up its report, Shepard Lee wrote to Baldwin, declaring, "One thing emerges clearly. You were the hero of the era." The report would find, Lee explained, "that according to all the evidence available to the commission, Roger Baldwin never applied to the FBI, or asked the FBI for clearance of any individual." Still, Lee felt compelled to seek reconfirmation from Baldwin: "Did you ever have occasion to request clearance of any individual from the FBI during your tenure with ACLU?"[30]

Somewhat testily, Baldwin stated that he had already made clear his disapproval "of raking up the unhappy past of some of our misguided officials." He was opposed to the hearing on the ACLU's association with the FBI because of its likely effect on both the ACLU and the individuals singled out for criticism. Baldwin then sharply argued,

> I do not think we gain anything for our public now in saying who are the good guys and who the bad. Of course we are the good guys, and those bad guys are all gone. But our members and board trusted them as they trust us now. Can we guarantee that all our staff will remain faithful to that trust? And future members of the staff also?
>
> You ask me to make a declaration of my own integrity. I must reply that I am not prepared to proclaim my innocence or my loyalty or my virtues; the mere suggestion to do so is offensive. It raises the suspicion that without such a declaration I might be guilty. I am sure that on reflection you would not wish to act on such an assumption.
>
> It is enough for me to say, as I have, that I was shocked that my colleagues asked the aid of the FBI to investigate our own members' political associations.
>
> I regret to say that I think no useful service is rendered by a report at this late date on the misdeeds of so long ago.[31]

The ACLU report pinpointed Freeman for the sharpest criticism but also asserted that Morris Ernst—from whom Baldwin had become estranged because of the attorney's relationship with Ramon Trujillo before he was deposed as dictator of the Dominican Republic—had "maintained a friendly and somewhat clubby relationship with the FBI." Furthermore, Ernst had delivered ACLU documents and information about organizational activities to J. Edgar Hoover. ACLU historian Sam Walker has charged that the report "pulled its punches on one point": the depiction of Baldwin's relationship with the FBI as "adversarial, otherwise cordial but distant." Walker correctly insists that Baldwin sought to maintain "a friendly relationship with Hoover." And he points to archival material, which "indicates that Baldwin actually identified someone to the Justice Department as a 'fellow traveler.'" Thus, as Walker sees it, "he did 'name names.'" Baldwin's actions were little different, the report failed to acknowledge, than those of the ACLU figures it criticized.[32]

Baldwin's public image meant a great deal to him, as attested by his determination to shape the historical record. For decades he painstakingly compiled papers associated with numerous organizational activities, especially civil liberties groups. He also produced multiple, and sometimes varied, accounts of individuals, events, and developments of both a professional and personal nature. His versions of lifetime experiences were sometimes insightful but were frequently sanitized and dispassionately delivered. Baldwin obviously appreciated the magnitude of certain campaigns he was involved with and was fully aware of his own importance as an epochal figure in the pantheon of American liberalism and radicalism.

CHAPTER TWENTY-SIX

Traveling Hopefully

While the ACLU's special commission was examining its ties to the FBI, controversy beset the organization once more, but this time Baldwin was in full accord with decisions made by the organization's leadership. In late April 1977 the ACLU's Chicago office fostered a public outcry when staff attorney David Goldberger showed up in the Cook County Chancery Court representing Frank Collin, a member of the American Nazi Party determined to march through Skokie, Illinois. About thirty thousand Jews lived in the Chicago suburb, and the ACLU's defense of Collin on classic First Amendment grounds was troubling for many. Eventually, thousands resigned from the ACLU, and financial ruin threatened.[1]

In a twelve-page essay Baldwin reflected on the Skokie case. He opened by stating that the ACLU, since its inception, had been dedicated to defending the rights of all "without partisanship or favoritism." To Baldwin Skokie was yet another in a long line of ACLU cases that engendered great passion. Thus he was surprised that many members, Jews and non-Jews alike, had chosen to withdraw from the organization "in protest over an extreme but traditional test of principle," as Baldwin put it. For nearly six decades the ACLU had championed freedom of speech and assemblage for "all sorts of unpopular and hated people," including "Anarchists, Communists, Fascists, Nazis, Klansmen, religious bigots, or purveyors of smut," he noted. And American Jews had always backed the ACLU in its defense of such groups. National Jewish organizations generally had failed to oppose the ACLU defense of Fritz Kuhn and his German-American Bund in the 1930s, the anti-Semitic Gerald L. K. Smith and Father Charles Coughlin throughout World War II, or George Lincoln Rockwell and American Nazis during the postwar period.[2]

In Baldwin's estimation the Illinois ACLU, supported by the national office, had remained true to Voltaire's dictum: "I may detest what you say but I will defend to the death your right to say it." Baldwin also referred to Ben Franklin's observation: "Of course the abuses of free speech should be suppressed but to whom dare we entrust the power to do so?" Such a warning had been heeded by the ACLU, coupled with Thomas Jefferson's exhortation: "It is time enough for the rightful purposes of government to intervene when words break out into overt acts against peace and good order."[3]

In February 1978 a federal district court declared unconstitutional three Skokie ordinances that essentially sought to preclude the American Nazis from marching in that community. The First Amendment, the ruling asserted, "means that government has no power to restrict expression because of its message, its ideas, its subject matter, or its content." After the appellate court affirmed that decision, Collin backed down, opting instead to gather with his fellow Nazis at Chicago's Federal Plaza. Thoroughly outnumbered by angry opponents, the Nazis and their demonstration lasted a mere fifteen minutes.[4]

In the midst of the Skokie controversy the ACLU hosted the National Convocation on Free Speech, on June 13, 1978, at the New York Hilton, attended by senators Edward M. Kennedy of Massachusetts and Jacob Javits of New York, and former U.S. attorney general Ramsey Clark, among others. The highlight of the gathering was a stirring address delivered by Baldwin that was filmed by John Avildsen, director of the immensely popular film *Rocky*.

Avildsen had called the New York chapter office and offered, "If there's anything I can do." Eventually, he shot hundreds of thousands of feet of film, which he used for a documentary, *Traveling Hopefully*. While he initiated the project intending to provide a broad overview of the ACLU, he quickly determined that its founder was more interesting still. *Traveling Hopefully* included interviews with Baldwin conducted by the Hollywood producer Norman Lear, the author Gail Sheehy, and Arthur Schlesinger Jr. In the film Baldwin defiantly informs Sheehy, "I'm a radical in the sense that the Bill of Rights is radical" and because he was a pacifist. Somewhat disingenuously, he denied the long-standing charge that the ACLU was originally designed to protect unions and the Left. He spoke of freedom of speech, of the press, and of association as deriving from natural rights.[5]

Baldwin tells Lear, "I confine my religious beliefs to humanity." At the same time he terms the Sermon on the Mount a "great declaration of love" and the fount of all pacifism. Demonstrating what still made him vibrant at the age of ninety-five, he insists, "Every day you have to live with hope for the next day." He expresses some pride in having beaten insurance company actuarial predictions and declares, "I think you have to have a basic sense of wonder about life." The film closes with Baldwin quoting Robert Louis Stevenson's belief in the importance of an optimistic outlook, followed by his own declaration: "I've been traveling hopefully with you for all these years. I'm still traveling hopefully. So is the ACLU." He expresses his belief that humankind is "beginning to approach a tolerable world of peace, order, and justice."[6]

Operating behind the scenes, supposedly in an unobtrusive manner, Baldwin maintained his efforts to influence the direction of the organization he had founded. In 1978 Aryeh Neier resigned as executive director, and Ira Glasser, then head of the ACLU's New York branch, became a candidate to succeed him. Supported by many ACLU insiders, Glasser possessed "a well-deserved reputation for flaunting a sort of New York street kid persona," as he put it. Consequently, there were concerns about how Glasser would play in Peoria.[7]

Although no one directly expressed concerns that he was Jewish, Glasser later reflected that parochialism suffused the supposedly sophisticated New York crowd. Some wondered whether a Jew could lead an already unpopular organization and communicate forcefully and effectively with different groups. Glasser heard through the grapevine—although not directly from Baldwin—that Baldwin "had quietly—which was the way he did it—raised the question with some of the leadership on the board. As they put it: 'Is he too New York?'" There were those who, long familiar with Baldwin's machinations, believed that they could discern his fine hand in the question about Glasser. But Glasser never found any evidence of such an attitude in his relationship with Baldwin, finding it only to be "sweet, cordial, friendly."[8]

As Glasser said, Baldwin clearly "was not somebody to disengage very easily, he was around all the time." When Glasser first was named ACLU executive director in the fall of 1978, Baldwin invited him to lunch from time to time. "There are a number of things I have to talk to you about!" Baldwin would exclaim over the phone. He would be happy, Glasser responded, to go down to Greenwich Village to meet Baldwin, who invariably fired back, "Oh, no! I'll walk." He then proceeded on to midtown to the ACLU national head-quarters. When he arrived he would ask Glasser, "Do you like Chinese food?" At the restaurant Baldwin would read the menu without glasses and order the spiciest dishes. Always, he showed up in a three-piece suit with a watch fob, very much the man of the 1920s. Baldwin never understood Glasser's more casual appearance, "never quite trusted it," Glasser said. At lunch Baldwin inevitably took from his vest pocket a small slip of paper that contained a list of issues to discuss with his guest. Some involved substantive matters, but most related to the structure or financial status of the organization he was so identified with.[9]

In 1979, in the midst of a spiraling New York real estate market, the ACLU board paid $750,000 for a terribly dilapidated building in Times Square that had been unoccupied for three years. The rent for the ACLU offices was about to be raised from $5.50 a square foot, which covered cleaning and electricity, to $25 a square foot, for the space alone. A similar situation compelled the NAACP to relocate to Baltimore. Shortly after Glasser became executive director, the ACLU leadership too began searching for a new location. Edward Ennis, former board chairman, had offered $250,000 as seed money, but the Times Square building eventually required renovations that amounted to more than $1 million. Nervous about Glasser's decision, Baldwin asked, "Can you afford it?" On various occasions, still distrustful of the organization's growth, he would drop in to Glasser's office, remind him, "Stay solvent!" and depart.[10]

Glasser was always impressed by Baldwin's continued interest in ACLU operations, which the younger man considered the key to Baldwin's longevity and passion. He would phone Glasser and ask, "Ira, do you see what they're doing? What are we doing about it?" Or he would call and exclaim, "Now, keep me posted!" However, Glasser recalled, Baldwin never showed up at meetings to complain, "You're not doing enough." To Glasser, "he was just very engaged up until the very end, and that was a tremendously endearing and inspiring kind of quality to see, as a young person, in a man that old. There was no flagging of interest or passion." As befitting someone who had created the kind of organization he had, Baldwin seemed to possess "a strength and a resolve and a persistence and a stamina and an energy and qualities of relentlessness that I don't think ordinary people have," Glasser said.[11]

When Glasser informed others who had known Baldwin far longer that he "never felt blindsided or anything," they inevitably "would grin at me with a knowing look and tell me some anecdote about, 'Well, he wasn't so sweet and benign back then!'" Glasser heard "tales that this sweet old man . . . was really quite ruthless and authoritarian in the way he ran the organization. There were a lot of people who didn't like him."[12]

When he had turned eighty-six, Baldwin had yet to experience aches, pains, or disabilities and reported being "ridiculously healthy." He admitted to having "slowed down a bit" and to be suffering from a shortness of breath on climbing too many stairs—the by-product of emphysema, induced by a near-lifetime of smoking. He no longer skated, having broken his leg doing so back in 1961. Nevertheless, he still hiked, rode horses, and swam on occasion. Within two years he reported having lost fifteen pounds and regaining stamina in climbing or walking around town. His eyesight remained astounding and his hearing "good enough," although his wrinkled skin led him to resort more to long-sleeved clothing. He was troubled by somewhat more frequent memory lapses. Still, Trude Lash considered him "really remarkable in the way he does not give in to infirmities."[13]

Baldwin's brothers Herb and Bob both viewed him as constantly on the go. When Roger visited his home, Bob asked him, "When are you going to stop long enough to reflect?" Bob thought that his oldest brother demanded an audience. Herb contended that Roger—to whom he referred as "quite an energetic rascal"—was "awfully proud of his energy—of his age. [He] will say, 'No pill.' He may be too proud to admit he has low moments." Roger strove to dominate conversations, Herb believed, by talking "twice as loud." Bob's children thought their uncle was terrific but considered him "quite a name-dropper." Bob believed this was nothing new: "He did like big names. He always liked them."[14]

Joseph Lash saw other contradictions abounding in Baldwin. In his advancing years Baldwin, Lash said, had "reverted to a personal style that was appropriate to a Back Bay Yankee." His disdain for nude bathing along the beach at Chilmark could be viewed as "arbitrary and outrageous." And Lash thought Baldwin behaved like the protagonist in *Life with Father*.[15]

Increasingly, monetary and health concerns, which had little troubled Baldwin, began to crop up. On a few occasions in the 1970s he asked for a readjustment in his $3,600 annual salary, which had not withstood the ravages of runaway inflation. On November 1, 1973, Associate Director Alan Reitman acknowledged that the ACLU had been remiss in not making some kind of adjustment. The executive committee, he informed Baldwin, had upped the salary to $6,000, with an additional $1,000 allocated for expenses. At one point Baldwin sought to have the issue of increased compensation withdrawn in order that his personal finances not be examined. The salary increase went through, but within five years Baldwin again sought an adjustment to his now $7,200 salary because of the double-digit inflation that the United States had experienced throughout much of the decade. He hoped for another $2,400 increase.[16]

On turning ninety Baldwin announced that his shortness of breath had returned. Now he was unable to walk more than thirty stairs or a mile without taking a break. On the other hand, he no longer experienced the recurring leg cramps that had pained him for some time, and medication was helping the edema in his ankles and legs. His memory also seemed sharper than it had been for some time.[17]

Three years later Baldwin both expressed satisfaction with "so little loss of powers" and acknowledged that his physical activities had slackened. He was short of breath whenever he climbed stairs, went on extended walks, lifted anything, or even stood for more than a few minutes. Happily, his spirits were invariably good, although he was often lonely and "am too often alone" since Evie Baldwin's death. Still, he retained his enthusiasm and interest in his life's work: "the drama for human rights."[18]

Having reached ninety-four, however, Baldwin now referred to himself as a semi-invalid, incapacitated to a large degree by the emphysema. Beginning in November 1977, he had "been really crippled and under treatment," forced to stay for a couple of weeks in the hospital. His heart was weakened, placing a strain on his lungs, and his ankles were swollen. He still retained his great vitality, remaining "alert, interested in life," with his faculties as sharp as ever. He was, he recognized, "just lucky to survive so long so well. If there is reason in it maybe it is just a cheerful nature, an optimism, and an acceptance of life and death—and—old age—without fear." In an interview with the *Los Angeles Times* in April 1978 he said he was still able to canoe and ride horseback but could no longer climb mountains. On February 2, 1979, in an interview with Robert MacNeil and Jim Lehrer of PBS, Baldwin demonstrated his continued feistiness and dedication to the civil liberties movement. Near the end of the program Baldwin said that he cared about unresolved civil liberties issues. But, as he acknowledged, "I don't have to act and do anything about it and demonstrate it, the way I used to have to do it. Any time any of these incidents happened, I used to run to the fire right away. I was my own fire department." Later that year Norman Dorsen, the ACLU chairman, said that "(true to his form) Roger has not hesitated to raise questions about the way things are going at the ACLU." Baldwin continued to exclaim on numerous occasions, "I was present at the creation!" lest anyone forget he had been in on the founding of the organization.[19]

He remained a conservative force within the ACLU, as he "resisted modernization with every fiber of his being," Florence Isbell recalled. In the spring of 1979 Isbell wanted to send out a fund-raising letter over his signature. Then she had second thoughts and told Ira Glasser, "Let's not do this. We'll never get him to sign off on it." She then remembered how Baldwin edited press releases. "He'll sit down and write something himself and it will be terrible, because he doesn't know anything about fund-raising." Nevertheless, Glasser sent Isbell to show Baldwin the copy and obtain his signature. Baldwin examined the letter and scrawled comments and questions. As she had forewarned, he exclaimed, "That's ridiculous! You ought to get rid of these people and just keep the influential ones." The four-and-a-half page document was too long. "If you reduce it to one page," he promised, "I'll sign it, no matter what it says on the one page." She refused to do so, telling him, "I'm not going to do that. That isn't the way it's done. We've got scientific studies that show that this works better than that." Baldwin became quite angry and defensive, and Isbell thought that he was going to call her a whippersnapper, as in times past.[20]

In May 1979 Baldwin suffered a crushing blow with the death of his daughter, Helen, at only forty-one years of age, of kidney cancer. Three months of chemotherapy had followed an unsuccessful operation. Like her mother, Helen asked that her ashes be buried at the Windy Gates estate.[21]

In one sense Baldwin seemed to possess "an unusual capacity to keep going, not to let up and not stop," his stepson Carl said. Such an approach, Carl suggested, "saved his sanity." But then, Roger Baldwin was not "the kind of person to allow feelings to really take over." Still, the loss of Helen was devastating, and the depression that had afflicted him at earlier points now recurred. As Norman Dorsen recalled, "The only time I ever heard him with defeat in his voice was when he called to tell me . . . 'My baby is dying.'"[22]

His older granddaughter, Francesca Mannoni, eloquently recalled how her mother's fatal illness affected her grandfather:

> He just seemed incredibly tired, much quieter, very sort of sullen and withdrawn. Sort of introverted, which he was not. He was an extrovert. He was a big, loud, social, humanly connected person.

He was about community, interconnections with people. If he didn't have that dynamic at home, he was looking for it in some place, like the Barn House. And that period in the hospital . . . I don't think he could really face it. His energies were just inside. He didn't try to console anyone else. . . . It was just the last straw.[23]

In addition, a draining legal battle ensued over possession of the Greenwich Village townhouse; it pitted Piero Mannoni against Roger Baldwin and Bill Butler, executor of Helen's estate. Her will granted Mannoni only a modest sum of cash, with the remainder left in trust to their two daughters. An enraged Mannoni, who undoubtedly had hoped that at long last he would be able to remove Baldwin from West 11th Street, determined to contest the will. That only infuriated Baldwin, who reasoned, "This is what Helen wanted. If Helen wanted it, that must be respected." Moreover, her father believed there was a common understanding that he would be allowed to live in the apartment until his own death. He became very upset when Mannoni, in Baldwin's words, "threw him out." Thus family feelings were unfolding, Francesca believed, "at sort of a fever pitch." Mannoni's initial move to seek legal counsel also disturbed Butler, who did not consider it "a very New England way" of handling matters. Unfortunately for Mannoni, he had earlier agreed to a quasi-prenuptial contract that Baldwin and Butler had convinced Helen to demand. Mannoni, who might have been able to claim some kind of life estate in the property, finally decided not to pursue the matter. As a consequence, Butler, as executor of the estate, retained control of the townhouse. Unhappy about it all, Mannoni returned to Europe, where he worked as an art restorer, spending most of his time in Rome or Sardinia. Baldwin stayed with Carl for about five weeks, then took up residence at the New Jersey farm in Oakland, with Roger Jr. and his wife, Pat.[24]

The death of her mother and the departure of her grandfather from the Greenwich Village townhouse were unsettling to Francesca Mannoni. Having dealt with her grandfather intimately on an everyday basis, she now talked to him infrequently. Yet she knew that her father and grandfather could not get along. More clearly than before, she thought to herself, "Grandpa's not just Grandpa. He's this man who got in my father's way."[25]

Baldwin continued his annual excursion to the Caribbean, but students less often spotted him at breakfast in the cafeteria at the student center or at the faculty club. He continued to buy the *New York Times* and the *San Juan Star* at the law school. However, his seminar on civil rights had not been offered since the winter of 1975; his friend Jaime Benitez was no longer university president. For a time Baldwin continued to work for the Puerto Rican Civil Rights Commission. At first he took lunch wherever he could and looked forward to dinners with friends. On weekends he could be found on the beaches or in the mountains, usually with one or another of the families that viewed him as a kind of adopted grandfather. The American kids referred to him as "Roger," while the Puerto Ricans called him "Professor." His Spanish, he confessed, was "still low-grade"; he could read it easily enough but half the time was unable to comprehend answers to questions he had himself posed.[26]

Now, in the winter after Helen's death, he was back in Puerto Rico and reported to friends, "I feel completely at home after 25 years of winter visits." He was fortunate to have been befriended by Herbert and Nancy Brown, a young couple who had invited him to stay with them as he had the previous year. "My machinery still works well enough not to burden anyone," Baldwin wrote, although he was experiencing increased shortness of breath due to circulatory problems. Now he could walk no more than a block without having to take a break. Luckily, cars and taxis were plentiful, "so I get around."[27]

His day opened with breakfast on the Browns' front porch, which faced Santurce from a hilly vantage point. Birds, trees bedecked with flowers, and palms surrounded the two-story concrete house, which contained a downstairs bedroom and bath for Baldwin. The Browns and Baldwin watched the *CBS Evening News* and read the *San Juan Star* before Herbert Brown headed for his law office, and Nancy Brown, a flight attendant, took off for a flight to New York. Baldwin would spend the day reading, writing letters, meeting with the Puerto Rican Civil Rights Commission, or visiting the nearby university library. In the evenings the three shared drinks and dined in or went to eat at a restaurant. Afterward they listened to records, attended a movie or symphony concert, or simply talked. On weekends they visited Herbert Brown's parents, who lived in the mountains. Baldwin also saw old friends, forty of whom came to his ninety-sixth birthday party. Occasionally, he went to the beach but now could be heard to say, "I do better on land than water."[28]

By the end of the year the chronic emphysema had confined him to his farm; his voice was raspier than ever, his hands more gnarled, and his face more weathered. Nevertheless, a reporter insisted, "His mind is as active and as clear as the river his home overlooks." And Baldwin readily criticized the existing political and economic system in the United States, just as he had back in the 1920s: "It is not defensible, it's a system of greed and personal power, it's a very selfish system."[29]

In January 1981 an ailing Baldwin received the Medal of Freedom Award, along with veteran CBS anchorman Walter Cronkite, among others. The citation read, "Roger Nash Baldwin is a leader in the field of civil rights and a leader in the field of civil liberties. He is a national resource, and an international one as well, an inspiration to those of us who have fought for human rights, a saint to those for whom he has gained them." Cronkite told Baldwin that he deemed it "far more important [than the medal] that I was in the same 'class' of Medal recipients as yourself." Next to Baldwin's accomplishments, Cronkite observed, "the rest of your fellow honorees pale in significance. There should be an even more special award for you."[30]

Baldwin, of course, remained as testy as ever. On hearing that Baldwin was to receive the Medal of Freedom, Bill Preston congratulated him and asked, "Well, how are you feeling?" Baldwin replied, "Well, Bill, as good as expected for a man with four fatal illnesses."[31]

He had recently been hospitalized because of double pneumonia and was distressed that his hair had entirely whitened and that he now needed a cane to walk. He moved slowly and painfully, his face was "a patchwork of lines," the Los Angeles Times reported, and his voice rasped even more than before.[32]

Because of his health, a ceremony honoring him as a Medal of Freedom recipient was held at his New Jersey farm. Bill Butler, now chairman of the International Commission of Jurists in Geneva, spoke of Baldwin's mesmerizing influence that had led Butler to become involved in the human rights crusade and called Baldwin "the father of us all, the Dean of the Human Rights convention."[33]

Bill vanden Heuvel—who had just completed a term as deputy U.S. ambassador to the UN in Geneva—referred to Baldwin's life as one "filled with honor, challenge, love, commitment, adventure, idealism, struggle and singular energy." Now the Medal of Freedom was being bestowed on "this son of New England who sang for Harvard with the diction of a Brahmin, the gusto of a revolutionary, and who took the seed of Thoreau's thought and Emerson's wisdom and caused it to grow in the soil of the 20th Century," vanden Heuvel said.[34]

After Baldwin expressed appreciation to President Jimmy Carter for having honored him so, Dorsen spoke briefly. Reading from a 1921 report, he quoted Baldwin on the disillusionment of liberals, revolutionaries, and reactionaries with the ACLU. No matter, Baldwin had written, the ACLU would strive "more vigorously than ever, confident in the soundness of our position."[35]

The ushering in of the Reagan administration depressed many younger civil liberties proponents, including Ira Glasser, who despaired that the Warren Court was over, whereas former segregationist Strom Thurmond now headed the Senate Judiciary Committee. Like his younger colleagues, Baldwin eloquently and passionately expressed concerns about the present state of affairs. At the same time he possessed an optimism that Glasser saw as "the wellspring of his life. It came from his having had a longer perspective than the rest of us." Baldwin looked back to bleaker times still, such as the 1920s when the ACLU had originated, Jim Crow was entrenched, the U.S. Supreme Court had yet to strike down any legislation infringing on the First Amendment, and the right of workers to organize was in question. Thus, no matter how threatening present circumstances appeared, Baldwin "was looking at a tide that was so clearly and irreversibly, it seems, in his direction, that the changes that—that anyone that he had fought with, in 1920, over these issues—that other person was the one to be pessimistic, not he," Glasser said.[36]

Baldwin's optimism was energizing to young vulnerable ACLU members. He told them of the organization's founding, when forty or so people had gathered in a cold New York hotel room, determined to safeguard the Bill of Rights. With little support, a hostile Court, and unfavorable popular sentiments prevailing, they determined to act. Consequently, if the founders had not been depressed or prone to inaction, the newer generation had no right to be, "a momentary setback in a panorama of victory" notwithstanding. To Glasser, Baldwin "was just terrific at laying that out, you know, without being overbearing about it. It was just part of what he projected. He was bright-eyed."[37]

In March 1981 Glasser arrived at his office shortly after nine in the morning to discover his phone ringing. "Ira, it's Roger!" the voice on the other line bellowed out. "Did you see what they did in Arkansas?" He was referring to the passage of a creation statute by the Arkansas legislature. Glasser replied in the affirmative, and Baldwin demanded, "Well, what are you doing about it?" Glasser responded, "Roger, it's only ten after nine!" For Glasser, because of Baldwin's earlier involvement with the Scopes case, this "was sort of like getting a call in the middle of the night from Thomas Jefferson telling you that you had been insufficient in your protection of his First Amendment." The ACLU eventually challenged the Arkansas legislation, and Glasser had Baldwin deliver the statement at the press conference.[38]

A few months later Baldwin again called Glasser to find out how the case was unfolding. Glasser answered, "Well, you know, this case is actually a little more complicated than the Tennessee case." Arkansas had required that Genesis be taught alongside evolution in science classes. Informed that ten lawyers were working on the case, Baldwin cried out, "Ten lawyers! We only needed two!" Glasser said, "Yeah, Roger, but you lost." Baldwin laughed, harrumphed, and bellowed, "Well, keep me posted!" and banged the receiver down. In early 1982 the 8th U.S. Circuit Court of Appeals deemed the Arkansas law unconstitutional, declaring that it was intended to bring "the Biblical version of creation into the public school curricula." As Sam Walker has written, the issue was hardly settled—a similar measure soon appeared on the books in Louisiana. The U.S. Supreme Court, in *Edwards v. Aguillard* (1987), struck it down too.[39]

During his last visit, Glasser found Baldwin sitting in his easy chair, reading Henry Kissinger's massive autobiography. Although considerably more infirm than before, Baldwin insisted on getting up to pour sherry. Glasser asked him, "So, Roger, how you doing?" "I'm fine," he replied. "I'm having a little trouble breathing, but other than that I'm fine."[40]

In the last few months of his life Baldwin had orchestrated his memorial service, to be held at the Community Church on East 35th Street. A Unitarian-Congregationalist-Transcendentalist church, it was fitting for one who was both a self-professed agnostic and "a class-B Christian," Bill Butler claimed. Butler was with Baldwin when he wrote a speech to be delivered at the service. Baldwin told Butler, "Let everyone say all these nice things about me, and when the last guy says the last word, I want you to stand up, and say, 'Just a minute. Roger has asked me to give you this message,' and read it."[41]

On Wednesday, August 26, 1981, at 7:50 A.M. Roger Baldwin died at the age of ninety-seven at Valley Hospital in Ridgewood, New Jersey, near Dell Brook. He had been hospitalized since Sunday. Bill vanden Heuvel believed that his friend—in typical fashion—had orchestrated his own death: Roger "came to the conclusion that he didn't want to live any longer."[42]

In its obituary the *New York Times* termed Baldwin "the country's unofficial agitator for, and defender of, its civil liberties." And the *New Republic*, the *National Review*, the *New Leader*, and *Dissent* delivered appropriate plaudits.

The eulogy that Baldwin would have especially loved came from *Inquiry*, published by the Libertarian Review Foundation. It praised his lifelong campaign "to protect, defend, and extend the guarantees of the First Amendment." The ACLU and Baldwin had transformed "American life as perhaps no single individual or organization in the modern history of the republic."[43]

Memorial services were held for Baldwin on Martha's Vineyard and in New York City. Found among his papers were instructions regarding who should speak at the Community Church in Manhattan, in what order they should talk, and how much time each should be allotted. As Ira Glasser recalled, "People really made a joke about that: that's how controlling a character Roger was, that he even made an attempt to control his own funeral service!"[44]

The Community Church memorial was packed, with two hundred in attendance, including many of Baldwin's compatriots from the United Nations, the ACLU, and the International League for Human Rights. Baldwin's own well-planned speech closed the proceeding, leaving the impression that he was announcing, "I'm off on a new adventure," still traveling hopefully. Baldwin had instructed Butler to read as the farewell: "All I can say is that I have enjoyed immensely the experience of living with the fulfillment of my capacities and desires. I have the sense of having lived happily, despite the inevitable downs, always with optimism and hope." Baldwin insisted he had not feared death at all, and "I would not have missed my life for the world." He went on to say, "If I have stood for anything distinctive it is for my consistency in sticking to the principles I so profoundly believe in—nonviolence, freedom, equality, law and justice."[45]

During the six-decade span of his involvement with the modern civil liberties movement, Baldwin witnessed expanded protection for key portions of the Bill of Rights. In 1917, when he initiated the civil liberties campaign, those constitutional guarantees hardly amounted to anything for little-liked groups such as conscientious objectors, socialists, and Wobblies. Along the way, others, including communists, American fascists, aliens, and Japanese Americans, also suffered civil liberties deprivations. Baldwin and the ACLU, often at his behest, generally defended the rights of those same groups when few others proved willing to do so. The ACLU leaders, guided by their longtime executive director, waged public relations wars, undertook groundbreaking litigation, and wrestled with public officials, while demanding an expansive interpretation of the Bill of Rights.

Consequently, by the close of Baldwin's life, First Amendment provisions involving freedom of speech, the press, assemblage, and religion had been brought closer to actuality than at any point in American history. Similarly, the rights of criminal defendants were far better safeguarded than they had been when the civil liberties campaign was initiated.

Much of the credit resides with Roger Nash Baldwin, that man of multiple contradictions who lived a patrician existence of a rather unconventional cast. A genuine democrat in the political realm, he was a classic authoritarian at home and at the ACLU national office. A moralist and a bit of a puritan as well, he was a notorious philanderer. A firm believer that nongovernment forces had to keep a watch on official misconduct, Baldwin sometimes desperately sought connections to the political high and mighty. While beginning his career as a progressive reformer, he headed leftward, becoming one of America's leading Popular Fronters, before ending up in the liberal anticommunist camp.

But through it all Baldwin remained nearly true to his original, absolutist vision of an unfettered application of the Bill of Rights. Yes, compromises and mistakes occurred along the way, strewing the civil libertarian path with bumps and some would argue even wreckages. Nevertheless, Mr. ACLU, more than any other individual, helped to implant the gospel and the reality of civil liberties into U.S. law and society.

Notes

1. Growing up in Wellesley Hills

1. Peggy Lamson, *Roger Baldwin: Founder of the American Civil Liberties Union: A Portrait* (Boston: Houghton Mifflin, 1976), p. 1; Roger Baldwin, "Some Notes," November 1964, Roger Nash Baldwin Papers, Public Policy Papers, Department of Rare Books and Special Collections, Princeton University Libraries; Robert L. Duffus, "The Legend of Roger Baldwin," *American Mercury*, August 25, 1925, p. 408; Travis Hoke, "Red Rainbow," *North American Review* 234 (November 1932): 432. Box numbers for the Baldwin Papers are not listed, because Mudd Library archivists renumbered those materials while this book was being completed.

2. Lamson, *Roger Baldwin*, p. 1; Roger Baldwin, "The Reminiscences of Roger Nash Baldwin," 1954, p. 6, Columbia University Oral History Collection; Baldwin, "*The Roger Baldwin Story*: A Prejudiced Account by Himself," 1971, p. 1, Baldwin Papers; Duffus, "The Legend of Roger Baldwin," p. 408.

3. Peggy Lamson, "Transcripts of Interviews with Roger Baldwin," p. 18, Peggy Lamson Collection on Roger Baldwin, Public Policy Papers, Department of Rare Books and Special Collections, Princeton University Libraries; Lamson, *Roger Baldwin*, p. 7; Dwight Macdonald, "The Defense of Everybody—II," *New Yorker*, July 18, 1953, p. 32.

4. Booker T. Washington, *The Booker T. Washington Papers*, vol. 5, 1899–1900, ed. Louis R. Harlan and Raymond W. Smock (Urbana: University of Illinois Press, 1976), p. 529; Lamson, *Roger Baldwin*, pp. 7–9; Samuel Walker, *In Defense of American Liberties: A History of the ACLU* (New York: Oxford University Press, 1990), p. 31; Macdonald, "The Defense of Everybody—II," p. 23; Baldwin, "Reminiscences," p. 9; Baldwin, "A Memo by RNB on My Travels," November 1964, p. 1, Baldwin Papers; Baldwin, "A Memo on My Monthly Public Activities," February 1974, p. 1, Baldwin Papers;

Joseph P. Lash interview with Roger Baldwin, November 4, 1971, Box 49, Joseph P. Lash Papers, Franklin Delano Roosevelt Presidential Library, Hyde Park, N.Y.; Charles Lam Markmann, *The Noblest Cry: A History of the American Civil Liberties Union* (New York: St. Martin's, 1965).

5. Lamson, *Roger Baldwin*, p. 1; Duffus, "The Legend of Roger Baldwin," p. 409 (Duffus quoted many people whom he did not identify); Baldwin, "Some Facts About the More Personal Life of Roger N. Baldwin (for possible posthumous inquiries)," 1961, p. B-3, Baldwin Papers.

6. Baldwin, "Reminiscences," pp. 17–18; Lamson, *Roger Baldwin*, pp. 12–13; Duffus, "The Legend of Roger Baldwin," p. 409; Lamson, "Transcripts," p. 5, Lamson Collection; Lash interview with Roger Baldwin's brothers, Herbert and Robert Baldwin, October 26, 1971, Box 49, Lash Papers; Lash interviews with Roger Baldwin, January 8, 1972, May 17, 1972, and November 4, 1971, Box 49, Lash Papers.

7. Lash interview with Roger Baldwin, January 8, 1972, Lash Papers.

8. Ibid.; Baldwin, "Reminiscences," pp. 17–18; Lash interview with Herbert Baldwin and Robert Baldwin, October 26, 1971, Lash Papers; Lamson, *Roger Baldwin*, pp. 12–13; Lash interview with Roger Baldwin, January 12, 1972, Box 49, Lash Papers; Duffus, "The Legend of Roger Baldwin," p. 409; Lamson, "Transcripts," p. 5, Lamson Collection.

9. Baldwin, "Some Notes by Roger Baldwin for Memoirs Not Covered in the Oral History," November 1964, p. F-1, Baldwin Papers; Lamson, *Roger Baldwin*, pp. 1–2, 20–21; Lash interview with Herbert Baldwin and Robert Baldwin, October 26, 1971, Lash Papers; Lash interview with Lawrence Grose, October 25, 1971, Box 49, Lash Papers; Baldwin, "Memo on My Interests in Nature," November 1964, p. 1, Baldwin Papers; Baldwin, "A Memo on My Mostly Public Activities," February 1974, p. 1, Baldwin Papers; Lash interview with Roger Baldwin, November 4, 1971, Lash Papers.

10. Baldwin, "Reminiscences," pp. 13–14; Cleveland Amory, *The Proper Bostonians* (New York: Dutton, 1947), p. 11; Lamson, *Roger Baldwin*, p. 8; Baldwin, "A Memo on My Mostly Public Activities," February 1974, p. 1, Baldwin Papers.

11. Baldwin, "A Memo by RNB on My Travels," November 1964, p. G-2; Baldwin, "A Memo on Some of My Older Friends," March 1974, p. 1, both in Baldwin Papers; Lash interview with Roger Baldwin, November 4, 1971, Lash Papers.

12. Baldwin to Charlotte M. Ryman, April 18, 1898; Baldwin, "Post-script to the More Personal Account," November 1961, p. B-6, both in Baldwin Papers.

13. Baldwin to Charlotte M. Ryman, February 11, 1899, Baldwin Papers.

14. Baldwin to Booker T. Washington, April 30, 1899, *Booker T. Washington Papers*, vol. 5, p. 95.

15. Baldwin to Charlotte M. Ryman, July 27, 1899, Baldwin Papers.

16. Baldwin to Charlotte M. Ryman, September 9, 1898; December 21, 1898; February 11, 1899, both in Baldwin Papers.

17. Baldwin to Charlotte M. Ryman, July 27, 1899; Baldwin to Charlotte M. Ryman, August 12, 1899, both in Baldwin Papers.

18. Baldwin to Charlotte M. Ryman, February 27, 1900; Baldwin to Charlotte M. Ryman, June 1, 1900, both in Baldwin Papers.

19. Baldwin, "Memo for Biographical Notes: On Religion and Ethics," December 1964, p. I-1, Baldwin Papers; Macdonald, "The Defense of Everybody—II," p. 34; Baldwin, "Reminiscences," p. 14; Lamson, *Roger Baldwin*, p. 6; Baldwin, "*The Roger Baldwin Story*: A Prejudiced Account by Himself," 1971, p. 1, Baldwin Papers; Lamson, "Transcripts," p. 4, Lamson Collection.

20. Baldwin, "Reminscences," pp. 15–16.

21. Lash interviews with Roger Baldwin, October 21, 1971, November 11, 1971, and December 21, 1971, Box 49, Lash Papers.

22. Lash interview with Herbert Baldwin and Robert Baldwin, October 26, 1971, Lash Papers.

23. Baldwin, "Post-script to the More Personal Account," November 1961, p. B-5, Baldwin Papers; Baldwin, "Some Notes by Roger Baldwin for Memoirs Not Covered in the Oral History," November 1964, p. F-1, Baldwin Papers; Lamson, *Roger Baldwin*, pp. 20–21.

24. Baldwin, "Post-script to the More Personal Account," November 1961, p. B-5; Baldwin, "Memo on My Interests in Nature," November 1964, p. H-1, Baldwin Papers; Baldwin, note on Lawrence Rich Grose, all in Baldwin Papers; Lamson, *Roger Baldwin*, p. 2.

25. Baldwin, "Memo on My Interests in Nature," November 1964, p. 1, Baldwin Papers; Lamson, *Roger Baldwin*, p. 4.

26. Baldwin, "Memo on My Interests in Nature," November 1964, pp. 1–2, Baldwin Papers.

27. Lash interview with Herbert Baldwin and Robert Baldwin, October 26, 1971, Lash Papers; Baldwin, "Post-script to the More Personal Account," November 1961, p. B-5, Baldwin Papers; Baldwin, note on Grose, Baldwin Papers; Lash interview with Roger Baldwin, November 11, 1971, Lash Papers.

28. Lash interview with Roger Baldwin, November 11, 1971, Lash Papers.

29. Baldwin, "Reminiscences," pp. 16–17; Lamson, *Roger Baldwin*, p. 4; Macdonald, "The Defense of Everybody—II," p. 34; Lash interviews with Baldwin, October 30, 1971, and November 11, 1971, Lash Papers.

30. Lash interview with Baldwin, October 30, 1971, Box 49, Lash Papers.

31. Baldwin, "Post-script to the More Personal Account," November 1961, p. 1; Baldwin, "Reminiscences," p. 15; Baldwin, note on Grose; Baldwin to Charlotte M. Ryman, September 9, 1898, all in Baldwin Papers; Lash interview with Grose, October 25, 1971, Box 49, Lash Papers; Lash interviews with Roger Baldwin, October 30, 1971, November 4, 1971, November 11, 1971, and December 14, 1971, Box 49, Lash Papers.

32. Lamson, *Roger Baldwin*, pp. 3–4.

33. Lash interview with Grose, October 25, 1971, Box 49; Lash interview with Roger Baldwin, November 11, 1971, both in Lash Papers.

34. Lash interview with Grose, October 25, 1971, Box 49; Lash interview with Herbert Baldwin and Robert Baldwin, October 26, 1971, both in Lash Papers.

35. Lash interview with Grose, October 25, 1971, Box 49; Lash interview with Herbert Baldwin and Robert Baldwin, October 26, 1971, both in Lash Papers.

36. Lash interview with Grose, October 25, 1971, Box 49; Lash interviews with Roger Baldwin, November 11, 1971, and January 12, 1972, all in Lash Papers.

2. *The Inevitable Harvard and Beyond*

1. Baldwin, "*The Roger Baldwin Story*: A Prejudiced Account by Himself," 1971, p. 1, Roger Nash Baldwin Papers, Public Policy Papers, Department of Rare Books and Special Collections, Princeton University Libraries; Peggy Lamson, *Roger Baldwin: Founder of the American Civil Liberties Union: A Portrait* (Boston: Houghton Mifflin, 1976), pp. 14–15; Peggy Lamson, "Transcripts of Interviews with Roger Baldwin," pp. 7–8, Peggy Lamson Collection on Roger Baldwin, Public Policy Papers, Department of Rare Books and Special Collections, Princeton University Libraries.

2. Baldwin, "A Memo on My Mostly Public Activities," February 1974, pp. 4–5, Baldwin Papers; Lamson, *Roger Baldwin*, p. 20; "Jail for Man Known as Aristocrat at Harvard," *Boston Globe*, 1924, Madeleine Z. Doty Papers, Smith College; Baldwin, "Some Facts About the More Personal Life of Roger N. Baldwin," 1961, p. B-1, Baldwin Papers; Baldwin, "Post-script to the More Personal Account," November 1961, p. B-5, Baldwin Papers; Joseph P. Lash interview with Roger Baldwin, December 14, 1971, Joseph P. Lash Papers, Franklin Delano Roosevelt Presidential Library, Hyde Park, N.Y.; Lash, "Conforming Harvard Man," p. 1, unpublished manuscript, Box 50, Lash Papers.

3. Lash interview with Lawrence Grose, October 25, 1971, Box 49; Lash interview with Herbert Baldwin and Robert Baldwin, October 26, 1971; Lash interview with Roger Baldwin, December 21, 1971, all in Lash Papers.

4. Baldwin, "Post-script to the More Personal Account," November 1961, pp. B-5–6, Baldwin Papers; Robert L. Duffus, "The Legend of Roger Baldwin," *American Mercury*, August 25, 1925, p. 409; Lamson, *Roger Baldwin*, p. 19; Lash interviews with Roger Baldwin, September 24, 1971, and October 11, 1971, Box 49, Lash Papers.

5. Baldwin, "A Memo on My Mostly Public Activities," February 1974, p. 4; Baldwin, "Some Facts About the More Personal Life of Roger N. Baldwin," 1961, p. B-1; Baldwin, "Memo on My Interests in Nature," November 1964, p. H-2, all in Baldwin Papers; Lash interview with Roger Baldwin, November 10, 1971, Box 49, Lash Papers.

6. Lash interviews with Roger Baldwin, October 11, 1971, and December 21, 1971, Lash Papers; Duffus, "The Legend of Roger Baldwin," p. 409; Baldwin, "Post-script to

the More Personal Account," November 1961, pp. B-5–6, Baldwin Papers; Lamson, "Transcripts," p. 7, Lamson Collection; Lamson, *Roger Baldwin*, pp. 18–19.

7. Lash interview with Roger Baldwin, December 21, 1971, Lash Papers.

8. Baldwin, "A Memo on My Mostly Public Activities," February 1974, p. 4, Baldwin Papers; Baldwin, "Post-script to the More Personal Account," November 1961, p. B-6, Baldwin Papers; Lamson, *Roger Baldwin*, p. 22.

9. Roger Baldwin, "The Reminiscences of Roger Nash Baldwin," 1954, pp. 6–7, Columbia University Oral History Collection; Lamson, "Transcripts," p. 9, Lamson Collection; Duffus, "The Legend of Roger Baldwin," p. 409; Richard Norton Smith, *The Harvard Century: The Making of a University to a Nation* (New York: Simon and Schuster, 1986), p. 50; Lash interviews with Roger Baldwin, September 24, 1971, and September 29, 1971, Box 49, Lash Papers; Lamson, *Roger Baldwin*, p. 17; "Jail for Man."

10. Harvard College transcripts of Roger Baldwin, 1901–1905, Harvard Archives; Lash, "Conforming Harvard Man," pp. 4, 6, 12–14, Lash Papers; Baldwin, "Some Notes by Roger Baldwin for Memoirs Not Covered in the Oral History," November 1964, p. F-1, Baldwin Papers; Baldwin, "A Memo on My Mostly Public Activities," February 1974, p. 3, Baldwin Papers; Baldwin, "Memo on My Interests in Nature," November 1964, p. II-3, Baldwin Papers; Lamson, *Roger Baldwin*, p. 17; Lash interviews with Roger Baldwin, October 30, 1971, and November 11, 1971, Lash Papers.

11. Lee Simonson, "My College Life Was an Inner One," in *The Harvard Book: Selections from Three Centuries*, rev. ed. (Cambridge, Mass.: Harvard University Press, 1982), p. 280; Baldwin, "Reminiscences," p. 19; Lash interview with Grose, October 25, 1971, Box 49, Lash Papers; Lash interview with Roger Baldwin, November 11, 1971, Lash Papers.

12. Baldwin, "A Memo on My Mostly Public Activities," February 1974, p. 5; Baldwin, "A Memo by RNB on My Travels," November 1964, pp. G-2–3, both in Baldwin Papers.

13. Baldwin, "A Memo on My Mostly Public Activities," February 1974, p. 5; Baldwin, "A Memo by RNB on My Travels," November 1964, p. G-3, both in Baldwin Papers.

14. "Jail for Man"; Baldwin, "A Memo by RNB on My Travels," November 1964, p. G-3, Baldwin Papers; Baldwin, "A Memo on My Mostly Public Activities," February 1974, pp. 3–4, Baldwin Papers; Travis Hoke, "Red Rainbow," *North American Review* 234 (November 1932): 433; Lash, "Conforming Harvard Man," p. 17, Lash Papers.

15. Baldwin, "Reminiscences," pp. 20, 6; Baldwin, "Some Notes by Roger Baldwin for Memoirs Not Covered in the Oral History," November 1964, p. F-1, Baldwin Papers; Lash interview with Roger Baldwin, November 11, 1971, Lash Papers.

16. Baldwin, "Some Notes by Roger Baldwin for Memoirs Not Covered in the Oral History," November 1964, p. F-1; Baldwin, "A Memo by RNB on My Travels," November 1964, p. G-3–4; Baldwin, "Record of the More Public Activities of Roger

N. Baldwin," November 1961, p. C-1, all in Baldwin Papers; Lamson, *Roger Baldwin*, p. 22.

17. Baldwin, "A Memo by RNB on My Travels," November 1964, p. G-4, Baldwin Papers; Lamson, *Roger Baldwin*, pp. 22–24; Lash interviews with Roger Baldwin, November 11, 1971, and December 21, 1971, Lash Papers.

18. Lash interview with Herbert Baldwin and Robert Baldwin, October 26, 1971, Lash Papers; Baldwin, "A Memo by RNB on My Travels," November 1964, p. G-4, Baldwin Papers; Lamson, *Roger Baldwin*, pp. 25–26.

19. Baldwin, "A Memo by RNB on My Travels," November 1964, pp. G-4–5, Baldwin Papers; Lamson, *Roger Baldwin*, p. 26; Baldwin, "Reminiscences," p. 20; Baldwin, "Some Notes by Roger Baldwin for Memoirs Not Covered in the Oral History," November 1964, p. F-2, Baldwin Papers; Lash interview with Roger Baldwin, October 30, 1971, Lash Papers.

20. Lash interview with Roger Baldwin, October 30, 1971; Lash interview with Roger Baldwin, December 14, 1971; Lash interview with Herbert Baldwin and Robert Baldwin, October 26, 1971, Box 49, all in Lash Papers.

21. Baldwin, "Some Notes by Roger Baldwin for Memoirs Not Covered in the Oral History," November 1964, p. F-1; Baldwin, "Some Facts About the More Personal Life of Roger N. Baldwin," 1961, p. B-3, both in Baldwin Papers; Lash interview with Roger Baldwin, December 14, 1971, Lash Papers.

22. Lash interview with Roger Baldwin, December 14, 1971, Lash Papers; Alfred Steinberg, "Roger Baldwin," n.d., p. 12, Baldwin Papers.

23. Baldwin, "Reminiscences," pp. 9–11; Baldwin, "Post-script to the More Personal Account," November 1961, p. B-6, Baldwin Papers; Baldwin, "A Memo on Some of My Older Friends," March 1974, p. 2, Baldwin Papers; Lamson, *Roger Baldwin*, p. 27; Lash interview with Roger Baldwin, March 7, 1972, Box 49, Lash Papers.

24. Baldwin, "Record of the More Public Activities of Roger N. Baldwin," November 1961, p. C-1, Baldwin Papers; Lamson, *Roger Baldwin*, pp. 27–28.

25. Baldwin, "Reminiscences," pp. 11–12.

26. Ibid., p. 10.

27. Ibid., p. 12; Baldwin, "Record of the More Public Activities of Roger N. Baldwin," November 1961, p. C-1, Baldwin Papers.

3. The Progressive as Social Worker

1. Roger Baldwin, "Some Notes by Roger Baldwin for Memoirs Not Covered in the Oral History," November 1964, p. F-2, Roger Nash Baldwin Papers, Public Policy Papers, Department of Rare Books and Special Collections, Princeton University Libraries; Joseph P. Lash interview with Roger Baldwin, December 21, 1971, Joseph P. Lash Papers, Franklin Delano Roosevelt Presidential Library, Hyde Park,

N.Y.; Baldwin, "Highlights of Roger Baldwin's Private Life," ca. 1972, Baldwin Papers.

2. Baldwin, "Memo on the Beginning of the St. Louis Juvenile Court," 1966, p. 1; Baldwin, "Record of the More Public Activities of Roger N. Baldwin," November 1961, p. C-1, both in Baldwin Papers; Peggy Lamson, *Roger Baldwin: Founder of the American Civil Liberties Union: A Portrait* (Boston: Houghton Mifflin, 1976), pp. 30, 39; Travis Hoke, "Red Rainbow," *North American Review* 234 (November 1932): 433; Baldwin, "Some Facts About the More Personal Life of Roger N. Baldwin," 1961, p. B-1, Baldwin Papers; Baldwin, "Some Notes by Roger Baldwin for Memoirs Not Covered in the Oral History," November 1964, p. F-2, Baldwin Papers; Baldwin, "Highlights of Roger Baldwin's Private Life," ca. 1972, Baldwin Papers.

3. Baldwin, "Memo on My Interests in Nature," November 1964, p. H-3; Baldwin, "Highlights of Roger Baldwin's Private Life," ca. 1972, both in Baldwin Papers; Lash interview with Roger Baldwin, December 21, 1971, Lash Papers; Baldwin, "Memo on My Interests in Nature," November 1964, p. H-3, Baldwin Papers; Baldwin, "Postscript to the More Personal Account," November 1961, p. B-6, Baldwin Papers; Lash interview with Roger Baldwin, October 4, 1971, Box 49, Lash Papers.

4. Lash interview with Roger Baldwin, January 8, 1972, Lash Papers.

5. Baldwin, "Highlights of Roger Baldwin's Private Life," ca. 1972, Baldwin Papers; Lamson, *Roger Baldwin*, p. 56.

6. Baldwin, "Memo for Mrs. Lamson on My Attitude to Money," April 1974, p. 1, Baldwin Papers; Roger Baldwin, "The Reminiscences of Roger Nash Baldwin," 1954, p. 324, Columbia University Oral History Collection.

7. Baldwin, "Highlights of Roger Baldwin's Private Life," ca. 1972; Baldwin, "Some Notes by Roger Baldwin for Memoirs Not Covered in the Oral History," November 1964, pp. F-5–6; Baldwin, "A Memo on My Love Life," February 1974, pp. 1–2, all in Baldwin Papers; Lamson, *Roger Baldwin*, pp. 40, 42–43; Virginia Gardner, *"Friend and Lover": The Life of Louise Bryant* (New York: Horizon, 1982), p. 154.

8. Baldwin, "Some Notes by Roger Baldwin for Memoirs Not Covered in the Oral History," November 1964, p. 6; Baldwin, "A Memo on My Love Life," February 1974, pp. 1–2, both in Baldwin Papers; Lash interview with Roger Baldwin, January 8, 1972, Lash Papers; "Suffragism Has Crawled," n.d. (apparently a photocopy of a news article), Box 49, Lash Papers; Lamson, *Roger Baldwin*, pp. 40–41.

9. Edwin C. McReynolds, *Missouri: A History of the Crossroads State* (Norman: University of Oklahoma Press, 1962), pp. 316–17; Lash interview with Roger Baldwin, December 21, 1971, Lash Papers; Baldwin, "Reminiscences," pp. 22–23.

10. Lash interview with Roger Baldwin, January 12, 1972, Lash Papers; Baldwin, "Record of the More Public Activities of Roger N. Baldwin," November 1961, p. C-1, Baldwin Papers; Roger Baldwin and Alan Westin, "Recollections of a Life in Civil Liberties—I," *Civil Liberties Review* 1 (Spring 1975): 41.

11. Baldwin, "Reminiscences," pp. 22–23; Baldwin to George W. Pieksen, March 27, 1909, pp. 1–2, Baldwin Papers; Lash interview with Roger Baldwin, December 21, 1971, Lash Papers.

12. Baldwin and Westin, "Recollections of a Life in Civil Liberties—I," pp. 49–50; Committee for Social Service Among Colored People, "A Statement of the Work of the Committee for Social Service Among Colored People," May 1911, p. 1, Baldwin Papers.

13. Baldwin to David F. Houston, August 4, 1911; Baldwin to David F. Houston, August 28, 1911; "The Local Segregation of Negroes in Saint Louis," January 1913, all in Baldwin Papers.

14. Baldwin, "Reminiscences," p. 24.

15. Ibid., pp. 24–28; Baldwin, "Memo on the Beginnings of the St. Louis Juvenile Court," 1966, pp. 1–2, Baldwin Papers; Baldwin, "Record of the More Public Activities of Roger N. Baldwin," November 1961, p. C-1, Baldwin Papers; Lamson, *Roger Baldwin*, p. 35.

16. Baldwin to David F. Houston, March 20, 1909, Baldwin Papers; Baldwin, "Reminiscences," pp. 28–29; Baldwin, "Memo on the Beginnings of the St. Louis Juvenile Court," 1966, p. 2, Baldwin Papers.

17. Baldwin, "Reminiscences," p. 29.

18. Ibid., pp. 29–30; 35; Baldwin, "Memo on the Beginnings of the St. Louis Juvenile Court," 1966, p. 3, Baldwin Papers; Lash interview with Roger Baldwin, January 8, 1972, Lash Papers.

19. Baldwin, "Record of the More Public Activities of Roger N. Baldwin," November 1961, p. C-1; Baldwin, "Some Facts about the More Personal Life of Roger N. Baldwin," 1961, p. B-4, both in Baldwin Papers; Dwight Macdonald, "The Defense of Everybody—II," *New Yorker*, July 18, 1953, p. 34; Baldwin, "Some Notes by Roger Baldwin for Memoirs Not Covered in the Oral History," November 1964, pp. F-2–3, Baldwin Papers.

20. Lamson, *Roger Baldwin*, pp. 37–39.

21. Lash interview with Roger Baldwin, January 8, 1972, Lash Papers.

22. Baldwin and Westin, "Recollections of a Life in Civil Liberties—I," pp. 5–6; Baldwin, "Record of the More Public Activities of Roger N. Baldwin," November 1961, p. C-2, Baldwin Papers.

23. Baldwin, "Reminiscences," p. 36; Lash interview with Roger Baldwin, October 11, 1971, Lash Papers; Baldwin and Westin, "Recollections of a Life in Civil Liberties—I," p. 43.

24. Baldwin, "Reminiscences," pp. 36–37; James Neal Primm, *Lion of the Valley: St. Louis, Missouri* (Boulder, Colo.: Pruett, 1981), p. 390.

25. Baldwin, "Reminiscences," pp. 37–38; Robert L. Duffus, "The Legend of Roger Baldwin," *American Mercury*, August 25, 1925, p. 410; Macdonald, "The Defense of Everybody—II," p. 34; Lamson, *Roger Baldwin*, pp. 58–59; Roger Baldwin, "The Immorality of Social Work," *World Tomorrow* 5 (February 1922): 44–45.

26. Emma Goldman, *Living My Life* (Garden City, N.Y.: Garden City Publishing, 1931), p. 477.

27. Emma Goldman to Roger Baldwin, September 10, 1909, pp. 1–2, Microfilm, Reel 3, Emma Goldman Papers, New York University; Baldwin to Goldman, September 20, 1909, Baldwin Papers; Baldwin to E. H. Wuerpel, January 12, 1910, Baldwin Papers; Samuel Walker, *In Defense of American Liberties: A History of the ACLU* (New York: Oxford University Press, 1990), p. 34; Macdonald, "The Defense of Everybody—II," p. 34.

28. Baldwin, "*The Roger Baldwin Story:* A Prejudiced Account by Himself," 1971, p. 3, Baldwin Papers; Baldwin, "Reminiscences," pp. 37–38; Baldwin and Westin, "Recollections of a Life in Civil Liberties—I," p. 43; Baldwin, "Recollections of Debs," March 1964, p. 1, Baldwin Papers.

29. Baldwin and Westin, "Recollections of a Life in Civil Liberties—I," pp. 43–44; Lamson, *Roger Baldwin*, p. 63; Goldman to Baldwin, December 7, 1910, pp. 1–2, Reel 4, Goldman Papers; Baldwin to Goldman, December 10, 1910, Reel 4, Goldman Papers.

30. Baldwin, "Record of the More Public Activities of Roger N. Baldwin," November 1961, p. C-2, Baldwin Papers; Duffus, "The Legend of Roger Baldwin," p. 409; Baldwin, "Reminiscences," pp. 30–31, 33–34.

31. Roger Baldwin, "Statistics Relating to Juvenile Delinquents," *Proceedings of the National Conference of Charities at Corrections* (Ft. Wayne, Ind.: Archer, 1910), pp. 523–24.

32. Baldwin, "Reminiscences," p. 34; Lamson, *Roger Baldwin*, pp. 35–36; Bernard Flexner and Roger N. Baldwin, *Juvenile Courts and Probation* (New York: Century, 1914), pp. 68, 80–81.

33. Baldwin, "Reminiscences," pp. 31–33.

34. Lucille Milner, *Education of an American Liberal: An Autobiography* (New York: Horizon, 1954), pp. 17, 31, 50–52.

35. Ibid., p. 52.

4. The Civic League

1. Roger Baldwin, "The Reminiscences of Roger Nash Baldwin," 1954, pp. 38, 324, Columbia University Oral History Collection.

2. Ibid., pp. 38–39; Peggy Lamson, *Roger Baldwin: Founder of the American Civil Liberties Union: A Portrait* (Boston: Houghton Mifflin, 1976), p. 46.

3. Baldwin, "Reminiscences," p. 48; Lamson, *Roger Baldwin*, p. 44.

4. Lamson, *Roger Baldwin*, pp. 44–46, 52; Joseph P. Lash interview with Roger Baldwin, March 4, 1972, Box 49, Joseph P. Lash Papers, Franklin Delano Roosevelt Presidential Library, Hyde Park, N.Y.

5. Lash interview with Roger Baldwin, March 6, 1972, Box 49, Lash Papers.

6. James Neal Primm, *Lion of the Valley: St. Louis, Missouri* (Boulder, Colo.: Pruett, 1981), p. 424.

7. Baldwin, "Reminiscences," pp. 43–47. To avoid economic inequities, George called for taxing the "unearned increment," the increase in land values that resulted from market forces alone and not because of the owner's labor.

8. Ibid., 39; Baldwin, "Record of the More Public Activities of Roger N. Baldwin," November 1961, p. C-2, Baldwin Papers; Primm, *Lion of the Valley*, pp. 424–25.

9. Baldwin, "Reminiscences," pp. 39–40.

10. Dwight Macdonald, "The Defense of Everybody—II," *New Yorker*, July 18, 1953, p. 34; Baldwin, "Reminiscences," pp. 40–41; Primm, *Lion of the Valley*, pp. 369, 425–26.

11. Baldwin, "Reminiscences," p. 41; Primm, *Lion of the Valley*, p. 427; Roger Baldwin, "The St. Louis Pageant and Masque: Its Civic Meaning," *Survey* 32 (April 11, 1914): 52.

12. Baldwin, "The St. Louis Pageant and Masque," pp. 52–53.

13. Baldwin, "Reminiscences," pp. 41–42; Primm, *Lion of the Valley*, pp. 427, 419.

14. Baldwin, "Reminiscences," p. 42; Roger Baldwin, "St. Louis' Successful Fight for a Modern Charter," *National Municipal Review* 3 (October 1914): 720–21, 724.

15. Baldwin, "Reminiscences," p. 42; Primm, *Lion of the Valley*, pp. 434–35, 430; Lamson, *Roger Baldwin*, p. 48; Baldwin, "St. Louis' Successful Fight," pp. 720–21.

16. Baldwin, "St. Louis' Successful Fight," p. 724; Primm, *Lion of the Valley*, pp. 421–25; Roger Baldwin, "The Use of Municipal Ownership to Abolish Trans-Mississippi Freight and Passenger Tolls," *National Municipal Review* 4 (July 1915): 472.

17. Primm, *Lion of the Valley*, pp. 435–36.

18. Ibid., pp. 436–38.

19. Ibid., pp. 437–38; Luther Ely Smith, petition of the Citizens' Committee Opposed to the Legal Segregation of Negroes, January 25, 1916, Baldwin Papers.

20. Primm, *Lion of the Valley*, pp. 438–40; Baldwin, letter regarding the segregation ordinance, n.d., Baldwin Papers.

21. Baldwin, letter regarding the segregation ordinance, n.d., Baldwin Papers; Primm, *Lion of the Valley*, pp. 438–40.

22. Macdonald, "The Defense of Everybody—II," p. 34; Baldwin, "Reminiscences," pp. 40–41; Primm, *Lion of the Valley*, pp. 435–39.

23. Baldwin, "Reminiscences," p. 50; Baldwin, "Record of the More Public Activities of Roger N. Baldwin," January 1961, p. C-2, Baldwin Papers; Lamson, *Roger Baldwin*, p. 49; Roger Baldwin and Alan Westin, "Recollections of a Life in Civil Liberties—I," *Civil Liberties Review* 1 (Spring 1975): 48.

24. Baldwin, "Reminiscences," pp. 48–49.

25. Lamson, *Roger Baldwin*, p. 55; Lash interview with Roger Baldwin, March 4, 1972, Lash Papers; Baldwin, "*The Roger Baldwin Story*: A Prejudiced Account by Him-

self," 1971, p. 3, Baldwin Papers; Robert L. Duffus, "The Legend of Roger Baldwin," *American Mercury*, August 25, 1925, p. 410.

26. Baldwin, "Reminiscences," pp. 50–51; Baldwin and Westin, "Recollections of a Life—I," p. 59; Lash interview with Phil Taft, October 12, 1972, Box 49, Lash Papers.

27. Lash interview with Lucille Milner, March 22, 1972, Box 49, Lash Papers.

28. Lash interview with Roger Baldwin, March 4, 1972, Lash Papers; Samuel Walker, *In Defense of American Liberties: A History of the ACLU* (New York: Oxford University Press, 1990), pp. 35–36; Baldwin to Frank P. Walsh, September 15, 1915, Baldwin Papers.

29. Baldwin and Westin, "Recollections of a Life—I," pp. 50–51; Baldwin, "Reminiscences," p. 51.

5. Early Civil Liberties Career

1. Baldwin to George W. Foley, June 12, 1916, Roger Nash Baldwin Papers, Public Policy Papers, Department of Rare Books and Special Collections, Princeton University Libraries.

2. Roy Smith Wallace to Baldwin, March 7, 1917, pp. 1–2, Baldwin Papers.

3. Baldwin to Wallace, March 9, 1917, Baldwin Papers.

4. Roger Baldwin and Alan Westin, "Recollections of a Life in Civil Liberties—I," *Civil Liberties Review* 1 (Spring 1975): 52.

5. Ibid.; Peggy Lamson, *Roger Baldwin: Founder of the American Civil Liberties Union* (Boston: Houghton Mifflin, 1976), pp. 65–66; C. Roland Marchand, *The American Peace Movement and Social Reform, 1898–1918* (Princeton: Princeton University Press, 1972), pp. 223–27, 231–34, 238–40; Baldwin and Westin, "Recollections of a Life—I," p. 51; Samuel Walker, *In Defense of American Liberties: A History of the ACLU* (New York: Oxford University Press, 1990), p. 36.

6. Charles Lamm Markmann, *The Noblest Cry: A History of the American Civil Liberties Union* (New York: St. Martin's, 1965), p. 20; Robert L. Duffus, "The Legend of Roger Baldwin," *American Mercury*, August 1925, p. 41; Baldwin, "Record of the More Public Activities of Roger N. Baldwin," November 1961, p. C-1, Baldwin Papers; Baldwin, "The Reminiscences of Roger Nash Baldwin," 1954, p. 52, Columbia University Oral History Collection; Lamson, *Roger Baldwin*, pp. 66–68; Joseph P. Lash interview with Roger Baldwin, March 4, 1972, Joseph P. Lash Papers, Franklin Delano Roosevelt Presidential Library, Hyde Park, N.Y.; Peggy Lamson, "Transcripts of Interviews with Roger Baldwin," p. 28, Box 3, Peggy Lamson Collection on Roger Baldwin, Public Policy Papers, Department of Rare Books and Special Collections, Princeton University Libraries; Baldwin and Westin, "Recollections of a Life—I," p. 51; Baldwin, "Memo for Peggy Lamson from Roger Baldwin on Moving East," June 1975, p. 1, Baldwin Papers.

7. Baldwin, "Memo for Peggy Lamson from Roger Baldwin on Moving East," June 1975, p. 2, Baldwin Papers.

8. Baldwin, "Highlights of Roger Baldwin's Private Life," ca. 1972; Baldwin, "Some Facts about the More Personal Life of Roger N. Baldwin Not Covered in the Oral History," November 1964, p. B-1, both in Baldwin Papers; Baldwin and Westin, "Recollections of a Life," p. 53; Lamson, *Roger Baldwin*, p. 87.

9. Baldwin, "Reminiscences," pp. 52–53; Baldwin and Westin, "Recollections of a Life—I," pp. 52–53.

10. Baldwin and Westin, "Recollections of a Life—I," p. 53; Lash interview with Roger Baldwin, March 4, 1972, Lash Papers; Baldwin, "Reminiscences," pp. 53–54; Baldwin, "A Memo on My International Associations," March 1974, p. 11, Baldwin Papers.

11. David M. Rabban, *Free Speech in Its Forgotten Years* (Cambridge: Cambridge University Press, 1997), pp. 25, 44–50, 57–76, 93–94, 111, 119; Walker, *In Defense*, pp. 22–23.

12. Walker, *In Defense*, pp. 132–33; Rabban, *Free Speech in Its Forgotten Years*, pp. 177–210.

13. Baldwin and Westin, "Recollections of a Life—I," pp. 53–54; Baldwin, "Reminiscences," pp. 54–55.

14. Baldwin and Westin, "Recollections of a Life—I," p. 53; Baldwin, "Reminiscences," p. 53; Lamson, *Roger Baldwin*, pp. 67–68; Lamson, "Transcripts," pp. 28–29, Lamson Collection.

15. William Preston, "By Life Possessed: The Dissenter as Hero," Fall 1976, pp. 2–3, 10, courtesy of William Preston.

16. Lash interview with Baldwin, May 24, 1972, Lash Papers; Lamson, *Roger Baldwin*, p. 212; Lash interview with Baldwin, May 24, 1972, Lash Papers.

17. Lamson, *Roger Baldwin*, p. 38, "Reminiscences," p. 54; Lash interviews with Roger Baldwin, May 24, 1972, and May 17, 1972, Box 49, Lash Papers.

18. Roger Baldwin to Rudolph Spreckles, April 14, 1917, p. 24, vol. 3, American Civil Liberties Union Papers, Mudd Library, Princeton University.

19. Baldwin to Jane Addams, April 27, 1917, Microfilm, Reel 10, Jane Addams Papers, Swarthmore College Peace Collection; Norman Thomas and Roger Baldwin, "To the Conference Committee on the Army Bill," May 1, 1917, pp. 263–64, vol. 3, ACLU Papers; Baldwin to Jane Addams, May 10, 1917, p. 45, vol. 3, ACLU Papers.

20. American Union Against Militarism (hereafter AUAM), "Conscription and the Conscientious Objector to War," May 1917, Baldwin Papers; Baldwin to Dear Sir, May 23, 1917, Baldwin Papers; AUAM, "To Men of Military Age Opposed to War!" n.d, Baldwin Papers; Baldwin to Austin Lewis, July 2, 1917, Box Correspondence, Austin Lewis Papers, Bancroft Library, University of California–Berkeley; Baldwin to Dear Sir, May 23, 1917, Reel 10.1, AUAM Papers, Swarthmore College.

21. Baldwin to Frederick D. Keppel, May 18, 1917, p. 142, vol. 2, ACLU Papers.

22. See especially Marchand, *American Peace Movement*, pp. 266–306; Baldwin, "Reminiscences," p. 56; Baldwin and Westin, "Recollections of a Life—I," p. 54; Baldwin to Benjamin Diamond, January 18, 1974, Baldwin Papers.

23. "Minutes of Special Meeting," June 1, 1917, Reel 10.1, AUAM Papers.

24. Lamson, *Roger Baldwin*, p. 75; Baldwin to Frederick D. Keppel, June 2, 1917, vol. 2, ACLU Papers; Baldwin to Newton D. Baker, June 15, 1917, vol. 2, ACLU Papers.

25. Baldwin, memo of interview with Secretary Baker, June 22, 1917, p. 5, vol. 2, ACLU Papers.

26. Lash interview with Roger Baldwin, May 17, 1972, Lash Papers.

27. "Meeting, June 4," June 4, 1917, Reel 10.1, AUAM Papers.

28. Untitled document, June 15, 1917, p. 1, Reel 10.1, AUAM Papers.

29. Lamson, *Roger Baldwin*, p. 72; Lillian Wald to Jane Addams, August 14, 1917, pp. 1–2, Reel 11, Addams Papers; Crystal Eastman Fuller, notes of AUAM meeting, June 15, 1917, p. 4, Reel 10.1, AUAM Papers.

30. AUAM, "Constitutional Rights in War Time," July 1917, pp. 1–8; AUAM, "The American Union Against Militarism," n.d., both in Baldwin Papers.

31. Baldwin to Baker, June 30, 1917, vol. 2, pp. 6–7, ACLU Papers.

32. Charles Chatfield, *For Peace and Justice: Pacifism in America, 1914–1941* (Boston: Beacon, 1973), p. 57; Baldwin to Baker, June 30, 1917, vol. 2, p. 7, ACLU Papers.

33. "For Immediate Release," July 2, 1917, Reel 10.1, AUAM Papers; Civil Liberties Bureau, "Conscription and the 'Conscientious Objector,'" July 1917, p. 1, Baldwin Papers.

34. Baldwin, "Reminiscences", pp. 56–60.

35. Lucille Milner, *Education of an American Liberal: An Autobiography* (New York: Horizon, 1954), pp. 67–69.

36. Marchand, *American Peace Movement*, pp. 253–55.

37. Baldwin's letter to Lochner can be found in New York Senate, Joint Legislative Committee Investigating Seditious Activities, *Revolutionary Radicalism: Its History, Purpose, and Tactics*, vol. 1 (Albany, N.Y.: J. B. Lyon, 1920), p. 1088.

38. Robert Justin Goldstein, *Political Repression in Modern America: From 1870 to the Present* (New York: Schenkman, 1978), pp. 105–135.

39. Baldwin to Maury Edlin, n.d., vol. 5, ACLU Papers; Baldwin, letter to the editor, *St. Louis Star*, August 23, 1917, pp. 125–27, vol. 3, ACLU Papers.

40. Baldwin to John H. Wigmore, September 14, 1917, p. 19, vol. 2; Baldwin to Wigmore, September 16, 1917, pp. 22–23, vol. 2, both in ACLU Papers.

41. Baldwin to Felix Frankfurter, September 29, 1917, p. 42, vol. 2; L. Hollingsworth Wood et al., to Woodrow Wilson, September 26, 1917, p. 26, vol. 3, both in ACLU Papers.

6. The National Civil Liberties Bureau

1. National Civil Liberties Bureau, "Proposed Announcement for Press," n.d., pp. 1–2, American Union Against Militarism Papers (hereafter AUAM), Swarthmore College; Roger Baldwin to Edmund C. Evans, October 6, 1917, vol. 3, ACLU Papers, Princeton University.

2. Roger Baldwin and Alan Westin, "Recollections of a Life in Civil Liberties—I," *Civil Liberties Review* 1 (Spring 1975): 54.

3. Ibid., pp. 54–55; Baldwin, "The Reminiscences of Roger Nash Baldwin," 1954, pp. 56–57, Columbia University Oral History Collection.

4. Baldwin and Westin, "Recollections of a Life—I," pp. 55–56; Baldwin, "Reminiscences," pp. 58–60; Marlise James, *The People's Lawyers* (New York: Holt, Rinehart and Winston, 1973), p. 5; Peggy Lamson, *Roger Baldwin: Founder of the American Civil Liberties Union: A Portrait* (Boston: Houghton Mifflin, 1976), p. 74.

5. Baldwin, "Uncle Sam's Military Prisons," n.d., pp. 1–12, Roger Nash Baldwin Papers, Public Policy Papers, Department of Rare Books and Special Collections, Princeton University Libraries.

6. Lamson, *Roger Baldwin*, p. 77; Baldwin, "Some Notes by Roger Baldwin for Memoirs Not Covered in the Oral History," November 1964, p. F-2, Baldwin Papers.

7. AUAM, "Minutes of the September 28 Meeting," Reel 10.1; J. P. Warbasse to Baldwin, October 10, 1917, p. 111, vol. 3; Baldwin to John S. Codman, October 11, 1917, p. 24, vol. 3, all in ACLU Papers.

8. Baldwin and Westin, "Recollections of a Life—I," pp. 56–58; Baldwin, "Reminiscences," pp. 62–65.

9. David Lawrence to Baldwin, October 24, 1917, p. 144, vol. 3; Baldwin to Edmund C. Evans, October 31, 1917, p. 25, vol. 3, both in ACLU Papers.

10. Baldwin and Westin, "Recollections of a Life—I," p. 55; Baldwin, "Reminiscences," pp. 58–59.

11. National Civil Liberties Bureau to Newton Baker, October 27, 1917, p. 51, vol. 3; Baldwin to Baker, November 22, 1917, vol. 2; Baldwin to Frederick D. Keppel, December 21, 1917, p. 21, vol. 2; Baldwin to John Dewey, December 26, 1917, p. 26, vol. 3, all in ACLU Papers.

12. Charles Lamm Markmann, *The Noblest Cry: A History of the American Civil Liberties Union* (New York: St. Martin's, 1965), p. 33; Paul L. Murphy, *World War I and the Origin of Civil Liberties in the United States* (New York: Norton, 1979), pp. 166–68; Baldwin to David Starr Jordan, January 13, 1918, Box 13, David Starr Jordan Papers, Hoover Institution, Stanford University.

13. Samuel Walker, *In Defense of American Liberties: A History of the ACLU* (New York: Oxford University Press, 1990), p. 37; National Archives, "Abstract from Report," February 16, 1918, Military Intelligence Division Documents (hereafter

MIDD), 10434-8-16; Joseph P. Lash interview with Roger Baldwin, March 9, 1972, Box 49, Joseph P. Lash Papers, Franklin Delano Roosevelt Presidential Library, Hyde Park, N.Y.

14. Baldwin and Westin, "Recollections of a Life—I," p. 62; Baldwin, "Reminiscences," pp. 66–67.

15. C. D. Millikin to Chief, Intelligence Section, War College, December 19, 1941, MIDD, 10434-8-1; R. H. Van Deman to Nicholas Biddle, December 31, 1917, MIDD, 10434-8-4.

16. Van Deman to Intelligence Officers, all divisions, February 6, 1918, MIDD, 10589-12-1; "Memorandum for Colonel Van Deman," February 19, 1918, pp. 1–2, MIDD, 10589-12-5.

17. C. L. Lloyd, "Report: Subject: Roger Baldwin," February 25, 1918, pp. 1–2, MIDD; Baldwin to Col. Edward M. House, January 22, 1918, p. 44, Lusk Committee Papers, New York State Archives, Albany; Baldwin to House, February 8, 1918, p. 47, Lusk Committee Papers; Baldwin to House, February 15, 1918, p. 48, Lusk Committee Papers.

18. Baldwin to the Conscientious Objectors on Hunger Strike at Camp Upton, N.J., February 13, 1918, vol. 2, ACLU Papers.

19. C. L. Lloyd, "Report: Subject: Roger N. Baldwin," March 6, 1918, pp. 1–3, MIDD, 10434-8-19; Keppel to Baldwin, February 26, 1918, p. 203, vol. 2, ACLU Papers.

20. Baldwin to Keppel, March 1, 1918, pp. 204–207, vol. 2, ACLU Papers.

21. Ibid., p. 207; Baldwin to Baker, March 2, 1918, p. 150, vol. 2; Baldwin to Keppel, March 4, 1918, p. 210, vol. 2, both in ACLU Papers; Keppel, "Memorandum for Colonel Van Deman," March 2, 1918, MIDD, 10589-12-33.

22. Baldwin to Jane Addams, March 7, 1918, Reel 11, Jane Addams Papers, Swarthmore College Peace Collection.

23. Van Deman to Biddle, March 7, 1918, MIDD, 10589-12-39; Baldwin to Maj. Nicholas Biddle, March 8, 1918, p. 316, Lusk Committee Papers; transcript of interrogation of Baldwin by Nicholas Biddle, March 8, 1918, Reel 9, *U.S. Military Intelligence Reports*, University of California–Davis; Biddle to Van Deman, March 6, 1918, MIDD, 10434-8-19.

24. Baldwin to Biddle, March 8, 1918, p. 317, Lusk Committee Papers; Memorandum from R. H. Van Deman for Mr. F. P. Keppel, March 9, 1918, n.p., Lusk Committee Papers.

25. Memorandum from R. H. Van Deman for Mr. F. P. Keppel, March 9, 1918, n.p., Lusk Committee Papers.

26. Baldwin to Keppel, March 13, 1918, p. 213, vol. 3, ACLU Papers; Baldwin to H. L. Rotzel, March 13, 1918, p. 1, MIDD, 10902-13-98.

27. Grant Squires to Nicholas Biddle, March 16, 1918, pp. 1–3, Reel 9, *U.S. Military Intelligence Reports*.

28. Office of Military Intelligence Section, 302 Broadway, New York, to Chief, Military Intelligence Branch, Executive Division, March 18, 1918, pp. 1–2, Reel 9, *U.S. Military Intelligence Reports.*

29. Baldwin to Edmund C. Evans, March 16, 1918, p. 56; Baldwin to Biddle, April 2, 1918, pp. 323–24, both in Lusk Committee Papers; Baldwin to Keppel, April 23, 1918, MIDD, 10902-13-65.

30. Baldwin to House, April 3, 1918, p. 52; Baldwin to Keppel, April 19, 1918, pp. 207–208, both in Lusk Committee Papers.

31. William H. Van Antwerp to Director of Naval Intelligence, April 11, 1918, pp. 1–2, MIDD, 10902-13-116; Biddle to Chief, Military Intelligence Branch, Executive Division, April 16, 1918, MIDD, 10902-13-76; "Memorandum to Mr. Bielaski," April 22, 1918, pp. 1–2, MIDD, 10962-13-48; Keppel to Van Deman, May 11, 1918, MIDD, 10902-13-66.

32. Roger Baldwin, *The Truth About the I.W.W.* (New York: National Civil Liberties Bureau, 1918), pp. 3, 8–10, 46–53.

33. Baldwin to Jessie Ashley, March 20, 1918, p. 22–23, Lusk Committee Papers; Donald Johnson, *The Challenge to American Freedoms: World War I and the Rise of the American Civil Liberties Union* (Lexington: University of Kentucky Press, 1963), p. 74.

34. Melvyn Dubofsky, *We Shall Be All: A History the Industrial Workers of the World* (New York: Quadrangle, 1969), p. 423; Baldwin and Westin, "Recollections of a Life—I," p. 60; Baldwin, "Reminiscences," p. 65; Roger Baldwin, "The IWW Trials," pp. 1–3, n.d., Baldwin Papers.

35. Baldwin, "The IWW Trials," pp. 3–4; Baldwin, "Reminiscences," pp. 290–91.

36. Baldwin and Westin, "Recollections of a Life—I," pp. 60–61; Baldwin, "Reminiscences," p. 287; Helen C. Camp, *Iron in Her Soul: Elizabeth Gurley Flynn and the American Left* (Pullman: Washington State University Press, 1995), p. 83.

37. A. B. Bielaski, "Memorandum for the Attorney General," May 13, 1918, pp. 1–2, FBI File, Baldwin Papers.

38. Van Deman to Keppel, May 15, 1918, p. 3, MIDD, 10902-13-69.

39. Keppel to Baldwin, May 19, 1918, p. 306, vol. 3, ACLU Papers; Keppel to L. Hollingsworth Wood, May 22, 1918, p. 308, Lusk Committee Papers.

40. Baldwin to Keppel, May 27, 1918, p. 310, Lusk Committee Papers; Baldwin to Van Deman, May 28, 1918, MIDD, 10902-13-106; Baldwin to Baker, June 6, 1918, p. 108, Lusk Committee Papers; Albert DeSilver et al., to Baker, July 6, 1918, pp. 1–5, vol. 2, ACLU Papers.

41. E. J. Hall, "Memorandum for M.I.B.," June 8, 1918, Reel 9, *U.S. Military Intelligence Reports.*

42. B. C. Decker to M.I.B. for Action, June 19, 1918, MIDD, 10902-12-120; Phillip J. Termini to J. E. Springarn, July 20, 1918, MIDD, 10902-13-131; Termini to Springarn, July 22, 1918, MIDD, 10902-13-140.

43. Baldwin to Keppel, August 3, 1918, p. 227, vol. 3, ACLU Papers; Keppel to Baldwin, August 13, 1918, MIDD, 10902-13-149.

44. Baldwin to Deman, August 17, 1918, p. 228, vol. 3, ACLU Papers.

45. Ibid.

46. Transcript of interview of Baldwin by Colonel Mastellar August 22, 1918, p. 9, Reel 9, *U.S. Military Intelligence Reports.*

47. See Keppel, Memorandum for Colonel Mastellar, August 26, 1918, MIDD, 10902-13-N-3-248; "The Activities of the National Civil Liberties Bureau," n.d., MIDD, 10902-13-N-12-248; Biddle to Chief, Military Intelligence Branch, Executive Division, August 26, 1918, MIDD, 10902-13-154.

48. "Copied from Captain Malone's Report," pp. 1–14, MIDD, 10902-13-155.

49. Ibid., pp. 3, 12.

50. W. H. Lamar to General M. Churchill, August 31, 1918, MIDD, 10902-13-33.

51. Biddle to Director, Military Intelligence Branch, Executive Division, August 31, 1918, pp. 1–2, MIDD, 10902-13-33.

52. Walker, *In Defense,* p. 38; Dubofsky, *We Shall Be All,* p. 436; Baldwin and Westin, "Recollections of a Life—I," p. 62; Baldwin, "Reminiscences," pp. 66–67; William H. Randolph to Commanding Officer, Corps of Intelligence Police, N.Y., September 3, 1918, MIDD, 10902-13-86.

7. The United States v. Roger Baldwin

1. Samuel Walker, *In Defense of American Liberties: A History of the ACLU* (New York: Oxford University Press, 1990), p. 38; John Haynes Holmes, *I Speak for Myself: The Autobiography of John Haynes Holmes* (New York: Harper, 1959), p. 191.

2. Walker, *In Defense,* pp. 38–39; Roger Baldwin and Alan Westin, "Recollections of a Life in Civil Liberties—I," *Civil Liberties Review* 1 (Spring 1975): 62; Baldwin, "The Reminiscences of Roger Nash Baldwin," 1954, p. 68, Columbia University Oral History Collection; Harry Fleischman, *Norman Thomas: A Biography* (New York: Norton, 1967), p. 69; Joseph P. Lash interview with Roger Baldwin, March 6, 1972, Joseph P. Lash Papers, Franklin Delano Roosevelt Presidential Library, Hyde Park, N.Y.

3. Baldwin, "How I 'Took the Veil': A Little Story for Friends," November 15, 1918, p. 1; Baldwin, letter to Local Board 129, September 12, 1918, both in Baldwin Papers; Walker, *In Defense,* p. 39.

4. Roger Baldwin, "Social Work and Radical Economic Movements," *Proceedings of the National Conference of Social Work* 45 (1918): 396–98; Roger Baldwin, "An Industrial Program After the War," *Proceedings of the National Conference of Social Work* 45 (1918): 428.

5. Baldwin to Frederick D. Keppel, September 16, 1918, Military Intelligence Division Documents (hereafter MIDD), 10902-13-86, National Archives.

6. M. Churchill to Intelligence Officer, Camp Wadsworth, S.C., September 24, 1918, MIDD, 10902-13.

7. Fleischman, *Norman Thomas*, pp. 69–70.

8. Walker, *In Defense*, p. 39; Nicholas Biddle to Director of Military Intelligence, October 11, 1918, MIDD, 10902-13. Frederick D. Keppel to Maj. Wrigley Brown, October 11, 1918, MIDD, 10902-13.

9. Baldwin, "How I 'Took the Veil,'" pp. 1–2; Baldwin to Francis G. Caffey, October 9, 1918, Baldwin Papers.

10. Baldwin, "How I 'Took the Veil,'" p. 2; Baldwin and Westin, "Recollections of a Life—I," pp. 62–63; Baldwin, "Reminiscences," p. 68; Peggy Lamson, *Roger Baldwin: : Founder of the American Civil Liberties Union: A Portrait* (Boston: Houghton Mifflin, 1976), p. 89; Baldwin, "The War-Time Bureau: Jail and Prison," n.d., p. 4A, Baldwin Papers.

11. Baldwin, "How I 'Took the Veil,'" p. 2; Baldwin and Westin, "Recollections of a Life—I," pp. 62–63; Baldwin, "Reminiscences," p. 68; Lamson, *Roger Baldwin*, p. 89.

12. Baldwin and Westin, "Recollections of a Life—I," p. 63; Baldwin, "Reminiscences," p. 70.

13. Baldwin, "How I 'Took the Veil,'" pp. 3–4; Baldwin, "Reminiscences," pp. 70–71.

14. Baldwin, "How I 'Took the Veil,'" pp. 4–5.

15. Baldwin, "Reminiscences," pp. 70–71; Baldwin, "The War-Time Bureau," n.d., p. 5A, Baldwin Papers.

16. Baldwin, "Reminiscences," pp. 71–72; Lamson, *Roger Baldwin*, p. 90; Baldwin and Westin, "Recollections of a Life—I," p. 64; Norman Thomas to H. W. Dana, October 15, 1918, pp. 1–110, Reel 71.1, Henry Wadsworth Longfellow Dana Papers, Swarthmore College Peace Collection; Baldwin, "The War-Time Bureau," n.d., p. 5A, Baldwin Papers; Baldwin to Lucy Baldwin, October 10, 1918, p. 1, Baldwin Papers; Lash interview with Roger Baldwin, March 6, 1972, Lash Papers.

17. John Haynes Holmes to Baldwin, October 17, 1918, p. 1, Baldwin Papers.

18. Baldwin, "Reminiscences," p. 73; Roger Baldwin, "Conscience at the Bar," *Survey* 41 (November 1918): 153; Walker, *In Defense*, p. 40; Lamson, *Roger Baldwin*, p. 91; Baldwin to Lucy Baldwin, October 31, 1918, p. 1, Baldwin Papers; Madeleine Z. Doty, unpublished autobiography, p. 2, chap. 12, Madeleine Z. Doty Papers, Smith College.

19. Lamson, *Roger Baldwin*, p. 91; Baldwin, "Conscience at the Bar," p. 153; Baldwin, "Recollections of Debs," March 1964, pp. 2–3, Baldwin Papers.

20. Baldwin, "Conscience at the Bar," p. 153.

21. Ibid.

22. Ibid.

23. Ibid., pp. 153–54.

24. Ibid., p. 154.

25. Ibid.

26. Julius M. Mayer, "Judge Mayer's Statement," *Survey* 41 (November 9, 1918): 154, 172–73.

27. Ibid., p. 173.

28. Lamson, *Roger Baldwin*, p. 93; "Pacifist Professor Gets Year in Prison," *New York Times*, October 31, 1918, p. 11; "He Chose Words in Haste," *New York Times*, November 1, 1918, p. 14.

29. Walker, *In Defense*, pp. 40–41; Baldwin to Lucy Baldwin, November 3, 1918, p. 1, Baldwin Papers; The Drifter, "In the Driftway," *Nation*, November 9, 1918, p. 555; Baldwin to Doty, October 31, 1918, p. 1, Baldwin Papers.

30. Baldwin, "Reminiscences," p. 96; Lamson, *Roger Baldwin*, pp. 94, 106; Lash interview with Herbert Baldwin and Robert Baldwin, October 26, 1971, Lash Papers; Frank Baldwin to Baldwin, November 13, 1918, pp. 1–2, Baldwin Papers; Margaret Baldwin to Baldwin, November 17, 1918, pp. 1–2, Baldwin Papers.

31. Baldwin, "Reminiscences," p. 96; Lamson, *Roger Baldwin*, pp. 94, 106; Margaret Baldwin to Baldwin, November 17, 1918, pp. 1–4, Baldwin Papers.

32. Crystal Eastman Fuller to Doty, cited in Doty, unpublished autobiography, p. 3, chap. 12, Doty Papers; Jane Addams to L. Hollingsworth Wood, November 6, 1918, Reel 11, Jane Addams Papers, Swarthmore College Peace Collection; Norman Thomas to Lucy Baldwin, October 30, 1918, Baldwin Papers; Julius M. Mayer to Baldwin, November 4, 1918, Baldwin Papers.

33. "Disloyalists Are United," duplicated in letter to the Friends and Subscribers of the Bureau (NCLB), November 18, 1918, pp. 1–2, Baldwin Papers.

8. Prison Life

1. Roger Baldwin to Fay Lewis, February 7, 1918, vol. 5, ACLU Papers, Princeton University; R. W. Finch, "IN RE: RADICAL DISTURBANCE, Talk of 'Revolution' in U.S.," October 21, 1918, p. 2, Military Intelligence Division Documents (hereafter MIDD), 10901-13-86X, National Archives.

2. Finch, "IN RE: RADICAL DISTURBANCE," October 21, 1918, pp. 1–2.

3. Finch, "IN RE: ROGER N. BALDWIN, EX-DIRECTOR, NATIONAL CIVIL LIBERTIES BUREAU, November 4, 1918, pp. 1–4, MIDD, 10902-13.

4. Ibid., p. 4.

5. "Jail for Man Known as Aristocrat at Harvard," *Boston Globe*, 1924, Madeleine Z. Doty Papers, Smith College.

6. Baldwin, "How I 'Took the Veil': A Little Story for Friends," November 15, 1918, pp. 5–7, Roger Nash Baldwin Papers, Public Policy Papers, Department of Rare Books and Special Collections, Princeton University Libraries.

7. Ibid.; Baldwin, "My Vacation on the Government: A Little Account of Jail Life for Friends," n.d., pp. 1, 4; Baldwin to Lucy Baldwin, November 12, 1918, p. 1; Baldwin to Lucy Baldwin, November 16, 1918, pp. 1–2; Baldwin, "To a Sycamore," March 1919; Baldwin, "Walls," 1919; Baldwin, "To a Purple Finch," May 1919; Baldwin, "The Gray Enchanter," June 1919, all in Baldwin Papers.

8. Herb Baldwin to Baldwin, November 20, 1918, pp. 1–6; Bob Baldwin to Baldwin, January 18, 1919, pp. 1–12, both in Baldwin Papers.

9. Brownie Brown to Baldwin, December 26, 1918, Baldwin Papers.

10. Baldwin, "How I 'Took the Veil,'" November 15, 1918, p. 7; Roger Baldwin, "The Reminiscences of Roger Nash Baldwin," 1954, pp. 97–98, Columbia University Oral History Collection; Baldwin, "My Vacation on the Government," n.d., pp. 1–5, Baldwin Papers; Baldwin to Lucy Baldwin, November 12, 1918, pp. 1–2, Baldwin Papers.

11. Baldwin, "My Vacation on the Government," n.d., pp. 2–3, 5; Baldwin to Lucy Baldwin, November 12, 1918, pp. 1–2, both in Baldwin Papers.

12. Baldwin, "How I 'Took the Veil," November 15, 1918, p. 7, Baldwin Papers; Baldwin, "Reminiscences," pp. 97–98; Baldwin, "My Vacation on the Government," n.d., pp. 1–5, Baldwin Papers; Baldwin to Lucy Baldwin, November 22, 1918, pp. 1–2, Baldwin Papers; Baldwin, "To a Sycamore," March 1919, Baldwin Papers; Baldwin, "Walls," 1919, Baldwin Papers; Baldwin, "To a Purple Finch," May 1919, Baldwin Papers; Baldwin, "The Gray Enchanter," June 1919, Baldwin Papers.

13. Baldwin to Scott Nearing, November 18, 1918, pp. 1–3, Baldwin Papers.

14. Baldwin to DeSilver, March 5, 1919, pp. 1–3; Baldwin, "My Vacation on the Government," n.d., p. 3, both in Baldwin Papers.

15. Baldwin to John J. Hanley, December 17, 1918, p. 1, Baldwin Papers; Baldwin, "Reminiscences," pp. 98–99; Finch, "ROGER N. BALDWIN, Ex. Director, Natl. Civil Liberties Bureau: Intellectual Radical Activities," p. 3.

16. Baldwin, "The War-Time Bureau: Jail and Prison," n.d., p. 7A, Baldwin Papers; Baldwin, "Reminiscences," p. 99; Baldwin to My Friends, May 26, 1919, Baldwin Papers; Baldwin, "Some Penitentiary," n.d., p. 1, Baldwin Papers; Peggy Lamson, *Roger Baldwin: Founder of the American Civil Liberties Union: A Portrait* (Boston: Houghton Mifflin, 1976), pp. 101–102.

17. Baldwin, "The War-Time Bureau," n.d., p. 7A; Baldwin to My Friends, May 26, 1919; Baldwin, "Some Penitentiary," n.d., pp. 1–3, all in Baldwin Papers; Baldwin, "Reminiscences," pp. 100–101.

18. Baldwin, "Some Penitentiary," n.d., pp. 2–3, Baldwin Papers.

19. Baldwin to My Friends, May 26, 1919; Baldwin, "Some Penitentiary," n.d., p. 3, both in Baldwin Papers.

20. Baldwin, "Some Penitentiary," n.d., p. 3, Baldwin Papers.

21. Ibid., pp. 1–3; Lamson, *Roger Baldwin*, p. 104; Arthur Dunham, interview by Vida S. Grayson, July 19, 1979, pp. 93–95, Columbia University Oral History Project.

22. Lamson, *Roger Baldwin*, pp. 104–105.

23. Baldwin, "The Immorality of Social Work," *World Tomorrow* 5 (February 1922): 44–45.

24. Baldwin, "Reminiscences," pp. 101–102; Brownie Brown to Baldwin, April 16, 1919, Baldwin Papers; Baldwin to My Friends, July 31, 1919, Baldwin Papers.

25. "Baldwin Quits Pacifist Cell to Join I.W.W.," *New York Herald Tribune*, n.d., Baldwin Papers.

26. Ibid.

27. Baldwin to My Friends, July 31, 1919, Baldwin Papers; Lucille Milner, *Education of an American Liberal: An Autobiography* (New York: Horizon, 1954), pp. 119–20.

28. Ibid., p. 120.

29. Oswald Garrison Villard, "On Being in Jail," *Nation*, August 2, 1919, pp. 142–43.

30. Baldwin, "Reminiscences," pp. 137–39.

9. An Unconventional Marriage

1. Roger Baldwin, "*The Roger Baldwin Story*. A Prejudiced Account by Himself," 1979, p. 4; Baldwin, "A Memo on Madeleine Zabriskie Doty for the Files at Smith College," October 1978, p. 1, both in Roger Nash Baldwin Papers, Public Policy Papers, Department of Rare Books and Special Collections, Princeton University Libraries.

2. Baldwin, "A Memo on Madeleine Zabriskie Doty," October 1978, p. 2; Peggy Lamson, *Roger Baldwin: Founder of the American Civil Liberties Union: A Portrait* (Boston: Houghton Mifflin, 1976), p. 115; Madeleine Z. Doty, unpublished autobiography, pp. 1–2, chap. 12, Doty Papers, Smith College.

3. Baldwin, "A Memo on Madeleine Zabriskie Doty," October 1978, p. 2, Baldwin Papers.

4. Ibid.; Baldwin to Doty, September 26, 1918, p. 1; Baldwin to Doty, October 14, 1918, p. 1; Baldwin to Doty, October 31, 1918, pp. 1–2, all in Baldwin Papers.

5. Baldwin to Doty, January 6, 1919, pp. 1–3, Baldwin Papers.

6. Doty, unpublished autobiography, pp. 2, 4, 7, chap. 12, Doty Papers; Baldwin, "A Memo on Madeleine Zabriskie Doty," October 1978, p. 2, Baldwin Papers; Baldwin to Doty, March 1919, p. 1, Baldwin Papers.

7. Baldwin to Doty, March 31, 1919, pp. 1–3; Baldwin, "Some Facts about the More Personal Life of Roger N. Baldwin," 1961, p. B4; Baldwin, "Some Notes by Roger Baldwin for Memoirs Not Covered in the Oral History," November 1964, pp. F-3–F-4, all in Baldwin Papers.

8. Baldwin to Doty, April 4, 1919; Baldwin to Doty, July 1919, both in Baldwin Papers.

9. Lamson, *Roger Baldwin*, p. 114; Doty, unpublished autobiography, pp. 30–31, chap. 12, Doty Papers; Baldwin to Doty, July 1919, p. 3, Baldwin Papers; Baldwin, "*The Roger Baldwin Story*," 1979, p. 4, Baldwin Papers; Baldwin, "The War-Time Bureau: Jail and Prison," n.d., p. 8A, Baldwin Papers; Baldwin, "Highlights of Roger Baldwin's Private Life," ca. 1972, Baldwin Papers; Baldwin, "A Memo on Madeleine Zabriskie Doty," October 1978, p. 2, Baldwin Papers; Joseph P. Lash interview with Herbert Baldwin and Robert Baldwin, October 26, 1971, Joseph P. Lash Papers, Franklin Delano Roosevelt Presidential Library, Hyde Park, N.Y.; Lash interview with Roger Baldwin, March 6, 1972, Lash Papers.

10. Doty, "Today We Start," August 8, 1919, pp. 1–2, Doty Papers.

11. Baldwin, "Roger Baldwin, 1920s," n.d., pp. 1–2, Doty Papers.

12. Baldwin, "*The Roger Baldwin Story*," 1979, p. 4; Baldwin, "The War-Time Bureau," n.d., p. 8A; Baldwin, "Highlights of Roger Baldwin's Private Life," ca. 1972; Baldwin, "A Memo on Madeleine Zabriskie Doty," October 1978, p. 2, all in Baldwin Papers; Lamson, *Roger Baldwin*, p. 121; Doty, unpublished autobiography, pp. 32–33, chap. 12, Doty Papers.

13. Baldwin, "A Memo on the Old Greenwich Village by Roger Baldwin for Robert Humphrey," May 1972, pp. 1–2, Baldwin Papers.

14. Robert A. Rosenstone, *Romantic Revolutionary: A Biography of John Reed* (New York: Vintage, 1981), pp. 99–105; Henry F. May, *The End of American Innocence: A Study of the First Years of Our Own Time, 1912–1917* (Chicago: Quadrangle, 1964), pp. 283–85; Robert E. Humphrey, *Children of Fantasy: The First Rebels of Greenwich Village* (New York: Wiley, 1978); June Sochen, *The New Woman: Feminism in Greenwich Village, 1910–1920* (New York: Quadrangle, 1972); Leslie Fishbein, *Rebels in Bohemia: The Radicals of the* Masses, *1911–1917* (Chapel Hill: University of North Carolina Press, 1982).

15. Lamson, *Roger Baldwin*, p. 118; Nearing to Baldwin, May 5, 1919, pp. 2–3, Baldwin Papers.

16. Roger Baldwin, "The Reminiscences of Roger Nash Baldwin," 1954, p. 103, Columbia University Oral History Collection.

17. Evan Thomas to Baldwin, May 30, 1919, pp. 1–3; Harold L. Varney to Baldwin, July 24, 1919, both in Baldwin Papers.

18. Baldwin to Bill Haywood, September 15, 1919; Haywood to Baldwin, September 17, 1919, both in Baldwin Papers.

19. Baldwin, "Reminiscences," pp. 104–105.

20. Baldwin to Doty, October 2, 1919, pp. 1–2, Doty Papers.

21. Baldwin, "Reminiscences," pp. 105–106; Lamson, *Roger Baldwin*, p. 119; National Archives, "Radicalism in St. Louis: Industrial Workers of the World," October 7, 1919, Military Intelligence Division Documents (hereafter MIDD), 10110-1146-203; Baldwin, "I Used to Flatter Myself," n.d., p. 1, Baldwin Papers.

22. Baldwin, "Reminiscences," pp. 106–109; Lamson, *Roger Baldwin*, p. 119; Baldwin to Haywood, November 10, 1919, Baldwin Papers; Industrial Workers of the World receipt, November 18, 1919, Baldwin Papers.

23. Baldwin, "Reminiscences," pp. 109–11; Baldwin, "I Used to Flatter Myself," n.d., p. 2, Baldwin Papers.

24. Baldwin, "Reminiscences," pp. 111–12.

25. Lucy Baldwin to Doty, October 24, 1919, pp. 1–2, Doty Papers.

26. Doty, unpublished autobiography, chap. 12, p. 33; Baldwin, "Madeleine Doty, A Post-Script," n.d., p. 1, both in Doty Papers.

27. Doty, unpublished autobiography, chap. 12, pp. 33–34, Doty Papers; Lamson, *Roger Baldwin*, p. 121.

28. Doty, unpublished autobiography, chap. 12, pp. 35–36, Doty Papers.

29. Ibid., p. 35; Beulah Powers, "Hubby Pays Wife for Doing Housework in Happy Doty-Baldwin 50-50 Marriage," *New York Evening Mail*, September 15, 1920, Doty Papers.

30. Travis Hoke, "Red Rainbow," *North American Review* 234 (November 1932): 437–38; Doty, unpublished autobiography, chap. 12, pp. 36–37, Doty Papers.

31. Baldwin, "A Memo on Madeleine Zabriskie Doty," October 1978, p. 2A, Baldwin Papers; Baldwin, "Madeleine Doty, A Post-Script," n.d., p. 2, Doty Papers; Lamson, *Roger Baldwin*, pp. 122, 150; Doty, unpublished autobiography, chap. 12, p. 37, Doty Papers.

32. Lash interviews with Roger Baldwin, March 6, 1972, and October 21, 1971, Lash Papers.

33. Doty, unpublished autobiography, chap. 12, p. 38; Baldwin to Doty, June 14, 1921, pp. 1–2, both in Doty Papers.

34. Baldwin to Doty, May 20 (year uncertain), pp. 1–3, Doty Papers.

35. Baldwin to Doty, July 27, 1921, pp. 1–2, 4, Doty Papers.

36. Doty, unpublished autobiography, chap. 12, pp. 38–39, Doty Papers.

37. Ibid., pp. 39–41.

38. Baldwin to Mary E. Buckley, July 17, 1922, pp. 1–3, Baldwin Papers.

39. Doty, unpublished autobiography, chap. 12, pp. 41–42, Doty Papers.

40. Ibid., pp. 40–41.

41. Lucy Baldwin to Roger Baldwin, 1923 (date uncertain), Doty Papers.

42. Doty, unpublished autobiography, chap. 12, pp. 41–45, Doty Papers; Baldwin, "A Memo on Madeleine Zabriskie Doty," p. 2A, Baldwin Papers; Lamson, *Roger Baldwin*, pp. 150–53.

43. Doty, unpublished autobiography, chap. 12, p. 45, Doty Papers.

44. Ibid., pp. 43–46; Baldwin, "A Memo on Madeleine Zabriskie Doty," October 1978, p. 2A, Baldwin Papers; Baldwin to Doty, July 9, 1925, Doty Papers.

45. Baldwin to Doty, July 9, 1925, Doty Papers.

46. Lash interview with Lucille Milner, March 22, 1972, Lash Papers.

47. Doty, unpublished autobiography, chap. 12, pp. 46–47, Doty Papers.

48. Baldwin, "A Memo on Madeleine Zabriskie Doty," October 1978, p. 2A, Baldwin Papers; Lamson, *Roger Baldwin*, pp. 175–80; Doty to Baldwin, 1927, Baldwin Papers; Baldwin, "A Memo on Madeleine Zabriskie Doty," October 1978, p. 3, Baldwin Papers; Baldwin, "Madeleine Doty, a Post-Script," n.d., p. 3, Baldwin Papers.

49. Malini Pethick-Lawrence to Baldwin, July 5, 1927, pp. 1–5, Baldwin Papers.

10. The American Civil Liberties Union

1. "Sixty-two Are Named in 'Who's Who' of Pacifism," *New York Tribune*, January 25, 1919, p. 4.

2. W. A. Swanberg, *Norman Thomas: The Last Idealist* (New York: Scribner's, 1976), p. 73; "Who's Who in Leadership of Organized Bolshevik Movement in the U.S.," 1919, Roger Nash Baldwin Papers, Public Policy Papers, Department of Rare Books and Special Collections, Princeton University Libraries.

3. Department Intelligence Office, Chicago, "Report: The Fellowship of Reconciliation," September 23, 1919, Military Intelligence Division Documents (hereafter MIDD), 10902-13.

4. A fine summary of the postwar Red Scare can be found in Samuel Walker, *In Defense of Civil Liberties: A History of the American Civil Liberties Union* (New York: Oxford University Press, 1990), pp. 42–44.

5. Peggy Lamson, *Roger Baldwin: Founder of the American Civil Liberties Union* (Boston: Houghton Mifflin, 1976), p. 123; Baldwin, "The Reminiscences of Roger Nash Baldwin," 1954, p. 115, Columbia University Oral History Collection; Joseph P. Lash interview with Roger Baldwin, March 6, 1972, Joseph P. Lash Papers, Franklin Delano Roosevelt Presidential Library, Hyde Park, N.Y.

6. Baldwin to Albert DeSilver, August 12, 1919, Baldwin Papers; Lamson, *Roger Baldwin*, pp. 123–24; Walker, *In Defense*, p. 46; Baldwin to H. Austin Simons, December 8, 1919, Baldwin Papers.

7. Lamson, *Roger Baldwin*, p. 124; Joseph Freeman, *An American Testament: A Narrative of Rebels and Romantics* (New York: Octagon, 1973), p. 242.

8. Lamson, *Roger Baldwin*, p. 46.

9. Baldwin, "Reminiscences," pp. 115–16.

10. Ibid., pp. 115–17, 123–24; Donald Johnson, *The Challenge to American Freedoms: World War I and the Rise of the American Civil Liberties Union* (Lexington: University of Kentucky Press, 1963), p. 147; Eugene Lyons, *The Red Decade: The Stalinist Penetration of America* (Indianapolis, Ind.: Bobbs-Merrill, 1941).

11. Baldwin, "Reminiscences," pp. 156, 126–27.

12. Ibid., p. 58, 127–28; Baldwin, introduction to *American Civil Liberties Union: Annual Reports*, vol. 1 (New York: Arno Press and the *New York Times*, 1970); "Albert

DeSilver," in ACLU, *Free Speech in 1924*, annual report (New York: ACLU, 1925), p. 2.

13. Lash interview with Lucille Milner, March 22, 1972, Lash Papers.

14. Baldwin, "Reminiscences," pp. 130–37; Lash interview with Morris Ernst, February 7, 1972, Box 49, Lash Papers.

15. Baldwin, "Reminiscences," pp. 153–55, 165–66.

16. Ibid., pp. 155, 163–64; Walker, *In Defense*, pp. 69–70, 67.

17. Walker, *In Defense*, pp. 51, 68–69.

18. Baldwin, "Reminiscences," pp. 155–57.

19. Ibid., pp. 157–58; Eugene Lyons, *The Red Decade: The Stalinist Penetration of America* (Indianapolis: Bobbs-Merrill, 1941), pp. 148, 372.

20. Joseph Freeman, *An American Testament: A Narrative of Rebels and Romantics* (New York: Octagon, 1973), pp. 327–28.

21. Walker, *In Defense*, p. 69.

22. Lash interview with Philip Taft, October 12, 1972, Lash Papers.

23. Lash interview with Anna Friedkin, January 16, 1972, Box 49, Lash Papers.

24. Lash interview with Morris Ernst, February 7, 1972, Lash Papers.

25. Baldwin, "Memorandum on Conditions Observed on Trip Throughout U.S. in May and June 1920," vol. 23, ACLU Papers, Princeton University; Helen C. Camp, *Iron in Her Soul: Elizabeth Gurley Flynn and the American Left* (Pullman: Washington State University, 1995), p. 164.

26. Roger Baldwin, "Freedom of Opinion," *Socialist Review* 9 (August 1920): 115.

27. Ibid.

28. ACLU, *The Fight for Free Speech*, annual report (New York: ACLU, 1921), pp. 3–4.

29. Ibid., pp. 4–8, 15–18.

30. Baldwin to Dr. Cabot, March 7, 1922, Baldwin Papers; Roger Baldwin, "How Shall We Escape Private Property?" *World Tomorrow* (April 1922): 109–10.

31. Baldwin, "Who's Got Free Speech?" 1923, p. 3, Baldwin Papers.

32. Baldwin, "Garland's Million," ca. 1934, pp. 1–3; Baldwin, "A Memo on Charles Garland," February 1975, p. 1, both in Baldwin Papers; Merle Curti, "Subsidizing Radicalism: The American Fund for Public Service, 1921–1941," *Social Service Review* 33 (September 1959): 275–77; Walker, *In Defense*, p. 70; Baldwin, "Reminiscences," pp. 324–26. See Gloria Garrett Samson, *The American Fund for Public Service: Charles Garland and Radical Philanthropy, 1922–1941* (Westport, Conn.: Greenwood, 1996).

33. "[American Fund] Board of Directors: Correspondence, 1922–1923," Box 1, American Fund for Public Service Papers, New York Public Library; Baldwin, "Reminiscences," p. 326; Curti, "Subsidizing Radicalism," p. 276.

34. Baldwin, "Garland's Million," ca. 1934, pp. 2–4, Baldwin Papers.

35. Lash interview with Roger Baldwin, March 6, 1972, Lash Papers; Baldwin to Goldman, September 12, 1922, p. 2, Emma Goldman Papers, New York University;

Baldwin to Goldman, February 12, 1923, p. 2, Goldman Papers; Baldwin to Goldman, November 20, 1923, Goldman Papers.

36. Baldwin to the Board of Directors of the American Fund for Public Service, Inc., June 22, 1925, Box 1, Charles Garland Papers, New York Public Library.

37. Baldwin, "Garland's Million," ca. 1934, pp. 6–7, Baldwin Papers.

38. Ibid., pp. 7–9; Lamson, *Roger Baldwin*, p. 149; Constance Ashton Myers, *The Prophet's Army: Trotskyists in America, 1928–1941* (Westport, Conn.: Greenwood, 1977), p. 72; Curti, "Subsidizing Radicalism," p. 281.

39. Baldwin, "Garland's Million," ca. 1934, pp. 7–9, Baldwin Papers.

40. Ibid.; Curti, "Subsidizing Radicalism," p. 292.

41. Baldwin, "Garland's Million," ca. 1934, p. 10, Baldwin Papers; Freeman, *American Testament*, pp. 338–39.

42. Baldwin, "Garland's Million," ca. 1934, p. 10, Baldwin Papers; Baldwin to the board of directors of the American Fund for Public Service, October 17, 1923, Box 1, Garland Papers; Baldwin, "Summary of Nineteen Years of Operation: July 5, 1923–June 30, 1941," Baldwin Papers.

43. Lash interview with Ernst, February 7, 1972, Lash Papers.

44. Baldwin, "A Memo on Charles Garland," ca. 1934, p. 2, Baldwin Papers; Baldwin, "Reminiscences," pp. 330–31.

11. *The ACLU Under Suspicion*

1. Col. Gordon Johnston and Capt. John B. Campbell to Intelligence Officer, U.S. Disciplinary Barracks, Ft. Leavenworth, Kansas, May 3, 1920, Military Intelligence Division Documents (hereafter MIDD), 10902-13, National Archives; New York Senate, *Revolutionary Radicalism: Its History, Purpose, and Tactics* (Albany: J. B. Lyon, 1920), vol. 1, pp. 1021–23.

2. New York Senate, *Revolutionary Radicalism*, vol. 1, p. 1088.

3. "Civil Liberty Union Record Investigated," *Stroudsburg* (Pa.) *Sun*, April 18, 1931, pp. 1–2, vol. 464, ACLU Papers, Princeton University.

4. Richard Gid Powers, *Not Without Honor: The History of American Anticommunism* (New York: Free Press, 1995), p. 30, and *Secrecy and Power: The Life of J. Edgar Hoover* (New York: Free Press, 1987), p. 108.

5. Curt Gentry, *J. Edgar Hoover: The Man and His Secrets* (New York: Norton, 1991), p. 140; Roger Baldwin, "The ACLU and the FBI: 'They Never Stopped Watching Us,'" *Civil Liberties Review* 4 (November–December 1977): 20–21; David Williams, "The Bureau of Investigation and Its Critics, 1919–1921: The Origins of Federal Political Surveillance," *Journal of American History* 68 (December 1981): 560–79.

6. Gentry, *J. Edgar Hoover*, p. 140.

7. Ibid., pp. 140–41; Baldwin, "The ACLU and the FBI," p. 21; Theodore Draper, *The Roots of American Communism* (Chicago: Ivan R. Dee, 1989), p. 371.

8. R. M. Whitney, *Reds in America: The Present Status of the Revolutionary Movement in the United States Based on Documents Seized by the Authorities in the Raid upon the Convention of the Communist Party at Bridgman, Michigan, August 22, 1922, Together with Descriptions of Numerous Connections and Associations of the Communists Among the Radicals, Progressives and Pinks* (Boston: Western Islands Publishers, 1924), pp. 181–84; Draper, *Roots of American Communism*, pp. 371–72.

9. E. B. Harrigan, "Roger Baldwin," February 11, 1922, p. 1–2, FBI File, 100-49565-X2; J. Edgar Hoover to Mr. Rush, November 21, 1922, FBI File, 100-49565-X3; "Memorandum. In Re: Roger Nash Baldwin," December 15, 1922, FBI File, 100-49565-X6.

10. Wilbur F. Crafts to the Attorney General, September 8, 1922, Box 3165, Department of Justice Straight Numerical Files, National Archives.

11. "In Re," October 26, 1923, FBI File; Donald Johnson, *The Challenge to American Freedoms: World War I and the Rise of the American Civil Liberties Union* (Lexington: University of Kentucky Press, 1963), p. 165.

12. William J. Burns to Lawrence Richay, November 3, 1923, FBI File, 100-49565-X8; Burns to E. J. Brennan, November 4, 1923, FBI File, 100-49565-X9; "Memorandum for Spec. Agt. in Charge Brennan: Re: Roger N. Baldwin, Attempt to Broadcast Radical Speech Via Radio," November 7, 1923, pp. 1–2, FBI File, 100-49565-X106.

13. [Name of sender blotted out by FBI] to Burns, February 19, 1924, FBI File, 100-49565-X14; Burns to [recipient blotted out by FBI], February 26, 1924, FBI File, 100-49565-X14.

14. Baldwin to Lauck, March 28, 1924, vol. 38; Baldwin to Lauck, April 2, 1924, vol. 38, both in ACLU Papers.

15. Baldwin to W. Jett Lauck, February 11, 1924, vol. 38; Baldwin, "Memorandum," vol. 38, both in ACLU Papers.

16. Baldwin, "The Reminiscences of Roger Nash Baldwin," 1954, pp. 180–81, Columbia University Oral History Collection; Baldwin to Harlan F. Stone, April 4, 1924, vol. 38, ACLU Papers; Samuel Walker, *In Defense of American Liberties: A History of the ACLU* (New York: Oxford University Press, 1990), p. 65.

17. Baldwin to the Committee on Appropriations, April 26, 1924, vol. 38, ACLU Papers.

18. Ibid., p. 3.

19. Baldwin to Stone, May 21, 1924, vol. 38; Baldwin to Stone, June 19, 1924, vol. 38; Baldwin to William B. Colver, September 9, 1924, vol. 83, all in ACLU Papers; Eugene Lyons, *The Red Decade: The Stalinist Penetration of America* (Indianapolis, Ind.: Bobbs-Merrill, 1941), pp. 148, 372.

20. Baldwin, "The ACLU and the FBI," pp. 22, 24; Gentry, *J. Edgar Hoover*, pp. 138–39; Athan G. Theoharis and John Stuart Cox, *The Boss: J. Edgar Hoover and the Great American Inquisition* (New York: Bantam, 1990), pp. 98–99.

21. Baldwin to Stone, August 7, 1924, vol. 38; Baldwin to Stone, August 11, 1924, vol. 38, both in ACLU Papers; Johnson, *Challenge to American Freedoms*, p. 175; Baldwin, "Memorandum on the Department of Justice–Bureau of Investigation," October 17, 1924, vol. 38, ACLU Papers.

22. Gentry, *J. Edgar Hoover*, pp. 139–40; Frank J. Donner, *The Age of Surveillance: The Aims and Methods of America's Political Intelligence System* (New York: Vintage, 1981), pp. 145–46.

23. Stone to Baldwin, January 17, 1925, vol. 38; Baldwin to M. C. Harrison, January 19, 1925, vol. 38, both in ACLU Papers.

24. Walker, *In Defense*, p. 57; Baldwin, "Reminiscences," p. 166; Baldwin, "The Professional Patriots Racket," n.d., pp. 1–3, Baldwin Papers.

25. Powers, *Not Without Honor*, pp. 75–78; Whitney, *Reds in America*, pp. 59, 121.

26. Whitney, *Reds in America*, pp. 124, 126–27.

27. Ibid., pp. 128–29.

28. Blair Coan, *The Red Web* (Chicago: Northwest, 1925), pp. 91, 93–94, 118; Powers, *Not Without Honor*, p. 72.

29. Baldwin to William Z. Foster, January 31, 1925, vol. 41, ACLU Papers.

30. Baldwin, letter to editor, *Daily Worker*, February 10, 1925, vol. 41, ACLU Papers.

31. Earl Browder to Baldwin, February 17, 1925, vol. 41; Baldwin to Browder, February 21, 1925, vol. 41; William F. Dunne to Baldwin, March 7, 1925, vol. 41; Baldwin to Dunne, March 11, 1925, pp. 1–2, vol. 41, all in ACLU Papers.

32. Baldwin to Browder, March 3, 1925, pp. 1–2, vol. 41; Baldwin to Browder, March 11, 1925, vol. 41; Baldwin and John Haynes Holmes to Browder, March 11, 1925, vol. 41; Browder to Baldwin, March 12, 1925, pp. 1–2, vol. 41, all in ACLU Papers.

33. Baldwin to Robert Morss Lovett, March 14, 1925, vol. 41; Baldwin to Browder, March 14, 1925, vol. 41, both in ACLU Papers.

34. Ernst to Baldwin, March 19, 1925, vol. 41, ACLU Papers.

35. John Haynes Holmes et al. to the Central Executive Committee, Workers Party of America, March 19, 1925, pp. 1–2, vol. 41; Browder to Friends, April 2, 1925, pp. 1–2, vol. 41, both in ACLU Papers.

36. Baldwin to Browder, April 5, 1925, vol. 41, ACLU Papers.

37. George Maurer to Baldwin, May 30, 1925, vol. 41; Baldwin to Maurer, June 2, 1925, pp. 1–3, vol. 41; ACLU to Robert Morss Lovett, June 4, 1925, vol. 41; Maurer to Baldwin, June 4, 1925, pp. 1–2, vol. 41; Baldwin to Maurer, June 6, 1925, vol. 41; Baldwin to Edward C. Wentworth, June 6, 1925, vol. 41; Maurer to Baldwin, June 12, 1925, pp. 1–2, vol. 41; Baldwin to Emil E. Holmes, June 15, 1925, vol. 41; Baldwin to Wentworth, June 12, 1925, pp. 1–2, vol. 41, all in ACLU Papers.

38. Baldwin to Wentworth, June 19, 1925, vol. 41; Baldwin to Friends, June 17, 1925, vol. 41; Baldwin to Maurer, June 19, 1925, pp. 1–2, vol. 41, all in ACLU Papers.

39. Baldwin to Maurer, July 20, 1925, vol. 41, ACLU Papers; Baldwin to Eugene Debs, July 13, 1925; and Baldwin to Eugene Debs, July 22, 1925, both in ACLU Papers.

40. Roger Baldwin, "Where Are the Pre-War Radicals?" *Survey* 55 (February 1, 1926): 560.

41. Robert L. Duffus, "The Legend of Roger Baldwin," *American Mercury*, August 1925, pp. 408–14.

42. Ibid., pp. 413–14.

43. "Roger N. Baldwin," April 12, 1926, pp. 1–2, MIDD, 10902-13; Col. Perry Weidner, "Extra Special: Roger N. Baldwin," April 13, 1926, MIDD, 10902-13.

44. "Memorandum to: The Assistant Chief of Staff, G-2," June 8, 1926, pp. 1–4, MIDD, 10902-13.

12. Turning to the Courts

1. Roger Baldwin, "The Reminiscences of Roger Nash Baldwin," 1954, pp. 151, 169, Columbia University Oral History Collection.

2. Ibid., pp. 173–74; Samuel Walker, *In Defense of American Liberties: A History of the ACLU* (New York: Oxford University Press, 1990), p. 77; Peggy Lamson, *Roger Baldwin: Founder of the American Civil Liberties Union* (Boston: Houghton Mifflin, 1976), p. 159; Baldwin to Our Friends, October 9, 1924, vol. 37, ACLU Papers, Princeton University; Charles J. Pirole acknowledgment, October 9, 1924, vol. 37, ACLU Papers; ACLU, *Free Speech in 1924*, annual report (New York: ACLU, 1925), p. 23.

3. Baldwin, "Reminiscences," p. 243.

4. Ibid., p. 244; "Here's What Really Happened," vol. 37, ACLU Papers; Oliver Jensen, "The Persuasive Roger Baldwin," *Harper's*, September 1951, p. 51.

5. Baldwin, "Reminiscences," pp. 244–45; "Testimony of Roger N. Baldwin Before Judge Joseph A. Delaney of the Paterson Court of Common Pleas," December 17, 1924, p. 4, ACLU Papers; Baldwin, "Memorandum of Conversation Between Roger N. Baldwin and Chief of Police John M. Tracey," December 12, 1924, pp. 1–3, vol. 37, ACLU Papers.

6. Baldwin, "Reminiscences," pp. 244–45; "Here's What Really Happened," vol. 37, ACLU Papers; ACLU, *Free Speech in 1924*, p. 26.

7. Baldwin, "Reminiscences," pp. 245–46; "Here's the Grand Jury Indictment," vol. 37, ACLU Papers; Charles Lamm Markmann, *The Noblest Cry: A History of the American Civil Liberties Union* (New York: St. Martin's, 1965), p. 71; "Jail for Man Known as Aristocrat at Harvard," *Boston Globe*, 1924, Madeleine Z. Doty Papers, Smith College; John Haynes Holmes to Baldwin, November 28, 1924, vol. 37, ACLU Papers; ACLU, *Free Speech in 1924*, p. 26.

8. Baldwin, "Reminiscences," pp. 246–47; "Testimony of Roger N. Baldwin Before Judge Joseph A. Delaney," pp. 1–9; Joseph Freeman, "News Release," December 15–16, 1924, p. 1, vol. 37, ACLU Papers.

9. Lamson, *Roger Baldwin*, pp. 160–61; ACLU, *Free Speech in 1924*, pp. 26–27.

10. Baldwin, "Reminiscences," pp. 247–48; "Baldwin Cleared in Textile Strike," *New York Times*, May 15, 1928, Doty Papers, Smith College; Elizabeth Gurley Flynn to Friend, September 3, 1925, Box 1, Garland Fund Papers, New York Public Library; Walter Nelles to Scott Nearing and Elizabeth Gurley Flynn, September 1, 1925, Box 1, Garland Fund Papers; Walter Nelles to John Haynes Holmes, September 1, 1925, Box 1, Garland Fund Papers; Walter Nelles to Elizabeth Gurley Flynn, September 8, 1925, pp. 1–2, Box 1, Garland Fund Papers.

11. "Baldwin Cleared in Textile Strike"; Walker, *In Defense*, p. 79; "There Are Judges in Trenton," *New York Times*, May 16, 1928, p. 24.

12. Lamson, *Roger Baldwin*, pp. 163–65; Walker, *In Defense*, p. 72.

13. Lamson, *Roger Baldwin*, pp. 165–66; John T. Scopes and James Presley, *Center of the Storm: Memoirs of John T. Scopes* (New York: Holt, Rinehart and Winston, 1967), pp. 66–67.

14. Scopes and Presley, *Center of the Storm*, p. 70; Walker, *In Defense*, p. 73; Lamson, *Roger Baldwin*, p. 166.

15. Lamson, *Roger Baldwin*, p. 167; Walker, *In Defense*, pp. 74–75.

16. Lamson, *Roger Baldwin*, pp. 167–68; Baldwin, "How Did the Union Get Involved in the Tennessee Evolution Case?" n.d., pp. 1–3, Roger Nash Baldwin Papers, Public Policy Papers, Department of Rare Books and Special Collections, Princeton University Libraries.

17. Baldwin, "Reminiscences," pp. 229, 231–33, 236–37; Baldwin, "Memo on Sacco and Vanzetti," 1974, Baldwin Papers.

18. Baldwin, "Memo on Sacco and Vanzetti"; Baldwin, "Reminiscences," pp. 229–230; Joseph P. Lash interview with Herbert and Robert Baldwin, October 26, 1971, Joseph P. Lash Papers, Franklin Delano Roosevelt Presidential Library, Hyde Park, N.Y.; Roberta Strauss Feuerlicht, *Justice Crucified: The Story of Sacco and Vanzetti* (New York: McGraw-Hill, 1977), p. 192.

19. Baldwin, "Reminiscences," pp. 234–35.

20. Baldwin, "Memorandum for the Sacco-Vanzetti Defense Committee," October 12, 1924, p. 3, vol. 37; Baldwin to Sanford Bates, October 15, 1924, vol. 37, both in ACLU Papers.

21. Fred H. Meyer to Baldwin, October 17, 1924, pp. 1–3, vol. 37; Baldwin, "Memorandum for the Sacco-Vanzetti Defense Committee," October 12, 1924, pp. 1–3, both in ACLU Papers.

22. Baldwin, "Reminiscences," p. 235; Gardner Jackson, inteview by Dean Albertson, 1955, p. 210, Columbia University Oral History Project.

23. Robert H. Montgomery, *Sacco-Vanzetti: The Murder and the Myth* (New York: Devin-Adair, 1960), pp. 76–78.

24. Baldwin, "Reminiscences," p. 231; Bartolomeo Vanzetti to Baldwin, June 25, 1927, pp. 1–3, Baldwin Papers.

25. Baldwin, "Reminiscences," pp. 232–33.

26. Baldwin, "Abstract of Speech of Roger N. Baldwin," 1928, p. 4, Baldwin Papers.

27. Baldwin, "Reminiscences," pp. 222–23.

28. Baldwin to Mary Fleisher, January 28, 1929, pp. 1–2; Baldwin to Austin Lewis, April 22, 1929, pp. 1–2; Baldwin to Lewis, April 30, 1929, pp. 1–3; Warren K. Billings to Baldwin, May 12, 1929, pp. 1–2, all in Box Correspondence, Austin Lewis Papers, Bancroft Library, University of California–Berkeley.

29. Roger Baldwin, "While California's Governor Deliberates," *Unity*, August 12, 1929, pp. 329–30.

30. Baldwin, "Reminiscences," pp. 224–25; Harvey Klehr, *The Heyday of American Communism: The Depression Decade* (New York: Basic, 1984), p. 102.

31. Baldwin, "Reminiscences," p. 238; Dan T. Carter, *Scottsboro: A Tragedy of the American South* (New York: Oxford University Press, 1971); James Goodman, *Stories of Scottsboro* (New York: Vintage, 1995); Baldwin to Charles Erskine Wood, February 29, 1932, vol. 557, ACLU Papers; Baldwin to Walter White, January 5, 1932, vol. 557, ACLU Papers; Baldwin to White, March 15, 1932, p. 1, vol. 557, ACLU Papers; Baldwin to White, March 19, 1932, vol. 557, ACLU Papers; Baldwin to White, August 17, 1932, vol. 557, ACLU Papers.

32. Baldwin, "Reminiscences," p. 239.

33. Ibid., pp. 240–41.

34. Arthur Hays to Baldwin, March 5, 1932, vol. 557; Clarence Darrow to White, March 10, 1932, vol. 557, both in ACLU Papers.

35. Martha Gruening to Baldwin, May 11, 1932, vol. 557, ACLU Papers.

36. Baldwin to William C. Biddle, August 12, 1932, vol. 557, ACLU Papers.

37. Baldwin to White, August 17, 1932, vol. 557; White to Baldwin, August 23, 1932, p. 1, vol. 557, both in ACLU Papers.

38. Klehr, *Heyday of American Communism*, p. 338.

39. Walker, *In Defense*, pp. 81–82; "A Fraud Exposed," *Chicago Daily Tribune*, April 13, 1933, vol. 630, ACLU Papers.

40. "A Fraud Exposed."

41. Baldwin, letter to editor, *Chicago Tribune*, April 14, 1933, pp. 1–2, vol. 613; Baldwin, "Civil Liberties," *Chicago Tribune*, April 24, 1933, p. 1, vol. 613, both in ACLU Papers.

42. ACLU, Board of Directors Minutes, November 26, 1934, Reel 5, ACLU Papers.

43. Baldwin to Mr. Rockey, June 21, 1966, Baldwin Papers.

44. Roger Baldwin to Ernest Boyer, February 23, 1966, Baldwin Papers; Walker, *In Defense*, pp. 82–83; Lash interview with Roger Baldwin, March 6, 1972, Lash Papers.

45. Walker, *In Defense*, p. 83; Lash interview with Roger Baldwin, March 6, 1972, Lash Papers.

46. Walker, *In Defense*, p. 83; Zechariah Chafee Jr., *Censorship in Boston*. Boston: Civil Liberties Union of Massachusetts, 1929.

47. ACLU, Board of Directors Minutes, October 21, 1929, Reel 2, ACLU Papers.

48. Walker, *In Defense*, pp. 85–86.

49. "Drive for Fascism Charged by Ickes," *New York Times*, December 9, 1937, pp. 1, 20; "Baldwin Accuses Hague of Tyranny," *New York Times, December* 16, 1937, p. 3; "Jersey Labor Party Denounced by Hague," December 18, 1937, *New York Times*, p. 5; ACLU, *Eternal Vigilance!* annual report (New York: ACLU, 1938), pp. 35–37.

13. International Human Rights

1. Roger Baldwin, "A Memo on My International Associations," pp. 1–2, March 1974, p. 1, Roger Nash Baldwin Papers, Public Policy Papers, Department of Rare Books and Special Collections, Princeton University Libraries; Peggy Lamson, *Roger Baldwin: Founder of the American Civil Liberties Union* (Boston: Houghton Mifflin, 1976), pp. 144–46; Baldwin to Mr. Saran, November 22, 1971, Baldwin Papers; Baldwin, "Recollections of Jawaharlal Nehru," 1967, p. 1, Baldwin Papers; Baldwin, "The Reminiscences of Roger Nash Baldwin," 1954, pp. 412–13, Columbia University Oral History Collection.

2. Baldwin, "Reminiscences," p. 378; Alan Westin and Roger Baldwin, "Recollections of a Life in Civil Liberties—II: Russia, Communism, and United Fronts, 1920–1940," *Civil Liberties Review* 2 (Fall 1975): 11.

3. Baldwin, "Reminiscences," p. 379; Baldwin, "A Memo on My International Associations," March 1974, p. 1, Baldwin Papers.

4. Baldwin, "A Memo on My International Associations," March 1974, p. 2, Baldwin Papers; Baldwin, "Reminiscences," p. 383.

5. "Friends of Soviet Russia Cleared in Probers' Report," October 18, 1922, pp. 1–2, unidentified clipping in Baldwin Papers; "Report of the Investigating Committee of Five to the Friends of Soviet Russia," committee report, 1922, Baldwin Papers.

6. Baldwin, "Statement Released by Mr. Baldwin Today," 1922, Baldwin Papers.

7. Baldwin, "A Memo on My International Associations," March 1974, p. 2; Baldwin, "Reminiscences," pp. 379–80; "Statute A.I.C. Kuzbas"; Baldwin, "A Memo on the Kuzbas Industrial Colony," March 1974, p. 1, all in Baldwin Papers.

8. Baldwin, "A Memo on the Kuzbas Industrial Colony," March 1974, p. 1; Baldwin to Tom Reese, April 5, 1923, both in Baldwin Papers.

9. Baldwin, "A Memo on the Kuzbas Industrial Colony," March 1974, p. 1; Westin and Baldwin, "Recollections of a Life—II," p. 12; Baldwin, "Reminiscences," p. 380; ACLU Executive Committee, "A Statement from the Executive Committee of the American Civil Liberties Union Regarding the Prosecution of Roger N. Baldwin," April 28, 1923, pp. 1–2, Baldwin Papers.

10. ACLU Executive Committee, "A Statement from the Executive Committee," April 28, 1923, pp. 1–3; John H. Gundlach to Baldwin, May 7, 1923, both in Baldwin Papers.

11. "Mr. Baldwin's Statement," April 28, 1923, p. 3, Baldwin Papers.

12. Baldwin, deposition of May 28, 1923, Baldwin Papers.

13. Baldwin, "A Memo on the Kuzbas Industrial Colony," March 1974, pp. 1–2; Harry F. Ward to Members of the American Civil Liberties Union, December 31, 1923, both in Baldwin Papers.

14. Thomas Reese to Baldwin, December 26, 1923; Baldwin to Thomas Reese, n.d.; Baldwin to S. J. Rutgers, December 31, 1923, pp. 1–2, all in Baldwin Papers.

15. Westin and Baldwin, "Recollections of a Life—II," pp. 12–13; Baldwin, "Reminiscences," p. 381. Whittaker Chambers, as Richard Gid Powers reports, later accused Ware of heading an "underground Communist cell of government employees" during the New Deal era. See Powers, *Not Without Honor: The History of American Anticommunism* (New York: Free Press, 1995), p. 222.

16. Baldwin, "Reminiscences," p. 382.

17. Ibid.

18. Baldwin to Goldman, February 12, 1923, p. 2; Baldwin to Goldman, November 20, 1924, both in Baldwin Papers.

19. Goldman to Baldwin, March 18, 1924, pp. 1–2, Baldwin Papers.

20. Baldwin to Goldman, April 23, 1924, Baldwin Papers.

21. Baldwin to Goldman, May 15, 1924, Baldwin Papers.

22. Goldman to Baldwin, June 3, 1924, p. 1, Emma Goldman Papers, New York University.

23. Goldman to Baldwin, November 6, 1924, pp. 2–3, Goldman Papers.

24. Ibid., pp. 3–5.

25. Baldwin to Goldman, November 24, 1924, p. 2, Goldman Papers.

26. Ibid.

27. Baldwin to Goldman, March 27, 1925, p. 1; Goldman to Baldwin, April 20, 1925, pp. 1–2, both in Goldman Papers.

28. Lamson, *Roger Baldwin*, pp. 138–40; International Committee for Political Prisoners, "Members—Actual and Perspective [sic]," March 17, 1925, ICPP Papers, Columbia University; Baldwin, "Reminiscences," pp. 616.

29. Baldwin, "Summary of Remarks of Roger N. Baldwin Before the Foreign Policy Association . . . on Russian Political Prisoners," January 17, 1925, vol. 40, ACLU Papers; Alice Wexler, *Emma Goldman in Exile: From the Russian Revolution to the Spanish Civil War* (Boston: Beacon, 1989), pp. 105–106.

30. Baldwin, "Summary of Remarks of Roger N. Baldwin," January 17, 1925, pp. 2–3, vol. 40, ACLU Papers.

31. Ibid., pp. 3–4.

32. Westin and Baldwin, "Recollections of a Life—II," p. 14.

33. Baldwin, introduction to International Committee for Political Prisoners, *Letters from Russian Prisons: Consisting of Reprints of Documents by Political Prisoners in Soviet Prisons, Prison Camps and Exile, and Reprints of Affidavits Concerning Political Persecution in Soviet Russia, Official Statements by Soviet Authorities, Excerpts from Soviet Laws Pertaining to Civil Liberties, and Other Documents* (Westport, Conn.: Hyperion, 1977), pp. xiii–xiv.

34. Ibid., pp. xiv–xv.

35. Ibid., pp. xv, xviii–xix.

36. Baldwin, letter to editor, *New Leader*, March 18, 1926, Jay Lovestone Papers, Hoover Institution, Stanford University.

14. A European Sabbatical

1. Joseph P. Lash interviews with Roger Baldwin, March 6, 1972, and May 24, 1972, both in Joseph P. Lash Papers, Franklin Delano Roosevelt Presidential Library, Hyde Park, N.Y.

2. Lash interview with Baldwin, March 6, 1972.

3. Baldwin to Peggy Lamson, March 5, 1974, Roger Nash Baldwin Papers, Public Policy Papers, Department of Rare Books and Special Collections, Princeton University Libraries.

4. Baldwin to Madeleine Doty, November 8, 1925, pp. 1–4, Madeleine Z. Doty Papers, Smith College.

5. Baldwin to Harry Ward, December 4, 1926, Baldwin Papers; ACLU, Board of Directors Minutes, December 20, 1926, pp. 1–2, Reel 1, ACLU Papers, Princeton University; Lash interview with Lucille Milner, March 22, 1972, Lash Papers; Roger Baldwin, "The Reminiscences of Roger Nash Baldwin," 1954, p. 162, Columbia University Oral History Collection.

6. Baldwin to Ward, December 4, 1926, Baldwin Papers.

7. Peggy Lamson, *Roger Baldwin: Founder of the American Civil Liberties Union* (Boston: Houghton Mifflin, 1976), p. 173; Baldwin to Mary Buckley, July 16, 1926, pp. 1–2, Baldwin Papers.

8. Lamson, *Roger Baldwin*, pp. 174–75; Alan Westin and Roger Baldwin, "Recollections of a Life in Civil Liberties—II: Russia, Communism, and United Fronts, 1920–1940," *Civil Liberties Review* 2 (Fall 1975): 30.

9. Baldwin to Lucy Baldwin, January 26, 1927, Baldwin Papers.

10. Ibid.; Baldwin to Lucy Baldwin, February 18, 1927, Baldwin Papers; Lamson, *Roger Baldwin*, p. 177; Baldwin, "A Memo on My International Associations," March 1974, p. 3, Baldwin Papers; Baldwin, "To Our Friends," March 7, 1927, no. 2, p. 1, Baldwin Papers; *Ligue Contre L'Oppression Coloniale*, "*Liste des organisations et délégués*

apportant leur concours au Congrès International contre l'oppression coloniale et l'im-périalisme," February 10–14, 1927, Baldwin Papers; Baldwin, "Recollections of Jawa-harlal Nehru," 1967, p. 4, Baldwin Papers.

11. Baldwin, "To Our Friends," February 13, 1927, pp. 1, 4; Baldwin to Lucy Baldwin, February 18, 1927; "Memo on the Matter of Roger N. Baldwin," n.d.; ACLU memo, note on Roger N. Baldwin, March 23, 1927, all in Baldwin Papers; Baldwin, "Reminiscences," pp. 423–24.

12. Baldwin to Lucy Baldwin, March 6, 1927, Baldwin Papers; Baldwin to Lucy Baldwin, March 20, 1927, Baldwin Papers; "George Lansbury Dead; British Pacifist, 81," *New York Times*, May 8, 1940, p. 23; Baldwin, "To Our Friends," April 9, 1927, no. 3, p. 1, Baldwin Papers.

13. Baldwin to Lucy Baldwin, March 20, 1927; ACLU memo, note on Roger N. Baldwin, March 23, 1927; Baldwin to Lucy Baldwin, April 5, 1927, all in Baldwin Papers.

14. Baldwin to Lucy Baldwin, April 5, 1927 and March 30, 1927, all in Baldwin Papers; Lash interview with Herbert and Robert Baldwin, October 26, 1971, Lash Papers; Joseph Freeman, *An American Testament: A Narrative of Rebels and Roman-tics* (New York: Octagon, 1973), p. 636.

15. Baldwin to Lucy Baldwin, April 15, 1927; Baldwin, "To Our Friends," May 12, 1927, no. 4, pp. 2–3, both in Baldwin Papers.

16. Baldwin, "To Our Friends," May 12, 1927, no. 4, pp. 2–4, Baldwin Papers.

17. Baldwin to Lucy Baldwin, May 17, 1927, and June 11, 1927, p. 1; Baldwin, "To Our Friends," August 10, 1927, no. 5, p. 1, all in Baldwin Papers; Lash interview with Herbert and Robert Baldwin, October 26, 1971, Lash Papers.

18. Baldwin to Lucy Baldwin, June 11, 1927, pp. 1; Baldwin, "To Our Friends," August 10, 1927, no. 5, p. 2, both in Baldwin Papers.

19. Baldwin to Lucy Baldwin, June 11, 1927, p. 2; Baldwin, "To Our Friends," August 10, 1927, no. 5, p. 2; Baldwin to Lucy Baldwin, July 4, 1927, p. 1, all in Baldwin Papers; Lamson, *Roger Baldwin*, p. 181–83; Baldwin, "After a Sabbatical Year of Study . . . ," 1928, p. 4, Baldwin Papers; Baldwin, "Reminiscences," p. 386.

20. Lamson, *Roger Baldwin*, p. 184; Baldwin to Lucy Baldwin, July 23, 1927, pp. 1–2, Baldwin Papers.

21. Baldwin, "Reminiscences," pp. 389, 405, 407; Baldwin, "A Memo on My Inter-national Associations," March 1974, p. 5, Baldwin Papers. See James William Crowl's *Angels in Stalin's Paradise: Western Reporters in Soviet Russia, 1917 to 1937, a Case Study of Louis Fischer and Walter Duranty* (Washington, D.C.: University Press of America, 1982), and S. J. Taylor's *Stalin's Apologist: Walter Duranty: The* New York Times's *Man in Moscow* (New York: Oxford University Press, 1990).

22. Baldwin, "Reminiscences," pp. 405–406; Leonard Wilcox, *V. F. Calverton: Rad-ical in the American Grain* (Philadelphia: Temple University Press, 1992), p. 60.

23. Baldwin to Lucy Baldwin, July 23, 1927, p. 1, Baldwin Papers.

24. Baldwin and Westin, "Recollections of a Life—II," pp. 19–20.

25. Baldwin to Lucy Baldwin, August 13, 1927, Baldwin Papers.

26. Baldwin, "To Our Friends," September 23, 1927, no. 6, p. 1, Baldwin Papers.

27. Ibid., pp. 1–3.

28. Ibid.

29. Ibid.

30. Baldwin, "Memorandum Situations in Georgia: Confidential. Not for Publication," October 14, 1927, p. 4, Baldwin Papers; Peter Kropotkin, *Kropotkin's Revolutionary Pamphlets: A Collection of Writings by Peter Kropotkin*, ed. Roger N. Baldwin (New York: Dover, 1970), pp. 1–12, 28; Lash interview with Roger Baldwin, October 4, 1971, Lash Papers.

31. Baldwin to Lucy Baldwin, October 18, 1927, Baldwin Papers; Lamson, *Roger Baldwin*, p. 186.

32. Baldwin to Doty, October 18, 1927, Baldwin Papers.

33. R. Abramowitsch to Baldwin, December 4, 1927, Baldwin Papers.

34. Baldwin to Lucy Baldwin, October 18, 1927, Baldwin Papers.

35. Baldwin, "Abstract of Speech of Roger N. Baldwin, Director of American Civil Liberties Union, New York, on 'Liberty Under the Soviets,'" n.d., p. 1, Baldwin Papers.

36. Ibid, p. 4.

37. Baldwin, "After a Sabbatical Year of Study," 1928, p. 1, Baldwin Papers.

38. Goldman to Baldwin, May 3, 1928, p. 3; Baldwin to Goldman, June 1, 1928, p. 1, both in Baldwin Papers.

39. Willi Münzenberg to Baldwin, May 7, 1928, pp. 1–3, Baldwin Papers.

40. Baldwin to Münzenberg, May 24, 1928, p. 1; Baldwin to My Friends of the Executive Committee, June 20, 1928, both in Baldwin Papers.

41. Baldwin to Münzenberg, May 24, 1928, pp. 1–2; Baldwin to V. Chattopadhyaya, May 17, 1928, pp. 1–2, both in Baldwin Papers.

42. Roger Baldwin, *Liberty Under the Soviets* (New York: Vanguard, 1928), pp. 2–3; Peter G. Filene, *Americans and the Soviet Experiment, 1917–1933* (Cambridge, Mass.: Harvard University Press, 1967), p. 149.

43. Baldwin, *Liberty Under the Soviets*, pp. 4, 60–61, 272.

44. Ibid., pp. 136, 177, 186, 194–95, 175.

45. Frank A. Warren III, *Liberals and Communism: The "Red Decade" Revisited* (Westport, Conn.: Greenwood, 1976), pp. 63–65.

46. "Soviet Tyranny," *Leader*, January 5, 1929; B. Charney Vladeck, "Americans and Russia," *Bookman*, January 1929; "Radical Author Emphasizes Sincerity of Sovietism in Book About Modern Russia," *Missourian*, February 23, 1929; Bernard Smith, "Limitations of Liberty and Education Under the Soviet Regime," *New York World*, March 3, 1929; J.S.S., "Liberty and Russia," (Boston) *Transcript*; "Daniel in Russia," *New York Herald Tribune*, April 21, 1929, all in Baldwin Papers.

47. Goldman to Baldwin, April 7, 1930; Baldwin to Goldman, April 21, 1930, both in Baldwin Papers.

48. Baldwin to Lillian D. Wald, March 28, 1928, File 1; Baldwin to our friends, draft, n.d., File 1, both in Wald Papers, Columbia University.

49. Westin and Baldwin, "Recollections of a Life—II," p. 30.

50. Lamson, *Roger Baldwin*, pp. 195–96; Westin and Baldwin, "Recollections of a Life—II," p. 31; Baldwin, "Reminiscences," pp. 420, 427–28.

51. Baldwin to Goldman, November 27, 1931, Emma Goldman Papers, New York University.

15. Free Speech and the Class Struggle

1. Roger Baldwin to Members of the National Committee, February 7, 1929, p. 1; ACLU, Board Minutes, April 1, 1929, p. 2, Reel 2, both in ACLU Papers, Princeton University.

2. Baldwin to Members of the National Committee, February 7, 1929, pp. 1–2, ACLU Papers.

3. Baldwin, "After a Sabbatical Year of Study . . . ," 1928, pp. 12–13; Baldwin, "Five Days Among the Black Shirts," 1929, pp. 1–3, both in Roger Nash Baldwin Papers, Public Policy Papers, Department of Rare Books and Special Collections, Princeton University Libraries.

4. Baldwin, "After a Sabbatical Year of Study . . . ," 1928, pp. 15–17, Baldwin Papers.

5. Ibid., pp. 17–18.

6. Ibid., p. 18.

7. Baldwin, "Free Speech and the Communists," 1930, p. 3; Baldwin, "Free Speech and the Class Struggle," p. 1, both in Baldwin Papers.

8. Baldwin to Earl Browder, January 23, 1930; Browder to Baldwin, January 27, 1930; Baldwin to Browder, January 28, 1930; "Proposed Statement by the Civil Liberties Union," n.d., pp. 1–3, all in Earl Browder Papers, Syracuse University.

9. Harry F. Ward and Baldwin to Browder, January 26, 1930; Browder to Ward and Baldwin, January 27, 1930; Baldwin to Browder, January 28, 1930 (second letter), all in Browder Papers; ACLU Board of Directors Minutes, November 3, 1930, Reel 2, ACLU Papers.

10. Transcript, "From Testimony of Roger N. Baldwin Before the Special Committee to Investigate Communist Activities in the United States, Headed by Hamilton Fish, Jr.," December 5, 1930, pp. 1–3, vol. 774, ACLU Papers; "Foster and His Aides Put Red Flag First," *New York Times*, December 6, 1930, pp. 1, 12.

11. "Outlaw Reds as Foes of U.S. Is Fish's Plan," *New York World*, January 18, 1931, vol. 464, ACLU Papers.

12. William Morris, "The News To-day: Mr. Fish Reports," January 20, 1931, vol. 464, ACLU Papers; "The American Civil Liberties Union Sticks out Its Tongue," *Law*

and Labor (January 1931): 7; "Communistic Propaganda," *Argos* (Rock Island, Illinois), February 9, 1931, vol. 464, ACLU Papers.

13. Baldwin to State Correspondents in States Where Legislatures Are Meeting, February 7, 1931, vol. 466; Ward to the Honorable Members of the Senate and House of Representatives, February 21, 1931, pp. 1–4, vol. 467, both in ACLU Papers.

14. Roger Baldwin, "The Myth of Law and Order," in *Behold America!* ed. Samuel D. Schmalhausen (New York: Farrar and Rinehart, 1931), pp. 657–71.

15. Ibid., pp. 660, 662, 670–71.

16. Ibid., p. 671.

17. ACLU, *The Fight for Civil Liberty*, annual report (New York: ACLU, 1931), pp. 4, 11; Winchell Taylor, "'Depression Means Repression,' Civil Liberties Union Head Says," *New York World*, February 1, 1931, vol. 464, both in ACLU Papers.

18. "Baldwin Fears Revolution May Strike America," *E. Union* (Springfield, Mass.), April 15, 1932, vol. 541, ACLU Papers.

19. Baldwin to Managing Editor, *Chicago Tribune*, May 5, 1932, vol. 542, ACLU Papers.

20. "Link Evanston Leaders with Radical Group," June 8, 1932, *(Evanston, Ill.) News Index*, vol. 541, ACLU Papers.

21. James P. Cannon to Baldwin, August 9, 1932, p. 1, Baldwin Papers.

22. Ibid., p. 2.

23. Baldwin to Cannon, August 12, 1932, Baldwin Papers.

24. Baldwin to Miss Campbell, August 18, 1932, p. 1, Baldwin Papers.

25. Ibid., p. 2.

26. Guenter Lewy, *The Cause That Failed: Communism in American Political Life* (New York: Oxford University Press, 1990), pp. 169–70.

27. "Galahad of Freedom," *World Tomorrow* 13 (January 1930): 33, 36; Travis Hoke, "Red Rainbow," *North American Review* 234 (November 1932): 433, 437–38.

28. Hoke, "Red Rainbow," pp. 438–39.

29. Baldwin to Bettina Warburg, January 17, 1933, vol. 700, ACLU Papers.

30. George L. Willets to Baldwin, February 1, 1933, vol. 630; Baldwin to Willets, February 3, 1933, vol. 630; Baldwin to Falkenberg, February 20, 1933, vol. 630, all in ACLU Papers.

31. "Whad'ye Mean—Class Struggle?" *Student Outlook* (March 1933): 6.

32. "15,000 Reds Cheer Attacks on Hitler," *New York Times*, April 6, 1933, p. 10; "Knocks for Everybody," *New York Times*, April 7, 1933, p. 18.

33. Baldwin, letter to editor, *Christian Science Monitor*, April 21, 1933, vol. 613, ACLU Papers.

34. Baldwin to Maury Maverick, November 28, 1933, vol. 630, ACLU Papers; Baldwin, "Free Speech for Nazis?" *World Tomorrow* 16 (November 1933): 613; Baldwin to Israel Davidson, January 5, 1934, vol. 700, ACLU Papers; Baldwin to Dr. William J. Robinson, January 5, 1934, vol. 700, ACLU Papers.

16. From the United Front to the Popular Front

1. Guenter Lewy, *The Cause That Failed: Communism in American Political Life* (New York: Oxford University Press, 1990), p. 145; Walter Goodman, *The Committee: The Extraordinary Career of the House Committee on Un-American Activities* (New York: Farrar, Straus and Giroux, 1968), p. 36; J. B. Matthews, *Odyssey of a Fellow Traveler* (New York: Mt. Vernon, 1938), p. 119.

2. Samuel Walker, *In Defense of American Liberties: A History of the American Civil Liberties Union* (New York: Oxford University Press, 1990), pp. 87–88.

3. Baldwin to William N. Doak, April 1, 1932, pp. 1–2, vol. 527; Doak to Baldwin, April 5, 1932, vol. 527; Baldwin to Doak, April 7, 1932, vol. 527; Baldwin to Henry L. Stimson, December 2, 1932, vol. 527; Stimson to Baldwin, December 5, 1932, pp. 1–3, vol. 527; Baldwin to Stimson, December 6, 1932, vol. 527, all in ACLU Papers, Princeton University.

4. ACLU, Board of Directors Minutes, January 11, 1932, Reel 3, ACLU Papers; Baldwin, "Memo on Relations with Government Officials," April 1974, pp. 1–2, Roger Nash Baldwin Papers, Public Policy Papers, Department of Rare Books and Special Collections, Princeton University Libraries; Baldwin, "The Reminiscences of Roger Nash Baldwin," 1954, pp. 181–82, Columbia University Oral History Collection; ACLU, *Land of the Pilgrim's Pride*, annual report (New York: ACLU, 1933), pp. 3–4.

5. Thomas Doyle to Baldwin, August 2, 1933, vol. 609; Baldwin to Doyle, August 3, 1933, vol. 609; Doyle to Baldwin, August 16, 1933, vol. 609; Baldwin to Doyle, August 17, 1933, vol. 609, all in ACLU Papers.

6. Baldwin to Edmund D. Campbell, August 23, 1933, vol. 608; Campbell to Baldwin, August 28, 1933, vol. 608; Baldwin to Bruce Bliven, August 29, 1933, vol. 608, all in ACLU Papers.

7. Baldwin to J. Edgar Hoover, October 2, 1933, vol. 608; Hoover to Baldwin, October 12, 1933, vol. 608; Baldwin to Hoover, October 13, 1933, vol. 608, all in ACLU Papers.

8. ACLU, *Liberty Under the New Deal*, annual report (New York: ACLU, 1934), pp. 1–10.

9. "Report of the Commission of Inquiry to the Board of Directors," February 1934, p. 2, Box 38, Arthur Garfield Hays Papers, Princeton University.

10. Ibid., pp. 3–5.

11. Baldwin to J. B. Matthews, February 20, 1934.

12. Alan Westin and Baldwin, "Recollections of a Life in Civil Liberties—II: Russia, Communism, and United Fronts, 1920–1940," *Civil Liberties Review* 2 (Fall 1975): 31–33; Dwight Macdonald, "The Defense of Everybody—I," *New Yorker*, July 11, 1953, p. 44.

13. Baldwin, transcript of "Address Delivered at the Presentation of 'The Case of Civilization against Hitlerism' at Madison Square Garden," March 7, 1934, pp. 1–3, Baldwin Papers.

14. Baldwin to Secretary, League Against War and Fascism, March 10, 1934, Baldwin Papers; Westin and Baldwin, "Recollections of a Life—II," p. 33; Baldwin, "What Tactics for United Front?" 1934, pp. 1–3, Baldwin Papers.

15. Baldwin, "What Tactics for United Front?" 1934, pp. 3–6, Baldwin Papers.

16. Ibid., p. 6; ACLU, Board of Directors Minutes, May 28, 1934, Reel 5, ACLU Papers; Westin and Baldwin, "Recollections of a Life—II," p. 33; Dwight Macdonald, "The Defense of Everybody—II," *New Yorker*, July 18, 1953, p. 33; Baldwin to Earl Browder, July 14, 1934, Baldwin Papers.

17. Baldwin to Norman Thomas, July 22, 1934, Baldwin Papers.

18. Roger Baldwin, "Freedom in the U.S.A. and the U.S.S.R.," *Soviet Russia Today* 3 (September 1934): 11.

19. Ibid.

20. Ibid.

21. Ibid.

22. Ibid.

23. Baldwin to Joseph Wood Krutch, January 2, 1935, vol. 785; Baldwin memo for Krutch, January 5, 1935, vol. 785, both in ACLU Papers.

24. Baldwin et al. to Alexander A. Troyanovsky, January 18, 1935, p. 1, Box 39, Hays Papers.

25. Ibid.

26. Ibid., pp. 1–2.

27. Baldwin, letter to editor, *Daily Worker*, February 15, 1935, Box 39, Hays Papers.

28. Baldwin, "From the Harvard Classbook," June 1935, vol. 763, ACLU Papers.

29. Baldwin, "Minutes of the Conference on Civil Liberties Under the New Deal to Discuss Proposals for Legislation in the Forthcoming Congress and to Enlist Support for Them," December 1934, RG 233, Box 142, "ACLU Exhibits, Evidence, and Other Records . . . ," Dies Committee Papers, National Archives.

30. ACLU, Board of Directors Minutes, May 6, 1935, Reel 5; Baldwin to Robert F. Wagner, April 1, 1935, vol. 780, both in ACLU Papers; Cletus E. Daniel, *The ACLU and the Wagner Act: An Inquiry into the Depression-Era Crisis of American Liberalism* (Ithaca: Cornell University Press, 1980); ACLU, *How Goes the Bill of Rights?* annual report (New York: ACLU, 1936), p. 7; ACLU, *Let Freedom Ring!* annual report (New York: ACLU, 1937), p. 3.

31. Baldwin, "For the *Daily Worker*," July 18, 1935, pp. 1–2, vol. 785, ACLU Papers.

32. Ward, Mary van Kleeck, and Baldwin to Editor-in-Chief, Hearst Newspapers, "An Answer from American liberals to an Open Letter by Fred E. Beal Introducing a

Series of Articles on the Soviet Union in the Hearst Press," July 18, 1935, p. 1, Baldwin Papers.

33. Baldwin, letter to editor, *San Francisco Daily News*, October 21, 1935, p. 1, vol. 772, ACLU Papers.

34. Baldwin to Laurance Labadie, August 17, 1936, Baldwin Papers; Baldwin, "Statement by Roger N. Baldwin for the National Student Federation," August 18, 1936, vol. 904, ACLU Papers; Baldwin, "Who Is for Democracy?" November 27, 1936, pp. 2–3, vol. 904, ACLU Papers.

35. Baldwin to Joseph Levenson, December 5, 1936; Baldwin, note on Dr. Sidney Gullick, n.d., both in Baldwin Papers.

36. Baldwin to Maj. Gen. Smedly D. Butler, December 11, 1936, Baldwin Papers.

37. Baldwin, "Abstract of Address of Baldwin Before the Community Church, Boston, Sunday, December 13th on 'Liberty in the U.S.A. and the U.S.S.R.,'" December 14, 1936, vol. 904, ACLU Papers.

38. Ibid., pp. 1–2.

39. Ibid., p. 3.

40. Baldwin, "Revolution and Evolution in Social Change," address delivered at the Eastern Sociological Conference, New Haven, Conn., 1936, p. 1, Baldwin Papers.

41. Ibid., pp. 4–5.

42. Ibid., pp. 5–7.

43. Baldwin to Paul M. Reid, August 26, 1937, vol. 990, ACLU Papers.

44. Peggy Lamson, *Roger Baldwin: Founder of the American Civil Liberties Union: A Portrait* (Boston: Houghton Mifflin, 1976), pp. 200–201.

45. Baldwin to Mary Buckley, August 14, 1937, Baldwin Papers; Baldwin to Madeleine Doty, October 18, 1937, Madeleine Z. Doty Papers, Smith College.

46. Harry Fleischman, *Norman Thomas: A Biography* (New York: Norton, 1967), p. 175; Baldwin to Buckley, November 4, 1936, Baldwin Papers; Lamson, *Roger Baldwin*, pp. 202–203; Baldwin to Mr. Wetzel, March 20, 1967, Baldwin Papers.

47. Baldwin to William B. Spofford, January 25, 1938, Baldwin Papers.

48. Baldwin to Leonard Bright, July 12, 1938, Baldwin Papers.

17. The Home Front

1. Madeleine Doty to Jane Addams, March 6, 1929, Reel 20, Jane Addams Papers, Swarthmore College Peace Collection.

2. Roger Baldwin to Homer Folks, August 1, 1929, pp. 1–2, Roger Nash Baldwin Papers, Public Policy Papers, Department of Rare Books and Special Collections, Princeton University Libraries; Joseph P. Lash interview with Roger Baldwin, January 8, 1972, Joseph P. Lash Papers, Franklin Delano Roosevelt Presidential Library, Hyde Park, N.Y.

3. Baldwin to Peggy Lamson, March 5, 1974, Baldwin Papers; Peggy Lamson, *Roger Baldwin: Founder of the American Civil Liberties Union* (Boston: Houghton Mifflin, 1976), p. 209.

4. Baldwin, "I Have Just Been Shocked," p. 1, February 13, 1930, Baldwin Papers.

5. Ibid.; Otto Stolz, "Be It Remembered," September 11, 1929; Frank Bryson to Baldwin, February 27, 1930; Bryson to Baldwin, March 20, 1930, all in Baldwin Papers.

6. Lamson, *Roger Baldwin*, pp. 207–208; Frances Bowen to Baldwin, August 17, 1930, pp. 1–4, Baldwin Papers; Oral James to Baldwin, February 20, 1930, Baldwin Papers.

7. Lamson, *Roger Baldwin*, p. 208; Baldwin to Harold Z. "Brownie" Brown, August 17, 1928, Baldwin Papers; Baldwin to Brown, October 13, 1928, Baldwin Papers.

8. Lamson, *Roger Baldwin*, pp. 208–209; Baldwin, "Harold Z. Brown, 1902–1930," n.d., Baldwin Papers; Baldwin to Buckley, March 26, 1930, p. 1–4, Baldwin Papers.

9. Lash interview with Anna Friedkin, January 16, 1972; Lash interview with Roger Baldwin, May 24, 1972; Lash interview with Phil Taft, October 12, 1972; Lash interview with Lucille Milner, March 22, 1972, all in Lash Papers.

10. Lash interview with Friedkin, January 16, 1972, Lash Papers.

11. Lash interview with Roger Baldwin, May 24, 1972, Lash Papers; Baldwin, "Appendix to My Memo on Evie and myself," 1962, p. A-8, Baldwin Papers; Baldwin, "Notes on the Ramapo Valley Around Old Midvale Road, 1947," Baldwin Papers; Baldwin, "Notes on the History of Dell Brook," November 1964, pp. 2, 5, Baldwin Papers; photograph of plaque of "Dell Brook Estate, Baldwin Residence," courtesy William Preston.

12. Baldwin, "History of Dell Brook, 1980," pp. 1, 5, Baldwin Papers.

13. Baldwin, note on Madeleine Doty correspondence, n.d.; Baldwin, "For the Children and Grand-Children and Their Kin," 1962, pp. A-1–A-2; Baldwin, "*Evie*: For the Children," July 1978, p. 1, all in Baldwin Papers; author's interview with Carl Baldwin, August 12, 1996, New York City; "Evelyn Preston Baldwin," memorial pamphlet, p. 1, File 1, Charles Ascher Papers, Columbia University, Rare Books and Manuscript Library; "Geraldine M. Thompson Dies," *New York Times*, September 10, 1967; Carl Baldwin interview; author's interview with William Preston, October 17, 1996, Detroit.

14. Baldwin, note on Doty correspondence, n.d., Baldwin Papers; Baldwin, "For the Children and Grand-Children," 1962, pp. A-1–A-2, Baldwin Papers; Lamson, *Roger Baldwin*, p. 205; Baldwin, "*Evie*: For the Children," July 1978, p. 1, Baldwin Papers; Henry Beetle Hough, "Mr. Baldwin Was Friend of Vineyard," 1981, p. 1, Box 50, Lash Papers; Arthur R. Railton, "The Barn House: What Is It?" *Dukes County Intelligencer*, August 1990, p. 32; Thomas Hart Benton, *An American in Art: A Professional and Technical Autobiography* (Lawrence: University Press of Kansas, 1969), p. 52; William Preston interview; Arthur R. Railton, "Artists and Other Free Spirits at Chilmark's Barn House," *Dukes County Intelligencer*, August 1995, pp. 3–7, 12.

15. Railton, "Artists and Other Free Spirits," pp. 26–27.

16. Baldwin, "For the Children and Grand-Children," 1962, p. A-1, Baldwin Papers; Lamson, *Roger Baldwin*, p. 206; Baldwin, "*Evie*: For the Children," July 1978, pp. 1–2, Baldwin Papers; Lash interview with Roger Baldwin, September 24, 1971, Lash Papers.

17. Baldwin, "For the Children and Grand-Children," 1962, pp. A-1–A-2, Baldwin Papers; "Evelyn Preston Baldwin," memorial pamphlet, Ascher Papers; "A Tribute by Dorothy Kenyon," memorial pamphlet, p. 2; Carl Baldwin interview.

18. Baldwin, "For the Children and Grand-Children," 1962, p. A-2; Baldwin, "*Evie*: For the Children," July 1978, p. 3, both in Baldwin Papers; Lamson, *Roger Baldwin*, pp. 210, 212–13; Lash interview with Roger Baldwin, March 6, 1972, Lash Papers; Baldwin, "Appendix to My Memo on Evie and Myself," 1962, p. A-8, Baldwin Papers; Baldwin, "Notes on the History of Dell Brook," November 1964, p. 1, Baldwin Papers.

19. Baldwin to Buckley, July 6, 1934, pp. 1–2, Baldwin Papers.

20. Baldwin, "A Memo on Madeleine Zabriskie Doty for the Files at Smith College," October 1978, p. 3, Baldwin Papers; Lamson, *Roger Baldwin*, p. 210; Baldwin, "*Evie*: For the Children," July 1978, p. A-2, Baldwin Papers; Arthur Garfield Hays to Baldwin, December 18, 1934, Baldwin Papers; Lucy Baldwin to Baldwin, November 2, 1934, pp. 1–4, Madeleine Z. Doty Papers, Smith College.

21. Baldwin, "*Evie*: For the Children," July 1978, p. A-3, Baldwin Papers; Baldwin, "Declaration of Roger N. Baldwin in Favor of Madeleine Z. Doty," September 1935, Doty Papers; Baldwin, "A Memo on Madeleine Zabriskie Doty for the Files at Smith College," October 1978, p. 4, Baldwin Papers; Lash interview with Roger Baldwin, March 6, 1972, Lash Papers.

22. Baldwin, "*Evie*: For the Children," July 1978, p. A-3, Baldwin Papers; author's interview with William Butler, September 27, 1996, New York City; Baldwin, "Notes on the History of Dell Brook," November 1964, p. 1, Baldwin Papers; "Roger Nash Baldwin," September 5, 1946, p. 3, FBI File #100-49565-43.

23. Baldwin, "*Evie*: For the Children," July 1978, p. A-3, Baldwin Papers; Lamson, *Roger Baldwin*, pp. 210–11.

24. Lash interview with Osmond Fraenkel, n.d.; Lash interview with Milner, March 22, 1972, both in Lash Papers.

25. Baldwin to the Librarian, Smith College, November 30, 1978; Malini Pethick-Lawrence to Baldwin, August 23, 1938, pp. 1–5; Pethick-Lawrence to Baldwin, November 3, 1938, pp. 1–2; Doty to Baldwin, November 15, 1938; "N.Y. Woman Wins Degree at Geneva," n.d., all in the Baldwin Papers.

26. Baldwin, "*Evie*: For the Children," July 1978, pp. A-3, A-7; Baldwin, "For the Children and Grand-Children," 1962, pp. 2, 4, both in Baldwin Papers; Carl Baldwin interview; Baldwin to Buckley, January 7, 1938, Baldwin Papers; Baldwin to Doty, May 5, 1938, Doty Papers.

27. Baldwin, "*Evie*: For the Children," July 1978, pp. A-3, A-6; Baldwin, "For the Children and Grand-Children," 1962, p. 5, both in Baldwin Papers.

28. Baldwin, "*Evie*: For the Children," July 1978, p. A-4, Baldwin Papers; Lamson, *Roger Baldwin*, p. 213; Carl Baldwin interview.

29. Baldwin, "*Evie*: For the Children," July 1978, p. A-5, Baldwin Papers.

30. Lash interview with Helen Mannoni, October 31, 1971, Box 49, Lash Papers.

31. Dorothy Kenyon, reflections on Evelyn Preston Blackwell, pp. A-6–A-7, Baldwin Papers; Lash interview with Roger Baldwin, March 6, 1972, Lash Papers; Lash interview with William Butler, December 5, 1971, Box 49, Lash Papers.

32. Carl Baldwin interview.

33. Ibid.

34. Ibid.

35. Ibid.

36. Ibid.

37. Ibid.

38. Lamson, *Roger Baldwin*, p. 282.

39. Carl Baldwin interview.

40. Ibid.

41. Ibid.

42. Ibid.

43. Ibid.

44. Ibid.

45. Baldwin, "Notes on the History of Dell Brook," November 1964, pp. 2–4, Baldwin Papers.

46. Carl Baldwin interview.

47. Ibid.

48. Ibid.

49. Ibid.

50. Ibid.; Lash interview with Roger Baldwin, March 6, 1972, Lash Papers.

51. Carl Baldwin interview; Peggy Lamson, *Roger Baldwin*, p. 279; "Roger Nash Baldwin," *Current Biography* (1940): 44.

52. Carl Baldwin interview.

53. Ibid.; Lash interview with Roger Baldwin, March 6, 1972, Lash Papers.

54. Lamson, *Roger Baldwin*, pp. 279–82.

55. Ibid., p. 280.

18. Controversies on the Path from Fellow Traveling to Anticommunism

1. Elizabeth Dilling, *The Red Network: A "Who's Who" and Handbook of Radicalism for Patriots* (Kenilworth, Ill.: Elizabeth Dilling, 1934), pp. 111–12; Elizabeth Dilling,

The Roosevelt Red Record and Its Background (Kenilworth, Ill.: Elizabeth Dilling, 1936), pp. 130–33.

2. Harold Lord Varney, "The Civil Liberties Union," *American Mercury*, December 1936, pp. 385–99.

3. Baldwin to Ben Huebsch, December 2, 1936, Box 2, Benjamin Huebsch Papers, Library of Congress.

4. ACLU, *Let Freedom Ring!* annual report (New York: ACLU, 1937), pp. 14–15.

5. Ibid., pp. 47–48; Samuel Walker, *In Defense of American Liberties: A History of the American Civil Liberties Union* (New York: Oxford University Press, 1990), p. 128; ACLU Board of Directors Minutes, June 27, 1938, Reel 7, ACLU Papers, Princeton University; ACLU Board of Directors Minutes, July 25, 1938, Reel 7, ACLU Papers; H. L. Mencken, "The American Civil Liberties Union," *American Mercury*, October 1938, pp. 182–90; Dorothy D. Bromley et al. to H. L. Mencken, *American Mercury*, October 1938, pp. 191–92; ACLU, *The Bill of Rights—150 Years After*, annual report (New York: ACLU, 1939), p. 7.

6. Bromley et al. to Mencken.

7. Baldwin, "Civil Liberties comprise," *Social Work Year Book* 5 (1939): 76–77; ACLU, *Let Freedom Ring!* p. 3; ACLU, *Eternal Vigilance! The Story of Civil Liberty*, annual report (New York: ACLU, 1938), p. 3.

8. Roger Baldwin and Clarence E. Randall, *Civil Liberties and Industrial Conflict* (Cambridge, Mass.: Harvard University Press, 1938), pp. 7–8, 11–12.

9. Ibid., pp. 12–14.

10. The House Committee to Investigate un-American Activities operated under several variations of that title; it was best known from 1938 to 1945 as the Dies Committee and later, of course, as the House un-American Activities Committee, or HUAC. "Name-Calling Led by Ickes and Dies," *New York Times*, November 24, 1938, pp. 1, 32; "Calls Marcantonio Red Front Leader," *New York Times*, November 29, 1938, p. 9; John Haynes Holmes, B. W. Huebsch, and Baldwin, sworn deposition, December 31, 1938, p. 1, vol. 2064, ACLU Papers.

11. Jerold S. Auerbach, *Labor and Liberty: The La Follette Committee and the New Deal* (Indianapolis, Ind.: Bobbs-Merrill, 1966); ACLU, *How Goes the Bill of Rights?* annual report (New York: ACLU, 1936), p. 5; ACLU, *Let Freedom Ring!* p. 47; ACLU, *Eternal Vigilance!* p. 3.

12. Baldwin, sworn deposition, December 31, 1938, pp. 1–2, vol. 2064, ACLU Papers.

13. Ibid.

14. Ibid., p. 2.

15. Holmes, Huebsch, and Baldwin, sworn deposition, pp. 2–3, Roger Nash Baldwin Papers, Public Policy Papers, Department of Rare Books and Special Collections, Princeton University Libraries.

16. ACLU, Board of Directors Minutes, January 3, 1939, Reel 7; ACLU, Board of Directors Minutes, January 23, 1939, Reel 7, both in ACLU Papers.

17. Jerold Simmons, "The American Civil Liberties Union and the Dies Committee, 1938–1940," *Harvard Civil Rights–Civil Liberties Law Review* 17 (Spring 1982): 189; Baldwin, "Should the Dies Committee Die?" January 24, 1939, pp. 1–2, vol. 2360, ACLU Papers.

18. Baldwin, "Should the Dies Committee Die?" pp. 2–3.

19. ACLU, Board of Directors Minutes, January 30, 1939, Reel 7; ACLU, Board of Directors Minutes, February 13, 1939, p. 3, Reel 7, both in ACLU Papers.

20. Baldwin to Martin Dies, March 8, 1939, vol. 2075; transcript of testimony delivered by Baldwin before Rhea Whitley and J. B. Matthews of the House Committee to Investigate un-American Activities, March 31, 1939, pp. 1–3, vol. 2075, both in ACLU Papers.

21. Transcript of Baldwin testimony, March 31, 1939, pp. 10, 12, vol. 2075, ACLU Papers.

22. Ibid., pp. 13–14.

23. Ibid., pp. 14–15.

24. Ibid., p. 15.

25. Robert Justin Goldstein, *Political Repression in Modern America: From 1870 to the Present* (New York: Schenkman, 1978), p. 244.

26. Baldwin letter, May 9, 1939, vol. 2207, ACLU Papers; Alan Westin and Baldwin, "Recollections of a Life in Civil Liberties—II: Russia, Communism, and United Fronts, 1920–1940," *Civil Liberties Review* 2 (Fall 1975): 34; Peggy Lamson, *Roger Baldwin: Founder of the American Civil Liberties Union* (Boston: Houghton Mifflin, 1976), pp. 201; Baldwin, "The Reminiscences of Roger Nash Baldwin," 1954, p. 269, Columbia University Oral History Collection; Baldwin to the National Committee, American League for Peace and Democracy, October 17, 1939, pp. 1–2, Arthur Garfield Hays Papers, Princeton University.

27. "Liberties Parley Excludes No Group," *New York Times*, October 10, 1939, p. 14.

28. "Free Speech on Civil Rights," *New York Times*, October 11, 1939, p. 26.

29. Jerold S. Auerbach to Baldwin, January 7, 1971; Baldwin to Auerbach, January 11, 1971, both in Baldwin Papers; Mary S. McAuliffe, "The Politics of Civil Liberties: The American Civil Liberties during the McCarthy Years," in *Original Essays on the Cold War and the Origins of McCarthyism*, ed. by Robert Griffith and Athan Theoharis (New York: New Viewpoints, 1974), p. 316; Helen C. Camp, *Iron in Her Soul: Elizabeth Gurley Flynn and the American Left* (Pullman: Washington State University Press, 1995), p. 156.

30. Baldwin to Mary McLeod Bethune, November 22, 1939, Baldwin Papers.

31. "NLRB Challenged on Free Speech," *New York Times*, October 15, 1939, p. 2.

32. "Fight on Dr. Ward Hinted as Liberties Union Meets," *New York Post*, November 27, 1939, vol. 2064; "Move to Oust Ward Denied," *New York Herald-Tribune*, November 28, 1939, vol. 2064, both in ACLU Papers.

33. Robert A. Hoffman to Baldwin, December 1, 1939, Box 2064; Lillian Symes, "Hold That Line," *Call*, December 2, 1939, Box 2064, both in ACLU Papers.

34. Symes, "Hold That Line."

35. Ibid.

36. ACLU Board of Directors Minutes, December 4, 1939, Reel 7, ACLU Papers; John Haynes Holmes to Baldwin, December 13, 1939, John Haynes Holmes Papers, Reel 5, Library of Congress.

37. Auerbach to Baldwin, January 7, 1971; Baldwin to Cletus Daniel, March 8, 1981; Baldwin to Mr. Whitman, February 12, 1968, all in Baldwin Papers.

38. John Haynes Holmes to Baldwin, January 3, 1940, p. 1, Box 44, Hays Papers; Walker, *In Defense*, p, 130.

39. John Haynes Holmes to Baldwin, January 3, 1940, pp. 1–2, Hays Papers.

40. Baldwin, radio address, "Should the Dies Committee Be Continued?" NBC Blue Network, January 4, 1940, pp. 1–3, vol. 2181, ACLU Papers.

41. Lamson, *Roger Baldwin*, p. 224; John Nevin Sayre et al. to the Members of the National Committee, January 23, 1940, p. 1, Box 44, Hays Papers; Baldwin to Auerbach, January 12, 1971, Baldwin Papers; Baldwin to Mary S. McAuliffe, March 6, 1972, Baldwin Papers.

42. John Nevin Sayre et al. to the Members of the National Committee, January 23, 1940, pp. 1–2, Hays Papers.

43. R. W. Riis to Baldwin, January 20, 1940, pp. 1–3, Box 44, Hays Papers.

44. Oswald Garrison Villard to Baldwin, January 23, 1940, vol. 2163, ACLU Papers.

45. Walker, *In Defense*, pp. 130–31; Baldwin to Alexander Meiklejohn, February 13, 1940, Alexander Meiklejohn Papers, State Historical Society of Wisconsin, Madison; "Resolution Adopted by the Board of Directors and National Committee of A.C.L.U. at Annual Meeting of National Committee at Town Hall," February 5, 1940, Reel 8, ACLU Papers; ACLU, *In the Shadow of War*, annual report (New York: ACLU, 1940), pp. 48–50.

46. Baldwin to the Board of Directors, February 19, 1940, vol. 2166, ACLU Papers.

47. Riis to Baldwin, January 20, 1940, p. 2, Hays Papers; Baldwin to Harry Ward, July 12, 1938, Baldwin Papers; Walker, *In Defense*, p. 121; Baldwin to Robert A. Hoffman, December 4, 1939, vol. 2064, ACLU Papers.

48. ACLU, Board of Directors Minutes, March 13, 1933, Reel 4, ACLU Papers.

49. Arthur Garfield Hays to John Haynes Holmes, February 21, 1940, Box 44, Hays Papers; John Haynes Holmes to Margaret DeSilver, February 21, 1940, pp. 1–2, Reel 5, Holmes Papers.

50. Baldwin to our friends, February 1940, p. 1, Box 44, Hays Papers.

51. Ibid., pp. 1–2; John Haynes Holmes to Riis, March 19, 1940, p. 1, Reel 5, Holmes Papers.

52. I. F. Stone, "Dr. Robert Morss Lovett," March 18, 1940, Box 44, Hays Papers; Walker, *In Defense*, p. 131.

53. Lamson, *Roger Baldwin*, pp. 225–26; John Haynes Holmes to Elizabeth Gurley Flynn, March 20, 1940, pp. 1–2, Reel 5, Holmes Papers.

54. Camp, *Iron in Her Soul*, p. 159.

55. Baldwin is quoted in Corliss Lamont, ed., *The Trial of Elizabeth Gurley Flynn by the American Civil Liberties Union* (New York: Horizon, 1968), p. 13.

56. ACLU Board of Directors Minutes, April 8, 1940, Reel 8; ACLU Board of Directors Minutes, April 15, 1940, Reel 8, both in ACLU Papers.

57. Walker, *In Defense*, pp. 132–33; vote tabulations of motion to expel Elizabeth Gurley Flynn, vol. 2663, ACLU Papers; Lamson, *Roger Baldwin*, p. 223. See Lamont, *The Trial of Elizabeth Gurley Flynn*.

58. Harry Dana to Baldwin, May 16, 1940, vol. 2163, ACLU Papers.

59. Geoffrey Perrett, *Days of Sadness, Years of Triumph: The American People, 1939–1945* (Baltimore, Md.: Penguin, 1974), pp. 93–94; Leo P. Ribuffo, *The Old Christian Right: The Protestant Far Right from the Great Depression to the Cold War* (Philadelphia: Temple University Press, 1983), p. 219.

60. Joseph P. Lash interview with Corliss Lamont, September 28, 1972, Box 49, Joseph P. Lash Papers, Franklin Delano Roosevelt Presidential Library, Hyde Park, N.Y.; Lamont, *The Trial of Elizabeth Gurley Flynn*, p. 22.

61. Baldwin to Robert H. Jackson, March 7, 1940, pp. 1–2, vol. 2184, ACLU Papers; Goldstein, *Political Repression in Modern America*, p. 215; "Roger N. Baldwin: Communist," June 24, 1940, FBI File, #100-49565-X18; ACLU, Board of Directors Minutes, August 26, 1940, Reel 8, ACLU Papers.

62. Hoover memorandum for L. M. C. Smith, April 3, 1941, FBI File, #100-49565-X19; Hoover to Special Agent in Charge, October 21, 1941, pp. 1–2, FBI File, #100-49565-9.

63. Baldwin, "Memo re—J. Edgar Hoover, F.B.I.," October 20, 1941, pp. 1–2, vol. 2573, ACLU Papers; author's interview with Florence Isbell, August 13, 1996, Washington, D.C.; Hoover to Baldwin, November 1, 1941, FBI File #100-47565-5, p. 3.

64. G. A. Nicholson to Hoover, October 24, 1941, FBI File, #100-49565-7, pp. 1–2.

65. Baldwin to Hoover, October 28, 1941, FBI File, #100-49565-5; Hoover to Baldwin, November 1, 1941, pp. 1–4, FBI File, #100-49565-17.

66. Baldwin, draft of "Civil Rights and the F.B.I.," March 12, 1942, pp. 1–6, insert, Baldwin Papers.

67. Ibid., pp. 6–7.

68. Ibid., p. 7.

69. Baldwin, "Memo by Roger Baldwin for Files," July 1943, Baldwin Papers.

70. Hoover, "Roger Nash Baldwin: Security Matter-C" (New York File No. 100-8424), June 11, 1945, FBI File, #100-49565-41.

19. Civil Liberties During World War II

1. Samuel Walker, *In Defense of American Liberties: A History of the American Civil Liberties Union* (New York: Oxford University Press, 1990), p. 135; Roger Baldwin, "Extracts from Speech by Roger Baldwin, Director of the American Civil Liberties Union at the University of Chicago Law School, June 6, 1940, Speaking on 'National Defense and Civil Liberty,'" pp. 1–2, Roger Nash Baldwin Papers, Public Policy Papers, Department of Rare Books and Special Collections, Princeton University Libraries.

2. Walker, *In Defense*, pp. 150–51; ACLU, *Liberty's National Emergency*, annual report (New York: ACLU, 1941), p. 6.

3. ACLU, Board of Directors Minutes, August 12, 1940, Reel 8, ACLU Papers, Princeton University.

4. Walker, *In Defense*, pp. 149–150; Roger Baldwin, "Conscientious Objectors," *Nation*, October 12, 1941, p. 327; Roger Baldwin, "Conscience Under the Draft," *Nation*, August 9, 1941, p. 11; Baldwin, "Memorandum on Conscientious Objectors' Appeals on Religious Grounds," February 25, 1942, vol. 2352, ACLU Papers.

5. Baldwin, "Abstract of Remarks of Roger N. Baldwin, Director, American Civil Liberties Union, on 'Liberty in the Shadow of War,'" October 1941, pp. 1–2, Baldwin Papers.

6. "Propaganda and Censorship in Wartime," *Town Meeting*, December 15, 1941, pp. 4–5.

7. ACLU, Board of Directors Minutes, December 8, 1941, pp. 1–2, Reel 9, ACLU Papers.

8. Baldwin, "Peace-Time Sedition," January 12, 1942, pp. 1–4, vol. 2355, ACLU Papers.

9. Baldwin to Bruce Bliven, January 7, 1942, vol. 2386, ACLU Papers.

10. Edward A. Ross et al., to Francis Biddle, April 4, 1942, pp. 1–3, Box 47, Arthur Garfield Hays Papers, Princeton University.

11. Baldwin, letter to editor, *Nation*, April 11, 1942, p. 444; editors' response to Baldwin, *Nation*, April 11, 1942, p. 444.

12. Baldwin to John Haynes Holmes, April 20, 1942, pp. 1–2, vol. 2355, ACLU Papers.

13. Baldwin, transcript of "Our Wartime Rights and Liberties," radio address over station WMCA, May 6, 1942, pp. 1–3, Baldwin Papers.

14. Walker, *In Defense*, p. 143.

15. "Confidential Memorandum of Conversations with Officials at Washington on June 25, 1942, Arthur Garfield Hays, Dr. Alexander Meiklejohn and Roger Baldwin Representing the Union," July 1, 1942, pp. 1–3, vol. 2356, ACLU Papers.

16. Walker, *In Defense*, pp. 154–55; ACLU, *The Bill of Rights in War*, annual report (New York: ACLU, 1942), pp. 4–5.

17. Walker, *In Defense*, pp. 155–56.

18. Ibid., p. 156; ACLU, Notes on the Special Meeting, October 12, 1942, vol. 2355, ACLU Papers.

19. ACLU, Board of Directors Minutes, October 19, 1942, Reel 9, ACLU Papers.

20. Walker, *In Defense*, p. 157.

21. ACLU, Board of Directors Minutes, November 19, 1942, Reel 9; Baldwin to John Haynes Holmes, November 18, 1942, pp. 1–2, vol. 2355, both in ACLU Papers.

22. Baldwin, "The American Civil Liberties Union," January 30, 1943, pp. 1–2, Baldwin Papers.

23. Baldwin, "Abstract of Remarks of Roger N. Baldwin, Director of the American Civil Liberties Union, on 'War and the Bill of Rights,'" March 1943, p. 1, Baldwin Papers.

24. Ibid., pp. 1–2.

25. Ibid, pp. 2–4.

26. Baldwin to O. John Rogge, April 27, 1943, p. 1, vol. 2507; Baldwin to George Dession, December 15, 1942, vol. 2508, both in ACLU Papers; Baldwin to Max Lerner, July 25, 1944, Box 1, Max Lerner Papers, Yale University.

27. Baldwin to Rogge, April 27, 1943, pp. 1–2, Baldwin Papers.

28. Leo P. Ribuffo, *The Old Christian Right: The Protestant Far Right from the Great Depression to the Cold War* (Philadelphia: Temple University Press, 1983), p. 220; Peggy Lamson, *Roger Baldwin: Founder of the American Civil Liberties Union* (Boston: Houghton Mifflin, 1976), pp. 215–16.

29. Baldwin to Ernest Besig, January 20, 1942, MS 3580, Northern California Chapter of the American Civil Liberties Union Papers (hereafter NCCACLU Papers), California Historical Society, San Francisco. An excellent account of these events is contained in Peter Irons, *Justice at War: The Story of the Japanese-American Internment Cases* (New York: Oxford University Press, 1983); Baldwin, "The Reminiscences of Roger Nash Baldwin," 1954, pp. 184–85, Columbia University Oral History Collection.

30. Baldwin to Besig, February 21, 1942, MS 3580, NCCACLU Papers.

31. Besig to Baldwin, February 24, 1942, MS 3580; Baldwin to Besig, February 25, 1942, MS 3580, both in NCCACLU Papers.

32. ACLU, Board of Directors Minutes, March 2, 1942, Reel 9, ACLU Papers.

33. Walker, *In Defense*, p. 139; Alexander Meiklejohn to Baldwin, March 17, 1942, pp. 1–2, vol. 2363, ACLU Papers; Freda Kirchwey to Baldwin, March 18, 1942, vol. 2363, ACLU Papers; Joseph P. Lash interview with Osmond K. Fraenkel, n.d., Joseph P. Lash Papers, Franklin Delano Roosevelt Presidential Library, Hyde Park, N.Y.

34. Lash interview with Fraenkel, n.d., Lash Papers.

35. Edward Alsworth Ross et al., to Franklin D. Roosevelt, March 20, 1942, pp. 1–3, vol. 2363, ACLU Papers.

36. ACLU, Board of Directors Minutes, April 6, 1942, Reel 9; ACLU, Board of Directors Minutes, April 20, 1942, Reel 9; ACLU, Board of Directors Minutes, May 18, 1942, Reel 9; ACLU, Board of Directors Minutes, June 22, 1942, pp. 1, 3, Reel 9, all in ACLU Papers.

37. Richard Drinnon, *Keeper of Concentration Camps: Dillon S. Myer and American Racism* (Berkeley: University of California Press, 1987), pp. 112–17.

38. ACLU, Board Minutes, May 18 1942, Reel 9, ACLU Papers; Irons, *Justice at War*, p. 130; Baldwin to A. L. Wirin, June 24, 1942, vol. 2397, ACLU Papers.

39. Walter Frank, Fraenkel, and Baldwin to A. L. Wirin, July 2, 1942, MS 3580, NCCACLU Papers.

40. Thomas to Besig, July 8, 1942, p. 1, MS 3580, NCCACLU Papers.

41. Roger Baldwin, "Roger Baldwin Reviews the Japanese Evacuation Case," *Open Forum* 19 (August 15, 1942): 1–2; Roger Baldwin, "Japanese Americans and the Law," *Asia* 42 (September 1942): 518–19.

42. Drinnon, *Keeper of Concentration Camps*, pp. 124–25.

43. Ibid., p. 118.

44. Thomas to Baldwin, November 7, 1942, Norman Thomas Papers, New York Public Library.

45. Thomas to John Haynes Holmes, November 14, 1942, vol. 2355, ACLU Papers.

46. Holmes to Baldwin, December 14, 1942, vol. 2355, ACLU Papers.

47. ACLU, Board of Directors Minutes, October 26, 1942, Reel 9; ACLU, Board of Directors Minutes, December 14, 1942, Reel 9, both in ACLU Papers.

48. ACLU, *Freedom in Wartime*, annual report (New York: ACLU, 1943), pp. 3, 5.

49. Baldwin to Meiklejohn, November 17, 1943, Alexander Meiklejohn Papers, State Historical Society of Wisconsin, Madison; Baldwin to Wirin, May 27, 1944, p. 1, MS 3580, NCCACLU Papers; Baldwin to Wirin, June 2, 1944, MS 3580, NCCACLU Papers.

50. Besig to Baldwin, June 7, 1944, p. 1, MS 3580, NCCACLU Papers; Diane Garey, *Defending Everybody: A History of the American Civil Liberties Union* (New York: TV Books, 1998), p. 121.

51. Baldwin to Besig, June 13, 1944, MS 3580; Baldwin to Besig, June 21, 1944, p. 1, MS 3580, both in NCCACLU Papers.

52. Baldwin to D. S. Myer, June 23, 1944, MS 3580, NCCACLU Papers.

53. Baldwin to Meiklejohn, September 29, 1944, p. 1; Baldwin to Edward L. Parsons, October 17, 1944; Baldwin to Besig, November 1, 1944, p. 1, all in Meiklejohn Papers.

54. Korematsu v. United States, 323 U.S. 214 (1944).

55. Roger Baldwin, "The Japanese Americans in Wartime," *American Mercury*, December 1944, p. 666.

56. Drinnon, *Keeper of Concentration Camps*, pp. 129–30; Meiklejohn to Besig, September 14, 1945, p. 1, MS 3580, NCCACLU Papers.

57. Ibid., pp. 1–2.

58. Baldwin to Besig, September 17, 1945, MS 3580; Besig to Baldwin, September 21, 1945, MS 3580, both in NCCACLU Papers.

59. Myer to Baldwin, December 6, 1949, Baldwin Papers.

60. Baldwin, "Reminiscences," p. 168.

61. Lamson, *Roger Baldwin*, p. 240; Irons, *Justice at War*, pp. 360–61.

62. ACLU, *Liberty on the Home Front*, annual report (New York: ACLU, 1945), pp. 5, 24.

20. *"Quite a Dysfunctional Family"*

1. James M. Reid to Edward A. Lewsin, April 7, 1966, p. 1, Roger Nash Baldwin Papers, Public Policy Papers, Department of Rare Books and Special Collections, Princeton University Libraries; Joseph P. Lash interview with Corliss Lamont, September 28, 1972, Joseph P. Lash Papers, Franklin Delano Roosevelt Presidential Library, Hyde Park, N.Y.; Lash interview with Clifton Read, September 25, 1972, Box 49, Lash Papers.

2. James M. Reid to Lewsin, p. 2, Baldwin Papers.

3. Ibid., p. 3.

4. Walter Lippmann to Baldwin, June 30, 1937, pp. 1–2, Walter Lippmann Papers, Library of Congress; Lippmann to Baldwin, July 19, 1937, Walter Lippmann Papers, Yale University; Roger Baldwin, "The Reminiscences of Roger Nash Baldwin," 1954, pp. 338–40, Columbia University Oral History Collection.

5. Baldwin to Lippman, July 6, 1937, Lippmann Papers, Library of Congress; Baldwin to Lippmann, December 27, 1937, Lippmann Papers, Yale University; Lippmann to Baldwin, February 22, 1938, Lippmann Papers, Yale University; Baldwin to Lippmann, October 11, 1938, Lippmann Papers, Yale University; Baldwin to Lippmann, May 2, 1939, Lippmann Papers, Yale University; Baldwin to Lippmann, May 19, 1939, Lippmann Papers, Yale University; Baldwin, "Reminiscences," pp. 340–41.

6. Baldwin, "Reminiscences," pp. 343–44.

7. Ibid., pp. 347–51; Alvin Johnson to Baldwin, November 19, 1937, Baldwin Papers; Baldwin to Grenville Clark, December 24, 1937, Grenville Clark Papers, Dartmouth College.

8. Clifton Read, untitled diary entries, May–October 1933, Box 49; Lash interview with Clifton Read, September 25, 1972, both in Lash Papers.

9. Clifton Read, untitled diary entries, May–October 1933; Lash interview with Clifton Read, September 25, 1972, Box 49, both in Lash Papers.

10. Read to Lash, September 28, 1972, Box 49, Lash Papers.

11. Read to Lash, September 24, 1972, Box 49; Read to Lash, September 28, 1972, Box 49; Lash interview with Lucille Milner, March 22, 1972, all in Lash Papers.

12. Lash interview with Read, September 25, 1972; Lash interview with Osmond K. Fraenkel, n.d., both in Lash Papers.

13. Lash interview with Read, September 24, 1972; Lash interview with Milner, March 22, 1972, both in Lash Papers.

14. Read, notes, May–June 1933, Box 49, Lash Papers; Read to Lash, September 28, 1972, both in Lash Papers.

15. "Roger Nash Baldwin," *Current Biography, 1940* (New York: Wilson, 1941), p. 44.

16. Author's interview with Florence Isbell, August 13, 1996, Washington, D.C. Shactmanites supported Max Shactman, who condemned the "bureaucratic collectivism" that afflicted the Soviet Union.

17. Ibid.

18. Ibid.

19. Ibid.

20. Ibid.

21. Ibid.

22. Ibid.

23. Ibid.

24. Ibid.

25. Ibid.

26. Ibid.

27. Ibid.

28. Ibid.

29. Ibid.

30. Lash interview with Roger Baldwin, March 9, 1972, Lash Papers.

31. Isbell interview.

32. Ibid.

33. Lucille Milner, *Education of an American Liberal: An Autobiography* (New York: Horizon, 1954), pp. 295–308; Lash interview with Milner, March 22, 1972, Lash Papers.

34. Lash interview with Milner, March 22, 1972, Lash Papers.

35. Ibid.; Lash interview with Roger Baldwin, March 6, 1972, Lash Papers.

36. Baldwin to Mary Buckley, September 22, 1945, pp. 1–2, Baldwin Papers.

21. The Cold War, the Shogun, and International Civil Liberties

1. Transcript of Baldwin radio address, "Is Communism a Threat to the American Way of Life?," station WJZ, January 11, 1945, p. 1, Roger Nash Baldwin Papers, Public Policy Papers, Department of Rare Books and Special Collections, Princeton University Libraries.

2. Ibid., pp. 1–2.

3. Ibid.

4. Baldwin, "Abstract of Speech, by Roger N. Baldwin: 'Basic Human Rights and Group Tensions in the United States,'" 1946, pp. 1, 6, Baldwin Papers; Roger Baldwin, "Of All the Literature on Gandhi," *Voice of India* (June 1946): 309.

5. Baldwin, "American Liberties, 1945 and 1946," n.d., pp. 1–2, Baldwin Papers.

6. William Preston, "By Life Possessed," n.d., pp. 10–11, courtesy William Preston.

7. Ibid.

8. Samuel Walker, *In Defense of American Liberties: A History of the American Civil Liberties Union* (New York: Oxford University Press, 1990), pp. 175–76.

9. D. Donald Klous to Baldwin, January 9, 1947, p. 1, Baldwin Papers; ACLU Board of Directors Minutes, November 4, 1946, Reel 10, ACLU Papers, Princeton University; ACLU Board of Directors Minutes, November 18, 1946, Reel 10, ACLU Papers; Baldwin, "Confidential Memo for Officers of the Board," February 7, 1947, p. 1, Box International Civil Liberties 1, ACLU Papers; J. Edgar Hoover, "Roger Nash Baldwin—C" (New York File #100-8424), November 6, 1946, FBI File #100-49565-44.

10. Baldwin, "Confidential Memo for Officers of the Board," February 7, 1947, p. 1, ACLU Papers.

11. Roger Baldwin, "The Reminiscences of Roger Nash Baldwin," 1954, pp. 435–36, Columbia University Oral History Collection; Baldwin to J. Parnell Thomas, February 28, 1947, p. 1, Box 52, Arthur Garfield Hays Papers, Princeton University; Virginia Gardner, "Roger Baldwin: What Are You Hiding?" *New Masses*, May 20, 1947, pp. 3–4; Hoover, "Roger Nash Baldwin—C" (New York File #100-8424), November 6, 1946, FBI File #100-49565-44.

12. Robert Justin Goldstein, *Political Repression in Modern America: From 1870 to the Present* (Cambridge, Mass.: Schenkman, 1978), p. 299.

13. John Haynes Holmes to Richard S. Childs, March 12, 1947, Box International Civil Liberties 1, ACLU Papers; Baldwin, "Reminiscences," pp. 436–38.

14. Baldwin, "Reminiscences," pp. 436–37.

15. Gardner, "Roger Baldwin: What Are You Hiding?" pp. 3–4.

16. Liston M. Oak, "Roger Baldwin Gets the Axe," *New Leader*, May 24, 1947, Box International Civil Liberties 1, ACLU Papers; Baldwin to Friends, June 25, 1947, Baldwin Papers.

17. Baldwin, "Reminiscences," pp. 440–42; Baldwin to Friends, May 1, 1947, p. 1, Baldwin Papers; Peggy Lamson, *Roger Baldwin: Founder of the American Civil Liberties Union* (Boston: Houghton Mifflin, 1976), p. 243.

18. Baldwin to Friends, May 1, 1947, pp. 1–2, Baldwin Papers; Lamson, *Roger Baldwin*, p. 245; Baldwin, "Reminiscences," pp. 444–45.

19. Baldwin to Friends, May 1, 1947, p. 2, Baldwin Papers.

20. Ibid.

21. Baldwin to Douglas MacArthur, May 6, 1947, Box International Civil Liberties 1, ACLU Papers; Baldwin, "Memo for General MacArthur," May 6, 1947, Box International Civil Liberties 1, ACLU Papers.

22. Baldwin to the Board and National Committee, May 10, 1947, pp. 1–2, Alexander Meiklejohn Papers, State Historical Society of Wisconsin, Madison.

23. Baldwin, "More Impressions and Fun," May 16, 1947, pp. 1–2, Baldwin Papers; Baldwin, "Reminiscences," pp. 475–76.

24. Baldwin, "Reminiscences," pp. 476–78.

25. Ibid., pp. 478–79; Baldwin, press release, May 27, 1947, pp. 1–2, Box International Civil Liberties 1, ACLU Papers; Baldwin to Friends, June 4, 1947, pp. 1–2, Meiklejohn Papers.

26. Baldwin to Friends, June 4, 1947, p. 2, Meiklejohn Papers; Baldwin to Douglas MacArthur, June 8, 1947, Box International Civil Liberties 1, ACLU Papers.

27. Baldwin, "ACLU Director Reports on Japan, Korea Liberties Survey," 1947, pp. 1–3, Box International Civil Liberties 1, ACLU Papers; Baldwin, "Shogun and Emperor," 1947, pp. 1–5, Baldwin Papers.

28. Baldwin to Dick Deverall, May 15, 1952, Baldwin Papers.

29. Baldwin, "Reminiscences," p. 538; Baldwin, "At the Invitation of General Lucius Clay," August 20, 1948, pp. 1–2, Box International Civil Liberties 2, ACLU Papers.

30. Baldwin to Members of the Board, National Committee, and ACLU Friends, September 10, 1948, Baldwin Papers; Baldwin to Friends, October 29, 1948, pp. 1–3, Meiklejohn Papers.

31. Baldwin to Friends, November 4, 1948, pp. 1–2, Baldwin Papers.

32. Ibid., p. 3; Baldwin, "Can Democracy Succeed in Germany?" 1948, pp. 1–2, Baldwin Papers.

33. Roger Baldwin, "American Liberties, 1947–1948," *Art and Action: Tenth Anniversary Issue* (New York: Twice a Year Press, 1948), pp. 529–36; ACLU, Board of Directors Minutes, January 19, 1948, Reel 11, ACLU Papers; ACLU, Board of Directors Minutes, March 15, 1948, Reel 11, ACLU Papers.

34. Roger Baldwin, "Reds and Rights," *Progressive* 4 (June 1948): 5-6.

35. ACLU, *Our Uncertain Liberties*, annual report (New York: ACLU, 1948), pp. 26–28.

36. Baldwin, "Should Communists Be Allowed to Teach in Our Colleges?" pp. 7–8, transcript of ABC Radio broadcast, March 1, 1949, New York City, Baldwin Papers.

37. Ibid., pp. 8–9, 16, 19.

38. Roger Baldwin, "Communist Conspirators and the Bill of Rights," *Progressive* 5 (April 1949): 14.

39. ACLU, *In the Shadow of Fear*, annual report (New York: ACLU, 1949), p. 6; ACLU, *Our Uncertain Liberties*, p. 80.

40. Baldwin, "Memo on the Communist Party and Civil Liberties," November 10, 1949, pp. 1–2, Baldwin Papers.

41. Ibid., p. 2.

22. A Very Public Retirement in the Age of Anticommunism

1. ACLU, Board of Directors Minutes, August 9, 1948, Reel 11, ACLU Papers, Princeton University.

2. ACLU, Board of Directors Minutes, January 3, 1949, Reel 11; ACLU, Board of Directors Minutes, April 28, 1949, Reel 11, both in ACLU Papers; Samuel Walker, *In Defense of American Liberties: A History of the American Civil Liberties Union* (New York: Oxford University Press, 1990), pp. 204–205.

3. Walker, *In Defense*, pp. 203–205.

4. ACLU news release, October 27, 1949, pp. 1–2; Baldwin, "A Memo on My International Associations," March 1974, p. 11, both in Roger Nash Baldwin Papers, Public Policy Papers, Department of Rare Books and Special Collections, Princeton University Libraries.

5. "Prof. Patrick Malin Named New ACLU Director," December 26, 1949, Reel 12, ACLU Papers; Walker, *In Defense*, pp. 204, 206–207; Mary Sperling McAuliffe, *Crisis on the Left: Cold War Politics and American Liberals, 1947–1954* (Amherst: University of Massachusetts Press, 1978), p. 97; W. A. Swanberg, *Norman Thomas: The Last Idealist* (New York: Scribner's, 1976), p. 327; ACLU, *"We Hold These Truths . . .": Freedom Justice Equality: Report on Civil Liberties* (New York: ACLU, 1953); author's interview with Alan Reitman, September 28, 1996, Verona, N.J.

6. Arthur Schlesinger Jr. to Baldwin, November 28, 1949; A. J. Muste to Friends, November 4, 1949; Norman Thomas to Baldwin, November 17, 1949, all in Baldwin Papers.

7. Douglas MacArthur, "Roger Baldwin's Crusade," December 30, 1949; cartoon sketch by Bill Mauldin, n.d., both in Baldwin Papers.

8. John Haynes Holmes to Hoover, November 15, 1949, FBI File, #100-41565-46X2; An American to Hoover, April 23, 1949, pp. 1–6, FBI File, Federal Bureau of Investigation to director, "Would Director Like," FBI File #100-41565-46X2.

9. "Successful ACLU Conference, Dinner Held," February 27, 1950, p. 1, Reel 12, ACLU Papers; "Threat to Liberty Is Seen by Lehman," *New York Times*, February 23, 1950, p. 30.

10. "Threat to Liberty," p. 30; "Thirty Years of A.C.L.U.," *New York Times*, February 22, 1950, p. 28.

11. Baldwin, "Memorandum on Roger N. Baldwin's Arrangements After January 1, 1950, Baldwin Papers; author's interview with Arthur Schlesinger Jr., September 27, 1996, New York City; Reitman interview.

12. Patrick Murphy Malin to Ernest Angell, October 8, 1954, pp. 1–2, Baldwin Papers.

13. Swanberg, *Norman Thomas*, p. 341; McAuliffe, *Crisis on the Left*, p. 125. See Peter Coleman, *The Liberal Conspiracy: The Congress for Cultural Freedom and the Struggle for the Mind of Postwar Europe* (New York: Free Press, 1989), especially pp. 159–70.

14. Baldwin to Alexander Meiklejohn, August 22, 1950, Alexander Meiklejohn Papers, State Historical Society of Wisconsin; Baldwin, "Holmes: In the Middle of the Steady Explosion of Civil Rights," Baldwin Papers.

15. Baldwin to Samuel Reber, September 20, 1950, p. 1; Baldwin to Clinton S. Baldwin, "Memorandum by Roger N. Baldwin, National Chairman, American Civil Liberties Union, Concerning His Six-Month World Tour to Stimulate Civil Liberties, Which He Begins Saturday, July 1, 1950," p. 1, October 2, 1950, p. 2; Baldwin to Friends, October 30, 1950, pp. 2–3; ACLU news release, "Roger N. Baldwin, National Chairman," November 28, 1950, p. 1, all in Baldwin Papers.

16. "Appeal of 145 Calls for Fight on the 'Big Lie,'" *New York Herald Tribune*, January 20, 1951.

17. Roger Baldwin, Christopher Emmet, and Dwight Macdonald, "Statement on *The Fighting Group Against Inhumanity*," February 13, 1951, pp. 1–2, Baldwin Papers.

18. Oliver Jensen, "The Persuasive Roger Baldwin," *Harper's*, September 1951, p. 47.

19. Ibid., p. 48.

20. Ibid., pp. 48–49.

21. Ibid., p. 49.

22. Ibid., pp. 53, 55.

23. Frederic C. Smedley to Harry Truman, September 28, 1950, Harry S Truman Presidential Library, Independence, Mo.; Baldwin, "The Prospects for Freedom," the Annual Felix Adler Lecture, the Meeting House of the New York Society for Ethical Culture, May 12, 1952, pp. 4–8, 10–11, Baldwin Papers.

24. Ibid., pp. 6, 8–9.

25. ibid., pp. 9–10.

26. *Congressional Record*, May 26, 1952, pp. 5959–61.

27. Baldwin, "An American Liberal on the Rosenberg Case," January 1953, pp. 1–2, Baldwin Papers.

28. Baldwin to Dwight David Eisenhower, February 2, 1953, Baldwin Papers.

29. Baldwin to Friends, May 8, 1953, pp. 1–3; Baldwin, "Summary of Remarks on 'Congressional Investigations and Civil Liberties,'" May 21, 1953, both in Baldwin Papers.

30. Roger Baldwin, "The Reminiscences of Roger Nash Baldwin," 1954, pp. 630–31, Columbia University Oral History Collection; Roger Baldwin, ed., *A New Slavery: Forced Labor: The Communist Betrayal of Human Rights* (New York: Oceana, 1953), pp. 18–26.

31. Baldwin, *New Slavery*, pp. 18–20.

32. Ibid., pp. 20–22.

33. Baldwin to Harold Ross, July 22, 1951, p. 1, Baldwin Papers; Michael Wreszin, *A Rebel in Defense of Tradition: The Life and Politics of Dwight Macdonald* (New York: Basic, 1994), pp. 257–58; Joseph P. Lash interview with Roger Baldwin, October 21, 1971, Joseph P. Lash Papers, Franklin Delano Roosevelt Presidential Library, Hyde Park, N.Y.; Swanberg, *Norman Thomas*, p. 352; Norman Thomas to Baldwin, October 10, 1951, Baldwin Papers; Alan Reitman to Baldwin, June 25, 1953, Baldwin Papers; Baldwin, "Memo on Biographical Material About RNB," November 1970, Baldwin Papers.

34. Dwight Macdonald, "The Defense of Everybody—I," *New Yorker*, July 11, 1953, p. 31; Wreszin, *Rebel in Defense of Tradition*, p. 247.

35. Macdonald, "The Defense of Everybody—I," pp. 31–32, Wreszin, *Rebel in Defense of Tradition*, p. 247.

36. Macdonald, "The Defense of Everybody—I," pp. 31–35, 39–40.

37. Ibid., pp. 31, 54–55.

38. Lash interview with Roger Baldwin, October 21, 1971, Lash Papers; Baldwin, "Memo on Biographical Material About RNB," November 1970, Baldwin Papers.

39. Macdonald, "The Defense of Everybody—I," p. 55.

40. Maurice Isserman, *If I Had a Hammer . . .: The Death of the Old Left and the Birth of the New Left* (New York: Basic, 1987), p. 176.

41. Irwin Unger, *The Movement: A History of the American New Left, 1959–1972* (New York: Dodd, Mead, 1974), p. 13; Robert C. Cottrell, *Izzy: A Biography of I. F. Stone* (New Brunswick, N.J.: Rutgers University Press, 1992), p. 194; A. J. Muste to Baldwin, October 4, 1957, Baldwin Papers.

42. Baldwin to Muste, December 6, 1957, Baldwin Papers.

43. Baldwin to Robert R. Nathan, February 18, 1958, Baldwin Papers; Schlesinger interview.

44. Baldwin to My Dear Friends, May 15, 1979, File 1, Charles S. Ascher Papers, Columbia University; Baldwin, "Some Facts About the More Personal Life of Roger N. Baldwin (for Possible Posthumous Inquiries)," 1961, p. B2, Baldwin Papers; Baldwin, "A Memo by RNB on My Travels," November 1974, p. G-7, Baldwin Papers.

45. Baldwin to Friends, August 31, 1959, p. 2, Ralph Chaplin Papers, Washington State Historical Society, Tacoma; Baldwin, "Notes on Vietnam, from Talk with J. D. Montgomery Who Spent Two Years There Studying Administration and Use of Aid Funds (Michigan State Univ. Project)," August 1959, pp. 1–3, Baldwin Papers; Gil Jonas to Baldwin, September 10, 1959, Baldwin Papers.

46. Baldwin, "Notes on Vietnam," August 1959, p. 3, Baldwin Papers.

47. Baldwin, "A Report on a World Tour," October 1959, pp. 1–4, Baldwin Papers.

23. A Man of Contradictions

1. Marjorie M. Bitker, "The Underdog's Best Friend," *Milwaukee Journal*, September 19, 1961, Roger Nash Baldwin Papers, Public Policy Papers, Department of Rare Books and Special Collections, Princeton University Libraries.

2. Bitker, "Underdog's Best Friend."

3. *Congressional Record*, May 25, 1961, pp. 8966–67.

4. Bitker, "Underdog's Best Friend."

5. Ibid.

6. Ibid.

7. "Mrs. Roger Baldwin, 64, Dead; Was Fighter for Civil Liberties," *New York Times*, June 13, 1962, Madeleine Z. Doty Papers, Smith College; Peggy Lamson, *Roger Baldwin: Founder of the American Civil Liberties Union* (Boston: Houghton Mifflin, 1976), pp. 283–84; author's interview with Carl Baldwin, August 12, 1996, New York City; Baldwin, "Highlights of Public Life of Roger Baldwin," ca. 1972, p. 2, Baldwin Papers; Baldwin, "Memo for Mrs. Lamson on My Attitude to Money," April 1974, p. 2, Baldwin Papers.

8. Carl Baldwin interview.

9. Ibid.; "A Tribute by Dorothy Kenyon," in "Evelyn Preston Baldwin," memorial pamphlet, p. 1, File 1, Charles Ascher Papers, Columbia University, Rare Books and Manuscript Library; "A Tribute by William J. vanden Heuvel," p. 1, in "Evelyn Preston Baldwin," memorial pamphlet, Ascher Papers; "Evelyn Preston Baldwin: 1898 to 1962," in "Evelyn Preston Baldwin," memorial pamphlet, Ascher Papers.

10. Baldwin, "A Memo on Madeleine Zabriskie Doty for the Files at Smith College," October 1978, p. 4; Baldwin, "Some Notes by Roger Baldwin for Memoirs Not Covered in the Oral History," November 1964, p. F-5, both in Baldwin Papers; Baldwin to Doty, April 9, 1958, Doty Papers; Baldwin to Doty, March 7, 1959, Doty Papers.

11. Carl Baldwin interview; author's interview with William Preston, October 17, 1996, Detroit; author's interview with William Butler, September 26, 1996, New York City; author's interview with Francesca Mannoni, October 19, 1996, New York City; Baldwin to Norman Dorsen, May 11, 1963, Norman Dorsen Papers, New York University; Baldwin to Norman Dorsen, June 16, 1963, Dorsen Papers.

12. Butler interview.

13. Carl Baldwin interview; Francesca Mannoni interview; Baldwin, "Highlights of Public Life of Roger Baldwin," ca. 1972, p. 2, Baldwin Papers; Joseph P. Lash interview with Roger Baldwin, October 4, 1971, Joseph P. Lash Papers, Franklin Delano Roosevelt Presidential Library, Hyde Park, N.Y.

14. William Preston interview.

15. Carl Baldwin interview; author's interview with Florence Isbell, August 13, 1996, Washington, D.C.

16. Francesca Mannoni interview.

17. Ibid.

18. Butler interview.

19. Francesca Mannoni interview.

20. Ibid.

21. Ibid.

22. Ibid.

23. Carl Baldwin interview.

24. Francesca Mannoni interview.

25. Ibid.

26. Ibid.

27. Lash interviews with Helen Mannoni, October 31, 1971, and October 16, 1972; Lash interview with Butler, December 5, 1971, all in Lash Papers.

28. Lash interview with Helen Mannoni, October 16, 1972, Lash Papers.

29. Ibid.

30. Ibid; Lash interview with Butler, December 5, 1971, Lash Papers.

31. Lash interview with Helen Mannoni, October 16, 1972, Lash Papers.

32. Ibid.

33. Ibid.

34. Lash interview with Roger Baldwin, March 6, 1972, Lash Papers.

35. William Preston interview.

36. Lash interview with Helen Mannoni, October 16, 1972; Lash interview with Roger Baldwin, May 11, 1972, both in Lash Papers.

37. Francesca Mannoni interview.

38. Lash interview with Helen Mannoni, October 16, 1972, Lash Papers.

39. Ibid.; Lash interview with William Butler, May 11, 1972, Box 49, Lash Papers; Arthur R. Railton, "Artists and Other Free Spirits at Chilmark's Barn House," *Dukes County Intelligencer*, August 1995, pp. 10–11, 30–31.

24. Matters of Principle

1. Willie Morris, "Roger Baldwin," *New Republic*, January 25, 1964, pp. 8–9.

2. Ibid.

3. Ibid., p. 9.

4. Lyndon B. Johnson to Roger Baldwin, January 21, 1964, Roger Nash Baldwin Papers, Public Policy Papers, Department of Rare Books and Special Collections, Princeton University Libraries; Felix Frankfurter to Baldwin, May 5, 1964, File 14, Felix Frankfurter Papers, Library of Congress; Baldwin to Frankfurter, File 14, Frankfurter Papers.

5. Author's interview with Norman Dorsen, August 12, 1996, New York City.

6. Ibid.

7. Ibid.

8. Ibid.

9. Author's interview with Sheldon Ackley, New York City, August 12, 1996; author's interview with Alan Reitman, September 28, 1996, Verona, N.J.; author's interview with William Butler, September 26, 1996, New York City.

10. Author's interview with Ira Glasser, August 8, 1996, New York City.

11. Author's interview with Jack Pemberton, October 12, 1996, Monte Rio, California.

12. Ibid.

13. Ibid; Reitman interview.

14. Reitman interview.

15. ACLU, Board of Directors Minutes, June 8, 1964, p. 3, Reel 17, ACLU Papers, Princeton University; Guenter Lewy, *The Cause That Failed: Communism in American Political Life* (New York: Oxford University Press, 1990), p. 158.

16. "Background Information and Summary of Position Papers on the 1940 Resolution and Other Constitutional Issues," December 8, 1966, pp. 8–9, MS 3580, Northern California Chapter of the American Civil Liberties Union Papers (hereafter NCCACLU Papers), California Historical Society, San Francisco.

17. Ibid, p. 9; Reitman interview.

18. ACLU, "Minutes: Plenary Meeting of the Board of Directors," January 29–30, 1966, pp. 9–12, Reel 17, ACLU Papers; Lewy, *The Cause That Failed*, pp. 159–60.

19. Lewy, *The Cause That Failed*, p. 160; "Background Information and Summary of Position Papers," December 8, 1966, pp. 1–30, NCCACLU Papers; "Comment on the Draft Proposal for a Resolution of the Board," n.d., pp. 1–10, MS 3580, NCCACLU Papers.

20. Corliss Lamont to Ernest Besig, December 7, 1967, MS 3580, NCCACLU Papers.

21. Baldwin to Ed Lewin, February 6, 1968, Baldwin Papers.

22. Samuel Walker, *In Defense of American Liberties: A History of the American Civil Liberties Union* (New York: Oxford University Press, 1990), pp. 284–85.

23. Baldwin, "Random Notes: A Memo for My Colleagues in the ACLU," June 1969, pp. 1–4, Baldwin Papers.

24. Ibid., p. 3; Baldwin to Jack Pemberton, September 11, 1969, Baldwin Papers.

25. Baldwin, Stuart Chase, Henry Steele Commager, Ralph Fuchs, Milton Konvitz, and Arthur Schlesinger Jr. to Board of Directors, September 29, 1969, Baldwin Papers.

26. Baldwin to Norman Thomas, December 29, 1964; Wayne Morse to Baldwin, June 3, 1965; Baldwin to Thomas, August 25, 1965, all in Baldwin Papers.

27. Roger Baldwin, "Norman Thomas: A Combative Life," *New Republic*, January 13, 1968, p. 13; Baldwin to Will Bloch, November 11, 1965, Baldwin Papers.

28. Baldwin to Thomas, February 28, 1966; Thomas to Baldwin, March 2, 1966; Baldwin, *précis* of speech at the Student Center, University of Puerto Rico, April 24, 1966, all in Baldwin Papers.

29. Baldwin to Irma L. Hellinger, September 1, 1966; Floyd McKissick to Baldwin, September 7, 1966, p. 1, both in Baldwin Papers.

30. McKissick to Baldwin, September 7, 1966, pp. 1–2, Baldwin Papers.

31. Baldwin to James Farmer, December 22, 1966, Baldwin Papers.

32. Baldwin, "Report on the Geneva Conference for World Peace Through Law, July 1967," pp. 1–2; Baldwin, "I Returned to Moscow," August 1967, pp. 1–2, both in Baldwin Papers.

33. Baldwin, "I Returned to Moscow," August 1967, pp. 3–4, Baldwin Papers.

34. Ibid., p. 4; Baldwin, "One of My Purposes," August 1967, p. 1, Baldwin Papers.

35. Baldwin, "I Returned to Moscow," August 1967, p. 4, Baldwin Papers.

36. Baldwin, "A Memorandum on Pedro Albizu Campos," April 1972, pp. 1–3; Baldwin, "A Memo on a Visit to Pablo Casals," April 19, 1972, pp. 1–2; Baldwin, "Another Visit to Casals," March 1973, all in Baldwin Papers.

37. "Baldwin Hits LBJ in Local Speech," *San Juan Star*, March 7, 1968, pp. 2–3, Baldwin Papers.

38. Baldwin, "From Remarks of Roger Baldwin on 'Why Students Revolt,'" transcript of speech before St. Louis Ethical Society, December 15, 1968; Baldwin to Friends, April 15, 1968, p. 2, both in Baldwin Papers.

39. "A Tribute to Roger Nash Baldwin," presentation of the First Annual Human Rights Award of the International League for the Rights of Man, New York, December 6, 1968, pp. 1–3, Baldwin Papers.

40. Baldwin, "Norman Thomas," pp. 11–12.

41. Baldwin, "This Is a Report by the Civil Rights Commission of Puerto Rico," May 1970, Baldwin Papers.

42. Joseph Edwards, "At 86, A Civil Liberties Champion Retains His Optimism," *Paterson News*, October 7, 1970, p. 60.

25. The Public Image

1. Storer B. Lunt to Roger Baldwin, December 21, 1949, File A-B1; Baldwin to Lunt, December 22, 1949, File A-B1, both in W. W. Norton Papers, Columbia University, Rare Book and Manuscript Library; Joseph P. Lash to Gilbert A. Harrison, September 14, 1972, Gilbert A. Harrison Papers, Collections of the Manuscript Division, Library of Congress; Baldwin to Harrison, October 12, 1972, Harrison Papers; Lash to Harrison, October 16, 1972, Harrison Papers; Baldwin to Lash, October 19, 1972, Harrison Papers; Lash to Baldwin, October 23, 1972, Harrison Papers; author's interview with William Butler, September 26, 1996, New York City.

2. Baldwin, "These Folders Contain," November 1973, Roger Nash Baldwin Papers, Public Policy Papers, Department of Rare Books and Special Collections, Princeton University Libraries.

3. Author's interview with William Preston, October 17, 1996, Detroit; author's interview with William vanden Heuvel, September 26, 1996, New York City.

4. Lash interview with Herbert and Bob Baldwin, October 26, 1971, Cambridge, Mass., Joseph P. Lash Papers, Franklin Delano Roosevelt Presidential Library, Hyde Park, N.Y.; Lash interview with Phil Taft, October 12, 1972, New York City.

5. Author's interview with Alan Reitman, September 28, 1996, Verona, N.J.; Preston interview; vanden Heuvel interview; Butler interview; author's interview with Arthur M. Schlesinger Jr., September 27, 1996, New York City.

6. Butler interview; Schlesinger interview.

7. Baldwin to Ramsey Clark, February 25, 1972, Baldwin Papers.

8. Samuel Walker, *In Defense of American Liberties: A History of the ACLU* (New York: Oxford University Press, 1990), pp. 292 94.

9. Baldwin to Edward J. Ennis, November 5, 1973, Baldwin Papers.

10. Baldwin, "Baldwin's Brief," *Star* (where this paper was published is not clear), March 17, 1974, Baldwin Papers.

11. Ibid.

12. Jerold S. Auerbach, "The Depression Decade," in Alan Reitman, ed., *The Pulse of Freedom: American Liberties, 1920–1970s*, (New York: Norton, 1975), 65–104; Baldwin, "As the Executive Director," in Reitman, *Pulse of Freedom* (New York: New American Library, 1976), pp. 70–71.

13. Baldwin, "As the Executive Director," pp. 70–71.

14. Ibid., p. 71.

15. Ibid.

16. Preston interview.

17. Baldwin, "Why the Last Twenty-five Years of My Life," 1975, pp. 1–4; Baldwin, "A Postscript to the Memo of My Last Twenty-five Years," n.d., both in Baldwin Papers.

18. Sadie Alexander et al. to Board of Directors, February 1, 1974; Baldwin to Norman Dorsen, April 1, 1976, both in Baldwin Papers; author's interview with Frank Haiman, September 14, 1996, Oakland, Calif.; Alan Reitman telegram to Baldwin, April 12, 1976, Baldwin Papers.

19. Alexander, Baldwin, et al. to Board of Directors, February 1, 1974, Baldwin Papers; Lewy, *The Cause That Failed*, pp. 161–62.

20. Lewy, *The Cause That Failed*, pp. 162–63; Baldwin to Ennis, February 23, 1976, Baldwin Papers; Baldwin to Norman Thomas, April 1, 1976, Baldwin Papers.

21. Lewy, *The Cause That Failed*, p. 162; Aryeh Neier to Baldwin, April 28, 1976, Baldwin Papers; Alan Westin to Baldwin, May 3, 1976, Baldwin Papers.

22. Peggy Lamson, *Roger Baldwin: Founder of the American Civil Liberties Union* (Boston: Houghton Mifflin, 1976).

23. Baldwin to Dorothy Kenyon, March 4, 1979, Baldwin Papers.

24. Walker, *In Defense*, p. 333; Michael Baumann, "Civil Liberties Union a Target of FBI Since 1920," *Intercontinental Press* (July 4, 1977): 764.

25. Roger Baldwin, "The ACLU and the FBI: 'They Never Stopped Watching Us,'" *Civil Liberties Review* 4 (November–December 1977): 25.

26. Ibid.

27. Walker, *In Defense*, p. 333; Baldwin to Reitman, October 27, 1977, Baldwin Papers; Baldwin, "The ACLU and the FBI," p. 17.

28. Baldwin, "Memo for the Special Committee," May 5, 1978, Baldwin Papers.

29. Ibid.

30. Shepard Lee to Baldwin, January 22, 1979, Baldwin Papers.

31. Baldwin to Lee, January 29, 1979, Baldwin Papers.

32. ACLU, Report of ACLU Special Commission on the FBI Files to the ACLU Board of Directors, October 2, 1979, ACLU Papers; Walker, *In Defense*, pp. 333–34.

26. Traveling Hopefully

1. Samuel Walker, *In Defense of American Liberties: A History of the American Civil Liberties Union* (New York: Oxford University Press, 1990), p. 323.

2. Roger Baldwin, "Reflections on the Skokie Case," 1978, pp. 1–2, Roger Nash Baldwin Papers, Public Policy Papers, Department of Rare Books and Special Collections, Princeton University Libraries.

3. Ibid., p. 3.

4. Walker, *In Defense*, pp. 325–27.

5. "National Convocation on Free Speech," June 13, 1978, Norman Dorsen Papers, New York University School of Law; author's interview with Ira Glasser, August 12, 1996, New York City; *Traveling Hopefully*, Arnuthfonyus Films, Inc., 1982, Wilmette, Ill.

6. *Traveling Hopefully*.

7. Glasser interview.

8. Ibid.

9. Ibid.

10. Ibid.

11. Ibid.

12. Ibid.

13. Baldwin to Dorothy Kenyon, January 4, 1971; Baldwin, "A Note for the Files," April 3, 1972, both in Baldwin Papers; Joseph P. Lash interviews with Roger Baldwin, November 5, 1971, and May 11, 1972, Box 49, Joseph P. Lash Papers, Franklin Delano Roosevelt Presidential Library, Hyde Park, N.Y.

14. Lash interview with Herbert Baldwin and Robert Baldwin, October 26, 1971, Lash Papers.

15. Lash to Ira Glasser and Art Kopivaara, November 3, 1981, Box 50, Lash Papers.

16. Baldwin to William Butler, October 5, 1973; Alan Reitman to Baldwin, November 1, 1973; Baldwin to Reitman, November 16, 1973; Baldwin to Aryeh Neier, June 15, 1978, all in Baldwin Papers; author's interview with Frank Haiman, September 14, 1996, Oakland, Calif.

17. Baldwin, "Another Memo on Aging—at 90," 1974, Baldwin Papers.

18. Baldwin, "Another Memo on Old Age," May 1977, Baldwin Papers.

19. Baldwin, "A Memo on Aging for the Files," February 1978; Baldwin, "*The Roger Baldwin Story*: A Prejudiced Account of Himself," 1971, p. 9, both in Baldwin Papers; Judith Michaelson, "Grand Old Man of ACLU: Still Scrapper at 94," *Los Angeles Times*, pt. 2, April 12, 1978, p. 2; Haiman interview; Public Broadcasting System, "Roger Baldwin Interview," *The MacNeil/Lehrer Report*, February 2, 1979, transcript, Dorsen Papers; Dorsen to Glasser, Florence Isbell, and Carol Pitchersky, October 16, 1979, Dorsen Papers.

20. Author's interview with Florence Isbell, August 13, 1996, Washington, D.C.; Robert M. Smith to Dorsen, May 29, 1979, Dorsen Papers; Norman Dorsen to Members, May 1, 1979, Dorsen Papers.

21. Author's interview with Carl Baldwin, September 26, 1996, New York City; Baldwin to My Dear Friends, May 15, 1979, Baldwin Papers.

22. Carl Baldwin interview; Norman Dorsen, "Roger Baldwin: 'Traveling Hopefully,'" *Harvard Magazine*, January–February 1982, p. 77; author's interview with Norman Dorsen, August 12, 1996, New York City.

23. Author's interview with Francesa Mannoni, October 19, 1996, New York City.

24. Carl Baldwin interview; author's interview with William Butler, September 26, 1996, New York City; Baldwin to My Dear Friends, May 15, 1979, Baldwin Papers; Isbell and Francesa Mannoni interviews.

25. Francesa Mannoni interview.

26. Baldwin to Folks, March 1975, pp. 1–2, Baldwin Papers.

27. Baldwin to My Dear Folks and Friends at Home, February 1980, Dorsen Papers.

28. Ibid.

29. Miriam Lacob, "First Man of First Amendment" (Passaic County, N.J.), *News*, October 28, 1980, pp. 1, 6.

30. "Carter Gives Medal of Freedom to His Mentor, Rickover, and 13 Others," undated *New York Times* clipping, Dorsen Papers; editorial, *New York Times*, August 28, 1981; Walter Cronkite to Baldwin, January 26, 1981, Baldwin Papers.

31. William Preston, "Roger Was My Uncle," in *Roger Baldwin: In Remembrance* (Martha's Vineyard, Mass.: Tashmoo Press, 1982), pp. 27–28.

32. Marlene Cimons, "ACLU Founder Has a Mind Untouched by Time," *Los Angeles Times*, February 23, 1981, pt. 5, p. 1.

33. Butler, "Roger, Bill, Norman and All Our Friends," 1981, pp. 1–2, transcript, Dorsen Papers.

34. William vanden Heuvel, "As Far as I Can Tell," 1981, pp. 1, 3, transcript, Dorsen Papers.

35. Norman Dorsen, "There Is Really Very Little," 1981, pp. 1–2, transcript, Dorsen Papers.

36. Glasser interview.

37. Ibid.

38. Ibid.

39. Ibid.; Walker, *In Defense*, p. 342–43.

40. Glasser interview.

41. Author's interview with William vanden Heuvel, September 26, 1996, New York City; Butler interview.

42. Vanden Heuvel interview.

43. Ibid.; "The Baldwin Century," *New Republic*, September 23, 1981, p. 6; "Roger Baldwin, RIP," *National Review*, September 18, 1981, p. 1065; John P. Roche, "Perspectives: Remembering Roger Baldwin," *New Leader*, September 21, 1981, p. 14; Gordon Haskell, "Roger Baldwin, 1884–1981," *Dissent*, Winter 1982, p. 102; "A Legacy of Freedom: Remembering Roger Baldwin," *Inquiry*, October 19, 1981, p. 3.

44. Glasser interview.

45. Butler and vanden Heuvel interviews; Baldwin, "Last Words," in *Roger Baldwin: A Remembrance* (New York: American Civil Liberties Union, 1981), pp. 18–19.

Collections, Oral Histories, and Interviews

Manuscript Collections

Jane Addams Papers, Swarthmore College
Devere Allen Papers, Swarthmore College
American Civil Liberties Union Papers, Princeton University
American Civil Liberties Union Papers, Swarthmore College
American Fund for Public Service Papers, New York Public Library
American Labor Conference on International Affairs, New York University
American Union Against Militarism Papers, Swarthmore College
Charles S. Ascher Papers, Columbia University
Roger Nash Baldwin Papers, Princeton University
Joseph Barnes Papers, Columbia University
Erik Barnouw Papers, Columbia University
John Beffel Papers, Library of Congress
Eleanor Robson Belmont Papers, Columbia University
Chester Bowles Papers, Yale University
Earl Browder Papers, Syracuse University
Raymond Leslie Buell Papers, Library of Congress
Charles C. Burlingham Papers, Harvard University Law School
V. F. Calverton Papers, New York Public Library
Carnegie Council on Ethics and International Affairs Papers, Columbia University
Ralph Chaplin Papers, Washington State Historical Society, Tacoma
Grenville Clark Papers, Dartmouth College
Columbia University Forum Papers, Columbia University
Committee on Militarism in Education Papers, Swarthmore College
Henry Wadsworth Longfellow Dana Papers, Swarthmore College

Lawrence Dennis Papers, Hoover Institution, Stanford University
Dorothy Detzer Papers, Swarthmore College
Dies Committee Papers, National Archives
Joseph Dorfman Papers, Columbia University
Norman Dorsen Papers, New York University School of Law
Madeleine Z. Doty Papers, Smith College
Christopher Emmet Jr. Papers, Hoover Institution, Stanford University
Morris Ernst Papers, University of Texas
Federal Bureau of Investigation File on Roger Nash Baldwin, Princeton University
Fellowship of Reconciliation Papers, Swarthmore College
James L. Fly Papers, Columbia University
Elizabeth Gurley Flynn Papers, New York University
Elizabeth Gurley Flynn Papers, State Historical Society of Wisconsin, Madison
Osmond K. Fraenkel Papers, Princeton University
Felix Frankfurter Papers, Library of Congress
Joseph Freeman Papers, Hoover Institution, Stanford University
Varian Fry Papers, Columbia University
Charles Garland Papers, New York Public Library
Garland Fund Papers, New York Public Library
Maurice Goldbloom Papers, University of Oregon
Emma Goldman Papers, New York University
Thomas W. Gregory Papers, Library of Congress
James Gutmann Papers, Columbia University
Gilbert Harrison Papers, Library of Congress
Arthur Garfield Hays Papers, Princeton University
Granville Hicks Papers, Syracuse University
Laura Zametin Hobson Papers, Columbia University
John Haynes Holmes Papers, Library of Congress
Sidney Hook Papers, Hoover Institution, Stanford University
Henry Beetle Hough Papers, Columbia University
Edward M. House Papers, Yale University
Sidney Coe Howard Papers, University of California–Berkeley
Benjamin Huebsch Papers, Library of Congress
International Committee for Political Prisoners, New York Public Library
Gardner Jackson Papers, Franklin Delano Roosevelt Presidential Library, Hyde Park, N.Y.
Oszkar Jaszi Papers, Columbia University
Alvin S. Johnson Papers, Yale University
David Starr Jordan Papers, Hoover Institution, Stanford University
William Kent Papers, Yale University

Dorothy Kenyon Papers, Smith College
Harry Lees Kingman Papers, University of California–Berkeley
Corliss Lamont Papers, Columbia University
Joseph Lash Papers, Franklin Delano Roosevelt Presidential Library, Hyde Park, N.Y.
Harold Laski Papers, Syracuse University
Max Lerner Papers, Yale University
Austin Lewis Papers, University of California–Berkeley
Samuel McClure Lindsay Papers, Columbia University
Walter Lippmann Papers, Yale University
Lewis Levitzki Lorwin Papers, Columbia University
Jay Lovestone Papers, Hoover Institution, Stanford University
Lusk Committee Papers, New York State Archives
Dwight Macdonald Papers, Yale University
Alexander Meiklejohn Papers, State Historical Society of Wisconsin, Madison
Military Intelligence Division Papers, National Archives
Wesley Clair Mitchell Papers, Columbia University
Ivan I. Morris Papers, Columbia University
A. J. Muste Papers, Swarthmore College
Scott Nearing Papers, Swarthmore College
New York Bureau of Legal Advice Papers, New York University
John Francis Neylan, University of California–Berkeley
Northern California Chapter of the ACLU, California Historical Society,
    San Francisco
W. W. Norton Papers, Columbia University
Pacific Relations Institute Papers, Columbia University
Guichard Auguste Bolivar Parris Papers, Columbia University
People's Council of America Papers, Swarthmore College
Fred Rodell Papers, Haverford College
Margaret Sanger Papers, Library of Congress
John Nevin Sayre Papers, Swarthmore College
Theodore Schroeder Papers, Southern Illinois University
M. Lincoln Schuster Papers, Columbia University
Frederic C. Smedley Papers, Columbia University
Socialist Party Papers, Duke University
Society for the Prevention of Crime Papers, Columbia University
Lincoln Steffens–Ella Winters Papers, Columbia University
I. N. P. Stokes Papers, Yale University
James Graham Phelps Stokes Papers, Columbia University
Benjamin Stolberg Papers, Columbia University
Sydney Dix Strong Papers, Swarthmore College

W. A. Swanberg Papers, Columbia University
Norman Thomas Papers, New York Public Library
Harry S Truman Papers, Harry S Truman Presidential Library, Independence, Mo.
Rexford Tugwell Papers, Franklin Delano Roosevelt Presidential Library,
    Hyde Park, N.Y.
U.S. Department of Justice Papers, National Archives
U.S. Military Intelligence Reports, University of California–Davis
Mary Van Kleeck Papers, Smith College
Oswald Garrison Villard Papers, Harvard University
Lillian Wald Papers, Columbia University
Lillian Wald Papers, New York Public Library
John Hunter Walker Papers, Illinois Historical Society, Urbana
Booker T. Washington Papers, Library of Congress
Harry Weinberger Papers, Yale University
L. Hollingsworth Wood Papers, Columbia University

Columbia University Oral History Project

Roger Baldwin
Algernon D. Black
Arthur Dunham
John W. Edelman
Luther Evans
Osmond K. Fraenkel
Walter Gellhorn
Alvin Grauer
Richard G. Green
James Gutmann
John R. Harold
Burton J. Hendrick
Quincy Howe
Gardner Jackson
Corliss Lamont
Mary Lord
Herbert L. May
H. L. Mitchell
A. J. Muste
Douglas W. Overton
Louis H. Pink
Justine Wise Polier
I. D. Robbins

Edwin Seaver
W. A. Swanberg
Philip Taft
Norman Thomas
Colston Warne
Palmer Weber
Frances Witherspoon and Tracy D. Mygatt

Interviews by Author

Ackley, Sheldon, August 12, 1996, New York City
Baldwin, Carl, August 12, 1996, New York City
Butler, William, September 26, 1996, New York City
Dorsen, Norman, August 12, 1996, New York City
Glasser, Ira, August 8, 1996, New York City
Haiman, Frank, September 14, 1996, Oakland, Calif.
Isbell, Florence, August 13, 1996, Washington, D.C.
Mannoni, Francesca, October 19, 1996, New York City
Miller, Jay, September 4, 1996, telephone
Pemberton, Jack, October 12, 1996, Monte Rio, Calif.
Preston, William, October 17, 1996, Detroit
Reitman, Alan, September 28, 1996, Verona, N.J.
Schlesinger, Arthur Jr., September 27, 1996, New York City
vanden Heuvel, William, September 26, 1996, New York City

Interviews by Joseph Lash

Baldwin, Herbert and Robert, October 26, 1971, Cambridge, Mass.
Baldwin, Roger, multiple
Butler, William, December 5, 1971, New York City
Ernst, Morris, February 7, 1972, New York City
Fraenkel, Osmond, n.d., New York City
Friedkin, Anna, January 16, 1972, New York City
Gross, Lawrence, October 25, 1971, Amherst, Mass.
Lamont, Corliss, September 28, 1972, New York City
Mannoni, Helen, October 13, 1971, October 16, 1972, New York City
Milner, Lucille, March 22, 1972, New York City
Read, Clifton, September 25, 1972, New York City
Taft, Philip, October 1972, New York City

Bibliography

Abbott, Philip. *Leftward Ho! V. F. Calverton and American Radicalism*. Westport, Conn.: Greenwood, 1993.

Abrahams, Edward. *The Lyrical Left: Randolph Bourne, Alfred Stieglitz, and the Origins of Cultural Radicalism in America*. Charlottesville: University Press of Virginia, 1988.

American Civil Liberties Union. *American Civil Liberties Union: Annual Reports*. 6 Vols. New York: Arno Press and *New York Times*, 1970.

ACLU. *The Fight for Free Speech*. Annual report. New York: ACLU, 1921.

———. *A Year's Fight for Free Speech*. Annual report. New York: ACLU, 1923.

———. *Free Speech in 1924*. Annual report. New York: ACLU, 1925.

———. *The Fight for Civil Liberty*. Annual report. New York: ACLU, 1931.

———. *"Land of Pilgrim's Pride."* Annual report. New York: ACLU, 1933.

———. *Liberty under the New Deal*. Annual report. New York: ACLU, 1934.

———. *How Goes the Bill of Rights?* Annual report. New York: ACLU, 1936.

———. *Let Freedom Ring!* Annual report. New York: ACLU, 1937.

———. *Eternal Vigilance! The Story of Civil Liberty, 1937–1938*. Annual report. New York: ACLU, 1938.

———. *The Bill of Rights—150 Years After, June 1939*. Annual report. New York: ACLU, 1939.

———. *In the Shadow of War*. Annual report. New York: ACLU, 1940.

———. *Liberty's National Emergency*. Annual report. New York: ACLU, 1941.

———. *The Bill of Rights in War*. Annual report. New York: ACLU, 1942.

———. *Freedom in Wartime*. Annual report. New York: ACLU, 1943.

———. *Liberty on the Home Front*. Annual report. New York: ACLU, 1945.

———. *Our Uncertain Liberties*. Annual report. New York: ACLU, 1948.

——. *In the Shadow of Fear.* Annual report. New York: ACLU, 1949.

——. *"We Hold These Truths . . .": Freedom Justice Equality: Report on Civil Liberties.* Annual report. New York: ACLU, 1953.

"The American Civil Liberties Union Sticks out Its Tongue." *Law and Labor* (January 1931): 7.

Amory, Cleveland. *The Proper Bostonians.* New York: Dutton, 1947.

"Appeal of 145 Calls for Fight on the 'Big Lie.'" *New York Herald Tribune,* January 20, 1951.

Auerbach, Jerold S. *Labor and Liberty: The La Follette Committee and the New Deal.* Indianapolis, Ind.: Bobbs-Merrill, 1966.

——. "The Depression Decade." In Alan Reitman, ed., *The Pulse of Freedom: American Liberties, 1920–1970s.* New York: Norton, 1975.

"Baldwin Accuses Hague of Tyranny." *New York Times,* December 16, 1937, p. 3.

"The Baldwin Century." *New Republic,* September 23, 1981, p. 6.

Baldwin, Roger. "Statistics Relating to Juvenile Delinquents." *Proceedings of the National Conference of Charities at Corrections.* Ft. Wayne, Ind.: Archer, 1910.

——. "The St. Louis Pageant and Masque: Its Civic Meaning." *Survey* 32 (April 11, 1914): 52–53.

——. "St. Louis' Successful Fight for a Modern Charter." *National Municipal Review* 3 (October 1914): 720–21, 724.

——. "The Use of Municipal Ownership to Abolish Trans-Mississippi Freight and Passenger Tolls." *National Municipal Review* 4 (July 1915): 468–72.

——. "Conscience at the Bar." *Survey* 41 (November 1918): 253.

——. "An Industrial Program After the War," *Proceedings of the National Conference of Social Work* 45 (1918): 426–29.

——. "Social Work and Radical Economic Movements." *Proceedings of the National Conference of Social Work* 45 (1918): 396–98.

——. *The Truth About the I.W.W.* New York: National Civil Liberties Bureau, 1918.

——. "Freedom of Opinion." *Socialist Review* 9 (August 1920): 115.

——. "The Immorality of Social Work." *World Tomorrow* 5 (February 1922): 44–45.

——. "How Shall We Escape Private Property?" *World Tomorrow* (April 1922): 109–10.

——. "Where Are the Prewar Radicals?" *Survey* 55 (February 1, 1926): 560.

——. *Liberty Under the Soviets.* New York: Vanguard, 1928.

——. "While California's Governor Deliberates." *Unity,* August 12, 1929, pp. 329–30.

——. "The Myth of Law and Order." In Samuel D. Schmalhausen, ed., *Behold America!* New York: Farrar and Rinehart, 1931.

——. "Free Speech for Nazis?" *World Tomorrow* 16 (November 1933): 613.

——. "Freedom in the U.S.A. and the U.S.S.R." *Soviet Russia Today* 3 (September 1934): 11.

——. "Civil Liberties comprise." *Social Work Year Book* 5 (1939): 76–77.

——. "Conscience Under the Draft." *Nation*, August 9, 1941, pp. 114–16.

——. "Conscientious Objectors." *Nation*, October 12, 1941, pp. 326–28.

——. "Roger Baldwin Reviews the Japanese Evacuation Case." *Open Forum* 19 (August 15, 1942): 1–2.

——. "Japanese Americans and the Law." *Asia* 42 (September 1942): 518–19.

——. "The Japanese Americans in Wartime." *American Mercury*, December 1944, pp. 664–70.

——. "Of All the Literature on Gandhi," *Voice of India* (June 1946): 309.

——. "American Liberties, 1947–1948." *Art and Action: Tenth Anniversary Issue* (New York: Twice a Year Press, 1948).

——. "Reds and Rights." *Progressive* 4 (June 1948): 5–6.

——. "Communist Conspirators and the Bill of Rights." *Progressive* 5 (April 1949): 14.

——. "The Prospects for Freedom." Felix Adler Lecture, American Ethical Union, New York, 1952.

——. "Norman Thomas: A Combative Life." *New Republic*, January 13, 1968, pp. 11–12.

——. "Recollections of a Life in Civil Liberties—I." *Civil Liberties Review* 1 (Spring 1975): 39–63.

——. "Recollections of a Life in Civil Liberties—II: Russia, Communism, and United Fronts, 1920–1940." *Civil Liberties Review* 2 (Fall 1975): 10–40.

——. "As the Executive Director." In Alan Reitman, ed., *Pulse of Freedom: American Liberties, 1920–1970s.* New York: New American Library, 1976.

——. Introduction to International Committee for Political Prisoners, *Letters from Russian Prisons: Consisting of Reprints of Documents by Political Prisoners in Soviet Prisons, Prison Camps and Exile, and Reprints of Affidavits Concerning Political Persecution in Soviet Russia, Official Statements by Soviet Authorities, Excerpts from Soviet Laws Pertaining to Civil Liberties, and Other Documents.* Westport, Conn.: Hyperion, 1977.

Baldwin, Roger and Clarence B. Randall. *Civil Liberties and Industrial Conflict.* Cambridge, Mass.: Harvard University Press, 1938.

Baldwin, Roger and Alan Westin. "The ACLU and the FBI: 'They Never Stopped Watching Us.'" *Civil Liberties Review* 4 (November–December 1977): 17–25.

Baldwin, Roger, ed. *A New Slavery: Forced Labor: The Communist Betrayal of Human Rights.* New York: Oceana, 1953.

——. *Kropotkin's Revolutionary Pamphlets: A Collection of Writings by Peter Kropotkin.* New York: Dover, 1970.

Baumann, Michael. "Civil Liberties Union a Target of FBI Since 1920." *Intercontinental Press*, July 4, 1977, p. 764.

Beaver, Daniel R. *Newton D. Baker and the American War Effort, 1917–1919*. Lincoln: University of Nebraska Press, 1966.

Belknap, Michael R. *Cold War Political Justice: The Smith Act, the Communist Party, and American Civil Liberties*. Westport, Conn.: Greenwood, 1977.

Bennett, David H. *The Party of Fear: From Nativist Movements to the New Right in American History*. New York: Vintage, 1995.

Benton, Thomas Hart. *An American in Art: A Professional and Technical Autobiography*. Lawrence: University Press of Kansas, 1969.

Biel, Steven. *Independent Intellectuals in the United States, 1910–1945*. New York: New York University Press, 1992.

Blanchard, Margaret A. *Revolutionary Sparks: Freedom of Expression in Modern America*. New York: Oxford University Press, 1992.

Bosworth, Allan R. *America's Concentration Camps*. New York: Norton, 1967.

Boyer, Paul S. *Purity in Print: The Vice Society and Book Censorship in America*. New York: Scribner's, 1968.

Buckley, William F. Jr. and L. Brent Bozell. *McCarthy and His Enemies*. Chicago: Regnery, 1954.

Budenz, Louis Francis. *This Is My Story*. New York: McGraw-Hill, 1947.

Buhle, Mari Jo, Paul Buhle, and Dan Georgakas, eds. *Encyclopedia of the American Left*. New York: Garland, 1990.

"Calls Marcantonio Red Front Leader." *New York Times*, November 29, 1938, p. 9.

Camp, Helen C. *Iron in Her Soul: Elizabeth Gurley Flynn and the American Left*. Pullman: Washington State University Press, 1995.

Cantor, Milton. *The Divided Left: American Radicalism, 1900–1975*. New York: Hill and Wang, 1978.

Carter, Dan T. *Scottsboro: A Tragedy of the American South*. New York: Oxford University Press, 1971.

Casper, Jonathan D. *The Politics of Civil Liberties*. New York: Harper and Row, 1972.

Caute, David. *The Fellow Travelers: A Postcript to the Enlightenment*. New Haven: Yale University Press, 1988.

——. *The Great Fear: The Anticommunist Purge Under Truman and Eisenhower*. New York: Simon and Schuster, 1979.

Chafee, Zechariah Jr. *The Censorship in Boston*. Boston: Civil Liberties Union of Massachusetts, 1929.

Chalberg, John. *Emma Goldman: American Individualist*. New York: Harper Collins, 1991.

Chatfield, Charles. *For Peace and Justice: Pacifism in America, 1914–1941*. Boston: Beacon, 1973.

——. *The American Peace Movement: Ideals and Activism*. New York: Twayne, 1992.

Cimons, Marlene. "ACLU Founder Has a Mind Untouched by Time." *Los Angeles Times*, February 23, 1981, pt. 5, p. 1.

Coan, Blair. *The Red Web: An Underground Political History of the United States from 1918 to the Present Time Showing How Close the Government Is to Collapse and Told in an Understandable Way*. Chicago: Northwest, 1925.

Coleman, Peter. *The Liberal Conspiracy: The Congress for Cultural Freedom and the Struggle for the Mind of Postwar Europe*. New York: Free Press, 1989.

Cook, Fred J. *The FBI Nobody Knows*. New York: Macmillan, 1965.

———. *The Nightmare Decade*. New York: Random House, 1971.

Cortner, Richard C. *The Supreme Court and the Second Bill of Rights: The Fourteenth Amendment and the Nationalization of Civil Liberties*. Madison: University of Wisconsin Press, 1981.

Cottrell, Robert C. *Izzy: A Biography of I. F. Stone*. New Brunswick, N.J.: Rutgers University Press, 1992.

Crawford, Alan. *Thunder on the Right: The "New Right" and the Politics of Resentment*. New York: Pantheon, 1980.

Crossman, Richard, ed. *The God That Failed*. New York: Bantam, 1965.

Crowl, James William. *Angels in Stalin's Paradise: Western Reporters in Soviet Russia, 1917 to 1937, a Case Study of Louis Fischer and Walter Duranty*. Washington, D.C.: University Press of America, 1982.

Curti, Merle. "Subsidizing Radicalism: The American Fund for Public Service, 1921–1941." *Social Service Review* 33 (September 1959): 275–77.

Daniel, Cletus E. *The ACLU and the Wagner Act: An Inquiry into the Depression-Era Crisis of American Liberalism*. Ithaca: Cornell University Press, 1980.

Diggins, John P. *Mussolini and Fascism: The View from America*. Princeton: Princeton University Press, 1975.

———. *Up from Communism: Conservative Odysseys in American Intellectual History*. New York: Harper and Row, 1975.

———. *The Rise and Fall of the American Left*. New York: Norton, 1992.

Dilling, Elizabeth. *The Red Network*. Kenilworth, Ill.: Elizabeth Dilling, 1934.

———. *The Roosevelt Red Record and Its Background*. Kenilworth, Ill.: Elizabeth Dilling, 1936.

Donner, Frank J. *The Age of Surveillance: The Aims and Methods of America's Political Intelligence System*. New York: Vintage, 1981.

Donohue, William A. *The Politics of the American Civil Liberties Union*. New Brunswick, N.J.: Transaction, 1990.

———. *Twilight of Liberty: The Legacy of the ACLU*. New Brunswick, N.J.: Transaction, 1994.

Dorsen, Norman. "Roger Baldwin: 'Traveling Hopefully.'" *Harvard Magazine*, January–February 1982, p. 77.

Downs, Donald Alexander. *Nazis in Skokie: Freedom, Community, and the First Amendment.* South Bend, Ind.: University of Notre Dame Press, 1985.

Draper, Theodore. *American Communism and Soviet Russia.* New York: Vintage, 1986.

——. *The Roots of American Communism.* Chicago: Ivan R. Dee, 1957.

The Drifter. "In the Driftway." *Nation,* November 9, 1918, p. 555.

Drinnon, Richard. *Keeper of Concentration Camps: Dillon S. Myer and American Racism.* Berkeley: University of California Press, 1987.

——. *Rebel in Paradise: A Biography of Emma Goldman.* Boston: Beacon, 1961.

"Drive for Fascism Charged by Ickes." *New York Times,* December 9, 1937, pp. 1, 20.

Dubofsky, Melvyn. *We Shall Be All: A History of the Industrial Workers of the World.* New York: Quadrangle, 1969.

Duffus, Robert L. "The Legend of Roger Baldwin." *American Mercury,* August 25, 1925, pp. 408–14.

Edwards, Joseph. "At 86, A Civil Liberties Champion Retains His Optimism." *Paterson* (N.J.) *News,* October 7, 1970, p. 60.

Ernst, Morris L. *The Best Is Yet . . .* New York: Harper, 1945.

Feuerlicht, Roberta Strauss. *Justice Crucified: The Story of Sacco and Vanzetti.* New York: McGraw-Hill, 1977.

Fiedler, Leslie. *An End to Innocence: Essays on Culture and Politics.* Boston: Beacon, 1955.

"15,000 Reds Cheer Attacks on Hitler." *New York Times,* April 6, 1933, p. 10.

Filene, Peter G. *Americans and the Soviet Experiment, 1917–1933.* Cambridge, Mass.: Harvard University Press, 1967.

Fishbein, Leslie. *Rebels in Bohemia: The Radicals of the Masses, 1911–1917.* Chapel Hill: University of North Carolina Press, 1982.

Fleischman, Harry. *Norman Thomas: A Biography.* New York: Norton, 1967.

Flexner, Bernard and Roger Baldwin. *Juvenile Courts and Probation.* New York: Century, 1914.

Flynn, Elizabeth Gurley. *The Rebel Girl: An Autobiography: My First Life, 1906–1926.* New York: International, 1973.

"Foster and His Aides Put Red Flag First." *New York Times,* December 6, 1930, pp. 1, 12.

Freeman, Joseph. *An American Testament: A Narrative of Rebels and Romantics.* New York: Octagon, 1973.

"Free Speech on Civil Rights." *New York Times,* October 11, 1939, p. 26.

Fried, Richard M. *Nightmare in Red: The McCarthy Era in Perspective.* New York: Oxford University Press, 1990.

"Galahad of Freedom," *World Tomorrow* 13 (January 1930): 33, 36.

Gallagher, Dorothy. *All the Right Enemies: The Life and Murder of Carlo Tresca.* New York: Penguin, 1989.

Gardner, Virginia. "Roger Baldwin: What Are You Hiding?" *New Masses* (May 20, 1947): 3–4.

———. *"Friend and Lover": The Life of Louise Bryant.* New York: Horizon, 1982.

Garey, Diane. *Defending Everybody: A History of the American Civil Liberties Union.* New York: TV Books, 1998.

Gentry, Curt. *J. Edgar Hoover: The Man and His Secrets.* New York: Norton, 1991.

Gibson, James L. and Richard D. Bingham. *Civil Liberties and Nazis: The Skokie Free-Speech Controversy.* New York: Praeger, 1985.

Gillon, Steven M. *Politics and Vision: The ADA and American Liberalism, 1947–1985.* New York: Oxford University Press, 1987.

Ginger, Ray. *Six Days or Forever? Tennessee v. John Thomas Scopes.* New York: Oxford University Press, 1958.

Glasser, Ira. *Visions of Liberty: The Bill of Rights for All Americans.* New York: Arcade, 1991.

Goldberg, Robert A. *Grassroots Resistance: Social Movements in Twentieth-Century America.* Belmont, Calif.: Wadsworth, 1991.

Goldman, Emma. *Living My Life.* Garden City, N.Y.: Garden City Publishing, 1931.

Goldstein, Robert Justin. *Political Repression in Modern America: From 1870 to the Present.* New York: Schenkman, 1978.

Goodman, James. *Stories of Scottsboro.* New York: Vintage, 1995.

Goodman, Walter. *The Committee: The Extraordinary Career of the House Committee on Un-American Activities.* New York: Farrar, Straus and Giroux, 1968.

Gornick, Vivian. *The Romance of American Communism.* New York: Basic, 1977.

Graber, Mark A. *Transforming Free Speech: The Ambiguous Legacy of Civil Libertarianism.* Berkeley: University of California Press, 1991.

Griffith, Robert. *The Politics of Fear: Joseph R. McCarthy and the Senate.* Lexington: University Press of Kentucky, 1970.

Griffith, Robert and Athan Theoharis, eds. *The Specter: Original Essays on the Cold War and the Origins of McCarthyism.* New York: New Viewpoints, 1974.

Guttmann, Allen. *The Wound in the Heart: America and the Spanish Civil War.* New York: Free Press of Glencoe, 1962.

Hall, Kermit L. *The Magic Mirror: Law in American History.* New York: Oxford University Press, 1989.

Hamby, Alonzo L. *Beyond the New Deal: Harry S Truman and American Liberalism.* New York: Columbia University Press, 1973.

Hamlin, David. *The Nazi-Skokie Conflict: A Civil Liberties Battle.* Boston: Beacon, 1980.

Hapgood, Norman. *Professional Patriots.* New York: Albert and Charles Boni, 1927.

Haskell, Gordon. "Roger Baldwin, 1884–1981." *Dissent,* Winter 1982, p. 102.

Hays, Arthur Garfield. *Let Freedom Ring.* New York: Boni and Liveright, 1928.

———. *Trial by Prejudice*. New York: Covici, Friede, 1933.

———. *City Lawyer*. New York: Simon and Schuster, 1942.

Heale, M. J. *American Anticommunism: Combating the Enemy Within, 1830–1970*. Baltimore.: Johns Hopkins University Press, 1990.

"He Chose Words in Haste." *New York Times*, November 1, 1918, p. 14.

Hoke, Travis. "Red Rainbow." *North American Review* 234 (November 1932): 433–39.

Hollander, Paul. *Political Pilgrims: Travels of Western Intellectuals to the Soviet Union, China, and Cuba, 1928–1978*. New York: Harper Colophon, 1983.

———. *Anti-Americanism: Critiques at Home and Abroad, 1965–1990*. New York: Oxford University Press, 1992.

Holmes, John Haynes. *I Speak for Myself: The Autobiography of John Haynes Holmes*. New York: Harper, 1959.

Howe, Irving and Lewis Coser. *The American Communist Party: A Critical History*. New York: Praeger, 1962.

Humphrey, Robert E. *Children of Fantasy: The First Rebels of Greenwich Village*. New York: Wiley, 1978.

Irons, Peter. *Justice at War: The Story of the Japanese-American Internment Cases*. New York: Oxford University Press, 1983.

———. *The Courage of Their Convictions*. New York: Free Press, 1988.

Isserman, Maurice. *Which Side Were You On? The American Communist Party During the Second World War*. Middletown, Conn.: Wesleyan University Press, 1982.

———. *If I Had a Hammer . . .: The Death of the Old Left and the Birth of the New Left*. New York: Basic, 1987.

Jaffe, Julian F. *Crusade Against Radicalism: New York During the Red Scare, 1914–1924*. Port Washington, N.Y.: Kennikat, 1972.

James, Marlise. *The People's Lawyers*. New York: Holt, Rinehart and Winston, 1973.

Jeansonne, Glen. *Gerald L. K. Smith: Minister of Hate*. New Haven: Yale University Press, 1988.

Jensen, Oliver. "The Persuasive Roger Baldwin." *Harper's*, September 1951, pp. 47–55.

"Jersey Labor Party Denounced by Hague." *New York Times*, December 18, 1937, p. 5.

Johnson, Donald. *The Challenge to American Freedoms: World War I and the Rise of the American Civil Liberties Union*. Lexington: University of Kentucky Press, 1963.

Josephson, Matthew. *Infidel in the Temple: A Memoir of the 1930s*. New York: Knopf, 1967.

Joughin, G. Louis and Edmund M. Morgan. *The Legacy of Sacco and Vanzetti*. New York: Harcourt, Brace, 1948.

Kalven, Harry. *A Worthy Tradition: Freedom of Speech in America*. New York: Harper and Row, 1988.

Katz, Milton S. *Ban the Bomb: A History of SANE, the Committee for a Sane Nuclear Policy, 1957–1985*. New York: Greenwood, 1986.

Kazin, Alfred. *Starting out in the Thirties*. New York: Vintage, 1980.

Keller, William W. *The Liberals and J. Edgar Hoover*. Princeton: Princeton University Press, 1989.

Klehr, Harvey. *The Heyday of American Communism: The Depression Decade*. New York: Basic, 1984.

——. *The American Communist Movement: Storming Heaven Itself*. New York: Twayne, 1992.

Kluger, Richard. *Simple Justice*. New York: Vintage, 1977.

"Knocks for Everybody." *New York Times*, April 7, 1933, p. 18.

Kovel, Joel. *Red Hunting in the Promised Land: Anticommunism and the Making of America*. New York: Basic, 1994.

Kropotkin, Peter. *Kropotkin's Revolutionary Pamphlets: A Collection of Writings by Peter Kropotkin*. Ed. Roger N. Baldwin. New York: Dover, 1970.

Kutler, Stanley I. *The American Inquisition: Justice and Injustice in the Cold War*. New York: Hill and Wang, 1982.

Kutulas, Judy. *The Long War: The Intellectual People's Front and Anti-Stalinism, 1930–1940*. Durham: Duke University Press, 1995.

Lacob, Miriam. "First Man of First Amendment." (Passaic County, N.J.) *News*, October 28, 1980, pp. 1, 6.

Lader, Lawrence. *Power on the Left: American Radical Movements Since 1946*. New York: Norton, 1979.

Lamont, Corliss, ed. *The Trial of Elizabeth Gurley Flynn by the American Civil Liberties Union*. New York: Horizon, 1968.

Lamont, Corliss. *Yes to Life*. New York: Horizon, 1981.

Lamson, Peggy. *Roger Baldwin: Founder of the American Civil Liberties Union: A Portrait*. Boston: Houghton Mifflin, 1976.

Larson, Edward J. *Trial and Error: The American Controversy over Creation and Evolution*. New York: Oxford University Press, 1985.

Lasch, Christopher. *The American Liberals and the Russian Revolution*. New York: Columbia University Press, 1962.

Lavine, Harold. *Fifth Column in America*. New York: Doubleday, 1940.

Lawson, R. Alan. *The Failure of Independent Liberalism, 1930–1941*. New York: Putnam's, 1971.

"A Legacy of Freedom: Remembering Roger Baldwin." *Inquiry*, October 19, 1981, p. 3.

Leuchtenburg, William E. *Franklin D. Roosevelt and the New Deal, 1932–1941*. New York: Harper and Row, 1963.

——. *The Supreme Court Reborn: The Constitutional Revolution in the Age of Roosevelt*. New York: Oxford University Press, 1995.

Levanson, Leah and Jerry Natterstad. *Granville Hicks: The Intellectual in Mass Society*. Philadelphia: Temple University Press, 1993.

Lewis, Felice Flanery. *Literature, Obscenity, and Law*. Carbondale: Southern Illinois University Press, 1976.

Lewy, Guenter. *The Cause That Failed: Communism in American Political Life*. New York: Oxford University Press, 1990.

"Liberties Parley Excludes No Group." *New York Times*, October 10, 1939, p. 14.

Lottman, Herbert. *The Left Bank: Writers, Artists, and Politics from the Popular Front to the Cold War*. San Francisco: Halo, 1991.

Ludington, Townsend. *Twentieth-Century Odyssey: The Life of John Dos Passos*. New York: Dutton, 1989.

Lyons, Eugene. *The Red Decade: The Stalinist Penetration of America*. Indianapolis, Ind.: Bobbs-Merrill, 1941.

McAuliffe, Mary S. "The Politics of Civil Liberties: The American Civil Liberties Union During the McCarthy Years." In Robert Griffith and Athan Theoharis, eds., *Original Essays on the Cold War and the Origins of McCarthyism*. New York: New Viewpoints, 1974.

———. *Crisis on the Left: Cold War Politics and American Liberals, 1947–1954*. Amherst: University of Massachusetts Press, 1978.

Macdonald, Dwight. "The Defense of Everybody—I." *New Yorker*, July 11, 1953, pp. 31–32, 34–36, 38–46, 48–55.

———. "The Defense of Everybody—II." *New Yorker*, July 18, 1953, pp. 29–32, 34–36, 38–40, 42, 44–59.

McReynolds, Edwin C. *Missouri: A History of the Crossroads State*. Norman: University of Oklahoma Press, 1962.

Marchand, C. Roland. *The American Peace Movement and Social Reform, 1898–1918*. Princeton: Princeton University Press, 1972.

Margulies, Sylvia R. *The Pilgrimage to Russia: The Soviet Union and the Treatment of Foreigners, 1924–1937*. Madison: University of Wisconsin Press, 1968.

Markmann, Charles Lamm. *The Noblest Cry: A History of the American Civil Liberties Union*. New York: St. Martin's, 1965.

Markowitz, Norman D. *The Rise and Fall of the People's Century: Henry Wallace and American Liberalism, 1941–1948*. New York: Free Press, 1973.

Matthews, J. B. *Odyssey of a Fellow Traveler*. New York: Mt. Vernon, 1938.

Matusow, Allen J. *The Unraveling of America: A History of Liberalism in the 1960s*. New York: Harper and Row, 1984.

May, Gary. *Un-American Activities: The Trials of William Remington*. New York: Oxford University Press, 1994.

May, Henry F. *The End of American Innocence: A Study of the First Years of Our Own Time, 1912–1917*. Chicago: Quadrangle, 1964.

Mayer, Julius M. "Judge Mayer's Statement." *Survey* 41 (November 9, 1918): 154, 172–73.

Meier, August and Elliot Rudwick. *CORE: A Study in the Civil Rights Movement, 1942–1968*. New York: Oxford University Press, 1973.

Mencken, H. L. "The American Civil Liberties Union." *American Mercury*, October 1938, pp. 182–90.

Michaelson, Judith. "Grand Old Man of ACLU: Still Scrapper at 94." *Los Angeles Times*, April 12, 1978, pt. 2, p. 2.

Milner, Lucille. *Education of an American Liberal: An Autobiography*. New York: Horizon, 1954.

Mitford, Jessica. *The Trial of Doctor Spock*. New York: Knopf, 1969.

Montgomery, Robert H. *Sacco-Vanzetti: The Murder and the Myth*. New York: Devin-Adair, 1960.

Morgan, Charles Jr. *One Man, One Voice*. New York: Holt, Rinehart and Winston, 1979.

Morris, Willie. "Roger Baldwin." *New Republic*, January 25, 1964, pp. 8–10.

Murphy, Paul L. *The Constitution in Crisis Times, 1918–1969*. New York: Harper and Row, 1972.

———. *The Meaning of Freedom of Speech*. Westport, Conn.: Greenwood, 1972.

———. *World War I and the Origin of Civil Liberties in the United States*. New York: Norton, 1979.

Murray, Robert K. *Red Scare: A Study in National Hysteria, 1919–1920*. New York: McGraw-Hill, 1964.

Myers, Constance Ashton. *The Prophet's Army: Trotskyists in America, 1928–1941*. Westport, Conn.: Greenwood, 1977.

"Name-Calling Led by Ickes and Dies." *New York Times*, November 24, 1938, pp. 1, 32.

Navasky, Victor S. *Naming Names*. New York: Penguin, 1981.

Neier, Aryeh. *Defending My Enemy: American Nazis, the Skokie Case, and the Risks of Freedom*. New York: Dutton, 1979.

———. *Only Judgment: The Limits of Litigation in Social Change*. Middletown, Conn.: Wesleyan University Press, 1982.

Nelles, Walter. *A Liberal in Wartime: The Education of Albert DeSilver*. New York: Norton, 1940.

New York Senate. Joint Legislative Committee Investigating Seditious Activities. *Revolutionary Radicalism: Its History, Purpose, and Tactics*. 4 Vols. Albany, N.Y.: J. B. Lyon, 1920.

"NLRB Challenged on Free Speech." *New York Times*, October 15, 1939, p. 2.

Ogden, August Raymond. *The Dies Committee: A Study of the Special House Committee for the Investigation of Un-American Activities, 1938–1944*. Washington, D.C.: Catholic University of America Press, 1945.

O'Neill, William A. *Coming Apart: An Informal History of America in the 1960s*. New York: Times Books, 1971.

———. *The Last Romantic: A Life of Max Eastman*. New York: Oxford University Press, 1978.

———. *A Better World: The Great Schism: Stalinism and the American Intellectuals*. New York: Simon and Schuster, 1982.

O'Reilly, Kenneth. *Hoover and the Un-Americans: The FBI, HUAC, and the Red Menace*. Philadelphia: Temple University Press, 1983.

Oshinsky, David M. *A Conspiracy So Immense: The World of Joe McCarthy*. New York: Free Press, 1983.

Ottanelli, Fraser M. *The Communist Party of the United States: From the Depression to World War II*. New Brunswick, N.J.: Rutgers University Press, 1991.

"Pacifist Professor Gets Year in Prison." *New York Times*, October 31, 1918, p. 11.

Parenti, Michael. *The Anticommunist Impulse*. New York: Random House, 1969.

Perrett, Geoffrey. *Days of Sadness, Years of Triumph: The American People, 1939–1945*. Baltimore, Md.: Penguin, 1974.

Peterson, H. C. and Gilbert C. Fite. *Opponents of War, 1917–1918*. Seattle: University of Washington Press, 1968.

Polenberg, Richard. *Fighting Faiths: The Abrams Case, the Supreme Court, and Free Speech*. New York: Penguin, 1989.

Post, Louis F. *The Deportations Delirium of 1920: A Personal Narrative of an Historic Official Experience*. New York: Da Capo, 1970.

Powers, Richard Gid. *Secrecy and Power: The Life of J. Edgar Hoover*. New York: Free Press, 1987.

———. *Not Without Honor: The History of American Anticommunism*. New York: Free Press, 1995.

Preston, William Jr. *Aliens and Dissenters: Federal Suppression of Radicals, 1903–1933*. Urbana: University of Illinois Press, 1994.

Primm, James Neal. *Lion of the Valley: St. Louis, Missouri*. Boulder, Colo.: Pruett, 1981.

Rabban, David M. *Free Speech in Its Forgotten Years*. Cambridge: Cambridge University Press, 1997.

Railton, Arthur R. "The Barn House: What Is It?" *Dukes County Intelligencer*, August 1990, pp. 9–33.

———. "Artists and Other Free Spirits at Chilmark's Barn House." *The Dukes County Intelligencer*, August 1995, pp. 3–28.

Reitman, Alan, ed. *The Price of Liberty: Perspectives on Civil Liberties by Members of the ACLU*. New York: Norton, 1968.

———. *The Pulse of Freedom: American Liberties, 1920–1970s*. New York: New American Library, 1976.

———. *The Pulse of Freedom: American Liberties, 1920–1970s*. New York: Norton, 1975.

Rembar, Charles. *The End of Obscenity*. New York: Random House, 1968.

Ribuffo, Leo P. *The Old Christian Right: The Protestant Far Right from the Great Depression to the Cold War*. Philadelphia: Temple University Press, 1983.

Rice, Elmer. *Minority Report: An Autobiography*. New York: Simon and Schuster, 1963.

Robins, Natalie. *Alien Ink: The FBI's War on Freedom of Expression*. New York: Morrow, 1992.

Robinson, Jo Ann. *Abraham Went Out: A Biography of A. J. Muste*. Philadelphia: Temple University Press, 1981.

Roche, John P. *The Quest for the Dream: The Development of Civil Rights and Human Relations in Modern America*. Chicago: Quadrangle, 1963.

——. "Perspectives: Remembering Roger Baldwin." *New Leader*, September 21, 1981, p. 14.

Roger Baldwin: A Remembrance. New York: ACLU, 1981.

"Roger Nash Baldwin." *Current Biography, 1940*. New York: Wilson, 1941.

"Roger Baldwin, RIP." *National Review*, September 18, 1981, p. 1065.

Rosenstone, Robert A. *Romantic Revolutionary: A Biography of John Reed*. New York: Vintage, 1981.

Saltmarsh, John A. *Scott Nearing: An Intellectual Biography*. Philadelphia: Temple University Press, 1991.

Samson, Gloria Garrett. *The American Fund for Public Service: Charles Garland and Radical Philanthropy, 1922–1941*. Westport, Conn.: Greenwood, 1996.

Schlesinger, Arthur M. Jr. *The Vital Center: The Politics of Freedom*. Boston: Houghton Mifflin, 1949.

——. *The Age of Roosevelt: The Crisis of the Old Order, 1919–1933*. Boston: Houghton Mifflin, 1957.

Schrecker, Ellen. *No Ivory Tower: McCarthyism and the Universities*. New York: Oxford University Press, 1986.

Schultz, Bud and Ruth Schultz. *It Did Happen Here: Recollections of Political Repression in America*. Berkeley: University of California Press, 1989.

Schwartz, Jordan A. *Liberal: Adolph A. Berle and the Vision of an American Era*. New York: Free Press, 1987.

Scopes, John T. and James Presley. *Center of the Storm: Memoirs of John T. Scopes*. New York: Holt, Rinehart and Winston, 1967.

Shannon, David A. *The Decline of American Communism: A History of the American Communist Party of the United States Since 1945*. New York: Harcourt, Brace, 1959.

Sheehy, Gail. *Pathfinders*. New York: Bantam, 1981.

Shi, David E. *Matthew Josephson: Bourgeois Bohemian*. New Haven: Yale University Press, 1981.

Simmons, Jerold. "The American Civil Liberties Union and the Dies Committee, 1938–1940." *Harvard Civil Rights–Civil Liberties Law Review* 17 (Spring 1982): 183–207.

———. *Operation Abolition: The Campaign to Abolish the House Un-American Activities Committee, 1938–1975.* New York: Garland, 1986.

Simon, Rita James, ed. *As We Saw the Thirties: Essays on Social and Political Movements of a Decade.* Urbana: University of Illinois Press, 1969.

Simonson, Lee. "My College Life Was an Inner One." In *The Harvard Book: Selections from Three Centuries,* rev. ed. Cambridge, Mass.: Harvard University Press, 1982.

"Sixty-two Are Named in 'Who's Who' of Pacifism." *New York Tribune,* January 25, 1919, p. 4.

Smith, Richard Norton. *The Harvard Century: The Making of a University to a Nation.* New York: Simon and Schuster, 1986.

Sochen, June. *The New Woman: Feminism in Greenwich Village, 1910–1920.* New York: Quadrangle, 1972.

Souraf, Frank. *The Wall of Separation: The Constitutional Politics of Church and State.* Princeton: Princeton University Press, 1976.

Spivak, John L. *A Man in His Time.* New York: Horizon, 1967.

Starobin, Joseph R. *American Communism in Crisis, 1943–1957.* Cambridge, Mass.: Harvard University Press, 1972.

Steinberg, Peter. *The Great 'Red Menace': United States Prosecution of American Communists, 1947–1952.* Westport, Conn.: Greenwood, 1984.

Straight, Michael. *After Long Silence.* New York: Norton, 1983.

Svonkin, Stuart. *Jews Against Prejudice: American Jews and the Fight for Civil Liberties.* New York: Columbia University Press, 1997.

Swanberg, W. A. *Norman Thomas: The Last Idealist.* New York: Scribner's, 1976.

Taylor, S. J. *Stalin's Apologist: Walter Duranty: The* New York Times*'s Man in Moscow.* New York: Oxford University Press, 1990.

Theoharis, Athan G. and John Stuart Cox. *Seeds of Repression: Harry S Truman and the Origins of McCarthyism.* New York: Quadrangle, 1977.

———. *Spying on Americans: Political Surveillance from Hoover to the Huston Plan.* Philadelphia: Temple University Press, 1978.

———. *The Boss: J. Edgar Hoover and the Great Inquisition.* New York: Bantam, 1990.

"Thirty Years of A.C.L.U." *New York Times,* February 22, 1950, p. 28.

Thomas, Norman. *The Conscientious Objector in America.* New York: Huebsch, 1923.

"Threat to Liberty Is Seen by Lehman." *New York Times,* February 23, 1950, p. 30.

Unger, Irwin. *The Movement: A History of the American New Left, 1959–1972.* New York: Dodd, Mead, 1974.

Varney, Harold Lord. "The Civil Liberties Union." *American Mercury,* December 1936, pp. 385–99.

Villard, Oswald Garrison. "On Being in Jail." *Nation,* August 2, 1919, pp. 142–43.

Viorst, Milton. *Fire in the Streets.* New York: Simon and Schuster, 1979.

Wald, Alan M. *James T. Farrell.* New York: New York University Press, 1978.

Walker, Samuel. *In Defense of American Liberties: A History of the American Civil Liberties Union*. New York: Oxford University Press, 1990.

———. *The American Civil Liberties Union: An Annotated Bibliography*. New York: Garland, 1992.

Warren, Frank A. *An Alternative Vision: The Socialist Party of the 1930s*. Bloomington: Indiana University Press, 1974.

———. *Liberals and Communism: The "Red Decade" Revisited*. Westport, Conn.: Greenwood, 1976.

Washington, Booker T. *The Booker T. Washington Papers*. Vol. 5, 1899–1900, ed. Louis R. Harlan and Raymond W. Smock. Urbana: University of Illinois Press, 1976.

Weinstein, Allen. *Perjury: The Hiss-Chambers Case*. New York: Knopf, 1978.

Weglyn, Michi. *Years of Infamy: The Untold Story of America's Concentration Camps*. New York: Morrow, 1976.

Wexler, Alice. *Emma Goldman in Exile: From the Russian Revolution to the Spanish Civil War*. Boston: Beacon, 1989.

"Whad'ye Mean—Class Struggle?" *Student Outlook* (March 1933): 6.

Whipple, Leon. *The Story of Civil Liberty in the United States*. New York: Vanguard, 1927.

Whitfield, Stephen J. *The Culture of the Cold War*. Baltimore: Johns Hopkins University Press, 1991.

———. *Scott Nearing: Apostle of American Radicalism*. New York: Columbia University Press, 1974.

Whitney, Richard M. *Reds in America: The Present Status of the Revolutionary Movement in the United States Based on Documents Seized by the Authorities in the Raid upon the Convention of the Communist Party at Bridgman, Michigan, August 22, 1922, Together with Descriptions of Numerous Connections and Associations of the Communists Among the Radicals, Progressives and Pinks*. Boston: Western Islands Publishers, 1924.

Wilcox, Leonard. *V. F. Calverton: Radical in the American Grain*. Philadelphia: Temple University Press, 1992.

Williams, David. "The Bureau of Investigation and Its Critics, 1919–1921: The Origins of Federal Political Surveillance." *Journal of American History* 68 (December 1981): 560–79.

Wittner, Lawrence S. *Rebels Against War: The American Peace Movement, 1933–1983*. Philadelphia: Temple University Press, 1984.

Wolfskill, George and John Hudson. *All but the People: Franklin D. Roosevelt and His Critics, 1933–1939*. Toronto: Macmillan, 1969.

Wreszin, Michael. *A Rebel in Defense of Tradition: The Life and Politics of Dwight Macdonald*. New York: Basic, 1994.

Zaroulis, Nancy and Gerald Sullivan. *Who Spoke Up? American Protest Against the War in Vietnam, 1963–1975*. Garden City, N.Y.: Doubleday, 1984.

Subject Index

Index of Names